Equity
and the
Law of Trusts
in the
Republic of Ireland

Equity
and the
Law of Trusts
in the
Republic of Ireland

The Hon Mr Justice Ronan Keane
BA (NUI), of Lincoln's Inn, Barrister
Judge of the High Court
President of the Law Reform Commission

London, Edinburgh
Butterworths
1988

United Kingdom	Butterworth & Co (Publishers) Ltd, 88 Kingsway, London WC2B 6AB and 61A North Castle Street, Edinburgh EH2 3LJ
Australia	Butterworths Pty Ltd, Sydney, Melbourne, Brisbane, Adelaide, Perth, Canberra and Hobart
Canada	Butterworths. A division of Reed Inc., Toronto and Vancouver
New Zealand	Butterworths of New Zealand Ltd, Wellington and Auckland
Singapore	Butterworth & Co (Asia) Pte Ltd, Singapore
USA	Butterworths Legal Publishers, St Paul, Minnesota, Seattle, Washington, Boston, Massachusetts, Austin, Texas and D & S Publishers, Clearwater, Florida

British Library Cataloguing in Publication Data

Keane, Ronan
  Equity and the law of trusts in the Republic of Ireland
  1. (Republic) Ireland. Law. Equity
  2. (Republic) Ireland. Trusts. Law
  I. Title
  344. 1706' 04

  ISBN 0 406 10270 8

Typeset by Irish Typesetters, Galway, Ireland
Printed and bound in Great Britain by Billing & Sons Ltd, Worcester

For Madeleine, Timothy and Justine

Preface

A vast appendix to the volumes of the common law was how Maitland saw the law of equity. But more than a century has passed since the Judicature Acts put an end to the system under which the two great legal jurisdictions were administered by judges sitting in different courts assisted by separate bars of common law and chancery advocates and much has changed. Now equity flourishes as never before in almost every court and the young junior applying for an injunction on a Monday morning hardly thinks of himself as a successor to the chancery lawyers of the last century with their thirst for the intricacies of legal argument and dislike of the rhetorical excesses of their brethren at *nisi prius*. Even their most revered institution, the trust, has long been freed from what some regarded as its medieval constraints and emerges in unexpected places in the guise of 'new model' constructive trusts and the like.

Yet only one attempt has been made to provide an Irish guide to the law of equity to which our lawyers have made, and are continuing to make, a unique contribution. The late Mr O'Neill Kiely's *Principles of Equity* was an invaluable aid to generations of students. But it was produced over fifty years ago and it is an understatement to say that much has changed in the legal world since then.

The need for a modern textbook is thus obvious, but it is important to acknowledge at the outset the debt I owe to those who have already been at work. Professor Wylie's encyclopedic works on land and conveyancing law and his casebooks contain much valuable material for the student and practitioner. The standard English works, most notably Hanbury, Pettit, Snell and Keeton and Sheridan (the last named containing much of Irish interest) have been a constant source of enlightenment and stimulation. And I have benefited more than I can say from the absorbing Australian textbook, Meagher Gummow and Lehane, with its fascinating blend of reverence for tradition and a healthily sceptical approach to certain aspects of contemporary English 'equitable' jurisprudence. (I think they would approve of the quotation marks.)

The question of what to include and what to leave out presents peculiar problems in a book on modern equity and it is impossible to please everyone. Doctrines such as satisfaction and conversion hardly trouble the practitioner of to-day with much frequency. But examiners retain a fondness for them and I have also borne in mind the old folk wisdom of the law library: 'one case and the book is paid for'. Mortgages present a greater problem but ultimately I concluded that they are so extensively and admirably treated by Professor Wylie that I could reasonably omit them.

Preface

I am grateful to my publishers for their understanding and patience when my appointment as President of the Law Reform Commission meant an unexpected delay in the delivery of a final manuscript and for taking responsibility for the compilation of the tables and index. Mr. Garrett Gill S.C. and Professor G.J. Hand read substantial portions of the book and made most helpful comments. I should also like to thank the following for assistance in various forms: Professor J.C. Brady, Miss Justice Mella Carroll, Dr. Robert Clarke, Mr. Eamonn Mongey and Mr. Roderick Murphy, Barrister-at-Law. I am indebted to the staffs of the following libraries for their courtesy and co-operation: the King's Inns, the Judges' Library in the Four Courts, the Law Library, the National Library, Trinity College and Lincoln's Inn.

I am grateful to my daughter, Justine, who gave up much of her summer vacation to reducing my untidy manuscript to polished and professional form.

The responsibility for errors and omissions is entirely mine. I will be extremely grateful to have them identified so that they can be remedied, I would hope, in a later edition.

The law is stated as of 1 September 1987. However, where possible, recent developments have been incorporated at proof stage.

Ronan Keane
Four Courts
Dublin

Addenda

Four recent decisions, which could not be incorporated in the text, should be noted. Three of them arise out of the protracted 'Spycatcher' litigation.

In Australia, the decision at first instance to refuse an injunction to the English Attorney General restraining publication of Mr Wright's memoirs in that jurisdiction has been upheld on appeal: para 30.09.

In England, the Court of Appeal in *A-G v Newspaper Publishing plc* [1987] 3 All ER 276 have held, reversing Browne-Wilkinson V-C, that it is a contempt of court, in the sense of knowingly interfering with the course of justice, for a person who is not prohibited by an order to do something which is forbidden by the order, even where he is not 'aiding and abetting' the person named in the order: para 15.44.

The Court of Appeal in England has refused to grant the Attorney General a permanent injunction restraining the publication of Mr Wright's memoirs, holding that the duty of confidentiality was outweighed by the public interest in disclosure: *A-G v Observer Ltd* (1988) Times, 11 February. Leave to appeal to the House of Lords has been granted.

In *Webb v Ireland* (unreported; judgment delivered 16 December 1987), the Supreme Court held that the finders of the valuable antiquities known as the 'Derrynaflan Hoard', which they had deposited with the National Museum for safe keeping pending the determination of their legal ownership, were entitled to rely on an assurance by the Director of the Museum that the finders would be 'honourably treated' and were accordingly entitled to a reasonable reward. The court based its conclusion on a doctrine of 'legitimate expectation' which, it said, was an aspect of the equitable doctrine of promissory estoppel (Chapter 28). It might be premature to regard this decision as a rejection of the limitations which have been said to attach to the doctrine of equitable estoppel: paras 28.05 to 28.11 inclusive.

Finally, it should be noted that section 27(5) of the Status of Children Act 1987 repeals the common law rule which rendered void trusts in favour of future illegitimate children in the case of wills or settlements made after the commencement of the Act. It is suggested in the text that it is at least doubtful whether the common law rule survived the enactment of the Constitution: para 14.03.

Contents

Abbreviations

HANBURY	Hanbury and Maudsley *Modern Equity* (12th edn,) ed Martin
MEAGER GUMMOW AND LEHANE	Meagher Gummow and Lehane *Equity Doctrines and Remedies* (2nd edn)
PETTIT	Philip Pettit *Equity and the Law of Trusts* (5th edn)
SNELL	*Snell's Principles of Equity* (28th edn) ed Baker and Langan
UNDERHILL	*Underhill's Law of Trusts* (13th edn) ed Hayton
WYLIE LAND LAW	J C W Wylie *Irish Land Law* (2nd edn)
WYLIE CONVEYANCING	J C W Wylie *Irish Conveyancing Law*
WYLIE CASEBOOK	J C W Wylie *Casebook on Equity and Trusts*
CLJ	Cambridge Law Journal
DULJ	Dublin University Law Journal
Ir Jur (n.s)	Irish Jurist (new series)
LQR	Law Quarterly Review
MLR	Modern Law Review

Table of statutes

Table of cases

G

O

The Arthur Cox Foundation

Arthur Cox, solicitor, classical scholar and former President of the Incorporated Law Society of Ireland, was associated with the setting up of many Irish companies, not least the E.S.B. He was a specialist in company law and was a member of the Company Law Reform Committee which sat from 1951 and reported to the Government in 1958, ultimately giving rise to the Companies Act, 1963. When he decided to retire from practice as a solicitor in 1961 a number of his clients, professional colleagues and other friends, in recognition of his outstanding contribution to Ireland and his profession, thought that a fund should be established as a tribute to him, which fund would be used to encourage the writing and publication of legal text books. There was a generous response to this appeal.

After his retirement he studied for the priesthood and was ordained in 1963. He went to Zambia to do missionary work. He died there in 1965 as a result of a car accident.

The Foundation was established to honour Arthur Cox and was for many years administered by Mr Justice John Kenny in conjunction with the Law Society. In paying tribute to the memory of Arthur Cox it is appropriate that tribute should also be paid to Mr Justice John Kenny, who died on 25 March 1987. John Kenny was a close personal friend of Arthur Cox and, like Arthur Cox, graced with distinction his own barristers' profession as a chancery practitioner, and both the High Court and Supreme Court as a judge. John Kenny was the encouraging force behind the publication of a number of Irish legal textbooks. Without his quiet drive and enthusiasm there would have been no Foundation. To both Arthur Cox and John Kenny we pay tribute.

The Law Society, as the continuing trustee of the Foundation, is pleased to have been able to assist Mr Justice Ronan Keane in the writing of his book.

Thomas D Shaw
President,
The Incorporated Law Society of Ireland.

liii

Part one

The nature of equity

Chapter 1

Introduction

1.01 All Irish law derives its validity from the Constitution enacted by the people in 1937. That law takes the form of statutes enacted by parliament and cases decided by courts. But apart from Acts passed by the Oireachtas since the enactment of the Constitution, and cases decided by the courts established under the Constitution, the law in force also includes statutes passed before the enactment of the Constitution and cases decided by the courts which were responsible for the administration of justice before the establishment of the present hierarchy of courts. Such statutes and cases— many of them dating from before the establishment of the Irish Free State in 1921 when Ireland was still a part of the United Kingdom—remain part of our law by virtue of the Constitution, unless they are inconsistent with that Constitution.[1]

The Irish legal system, accordingly, is broadly similar to the legal systems which exist in the United Kingdom, the United States and many of the present and former member states of the British Commonwealth. The law is contained not merely in the statutes passed by parliament, but in the corpus of judicial decisions, some of them concerned with the interpretation of statutes and others with the evolution of legal principles to be applied to situations for which the legislature has not provided. That corpus of law in turn consists of two great sections: the common law and the law of equity.

1 Article 50.1.

1.02 The common law of England which, in the centuries following the Norman invasion of Ireland in 1169, was also applied by the courts which were established in the 'lordship of Ireland' was seen in medieval times to suffer from three major defects. In the first place, a litigant might find himself deprived of justice simply because his opponent was too powerful or unscrupulous in the methods he employed or because the neighbourhood was in too disturbed a state for the courts to function effectively: in the formative days of the common law, there did not exist the highly centralised machinery of courts and enforcement agencies, such as the police, which we take for granted to-day. In the second place, the common law became with the passage of time too rigid: if a litigant could not frame his action within the constraints of the existing forms of procedure, the injustice of which he complained might remain without remedy. In the third place, even where there was a remedy, it was very often confined to an award of damages which might not be adequate to redress the wrong of which the litigant complained.

It was against this background that the practice developed under which dissatisfied litigants presented petitions seeking the justice which had been denied to them to the king's most powerful officer, the Chancellor. In those days, he was invariably an eminent churchman and thus combined in a formidable manner the power of both church and state. Equipped as he was with the highest authority in the land next to the king and with an efficient administration at his disposal—the chancery—he was seen as the obvious person to remedy the inadequacies of the common law courts. But he did so, not by overturning the common law, but by requiring the litigants who came before him to obey the dictates of conscience. Thus a jurisdiction evolved which was essentially supplementary to the common law and which came to be known as the law of 'equity' or 'chancery' after the great officer who administered it.

Equity then in Maitland's famous aphorism came 'not to destroy the law but to fulfil it.'[1] This all important feature of the Chancellor's jurisdiction is seen at its most characteristic in the most celebrated of equitable institutions, the trust. Where one person—a trustee—held property on behalf of another—a beneficiary—the Chancellor treated the trustee, as did the common law courts, as the legal owner of the property. He did not purport to divest the trustee of that legal ownership and transfer it to the beneficiary. But he did prevent the trustee from acting in breach of the trust he had undertaken. Thus the trustee could be compelled by the intervention of the court of equity to acknowledge that, although the legal ownership was vested in him, he held the property on behalf of the beneficiary.

1 Maitland, *Equity*, p 17.

1.03 As we shall see in the next chapter, from these roots there developed in both England and Ireland—and the various jurisdictions throughout the world to which the common law system was exported—the separate jurisdiction of equity with its own courts and corpus of law. Not merely the concept of the trust owed its vitality to equity: from these courts emerged a whole range of remedies and doctrines in the great formative period of equity which is generally seen as extending from the end of the seventeenth to the beginning of the nineteenth centuries. These included some of the most effective weapons in the armoury of the law, such as the injunction, and in the course of time the courts of equity also extended their protection to those members of the community who were thought to be peculiarly incapable of defending their own legal rights, such as infants, persons of unsound mind and married women.

1.04 By the mid-nineteenth century, it had become obvious that, although equity had come to play an indispensable role in the legal system of the United Kingdom, its administration by a separate system of courts was an anachronism and an anomaly which could no longer be justified. It offended common sense that a litigant could be told that his complaint was fully justified but that he would have to go to another court to have it remedied. The result was the legislative process which culminated in the Judicature Acts (that applicable to Ireland being passed in 1877) under which the courts of law and equity were fused. Henceforth in both jurisdictions the principles of law and equity were to be applied by all courts and where they conflicted those of equity were to prevail. There remained separate divisions of the High Court, so that a litigant seeking equitable relief, such as the enforcement of a trust or the obtaining of an injunction, would begin his proceedings in the Chancery Division. But whether he was proceeding at common law or in chancery, the court would be bound to recognise and apply both legal and equitable principles. With the establishment of the High Court of the newly independent Irish Free State, the distinctions between the common law and chancery divisions were abolished, but the corpus of equity law remained and continues to exist as a separate and identifiable body of doctrines and remedies in the system of law established under the Constitution in 1937.

1.05 How then should we define equity to-day? We can probably find no better words than those Maitland used eighty years ago:

> 'That body of rules administered by our...courts which, were it not for the operation of the Judicature Acts, would be administered only by those Courts which would be known as Courts of Equity.'[1]

It is now, as then, 'a poor thing to call a definition', but then as now nothing better is possible. This is because equity is essentially, as he put it, 'a collection of appendixes'[2] to the common law rather than a self-contained system.

But his definition requires three important qualifications. First, no equitable doctrine or remedy will be regarded as part of our law if it is inconsistent with the Constitution. Second, the absence of an equitable remedy will be regarded by the courts as irrelevant if the protection or vindication of a right guaranteed by the Constitution is required.[3] Third, the law of equity was not petrified by the passing of the Judicature Acts: it continued to develop and the process went on after independence.

1 Maitland, *Equity*, p 18.
2 Ibid, p 19.
3 See para 3.05,infra.

1.06 We retain, accordingly, as part of our law a separate body of doctrines and remedies which are to be found at work in almost every area of the law, except the criminal law, which owe their birth and evolution not to any statute but to the development of the law by judges and which we compendiously call 'equity'.

The question may be asked: why do we continue to treat equity as a separate system of law? Can we not to-day regard all law, other than that contained in the Constitution and legislation, as the body of law developed by the courts and discard the distinction between the common law and equity as irrelevant to contemporary jurisprudence? Such an approach has, to the accompaniment of severe criticism, received weighty judicial endorsement in recent times.[1] Before examining that problem in more detail, however, it is as well to place the present Irish law of equity in its historical perspective.

1 See para 2.20,infra.

Chapter 2

The historical background

2.01 An understanding of the historical development of equity is important for the student. But at the outset a warning note must be sounded. The materials available for someone anxious to acquaint himself with how equity developed in Ireland are far scantier than those to which the student of English legal history has access. There are three principal reasons for this. First, the calamitous destruction of the Public Records Office in the Four Courts during the civil war in 1922 meant the disappearance of much of the primary sources on which such a history could be based. Secondly, reporting of law cases in Ireland did not begin on any serious or systematic basis until the nineteenth century. Thirdly, Irish legal history still has to find, in Professor F H Newark's words, 'its Reeves or its Holdsworth'.[1]

It should also be born in mind that the formative period of the modern law of equity is generally acknowledged to be that which began with the chancellorship of Lord Nottingham, sometimes called 'the father of modern equity' in 1672 and ended with that of Lord Eldon who was chancellor from 1801 to 1806 and 1807 to 1827. While it is true that some of the most characteristic features of equity, including the institution of the trust, can be traced to much earlier times, it is in this period that the body of equitable jurisprudence with which the modern lawyer is required to be familiar was developed. It was also during the seventeenth century that the extension of English law to the whole island of Ireland was completed. The history of the development of the modern law of equity is accordingly largely the history of the application of the evolving English doctrines to Ireland. These doctrines were in the main fully established by the end of Lord Eldon's long reign and while they were to be developed and refined by many judges since then, including Irish judges, they remain the essential law of equity to-day.

1 There are excellent short accounts of the development of equity in England in J H Baker, *An Introduction to English Legal History*, 2nd edn. (especially chapter 6) and *Radcliffe and Cross: The English Legal System*, ed G J Hand and D J Bentley (6th edn) (especially Chapters 8 and 9). As a comprehensive history, Holdsworth's monumental *History of English Law* remains unique, although it is inevitably out of date in some respects.

For the reasons mentioned, the Irish literature is much sparser, although the situation has improved dramatically in recent years. O'Flanagan's *Lives of the Irish Lord Chancellors* and Ball's *The Judges in Ireland* have the advantage that the authors had access to the records subsequently destroyed in the civil war, but the former has been criticised as in many respects unreliable: see G J Hand, 'A Note on the Early Irish Chancery', 5 Ir Jur (ns) 291. On the early medieval period, Professor Hand's pioneering work *English Law in Ireland 1290-1324* is invaluable. There is also useful material on the development of the equity jurisdiction in Ireland in Richardson and Sayles, *The Irish Parliament in the Middle*

Ages, the same authors' *The Administration of Ireland 1172/1377* and two recent works by S G Ellis, *Tudor Ireland: Crown, Community and the Conflict of Cultures, 1470-1603* and *Reform and Revival: English Government in Ireland, 1470-1534* (especially Chapter 4 in the latter). Another important recent work is *Sir John Davies and the conquest of Ireland: a study in legal imperialism* by H J Pawlisch. Excellent shorter studies can be found in three essays by Professor Newark in *Elegantia Juris*, pp 185/228 and A C Donaldson, *Some comparative aspects of Irish Law*. Material on the later period will be found in Daire Hogan, *The Legal Profession in Ireland 1790-1921*.

Modern Irish legal historiography is comprehensively surveyed in W N Osborough, *Recent Writing on Modern Irish Legal History* (Vienna 1986).

The origins of equity in England

2.02 After the Norman conquest, a system of courts developed in England which applied a body of law consisting partly of statutes and partly of the law regarded as generally applicable to Englishmen and known as the *ius commune* or common law. These were the courts of King's Bench, Common Pleas and Exchequer.

In order to bring his grievance before the courts, the litigant was obliged to make use of the document known as a *writ*. This could only be issued under the king's great seal which was in the custody of the chancellor. The latter was indeed effectively in charge of the royal secretariat and his power and prestige was such that in at least two European countries—West Germany and Austria—the head of government is still described as the 'chancellor' rather than the 'prime minister'. In the later thirteenth century, attempts were made to curb his powers, culminating in the Second Statute of Westminster in 1285. This permitted the issuing of new writs only *in consimilu casu*, which meant that the chancellor was effectively confined to varying the form of existing writs.[1]

The fact that the litigant might not be able to obtain a writ tailored to his specific grievance was not the only difficulty with which he might be faced. The courts in which he sued were so unlike our own that we would have difficulty in recognising them as courts. Not only were the parties unable to give evidence, a feature which persisted in common law courts until well into the nineteenth century: witnesses in the modern sense were unknown in medieval times. The jury, whose verdicts were of paramount import-ance, arrived at them, not on the basis of evidence as we would understand the word, but from their own local knowledge of the parties and the background to the dispute. In an age when there was no police force, it was relatively easy for a powerful and unscrupulous litigant to intimidate juries—or his opponent—with a view to getting the result he wanted. The courts moreover adopted an unyielding approach to their application of the law. A striking example is the unfortunate debtor who paid off his debt but omitted to have the bond which secured it cancelled. If his creditor unblushingly sued for the amount already paid, the court would give it him because the debtor was unable to show that the bond had been cancelled.[2]

1 Holdsworth, op cit Vol 1, pp 396/8.
2 Baker, op cit pp 87/8.

2.03 It was against this background that the practice developed of presenting petitions—or 'bills' as they came to be known—to the king or the king's council seeking the justice which the courts seemed unable to effect. The chancellor was the great officer who saw to the formulation of whatever remedy might be available to the distressed litigant, as he presided over the department which kept custody of the great seal and acted as the royal secretariat. And so it is not surprising to find him playing an increasingly important role in dealing with such petitions.

The chancellor was almost invariably a churchman until Tudor times and this is reflected to some extent in the form of the petitions with their emphasis on the demands of 'conscience' and their concluding rubric 'your petitioner will every pray (sc. for the soul of the chancellor)' with which petitions in our own courts ended until recent times. But the extent of the chancellor's spiritual influence should not be exaggerated, although to it has been traditionally ascribed the concern of equity with restraining 'unconscionable' conduct. Of undoubted significance, and also deriving from his ecclesiastical status, was the influence of the canon law on the evolving chancery jurisdiction: this in turn reflected the Roman law which was the basis of so much of the civil law of continental Europe. As a result the chancery developed a consensual approach to questions of contract at a time when the common law had still to escape from the constraints of the action for debt and evolve its own doctrines of offer and acceptance as the basis of contract.

The petitions to the chancellor frequently employ the word 'equity' to denote the fair dealing which the petitioner seeks. These petitions were dealt with on the 'equity' side of the chancery: it had also a common law side, principally invoked when the king himself was alleged to have acted oppressively. But it was the equity side which was to be of permanent importance in legal history.

The original equity jurisdiction has to some extent in modern eyes a distinctly criminal appearance and it could be said, albeit crudely and simplistically, that the chancellor was endeavouring to ensure that what modern politicians like to call 'law and order' replaced the lawlessness and near anarchy which disfigured so much of the king's realm. But as the monarchy grew more powerful and its administration more centralised, this role of equity became of less importance until in the time of the Tudors it is virtually taken over by the King's Council and the Court of Star Chamber.[1]

The chancellor's jurisdiction was in the early period of equity characteristically exercised by the issue of a *sub poena:* the defendant is required under pain of a fine or some other punishment to attend and be examined concerning the subject matter of the plaintiff's complaint. In exercising this power of summoning a party to be examined on oath in the manner of a witness to-day, equity was again parting company with the common law. It was not until the fifteenth century, however, that the Chancery emerges as what we should recognise as a court. And as it developed into something approaching its modern form, it was in the area of uses and trusts that its jurisdiction became of the greatest significance.

1 Holdsworth, op cit Vol 1, pp 405/6.

2.04 The modern trust is the descendant of the ancient *use*, which is thought to have existed in England even before the Norman conquest in 1066. Put at its simplest, it meant that the owner of land gave it to someone else to hold on his behalf. If he were going on a crusade, for example, he would grant the land to another 'to his (the owner's) use'[1] (the word 'use' itself may have been derived from the Latin *opus*).[2] To understand how it evolved into the trust, however, we must say something first about the medieval system of land ownership after the Norman conquest.

The feudal system of land ownership meant that the owner of land held it as tenant from his immediate lord. The only person in the realm who did not hold land from someone else was the king. He was at the apex of the feudal pyramid and was the owner of all land. As with any other lord, his immediate tenant had to render the king the appropriate service in return for which he held the land, one of the most common being military service. In turn, by the process called *subinfeudation*, other tenants would hold from the king's tenant and so on down to the base of the pyramid. Failure to render the service would result in the land reverting to the king or lord under the process called *escheat*.

Under the feudal system, then, all land was held directly or indirectly from the king and although the crown has vanished from our law this system of *tenure* is still an essential feature of our law of property. Its complexities belong more properly to land law: here we content ourselves with observing that it was accompanied by another feature which determined the nature of ownership, the concept of *estates*. No one, whatever tenure he enjoyed, whether based on military service or some other kind, owned his land absolutely, since that would conflict with the central ·concept of feudalism, that all land was held ultimately from the king. But with that qualification, he and his descendants could enjoy the effective ownership of the land forever by having the estate known as the *fee simple*. He might not own the lands in perpetuity, however: he might be entitled to them only for his lifetime in which case he had a *life estate*. Or his interest in the lands might be limited to the life of another person, in which case he had an estate *pur autre vie*. Or he might have the form of estate known as a *fee tail* which essentially confined the inheritance of the estate to the lineal descendants of the owners, the form of ownership which for centuries played such an important part in land ownership and was known as the *entail*. All of these were *freehold* or *real* estates and they are to be distinguished from the other great category of estates, the *leasehold*, under which the land was held, not in perpetuity, but for a limited period such as a term of 99 years and from which the periodic tenancies—yearly, monthly or weekly—which are features of our modern law of landlord and tenant are derived.

1 Maitland, p 23.
2 Ibid, p 24.

2.05 The owner of a freehold estate was said to be *seised* of the land and it was only to *seisin* that the institution of the use applied. A person was said to be seised of the land to the use of another and the nature of the feudal system made such uses extremely popular. In the first place, the owner of the land, A, by granting the land to B to hold it to the use of A could avoid the burden of military service or whatever other form of service might be required of him. He could also avoid the consequences of another essential feature of the feudal system, i e *primogeniture* or the right of the eldest male son of the owner, the *heir*, to succeed to the estate on his father's death. If the heir was an infant, there could be no immediate succession and under the doctrine of *wardship*, the lord stepped in and took the land until he came of age. The owner could prevent this happening by conveying the land to be held to the use of a number of adults. They held the land on the death of the owner as joint tenants and the land thereafter devolved on the survivors in turn. Secondly, it enabled the owner to ensure that the ownership of the land went on his death to the person of his choice by conveying it to the use of that person. He thus achieved what at a later period of legal history was the result of a *will*: it was not until 1540 in England and 1634 in Ireland that it was possible to make a devise of land by a will.[1] Thirdly, it enabled land to be transferred to *corporations*, i e groups of people rather than individuals. One of the most important examples in medieval times of the corporations were religious communities. Landowners frequently wished to benefit such bodies for the good of their own souls. To do so, however, would deprive the feudal lord of his dues and there were statutes, known as the Mortmain Acts, which rendered this unlawful. Finally, conveyances to uses were frequently availed of in order to keep the land out of the reach of the owner's creditors.

The Chancellor was prepared to enforce such uses where he considered it unconscionable of the legal owner to deny the use—or 'trust' as it came to be called—upon which he held the land. It should be noted that in doing so he was in essence requiring the parties to perform their *agreement* and this at a time when the common law courts had yet to develop a law of contract based on any such consensual theory.[2]

1 Statute of Wills 1540; Statute of Wills (Ireland) 1634.
2 Maitland, p 29.

2.06 However, while such uses were popular with the Chancellor, they were frowned upon by those lords who were deprived of their services or of profitable opportunities provided by escheats and wardships. They were most unpopular of all with the king who had most to lose. Hence the enactment of the Statute of Uses in England in 1535 and its Irish counterpart in 1634. (It has been pointed out that by the time the Irish statute was passed the military service aspect of feudalism had ceased to be of any real importance and that its enactment was probably prompted by a desire to secure uniformity in the laws of the two islands.[1] But it has also been suggested that the object of one of the Statutes of Kilkenny (passed a few years before the English statute) may well have been the avoidance of such uses.[2])

The manner in which the Statute of Uses sought to achieve its object was relatively simple. It was usual to grant the land 'unto A and his heirs to the use of B and his heirs'. Today we should speak of A as the legal owner and B as the *equitable* or *beneficial* owner. We would also refer to A as the *trustee* since he held the land in trust for B. In the Norman French terminology in which such concepts were described in medieval England, A was the *feoffee to uses* and B the *cestui que use*. The Statute of Uses provided that all such uses should be immediately *executed*, i e B would become both the legal and equitable owner and A would drop out of the picture. The only exception was where the feoffee had active duties to perform: in such a case the law had to recognise the continuing use.

Prior to the Statute, it had been held by the common law courts that one could not have a second use in a conveyance of freehold land. Thus if land was conveyed 'unto A and his heirs to the use of B and his heirs to the use of C and his heirs', the common law simply ignored the use to C: there could not be 'a use upon a use'. In *Jane Tyrrel's Case*,[3] it was held that the enactment of the Statute had not affected this principle: the second use was still ineffectual. But the Chancellor was prepared to enforce it if the requirements of equity so demanded and thus the formula for creating a trust emerged in its final form: a conveyance 'unto and to the use of A and his heirs in trust for B and his heirs'. A was at law the owner, the first use being executed by force of the statute, but equity enforced the second use or trust.[4]

1 Wylie, *Land Law*, p 81.

2 Hand, 'The Forgotten Statutes of Kilkenny: A Brief Survey', 1 Ir Jur (ns) 299.
3 (1557) 2 Dyer 155a.
4 It is sometimes said that as a result the only practical effect of the Statute of Uses was to add three words to a conveyance, i e 'to the use', but this is not thought to be correct: see Maitland, p 41.

2.07 As we have mentioned, the *contractual* nature of the trust was of major significance in the development of equity. The common law doctrine of contract only emerged when the action for debt was supplemented by the form of action known as trespass on the case or *assumpsit*. [1] But equity at an early stage assumed a jurisdiction to enforce contracts by means of the order of specific performance or the injunction which was to be of lasting importance.

All this reflected the chancellor's preoccupation with ensuring that people obeyed the dictates of conscience. And he was also vigilant in protecting litigants against what was seen as fraudulent conduct: not necessarily actions which were dishonest, let alone criminal, but those which in his eyes constituted unfair use by someone of his position. Nor was the equitable jurisdiction confined to relieving the victims of *fraud* in this extended sense: it also came to the aid of those who by some *accident* found themselves in a position of disadvantage from which the common law courts could not rescue them. Equity from an early stage is prepared to depart from the strict letter of written instruments, and even ultimately of statutes themselves, where to adhere to them could cause injustice. [2]

There is one other feature of the chancellor's approach to trusts in particular which deserves emphasis at this point: his jurisdiction was exercised *in personam*. He did not see himself as creating a new estate or interest in the land, but as simply compelling the legal owner to acknowledge and carry out the trust which he had freely assumed. As the law developed, however, so did the concept of the equitable estate as an interest in the land which could be bought and sold or transmitted by will in the same way as the legal estate. And as the concept of the trust took root in the equity jurisprudence, this concept of dual ownership provided the basis for the *settlement*, i e the ownership of property in succession by different people, the legal ownership being vested in the trustees and the equitable ownership in the successive owners or *cestuis que trust*.

1 Cheshire, Fifoot & Furmston, *Law of Contract*, 11th edn, p 4 et seq.
2 See para 2.12, infra.

2.08 In time, the position of the chancellor came to be occupied exclusively by lawyers rather than churchmen. The last of the ecclesiastical chancellors was Cardinal Wolsey and the first lay chancellor in the modern mould of lawyer was St Thomas More. But although the clerical chancellors were not themselves lawyers, they frequently consulted the judges and a harmonious relationship developed between the chancellor and the common law judges.

As the Tudors gave way to the Stuarts, however, the development of a powerful equitable jurisdiction presided over by a great officer of state who had the ear of the king was viewed with increasing misgivings by the common law judges and these tensions eventually erupted in a series of bitter clashes between the great common lawyer, Sir Edward Coke, chief justice under James I, and the chancellor, Ellesmere. The actual point at issue was the assertion by the chancellor of a jurisdiction to restrain by injunction the enforcement of decrees of the common law courts which he considered unconscionable. So acute did the controversy become, culminating in the *Earl of Oxford's Case,*[1] that the king was eventually obliged to intervene. He resolved the dispute decisively in favour of the chancellor and thereafter the jurisdiction of the court of equity, consolidated under Ellesmere's great successor, Francis Bacon, was unchallenged.

So as the era of the Stuarts was succeeded by the commonwealth and the restoration, equity was established on a sure footing in England. It is now time to retrace our footsteps and examine its development in the neighbouring island.

1 (1615) 1 Rep Ch 1. See Baker, 'The Common Lawyers and the Chancery', 4 Ir Jur (ns) 368.

The early history of equity in Ireland

2.09 It must be a long time since any educated person entertained the naive belief that Ireland was conquered by the Normans in the twelfth century and that the law of England was in force throughout the length and breadth of the country from that time onwards.[1] The reality was, of course, much different. The Norman adventurers who invaded Ireland in 1169 acknowledged Henry II as their feudal lord after a short lived attempt at independence reflected in Strongbow's assumption of the title of 'King of Leinster'. Henry subsequently gave the lordship of Ireland to his son John but, while the lordship was ultimately resumed by the English kings, it held sway until the age of the Tudors in part of the island only, most notably in Leinster and some of the coastal towns. Even within those areas, powerful 'liberties' were enjoyed by some of the local magnates, whether they were Norman barons or ecclesiastics. The area of the lordship contracted and expanded with the fluctuating fortunes of the two civilisations on the island, the Gaelic and the Anglo-Norman. They differed in race, language, societal organisation and not least in their systems of law. Between the areas where these contrasting cultures were dominant were the 'marches' where conflicts were at their most acute.

The law which prevailed in the Irish areas was the brehon law, which virtually disappeared from our law in the seventeenth century. This was a relatively advanced system of law, with its own written texts and commentaries on which modern scholarship, after some false starts in the last century, is throwing increased light.[2] It was, of course, the product of a less centralised society than feudal England and there are, moreover, sharp contrasts between some of its basic concepts and those of the common law. Primogeniture, for example, found no place in it: instead, it recognised the institution of tanistry whereby land descended to the eldest and worthiest male of the deceased's name and blood.

1 Although Fitzgibbon J felt obliged to refute it in detail in *Moore v A-G* [1934] IR 44.
2 Above all in the *Corpus Iuris Hibernici*, Vols I-VI, edited by Professor D A Binchy.

2.10 In the earliest period of the lordship of Ireland—during the time of John, in fact—we find the first vestigial traces of English law in Ireland in the form of some long extinct writs which he authorised to be issued in 1216.[1] The governor of the lordship was originally called the 'justiciar' and he was charged with ensuring that the laws and customs of England were obeyed throughout the lordship. To that end, itinerant justices travelled through the area of the lordship and in 1248 there is the first unambiguous reference to a sedentary bench at Dublin.[2] Thus the lordship acquired its own common bench or court of common pleas equivalent to that at Westminster.

These early courts were, however, administering English law in the lordship against a troubled background. The difficulties experienced by litigants in contemporary England were compounded in Ireland by the comparatively more lawless conditions which prevailed in what was then a remote province of the English crown. And the suitor who found himself frustrated in his attempts to seek justice in the court of common pleas, or the court of king's bench which emerged at a later stage, could not look to the chancery with the same confidence as his English counterpart.

There was, it is true, an Irish chancellor, the office dating from the institution of a separate royal seal for Ireland in 1232 and the first holder of the Irish great seal being Ralf Neville, the Bishop of Chichester.[3] (He was represented in Dublin by one Robert Luterel who on Neville's death in 1244 was recognised as the Irish chancellor.[4]) Thereafter until the sixteenth century the chancellors were frequently churchmen, as in England, and were also indeed usually Englishmen; but there the resemblance ended. Unlike the English chancery, the Irish chancery was poorly staffed: the Chancellor was assisted by a Keeper of the Rolls,[5] an office which was later to evolve into that of Master of the Rolls, but the chancery did not attract ambitious Englishmen and it suffered from the general neglect by the English kings of this distant part of their realm. It is not until the sixteenth century that the chancery takes on a role equivalent to that of the English chancery. In the medieval period, a significantly greater role in the administration of 'equity' is played by the court of the Exchequer, an institution which unlike the chancery was nurtured with some care by the crown.[6]

It was to parliament, however, that litigants seeking redress which the common law courts were not affording them most frequently turned in medieval Ireland. We must not, of course, think of that parliament in its early form as an especially representative, let alone democratic, assembly. In its earliest manifestations, indeed, it was more in the nature of an emanation of the king's council.[7] But by the fifteenth century, it had taken on a form more familiar to us with what were effectively three 'estates' consisting of peers, commons and lower clergy.[8] Petitions, which in England were addressed to the Chancellor, in Ireland were presented to these parliaments, and as in England they sought relief on many fronts.[9] Their theme, moreover, like that of the English petitions or bills, tends to be conscience: what has been done to the oppressed petitioner is 'against law and conscience', 'without conscience or reason', or 'without right, just title, conscience and law.'[10] The complaints of the petitioners reflect vividly the extent to which the common law courts had deteriorated. Within the pale itself, at Kildare, it is said

> 'the true liege people in these parts dare not appear in the king's courts in Ireland, nor any other of the true liege people there.......for dread to be slain, taken or spoiled of goods.'[11]

At this early stage of the development of English law in Ireland, it is not merely confined in its effective operation to the area of lordship: it is not universally available even within those boundaries, although the extent to which it was available to the native Irish has been the subject of much scholarly debate.[12] What is not in doubt is the disinclination of the English kings to allow English law in the lordship to go its own way: the judges who administered it were frequently Englishmen and it was not uncommon for causes in Irish courts to be removed to the court of King's Bench at Westminister by a writ of 'error'.

1 Hand, op cit, p 1.
2 Hand, op cit, p 7.
3 Richardson and Sayles, *The Administration of Ireland 1172/1377*, p 15.
4 Ibid, p 15.
5 Ibid, pp 17-18.
6 Hand, op cit, p 101.
7 Richardson and Sayles, *The Irish Parliament in the Middle Ages*, p 8.
8 Ibid, p 145.
9 Ibid, p 215.
10 Ibid, pp 215-216.
11 Ibid, p 175.
12 Hand, op cit, Chapter 10.

2.11 In the latter half of the fifteenth century, parliament continued to play a prominent part in the granting of equitable relief. But with the passing of Poynings' Law in 1494, its activities in this area were significantly reduced, the judicial work which it had formerly undertaken being carried out now by the King's Council and the developing court of chancery.[1] The judicial development of the latter is said by one historian to date from the appointment in 1494 of Bishop Deane of Bangor as chancellor.[2] With the appointment of Masters in Chancery and of leading clerics to the post of Keeper of the Rolls, its administrative shortcomings were to some extent remedied. The court heard a wide variety of cases: it enforced trusts and generally sought to supplement rather than supplant the common law. It was also prepared to enforce Gaelic customs, but not where the result was considered inequitable.[3] The position of chancellor was still held from time to time by ecclesiastics—such as the commanding figure of Archbishop Loftus in Tudor times and his nephew of the same name under the Stuarts—but from the sixteenth century it was increasingly common for the chancellor to be a lawyer.

More significant changes were under way in Ireland. After the ill starred experiment of 'surrender and regrant' under which the Gaelic chiefs were confirmed in the ownership of their lands in return for acknowledging that they held them from the crown, the Tudor monarchy embarked on its policy of bringing the entire island under its control by military force. Ulster was to prove the last redoubt of the old Gaelic world which collapsed with the flight of the earls, O'Neill and O'Donnell, in 1603. The brehon laws were replaced by English law, a process seen at work in the cases recorded by Sir John Davies, who was successively solicitor-general and attorney-general in Ireland from 1603 to 1619.[4] Most notably in the *Case of Tanistry*,[5] we find the court of King's Bench holding that the Gaelic custom was contrary to English law.

Thus in the seventeenth century, English law was extended to the whole island and from that time onwards, the history of equity in Ireland is essentially the history of the application of the developing English law of equity to the neighbouring island.

1 Ellis, *Tudor Ireland*, p 163.
2 Ellis, *Reform and Revival*, p 161. His patent of appointment specifically empowered him to determine 'plaints' moved in chancery.
3 Ellis, *Tudor Ireland*, p 164.
4 Davies' *Reports; A discovery of the true causes why Ireland was not entirely subdued*. Cf Pawlisch op cit.
5 Davies' *Reports*, p 78.

The development of the modern law of equity

2.12 It was during the chancellorship of Lord Nottingham (1673 - 1682) that the law administered in the court of chancery in England, and which was to be applied by the Irish court of chancery, began to take on the form of a body of fixed doctrines and principles, so much so that he is usually referred to as 'the father of modern equity.' Before his time, the chancellor's reliance on 'conscience' meant that cases in his court tended to be decided by reference to what the justice of the case seemed to require rather than any fixed principles. That justice reflected on occasions the religious aura of the office, as witness this outburst by Archbishop Morton:

'Every law should be in accordance with the law of God; and the law of God is that an executor who fraudulently misapplies the goods and does not make restitution will be damned in hell and to remedy this is to accord with conscience as I understand it.'[1]

The chancellor's dispensing of what lawyers came to call 'palm tree justice' prompted Selden's notorious jibe:

'Equity is a roguish thing: for Law, we have a measure, know what to trust to; Equity is according to the conscience of him that is Chancellor, and as that is larger or narrower, so is Equity. 'Tis all one as if they should make the standard for the measure we call the Foot, the Chancellor's foot: what an uncertain measure would be this. One Chancellor has a long foot, another a short foot, a third an indifferent foot: 'tis the same thing in the Chancellor's Conscience.'[2]

So the doctrine of precedent—under which general principles are extracted from particular cases and applied to resolve similar cases thereafter—was rarely used in the chancery before Nottingham's time: as late as 1670, Vaughan CJ was expressing surprise that precedents should be cited in a court of equity.[3] Nottingham, however, made it clear that he considered some of his decisions as being of general application. While his was a court of conscience, it was conscience as embodied in legal principles rather than any particular religious code, still less in the private conscience of the chancellor as it responded to individual cases.

Nottingham's stress on defining legal principles was of particular significance in the developing law of trusts. In *Cook v Fountain*,[4] we find the first systematic classification of different types of trusts: the distinction is drawn between *express trusts*, which are created by agreement between the parties or the unilateral declaration of the settlor and those trusts which are the result of the operation of the law and are usually divided into *resulting* and *constructive trusts*. A resulting trust is said to arise, for example, when property is conveyed to A but the purchase money is advanced by B: A is said to hold the property on a 'resulting' trust for B.[5] In his time, too, the *presumption of advancement* makes its first appearance in rebuttal of the presumption of a resulting trust: where B is A's father, it is presumed that he intended to make a gift of the property to his son.[6]

The significant part played by equity in the development of the mortgage—the borrowing of money on the security of land—is also evident in this period. Equity recognises the mortgagor's continuing interest in the land—the 'equity of redemption'—and treats it as an estate which can be transmitted to others. It insists, moreover, that the mortgagor cannot be fettered in his equitable right to redeem the mortgage on payment of the principal and interest, enshrined in the rule that 'there cannot be a clog upon the equity of redemption.'[7]

Equity's aversion to fraud takes even deeper root in this period. The principle appears in the law that a statute may not be used as an instrument as fraud: hence the Statute of Frauds (which requires certain agreements to be evidenced by writing before they can be enforced) will not be permitted in the chancery courts to be itself used as an engine of fraud. The doctrine of *part performance* thus makes its appearance for the first time in 1685, allowing a contract within the statute to be enforced despite the absence of writing where the plaintiff has done acts in performance of the contract which renders it inequitable for the purchaser to resist performance.[8] We can also see the beginnings of the doctrine of *undue influence*[9] in equity's attitude to 'catching bargains' with expectant heirs, i e transactions in which young men were persuaded to sell their future interest in their father's property at an undervalue. And the court of chancery's capacity to soften the sterner features of the common law is reflected in the evolution of such rules that *merger* of estates (the destruction of a lower estate, such as a leasehold, when its owner also becomes owner of freehold) will not take place where the result would be to destroy rights contrary to the intention of the parties;[10] or that the appointment of a debtor as an executor, which at common law released the debt,[11] will not do so in equity unless the creditor had forgiven the debt during his lifetime.

Equity also developed during this period a jurisdiction which was to give it a *protective* role in the legal system. In a time when married women could not dispose of their own property, the chancellor evolved rules designed to protect them. Similarly, infants—those under the age of twenty-one—became his special care after the Court of Wards ceased to exist. (The Irish court of wards lasted into the reign of James I.[12]) People of unsound mind were also under his protection, as were charities. In all this, the Lord Chancellor, and his Irish equivalent, were said to be acting on behalf of the king in his role as *parens patriae,* 'father of his country.'

In its fully developed condition, the court of chancery has a wide *administrative* jurisdiction and it is in this period that it begins to emerge. The granting of probate of wills and letters of administration of the estates of intestates was still the prerogative of the ecclesiastical courts and remained so, in theory at least, until 1857. The common law courts originally had an exclusive jurisdiction construing devises of realty and they also formulated rules as to the priority in which debts were to be paid out of the estate of the deceased. But equity, as ever supplementing rather than supplanting the common law, intervened when it was clear that the law was producing harsh results.[13] Thus, for example, it evolved the doctrine of *marshalling* under which where one creditor had two funds to resort to and simply availed of one, a second creditor with only one fund to resort to could attack the unexhausted fund. Equity also came to exercise a concurrent jurisdiction with the common law courts in construing devises of realty and—deriving from the ecclesiastical courts—personalty.[14] So too in cases of disputes between *partners* chancery had a special role to play, particularly as its machinery for taking accounts between the parties was more sophisticated than that of the common law.[15]

1 Lord Nottingham's Chancery Cases, ed Yale, Vol 1 p 39.
2 Selden, *Table Talk*, Equity, II.
3 Holdsworth, op cit, Vol VI p 669.
4 (1676) 3 Swan 585.
5 See Chapter 12, infra.
6 See Chapter 12, infra.
7 Holdsworth, op cit, Vol VI pp 663-665.
8 See Chapter 16, infra.

9 See Chapter 29, infra.
10 Holdsworth, op cit, Vol VI p 662.
11 Because he cannot sue himself.
12 H.F. Kearney, *The court of wards and liveries in Ireland 1622-1641*, R.I.A. proc., section C.LVII 29.
13 Holdsworth, op cit, Vol VI pp 652-657.
14 Ibid, pp 652-657.
15 Ibid, p 636.

2.13 By the close of the seventeenth century, then, equity was emerging as a systematised corpus of law. It was also apparent that it exercised a threefold jurisdiction. First, there was the *exclusive jurisdiction* where equity alone could make valid decrees, as in the enforcement of trusts. Second, there was the *concurrent jurisdiction* were both equity and the common law could make decrees, as in the case of contracts where equity could grant specific performance and the common law damages. Third, there was the *auxiliary jurisdiction*, where equity helped to ensure that common law rights were enforced, most notably in the granting of injunctions prohibiting interference with such rights.

The conflicts between the common law judges and the chancellor which had marked the era of Coke and Ellesmere now belonged to the past. It was indeed a feature of the formative period of equity in England that the great chancellors who dominated it were thoroughly versed in the common law, some of them having occupied the highest common law judgeships before becoming chancellor. (Ireland seems to have been less fortunate in this respect: Nottingham's contemporary, Archbishop Boyle of Armagh, the last ecclesiastic to occupy the Irish woolsack, had no legal training: nor had his successor, John Methuen.) Not surprisingly, they repeatedly insisted that the principles of the common law could not be overturned by courts of equity: 'equity follows the law' was one of the most important of the maxims of equity. But they also made full use of the more flexible nature of the equitable jurisdiction to provide remedies for injustice where the common law was deficient.

2.14 This process continued throughout the eighteenth century under the guidance of a succession of notable English chancellors of whom the most celebrated was Lord Hardwicke. His lengthy tenure of the woolsack saw the further systemisation of the corpus of equity. The doctrine of *notice* is now firmly established: equity recognises the special position of a person who purchases land without notice of any prior equitable rights. Where such a person acquires the legal ownership of the land, equity will permit his claim to take precedence over prior equitable claims of which he has no notice.[1] Here too we see the development of equity's emphasis on the importance of giving value: the purchaser of land for value is generally in a stronger position than he who receives it as a gift or in the language of the law is a *volunteer*. And side by side with this principle, Hardwicke develops an important corollary: that marriage is itself a consideration and that the parties to the marriage and their children are not volunteers.[2]

It was a central feature of the development of equity, as we have seen, that the jurisdiction of the chancellor was exercised *in personam*: the defendant was compelled by the court's decree to recognise the requirements of conscience. The striking consequences were illustrated in *Penn v Lord Baltimore*[3] in which Hardwicke decreed specific performance of an agreement determining the boundaries of the then American colonies of Maryland and Pennsylvannia. Where the common law could only award damages, equity was able to grant a decree affecting the title to land because it could punish the parties for failing to comply with its orders, and this even though the land was outside its jurisdiction. Equity acted *in personam* rather than *in rem*.

Hardwicke, moreover, repeatedly laid emphasis, as did the other chancellors in the eighteenth century, on the feature of equity which made it so uniquely flexible an instrument for securing justice, the fact that so much of the jurisdiction was *discretionary*. So while the court could ensure that a person did what he agreed to do by a decree of specific performance, it was by no means the case that it would do so in every case where there was an enforceable contract. It might refrain from doing so if this would be unduly harsh or because the plaintiff's own conduct had been in some sense inequitable.

In terms of remedies, however, it was probably in the granting of injunctions that equity was at its most effective. The land owner no longer had to bring an endless series of actions for damages to stop trespass or nuisance: he could obtain an order from the court restraining the offender and have him committed to prison or his assets sequestrated if the order was disobeyed.

During this period also the principles upon which equity would act in the exercise of its flexible and discretionary jurisdiction became embodied in what are sometimes called the *maxims of equity*. One of the earliest works which can lay claim to being a textbook of the law of equity was in fact a collection of such maxims by Richard Francis.

During the late seventeenth century the concept of the equitable estate as a separate interest in property capable of being alienated, transmitted to successors or mortgaged was firmly established. Hardwicke and his successors further refined the principles governing such estates and this, together with the increasing role played by equity in the law of mortgages, meant that land law became the province of the chancery rather than the common lawyers.

The eighteenth century also saw the development of other equitable doctrines some of which continue to be of significance while others have virtually ceased to be of much practical relevance. Still of some importance are the doctrines of *satisfaction* [4] and *ademption*:[5] a debtor who grants a benefit by his will to his creditor is presumed under certain conditions to have intended to satisfy the debt and a testator is also presumed not to have intended to benefit the same person twice over. So too is the doctrine of *election*[6] which compels a person to choose between particular benefits. Of less relevance to-day is the doctrine of *conversion* and *reconversion*[7] which derives much of its significance from the difference in the rules for the devolution on death of real and personal estates, rules which were abolished in Ireland by the Succession Act 1965. Of no relevance at all is the once celebrated 'restraint on anticipation' invented by one of Lord Hardwicke's most highly regarded successors, Lord Thurlow, to protect the wife, whose proprietorial rights were then solely the creation of equity, from handing over her future rights to property at her husband's behest.[8]

1 See para, 5.07, infra.
2 See para 8.04, infra.
3 (1750) I Ves Sen 444.
4 See Chapter 26, infra.
5 Ibid.
6 See Chapter 25, infra.
7 See Chapter 24, infra.
8 It was finally abolished in Ireland by the Married Women's Status Act 1957.

2.15 But although the eighteenth century was an era of major constructive innovation in the substantive law of equity, the same cannot be said of the procedures of the court of chancery during this period. As the law itself developed, so did the complexity of the proceedings and the possibilities of delays were multiplied.

In the second half of the century, moreover, a radical assault on equity's very foundations is mounted. Lord Mansfield, the great chief justice who presided over the common law courts from 1756 to 1788, was unwilling to accept that the principles of equity could not be applied in those courts and a similiar view was taken by Blackstone whose *Commentaries* were published in 1765. In a sense, their views anticipated the changes which were to be embodied in the Judicature Acts a century later.[1] But the equity judges firmly refused to countenance the suggestion of Mansfield and Blackstone that there was in essence no distinction between law and equity and the common law judges after Mansfield's time acknowledged that in this they were right. The differences between the two systems were still too great to permit of any easy merger: in the common law courts, the parties were still unable to give evidence themselves, for example, and those courts were still rigidly confined within the limits of the different forms of action.

1 See para 2.19, infra.

2.16 The third of the great Lord Chancellors who dominated the formative period of the English law of equity is Lord Eldon, with whom we reach the nineteenth century. He is generally credited with having worked out in detail the scope and application of the principles which Hardwicke had settled and of which Nottingham was the father. He played a leading part in the resistance to Lord Mansfield's advocacy of a fused system of law and equity, and made conspicuous contributions to the development of the law of trusts, including charitable trusts, and of the administration of the assets of deceased persons. He also enlarged the scope of the major equitable remedies, such as specific performance and injunctions.

Lord Eldon, however, also plays a less glorious part in the history of the law. His opposition to reform in virtually every sphere led Bagehot to say of him that 'he believed in everything which it is impossible to believe in— the danger of parliamentary reform, the danger of Catholic emancipation, the danger of altering the Court of Chancery......'[1] The ponderous manner in which he conducted his own court and the appalling delays which resulted, helped to bring the system of equity, which had arisen in the first place to remedy injustice, into disrepute as a frequent source of injustice.

1 Literary Studies, pp 6-7.

2.17 Because of the scarcity of law reports, it is not possible to trace in detail the application of the English law of equity in Ireland in this period. Such reports as we have are on the whole concerned with appeals from the Irish courts to the English House of Lords.[1] The very existence of that right of appeal indicates perhaps a uniformity of approach in the two jurisdictions: but it should be recorded in passing that the assertion by the English House of Lords of such an appellate jurisdiction met with vigorous opposition from the Irish House of Lords which, of course, remained in existence until the Act of Union in 1800. The English house in the *Bishop of Derry's Case*[2] in 1698 reversed an Irish chancery decision, but it was an appeal from the equity side of the Irish Exchequer which precipitated the final confrontation. In *Annesley v Sherlock*,[3] the Irish house went to the lengths of committing the Barons of the Exchequer for contempt in refusing to follow their rulings. But the Westminster parliament now intervened and passed the Act known as 'The Sixth of George the First' which prevented the Irish House of Lords from hearing such appeals: they now lay only to the English house. Grattan's parliament in the years 1782 and 1783 reasserted the exclusive appellate jurisdiction of the Irish house, but with the Act of Union that house passed into history.

It is also evident that the administration of the Irish equity jurisdiction was disfigured by the delays and inefficiencies which characterised the English system. Indeed, in one respect, matters were worse: from an early stage in England, the Lord Chancellor was freed of the burden of deciding all the cases in chancery by the establishment of the judicial office of Master of the Rolls. In Ireland, however, although such a position existed, its occupant did not discharge any judicial functions until 1801.

1 Such as Brown's Parliamentary Reports. See also: G.J. Hand: 'Rules and Orders to be observed in the proceedings of causes in the High Court of Chancery in Ireland, 1659,' 9 Ir Jur (ns) 110.
2 Newark, *Elegantia Juris*, p 215.
3 Ibid. Cf O'Flanagan, *Lives of the Lord Chancellors of Ireland*, Vol 2, Chapter 37.

The nineteenth century: decay and reform

2.18 By the end of Lord Eldon's tenure of the woolsack, the central features of the law of equity as we know them to-day were firmly in place. But so too were the elements in the system which were to bring it—and the law in general—into disrepute. By one of the stranger ironies in legal history, the very jurisprudence which owed its origin in part at least to the desire of litigants to escape from the technical fetters of the common law had itself become enmeshed in procedural complexities. The defects which had begun to emerge in Hardwicke's time were now a scandal. There were a number of reasons for this: the cumbersome and prolix method of pleading, and the fact that all the evidence was presented on affidavit were partly to blame.[1] So too was the fact that equity frequently resorted to the taking of accounts and the holding of inquiries as a method of resolving disputes, to which may be added the fact that the court officials were recruited in both England and Ireland by a system in which nepotism and patronage counted more than merit.[2] To be fair, many of equity's defects sprang from its anxiety to do complete justice between the parties, but in the nineteenth century the remedy showed signs of being as bad as the disease. Charles Dickens, drawing on his experiences as a young court reporter, has left us an unforgettable picture of the once great system in decline in *Bleak House*:

> 'This is the Court of Chancery: which has its decaying houses and its blighted lands in every shire: which has its worn out lunatic in every madhouse, and its dead in every churchyard: which has its ruined suitor with his slipshod heels and threadbare dress, borrowing and begging through the round of every man's acquaintance; which gives to monied might the means abundantly of wearing out the right; which so exhausts the finances, patience, courage, hope; so overthrows the brains and breaks the heart; that there is not an honourable man amongst its practitioners who would not give—who does not often give—the warning, "suffer any wrong that can be done you, rather than come here!"

But the early nineteenth century was also the age of reform. Under the influence of Jeremy Bentham and Lord Brougham, one of Lord Eldon's most controversial successors, the terrible blemishes of which Dickens wrote were at last being tackled. The abuses were not, of course, confined to the chancery court: the common law also laboured under archaic procedures. Some of these were tackled in a series of measures such as the Common Law Procedure Acts. The old forms of action were at last swept away and the parties to actions were made competent and compellable witnesses. One of the curses of the system—the absurdity of denying a suitor relief simply because he happened to be in one court rather than another—was recognised and to some extent alleviated by the Chancery Amendment Act 1858. Usually referred to as 'Lord Cairns' Act', after the great Irish lawyer who as lord chancellor[3] introduced it, this enabled the court of chancery for the first time to award damages where the plaintiff had claimed an injunction. The administrative shortcomings of the Irish jurisdiction were remedied to some extent by the elevation of the office of Master of the Rolls to a judgeship in 1801, the creation of a Court of Appeal in Chancery in 1856 and the establishment of the additional office of Vice-Chancellor in 1867.

1 Radcliffe and Cross, op cit pp 144-148.
2 Ibid, pp 153-154.
3 Hugh McCalmont Cairns, a graduate of Dublin University and the only Irishman to become Lord Chancellor of England.

2.19 This major reforming programme was crowned by the enactment of the Judicature Acts in 1873 and 1875, followed by their Irish counterpart in 1877.[1] The major provision of the new legislation was the abolition in both jurisdictions of the separate courts of common law and equity. Henceforth there was to be one Supreme Court only, consisting of a High Court and a Court of Appeal, and the principles of law and equity were to be applied in every case. Where there was any conflict, the rule in equity was to prevail.[2] Although the effect of the legislation in both jurisdictions was to establish one Supreme Court administering legal or equitable principles or both, depending on the nature of the case, it also provided for separate divisions in the new court. Thus in Ireland the High Court consisted of five divisions: chancery, queen's bench, common pleas, exchequer, and probate and matrimonial. As a result of further legislation, there were only two divisions by the end of the century, queen's bench and chancery. The great distinction introduced by the new system was that in each division the rules of both equity and the common law were to be applied whenever they were relevant to the particular case.

It should also be noted that during the nineteenth century a limited equity jurisdiction was enjoyed in Ireland by the local courts called 'civil bill courts'. This jurisdiction was redefined by the County Officers and Court (Ireland) Act, passed in the same year as the Irish Judicature Act, and was the forerunner of the equitable jurisdiction exercised to-day by the Circuit Court.

1 Judicature (Ireland) Act 1877.
2 Ibid, s 28 (11).

2.20 The view sometimes expressed that the Judicature Act effected a fusion of law and equity was generally regarded as erroneous until recent times. The Attorney-General who piloted the English Act through the House of Commons was emphatic in rejecting any suggestion that it was intended to effect such a fusion:

'If an Act were passed doing no more than fuse law and equity it would take twenty years of decisions and hecatombs of suitors to make out what parliament meant and had not taken the trouble to define. It was philosophical to admit the innate distinction between Law and Equity which you could not get rid of by Act of Parliament and to say, not that the distinction should not exist, but that the Courts should administer relief according to legal principles when these applied or else according to equitable principles. That was what the Bill proposed with the addition that, whenever the principles of Law and Equity conflicted, equitable principles should prevail.[1]

The textbook which was regarded for many years as the leading work on the subject, *Ashburner on Equity*, took the same view saying:

'the two streams of jurisdiction, though they run in the same channel, run side by side and do not mingle their waters.'[2]

Yet in 1977 the House of Lords unanimously concluded that the legislation had done precisely what its leading architects said was not its intention, namely effected a fusion of law and equity. In *United Scientific Holdings Ltd v Burnley Borough Council*,[3] Lord Diplock condemned the metaphor in *Ashburner* as 'mischievous' and 'deceptive'[4] and claimed, with the apparent concurrence of his brethren, that the systems had in truth been fused in 1875 and that the waters had long since mingled. His views, however, have provoked a storm of criticism and we shall return to the topic at the end of this chapter.

1 Hansard, second series, vol 216, 644-645.
2 2nd edn, p14.
3 [1978] AC 904, HL.
4 At pp 924-925.

Equity in Ireland since independence

2.21 Following the Anglo-Irish Treaty of 1921 and the enactment of the Constitution of the Irish Free State, a new system of courts was established under the Courts of Justice Acts 1924 providing for a High Court and a final court of appeal called the Supreme Court. In addition there were established new courts with local and limited jurisdiction, i e the Circuit Court and the District Court. Unlike its predecessor, the new High Court had no separate divisions. But it enjoyed broadly the same chancery jurisdiction as the High Court under the old regime.[1] Similarly, the circuit courts enjoyed a limited equitable jurisdiction corresponding to that of the county courts.[2] The jurisdiction of the Lord Chancellor over infants and persons of unsound mind was vested in the Chief Justice[3] and later transferred to the President of the High Court.[4]

The Constitution provided that to the extent that they were not inconsistent with the Constitution, the laws in force in the Irish Free State immediately prior to its enactment were to continue in force until they were either repealed or amended by the Oireachtas.[5] It was generally accepted by the judges of the new courts that the effect was to preserve in our law, not merely the statutes applicable to Ireland passed by the imperial parliament at Westminister, but also the corpus of common law and equity which had been administered in the Irish courts before the Constitution took effect, to the extent that it was consistent with the Constitution. When the present Constitution was enacted in 1937, it contained an article[6] which seemed designed to have the same effect, i e:

'Subject to this Constitution and to the extent to which they are not inconsistent therewith, the laws in force in Saorstat Eireann immediately prior to the coming into force of this Constitution shall continue to be of full force and effect until the same or any of them shall have been repealed or amended by the Oireachtas.'

In the same way, this Article was treated by the courts as having carried forward into post-1937 law the common law and equity system administered in the Irish Free State.[7] There has been some judicial support for the view that the article did no more than carry forward pre-1937 *legislation*,[8] but whatever may be the theoretical justification for that approach, in practice the courts established under the present Constitution have treated the corpus of the common law and equity as having been continued in existence. It might be said indeed that, even were the article to be interpreted otherwise, the Oireachtas by the terms in which it established the courts under both Constitutions and defined their respective jurisdictions adopted by implication as the substantive case law of the state the corpus of common law and equity in existence under the previous dispensation.[9]

1 Courts of Justice Acts 1924, s 17.
2 Ibid, s 48.
3 Ibid, s 19(1).
4 Courts of Justice Act 1936, s 9.
5 Article 73.
6 Article 50.
7 *Boylan v Dublin Corporation* [1949] IR 60, 77 per Black J SC; *Minister for Finance v O'Brien* [1949] IR 91, 116 per Murnaghan J SC.
8 *Gaffney v Gaffney* [1975] IR 133, 151 per Walsh J, SC. The learned judge took the view that the expression 'laws' in Article 50 and Article 73 could only refer to statute law, since any other interpretation would mean that the judge made law was petrified in 1921 and could not be developed by the courts. Professor J M Kelly has pointed out, however, that the carrying forward into post-1921 law of the existing corpus of law might reasonably be regarded as having brought with it the judicial capacity to develop the law which was an essential feature of that law *(The Irish Constitution*, 2nd edn, pp 712-713).
9 See, for example, Courts (Supplemental Provisions) Act 1961, Sch 3, Refs 1 and 6.

2.22 It must also be borne in mind, however, that while many aspects of the common law and equity are so deeply entrenched in our law at this stage that it would as a practical matter require legislation to alter them in any radical way, our courts are at liberty to depart from individual decisions of the Irish and English courts before independence whenever they consider that justice so requires. (It is, of course, the case that if they are inconsistent with the Constitution they never formed part of the present law in the first place.) Until 1964, the Supreme Court had taken the view that it was bound, not merely by its own decisions and those of the Supreme Court of the Irish Free State but also by decisions of the House of Lords prior to the treaty. In that year, however, in *Attorney-General v Ryan's Car Hire Ltd*[1] the court held that it was no longer the law that it was bound by its own decisions. The judgement of Kingsmill-Moore J suggests, as one would expect, that the same principle applied *a fortiori* to decisions of the Supreme Court of the Irish Free State and of the House of Lords prior to 1921, and this has recently been confirmed by McCarthy J (admittedly speaking *obiter*) in *Irish Shell Ltd v Elm Motors Ltd*.[2] But it has also been indicated that the freedom from the rigid application of *stare decisis* will be sparingly exercised.

The High Court, like the Supreme Court, exercises a similar freedom in relation to pre-1921 decisions, though it is of course bound by decisions of the Supreme Court and (it is thought)[3] decisions of the Supreme Court of the Irish Free State, save where the latter are inconsistent with the

Constitution. This indeed was the view taken by Gavan Duffy J even before *Ryan's Car Hire Ltd*, as the following trenchant passage demonstrates:

'In my opinion, judicial decisions in Ireland before the Treaty and English decisions which were followed here are binding upon this court only when they represent a law so well settled or pronounced by so weighty a juristic authority that they may fairly be regarded, in a system built up upon the principle of *stare decisis*, as having become established as part of the law of the land before the Treaty; and to bind they must, of course, not be inconsistent with the Constitution.....In my opinion, this Court cannot be fettered in the exercise of the judicial power by opinions of very different Courts under the old regime, unless those opinions must reasonably be considered to have had the force of law in Ireland so that they formed part of the code of law expressly retained....If before the Treaty a particular law was administered in a way so repugnant to the common sense of our citizens as to make the law look ridiculous, it is not in the public interest that we should repeat the mistake. The High Court must mould its own *cursus curiae*; in so doing I hold that it is free, indeed bound, to decline to treat any such absurdity in the machinery of administration as having been imposed on it as part of the law of the land; nothing is law here which is inconsistent with derivation from the People.'[4]

1 [1965] IR 642.
2 [1984] IR 200.
3 The point, however, has never been expressly decided.
4 *Exham v Beamish* [1939] IR 336, 348–349.

2.23 In practice, there have not been many occasions on which the Irish Courts since independence have departed from the settled principles of equity. Notable examples of when they have been prepared to do so are to be found in decisions of Gavan Duffy P and Dixon J in relation to charitable bequests and bequests conditional on the beneficiaries being brought up in specific religions.[1] On the other hand, some doctrines which might have been thought to be obsolete, such as the presumption of advancement as applied between husbands and wives remain,[2] although it is in some instances doubtful whether they would survive a challenge based on their possible inconsistency with the constitution.

The law of equity itself has been generally regarded in England as having reached the stage where it can be seen as a settled body of doctrines and principles which the courts should not seek to alter in any radical manner.[3] This view has been challenged by some and there have undoubtedly been areas, such as the doctrines of the *constructive trust*[4] and *promissory estoppel*,[5] where there have been significant changes in the law which to some extent have been accepted by the Irish courts. But in general it may be said that, given the greater readiness of the legislature to undertake changes in the law to-day and the existence of a statutory Law Reform Commission charged with the duty of examining the law in detail and proposing necessary alterations, the Irish courts will maintain their reluctance to indulge in any radical tampering with the existing corpus of equity law.

1 *Re Maguire* [1943] IR 238 and *Re Sheridan* [1957] IR 257 (gifts to religious orders), *Burke v Burke* [1951] IR 216 and *Re Blake* [1955] IR 89 (conditional gifts) and see para 11.16 and para 14.08, below.
2 *RF v MF* (unreported; judgement delivered October 1985).
3 Cf Pettit, pp 5–6.
4 See chapter 13, infra.
5 See chapter 28, infra.

2.24 On the fundamental question as to whether equity has survived as an independent body of law, there is as yet no authoritative Irish guidance. The opinion of the House of Lords in *United Scientific Holdings Ltd v Burnley Borough Council*[1] that the complete fusion of law and equity for which Mansfield and Blackstone yearned has taken place since the Judicature Act has attracted severe criticism.[2] Lord Diplock said that it had ceased to be part of English law just as much as the Statute of Uses and the Statute *Quia Emptores*, apparently overlooking the fact that the latter enactment was still on the English statute book. More crucially, neither his speech nor that of Lord Simon of Glaisdale offered any real illumination as to how the supposed fusion was to operate in practice. Thus, the approach of equity to the granting of relief has always been discretionary: where ? plaintiff seeks equitable remedies such as an injunction or specific performance the court will not grant him the relief automatically but will consider whether the application of such equitable principles as 'he who seeks equity must do equity' would disentitle him to the relief. This has no parallel in the common law system: a person who is negligently injured in a road accident is entitled to damages and the court is not concerned with the conduct of the parties.

While it has been said that the decision of the Supreme Court in *Hynes v Independent Newspapers Ltd*[3] indicates an acceptance that equity and the common law have also been fused in Ireland, it is submitted that this is not necessarily the case. The precise point at issue was admittedly the same as fell to be resolved in *United Scientific Holdings*, namely, as to whether time was of the essence for the taking of certain steps under a contract. It is also the case that O'Higgins CJ applied the decision in *United Scientific Holdings*, as did Kenny J, the former stating that he found the reasons for the English decision 'compelling'. O' Higgins CJ indeed expressly referred to the two systems as having been 'fused'.

But it should also be observed that the opinions expressed by the law lords as to the effect of the Judicature Acts were unnecessary for the decision in question and hence must be regarded as *obiter*. For this reason, it would be rash to assume that *Hynes* represents an unqualified acceptance by the Supreme Court of all that was said in *United Scientific Holdings*.The distinction between the two systems of law rests on solid foundations and remains part of our law until the Oireachtas or the only legal tribunal competent to do so has unequivocally announced its removal from our jurisprudence. Until then the observations of the English law lords are most safely regarded as in the nature of premature funeral orations.

1 [1978] AC 904, HL.
2 See P V Baker, 'The Future Of Equity' (1977) 93 LQR 529: Meagher, Gummow and Lehane, pp 65–66.
3 [1980] IR 204.

2.25 Equity then is a well defined body of doctrines and remedies found largely in the decisions of judges who have moulded its development since it first emerged in the middle ages. Like all human institutions, it is not perfect and some of the defects from which it undoubtedly suffers can be traced to the fact that juries played little part in its evolution, whereas their role in common law cases was central. The verdicts of juries did not have to be supported by reasons, unlike the decisions of the chancery judges. Such decisions became precedents which were occasionally applied in a rigid manner to cases where their application was unjustified. Sometimes the tendency was in the opposite direction and led to refinements and distinctions which swelled the reports and the textbooks in a way which benefited the chancery lawyers but hardly served the ends of justice. But these are defects which it is difficult to avoid in a legal system based on precedent; and equity remains with the common law, to which it has added an essential and enduring dimension, one of the world's great legal institutions.

Justice is the ideal to which all legal systems aspire, but in cases which come before our courts it must be justice according to law, whether it be the law declared by the Constitution itself, or to be found in legislation or the body of common law and equity which also forms part of that law. Individual judges are not free to depart from the law to meet what may seem to be a just result in a particular case. The very nature of the equitable jurisdiction gives a certain allure to the belief that there is some standard of 'fairness', of 'equity' indeed, which renders precedent superfluous. But it is the application of settled principles largely contained in precedent which gives the law of equity the virtues of certainty and consistency. It is as true to-day as in centuries past that hard cases make bad law and that the arbitrary abandonment of principle and precedent to meet what may seem to be the demands of justice in a particular context leads only to uncertainty, inconsistency and, in the end, injustice at a more profound level.

> 'There is another suggestion, which has been often repeated; and that is, that courts of equity are not, and ought not, to be bound by precedents; and that precedents, therefore, are of little or no use there; but that every case is to be decided upon circumstances, according to the arbitration or discretion of the judge, acting according to his notions, *ex aequo et bono*... If, indeed, a court of equity...did possess the unbounded jurisdiction which has been thus generally ascribed to it, of correcting, controlling, moderating, and ever superseding the law, and of enforcing all the rights, as well as the charities, arising from natural law and justice, and of freeing itself from all regard to former rules and precedents, it would be the most gigantic in its sway and the most formidable instrument of arbitrary power that could well be devised. It would literally place the whole rights and property of the community under the arbitrary will of the judge, acting, if you please, *arbitro bono judicis,* and, it may be, *ex aequo et bono,* according to his own notions and conscience, but still acting with a despotic and sovereign authority.'[1]

1 Story, *Equity Jurisprudence*, 3rd edn, pp 12-13.

Chapter 3

The maxims of equity

3.01 A number of aphorisms have been formulated since the emergence of equity as a separate jurisdiction which have come to be known collectively as 'the maxims of equity' or 'the principles of equity'. They do not provide a complete equitable code or anything like it. Some, moreover, are now of historic interest only and those which are still of practical relevance do not necessarily provide a definitive answer in cases where they might seem to be applicable. But their frequent invocation by judges over the centuries makes it clear that they have played an important role in the development of a number of features of the equitable jurisdiction (such as the area of priorities of interests in property). An understanding of them is still essential as a result to those who aspire to a comprehensive knowledge of equity.

The maxims of equity to-day are generally regarded as the following:

  (1) Equity follows the law.
  (2) Equity will not suffer a wrong to be without a remedy.
  (3) Equity acts *in personam.*
  (4) He who seeks equity must do equity.
  (5) He who comes into equity must come with clean hands.
  (6) Delay defeats equity.
  (7) Equality is equity.
  (8) Equity looks to the intent rather than the form.
  (9) Equity looks on that as done which ought to have been done.
 (10) Equity imputes an intention to fulfil an obligation.
 (11) Where the equities are equal, the first in time prevails.
 (12) Where the equities are equal, the law prevails.

Equity follows the law

3.02 It was an essential feature of equity that it did not seek to replace, still less to subvert, the common law: it was a supplement or appendix intended to modify the rigidity of that law. Hence, courts of equity followed the principles of the common law. But equally clearly equity could never have made its unique contribution to jurisprudence if it simply applied legal principles to cases, and the maxim must be understood subject to that important qualification. While equity did not seek to set aside the common law rules as such, it restricted or modified their application where it seemed equitable to do so.

We shall see in this book many examples of the refusal of equity to follow the law slavishly and in every case. But it is also to be observed that, applying the maxim, equity in the development of its own institutions, such as the trust, preferred to proceed by analogy with the common law.

3.03 This is most clearly illustrated in the different approach adopted by the courts of equity to *executed* and *executory* trusts. The former are trusts in which the settlor has specified precisely the limitations on which the property is to be held. As is sometimes said, in such cases the settlor has acted as his own conveyancer. The latter are trusts in which the settlor has indicated his general intentions as to how the property is to be disposed of, but has not spelled out the limitations precisely. In the case of executed trusts, equity followed the law and construed strictly the technical language used by the settlor for the purpose of ascertaining the interests of the beneficiary.[1] In the case of executory trusts, the court endeavoured to discover the actual intention of the settlor in ascertaining those interests.

The distinction is still of importance in Ireland where there has been no equivalent to the 1925 property legislation in England and where, accordingly, it is essential to use the appropriate words of limitation in a conveyance of freehold land in order to ensure that the ownership intended to be transferred is in law transferred. Until the Conveyancing Act 1881, the land had to be conveyed to 'A and his heirs' in order to pass the fee simple. After that Act, the words 'in fee simple' could be used instead of 'and his heirs.'[2] But any other form of words (eg to 'A in fee') would mean no more than a life estate passing.[3] This strict rule of construction was applied by equity to executed trusts.

In the leading Irish case, *Jameson and Another v McGovern*,[4] the intended husband had by a marriage settlement conveyed freehold premises to a trustee. After reserving a life interest to the husband, the settlement provided for a life estate for the intended wife and thereafter the property was to go to the children, if any, of the marriage. If there were no children, the property was to be held in trust for those to whom the husband might appoint it and, in default of appointment, for the survivor of the husband and wife 'absolutely'. There were no children of the marriage and no appointment by the husband, whom the wife survived. When the property was being sold, the purchaser objected to the title on the ground that the wife had a life interest only under the settlement.

This contention was upheld by the Supreme Court, which agreed with a decision to the same effect of the Court of Appeal in England in *Re Bostock's Settlement*.[5] Murnaghan J observed[6] that Lord Hardwicke had sought to construe *all* trusts according to the intention of the parties and to deny any distinction between executed and executory trusts,[7] but he considered that the distinction was too well established to be disregarded. He cited this comment by Lord Eldon, speaking of executed trusts:

'But these are cases where the testator has clearly decided what the trust is to be; and as equity follows the law, where the testator has left nothing to be done, but has himself expressed it, there the effect must be the same, whether the estate is legal or equitable.'[8]

Although there were a number of Irish cases in which it had been held that the rule of strict construction of technical words of limitation did not apply to the equitable interest where the result would be contrary to the intention of the settlor as inferred from the whole trust instrument,[9] the Supreme Court preferred to adopt the more traditional approach adopted in *Re Bostock's Settlement*. But they were also prepared to hold in the particular case that the wife had an equity independent of the settlement: since the husband had agreed in consideration of the marriage to settle the lands upon his wife absolutely if she survived him, this was sufficient to give her the equitable fee simple in the events that had happened. This approach was also adopted by Costello J in *Savage v Nolan*,[10] where the facts were broadly similar, save that it was the children of the marriage who were entitled to the equitable fee simple independently of the settlement. The learned judge held that, as persons within the marriage consideration, they were in the same position as the wife had been in *Jameson and Another v McGovern*.[11]

If technical words of limitation are not used, the rule in *Re Bostock's Settlement* and *Jameson v McGovern* will not apply. The difficulty is in deciding what are technical words in this context. In *Re Beer's Estate*[12] and *Re Arden*,[13] the Northern Ireland Court of Appeal and Clauson J respectively held that the words used were not technical and that effect could be given to the intention of the settlor. But in the latter case the words used were to 'A and B in [certain] shares absolutely' and the decision is thus irreconcilable with *Jameson and Another v McGovern* where the words were 'for the survivor of them......absolutely'.

1 *Re Bostock's Settlement* [1921] 2 Ch 469,CA; *Jameson v McGovern* [1934] IR 758, SC.
2 Conveyancing Act 1881, s 51.
3 *Re Ethel and Mitchell's and Butler's Contract* [1901] 1 Ch 945; cf *Re Ottley's Estate,* [1910] 1 IR 1.
4 See above.
5 See above.
6 At 773.
7 *Bagshaw v Spencer* (1748) 1 Ves Sen 142.
8 *Jervoise v Duke of Northumberland* [1820] 1 Jac & W 559.
9 These cases *Re Houston, Rodgers v Houston* [1909] 1 IR 319; *Re Stinson's Estate* [1910] 1 IR 47, *Re Cross's Trusts* [1915] 1 IR 304 and *In Re Murphy and Griffin's Contract* [1919] 1 IR 187 followed an English decision of *In Re Tringham's Trusts* [1904] 2 Ch 487 which was overruled by *Re Bostock's Settlement*. An earlier Irish decision of *Meyler v Meyler* (1884) 11 LR Ir 522 was to the same effect as *Re Bostock's Settlement* and *Jameson v McGovern*.
10 Unreported; judgement delivered 20 July 1978; Wylie, *Casebook on Land Law* p 122.
11 See para 8.09, below.
12 [1925] NI 191, CA.
13 [1935] Ch 326.

3.04 It was clearly the intention of the settlors in *Jameson and Another v McGovern* and *Savage v Nolan* that the wife in the former and the children in the latter case should take absolutely in the events which happened. In each case, the court was able to arrive at what would seem a just result by finding an independent equity on which the wife and children could rely. It must remain uncertain what the attitude of the Supreme Court would be if a case arose in which there was no such escape route. It might be that they would be prepared to hold that the rule should be modified to give effect to the intention of the settlor, for as Murnaghan J acknowledged[1] in *Jameson and Another v McGovern*.

'It may be that Lord Hardwicke was wiser than his successors and that equitable interests would have better flourished if they had not been measured so strictly by analogy to the common law.'

But the surer and more sensible road to reform would be to remove by legislation the archaic rules as to words of limitation which still surround our conveyancing law.

1 At 777.

Equity will not suffer a wrong to be without a remedy

3.05 It was because the common law frequently failed to provide an effective remedy for the violation of an undoubted legal right that the range of equitable remedies, such as the injunction and specific performance, developed. The maxim, accordingly, to this extent reflects an important feature of the equitable jurisdiction. But it does not mean that equity can supply a remedy in every case of apparent injustice. In the early development of equity, the courts sought to ensure that the parties before them acted in accordance with what were thought to be the requirements of conscience. But in its more systematised form, equity only came to the assistance of those who could show that recognised legal or equitable rights had been, or were in danger of being, violated. And in time, the range of equitable remedies themselves became limited to those which had been developed by the courts over the centuries. While there has been some attempt to extend their range in modern times—as in the case of so called 'new model constructive trusts'[1]—the orthodox view has been that in this area there is to-day no room for innovation. In the words of Lord Greene MR speaking for the Court of Appeal in England in *Re Diplock*:

'If (a) claim in equity exists, it must be shown to have an ancestry, founded in history and in the practice and precedents of courts administering equity jurisdiction. It is not sufficient that because we may think that the "justice" of the present case requires it, we should invent such a jurisdiction for the first time.'[2]

To this, however, one important qualification should be added. If a right guaranteed either expressly or by implication by the Constitution is attacked, the absence of an established statutory, common law or equitable remedy will be immaterial: in such cases, the courts are required to take whatever steps are necessary to protect and vindicate the right.[3]

1 See paras 13.10 to 13.14, below.
2 [1948] Ch 465, 481 to 482, CA.
3 *Educational Co of Ireland Ltd v Fitzpatrick (No 2)* [1961] IR 345 at 368; *Byrne v Ireland* [1972] IR 241, 281, SC; *Meskell v CIE* [1973] IR 12, SC; *A-G (Society for the Protection of the Unborn Child) v Open Door Counselling Ltd* (1987) ILRM 477.

Equity acts in personam

3.06 This maxim has long since ceased to be universally true. It reminds us that the jurisdiction of the court of chancery was originally exercised against the person—*in personam*—of the defendant rather than in relation to particular property—*in rem*. In the case of trusts, the court did not purport to deprive the legal owner of his property and transfer it to the beneficiary. But it could require the legal owner to acknowledge the right of the beneficiary and could enforce its decrees by punishment, including committal to prison for contempt and sequestration of the defendant's assets. But although the beneficiary's rights were properly described, because of this, as *iura in personam*. they have long since ceased to be exclusively such. The right of the beneficiary was recognised as one that could be transferred by him to another and transmitted on death, i.e. a proprietary right rather than a purely personal one. Ultimately, the legislature recognised that the *ius in personam* recognised by the court of equity had truly evolved into a *ius in rem* by enabling the courts to make orders vesting property which is subject to a trust in any person.[1] There are, it is true, many equitable rights which operate *in personam* only and they are usually referred to as 'equities' to distinguish them from equitable interests or estates proper. This distinction is more fully explored in the next chapter.

The maxim that equity acts *in personam*, while not of universal application, is of particular relevance where property out of the jurisdiction is concerned. Because its decrees are enforced personally against the defendant, it is not necessarily an objection to the court's jurisdiction to entertain a suit that the property is situated outside the jurisdiction, provided the defendant is within the jurisdiction or can be served outside the jurisdiction.[2] But the plaintiff must be asserting an equitable right: it is not sufficient that there is a question as to the legal entitlement to the property.[3] However, it seems that where the court is administering an estate or trust which includes property both in this country and abroad, it may make decrees affecting the overseas property even though no question of equitable rights is involved.[4] It should also be noted that even where an equitable claim to property situated abroad comes before the court and the defendant is within the jurisdiction or is capable of being served, the court may always decline jurisdiction if it considers it more convenient that the case should be decided by the foreign court.[5]

The application of the principle also means that the court may restrain a person from instituting proceedings in a foreign country. Thus in *Lett v Lett*,[6] a wife had settled divorce *a mensa et thoro* proceedings in Ireland. Her husband's property included property in the Argentine. She subsequently brought divorce proceedings in the Argentine claiming further relief which in effect amounted to a repudiation by her of the previous settlement. The Irish Court of Appeal upheld an injunction to restrain her from so doing, the lord chancellor, Sir Samuel Walker saying[7]

'Does it make any difference that the proceeding sought to be restrained is before a foreign tribunal? I think not, because the equity against her is founded not upon the tribunal to which she has resorted, but upon the personal contract binding her conscience. The jurisdiction asserted is not against the foreign tribunal but against the person within the jurisdiction, who has made a contract not to resort to proceedings; and whether such proceedings are in a foreign court or not is immaterial for the purpose of the equity on which the jurisdiction rests— an equity founded *in personam*.'

1 See para 9.12, below.
2 *Penn v Lord Baltimore* (1750) 1 Ves Sen 444.
3 *Re Hawthorne* [1883] 23 Ch D 743.
4 Snell, p 45.
5 *Ewing v Orr-Ewing* (1885) 10 App Cas 453, HL.

6 [1906] 1 IR 618.
7 At 635.

He who seeks equity must do equity

3.07 This is one of the most important of the maxims in practical terms. It emphasises a feature of the equitable jurisdiction which differentiates it sharply from the common law, i.e. its flexible and discretionary approach to the granting of relief. At common law, a person who is entitled to damages, the most characteristic of common law remedies, cannot generally be made to accept them subject to conditions. But this is what equity does, sometimes as a matter of course, when granting relief. The most frequent example in practice is the imposition of terms on the granting of an injunction, most notably at the interlocutory stage—where the court intervenes to preserve the status quo pending the trial of the action—and where it is invariable to require the defendant to give a personal undertaking to pay any damages that may be sustained by the plaintiff if it should emerge that the plaintiff was not entitled to the injunction sought.[1] Similarly, a person seeking specific performance of a contract can be required as a condition of granting relief to perform his part of the contract.[2]

Examples of the maxim can also be found in cases where the owner of land seeks to recover it from a person who has no title to it but has spent money on it to the owner's knowledge: the court applying equitable principles may allow the owner's title only if he is prepared to reimburse the person who has spent the money.[3] It is also applied where a mortgagor seeks to restrain the mortgagee from exercising the power of sale: the mortgagor can be required as a condition of obtaining relief to pay the amount of the mortgage debt and any interest due into court.[4] While the English authorities on which this principle is based were cases where an interlocutory injunction was being sought, it has been held in Australia that it also applies where final injunctive relief is claimed. The cases also suggest that there are two exceptions to the principle:

(a) where the amount claimed by the mortgagee is obviously wrong;
(b) where a question has arisen as to whether the power of sale has become exercisable at all.[5]

1 See para 15.26, below.
2 See para 16.11, below.
3 See para 28.13, below.
4 *Whitworth v Rhodes* (1850) 20 LJ Ch 105; *Warner v Jacob* (1882) 20 Ch D 220.
5 *Hickson v Darlow* (1883) 23 Ch D 690, CA; *Hotel Terrigal v Latec Investments (No 3)* [1969] 1 NSWLR 687; *Harvey v McWatters* (1949) 49 SR NSW 173.

He who comes into equity must come with clean hands

3.08 This is another very important maxim in practice. It is closely related to the one just discussed and, like that maxim, demonstrates the discretionary nature of equitable remedies. It differs from it essentially in that in this instance equity is having regard to the past conduct of the plaintiff rather than seeking to control it in the future. If the conduct of the plaintiff in relation to the particular matter in respect of which he is claiming relief has been inequitable, or tainted in some manner to which a court applying principles of equity should have regard, he may be refused relief. But this does not mean that the court will refuse the plaintiff relief simply because his conduct in some respects has been less than admirable: the inequitable behaviour relied on must relate in some way to the subject matter of the suit. So in *Argyll v Argyll*[1] where the Duchess of Argyll sought to restrain her former husband from publishing in a newspaper confidences of their married life, the plaintiff's previous sexual life was not a ground on which the court thought it right to refuse her relief.

A classic instance of where the maxim will apply is in actions for specific performances. If the plaintiff has procured the execution of the contract by means of a misrepresentation, even an innocent one, he may be refused a decree of specific performance on this ground, and this although the defendant has not exercised his right to rescind the contract.[2]

While the 'unclean hands' relied on must relate to the actual subject matter of the proceedings, it does not follow that the conduct in question must take the form of a breach of some duty owed to the plaintiff. It is clear that the court may refuse relief where the plaintiff has been guilty of conduct in respect of the particular transaction which the court could not countenance, although it may not have directly affected the plaintiff in any way. An interesting recent example is *Parkes v Parkes*.[3]

A husband had bought land at Tramore which seemed at the time to be of little value, and the conveyance was taken in his wife's name. When they subsequently were divorced (by which time the land had risen substantially in value), the husband claimed that the wife held the property on trust for him. He had advanced the entire purchase money and Costello J found as a fact that the only reason the property was taken in the wife's name was that she, unlike him, was an Irish citizen and under the provisions of the Land Act 1965 the consent of the Land Commission was required if the land was being conveyed to a non-Irish citizen. The husband was not anxious to go through the consent procedure and, to that end, not merely was the wife's name inserted in the conveyance but a certificate was also included (essential, if the consent was to be dispensed with) that the entire beneficial interest in the property was being acquired by an Irish citizen. The normal presumption of a resulting trust in favour of the husband was displaced by the presumption of an advancement to the wife,[4] but the husband claimed that the circumstances showed that no gift was intended and that hence the presumption of advancement had been rebutted. The learned judge, however, said that

'the court should not grant relief to a purchaser who has placed property in a wife's name dishonestly and by means of an illegal act performed for the purpose of evading the law relating to transfer of land.'

The husband had not come into equity with clean hands and hence his claim was dismissed.[5]

---

1 [1967] Ch 302.
2 *Cadman v Horner* (1810) 18 Ves 10. It has been suggested, however, that the modern approach is to treat such cases as instances where a decree of specific performance is refused on the ground of hardship: see Spry, *Equitable Remedies*, 3rd edn, 160.
3 Unreported; judgement delivered 1 July 1980; Wylie Casebook 74.
4 See para 12.03, below.
5 See also *Ardent Fisheries Ltd v Minister for Tourism* (1987) ILRM 528.

3.09 To the 'clean hands' doctrine, three exceptions have emerged. In the following cases 'unclean hands' will not be a ground for refusing relief:

(i) *Actions for delivery up and cancellation of documents*. In such cases, one object of the remedy is the wider public interest of ensuring that the public are not deceived by the circulation of a misleading document and the plaintiff's lack of merit is not a relevant consideration.[1]

(ii) *Suits to prevent multiplicity of actions*. Thus a plaintiff in a passing off action[2] might be able to establish fraud and hence to bring a common law action for damages to which his own 'unclean hands' would be no defence. But he will also be entitled to an injunction where the effect of refusing him one would be to result in a multiplicity of actions for damages.[3]

(iii) *Actions claiming purely statutory relief*. This clearly applies to actions claiming declaratory relief (including claims that a statute is constitutionally invalid) which is not strictly equitable relief, but also to any other claims where the relief is available under a statute.[4]

1 *St John v St John* 11 Ves 526. See Chapter 21, below.
2 An action in which the plaintiff claims that the defendant is falsely representing that goods sold by him are those of the plaintiff.
3 *Angelides v James Stedman Henderson's Sweets Ltd* (1927) 40 CLP 43.
4 See para 19.08, below.

Delay defeats equity

3.10 Equity has traditionally been reluctant to come to the aid of claimants who are unduly slow in asserting their rights, an attitude enshrined in the tag, *vigilantibus, non dormientibus, iura subveniunt*, ie 'the law assists the vigilant, not those who sleep.'[1] Hence delay, if it takes the form of what has come to be called *laches*, provides in certain circumstances a defence to equitable claims. But it would be dangerous to assume that even a lengthy period of inaction on the plaintiff's part, stretching over a number of years, will necessarily of itself lead to the dismissal of his claim.

In this context, the operation of the Statute of Limitations 1957 is important. Claims at common law have been affected by limitation periods imposed by statutes for centuries.[2] With one major exception which has emerged in recent years, it has generally been held by courts that, if such a claim is brought within the prescribed period, it cannot be defeated by a defence that there has been undue delay in instituting the proceedings. The exception is actions by minors in respect of personal injuries: since the decision of the Supreme Court in *O'Brien v Keogh*[3] that time does not begin to run against the minor until after he has attained his majority, such plaintiffs may have an effective limitation period of up to 21 years.[4] But the court has also held in *O Domhnaill v Merrick*[5] that 'inordinate and inexcusable delay' will bar such a claim even within the limitation period.

Historically, where there was no prescribed period within which a claim asserting an equitable right had to be brought (the usual position until comparatively modern times), equity applied the maxim we have already considered and followed the law: it acted by analogy with the statutes of limitations and applied whatever was the corresponding period of limitation at common law. But in the case of some of the most important equitable rights, the 1957 Act provided express periods of limitation, viz: -

(a) actions by beneficiaries to recover the trust property or in respect of any breach of trust;
(b) actions to recover the estates of deceased persons;
(c) actions for the recovery of land, including equitable interests in land;
(d) actions by a mortgagor to redeem a mortgage;
(e) actions by a mortgagee claiming an order for sale.

In the case of (a) and (b), the limitation period is six years[6] and in the case of (c), (d) and (e) 12 years.[7] In the case of actions against a trustee by a beneficiary, the limitation period does not apply where the action is based on a fraud to which the trustee was a party or privy, or claims to recover the trust property or its proceeds in the possession of the trustee or previously received by the trustee and converted to his own use.[8]

In these cases—where the statute provides a limitation period and the claim is brought within it—it has been held in England that laches will not afford a defence to a claim asserting an equitable right.[9] But in *O Domhnaill v Merrick,* Henchy J suggested a different approach:

'As to a plaintiff's right to proceed with an action brought before the period of limitation has run out, the Courts in the past have been reluctant to exercise their equitable jurisdiction to terminate stale claims at a time when the statutory period of limitation has yet to expire. However, the Statute of Limitations was enacted in a legal milieu which makes such reluctance to intervene inappropriate. Apart from implied constitutional principles of basic fairness of procedures[10] which may be invoked to justify the termination of a claim which places an inexcusable and unfair burden on the person sued, one must assume that the statute was enacted (there being no indication in it of a contrary intention) subject to the postulate that it would be construed and applied in consonance with the State's obligation under international law, including any relevant treaty obligations. The relevance of the rule of statutory interpretation in this case lies in the fact that article 6(1) of the (European) Convention for the Protection of Human Rights and Fundamental Freedoms (1950) provides:- "in the determination of his civil rights and obligations or of any criminal charge against him, every one is entitled to a fair hearing within a *reasonable time* by an independent and impartial tribunal established by law."

'While the Convention is not part of the domestic law of the State, still because the Statute of Limitations 1957 was passed after this State ratified the convention in 1953, it is to be argued that the statute, since it does not show any contrary intention, should be deemed to be in conformity with the Convention and should be construed and applied accordingly. However, I do not wish to express a concluded opinion on the point, as the application of the Convention in this case has not been argued.'[11]

Accordingly, in a case where the plaintiff had been guilty of 'inordinate and inexcusable delay' which deprived the defendant of the fair procedures guaranteed by the Constitution, the court applying this approach might non-suit the plaintiff, even though the limitation period had not expired. But it is unlikely that there would be much room for applying *O Domhnaill v Merrick* in cases other than those where the unusually extended limitation period applicable to personal injuries claims by minors was relevant. In such cases, not only is the limitation period unusually long: the prospects of a fair trial are more likely to be put at risk by the unavailability of witnesses or the unreliability of their recollection than would be the case in other actions.

1 *Smith v Clay* (1767) 3 Bros CL 639n at 640n.
2 See Brady and Kerr, *Limitation of Actions in the Republic of Ireland*.
3 [1972] IR 144, SC.
4 It was 24 years before the lowering of the age of majority to 18 by the Age of Majority Act 1985. The provision found unconstitutional was to the effect that the statute would run against a minor in the same manner as against an adult while the minor was in the custody of a parent. While doubts were expressed in a subsequent Supreme Court decision *(Moynihan v Greensmith* [1977] IR 55) as to the correctness of the decision in *O Brien v Keogh* the impugned provision was capable of producing anomalies, apart from any question of its constitutionality. The corresponding provision in the English Limitation Act 1939 has been repealed.
5 [1984] IR 151.
6 Statute of Limitations 1957, s 43 and s 45 as substituted by s 126 of the Succession Act 1965.
7 Ibid, s 13, s 34 and s 32.
8 Ibid, s 44.
9 *Re Pauling's Settlement Trusts* [1964] Ch 303 at 353.
10 Cf *Re Haughey* [1971] IR 217.
11 At pp 158 to 159.

3.11 Express periods of limitation are provided by s 11 of the 1957 Act for actions in contract and tort. But sub-s(9)(a) provides that

'this section shall not apply to any claim for specific performance of a contract or for an injunction or for other equitable relief.'

However, sub-s (9) (b) says that para (a)

'shall not be construed as preventing a Court from applying by analogy any provision of this section in like manner as the corresponding enactment repealed by this Act has heretofore been applied.'

Section 5 of the Act provides in addition that

'Nothing in this Act shall afford any equitable jurisdiction to refuse relief on the ground of acquiescence or otherwise.'

The effect of these statutory provisions would appear to be that, even where a common law right of action in contract or tort is barred by the statute, the court is not precluded from granting equitable relief by way of injunction, specific performance or otherwise. It may, however, in its discretion apply the statutory period by way of analogy where that appears appropriate.

Whether the equitable defence of laches will apply to a claim for equitable relief in respect of these common law rights in contract and tort where the common law claim is *not* barred by the statute is a more difficult question. Section 5 preserves the equitable jurisdiction to refuse equitable relief on the ground of 'acquiescence *or otherwise*' and it is clear that this was intended inter alia to preserve the equitable defence of laches. But in the case of an injunction sought in protection of a common law right, it had been held in England that laches afforded no defence where the cause of action was not statute barred.[1] It was also said that this applied as much after the Judicature Acts as before them. This was the view taken by Budd J in *Cahill v Irish Motor Traders' Association*,[2] where he said that

'mere delay will not of itself disentitle a plaintiff to an injunction in aid of his legal rights unless the claim to enforce the right is barred by a statute of limitations'.

More recently, however, the Court of Appeal in England in *Habib Bank Ltd v Habib Bank AG Zurich*[3] have brushed aside rather sweepingly the distinction between common law and equitable rights and have said that the defence of laches is now available whenever an injunction is sought. But their approach is redolent of the 'fusion' heresy discussed earlier[4] and it cannot be assumed that an Irish court will depart from the view of Budd J. It should, however, be said that. whatever may be the correct view as to the effect of laches on the granting of a *final* injunction in aid of common law rights, it is certainly a relevant consideration in the granting of all interlocutory injunctions.[5]

It should also be noted that in certain cases, irrespective of the application of a statutory period of limitation, special promptitude is required. This is so in cases of constructive trusts,[6] actions based on undue influence,[7] claims for specific performance[8] and rescission of contracts[9] and actions seeking to set aside allotments of shares.[10]

1 *Fullwood v Fullwood* (1878) 9 Ch D 176.
2 [1966] IR 430, at 449.
3 [1981] 2 All ER 650, at 666, CA.
4 See para 2.24, above.
5 See para 15.09, below.
6 *Beckford v Wade*, (1805) 17 Ves 87.
7 *Allcard v Skinner* (1887) 36 Ch D 145.
8 *Milward v Earl of Thanet* (1801) 5 Ves 720 n.
9 See para 17.16, below.
10 *Aaron's Reefs Ltd v Twiss* [1896] AC 273.

3.12 What constitutes the equitable defence of laches must next be considered. It should be noted at the outset that mere delay of itself, however substantial, does not amount to such laches. The following passage from the 27th edition of Snell[1] was cited with approval by Henchy J in *Murphy v A-G*:[2]

'Laches essentially consists of a substantial lapse of time, coupled with the existence of circumstances which make it inequitable to enforce the claim.'

Accordingly, where the defendant has altered his own position or acted to his detriment as a result of the plaintiff's inaction over a substantial period of time, the defence may be successfully pleaded. An example is *JH v WJH*,[3] where a widow had signed an agreement in January 1969 waiving her rights under the Succession Act 1965 to a share in her deceased husband's estate. The principle asset of the deceased, a 93 acre farm, had been left by his will to her son, the defendant, who agreed to pay her £1000 and £1.10s a week for the rest of her life in consideration of her releasing her statutory rights. The widow claimed to have the agreement set aside and Keane J found it to have been an improvident transaction which the court would normally set aside.[4] However, the proceedings had not been instituted until 1977, although the plaintiff had been aware of her rights since 1973 and Keane J held that it would be inequitable to allow the plaintiff relief. The defendant had invested 10 years of his life in working the farm and setting aside the instrument would involve him in raising a far more substantial sum to preserve his investment than would have been the case had the proceedings been instituted in 1973.[5]

1 See p 35.
2 [1982] IR 241 at 318, SC.
3 Unreported; judgement delivered 20 December 1979.
4 See Chapter 30, below.
5 Prices of agricultural land had risen sharply between 1973 and 1979.

3.13 The inaction on the plaintiff's part may also, depending on the circumstances, be of such a nature as to justify an inference that he has *acquiesced* in the violation by the defendant of his right. But the plaintiff must be aware of his rights, must not be under any disability and must be free to act (in the sense of not being subject to undue influence or other pressure).[1] It should be noted that while delay may thus enable an inference of acquiescence to be drawn which will provide a defence to an equitable claim, acquiescence as a defence is distinguishable from laches. Thus, without any element of serious delay, if A knowingly allows B to act in violation of his rights, he may not subsequently be allowed to assert them where B has acted to his own detriment in reliance on A's inaction.[2]

1 16 *Halsbury's Laws of England*, 4th edn, Vol 9, para 1478.
2 See Chapter 28.

Equality is equity

3.14 Equity's inclination to apply the principle of equality, wherever possible, is of long standing. It underlies the traditional equitable distaste for joint tenancies, the form of co-ownership of land in which each owner is regarded as owning the entire land (not simply an undivided share, as is the case with tenancies in common) and one of the consequences of which is that on the death of one joint tenant, the surviving joint tenant or tenants become entitled to the entire property. That the survivors should become so entitled to the exclusion of their co-owner's heirs or successors, simply because of the accident of longevity, was seen as fundamentally inequitable. If the property is vested in the owners without any indication as to the shares in which they are to enjoy it, there is no escaping the inference of a joint tenancy.[1] Similarly where the purchase money is contributed in equal shares, only a joint tenancy can result in the absence of any expression to the contrary.[2] But where the purchase money is contributed in unequal shares, equity is prepared to draw the inference that the purchasers are entitled as tenants in common in the same proportions, so that the shares of each descend to their successors. Similarly, equity refuses to treat partners as joint tenants: the principle of survivorship is inconsistent with the nature of the partnership relationship.[3] And where the money secured by a mortgage is advanced by two or more persons jointly, the presumption will be drawn that they are entitled to the mortgaged property as tenants in common and this even where they have contributed the money in equal shares.[4] (This led to the adoption of the 'joint account' clause intended to rebut this presumption: in many cases it was impractical for the mortgagees to own the property as tenants in common.) The principle of 'equality is equity' was also used to justify the distribution of property equally between the objects of a power of appointment in default of its exercise, but as we shall see in a later chapter the applicability of the maxim in this context has been restricted in a modern English decision.[5]

1 *Lake v Craddock* (1732) 3 P Wms 158, 24 ER 1011.
2 Ibid.
3 *Elliott v Brown* (1791) 3 Swan, 489 n.
4 *Petty v Styward* (1631) 1 Rep Ch 57.
5 See para 7.05, below.

3.15 Two further points should be noted. 'Equality' does not necessarily mean mathematical equality: the proper application of the maxim may require proportionate rather than mathematical equality. The following statement of the law in *Halsbury's Laws of England* was cited with approval by Megarry VC in *Re Steel*:[1]

'the maxim that 'equity is equality' expresses in a general way the object of both law and equity, namely, to effect a distribution of profits and losses proportionate to the several claims or to the several liabilities of the persons concerned. For equality in this connexion does not mean literal equality but proportionate equality.'[2]

The maxim was invoked in the past to justify the division of the matrimonial home in equal shares between husband and wife, although their respective contributions had not been equal. But in *Gissing v Gissing*,[3] a different approach was suggested in the House of Lords, ie a division in accordance with the respective contributions of the spouses and this has on the whole been the view which has prevailed in the Irish courts in recent years.[4]

1 [1979] Ch 218.
2 16 *Halsbury's Laws of England*, para 1301.
3 [1971] AC 886 at pp 897 and 907–9.
4 Eg *W v W* (1981) ILRM 202.

Equity looks to the intent rather than the form

3.16 Courts of equity do not disregard the words used in a written document, but they do seek to give effect to what was the intentions of the parties.[1] Hence, in the words of Romilly MR,

'If they... find that by insisting on the form, the substance will be defeated, they hold it to be inequitable to allow a person to insist on such form and thereby defeat the substance.'[2]

One classic instance was the mortgage: equity insisted on treating a transaction in which land was security for a loan as a mortgage,however it might be described. The maxim also underlay the growth of the remedy of rectification by which the courts sought to give effect to the real intention of the parties to an agreement.

1 *Parkin v Thorold* (1852) 16 Beav 59 at 66.
2 *Ibid* at 66–67.

39

3.17 A useful example of equity's preference for the substance to the form of agreements is to be found in its attitude to time clauses. In the case of contracts for the sale of land, to take one of the most important examples, the contract would frequently provide that it was to be completed by a specified date. There was not really any room for disagreement between courts of common law and equity as to what such a stipulation meant: equity, if anything, would defer to the opinion of the common law as to the proper interpretation of the contract. But the *consequences* of such a stipulation were different in equity. The time fixed for completion was not regarded as being of the essence of the contract, unless the parties expressly provided that it should be or there was something in the nature of the subject matter or the surrounding circumstances which would make it inequitable to interfere with the legal rights of the parties.[1] Hence, it was no defence to an action for specific performance to claim that the party seeking to enforce it had not been in a position to complete on the date fixed by the contract. Similarly, a party seeking to rescind a contract would not be allowed to do so in equity simply because the other party had failed to complete on the completion date. Equity in each case looked to the substance of the contract and did not permit a party to avoid performing his essential obligations by relying on the letter of the contract as to time for completion, unless it was an express term of the contract that time should be of the essence in that regard or there was some other feature which rendered time of the essence.[2]

This does not mean, however, that a party to such a contract can simply delay indefinitely its completion and still claim that the contract is binding on the other party. If, after the completion date has passed, he fails to complete within a reasonable time, the party not in default can by notice limit a reasonable time within which the contract is to be completed. At the end of that time, if the party in default has still failed to complete, the innocent party will be entitled to rescind the contract.[3]

1 *Stickney v Keeble* [1915] AC 386 at 416 per Lord Parker.
2 *Ibid*.
3 *Healy Ballsbridge Ltd v Alliance Property Corporation Ltd* [1974] IR 441 at 447. per Kenny J. See also Wylie, *Conveyancing*, pp 538–539.

Equity looks on that as done which ought to have been done

3.18 Where parties have entered into an enforceable agreement, the court will assess their legal rights and duties by reference to what their position would be had the agreement been legally implemented. Thus, ever since the leading case of *Walsh v Lonsdale*,[1] an agreement to enter into a lease has been treated as equivalent to a lease and the parties' rights and duties have been ascertained as if the lease had been actually executed. The principle also underlies the equitable doctrine of conversion which is discussed more fully in Chapter 24; and which arises most commonly where there has been an agreement for the sale of land. In such a case, the interest of the vendor in the land will be treated as being an interest in the purchase money as from the date of the contract, a distinction which was of more practical significance when the rules governing the devolution of real and personal estate were different. However, while the principle finds its most frequent application in practice in cases of contract, it is not confined to such cases but arises whenever there is a legal obligation on a party to perform a particular act, whether by virtue of a contract, a trust or otherwise.

1 [1882] 21 Ch D 9, CA.

Equity imputes an intention to fulfil an obligation

3.19 To put it another way, if one finds that A has performed a particular act which he was already obliged by law to do, it will be assumed that he has performed the act in fulfilment of that obligation. While its application in modern times is rare, this principle explains the development of the equitable doctrines of satisfaction, ademption and performance.[1]

1 See Chapters 26 and 27.

Where the equities are equal, the first in time prevails

Where the equities are equal, the law prevails

3.20 These two maxims attempt to encapsulate the principles which have in general been applied by the courts in determining the priorities between competing claims to property. Where the rival claims are purely equitable, the first of these maxims, frequently cited in its Latin form, *qui prior est tempore, potior est jure*, is applicable. Where one of the claimants is possessed of the legal estate, the second is applicable.

But this is to state the law in its baldest and most dangerously simple form. The law as to priorities between competing claims to property is one of extreme complexity and certainly cannot be stated solely in terms of the two maxims under discussion. At the outset, the phrase 'where the equities are equal' needs considerable elaboration. In particular, one must have regard to what is meant by 'equities' and the distinction frequently drawn between a mere 'equity' and an equitable interest. This distinction is dealt with in detail in the next chapter. Then in Chapter Five, in the light of that distinction, of the important doctrine of *notice* and the impact of the system of *registration,* we go on to consider the general law of priorities as it exists to-day.

Chapter 4

Equitable interests and 'equities'

4.01 The most distinctive of equitable institutions, the trust, began life as a purely personal remedy. The view also persisted with some writers that, since equity operated upon the conscience of the owner and always acted *in personam* and not *in rem,* equitable rights were not in their nature property rights. But we have also seen that, as the law developed, the interest of the beneficiary in the trust property was treated as something more than a simply personal right on his part to require the trustee to observe the trust. It was a right to the property itself which was capable of being devised by will or sold.[1] Thus the law ultimately recognised that there could exist *equitable interests* in property capable of being sold or mortgaged or transmitted by will in the same way as the legal interest. Nor were such equitable interests confined to land: they could exist in all species of property, real or personal. The evolution of the law was explained by Kingsmill Moore J speaking for the Supreme Court in *Re Cuff Knox deceased:*[2]

> 'Equity acts *in personam* and rights and interests evolved in equity were originally conceived as purely personal, binding only on the conscience of the individual and enforced against the individual if he acted contrary to good conscience. This view was expressed in *Sir Moyle Finch's Case.* But by the time of Charles I, Roll CJ was saying: "a trust is not a thing in action, but may be an inheritance or chattel as the case falls out"....
> 'Nevertheless the proposition that equitable interests are, in juristic theory, purely rights *in personam* found eminent champions, notably Maitland, who based his view on the fact that an equitable interest can never prevail against a purchaser for value without notice of the trust. But this view—that equitable interests convey no right *in rem*—cannot be squared with the right of the beneficiary to follow the trust property *in specie* into the hands of anyone except a purchaser for value without notice.....The existence of such rights has forced modern jurists to recognise that the rights of beneficiaries are not merely *iura in personam...*'

But a variety of remedies developed in equity, apart from the right of the beneficiary to the trust property. A party, for example, could claim to have a deed or contract set aside on the ground of fraud or undue influence. Or he could claim to have it rectified to accord with the real intentions of the parties. Such rights lacked the essentially proprietary characteristics of the interest of a beneficiary under a trust. They could not be disposed of in the market place in the same way. It is rights of this nature which are called *'equities'* to distinguish them from equitable interests. Considerable difficulty has been experienced, however, in drawing the boundary between equitable interests and equities. It is a distinction which can be of crucial importance in determining priorities between competing interests in property: an 'equity', even where earlier in time, will normally have to yield to a subsequent equitable estate acquired without notice of the equity.

1 Certainly not later than the Statute of Frauds (1677) 29 Car II c 3, which like its Irish counterpart, (1695) 7 William III c 12, requires assignments of equitable interests in land to be in writing.
2 [1963] IR 263 at 289.

What is meant by an 'equity'?

4.02 In *Allied Irish Banks Ltd v Glynn*,[1] Kenny J said

'The terms "equity" and "equitable estate" and "equitable interest" have been used in different senses in Acts of Parliament, in decided cases and in textbooks; the difference between them is not capable of complete definition. The main difference, I think, is that an "equity" does not create or give any estate in the land; it is a right against persons and is enforceable against those who were parties to the transactions which created it.'[2]

He also cited an observation of Lord Upjohn in *National Provincial Bank Ltd v Ainsworth*[3] that

'There are no doubt many cases where judges have said that a purchaser takes "subject to all the equities", but they meant "equitable interests"..........an equity to which a subsequent purchaser is subject must create an interest in the land.'[4]

These remarks, however, do not assist us in identifying the point at which an equity ceases to be a mere equity and generates the sort of interest which can be described as an equitable interest.

At one end of the scale, certain rights can be identified which are undoubtedly personal in their nature. A wife, for example, has a clear right, enforceable against her husband, to reside in the matrimonial home unless there has been a 'barring order'[5] or the right has been waived by a separation agreement. But it is also clear that this is an equity only as distinct from an equitable interest. (The spouse may, of course, enjoy such an equitable interest in addition, as where he or she has contributed to the purchase price of the home.)

It was argued on behalf of a deserted wife in *National Provincial Bank Ltd v Ainsworth* that her right to retain possession of the matrimonial home was binding on the plaintiff bank, who, it was said, had taken a mortgage on the property with knowledge of her rights. The Court of Appeal in England, led by Lord Denning, while acknowledging that such a right had never before been treated as having any proprietary characteristics which could affect third parties, held that the time had come to recognise it as having such an effect. The House of Lords, however, unanimously rejected this view: the right of the wife to reside in the matrimonial home derived solely from her marital status and was not necessarily dependent on her having any interest in the property. It was a right of a purely personal nature which could be enforced against her husband, but did not affect third parties, whether or not they had notice of the fact that it was a matrimonial home.

The precise point at issue in *National Provincial Bank Ltd v Ainsworth* has become somewhat academic in Ireland since the enactment of the Family Home Protection Act 1976. The Act invalidates any disposition of the family home by one spouse without the written consent of the other.[6] This right of veto is not dependent on there being any proprietary interest in the spouse whose consent is required. But circumstances may arise in which those in possession of property may have a similar right to that of a spouse to retain possession against the owner, a right which will be protected by equity but which is still an equity only and not binding on third parties. The most obvious example is of an unmarried couple living together: one of the partners will be unable to veto a disposition by the other and will have no more than at most a right to retain possession against that partner. Even that right will not necessarily exist in every such case. Circumstances have undoubtedly arisen in cases in Ireland and England where the courts have been able to infer the existence of a 'licence' from one party to the other to occupy a particular premises. But it would seem that, unless such a licence is ancillary to or dependent on an estate in the land, it will not be treated as affecting third parties, whether or not they have notice.[7]

1 [1973] IR 188.
2 At 192.
3 [1965] AC 1175, HL.
4 At 1237 to 1238.
5 Under s 2 of the Family Law (Protection of Spouses and Children) Act 1981.
6 S 3 (1). See Shatter, *Family Law in the Republic of Ireland,* 3rd edn, Chapter 16.
7 *National Provincial Bank Ltd v Ainsworth,* above, at p 1238 per Lord Upjohn.

4.03 There are, however, 'equities' which fall short of being fully fledged equitable estates and yet which are capable of affecting third parties who take with notice of them, and of being transmitted to others. They are thus superior to the equities dealt with in the preceding paragraph, leading some to describe the latter as 'naked equities'.[1] But although superior to the naked equity, they will still be postponed to later equitable interests acquired in good faith and without notice: here the equities in general are not equal and the priority in time is not decisive. These are, in general, rights which require to be enforced in proceedings before they mature into equitable estates, as an examination of the cases shows.

So, in *Bowen v Evans,*[2] Sir Edward Sugden, sitting as Lord Chancellor of Ireland, said that the right to set aside a deed for fraud was a mere equity, which could be displaced by a subsequent acquisition of the equitable estate for value and without notice of the fraud. He appears at first sight to have suffered a sea change, in more ways that one, when he was transported to the English woolsack, because we find him in *Stump v Gaby,*[3] as Lord St Leonards, opining that such a right was capable of being transmitted by will: the owner of the land conveyed by the fraudulent deed remained the owner in equity even before the deed was set aside by a court. But, as we shall see, the difference is more apparent than real. In *Phillips v Phillips,*[4] generally regarded as the *locus classicus* on this branch of the law, Lord Westbury was clearly of the view that this right was a mere equity, at least—and this is the important distinction—for the purpose of determining priorities. He said:

'where there are circumstances that give rise to an equity, as distinct from an equitable estate—as, for example, an equity to set aside a deed for fraud or correct it for mistake—and the purchaser under the instrument maintains a plea of purchaser for value without notice, the court will not interfere.'[5]

Phillips v Phillips has been generally regarded as correctly stating the law ever since, at least for the purpose of determining priorities and this was the principle applied by Kenny J in *Allied Irish Banks Ltd v Glynn*.

In that case, a father had conveyed land to his son, reserving a right of residence for himself. The son was registered as owner of the land and deposited the land certificate with the plaintiff bank to secure an advance, thus creating an equitable mortgage. Subsequently the father brought proceedings claiming that the conveyance of the land had been procured by the undue influence of the son. These proceedings were not defended and the deed was set aside by the Circuit Court which ordered the register to be rectified by the re-registration of the father as full owner. The plaintiff bank, who were not given notice of these proceedings, subsequently brought proceedings to enforce their equitable mortgage. Kenny J held that their equitable mortgage had priority over the father's right to have the deed set aside, which was not an equitable interest. At the same time, it was something more than a mere equity, in his view, since it would mature into an estate when proceedings were brought. But this could not elevate it into an equitable estate until that time and consequently it was displaced by the subsequent equitable mortgage.

That such a right is in the nature of an equity only in the context of determining priorities is further demonstrated by the Australian case of *Latec Investments Ltd v Hotel Terrigal Property Ltd*.[6] In that case, a company, L, had taken a mortgage of certain hotel property belonging to X. It purported to exercise its power of sale by selling the property to Y. Y in turn gave an equitable charge over the property to Z who ultimately sought to enforce his charge by appointing a receiver. Although it was five years since the purported sale by L to Y, X, the owner now for the first time sought to set aside the sale as having been an improper exercise of the power of sale. The court found that it was improper, but that the equity of X to have it set aside was postponed to Z's charge. They differed, however, in their reasons. Taylor J said[7] that in a case such as this X remained the owner in equity—thus applying the *Stump v Gaby* approach—but that he had lost his right to enforce his interest because of his delay. Menzies and Kitto JJ, however, treated the right of X as a mere equity which could not prevail over the equitable interest of Z even though the latter was later in time. Menzies J pointed out[8] that *Stump v Gaby* was capable of being reconciled with *Phillips v Phillips*: the former case was not dealing with priorities but with the right of the devisee of the land to succeed, as it were, to the right of the testator to have the deed set aside.

1 Ibid.
2 (1844) 6 Ir Eq R 569.
3 (1852) 2 De GM & G 623.
4 (1861) 4 De GF & J 208.
5 At 218.
6 (1965) 113 CLR 265.
7 At 282.
8 At 290 to 291.

4.04 We have already seen[1] that there are cases in which people in possession of land without any title to the land may be entitled to retain possession of the land against the owner. In such cases, the owner is usually prevented—under the doctrine of estoppel—from asserting that he is entitled to possession of the land. This may mean, depending on the particular circumstances, that the person in possession is not merely a licensee who can be expelled on reasonable notice, but a licensee who is entitled to retain possession indefinitely against the owner.[2] It may even mean that the licensee is entitled to an equitable interest in the land capable of being transferred or transmitted. In this last case—dependent on the form of estoppel known as *proprietary estoppel*—the 'equity' of the licensee may be converted into an equitable interest when he brings the necessary proceedings. These cases are dealt with in more detail in Chapter 29 below.

1 See para 4.02.
2 *Errington v Errington* [1952] 1 KB 290, CA *Cullen v Cullen* [1962] IR 268; *Inwards v Baker* [1965] 2 QB 29 CA; *Binions v Evans* [1972] Ch 359, CA;*Crabb v Arun District Council* [1976] Ch 179, CA; *Pascoe v Turner* [1979] 2 All ER 945, [1979] 1 WLR 431, CA; *McMahon v Kerry Country Council* (1981) ILRM 419.

4.05 The special position of beneficiaries under a will or an intestacy should be noted. It is clear that until such time as the personal representative assents to the bequest or, in the case of the residue, until he has completed the administration of the estate by paying all debts and legacies, the beneficiaries have no interest, legal or equitable, in the property comprised in the estate. The entire ownership until that time is vested in the personal representatives and the only right of the beneficiaries is their right to require them to complete the administration of the estate in accordance with the law. This was made clear by the House of Lords in *Lord Sudeley v Attorney General*[1] and has been reiterated in a number of cases since then.[2] It is true that under s10(3) of the Succession Act 1965, the personal representatives hold the estate 'as trustees for the persons by law entitled thereto.' But this simply illustrates the caution which must be exercised in attaching significance to the use of a particular expression such as 'trust': the context in which it is used must be borne in mind. Until the administration is completed, it is sometimes not possible to say who is the person entitled to the deceased's property: in the case of an insolvent estate, it will be his creditors and not the persons whom he sought to benefit by his will. The words in the Act simply make clear the statutory obligation on the personal representative to apply the estate in the manner required by law. If it is asked where the beneficial interest in the property is during the course of the administration, the authoritative answer is to be found in Viscount Radcliffe's judgement giving the advice of the judicial committee of the Privy Council in *Stamp Duties Comr (Queensland) v Livingstone* [3] where he rejected the suggestion that

'for all purposes and at every moment of time the law requires the separate existence of two different kinds of estate or interest in property, the legal and the equitable....Equity in fact calls into existence and protects equitable rights and interests in property only where their recognition has been found to be required in order to give effect to its doctrines.'[4]

1 [1897] AC 11 HL.
2 *Barnardo's Homes v Income Tax Special Comrs* (1921) AC 1, HL; *Moloney v Allied Irish Banks Ltd* [1986] IR 67. Cf *Re Cuff Knox deceased* (above) at 293 to 294.
3 [1965] AC 694 PC.

Equitable interests

4.06 It will be apparent from the foregoing that this is an area of the law in which tidy classifications into which every species of 'right' can be conveniently slotted are peculiarly difficult to achieve. It has been suggested, however, that the following four characteristics are of particular importance in determining whether a right is an equitable interest rather than a mere 'equity':

  (i) the right of the person entitled to recover the relevant property by proceedings;

  (ii) the fact that the right binds the property to which it relates in the hands of a third party to whom it is transferred;

  (iii) the ability of the person entitled to sell or transmit the right;

  (iv) the permanency of the right.[1]

It remains possible, however, for a right to have all these indicia and yet fall short of being an equitable interest. Another distinction which has been suggested is the *discretionary* nature of mere equities: so the court will not necessarily set aside a deed procured by undue influence, whereas it must give effect to the beneficiary's interest under a trust.[2] But it has also been pointed out that a purchaser's rights under a contract for the sale of land, although arguably more than a mere 'equity' are discretionary: the court will not necessarily decree the specific performance of the contract. In practice, the feature which probably most readily distinguishes the equitable interest is that it can be bought and sold in the market place, but, as Hanbury points out,[3] this is not entirely adequate, since the right of a person to enforce a restrictive covenant affecting land is accepted as an equitable interest and yet it cannot be sold detached from the estate for whose benefit it has been created.

The following interests have been identified by one writer as being equitable interests as distinct from mere equities:

  (a) the interest of a beneficiary under a trust;

  (b) equitable mortgages

  (c) a vendor's lien for the balance of the unpaid purchase money

  (d) restrictive covenants

  (e) 'estate contracts'.[4]

To this list, which was approved by Lord Upjohn in *National Provincial Bank Ltd v Ainsworth*[5] it has been suggested that one can add equitable easements and profits a prendre.[6]

The expression 'estate contracts' is taken from the English Land Charges Act 1972 and means a contract to convey or create a legal estate in land. It has no precise equivalent in Irish law. Whether the right of the purchaser under a contract for the sale of land constitutes an equitable estate or an equity only is not free from difficulty. There is no doubt that where he has paid any part of the purchase money he is entitled to a beneficial interest in the land of the same proportion as this bears to the entire purchase money.[7] In *Tempany v Hynes*,[8] a majority of the Supreme Court held that this was all he was entitled to and that a purchaser does not become entitled to the beneficial interest simply by virtue of the execution of the contract for sale: the vendor is a trustee for him only in the sense that he owes him a duty to take reasonable care of the property until the sale is completed.[9] But it can certainly be argued that, at least for the purpose of determining priorities, the purchaser's right is more than a mere equity.

At one stage in this country the list of equitable interests would have included rights of residence. It is a common practice in rural Ireland on a marriage or family settlement to reserve such a right to a parent, and it was held by the Supreme Court in *National Bank Ltd v Keegan*[10] that such a right was in the nature of an equitable interest. This position has, however, been reversed by legislation, the Registration of Title Act 1964 providing[11] that such a right

> 'shall be deemed to be personal to the person beneficially entitled thereto and to be a right in the nature of a lien for money's worth in or over the land and shall not operate to create any equitable estate in the land.'

1 Meagher, Lehane and Gummow, p 98.
2 Wade, (1955) CLJ 160/161.
3 At 756.
4 Crane, (1955) 19 Conv 343 at 346.
5 At 1238.
6 Pettit, p15.
7 *Rose v Watson* (1864) 10 HL Cas 672.
8 [1976] IR 101.
9 Per Kenny J at p 114. See further para 5.16 below and *Coffey v Brunel Construction* [1983] IR 36.
10 [1931] IR 344.
11 S 81.

4.07 The right of the beneficiary to the trust estate is unquestionably an equitable interest. A difficult problem arises, however, if the trustee, or one of the beneficiaries acting in fraud of his co-beneficiaries, wrongfully disposes of the trust property. Equity developed what came to be known as a 'tracing' remedy under which the beneficiary was entitled to follow the trust property into the hands of third parties. Such a right could not prevail against the claim of a purchaser of the legal estate without notice of the beneficiary's claim. But what of a subsequent equitable claimant? In *Cave v Cave*,[1] Fry J said that the beneficiary's right to follow the trust property was itself an equitable interest which came into being as soon as the trust property was misapplied. It followed that, when the property was subsequently made the subject of an equitable mortgage by deposit of the title deeds, the later incumbrancer, although acting in good faith and without notice, was postponed to the earlier interest of the beneficiary: the equities being equal, the first in time prevailed. But in *Re ffrench's Estate*,[2] decided by the Irish Court of Appeal some time after *Cave v Cave*, Porter MR took a different view: the right of the beneficiary to trace was, he said, a mere equity which was displaced by a subsequent equitable mortgage taken in good faith and without notice of the beneficiary's claim. It has been said by two leading commentators[3] that since *Re ffrench's Estate* has not been subsequently disapproved and has indeed been expressly applied in a number of cases, there is a clear divergence between Irish and English law in this area. A note of caution should be sounded, however: the other members of the Court of Appeal in *Re ffrench's Estate* did not rest their judgement on this ground and the general proposition that the tracing remedy operates *in personam* only and not *in rem* is clearly not reconcilable with subsequent Irish authority. This problem is discussed in more detail in Chapter 20 below.

1 (1880) 15 Ch D 639.
2 (1887) 21 LR Ir 283, CA.
3 Delaney, 'Equitable Interests and "Mere Equities" ' (1957) 21 Conv 195; Wylie *Land Law*, p 101.

Chapter 5

Priorities, registration and notice

Registration in Ireland

5.01 In order to determine priorities between competing interests in land, it is not sufficient simply to have regard to the two maxims already mentioned, *'where the equities are equal, the first in time prevails'* and *'where the equities are equal, the law prevails.'* In this area, the question of registration is of supreme importance in Ireland.

There are two systems of registration affecting land in Ireland, the first established by the Irish Registry Act[1] passed in the reign of Queen Anne and the second by the Local Registration of Title (Ireland) Act 1891, which has been replaced by the Registration of Title Act 1964.

1 6 Anne c 2.

5.02 Under the first system, all deeds, conveyances and wills affecting land may be registered in the Registry of Deeds in Dublin.[1] Registration of a deed or other instrument capable of registration has two main consequences:

(i) registered instruments rank in priority *inter se* according to the dates of their registration and not of their execution.[2] As between two such instruments, accordingly, the maxim 'where the equities are equal, the first in time prevails,' has no application.

(ii) a deed or conveyance of which a memorial is not registered is deemed fraudulent and void, as against a conveyance of which a memorial is registered.[3] But the person claiming under the registered deed must have given value. A voluntary deed will not be given priority over a prior unregistered deed for value.[4]

The effect of registration thus must always be taken into account in applying the two maxims in Ireland. As Christian LJ observed in *Agra Bank Ltd v Barry*:[5]

'The truth is that the part which registration law has played in England is insignificant compared with that which it has filled in Ireland.....Nothing but a general and inexorable law of registry could afford reasonable security against the cloud of secret, deceitful, evasive transactions that hovered over most incumbered properties (in Ireland). Such a law was the Act of Anne. We know how under its universal operation and more stringent clauses some of the doctrines which still possess all their original importance in English conveyancing have disappeared out of that of Ireland.'

(It should be said, in passing, that one factor which contributed to the prevalence of 'secret' and 'evasive' transactions was the penal laws which outlawed the owning of land by Catholics. The preamble refers to the 'forgeries and fraudulent....conveyances which have been frequently practised in this kingdom, especially by papists, to the great prejudice of the protestant interest thereof....'.)

1 Note that contracts in writing to convey or charge an interest in land are registrable instruments although not under seal: *Credland v Potter* (1874) 10 Ch App 8; *Re Stevenson's Estate* [1902] 1 IR 23 at 35.
2 6 Anne c 2 s 4.
3 Ibid, s 5.
4 *Re Flood* 13 Ir Ch R 312.
5 Ir R 6 Eq 128 at 161-2; affd LR 7HL 135.

5.03 Under the second system, the title to any land may be registered in the Land Registry under the Registration of Title Act 1964. The system in its present form was first established in 1891 and essentially provided for two types of registration, compulsory and voluntary. Land which was vested in tenant purchasers by the Irish Land Commission had to be registered: all other registration was voluntary. Under this registration system—which is found in many other jurisdictions where it is frequently referred to as a 'Torrens Title System' after its English pioneer—the title to the land is contained in the register maintained in the Land Registry rather than in a number of title deeds. All that a purchaser requires, broadly speaking, is that the vendor should be named in the register as the absolute owner and that no 'burdens' should appear on the register. He is not concerned, as is the purchaser of unregistered land, with examining all the transactions which have taken place for up to forty years in order to satisfy himself that the ownership of the land has devolved on the vendor. Nor need he search in the Registry of Deeds to see if there are any transactions affecting the land: the register is conclusive evidence of the title 'as appearing' therein.[1]

1 1964 Act, s 31(1).

Where the equities are equal, the first in time prevails

5.04 We shall confine the discussion of this maxim at this point to unregistered land. There are special considerations affecting registered land, which are dealt with below.[1] In the case of pure personalty—interests in property other than land—priorities are determined by the rule in *Dearle v Hall*,[2] rather than this maxim. In the case of unregistered land, the application of the maxim is confined in practice to competing claims between transactions one or more of which is incapable of registration, such as an equitable mortgage by deposit of title deeds. Such a mortgage is an extremely common form of security in Ireland: it means that where the title deeds of land are deposited with a person—usually a bank—to secure advances, a mortgage of the land is thereby created which enables the mortgagee to obtain an order for sale of the land, to secure repayment. Provided it is not accompanied by any writing, such a mortgage is regarded as incapable of registration in the Registry of Deeds. Hence, ever since the leading case of *Re Burke*,[3] it has been the law that such a deposit will be given priority over a subsequent equitable interest, even though the lattter is registered: here the maxim 'where the equitites are equal, the first in time prevails,' is fully applicable.

The maxim was thus stated by Kindersley V-C in his frequently cited judgement in *Rice v Rice*:[4]

'As between persons having only equitable interests, if their equities are in all other respects equal, priority of time gives the better equity, or *qui prior est tempore, potior est jure.*'

As equitable deed has, accordingly, been described as an 'innocent conveyance':[5] the transferor cannot give the transferee anything more than the beneficial interest which he actually has and if that interest is reduced, or displaced altogether, by an earlier equity, the transfer is affected to the same extent. For the maxim to apply, however, the equities must be equal and, as we saw in the last chapter, if the earlier equity is no more than an equity, it will be postponed to a subsequent equitable *interest* taken in good faith and without notice of the equity.[6] And where the contest is between two equitable interests, the court must have regard to all the circumstances, including the conduct of the parties, to determine who has the better equity.[7]

So, in *Re Lambert's Estate*,[8] A became entitled to lands by virtue of a deed. He left the lands to B, who mortgaged them to a bank to secure advances. This was an equitable mortgage which was effected by depositing the deed with the bank. B, however, retained the other title deeds to the lands and subsequently deposited these with C to secure further advances. C made all the enquiries that were reasonably necessary. Here there were two conflicting equitable interests, but the claim of C was held to be superior: the bank had been negligent in permitting B to retain the other title deeds. Moreover, the earlier mortgage, unlike the later, had been accompanied by a memorandum in writing and consequently was capable of registration. This again was held to be negligence on the bank's part, since a search would have brought it to light had it been registered. By contrast, in *National Bank v Keegan*[9] where the owner of a house agreed to give his aunt the right of residence in two rooms and subsequently created an equitable mortgage with the plaintiff bank, the aunt's equitable interest prevailed as being earlier in time, since here the equities were equal. (We have seen that the principle that such a right of residence amounts to an equitable estate has been reversed by the Registration of Title Act 1964.)[10]

1 Paras 5.11 to 5.14, below.
2 (1828) 3 Russ 1.
3 (1882) 9 LR Ir 24, CA.
4 (1854) 2 Drew 73.
5 Per Lord Westbury in *Phillips v Phillips* (1861) 4 de GF & J 208 at 215.
6 Para 4.03, above.
7 Per Kindersley V-C in *Rice v Rice* at 77.
8 (1884) 13 LR Ir 234.

9 [1931] IR 344.
10 Para 4.06, above.

5.05 It is clear, accordingly, that where the conduct of the first equitable owner has been such as to render it inequitable to allow his interest prevail over the interest of a subsequent equitable claimant, the equities will not be equal and the maxim will not apply. What is the position where there has been nothing in the conduct of the first equitable owner which would render it inequitable to give him the priority, but his trustee has been guilty of such conduct? To this difficult question, the Irish and English courts have given divergent answers.

The leading English case is *Shropshire Union Railways and Land Co v R.*[1] A director of a railway company secured advances on the strength of certificates of stock in the company which was registered in his name. In fact he was simply a trustee of the stock. The House of Lords rejected the argument that a trustee who was so armed with the documents of title to the trust estate could destroy the title of the beneficiary by purporting to confer an equitable interest on a third party. Only a transfer of the legal title to the property could have that effect, and, if a transfer had been executed, the directors could have refused to register the transferee, thereby preventing the legal title from passing. Lord Cairns acknowledged that there could be conduct on the part of the beneficiaries which would be sufficient to displace their equitable title. But allowing the trustee to have possession of the stock certificates was not such conduct.

The Irish Court of Appeal in *Re ffrench's Estate*[2] took a different view. In that case, land was purchased by the tenant for life under a marriage settlement, partly with money subject to the trusts of the settlement. The conveyance was taken in his name without any reference to the source of the monies and, although a deed was executed by him acknowledging that the land had been bought with trust monies, this deed was never registered. The trustees who had been persuaded to advance him the trust money thus failed to take the necessary steps to protect the interests of the other beneficiaries. Subsequently, the tenant for life raised money on the security of a legal mortgage of the land (of which he had then been in possession for many years) and was advanced further sums on the strength of an equitable mortgage. (Since he had parted with the legal estate, all he had left to mortgage was the equity of redemption.) The equitable mortgagee had no notice of the fact that the purchase had been made in part with trust funds many years before and there was nothing to put him on notice. When the land was being sold through the incumbered estates procedure, the children entitled under the marriage settlement claimed priority over the equitable mortgagee. Over sixty years had elapsed since the original misapplication of the trust funds and the Court of Appeal rejected emphatically the suggestion that a mortgagee could be defeated by a 'subterranean equity' of this nature of which he had no means of knowing and which had not been asserted by any of the beneficiaries during the previous sixty years.[3] Porter MR, as we have seen, thought that the right of the beneficiaries to trace the trust funds into the land was a mere equity which could not displace a subsequent equitable estate. But FitzGibbon and Barry LJJ preferred to rest their judgements on the conduct of the beneficiaries and the trustees. The former had failed to assert their rights with any expedition even when they became aware of them. But it is in their view of the consequences of the trustees' negligence that the real conflict between their approach and that of the House of Lords emerged. It was, in their view, the responsibility of beneficiaries to pick careful and honest trustees and where the chosen trustees acted in breach of duty, the loss could not fall on an innocent equitable incumbrancer.[4] This is plainly not reconcilable with the decision in *Shropshire Union Railways and Land Co* and since the latter decision was not cited to the court, the authority of *Re ffrench's Estate* must be open to question. Having regard to the hierarchy of courts which existed at the time, the Court of Appeal would have been bound by the House of Lords decision and hence their opposing pronouncements of the law were delivered *per incuriam*. But the decision was never reviewed by a court of co-ordinate or superior jurisdiction and judges at first instance felt obliged to apply it.[5] Should it come before the Irish courts to-day, they would not be bound either by the *Shropshire Union Railways and Land Co* or *Re ffrench's Estate*.[6] It is thought, however, that the reasoning in the latter case might still be regarded as more appropriate in Irish conditions: as Barry LJ remarked, the difference in practice in conveyancing in the two countries arising from the general registry system in force in Ireland is significant.[7] Hence the less weight attached in Ireland to getting in the legal estate and the greater reliance on equitable titles.

In any event, the exceptions to the principle laid down by Lord Cairns are numerous:[8] it is quite clear that it does not apply, for example, where the beneficiary vests the title in the trustee in order to enable him to deal with it on his behalf. In such a case, the parties' rights and liabilities are determined by the law of principal and agent and if the agent enters into a transaction—such as borrowing money on the strength of documents of title—which is beyond his authority, the principal will be bound by the transaction if the third party is unaware that it was beyond the agent's authority.[9]

1 (1875) LR 7HL 496.
2 (1887) 21 LR Ir 283.
3 Per Porter MR at 300.
4 Fitzgibbon LJ (at 319) appeared to think that the beneficiaries would be entitled to succeed it the trustee's conduct was *fraudulent* as opposed to merely negligent. This would have the odd result that the beneficiary who picked a clever rogue as trustee would be in a better position than one who picked an honest incompetent.
5 *Re Sloane's Estate* [1895] 1 IR 146; *Bank of Ireland v Cogry Spinning Co* [1900] 1 IR 219: In *Re Bobbett's Estate* [1904] 1 IR 461; *Scott v Scott* [1924] 1 IR 141.
6 In *Allied Irish Banks Ltd v Glynn* (1973) IR 188, Kenny J expressly declined to resolve the conflict, preferring to rest his decision on the patent superiority of the bank's equitable interest.
7 21 LR Ir at 337. See para 5.02, above.
8 See Meagher Gummow & Lehane, 218 to 227.
9 *Rimmer v Webster* [1902] 2 Ch 163.

Where the equities are equal, the law prevails.

5.06 Where there are competing equitable claims of equal merits, but one claimant is entitled to the legal estate, the latter's claim is preferred. But the applicability of this maxim is also restricted in Ireland by the registration system, which may render possession of the legal estate immaterial, just as it may render temporal priority immaterial. So, if A agrees to sell land to B and then, finding C is willing to pay a higher price, not only signs a contract but actually executes a conveyance in favour of C. B will still be given priority if he has registered his contract. C, it is true, has the legal estate, but B's contract is an instrument capable of registration and accordingly, will be given priority.

Where the maxim will apply, it will be again usually because of a conflict between an equitable interest not capable of registration—such as an equitable mortgage by deposit of title deed—and a legal interest. So, where the legal estate is acquired for value and there is a subsequent equitable mortgage, the legal owner will not be affected by the later transaction, unless he has been guilty of fraud or what has been called 'gross negligence'. Thus in *Re Greer's Estate*,[1] A granted a legal mortgage of land to B which was registered. B did not, however, obtain the title deeds from A and the latter subsequently deposited them with C to obtain a further advance. It was held that while B had been negligent in not obtaining possession of the title deeds, he had not been guilty of the 'gross negligence' which would have been necessary to deprive him of his security. The equities remain equal, in such a case, and the law prevails.

It should be noted that B's legal mortgage in that case had been registered. However, since the equitable mortgage was not capable of registration, the question of priorities was not strictly affected by registration. But Barton J did observe that in the case of a legal mortgage which had *not* been registered, a second mortgagee might be in a better position to contend that the non-possession of the deeds raised a prima facie case of negligence, placing on the legal mortgagee the burden of explaining why he had not got the deeds. It should also be pointed out that while the requirement that the equitable mortgagee prove 'gross negligence' has the imprimatur of Lord Eldon,[2] it may be questionable whether it would necessarily be applicable to-day. There has been considerable judicial scepticism as to whether the adjective 'gross' really adds anything to the concept of negligence.[3] The true position may be that in a case where the earlier dealing has been registered, the Court will certainly require positive evidence that the legal mortgagee was negligent, but if it can be shown that he had failed to take reasonable care to ensure that subsequent purchasers or lenders were not misled, he will be denied priority. If, for example, he never even asks the mortgagor to give him the title deeds, this would seem to amount to such a lack of reasonable care on his part as to render it unfair that the equitable mortgagee should suffer through his negligence. If, on the other hand, the mortgagor gives a reasonable explanation for retaining the deeds in his possession, there would seem no ground for postponing the legal mortgagee.

It was also at one time the law that the earlier mortgagee owed no duty of care to later incumbrancers or purchasers since there was no privity between them.[4] But this is clearly no longer so.

Where the equitable interest is earlier in time, it may still be defeated by the application of the maxim. This will happen where the legal estate is subsequently acquired by a bona fide purchaser for value without notice of the equitable interest. Here the equities are equal, but the law prevails. If the earlier interest is registered that, as we have seen, is sufficient to give priority. But where it is either not registered or is incapable of registration, acquisition of the legal estate for value without notice will defeat it. It may be thought that this would place at great risk an equitable deposit of title deeds, which of its nature cannot be registered if there is no instrument in writing, but in practice this is not so. The reason is that a bona fide purchaser for value—or someone advancing money—will invariably require the title deeds of the property to be produced. A failure by him to enquire for them would normally amount to his being fixed with notice: not actual notice, but the form of notice called constructive notice[5] which is dealt with in more detail below.[6]

1 [1907] 1 IR 57.
2 *Evans v Bicknell* (1801) 6 Ves 174 at 181.
3 In *Northern Bank Ltd v Henry* [1981] IR 1 Henchy J cited with approval (at 11) the view of Rolfe B in *Wilson v Brett* (1843) 11 M & W 133 that there was no difference between negligence and gross negligence: 'it is the same thing with the addition of a vituperative epithet.' See also the view of the same learned judge in *Banco Ambrosiano SPA v Ansbacher & Co Ltd* (unreported; judgements delivered 8 April 1987).
4 *Kelly v Munster and Leinster Bank* (1891) 29 LR Ir 19 at 44, CA.
5 See para 5.08, below.
6 It has been said that *Agra Bank Ltd v Barry* (above) suggests the contrary and would not be followed to-day (Wylie, *Land Law,* pp 70–71); but it is to be observed that in that case the earlier equitable mortgage by deposit was accompanied by a written instrument which should have been, but was not, registered.

Notice

5.07 It will be seen that, whether the contest is between competing equities or between equities and legal interests, the question of notice is often crucial. In general, it can be said that a person who acquires an interest, whether it be legal or equitable, with notice that it is subject to a prior claim, whether that be a legal or equitable claim, will not be permitted to deny that claim. To this, there are two major exceptions. As we have seen, a 'naked equity' such as the right of a spouse to possession will not be binding on a subsequent purchaser. And as we shall see later, the purchaser for value of registered land is unaffected by unregistered equitable claims, whether or not he has notice of them.

It would be surprising if, in a court required to apply equitable principles, a person who acquires property in the knowledge that another person has a recognised legal or equitable right to it would be permitted to deny that right. But what constitutes 'notice' of the earlier claim is a more difficult matter.

'Notice' in this area of the law can take three forms. It can be *actual* notice, where the person concerned is aware of his own knowledge of the previous claim. It can be *constructive* notice, where the person concerned is not himself aware, but would have become aware had he made proper inquiries. Or it can be *imputed* notice, where his agent as such in the course of the transaction has actual or constructive notice of the previous claim.[1]

1 *Bank of Ireland Finance Ltd v Rockfield Ltd* [1979] IR 21, SC.

5.08 Where the contest is between a registered instrument and an earlier unregistered instrument, which could have been registered, *actual* notice is essential to defeat the claim under the registered instrument. This principle was firmly established by the decision of the House of Lords in *Agra Bank Ltd and Others v Barry* and was applied by Costello J in more recent times in *Re Fuller and Co Ltd (in liquidation) O'Connor v McCarthy and Others*.[1] In that case, a liquidator had agreed to sell land to A, but on getting a better offer from B signed a second contract for sale with B. A's contract was not registered but B's was. Costello J found that B had no actual notice of the earlier contract and accordingly was entitled to priority because of his registration. Only actual notice—whether that of the claimant himself or notice of his agent which could be imputed to him—

would have been sufficient to defeat the priority of the registered instrument. It is also clear from the same decision that mere rumours or 'flying reports' will not amount to actual notice: Costello J adopted the test applied by Lord Cairns in *Lloyd v Banks*;[2]

> 'It must depend upon the facts of the case; but I am quite prepared to say that I think the Court would expect to find that those who alleged that the trustee had knowledge of the incumbrance had made it out, not by any evidence of casual conversations, much less by any proof of what would only be constructive notice—but by proof that the mind of the trustee has in some way been brought to an intelligent apprehension of the nature of the incumbrance which has come upon the property so that a reasonable man or an ordinary man of business would act upon the information and would regulate his conduct by it in the execution of the trust.'[3]

But while actual notice is thus essential to defeat the claim under the later registered instrument, it must not be thought that by deliberately shutting his eyes to the obvious a person can avoid having the sort of notice that might affect his interest. Again, Costello J applied the criterion proposed by Lord Cairns, this time in *Agra Bank Ltd and Others v Barry*:

> 'Of course, you may have.....conduct so reckless, so intensely negligent, that you are absolutely unable to account for it in any other way than this, that by reason of a suspicion entertained by the person whose conduct you are examining that there was a registered deed before his, he will abstain from inquiring into the fact, because he is so satisfied that the fact exists, that he feels persuaded that if he did enquire, he must find out.'

Such conduct amounts to what equity regards as a fraud and hence will never afford priority.

1 [1982] IR 161.
2 (1868) 3 Ch App 488.
3 At 490 to 491.

5.09 In other cases—ie where the earlier claim is not dependent on an unregistered instrument capable of registration—the later claimant will be affected by constructive notice. In the case of purchasers of unregistered land, the nature of the notice which will affect them is defined by statute in s 3 of the Conveyancing Act 1882 as follows:

> 'A purchaser shall not be prejudicially affected by notice of any instrument fact or thing unless—
>   (i) it is within his own knowledge or would have come to his knowledge if such inquiries had been made as ought reasonably to have been made by him; or
>   (ii) in the same transaction with respect to which a question of notice to the purchaser arises it has come to his knowledge or of his counsel as such or of his solicitor or other agent as such or would have come to the knowledge of his solicitor or other agent as such if such enquiries and inspections had been made as ought reasonably to have been made by the solicitor or other agent.'

It has been held by the Supreme Court in the leading modern Irish case on the topic, *Northern Bank Ltd v Henry and Others*,[1] that the test to be applied in determining whether reasonable inquiries have been made is an objective one. It is not material that, viewed in the light of the purchaser's own concerns, an inquiry might have been unnecessary. If a reasonable person in the position of a purchaser would have made the inquiry, then the purchaser will be affected by constructive notice, even though from his point of view an inquiry would not have been necessary. As a result, a purchaser is not entitled to confine his inquiries to matters which may affect his own interest in the property and then claim that he has not notice of matters which may affect third parties.

In *Northern Bank Ltd v Henry*, the defendant had acquired the house in which he and his wife lived in his own name. It was, however, decided in the subsequent litigation that he held it in trust for his wife, since its acquisition had been effected with her family monies.[2] The husband and wife having become estranged and separated, the husband sought advances from the plaintiff bank on the security of the title deeds to the house. The bank gave an advance on the security of a legal mortgage of the house. They were postponed to the wife's claim to the equitable ownership of the house, the High Court (McWilliam J) holding, and being upheld by the Supreme Court, that had the bank's solicitors made inquiries (in the form of requisitions on the title) as to whether the wife was claiming any equitable interest in the house, the nature of the wife's interest would have come to light. Henchy J put the matter thus in the Supreme Court:[3]

'In my judgement, the test of what inquiries and inspections ought to reasonably have been made is an objective test, which depends not on what the particular purchaser thought proper to do in the particular circumstances, but on what a purchaser ought reasonably to have done to acquire title to it.....
'The prudence of the worldly wise may justifiably persuade the purchaser that it would be unbusinesslike to stop and look more deeply into certain aspects of the title. But the reasonable man, in the eyes of the law will be expected to look beyond the impact of his decisions on his own affairs and consider whether they may unfairly and prejudicially affect his neighbour, in the sense in which that word has been given juristic currency by Lord Atkin in *Donoghue v Stevenson.*'[4]

The precise situation dealt with in *Northern Bank v Henry* should not arise again so long as the Family Home Protection Act 1976 remains on the statute book.[5] A purchaser or lender will now always require the consent of the spouse who is not the owner to a sale or mortgage, or evidence that the premises are not a family home. But the general principle which it lays down remains of importance: a purchaser, for example, who refrains from making inquiries as to who is in occupation of premises and why, either through carelessness or to avoid being saddled with embarrassing knowledge, may find himself affected by constructive notice of the rights of those in occupation.

1 [1981] IR 1.
2 See Chapter 12, below.
3 At 11 to 12.
4 [1932] AC 562.
5 See para 4.02, above.

5.10 The onus of proving that he had no notice rests on the person who claims that he took without notice. Thus, if a person claims that a prior equitable interest is to yield to his acquisition of the legal estate for value without notice, it is for him to prove that he had no notice.[1] He must, moreover, prove both elements: it is not sufficient for him to establish that he gave value and leave it to the prior claimant to prove that he had notice.[2]

1 *Re Nisbet and Pott's Contract* [1906] 1 Ch 386.
2 *Heneghan v Davitt and Rowley* [1933] IR 375, SC.

Priorities and notice in the case of registered land

5.11 The law as to priorities and notice is different in some important respects in the case of land the title to which is registered in the Land Registry under the provisions of the Registration of Title Act 1964 and this whether the land is registered compulsorily, because it is vested in a tenant under the Land Purchase Acts or is situated in one of the counties where registration is compulsory in all cases,[1] or is registered voluntarily.

In the first place, the register is conclusive evidence of the title 'as appearing' therein and under s 31(1):

'such title shall not, in the absence of actual fraud, be in any way affected in consequence of such owner having notice of any deed, document or matter relating to the land....'

The section goes on to provide for the rectification of the register by the court on the ground of actual fraud or mistake. Hence in the absence of actual fraud or mistake, the registered owner, a purchaser for value from him or a holder of a charge for value, is not affected by any equitable interest in the land whether or not he has notice of it. And this applies whether the notice is actual or constructive.[2] The 1964 Act also provides (in s 92) that notice of a trust is not to be entered in the register.

But it should not be thought that there cannot as a result be an effective trust of registered land. It is perfectly possible to create such a trust, even though the Act only recognises the registered owner and not any form of equitable interests. The 1964 Act, indeed, provides (in s 37(4) and s 44(4)) that nothing is to affect the registered owner's duties and liabilities as a trustee. A beneficiary who wishes to ensure that the registered owner/trustee does not dispose of the land in breach of his trust can protect his interest by entering a *caution* or *inhibition*. A caution prevents any dealing with the land on the part of the registered owner until notice has been given to the cautioner.[3] An inhibition prevents any such dealing until the occurrence of an event named in the inhibition or except with the consent of, or after notice, to named persons.[4]

Any person who buys land which is the subject of a caution or inhibition in the registry will be unable to secure registration himself as owner until the caution or inhibition has been removed. Until he is registered he is merely the equitable owner and hence priority will be given to the beneficiary whose interest is protected by the caution or inhibition, in accordance with the maxim 'where the equities are equal, the first in time prevails.'[5]

The 1964 Act also provides for the creation of 'rights' in or over any registered land.[6] It is clear from the terms of the Act and the decision of the Supreme Court in *Devoy v Hanlon*[7] that such rights will prevail against a voluntary transferee, but not against a purchaser for value or the holder of a charge for value.

1 Counties Carlow, Meath and Offaly.
2 *Re Michael Walsh* [1916] 1 IR 40.
3 1964 Act, s 97.
4 1964 Act, s 98.
5 Cf Kiely, *Principles of Equity*, p27.

6 1964 Act, s 68.
7 [1929] IR 246. Cf *Colreavy v Colreavy and Keenan* [1940] IR 71.

5.12 In the second place, in the case of registered land the evidence of the owner's title is contained in one document and not in a succession of title deeds proving the devolution of the title. When a person is registered as owner for the first time, he is issued with a document called the Land Certificate which must be produced to the Land Registry before any subsequent dealing with the land is registered. But although the evidence of title is contained in this single document, it resembles the title deeds to unregistered land in one important respect: its deposit with a lender to secure an advance creates an equitable charge, similar in its effect to the equitable mortgage by deposit of the title deeds.[1]

In accordance with the maxim 'where the equities are equal, the first in time prevails', this equitable charge is subject to any prior equitable interests. So, in *Tench v Molyneux*,[2] A, the registered owner, sold the land to B, who failed to get himself registered. A subsequently deposited the land certificate with C to secure a loan. It was held that the charge thus created was postponed to the earlier equitable interest of B under the contract. But such a charge would take priority over a *subsequent* sale: without the land certificate, a purchaser could not be registered and until registration would merely have an equitable interest in the land which would be postponed to the earlier equitable charge.

It should also be noted that, while a legal mortgage can be created of registered land, it is described as a 'charge'.[3] Such a charge is one of the burdens which may be registered on the folio. The priorities of such registered charges are determined by the dates of their registration. Where such a charge is made, as it frequently is, to secure both present and future advances, it will obtain priority in respect of the future advances over any intermediate charge of which the lender has no notice.[4]

1 1964 Act, s 105(5).
2 (1914) 48 ILTR 48, CA.
3 1964 Act, s 62.
4 1964 Act, s 75(1).

5.13 In the third place, while the only title which the Act acknowledges is that of the registered owner, that title itself may be merely a 'possessory' or 'qualified' title.[1] The register, it should be emphasised again, is only evidence of the title to the land 'as appearing' therein. A 'qualified' title is subject to estates or rights included in the qualification noted in the register. A 'possessory' title will be entered on the register where the person seeking registration cannot show any documentary title to the land. Such a registration does not affect or prejudice the enforcement of any right adverse to, or in derogation of, the registered owner's title and subsisting at the time of registration. A purchaser will thus be on notice of such rights and he will usually require that the title be converted into an 'absolute' title, which can be done in the Land Registry on the production of the appropriate evidence.

1 1964 Act, s 33(1).
2 1964 Act, s 38.
3 1964 Act, s 50.

5.14 In the fourth place, there are certain 'burdens' as already mentioned which affect registered land, even though they are not registered. They are specified in s 72 of the 1964 Act and include land purchase annuities, rights acquired under the Statute of Limitations 1957 (ie the right of a squatter to remain in possession of the land after the limitation period has expired)[1] tenancies for terms not exceeding twenty-one years where there is someone in occuption under the tenancies and

> 'the rights of every person in actual occupation of the land or in receipt of the rent and profits thereof, save where, upon enquiry made of such person, the rights are not disclosed.'

It will be seen, particularly from the last mentioned category, that as in the case of unregistered land, so also in the case of registered land, a purchaser cannot escape being fixed with notice simply by closing his eyes to the fact that there are people in occupation of the premises.

1 In the case of freehold land, the squatter will generally acquire a right to be registered at the expiration of the limitation period. It has also been suggested *obiter* by Walsh J in *Perry v Woodfarm Homes Ltd* [1975] IR 104 SC that the squatter on registered leasehold land acquires a similar right.

Judgement mortgages

5.15 A judgement mortgage is a method of recovering debts which has been an abundant source of litigation in Ireland. Essentially, a creditor who has recovered judgement for a money sum is entitled to convert it into a mortgage over any land of the debtor. He does so by filing in the court in which he obtained the judgement an affidavit setting out details of the judgement and then registering a copy of the affidavit in the Registry of Deed or the Land Registry. He thus makes himself a secured creditor with the usual rights of a conventional mortgagee, including the right to obtain an order for sale of the land.

In the case of unregistered land, such a mortgage is subject to all the equities which affected the land at the date of the registration of the judgement mortgage.[1] Hence the judgement mortgagee will be postponed to an earlier deed, even though it is unregistered.[2] There is an exception, however, for conveyances and transfers made *after* the date of the judgement and before registration, which would be void as against bona fide purchasers for value, ie dispositions intended to defeat creditors, and hence regarded as fraudulent.[3]

If the judgement creditor after registering his judgement as a mortgage gets a subsequent deed for value from his debtor which is registered, he will then be given priority over previous unregistered deeds. The subsequent registered deed, it is said, 'carries the judgement mortgage on its back.'[4] This only applies however, where there is a conflict between the earlier and the later deed.[5] While the rule has been described as 'peculiar', it seems logical: the reason a judgement mortgage simpliciter is subject to prior unregistered equities is that it is a form of security which is solely brought about by the creditor. He consequently takes the land comprised in it with all their imperfections, including any unregistered equities. But this should not apply where he takes a subsequent conveyance of the interest, since it then ceases to be such a security.

1 Judgment Mortgage (Ireland) Act 1850, s 6.
2 *Eyre v McDowell* (1861) 9 HL Cas 619.
3 Judgment Mortgage (Ireland) Act 1850, s 8; Voluntary Conveyances Act 1893, s 8.

4 *Murtagh v Tisdall* (1840) 3 Ir Eq 85 at 96.
5 *Latouche v Dunsany* (1803) 1 Sch & Lef 137 at 161.

5.16 In the case of registered land, the position is essentially the same. Section 71(4) of the 1964 Act provides that the charge created by the judgement mortgage is subject to existing registered burdens, burdens which affect the land without notice and 'all unregistered rights' subject to which the debtor held the land at the time of the registration.

However, the priority as between a judgement mortgagee and a purchaser of the land who has signed a contract but has not been registered as owner has given rise to difficulty. In *Re Murphy and McCormack's Contract,*[1] where the purchaser had actually paid his purchase money but had not been registered as owner at the time of the registration of the judgement mortgage, the Supreme Court was divided on the question as to whether the purchaser had priority, Kennedy CJ holding that he had and Murnaghan J that he had not. In that case, however, the affidavit leading to the registration of the judgement mortgage was defective and the purchaser was entitled to priority on that ground. Fitzgibbon J expressed no view on the point which divided his brethren. Subsequently, in *Re Strong,*[2] the court by a majority held that in such circumstances the purchaser had priority. There was no equivalent to s 71(4) in the 1891 Act, but O'Byrne J, speaking for the majority, said that the right of the purchaser was one of the 'rights' which by virtue of s 44(2) of that Act a registered owner was entitled to create. Such a right, in his view, was binding on voluntary transferees, although not on purchasers for value and holders of charges for value. Since it had been long established that a judgement mortgage was not a charge for value, but merely a process of execution, the right of the purchaser was binding on the judgement mortgagee. The question remained as to whether the same result followed where the purchaser had simply signed the contract but had not paid the purchase money.

This question came before the Supreme Court in *Tempany v Hynes.*[3] There the land was subject to a floating charge which crystallised on the appointment of a receiver. The receiver entered into a contract for the sale of the land, but before the purchase price was paid, a judgement mortgage was registered against the land. The purchaser refused to complete, but the Supreme Court held that he was obliged to do so, and granted a decree of specific performance. They differed, however, in their reasons.

Kenny J, with whom O'Higgins CJ agreed, held that the purchaser did not acquire any estate or interest in the land simply by virtue of the contract.[4] The beneficial ownership of the land, as well as the legal title, remained vested in the vendor. Hence it was properly the subject matter of a judgement mortgage which would continue in normal circumstances to affect the land after the completion of the sale. But in this case, the crystallisation of the floating charge had in any event created an equitable charge which took priority over the judgement mortgage and hence the purchaser was obliged to complete.

Henchy J took a different view as to the effect of the contract for sale: he thought that the beneficial ownership was thereby transferred to the purchaser and that the legal estate remaining in the vendor was all that could be captured by the judgement mortgage. Since that was a transient interest which disappeared on completion, the judgement mortgage would not affect the purchaser's title after completion. But in addition he pointed out that s 71 of the 1964 Act now made it clear that the judgement mortgagee's interest was subject to all 'unregistered rights' and said that this clearly included the rights of a purchaser, whether or not the purchase price had been paid. Since 'right' was defined as including any 'estate, interest, equity and power', the expression covered the right of the purchaser in that case.

The judgement of the majority in *Tempany v Hynes* represents, of course, the law, but it is thought that the decision is somewhat doubtful. Even if it is conceded that the beneficial interest in the land does not vest in the purchaser by virtue of the contract, it remains unclear why the right of the purchaser to specific performance of the contract does not qualify as a 'right' within the meaning of s 71 of the 1964 Act, particularly having regard to the view of O'Byrne J in *Re Strong* (not expressly dissented from in *Tempany v Hynes*) that in a similar context the expression should be interpreted broadly. This view is strengthened by the extended definition of the word 'right': even if it is the case that the purchaser's right to enforce the contract does not ripen into an equitable estate until the payment of the purchase money, it seems difficult to deny it the status at least of a mere 'equity'. Yet that is the word used in the definition of rights,[5] apparently in distinction to 'estate' and 'interest'. It should be noted that the judgement of Kenny J does not address the question as why the purchaser's rights should not be considered one of the 'rights' referred to in s 71.

Kenny J found it a puzzling concept to treat the judgement mortgage as surviving if the sale was abortive but extinct if it was completed.[6] However, this is not perhaps so difficult a concept, if it is acknowledged that the separation of the ownership into legal and equitable estates only takes place when the contract is signed and ceases to exist when the sale is completed, since at that stage, on any view, the legal and equitable ownership are vested in one person. Before then, even allowing that the equitable ownership is not vested in the purchaser until all the purchase price is paid, the duality of ownership may be necessary to reflect the different positions of the two parties. As Viscount Radcliffe made clear in *Commissioners of Stamp Duties v Livingstone*,[7] the concept of dual ownership is only invoked by the law where it is necessary to resolve specific problems and need not be seen as inhering in the property at all times.[8]

A decision by the Court of Appeal in *Re Kissock and Currie's Contract*[9] might seem to support the view of the majority in *Tempany v Hynes*. In that case, a purchaser who had signed a contract but had not taken a conveyance at the stage when the judgement mortgage was registered was held to have acquired the land subject to that mortgage and in the result the court refused to force the title on a subsequent purchaser. But there is a curious feature of the case: on the first sale, no money passed on the closing. The essence of the agreement was that the purchaser was to acquire the property , subject to incumbrances which he would pay off, and to releasing a debt due to him. The vendor was in effect transferring her equity of redemption to the first purchaser in return for being released from her debts. It seems unthinkable that in those circumstances, if no conveyance had ever been executed, the purchaser would have been treated as anything but the owner of the lands in equity subject to the mortgages. It is difficult to see how his position can be distinguished from the purchaser in *Re Strong* who had paid his purchase money. It would seem to follow that the case is not reconcilable with *Re Strong*, which as a later authority of the Supreme Court would seem to carry greater weight and that it should be treated as having been reversed *sub silentio* by the latter decision.

1 [1930] IR 322.
2 [1940] IR 382.
3 [1976] IR 101.
4 See para 4.06, above.
5 S 3(1).
6 At p 404.
7 [1965] AC 694.
8 See para 4.05, above.
9 [1916] 1 IR 393.

Personalty: the Rule in Dearle v Hall

5.17 So far we have been dealing with priorities and notice as they affect interests in land. Interests in personalty other than land—'pure personalty' as it is sometimes called—must next be considered.

In such cases, priorities are governed by the rule in *Dearle v Hall*.[1] Shortly stated, it means that where two or more persons are beneficially entitled to the same fund, the person who first gives notice to the fundholder of his interest is given priority. So where a person beneficially entitled to money held by a trustee assigns his interest to two persons in succession, the first assignee will lose his priority unless he gives notice to the trustee. The same result follows where a creditor assigns his debt to A and B in succession and A fails to notify the debtor. There are, however, additional requirements which must be met by the second assignee if he is to obtain priority.

First, he must have given value: the rule does not protect a subsequent voluntary assignee. Second, he must have had no notice, at the time of the assignment to him, of the earlier assignment. Third, he must give notice of his assignment to the trustee. Fourth, the trustee at the time of the assignment to him must have had no notice of the earlier assignment.[2]

1 (1828) 3 Russ 1.
2 *Re Holmes* (1885) 29 Ch D 786; Meagher Lehane & Gummon, p230.

5.18 The facts in *Dearle v Hall* itself were relatively simple. A was entitled to a life interest under a settlement. He borrowed money from B and C in succession, assigning his life interest to each of them as security. He subsequently advertised his life interest for sale and it was purchased by D. D's prudent solicitor had first inquired specifically of the executors of the will under which the settlement arose whether they knew of any earlier charges. They said they did not, as was the fact, since B and C had not notified them of their assignments. The solicitor was also told by A that the interest was unincumbered. When B and C tried to enforce their securities, they failed, Sir Thomas Plumer MR holding that they should have given notice to the executors of their interests and being upheld in this view by the Lord Chancellor, Lord Lyndhurst.

It was an important feature of the case that D's solicitor had done everything possible to protect his client, while B and C in contrast had failed to take the relatively simple precaution of notifying the executors. Obviously such a failure to give notice could only facilitate a fraudulent assignment by the beneficiary of an interest already mortgaged and it would seem patently unjust that the later innocent borrower who had taken every precaution should suffer. The Master of the Rolls not surprisingly treated it as a clear example of a case where the equities as a result were not equal and accordingly priority in time should not be decisive. But he also elected to buttress this relatively straightforward conclusion with some legal propositions which, as Lord Macnaghten was to demonstrate in a subsequent case,[1] were dubious. These deflected attention in later decisions from the crucial feature of the case—the superior equity of the later claimant—and led to a rigid application of the rule that the first claimant to give notice got priority which, in his words, produced on the whole 'at least as much injustice as justice.[2]' The major fallacy propounded in the judgement was that, in the case of choses in action, such as A's right to the income, the giving of notice by the assignee to the trustee or debtor was essential to perfect the assignee's title. But this was not so in equity: notice to the trustee or debtor was simply a sensible precaution which in the normal course would prevent a later fraudulent disposition by the assignor of the beneficial interest.[3]

The allegedly paramount importance of notice led to the strange development that in the absence of notice by the first assignee, a later assignee for value was protected. provided he gave notice to the trustee or debtor when he learnt of the earlier assignment. It would have seemed logical that he should give such notice *before* he took his assignment. Not merely was this not so: he was not required to make any inquiries at all of th trustee or debtor before he took the assignment.[4] It will be seen how far the law has travelled from the application of the maxim that where the equities are equal, the first in time should prevail.

1 *Ward v Duncombe* [1893] AC 369, HL.
2 Ibid at pp 393-394.
3 No formality is required for the assignment of a chose in action in equity: *William Brandt's Sons & Co v Dunlop Rubber Co Ltd* [1905] AC 454 at 462.
4 *Foster v Cockerell* (1835) 3 Cl & Fin 456; *Re Dallas* [1904] 2 Ch 385.

5.19 The application of the rule has led to some complicated law as to what constitutes notice to the trustee or debtor, the refinements being due in part to the anxiety of some judges to limit the ambit of what was increasingly seen as an unnecessarily rigid doctrine. No particular formalities are required for the notice: it need not even be in writing.[1] Clearly, if all the trustees are aware of the first interest, that will be sufficient to defeat the claims of any later assignees. But the same result follows where they die or retire and are replaced by new trustees, whether or not they have informed their successors.[2] Moreover, where there are two or more trustees and one only knows of the first claim, that is sufficient to preserve its priority, even where the knowledgeable trustee dies or retires without communicating his knowledge to the other trustees. It is not material that as a result of his death or retirement, none of the trustees is actually aware of the first claim: the second assignee's claims are not given a new lease of life by that fortuitous event.[3] This is certainly the case where the later claimant's interest comes into being while the knowledgeable trustee is still a trustee. The position as to interests which come into being after his death or retirement is not so clear: there is Irish and English authority[4] that in such circumstances the later claimant's interest is not affected by the knowledge of the dead or retired trustee. But Lord Macnaghten expressed strong reservations—admittedly *obiter*—in *Ward v Dunscombe*, as to whether the English decision usually relied on was in fact an authority for this proposition, adding that such a view would lead to a scramble for priority on the death or retirement of a trustee.[5] A later decision of Kekewich J[6] to the contrary effect must be of doubtful authority, since these *dicta* are not even referred to.

It has also been held by the House of Lords in *B S Lyle Ltd v Rosher*[7] that the rule does not apply where the later assignment is made by a person who himself holds his interest in trust for others. In that case, the assignor was beneficially entitled under settlement A but held the interest on the trusts of settlement B. The trustees of settlement A were not aware of settlement B. When the assignor made the assignment to moneylenders, they inquired of the trustees of settlement A whether they had notice of any prior charges and they said they had not. It was held that the trustees of settlement B were not affected by the later assignment. It was argued for the moneylenders that the trustees' claim rested on an illogical distinction. In the classic *Dearle v Hall* case, the beneficial owner had already parted with the beneficial interest when he came to make the second assignment and hence he was in no different position from someone who only had the legal estate to begin with. But the majority of the law lords were obviously swayed by the desire to confine the rule as far as possible. Lord Reid, while accepting that this distinction was untenable, was prepared to uphold the trustees' claim on the basis that *Dearle v Hall* did not deprive a person beneficially entitled of his priority where his interest was vested in a trustee. In such a case, he thought, the beneficiary should not be required to give notice to protect his interest. But it has been pointed out that this should not be relevant to the question of priorities: it is for the trustees of settlement B, and not the beneficiaries, to give notice to the trustees of settlement A.[8]

It should finally be emphasised again that in Ireland the rule is confined in its application to pure personalty and never applies to interests in land.[9] In England since 1925 it has applied to successive dealings with any equitable interests in property, real or personal.[10]

1 *Lloyd v Banks* (1868) 3 Ch App 488.
2 *Re Wasdale* [1899] 1 Ch 163.
3 *Ward v Dunscombe,* above.
4 *Timson v Ramsbottom* (1837) 2 Keen 35; *Re Hall* (1880) 7 LR Ir 180.
5 At 394–395.
6 *Re Phillips Trusts* [1903] 1 Ch 183.
7 [1958] 3 All ER 597.
8 Meagher, Gummow & Lehane p 238; see Elphinstone, 'The Mischief of Secret Trusts' (1961) 77 LQR 69.
9 *Rochard v Fulton* (1844) 7 I Eq R 131 at 141.
10 Snell, 67.

Part two

The trust

Chapter 6

The nature of a trust

6.01 The trust is the single most important contribution of equity to the law. As we have seen, it evolved from the concept of the use: the enforcement by the chancellor of the objects for which property had been assured was a consequence of his jurisdiction acting on the conscience of the legal owner. Equity would not permit a person who had accepted property for a particular purpose to repudiate the confidence reposed in him by the true owner. And as the concept of the trust developed in the formative period of equity, it ceased to be associated solely with land until eventually we find that there is no species of property which is incapable of being held in trust. Moreover, while in its origins its affinity with contract was strongly marked—almost invariably it arose because the trustee had agreed to hold the property not for his own benefit but for that of others—courts of equity became more prepared to acknowledge that the trust could exist without any real element of agreement between the owner and the trustee. It was sufficient that the circumstances were such that the court should draw the inference of a trust relationship and hence the development in our law of the idea of the *resulting* and *constructive trusts* which arose by operation of law and not by the express agreement of the parties.

What is a trust?

6.02 Many definitions of a trust have been attempted—by text-book writers rather than judges—but perhaps the most satisfactory is that of Underhill with the gloss added by Pettit:

'A trust is an equitable obligation, binding a person (who is called a trustee) to deal with property over which he has control (which is called the trust property) *either* for the benefit of persons (who are called the beneficiaries or *cestuis que trust*) of whom he himself may be one, and any one of whom may enforce the obligation, *or for a charitable purpose, which may be enforced at the instance of the Attorney-General, or for some other purpose permitted by law though unenforceable.*'[1]

A trust most characteristically arises because the owner of property disposes of it by will, or by an instrument intended to take effect in his lifetime, ie a disposition *inter vivos*. In the former case, the creator of the trust is called 'the *testator*', in the latter 'the *settlor*'. The property need not be land: it may be chattels or money. Or it may be such intangible species of property as *choses in action,* ie rights which can only be enforced by legal proceedings such as debts, shares in a company, copyrights and patents. Equitable estates themselves—the right of the beneficiary to the trust property—may themselves be held in trust, so that one can have a trust existing behind another trust.

The most obvious occasion for a trust to arise is because the owner of property wishes it to be enjoyed by persons in succession to one another. Thus, a testator may leave property to, or in trust for, his or her spouse for life and afterwards to his or her children. The legal ownership of the property will then be vested in the trustee who will pay the income to the spouse for his or her life after which the children will be entitled to both capital and income. Or a settlor may effect a similar object by deed. But this is far from being the only type of trust which can be created: in particular, the settlor or testator may wish to benefit charitable objects. Moreover, groups of persons who form themselves into clubs or societies will usually arrange to have the property of the club or society vested in trustees to be held by them for the objects of the group.

1 Underhill, p 1. The italicised words are added by Pettit (p 22) to cover charitable trusts and purpose trusts: as to the former see Chapter 11 and as to the latter Chapter 7. The Underhill definition was adopted with approval in *Re Marshall's Wills' Trusts* [1945] Ch 217.

6.03 It will be seen that the vesting of *property* in a trustee for the benefit of others is the distinguishing feature of the trust as a legal concept. A *contract* may confer benefits on persons who are not parties, but unless property is vested in one of the contracting parties for the benefit of those who are not parties, the latter will usually be unable to enforce the contract. Under our law, the doctrine of privity of contract means that only parties to the contract can enforce rights which it confers. If A agrees with B to pay C money and there is consideration for A's promise, B can sue A for his failure to perform the contract but C cannot.[1]

This doctrine can lead to injustice and the law has occasionally striven to avoid such consequences by treating B as a trustee of A's promise and C as a beneficiary who can enforce the promise. Such decisions in effect recognise Maitland's wider definition of a trust:

'Where a person has rights which he is bound to exercise on behalf of another or for the accomplishment of some particular purpose, he is said to have those rights in trust for another or for that purpose and he is called a trustee.'[2]

Thus in *Drimmie v Davies,*[3] a dentist took his son into partnership and the latter agreed in the partnership deed to pay certain annuities to his brothers and sisters on his father's death. (At that stage, the son was entitled to purchase the assets at a valuation.) When the father died, the son refused to pay the annuities and an action was brought against him by his father's executors and his brothers and sisters. It was held by the Irish Court of Appeal, upholding Chatterton V-C, that since the father would clearly have been entitled to sue had the annuities been payable in his lifetime, his executors were equally entitled to sue. But there are also *dicta*[4] in the Vice-Chancellor's judgement which suggest that the children would have had an independent right to sue, had the executors declined to do so, on the ground that they were beneficiaries, and the executors trustees, of the father's promise.

But the courts in modern times have shown on the whole little enthusiasm for the concept of a trust of a promise and it generally requires more than a simple conferring of a benefit on a third party for such a trust to arise. Cases such as *Re Schebsman,* [5] and *Green v Russell*[6] illustrate the difficulties that can arise: if A agrees with B to confer benefits on C, who is a minor, are A and B precluded from varying the terms of their agreement because of the existence of a trust?

In those cases, it was sought to establish that members of an insured person's family were entitled to the benefits of insurance policies maintained by him or his employer. The courts rejected the claim that the 'reasonable expectation' of the dependants that they would benefit under the policy was sufficient to create a trust in their favour. In *Re Irish Board Mills Ltd, McCann v Irish Board Mills Ltd,*[7] Barrington J accepted this as being the law, but concluded that on the facts in that case the company held the sum payable under the policy in trust for the employee's dependants.

A recent example of the judicial reluctance to revert to the 'cumbrous fiction'[8] of a trust is *Cadbury Ireland Ltd v Kerry Co-operative Creamery Ltd and Dairy Disposal Co Ltd.*[9] The plaintiffs sought to enforce a clause in an agreement between the two defendants which guaranteed that, following the sale of a number of creameries in Kerry by the second defendants to the first defendants, there would be no reduction in the supply of milk to the plaintiffs' chocolate crumb factory at Rathmore. Barrington J held that the concept of a trust should not be extended to cover such a case: there was no fiduciary relationship between the parties which justified such an inference.[10]

Some of the decisions in this area resulted in members of families being unable to recover monies payable under insurance policies admittedly entered into for their benefit. But under s 7 of the Married Women's Status Act 1957, life or endowment insurance policies effected by a spouse and expressed to be for the benefit of the other spouse or their children are held on trust for the persons so named in the policy. Moreover s 8 also provides that contracts expressed to be for the benefit of, or purporting to confer a benefit on, the wife, husband or child of the one of the contracting parties are enforceable by the third persons in their own names as if they were parties to the contract.

1 *Tweddle v Atkinson* (1861) 1 B & S 393; *Murphy v Bower.* IR 2 CL 506; *Beswick v Beswick* [1968] AC 58, HL.
2 Maitland, *Equity*, p 44.
3 [1899] 1 IR 176 at 186.
4 At p 182. Note that this case anticipated the decision of the House of Lords in *Beswick v Beswick* (above) that in such circumstances the personal representative may sue as the successor of the promisee.
5 [1944] Ch 83.
6 [1959] 2 QB 226.
7 (1980) ILRM 216.
8 Lord Wright's description in 55 LQR 189 at 208.
9 (1982) ILRM 77.
10 See also *Inspectors of Taxes Association v Minister for the Public Service*, the High Court, Murphy J, unreported, judgement delivered 24 March 1983.

6.04 A trust may also be distinguished from a *bailment*. The latter arises where one party (the bailor) leaves property in the custody of another (the *bailee.*) Sometimes the bailee takes care of the property for reward, as where I leave my suitcase in the left luggage office of a railway station.

Sometimes, the bailee pays for the use of the property, as where I hire a motor-car. And sometimes no money passes at all, as where I allow my neighbour to park his car in my driveway. But in all these cases, although the bailee is in possession of the property, the bailor remains the owner. It is true that the bailee has what is called a 'special property' in the object bailed, but while this enables him to resist the claims of others except the bailor, the latter remains the owner. By contrast, the trustee is the owner in law of the trust property and hence he is able to transfer the title to the property to a bona fide purchaser for value without notice of the trust. Except in special circumstances,[1] a bailee can give no title in the property to another, since he has none to give.

1 As to which, see *Benjamin's Sale of Goods*, 2nd edn p 230 et seq.

6.05 The trust relationship may also be distinguished from the relationship of *principal and agent*. This may exist, and frequently does, without any property being vested in the agent. It is enough to give rise to the relationship for one person to act on behalf of the other. Even though the agent may be in possession of property belonging to the principal, he is not a trustee of that property: the legal ownership remains in the principal. Agency also differs from a trust in that the agent is obliged to carry out his principal's instructions, whereas a trustee is not bound to comply with directions from the persons beneficially entitled to the property. He is simply bound to carry out the terms of his trust and perform any other obligations which the law imposes on him as a trustee. Moreover, an agent can incur liability on behalf of his principal to third parties, but a trustee cannot thus involve his beneficiary. Finally, an agency may be terminated when either principal or agent becomes incapable of continuing the contract of agency, because of death, bankruptcy or unsoundness of mind or because the agency agreement itself provides for its termination.[1] But a trust, it has been frequently said, will not fail for want of a trustee, although in the case of trustees becoming incapacitated for any reason, it may be necessary to replace them if the trust is not to become moribund.

1 I *Halsbury's Laws of England*, 4th edn, para 867.

6.06 Trusts should also be distinguished from *powers*. In particular, the difference between a trust and what is called a *power of appointment* must be appreciated. The latter is an authority given to a named person or persons—the *donees*—to nominate the persons who are to own particular property. Usually, the objects of the power must be chosen from a defined class and in its classic form the property is left in trust for A—generally the husband or wife—for his or her life with remainder to such of the children of A as he or she may by deed or will appoint. Generally, the settlor or testator will go on to provide for what is to happen in the event of A dying without having exercised the power. Thus, the instrument may provide that in default of appointment the property is to belong to the children of A in equal shares, i e there is a *gift over* in default of appointment.

The essential difference between a trust and such a power of appointment is that a trust is *imperative* and a power *discretionary*. A trustee, in other words, must carry out his trust. The donee of a power of appointment, if it is in truth no more than such a power, cannot be compelled to exercise the power. It is the logical consequence of this distinction that, unlike beneficiaries under a trust, the objects of a mere power of appointment—the class of persons among whom the appointment may be made—have no interest in the property until the appointment is made, or until any gift over in default of appointment takes effect. The beneficiaries under a trust, by contrast, have an interest in the trust property as soon as the trust takes effect and, if all *sui juris*, i e not suffering from any legal disability, can call upon the trustees to transfer the trust property to them.[1]

1 *Re Gulbenkian's Settlement Trusts* [1970] AC 508 at 525, HL.

6.07 There is a form of trust which more closely resembles a power of appointment than the conventional trust, i e a *discretionary trust*. Here the property is vested in trustees who have a discretion as to which members of a specified class, such as the children of the settlor or testator, they will pay the income of the trust property or transfer the capital to and in what proportions. In England a further distinction has been drawn between exhaustive and non-exhaustive discretionary trusts: in the former, the trustees are bound to distribute the whole income, while in the latter they may accumulate income instead of distributing it.

The difference between such a trust and a power of appointment is that the members of the class can always compel the performance of the trust, even though as a result of the exercise of the trustees' discretion, a particular member of the class may receive nothing. The donee of a power of appointment cannot be compelled to exercise it. Moreover, the members of the class also have an interest in the trust property, unlike the objects of a power of appointment. But it is an interest different in kind from that enjoyed by the beneficiaries under a conventional trust. It is not quantifiable in any way: it is right to be considered as a potential beneficiary and to have this right protected by the court in the exercise of its equitable jurisdiction.[1]

Discretionary trusts enjoyed a considerable vogue in the nineteen fifties and 'sixties in Ireland and England when they were seen by lawyers and accountants as providing a mechanism for avoiding death duties. Their popularity has faded as the legislation governing duties or tax payable on succession to property has altered radically. However, they can still offer a useful framework for property owners who wish to transfer or bequeath assets to their children or grandchildren but are concerned to ensure that they are not dissipated by youthful or foolish beneficiaries.

1 *Gartside v IRC* [1968] AC 553, HL. Because trustees in the case of a discretionary trust must exercise their powers although they cannot be required to exercise them in a particular way, their powers have sometimes been called 'trust powers' to distinguish them from bare powers. But the expression 'trust powers' has another significance explained in para 6.08 and its use should, it is thought, be confined to the cases there discussed. Cf Pettit, p 30.

6.08 It should also be noted that what appears to be no more than a power may on occasions be construed as being a power in the nature of a trust or, as it is sometimes called, a *trust power*. So if property is vested in trustees and they are empowered or directed to select one or more persons to enjoy the property from a specified class without any gift over in the event of their not doing so, it may construed as a trust for all the members of the class equally. This depends on the intention of the settlor or testator as it can be gathered from the whole trust instrument. While a gift over will always be treated as negativing the existence of a trust power, since it indicates that the testator contemplated that the power might *not* be exercised, the absence of a gift over is not necessarily conclusive in the other direction. There must be a clear indication that the testator or settlor intended the power to be in the nature of a trust.

The case usually cited as the authority on such trust powers is *Brown v Higgs*,[1] although it would appear that in that case there was no finding that the power was in the nature of a trust. A better example is *Borrough v Philcox*,[2] where the donee was given power 'to dispose of all my real and personal estates among my nephews or nieces or their children either all to one of them, or to as many of them as (the donee) shall think proper.' There was no gift over and Lord Cottenham held that the donee was under a duty to make a selection: where she did not, the court would not permit the objects of the power to suffer as a result, but fastened the property with a trust for their benefit. Similarly, in *Re Kieran, Matthews v Kieran*,[3] the testator left a farm and other property to his brother OK in trust for his (OK's) son, J, and in the event of J dying before he attained 21, 'upon trust for such other son of (OK) as (OK) shall appoint.' J in fact died before reaching 21 and OK died without having exercised the power. Pim J held that the three surviving sons of OK were entitled to the property equally.

A more modern example is *Re Parker's Will, Kilroy and Another v Parker*,[4] where a testator left the residue of his property to his executors in trust and directed them to divide the balance of the income from it after payment of a small annuity 'amongst such of my necessitous nieces and nephews (alive at the date of my death) and such of their children as my executors in their discretion may think fit.' Budd J held that this was a power in the nature of a trust which the court would, if necessary, execute itself.

The leading Irish case on the other side of the line is *Healy v Donnery*,[5] where the testator devised property to his daughter for her life with power to her by deed or will to dispose, devise or bequeath it to and among her children in such shares and proportions as she should think fit and proper. Pennefather B rejected the argument that this was a power coupled with a trust, saying that the cases where that inference was drawn turned upon the peculiar language of the power. His statement of the law was cited with approval by Romer J in *Re Weekes' Settlement*,[6] where the learned judge was at pains to dispel the misconception that there was a hard-and-fast rule in favour of the inference of a trust power where there was a gift to A for life with power to appoint among a class and no gift over in default of appointment. There must be an indication that the testator did intend the class or some of them to take. To the same effect is the decision of O'Connor MR in *Clibborn v Horan*.[7]

The importance of the distinction is the different approach adopted by the law in determining whether trusts and powers are void for uncertainty. The view in both Ireland and England until recent years was that in the case of a bare power, the power was not void for uncertainty if it was possible to identify individuals as belonging to the class to be benefited, but in the case of a discretionary trust or a trust power it was essential that *all* the potential beneficiaries could be ascertained with certainty. But the significance of the distinction has been eroded in England by the decision of the House of Lords in *Re Baden, McPhail v Doulton*[8] that the criteria of certainty are the same for bare powers and trust powers.[9]

1 (1799) 4 Ves 708; reheard (1800) 5 Ves 495; affd (1803) 8 Ves 561; on appeal (1813) 18 Ves 192.
2 (1840) 5 My & Cr 72.

3 [1916] 1 IR 289.
4 [1966] IR 309. Pettit suggests that this form of trust is better treated as a discretionary trust and that the term 'trust power' should be confined to cases where there is an implied trust in default of appointment (p 30).
5 (1853) 3 ICLR 213
6 [1897] 1 Ch 289.
7 [1921] 1 IR 93. See also *Robinson v Moore* (1623–3) Ir Jur Reps 29; *Re O'Toole, Bank of Ireland v O'Toole and Others*, unreported, Barrington J, judgement delivered 26 June 1980.
8 [1971] AC 424.
9 See para 7.05, below.

6.09 A *personal representative* is not, in the strict sense, a trustee simply by virtue of his office. Where the deceased was beneficially entitled to any property, the personal representative holds that property as trustee for the persons entitled thereto under the provisions of s 10(3) and s 45 of the Succession Act 1965. But it should be noticed that until such time as the estate is fully administered—i e until all assets have been collected and the debts and legacies paid—there is no one beneficially entitled to the residue of the estate. At that stage, the personal representative will become a trustee in the strict sense for those entitled to the residue of the estate.[1] (Until that time, he may simply have been holding the estate in trust for the deceased's creditors, since the estate may be insolvent.) It is not unusual however, for executors of wills to be appointed trustees in addition and this is desirable where the property is limited to different beneficiaries in succession, eg to a widow for her life and thereafter to her children. Where, however, no trustees have been appointed by the will in such a case, S 50(3) of the Succession Act 1965 provides that the personal representatives proving the will shall be deemed trustees of the settlement until trustees are appointed.

1 *Lord Sudeley v A-G* [1897] AC 11. See para 4.05, above.

Classification of trusts

6.10 A trust may arise because it is expressly created by the settlor or testator or because the law presumes it to have been created. In the first case, it is known as an *express trust*. Such trusts may be created either by instruments *inter vivos* or by wills, in which latter case, of course, they only become effective on the death of the testator. They may involve three sets of parties—the settlor or testator, the trustee and the beneficiary—or two, as where the settlor declares that he holds property in trust for the beneficiary and thus constitutes himself his own trustee.

In the second case—trusts arising by operation of law—they are variously described as *resulting, implied* or *constructive*. They arise not because of any express declaration by the settlor or testator as to his intention, or any agreement between him and the trustee, but because the law presumes that it was the intention of the settlor or testator to create a trust (in which case they are called resulting, or in some instances and by some writers, implied trusts) or the law considers it inequitable that the property should be held otherwise than on trust (in which case it is a constructive trust). These two categories are dealt with more fully in Chapters 12 and 13.

6.11 Trusts can be either *executed* or *executory trusts*. In the case of executed trusts, nothing remains to be done to make the trust effective: the deed or will sets out the limitations upon which the property is to be held. In the case of executory trusts, the settlor or testator, while indicating what his intentions are, has left them to be carried out by a further instrument which will spell out the precise limitations. The classic example of the executory trust in former times was the marriage articles which preceded the execution of the marriage settlement, but it can also be encountered in wills, as where the testator leaves property to someone who is unmarried with a direction that it is to be settled on his or her marriage.

As we have already seen,[1] the significance of the distinction is that in the case of executed trusts, 'equity follows the law' with the result that the language used is strictly construed and technical expressions are given their technical meaning. Where the trust is executory, however, the court may look to the intention of the settlor. Thus in the case of marriage articles, there is a presumption that the issue of the marriage are intended to benefit which will only be displaced by the expression of a contrary intention. This means that in the case of marriage articles, the rule in *Shelley's Case*[2] will not be applied. Under that hallowed precedent, where an estate in fee simple is conveyed or devised to A for life with remainder to his heirs, the words 'to his heirs' are words of limitation and not of purchase, with the result, manifestly contrary to the intention of the grantor, that A takes an absolute fee simple instead of a life estate.[3] The rule was abolished in England in 1925 but remains part of our law. In the result, the use of that expression in marriage articles—if they are ever employed in contemporary Ireland—will not be allowed to distort the settlor's intention, but its use in a settlement or will effectively negates the settlor's or testator's intentions.

Until 1965, a similar anomaly disfigured our law in the form of the rule in *Wild's Case.*[4] Under that rule, where an estate in fee simple was devised to A 'and his children' and A had no children when the will was made, A took an estate in fee tail, which he could subsequently bar and so become the absolute owner.[5] Again, this rule did not apply to marriage articles but did apple to wills. It was, however, abolished in the case of wills by the Succession Act 1965.[6]

1 Para 3.03, above.
2 (1581) 1 Co Rep 936.
3 Unless the testator uses words indicating an intention that specified persons should have the remainder, as contrasted with words of general import such as 'heirs', 'children' or 'issue'. See Wylie, *Land Law*, pp177–178.
4 (1599) 6 Co Rep 166.
5 *In Re Moyles' Estate* (1878) 1 LR Ir 155; *Clifford v Koe* (1880) 6 LR Ir 439.
6 S 95. See Wylie, *Land Law*, pp 226–227.

6.12 Trusts can be for the benefit of individuals (in which case they are usually called *private trusts*) or for charitable purposes (in which case they are called *charitable* or *public trusts*). It is possible in certain limited circumstances to create a trust for a purpose which is not in law charitable and is not for the benefit of an individual, such as a trust for the maintenance of a pet animal. Such trusts are called *purpose trusts*.

6.13 A settlor or testator may also create a *protective trust,* i e one in which the interest given to the beneficiary is determinable in the event of his alienating the interest or going bankrupt. The trust instrument normally provides that, in such an event, the interest is to be held on a discretionary trust, the objects usually being the former beneficiary and his family. Thus, the settlor or testator seeks to protect the trust property against its possible dissipation by the beneficiary. In England since 1925 it has been possible to create such protective trusts by the use of relatively simple language which brings a statutory protective trust into being, but there has been no corresponding legislation in this country.

6.14 Elaborate *statutory trusts* were created in England by the Law of Property Act 1925 which take effect in certain circumstances upon the death of a person beneficially entitled to property. There is no real equivalent to this form of statutory trust in Ireland, but, as we have seen, under the Succession Act 1965 all the property of the deceased person is held by his personal representatives in trust for those entitled thereto.

6.15 A modern variant of the traditional trust is the *unit trust*. This is essentially a method by which an investor seeks to reap the benefit of skilled management of a portfolio of securities. A number of securities are held by trustees in trust for a management company. These securities are divided into units and the public are invited to purchase whichever number of units they require. The purchasers of the units thus become entitled to the beneficial interest of the management company in the appropriate proportion of the securities and the purchase price is so calculated as to give the management company renumeration for their work in managing the trust. While it is possible to have a fixed unit trust, under which the investments cannot be varied, it is more common nowadays to allow the investments to be varied by the management company.

6.16 The trust has, it will be seen, shown itself a remarkably flexible instrument for dealing with a wide variety of circumstances which may arise in modern life. It has travelled far from its origins in the complexities of feudal land law and become a sophisticated technique for achieving a variety of ends: the holding of properties in succession by different members of a family, as in a will, the distribution of property so as to ensure that the tax burden is eased as much as possible and that those who are too immature to exercise responsible control over it do not enjoy it too soon (largely achieved through the discretionary trust) the facilitating of social, cultural and rectational activities and the advancement of charity. In addition, the development of the constructive trust has demonstrated the capacity of equity to reach broadly equitable solutions to the question of ownership of property even where the conventional structure of the trust does not exist at all.

Chapter 7

Express trusts: (1) the essential elements

7.01 No particular form of words is needed to create an express trust. It is not necessary to use the precise expression 'in trust for' or any other formula. But it has for long been the law that 'three certainties' must be present. They were originally laid down by Lord Langdale in *Knight v Knight*[1] and in *Chambers v Fahy*. O'Byrne J defined the three requirements for an express trust in these terms:

'It has been established that, in order that a trust may be created, the *subject matter* must be certain, the *objects* of the trust must be certain and the *words* relied on as creating the trust must have been used in an *imperative* sense so as to show that the testator intends to create an obligation.'[2]

We shall consider each of these requirements in some detail, but not in the order suggested in this passage.

1 (1840) 3 Beav 148.
2 [1931] IR 17, 21, SC.

Words relied on as creating a trust must be imperative

7.02 It is not enough that a person alleged to have created a trust should have simply expressed his desire or hope that the person to whom the property has been given should deal with it in a particular way. The words used must show that it was intended to impose an obligation on the person so to act: if an outright gift was intended, no trust will arise. At one time, so called 'precatory trusts' were allowed where the courts gave effect to what were obviously the wishes of a testator, even though it was also clear that he had not imposed any obligation on the alleged trustee to act in a particular way.[1] Such trusts have for long been disapproved of by the courts and the necessity stressed for the use of imperative language.[2] The expressions attached to gifts of property which have been held to be insufficient to create a trust include the following:

'*feeling confident* that she will act justly to our children in dividing the same when no longer required by her';[3]
'*in full confidence* that she will do what is right as to the disposal thereof between my children';[4]
'*in the fullest trust and confidence* that she will carry out my wishes in the following particulars';[5]

'*it is my desire* that she allows A an annuity of £25 during her lifetime.'[6]

But even though the words used may have been precatory in form. if the intention of a settlor or testator gathered from the instrument as a whole was to impose a trust, the courts will give effect to that intention.[7]

1 *Shaw v Lawless* (1838) 5 Cl & Fin 129.
2 *Re Humphrey's Estate* [1916] 1 IR 21; *Re Coulson* (1953) 87 ILTR 93; *Hillary v Sweeney* unreported, Hamilton J, 1974 374 Sp).
3 *Mussoorie Bank Ltd v Raynor* (1882) 7 App Cas 321.
4 *Re Adams and Kensington Vestry* (1884) 27 Ch D 394.
5 *Re Williams* [1897] 2 Ch 12.
6 *Re Diggles* (1888) 39 Ch D 253.
7 *Comiskey v Bowring–Hanbury* [1905] AC 84.

The subject matter must be certain

7.03 The settlor or testator must clearly identify the property which is to be subject to the trust and the exact shares to which the beneficiaries are to be entitled.

Thus, in *Re Jones*[1] there was a gift to a wife followed by a direction that, as to such parts of the estate as she should not have sold or disposed of, they should be held in trust for certain persons. It was held that the trust failed for uncertainty and the wife took absolutely. But provided that the property is *capable* of being quantified, the fact that it is not quantified in the will may not be fatal. In *Re Golay's Will Trusts*,[2] for example, Ungoed-Thomas J upheld a direction that a legatee was to receive a reasonable income, since the court would have no difficulty in determining what a reasonable income was.

In the case of property other than land, it may be unidentifiable because it has been mixed with other property. This can happen with money subject to a trust which is lodged to the trustee's own bank account. Or it can happen to goods which are subject to a 'reservation of title' clause under which the beneficial ownership in the goods is retained by the vendor until they are paid for, thus in effect making the purchaser a trustee. The goods may be mixed with other goods of the purchaser or may be used in the manufacture of other products. In all these cases it may still be possible to enforce the trust by 'tracing' the property into the property with which it has been mixed.[3]

1 [1898] 1 Ch 438.
2 [1965] 2 All ER 660.
3 See Chapter 20.

The objects must be certain

7.04 A trust will also fail for uncertainty if the objects intended to be benefited cannot be ascertained with precision. If I leave property in my will in trust for 'John Murphy', the trust may fail for uncertainty because it it impossible to say which John Murphy it was intended to benefit. But if I leave it in trust for 'John Murphy of 81 Ranelagh Avenue Dublin 4' and there was at the date of the will only one person of that name residing at that address, the trust will be valid.

Similarly, if the trust is for the benefit of a defined class of persons, the trust will be valid, provided the members of the class can be ascertained with certainty. Thus, if I leave property by my will in trust for such of my children as are living at the date of my death, it should be possible to ascertain at my death who belongs to the class without any difficulty. It may be, of course, that one of the children has gone to Australia years ago and not been heard of again, but that will present no insuperable obstacle: the trustees can always apply to the court for directions and the court may either allow the trustees to leave out the child in distributing the property[1] or pay his or her share into court. But if the class is so wide and vague that its membership cannot be ascertained with certainty, then the trust will fail. The test for ascertaining whether the class has been defined with sufficient certainty has been expressed in England as follows: if the trustees can compile a list of all the persons beneficially entitled at the inception of the trust without undue trouble or expense, the trust will not fail for uncertainty.[2]

1 *Re Benjamin* [1902] 1 Ch 723.
2 *Mc Phail v Doulton* [1971] AC 424 at 427, HL.

7.05 Trust powers have presented special problems in this context. It will be recalled that a trust power differs from a bare power in that the settlor's intention in the case of a trust power is that the objects of the power are to benefit whether an appointment is made or not.[1] To start with bare powers (where, of course, no trust arises in the first place), it is clear that, even if it is not possible to define the class from which the persons to benefit are to be selected with certainty by making a list of all the possible beneficiaries, the power will not fail for uncertainty, provided it is possible to identify individuals as belonging to the class.[2] If, for example, the donee of the power is entitled to vest the property in any one or more of the 'relatives' of the donor, the power will not fail for uncertainty, even though it would be difficult if not impossible to draw up a definitive list of relatives. (The list could differ almost endlessly, depending on how widely one was prepared to define the word 'relative'.) The donee will clearly be fulfilling the donor's intentions by distributing the property among, for example, his nearest blood relatives.

In the case of trust powers, a different principle was thought at one stage to apply. As we have seen, an essential difference between trusts and bare powers is that the former are imperative: the beneficiaries can always compel the performance of the trust. That could only be done, it was said, where the donee of a trust power had not exercised it, by applying the maxim 'equality is equity' and distributing the property equally between all the possible beneficiaries. Hence if all the beneficiaries were not ascertainable, the trust was not enforceable in accordance with the settlor's intentions. They would not be fulfilled, it was said, by confining the trust to a smaller group than that which he intended to benefit. This was the view taken by the Court of Appeal in *IRC v Broadways Cottages Trust*[3] and expressly approved of by Budd J in *Re Parker's Will, Kilroy v Parker*.[4] However, in the latter case, while holding that it was essential to the validity of the trust that the whole class of potential beneficiaries was ascertainable, the learned judge also took the view that the class in that case ('my necessitous nephews and nieces') was in fact ascertainable.

A different view of the law has been taken subsequently by the House of Lords in *McPhail v Doulton*[5] in which *IRC v Broadways Cottages Trust* was overruled. In that case, there was a gift to trustees of a fund which they were to apply 'in the making at their absolute discretion of grants to or for the benefit of any of the officers and employees or ex-officers or employees of the [named] company or to any relatives or dependants of any such persons in such amounts at such times and on such conditions (if any) as they think fit.'

The House of Lords, reversing the Court of Appeal, held that this was a trust power and not a bare power, but by a majority held that the same test was to be applied in determining whether it failed for uncertainty as applied in the case of a bare power. Although the language of the gift was such that it was not possible to list all the possible beneficiaries, there was no essential difficulty in deciding whether any particular person should be classified, for example, as a 'relative' of an officer or employee. Lord Wilberforce declined to accept that the law had become so fossilised in this area as to be incapable of further development: the settlor's intentions could be more effectively implemented by the abandonment of the former rule and by leaving it to the normal machinery of the chancery court to ensure that only persons who could be identified as being within the class were benefited. Adherence to the former rule would more surely frustrate the settlor's intentions by leading to the failure of the trust. He was able to underpin these conclusions by referring to earlier decisions from the formative period of equity and carried a majority of the law lords with him.[6]

There has been no reported Irish decision in this area since *Re Parker's Will, Kilroy v Parker*, but it would seem probable that the same approach as in *Re Baden* might be adopted in this jurisdiction. It is interesting to note that, although Budd J accepted the *Broadways Cottages* case as correctly stating the law, he succeeded in avoiding a finding of uncertainty by holding that there was no practical obstacle to the executors deciding whether any nephew or niece was at any time eligible and applying to the court for directions if they were in difficulties: a conclusion strikingly similar to that reached by Lord Wilberforce in the later English case.

1 See para 6.08, above.
2 *Re Bayley deceased* [1945] IR 224, SC. Cf *Re Gestetner's Settlement* [1953] Ch 672.
3 [1955] Ch 20.
4 [1966] IR 309.
5 [1971] AC 424, HL.
6 The case came before the Court of Appeal again in *Re Baden's Trust Deeds (No 2)* [1973] Ch 9. Differing views were expressed as to how the House of Lords test should be applied. The majority view was that the gift was valid if the class was 'conceptually certain', even though it might not be possible, for evidential reasons, to say whether a particular person fell within the class. A gift for 'relatives' on this view was valid, although in the case of a particular person, there might not be sufficient evidence to say whether he belonged to it or not. It would have been otherwise if, for example, the class consisted of 'my close friends': this would have been conceptually uncertain. Stamp LJ dissented, saying that the House of Lords test could only be satisfied if it was possible to say of any individual that he either belonged to the class or did not.

Purpose trusts

7.06 Trusts for purposes as distinct from individuals have caused particular problems. A private trust must be a trust in favour of individuals, either named or ascertainable as belonging to a class. In general a trust for a purpose ('the freedom of the press') or in favour of an inanimate object ('to erect and maintain a statue of myself') will fail. Such trusts may fail because they are uncertain. But they will also fail because they are not trusts for individuals. It is only where the trust is not private, ie where it is in law charitable, that it will be enforced.

Two basic reasons have been assigned by the courts for denying validity to such 'purpose' trusts where they are not charitable.

(1) *The trust cannot be enforced by the court.* If the trust is for a purpose or an inanimate object, there is no one who can call on the court to ensure its enforcement. In the words of Sir William Grant MR in the leading case of *Morice v Bishop of Durham*:[1]

> 'There can be no trust over the exercise of which the court will not assume control, for an uncontrolled power of disposition would be ownership and not trust. If there be a clear trust but for uncertain objects, the property that is the subject of the trust is undisposed of... But this doctrine does not hold good with regard to trusts for charities. Every other trust must have a definite object. There must be somebody in whose favour the court can decree specific performance.'[2]

(2) *The trust will violate the rule against perpetuities and against inalienability.* Both at common law and equity, a gift will be void unless the interest in the property vests in the donee within the perpetuity period, ie within a life or lives in being and a further period of twenty-one years.[3] If the duration of a private trust is measured by reference to a purpose or an inanimate object or even the life of an animal, it will violate this rule. Such a trust will also offend the rule against inalienability, which requires that property must not be frozen in the ownership of an individual for longer than the perpetuity period.

Neither of these difficulties arises where the trust is a charitable trust. The courts of equity at an early stage extended their protection to such trusts and allowed them to be enforced by the Attorney General. At a later stage, a statutory body was established with a special role in ensuring the proper administration of such trusts, the relevant functions in this country being discharged by the Commissioners for Charitable Donations and Bequests for Ireland. Such charitable trusts are also exempt from the rule against perpetuities and against inalienability. But as we shall see in Chapter 11, the legal definition of 'charity' is highly technical and a trust which might appear to the layman as charitable in its objects may fail because in the eyes of the law it is non-charitable and hence invalid as a purpose trust.

1 (1804) 9 Ves 399; on appeal (1805) 10 Ves 522.
2 9 Ves at 404/405.
3 A period for gestation must also be allowed. The rule remains in its pristine, unreformed state in this jurisdiction. The law has, of course, long since been altered in England and Northern Ireland. As to the rule in general, see Wylie, *Land Law*, pp 278-290, Morris and Leach, *The Rule Against Perpetuities* and Gray, *The Rule Against Perpetuities*.

7.07 As a result of the application of these principles, the courts have refused to carry out the intentions of testators or donors who have sought to benefit objects dear to their hearts but which are not in law charitable objects. One notable casualty was Bernard Shaw's bequest for the establishment of a new English alphabet on scientific lines and the publication of *Androcles and the Lion* in the new alphabet. It was held that this was not a charitable trust and hence failed as a purpose trust.[1] Similarly, the desire of the Astor family to establish a foundation for encouraging among other objects the freedom of the press was frustrated by the refusal of the law to recognise such a trust.[2]

The difficulty seen by the courts in enforcing such trusts might be met where the executor or trustee was prepared to go to the trouble—and saddle the estate with the expense—of applying to the court for 'directions' and undertaking to carry out the trust. But the difficulty remained, even where the trustee or executor gave such an undertaking, that the gift contravened the rule against perpetuities and inalienability. Such trusts of 'imperfect obligation', as they were called, appeared to present insuperable problems when it came to legal recognition. And it would have seemed logical that trusts for animals would encounter a similar fate—even where the trustees were prepared to go to court and undertake their enforcement, there would seem no escaping the difficulty presented by the rules against perpetuities and inalienability. A similar ineluctable problem would appear to be presented by gifts to inanimate objects, such as bequests for the upkeep of buildings or monuments.

There have, however, been cases—generally regarded as anomalous exceptions to the rule—where the courts have been prepared to enforce such trusts. They have been grouped under the following headings:

(1) trusts for the erection or maintenance of monuments or graves;
(2) trusts for the maintenance of particular animals;
(3) trusts for the benefit of unincorporated associations;
(4) miscellaneous cases.[3]

To this list is added, in other jurisdictions, trusts for the saying of masses. In Ireland, however, such trusts have been recognised as charitable since the decision in *O'Hanlon v Logue*[4] and accordingly need not be treated as an exception to the rule against purpose trusts.

The cases in which the courts have been prepared to accept trusts for the erection of monuments or graves or for the maintenance of animals have been described as 'concessions to human weakness or sentiment'[5] or even as occasions when 'Homer has nodded.'[6] It has repeatedly been emphasised that such anomalies should not be extended.

1 *Re Shaw, Public Trustee v Day* [1957] 1 All ER 745. But on appeal the matter was settled: [1958] 1 All ER 245n, CA.
2 *Re Astor's Settlement Trusts, Astor v Scholfield* [1952] Ch 534.
3 Morris and Leach, op cit, (1956) p298, cited with approval by Lord Evershed MR in *Re Endacott, Corpe v Endacott* [1960] Ch 232 at 246.
4 [1906] 1 IR 247, CA.
5 *Re Astor's Settlement Trusts, Astor v Scholfield*, (above), 547.
6 Per Harman LJ in *Re Endacott* (above) at 250.

7.08 Gifts for tombs and graves etc. up to a certain value were given charitable status by s 50 of the Charities Act 1961 and within those limits do not have to avail of the anomalous authorities discussed above. That section provides that

'(1) Every gift made after the commencement of this Act for the provision, maintenance or improvement of a tomb, vault, grave or of a tombstone or other memorial to a deceased person or persons which would not otherwise be charitable shall, to the extent provided by this section, be a charitable gift.
(2) Such a gift shall be charitable so far as it does not exceed
(a) in the case of income only, sixty pounds a year,
(b) in any other case, one thousand pounds in amount or value.'[1]

1 These amounts having been fixed over twenty-five years ago are presumably too low. It

would be a simple matter to provide that the Charity Commissioners should have power by order to fix the limits from time to time.

7.09 Gifts for animals would seem obviously vulnerable to the twofold objection that there is no one to enforce them and that they violate the perpetuity period. In *Re Kelly, Cleary v Dillon*,[1] where the testator left £100 for the purpose of spending four pounds on the support of each of his dogs per year, Meredith J did not have to deal with the first objection since none of the parties relied on it, accepting that the law had been settled in favour of giving such gifts exceptional treatment by the English decision of In *Re Dean, Cooper Dean v Stevens*.[2] He dismissed, however, in picturesque language the submission that the court should take judicial notice of the fact that dogs had a life expectancy of less than 21 years and that as a result the perpetuity period was not violated:

'The court does not enter into the question of a dog's expectation of life. In point of fact, neighbour's dogs and cats are unpleasantly long lived; but I have no knowledge of their precise expectation of life. Anyway the maximum period is exceeded by the lives even of specified butterflies and twenty-one years afterwards.....According to my decision—and, I confess, it displays this weakness on being pressed to a logical conclusion—the expiration of the life of a single butterfly, even without the twenty-one years, would be too remote, despite all the world of poetry that may thereby be destroyed...."Lives" means lives of human beings, not of animals or trees in California.'[3]

But he was able to uphold the gift by deciding that expenditure on the dogs for a period of 21 years following the testator's death did not violate the rule, although the theoretical provision for the period thereafter was void.

1 [1932] IR 255.
2 (1889) 41 Ch D 552.
3 At 260-261.

7.10 It is when one comes to gifts for unincorporated associations that the most extraordinary anomalies of all emerge. A gift to a body corporate presents no problems in this context. It can be enforced by the body and, since the body normally enjoys 'perpetual succession' it does not violate the perpetuity rule. Hence if a club or society is incorporated as a company limited by guarantee, there will be no problem about making a gift to it, even though its purposes are not charitable. But where it is not so incorporated, it has in law no separate personality and is simply a collection of individuals, the composition of which may change by death, retirement or the accession of new members. There seems no escaping the dilemma that a gift to such an association is either a gift for the purposes of the association—in which case there will be no one to enforce it—or a gift to the members of the association themselves, in which case it must logically extend to the members in the future, thus contravening the rule against perpetuities. In an effort to escape from this dilemma and to give effect to the obvious intentions of testators, courts have on occasions strained the language used in the relevant instrument to breaking point. It is not easy, or even possible, to reconcile the principal decisions, but they do indicate that careful drafting may still lead to the gift's being upheld. The court's task will be eased if there is an outright cash gift to one person, such as the superior of a religious order, or where the language used expressly limits the duration of the gift to the perpetuity period.

A series of decisions in the last century demonstrated the willingness of courts to construe gifts of this nature to religious communities as gifts to the individual members of the community alive at the testator's death. Such a construction, however foreign it might seem to the testator's real intentions, was essential if the gift was to be upheld, where the community was a contemplative order, as contrasted with an order engaged in nursing the sick or teaching. Because of the decision of Sir John Wigram VC in *Cocks v Manners*,[1] a gift to such an order was not in law charitable, but in that case the gift—to 'the Dominican convent at Carisbrook (payable to the superior for the time being)'—was treated as a gift to the superior of money to be placed by her at the disposal of the community and hence not affected by the perpetuity rule. The case was apparently irreconcilable with the earlier Irish decision of *Stewart v Green*[2] where the gift was 'to EB, Superioress of the Community......known as the Order of Mercy...to be used...by her as such superioress for the use and benefit of the said community' and was held to be invalid. However, in that case, despite the fact that the point was expressly raised by Christian LJ, counsel for the nuns declined to argue that it was a gift for their personal benefit. Emboldened presumably by *Cocks v Manners*, a different stance was adopted by counsel in *Re Delany*[3] where property was left 'in trust for the Sisters of Mercy at Bantry....for the benefit of the convent of Mercy at Bantry' and the gift was upheld as being one for the benefit of the dozen or so ladies comprising the community at the testator's death.

The question came before the Supreme Court in *Re Byrne deceased, Shaw v Attorney-General*[4] where the testator left his residuary estate in trust 'for the absolute use and benefit of the Jesuit Order in Ireland.' Kennedy CJ was prepared to uphold this as a charitable bequest, but declined to treat it as an absolute gift to the members of the Irish province of the Society of Jesus (to give it its proper name) living at the testator's death. He said:

> 'I can find nothing....to support the interpretation that he gave his property to the individual members of the Province in their natural capacities to do with it as they please. I cannot imagine anything further removed from the mind of the testator as evidenced by his will. It is clear to me that his bounty is directed to the benefit of the Province as a whole as of an indefinite future date, looked at in its quasi-corporate capacity, and I should find it very difficult to uphold that as a good bequest in law. It clearly tends to a perpetuity....'[5]

He distinguished the earlier cases—such as *Cocks v Manners* and *Re Delaney*—as being instances where the actual words used supported an interpretation that the gift was to the individual members of the community or the superior for the time being. Murnaghan J, however, with whom Fitzgibbon J agreed, while finding that the gift was not charitable, was prepared to uphold it as a gift for the benefit of an ascertainable class.

1 (1871) LR 12 Eq 574.
2 [1870] IR 5 Eq 470.
3 (1882) 9 LR Ir 226, CA.
4 [1935] IR 782.
5 At 809.

7.11 This case remains the leading Irish decision on the topic and it would seem reasonable to assume that the Irish courts will continue to apply the more benevolent approach favoured by the majority. In England, the tendency at one stage was to adopt the stricter construction favoured by

Kennedy CJ, the leading examples being *Re McCauley's Estate, McCauley v O'Donnell*[1] and *Leahy v A-G for New South Wales.*[2] In the former case, the gift was to the Folkestone Lodge of the Theosophical Society absolutely for the maintenance and improvement of the Theosophical Lodge at Folkestone. The House of Lords found the gift to be invalid, upholding the decision of Hanworth MR who had stated the recurring dilemma succinctly:

> 'If the gift is in truth to the present members of the society described by their society name so that they have the beneficial use of the property and can, if they please, alienate and put the proceeds in their own pocket, then there is a present gift to individuals which is good; but if the gift is intended for the good not only of the present but future members so that the present members are in the position of trustees and have no right to appropriate the property or its proceeds for their personal benefit, then the gift is invalid.'[3]

In *Leahy*, the gift was for the benefit of such order of nuns as the trustees might select. The trustees wished to be at liberty to apply the gift to a contemplative order of nuns, but the judicial committee of the Privy Council, following *Cocks v Manners,* held that this was not a charitable purpose. They also considered that the gift was, in the words of Viscount Simonds, 'not merely for the benefit of the existing members of the selected order but for its benefit as a continuing society and for the furtherance of its work.' The property could not accordingly be validly applied for the benefit of a contemplative order.

In recent years, however, this trend has been reversed in England and a distinctly more 'benevolent' approach has emerged. The principle decisions are extremely difficult to reconcile with *McCauley* and *Leahy,* the first major departure being *Re Denley's Trusts.*[4] In that case, Goff J upheld the validity of a gift of a sports ground for the benefit of the employees of a particular company: the mischief aimed at by the rule in *Morice v the Bishop of Durham* was removed in his view where, as in that case, the gift was not simply for an impersonal purpose but for the benefit of defined individuals who had the *locus standi* to enforce the trust. Since the gift was limited to a specified period within the perpetuity rule, the second ground of objection was also surmounted.

In *Re Recher's Will Trusts,*[5] a new concept was utilised to validate the gift, which in that case was to 'The Anti-Vivisection Society' at a specified address. Brightman J cited the view of Cross J in *Neville Estates v Madden,*[6] that a gift might, on its true construction, be a gift to the members of an association, subject to their contractual rights and liabilities towards one another. The share of each member would accrue to the other members on his death or resignation. But there would be no perpetuity, provided that the members were able to divide the gift at any time between themselves for their own benefit. Hence the gift to the Anti-Vivisection society was capable of being valid. A similar approach was adopted by Oliver J in *Re Lipinski's Trusts*[7] where a testator left half the residue of his estate to a Jewish association in Hull in memory of his wife 'to be used solely in the work of constructing the new building for the Association and/or improvements to the said building.'

It is unlikely that any of these decisions will survive scrutiny in the House of Lords, unless that tribunal is prepared to adopt a bold new approach to the venerable rule in *Morice v Bishop of Durham*. They are plainly at odds with the approach adopted in *Leahy*: it could as well have been said in that case that any contemplative order of nuns whom the trustees might have selected could have held the gift subject to the same implied terms. Viscount Simonds, it is true, expressed his doubts as to whether the constitution of any order the trustees might select would have permitted the division of the property among its members, but acknowledged that there was 'little or no evidence' on this matter, and this does not appear to have formed part of the *ratio decidendi*. Technically, this decision is not binding on English courts, but *McCauley*, with which they also appear to conflict, most certainly is. In particular, it is difficult to reconcile the decision in *Lipinski* with what was said by the law lords in *McCauley*. Oliver J stressed that in that case the gift was for the 'maintenance and improvement' of the lodge whereas in the instant case it was for 'construct-ing.....and/or improvements....' Whatever may be thought of the force of that distinction, it is very difficult to see how one gift (*McCauley*) was treated as unenforceable as a purpose trust and the other (*Lipinski*) as enforceable.

1 [1943] Ch 435n, HL.
2 [1959] AC 457, PC.
3 This passage does not appear in the official reports where the Court of Appeal judgements are not reported. (The House of Lords speeches are only reported by way of a footnote to another decision.) It was, however, extracted from the records in *Leahy v A-G for New South Wales* and cited with approval by Viscount Simonds.
4 [1969] 1 Ch 373.
5 [1972] Ch 526.
6 [1962] Ch 832.
7 [1976] Ch 235. Cf *Re Grant's Will Trusts* [1979] 3 All ER 359.

7.12 So far as contemplative orders of men or women are concerned, it will remain unclear whether they are now charitable gifts until s 45(2) of the Charities Act 1961 which has altered the law in this area is judicially construed.[1] The question thus remains of more than academic importance and it cannot be assumed that s 49 of that Act (which is discussed in detail in Chapter 11 below) provides an answer.

It can hardly be said that the present state of the law is satisfactory. It seems contrary to commonsense to attribute to testators an intention that the Anti-Vivisection Society and the Hull Judeans' Association were to feel perfectly free to spend the money they had been left on a round the world cruise for the members. Yet to such extremities has the law been driven in its perfectly understandable anxiety not to see testators' inten-tions frustrated. While *Morice v The Bishop of Durham* is so entrenched in the law that it would take a decision of the Supreme Court in this country or the House of Lords in England to dislodge it, there are clearly weighty reasons for re-examining the justification for retaining it in our law. It is unsatisfactory to adopt the approach that trusts of this nature can be enforced by the residuary legatee or other person entitled in default: no doubt he would have the necessary *locus standi*, but he would have no incentive to argue for the enforcement of a trust the failure of which would benefit him. It seems more sensible to adopt the straightforward approach of treating such gifts as more in the nature of powers conferred on trustees. In the event of the trustees not exercising the power and giving the property to the person entitled in default there would be no one to complain, but this seems unlikely to give rise to serious problems. This has been the law in the United States for many years as the *Restatement of Trusts* makes clear:

'Where the owner of property transfers it upon an intended trust for a specific non-charitable purpose, and there is no definite or definitely ascertainable beneficiary designated no trust is created; but the transferee has power to apply the property to the designated purpose, unless he is authorised so to apply the property beyond the period of the rule against perpetuities, or the purpose is capricious.[2]

1 See para 11.16, below.
2 Cited by Harman J in *Re Shaw* (above) at 759.

Chapter 8

Express trusts: (2) the formal requirements

8.01 Except in three cases, there are no formal requirements for the creation of an express trust. Provided the 'three certainties' dealt with in the preceding chapter are present, it can be created by deed, in writing or orally and no particular verbal formula is required.

The three cases where certain formalities are required are:

(a) where the subject matter of the trust is *land*, or an interest in land;
(b) where the trust is in consideration of marriage;
(c) where the trust is not to take effect until the death of the settlor, in which case it is in law a will and must comply with the requirements of the law as to such instruments.

8.02 (a) In the case of trusts of land, s 4 of the Statute of Frauds (Ireland) 1695 requires that the trust be evidenced in writing, signed by some person able to declare the trust, or by his will. As in the case of contracts for the sale of land, the statute does not require that the instrument itself be in writing: there must, however, be evidence in writing signed by the settlor of the existence of the trust, or it must be declared by his will. The section applies to all interests in land, whether freehold or leasehold.

Equity will not, however, permit the statute itself, designed as it is to prevent frauds, to be used as an instrument of fraud. Hence if it can be shown that a person is seeking to deprive a beneficiary of property which he holds in trust for him, the absence of writing will not defeat the beneficiary's claim. And as we shall see in Chapter 13 no writing is required in the case of constructive trusts. All this flows from the original concept of the trust which, as we have seen, developed because of equity's insistence that the owner of property should act in accordance with his conscience and acknowledge the title of the person on whose behalf he was holding the property. For this reason, a court will not allow a trustee to defeat the title of the beneficiary by reliance on the absence of evidence in writing, if such conduct would amount in law to a fraud on the beneficiary.

The leading English case establishing this principle is *Rochefoucald v Boustead*,[1] which was applied by Budd J in *McGillycuddy of the Reeks v Joy and Another*.[2] In the latter case, the plaintiff and the defendants agreed verbally that they would join in the purchase of a farm adjoining the plaintiff's land in Kerry. The price was to be paid as to one-third by the plaintiff and two-thirds by the defendants. It was also agreed, however, that all the negotiations would be conducted, and the contract ultimately signed, by one of the defendants. A contract was eventually signed by that defendant and the plaintiff paid his part of the purchase price. The defendants then repudiated their agreement with the plaintiff and claimed to be entitled to keep the farm for themselves. The plaintiff relied on a letter written by one on the defendants as being sufficient evidence for the purposes of the statute. Budd J, without deciding whether the letter was such evidence, held that the principle in *Rochefoucald v Boustead* applied, that the defendant had purchased part of the lands as trustee for the plaintiff and that his repudiation of the trust was a fraud on the plaintiff. The plaintiff accordingly succeeded. It should be noted that, in contrast to the facts in *Rochefoucald v Boustead*, no conveyance of the land had been executed in favour of the defendant, but Budd J concluded that the principle applied as much where there was a contract for sale as where there was a conveyance.

The principle to be applied in such cases must be distinguished from the doctrine of part performance under which the court will enforce an oral agreement for the sale of an interest in land where there have been acts by the plaintiff unequivocally referable to the existence of such an agreement. In such a case, the orthodox view is that the defendant is charged, not upon the contract itself which would be contrary to the statute, but upon the 'equities' arising from such acts of part performance.[3] In the cases under discussion, the defendant is charged upon his enforceable agreement with the plaintiff, because to allow him to retain the land would be to permit the statute to be used as an instrument of fraud. This has led to some misgivings as to the legitimacy of such decisions, one commentator going as far as to say that they represent

'the exercise by equity of a suspending or dispensing power denied the executive branch of government since the Bill of Rights 1689.'[4]

(b) The second exception is also provided for in the Statute of Frauds (Ireland) 1698. S 2 requires that contracts to create a trust in consideration of marriage must also be in writing.

(c) The third exception to the rule that no writing is required arises where the trust is created by will. In this case, the requirements of the Succession Act 1965 must be observed: ie:
  (i) the will must be in writing;
  (ii) it must be signed at the foot or end thereof by the testator or by some other person in his presence and at his direction;
  (iii) the testator's signature must be made or acknowledged in the presence of two or more witnesses present at the same time each of whom attests the testator's signature by his or her signature.[5]

It should also be noted that where a trust of any sort has been created, the Statute of Frauds requires that any *future* disposition of the equitable interest in the property be in writing. In this case it is not sufficient that it be simply evidenced in writing: the actual instrument disposing of the interest must be in writing. It should also be observed that this requirement is applicable to all trusts and not simply trusts of land.

1 [1897] 1 Ch 196.
2 [1959] IR 189.
3 *Maddison v Alderson* (1883) 8 App Cas 467. See para 16.14, below.
4 Meagher Gummow & Lehane, pp 337-338.
5 S 78. Note that the witnesses need not sign in each other's presence.

Secret and half-secret trusts

8.03 The insistence of equity that the statutes of wills (which preceded the Succession Act 1965), like the Statute of Frauds, should not be used as instruments of fraud, explains the recognition by the law of what are known as *secret trusts*. Since wills are published and any member of the public can inspect them in the Probate Office on payment of a small fee, it was inevitable that a testator in some instances would be concerned to avoid publicity, eg where he wished to provide for a mistress or an illegitimate child. Where a bequest is made to a person to whom the testator communicates his wish that the property in question should go to another and the devisee or legatee agrees, either expressly or tacitly, to hold it in trust for that other person, a trust arises which will be enforced by the courts. The same principle applies where the testator, in reliance on a similar undertaking, express or implied, by one of the next-of-kin, makes no will at all: the next-of-kin concerned hold his share in trust for the person whom the deceased wished to benefit.

Such trusts have provoked much academic discussion and indeed controversy, but it cannot be said that they have troubled practitioners that often and it seems likely that in modern conditions testators resort to them less frequently. However, the manner in which they have been approached by the courts illustrates some important principles applicable to the enforcement of trusts and the construction of wills generally which justify their extended treatment in the textbooks.

8.04 Such secret trusts have been recognised by the law for a long time, one of the earliest reported decisions[1] being by no less a person than Judge Jeffreys, of 'bloody assizes' fame, during his troubled reign as Lord Chancellor. As Lord Westbury explained in *McCormick v Grogan*[2] when the House of Lords were upholding the Irish Court of Appeal, they arose because of the refusal of courts of conscience to allow a man retain property which had been left to him on the faith of a promise, in reliance on which the testator might have refrained from changing his will or making a will at all.

> 'The Court of Equity has, from a very early period, decided that even an Act of Parliament shall not be used as an instrument of fraud; and if in the machinery of perpetrating a fraud an Act of Parliament intervenes (*sic*) the Court of Equity does not, it is true, set aside the Act of Parliament, but it fastens on the individual who gets a title under the Act and imposes upon him a personal obligation, because he applies the Act as an instrument for accomplishing a fraud. In this way, the Court of Equity has dealt with the Statute of Frauds and in this manner also it deals with the Statute of Wills.'[3]

But while the enforceability of secret trusts thus derives from the equitable aversion to fraud, it does not mean that fraud must be present in order to give rise to a secret trust. In a number of modern cases, the trust has arisen where the person alleged to be a trustee has acted perfectly honestly and may indeed be seeking the directions of the court as to whether a trust exists.

The essential ingredients of a secret trust to-day are

(a) a communication by A to B[4] that property which he is leaving to him by will or transferring to him by an instrument *inter vivos* is in fact intended to go to or benefit C, or

(b) a communication by A to B that he intends to die intestate in the expectation that B, being one of his next-of-kin, will transfer his share to C; and

(c) in either case, an express agreement by B to hold the property or share in trust for C or conduct by him (such as silence where he might reasonably be expected to respond)[5] from which the court may infer his acquiescence.

Neither the communication by the testator nor the acceptance of the trust by the legatee or beneficiary need be in writing. The standard of proof is the same as in any other case where it is sought to establish the existence of a trust: it must be proved upon the balance of probabilities. In *Re Snowden deceased*,[6] Megarry V-C accepted that where fraud arose—which it did not in that case—a higher standard of proof might be required. However, the Supreme Court have recently rejected the view that in civil cases an allegation of fraud imposes a higher burden of proof on the plaintiff: the burden of proof remains the same, although the nature of the evidence on which the court will act varies according to the gravity of the issue.[7]

1 *Crook v Brooking* (1688) 2 Vern 106.
2 (1869) LR 4HL 82.
3 At 97.
4 The communication must be made in the lifetime of A, because if B only learns of the trust after A's death, he will have acquired the property with a clear conscience: *Wallgrave v Tebbs* (1855) 2 K & J 313.
5 *Moss v Cooper* (1861) 1 John & H 352.
6 [1979] 2 All ER 172.
7 *Banco Ambrosiano SPA v Ansbacher & Co Ltd*, unreported, judgement delivered 8 April 1987.

8.05 A difficult problem arises if the property is left to two or more people and the secret trust has not been communicated to all of them. It has been held that whether the trust is binding on all of them depends on whether they are tenants in common or joint tenants. If they are tenants in common, the trust binds only those to whom it has been communicated. If they are joint tenants and the trust was communicated by the testator to one of them *before* the will was made, it will be binding on them all.[1] This is because the law would regard it as a fraud for the joint tenant who was privy to the secret to retain the beneficial ownership, and since there is only one estate in the case of a joint tenancy the other tenants cannot take the estate freed from the fraud. While logical, the distinction does not seem to produce a satisfactory result: it is surely anomalous that a court of equity should determine the respective rights of the trustee and the beneficiary by reference to the particular technical formula employed in the will. Wylie proposes the solution of treating the joint tenancy as severed by the creation of the secret trust and this would seem to produce a happier result.[2]

1 *Geddis v Semple* [1903] 1 IR 73.
2 Wylie, *Land Law*, p 477.

8.06 In the cases just discussed, there was no reference to the trust in the will or the instrument under which the property was vested in the trustee. Cases have also arisen in which it is made clear that the property is to be held on trust but the objects of the trust are not disclosed in the will. Where the objects are communicated to the trustee by the testator during his lifetime, such 'half-secret' trusts as they are called will be upheld. That this was the law in Ireland was made clear by Chatterton V-C in *Riordan v Banon*[1] where he said

'The result of the cases appears to me to be that a testator cannot by his will reserve to himself the right of disposing subsequently of property by an instrument not executed as required by the statute, or by parol; but that when, at thc time of making his will, he has formed the intention that a legacy thereby given shall be disposed of by the legatee in a particular manner, not thereby disclosed, but communicated to the legatee and assented to by him, at or before the making of the will, or probably, according to *Moss v Cooper*, subsequently to the making of it, the Court will allow such trust to be proved by admission of the legatee, or other parol evidence, and will, if it be legal, give effect to it. The same principle which led this Court, whether wisely or not, to hold that the Statute of Frauds and the Statute of Wills were not to be used as instruments of Fraud appears to me to apply to cases where the will shows that some trust was intended as well as to those where this does not appear upon it. The testator, at least when his purpose is communicated to and accepted by the proposed legatee, makes the disposition on the faith of his carrying out his promise and it would be a fraud on him to refuse to perform that promise. No doubt the fraud would be of a different kind if he could by means of it retain the benefit of the legacy for himself: but it appears that it would also be a fraud though the result would be to defeat the expressed intention for the benefit of the heir, next-of-kin or residuary donee.'[2]

Some features of the half-secret trust which emerge from this passage should be noted.

First, the court intervenes in this instance, not to prevent the trustee from retaining the property for himself, but to ensure that it goes to the real objects of the testator's benevolence and not the next-of-kin or residuary legatees. If the trust failed for uncertainty, the trustee could not retain it for himself since it was not the testator's intention that he should retain it and hence in accordance with the law applicable to resulting trusts, the property would revert to the testator's successors, i e the residuary legatee or, in the event of there being no residuary clause, the next-of-kin.

Secondly, while Chatterton V-C emphasises the origin of the principle in the equitable doctrine of fraud, it should not be thought that fraud is an essential element in the enforcement of a half-secret trust, any more than it is in the case of a secret trust. Indeed, precisely because the trustee will in this instance never derive any personal benefit, the element of fraud may be even more conspicuously absent. It may be noted that in England, where the enforceability of such trusts remained in doubt for a far longer period than in Ireland, Lord Sumner in *Blackwell v Blackwell*,[3] the case which finally laid such doubts to rest, stressed the inequity of a system which enforced the trust where the trustee was seeking to enrich himself unjustly but denied assistance to the honest trustee who wished to carry out his testator's intentions.

Thirdly, the communication by the testator of his wishes may be either oral or written. It is not necessary that he should sign any document: all that is required is that there should be evidence enabling the court to ascertain the objects of the trust with certainty.

Fourthly, Chatterton V-C refers to the possibility that such a half-secret trust may be enforceable, although the objects of the trust are not communicated to the trustee until *after* the making of the will. Since in that case, the testator had named the person whom he wished to benefit *before* the will was executed, the point did not have to be decided. Nor did it arise directly in *Blackwell v Blackwell*, although in his speech Lord Sumner expressed his clear view that they had to be communicated *before* the execution of the will. When the point did eventually come before the English Court of Appeal in *Re Keen*[4] they were unanimously of the same opinion. The judges' conclusion was based on their belief that to allow a testator to reserve to himself the right of declaring trusts by an instrument informally executed subsequent to the execution of his will would be to set aside all the statutory requirements as to the due execution, attestation and publication of wills.

The law is accordingly clear in England. It has been suggested more than once that the Irish courts have taken a different approach and have upheld half-secret trusts where the objects were communicated *after* the execution of the will.[5] It is thought that this is, to say the least, extremely doubtful. The passage already cited from the judgement of Chatterton V-C acknowledges at the outset the basic rule that the testator cannot reserve the right to dispose of property by an instrument to be executed subsequently and the principle was restated in almost identical language by Monroe J in *Re King's Estate*,[6] who added: 'that would be to repeal the Statute of Wills.' It is true that in the same case where the learned judge listed a number of principles applicable to secret and half-secret trusts, he said

> 'the rule applies when the communication is made subsequent to the execution of the will: *Moss v Taylor*.'

The citation of *Moss v Taylor* notwithstanding, Monroe J may have intended this comment to apply only to fully secret trusts. Whether that be so or not, *Re King's Estate* is no authority for the more general proposition, since in that case he found that the trust was a fully secret trust.

Nor is the later decision of Overend J, *Re Browne deceased*,[7] an authority for the proposition that the communication can be made after the execution of the will. In that case, the testator appointed a close friend as his executor and said

> 'I hereby give and bequeath unto (the executor) all my real and personal property of what nature or kind so ever, I relying on his carrying out the wishes which I have expressed to him and/or may do so hereafter.'

When the testator was dying, he sent for the executor and gave him the will and a document headed 'Instructions'. The executor did not read these at the time but their substance was explained to him by the testator and the executor was fully aware that the testator wished them to be carried out. He did not read the Instructions in full, however, until after the testator's death which took place later that day. The executor made no claim to any of the estate, except two small items which the testator had indicated that he wished him to have, but applied for directions as to whether the estate was to be distributed in accordance with the 'Instructions' or was to go to the next-of-kin. Overend J held that the reference in the will to the testator's wishes was so ambiguous that it could not be said that any trust was disclosed on the face of the will. As there had been a sufficient communication of his wishes during the testator's lifetime, the secret trust thus created would be enforced. Overend J seems certainly to have taken the view that the same result would have followed if he had found that the trust was a half-secret trust, but this was clearly *obiter* and it is respectfully suggested that the weight to be attached to the observation is lessened by the fact that, although *Re Keen* is referred to without apparent disapproval, it is, as we have seen, authority for a different view of the law.

The decision in the latter case and the dicta to the same effect of Lord Sumner in *Blackwell v Blackwell* were criticised by Holdsworth[8] and there has been some support from later commentators for his view. It is said that, as the essence of both the secret and the half secret trust is that they operate *dehors* the will, communication after as well as before execution should suffice. There is certainly force in that criticism, but there are also powerful policy reasons for rejecting a totally logical approach in this area: ultimately, the undesirability of allowing the statutory requirements as to the making of wills to be subverted and the public interest in ensuring that they are observed may be decisive considerations in Ireland as in England.

1 (1876) IR 10 Eq 469.
2 At pp 477-478.
3 [1929] AC 318.
4 [1937] Ch 236.
5 See for example Wylie, *Land Law*, 479. Professor Wylie has, however, moderated his view in the second edition.
6 [1888] 21 LR Ir 273.
7 (1944) IR 90.
8 'Secret Trusts', (1937) 53 LQR 501.

Incompletely constituted trusts

8.07 Once I have made a gift of property, I cannot recall it. But I must have actually transferred the property; if I simply make known my intention of presenting someone with the property, but do not take the necessary steps to vest its ownership in that person, the law will not enforce my promise. In the words of Johnston J in *Re Wilson, Grove-White v Wilson:*-[1]

'A gift is a gift and of course if a donor, while expressing an intention to give something and taking certain steps in the direction of giving it has not gone the whole way, the expectant donee has no equity to compel the completion of the gift. This is good sense and good law.'[2]

In the same way, if I wish to make a gift of property to be held in trust for someone, it is not enough to promise to do so or even to take steps towards doing so: I must do all that it is within my power to do to create the trust. Hence the legal principle evolved in the courts of equity that the law will not enforce an incompletely constituted trust of a voluntary nature, i e one for which no consideration has been given by the beneficiary. The law was thus stated by Turner LJ in *Milroy v Lord*: [3]

'I take the law of this Court to be well settled that, in order to render a voluntary settlement valid and effectual, the settlor must have done everything which, according to the nature of the property comprised in the settlement, was necessary to be done in order to transfer the property and render the settlement binding upon him. He may of course do this by actually transferring property to the persons for whom he intends to provide, and the provision will then be effectual, and it will be equally effectual if he transfers the property to a trustee for the purposes of the settlement, or declares that he himself holds it in trust for those purposes; and, if the property be personal, the trust may, as I apprehend, be declared either in writing or by parol; but in order to render the settlement binding one or other of these modes, must, as I understand the law of this Court, be resorted to, for there is no equity in the Court to perfect an imperfect gift.'[4]

We have already seen that an express trust may be created by a declaration on the part of the settlor that he holds the property in trust for the beneficiary. It is clear from this passage that, provided such a declaration is made, it is immaterial that there is no consideration given by the beneficiary. Thus, in the leading Irish case of *Miller v Harrison*[5]a person died intestate in the United States, leaving real and personal estate in New York City. At a meeting of his next-of-kin in Ireland, one of them, A, a naturalised US citizen, told the others that, as such, he was by the law of New York entitled to the whole of the real estate. The others disputed this and eventually A agreed that if two others of the next-of-kin, B and C, went to the US and recovered the property, he would relinquish his claim and allow the property to be divided equally, provided the others contributed to the expenses of sending B and C to the US. B and C duly went at the expense of the next of kin to the US where an action was in progress in relation to the property. B wrote to A saying that if A was still pressing his claim to be solely entitled to the property, B would have the case heard, but asking him, if he was adhering to the arrangement with the next-of-kin, to send out a deed so that it could be given effect to. A thereupon executed a deed declaring that if the US Court held him entitled to the property to the exclusion of the other next-of-kin, he would nevertheless share it equally with them. B and C, relying on the deed, allowed judgement to be given in favour of A in the action. A thereupon revoked the deed, but it was held by the Court of Appeal, upholding the decision of the Vice-Chancellor, that he could not do so. The execution by A of the deed in question constituted a declaration of trust which was 'clear, complete and final' and consequently the fact that it was a purely voluntary transaction was immaterial.[6]

1 [1933] IR 729.
2 At 739.
3 (1862) 4 De GF & J 264.
4 At 274-275.
5 (1871) IR 5 Eq 324.
6 It could be said, however, that in this case the forebearance of B and C from resisting A's claim constituted consideration for the deed.

8.08 The law is that the settlor must do all that is in his power to divest himself of his interest in the property and vest it in the trustees. But if there is some further requirement of the law to be met by the transferee, a trust will come into being, provided that the settlor has done everything which he can. In the case of shares in a company, for example, a person to whom the shares are transferred does not become in law a shareholder in the company until his name has been placed on the register of members. Where the shareholder has executed a transfer and handed it to the transferee together with the share certificates, he has done all he can to complete the transaction.

The applicability of the principle is illustrated by *Re Rose*.[1]In that case, it was held that a shareholder who wished to make a gift of shares and had executed a transfer but died before the transferee was registered as a member had created a valid trust. (The issue arose in a claim for death duties: if the donor was still the legal and equitable owner of the shares at the date of his death they formed part of his estate for death duties purposes.) The donor had done all that he could to transfer the property and although he remained in law the owner of the shares until the transferee was registered, he held them at the date of his death for the transferee.

It would also seem that in the case of registered land, this principle will apply where the registered owner had executed a transfer and delivered it to the transferee together with the Land Certificate. This would seem to be the clear implication of the decision in *Devoy v Hanlon*.[2] The views of the majority were, however, strictly *obiter* since the deed in that case had not been delivered. The same question has been considered in a number of cases in Australia dealing with registered land and the view most generally accepted appears to have been that in such circumstances the trust is complete.[3]

1 [1952] 1 Ch 499.
2 [1929] IR 246.
3 *Taylor v Deputy FCT* (1969) 123 CLR 206; *Cope v Keene* (1968) 118 CLR 1.

8.09 An incompletely constituted trust will, accordingly, fail unless there is consideration. By consideration is meant the conferring of some benefit on the settlor or the undergoing of some detriment by the beneficiary. It must, in other words, be *valuable consideration*—money or money's worth—and not merely 'good' consideration, i e natural love and affection. A trust created in consideration of marriage is, however, created for valuable consideration, since the consideration of marriage is the 'highest known to the law.'[1] But the settlement must be made before and in contemplation of the marriage: a settlement executed after the marriage is not supported by consideration, unless made pursuant to a pre-nuptial agreement to make such a settlement.[2]

In addition to the spouses, the issue of the marriage are also treated as being 'within the marriage consideration.' It follows that not merely the spouses but the issue of the marriage can enforce the settlement even though it is incompletely constituted.[3] But any other beneficiaries of the settlement, even though they may be blood relations of the spouses, are treated as volunteers, i e as not having given any consideration.

1 Per Walker LJ in *Re Downes* [1898] 2 IR 635 at 636.
2 *Re Greer* (1877) IR 11 Eq 502.
3 *Greenwood v Lutman* [1915] 1 IR 266.

8.10 We have seen[1] that occasions may arise on which the law will permit a stranger to a contract to enforce it on the ground that one of the parties has created a trust of his promise which the beneficiary can enforce. In such a case—where A agrees with B to confer a benefit on C—the true legal position is that B is a trustee of the chose of action represented by his contractual rights against A. But it is essential that A should have intended to create a trust of his promise in favour of C and, as we have already seen, the courts have been reluctant in modern times to draw the inference of such a trust from the mere fact of A agreeing with B to confer a benefit on C. Where such an intention can be inferred, however, the trust is completely constituted and there is nothing to prevent C from suing A for damages or specific performance, whichever is appropriate. But if there is simply an agreement to transfer property in the future, to C, then C will be unable to enforce the agreement. He cannot sue in contract because he is not a party. And he cannot sue as a beneficiary, unless he has given consideration, because the trust is incompletely constitued and equity will not assist a volunteer.

Where the agreement is under seal—i e where A *covenants* with B to confer a benefit on C—there is nothing *au fond* to prevent *B* from suing A, since the absence of consideration will not be a bar. Hence it has been suggested that the difficulty in C's way can be circumvented by B's suing as trustee in which case he would presumably hold any damages he recovered in trust for C. But the English authorities do not give much encouragement to this approach.

Two difficulties arise. First the trustee has suffered no damage by A's failure to fulfil his promise and hence can be awarded nominal damages only. Secondly, C cannot compel B to sue and there is even authority that, where B is willing himself to sue, he should not do so, the reason being that it is no part of a trustee's function to bestir himself in this fashion where his settlor, for whatever reason, elects not to proceed any further.[2]

So in a marriage settlement, where it is common for the settlor to covenant to settle after-acquired property, such a covenant will be enforceable by those within the marriage consideration, i e the spouses and children. But it will not be enforceable by other beneficiaries, since they are volunteers and the trust is incompletely constituted.[3]

An instance of where the court was prepared to enforce a trust at the behest of a volunteer is the old case of *Fletcher v Fletcher*[4] in which a father covenanted with trustees to pay a sum of money to his two natural sons. The deed did not come to light until after his death and the trustees, who apparently knew nothing about it, declined to sue his estate. But one of the sons did and was held entitled to recover. The case is only explicable on the basis that the father intended to create a trust of the covenant in favour of the sons, but is generally regarded as of somewhat doubtful authority since there seems to have been no satisfactory evidence that the father intended to create such a trust.[5]

1 Para 6.03, above.
2 *Re Pryce* [1917] 1 Ch 234.
3 *Re Kay's Settlement* [1939] Ch 329; *Re Cook's Settlement Trusts* [1965] Ch 902.
4 (1844) 4 Hare 67.
5 See generally on this topic Underhill, pp 110-122.

8.11 There are a number of exceptions to the rule that equity will not assist a volunteer in the case of an incompletely constituted trust. We now consider these in turn.

(a) *Where the settlor subsequently vests the legal title in the trustee or beneficiary, the trust is enforceable.* This is usually known as the rule in *Strong v Bird*[1] after the decision of Jessel MR which is generally cited as the *locus classicus* of the principle. It seems to have been thought at first that the case decided no more than that where a creditor forgives a debt during his lifetime, the appointment by him of the debtor as his executor makes the release enforceable at law. But it soon became apparent that he had used words of more general import. In *Re Stewart*[2] it was made clear that the principle was this: where a settlor manifests an intention of making a gift and subsequently vests the legal estate in the beneficiary or a trustee for the beneficiary, the trust is thereby completely constituted and is enforceable by the beneficiary.

The application of the rule was considered in *Re Wilson, Grove-White v Wilson*. In that case, a stockbroker agreed to transfer certain properties absolutely to his son or to bequeath them by his will. He appointed his son executor of his will and bequeathed some but not all of the property to him. Johnston J held that the agreement being both voluntary and incomplete could not be enforced and that the appointment of the son as executor did not render the trust completely constituted. The rule in *Strong v Bird* had no application where there was merely a promise of future testatmentary benefaction as opposed to an actual agreement to make a gift followed by the vesting of the legal estate.

The rule in *Strong v Bird* is applicable even though the executor is simply one of a number. It has also been held in England that it is applicable where the legal title is vested in the donee by virtue of his having become the administrator of the deceased,[3] but the correctness of this view was questioned in a subsequent decision and these doubts seem well founded. Where the settlor does all in his power to vest the legal estate in the donee and thereby completes the gift, as by making him the executor of his estate, it is logical that the trust should be regarded as completely constituted. But it is difficult to see why the same result should follow from the appointment of the donee as administrator, which is in no sense the act of the settlor and may well result from a series of fortuituous events which the settlor could not possibly have foreseen. Where, however, the property subsequently becomes vested in the trustee as trustee under some other settlement but in trust for the same beneficiary, the rule applies.

(b) *Donationes mortis causa.* These are gifts made by a person in contemplation of his death but which are revocable by the donor during his lifetime. They are thus incomplete gifts and if the general principle were applicable should be unenforceable by the donee. However, provided the actual subject matter of the gift, or something which enables the donee to exercise control over it, such as the key of a box in which it is contained, is handed over during the lifetime of the donor, such gifts are enforceable by the donee. They are considered in more detail in Chapter Thirty Three.

(c) *Proprietary estoppel.* If the owner of land either expressly or impliedly promises another person that he will give him an interest in the land and the latter in reliance on the promise spends money on the land or acts to his own detriment in some other manner, the owner of the land may be required to fulfill his promise even though it is not supported by consideration and the promisee is thus a volunteer. This is a form of what is called *proprietary estoppel* and is considered in more detail in Chapter Twenty Eight.

1 (1874) LR 18 Eq 315.
2 [1908] 2 Ch 251.
3 *Re James* [1935] Ch 449.

Chapter 9

The office of trustee

9.01 Professor Frances Moran, the formidable lady who for many years lectured on Equity to the students of King's Inns, used to tell her (in those days) all male classes: 'there are three roads to ruin in life, wine, women and becoming a trustee. The first two are at least enjoyable.' She was also wont to enquire rhetorically: 'what is the first duty of a trustee?' and answer her own question succinctly: 'retire.'

This was not merely cynicism. The office of trustee is one which generally offers few advantages, material or otherwise. It can be time consuming, tedious and, where the beneficiaries are difficult, importunate or quarrelsome, as they frequently are, positively distasteful. And, on top of all this, it may involve the holder in legal liability and that in circumstances where he or she has done nothing remotely dishonourable.

Why then do people agree to become trustees? Frequently because they are members of the settlor's family and sometimes because of long-standing friendship. In the case of charitable trusts, those who are interested in the particular charity may be prepared to give practical assistance by agreeing to act as trustees. And while a trustee as such is not entitled to any remuneration, and indeed is precluded from making any profit out of his office, there is nothing to prevent the trust instrument from providing that he is to be remunerated for any work in which he is involved. To-day settlors and testators commonly appoint a bank to act as trustee and executor but the bank will only agree to act if the instrument provides that it is to be entitled to charge its normal remuneration. Similarly, a solicitor who is appointed trustee usually is empowered to charge his normal professional fees for any work as solicitor which is involved in his trusteeship. (But it should be noted that this will be regarded in law as a legacy in the case of a trust created by a will and accordingly the solicitor should not witness the will since this will prevent him from charging his fees.)

Those who can be appointed trustee

9.02 With one exception, anyone can be appointed a trustee. The exception is a corporation which is prohibited by its constitution from being a trustee. Provided its constitution expressly authorises it so to act, a corporation (including a limited company) may act as a trustee.[1] And there is nothing to prevent a minor, ie someone under the age of 18, from being appointed a trustee, since there is no equivalent in Ireland to s 20 of the English Law of Property Act 1925 which rendered such an appointment void in the case of an express trust. Nor in theory is there anything to stop the settlor appointing a person of unsound mind, even where he has been so found, to be a trustee. But since a trustee is expected to play more than a merely passive and honorary role and to exercise at least some discretion, the sensible course is to appoint a person who is mature and responsible. Moreover, while unsoundness of mind does not in theory disqualify a person from being a trustee, it will always be a good ground for his removal from office. Again it is possible to appoint a bankrupt as trustee, but where a person appointed is subsequently adjudicated a bankrupt this will be a ground for his removal, save in exceptional circumstances.[2]

A beneficiary may be a trustee, but it is undesirable that he should be in any case where a conflict of interest is likely to arise. In practice, beneficiaries are frequently appointed, if for no other reason than that it is hard to find persons willing to act who are not going to benefit. This is perfectly lawful, but the possibility of a conflict of interest arising should always be borne in mind.

Local authorities would also appear to be capable of acting as trustees: they are specifically empowered to accept gifts under the Local Authorities (Acceptance of Gifts) Act 1945 and presumably would be regarded as holding property donated to them in trust for the ratepayers.

1 *Re Munster & Leinster Bank Ltd* [1907] I IR 237.
2 As where he has no money to deal with: *Re Barker's Trusts* (1875) 1 Ch D 43.

9.03 There is no doubt as to the capacity of the State to hold property. The principle that the State is a juristic person, correctly described as 'Ireland', or 'the Republic of Ireland', was firmly established in our law in *Comyn v Attorney General*.[1] As such a juristic person, it is capable of holding property and the machinery by which it does so is to be found in the State Property Act 1954. Clearly there is nothing to prevent the State from being a trustee of any property which is vested in it, but it does not necessarily follow that because property is vested in the State for the benefit of named persons, it becomes in law a trustee of that property for the persons so named, thus entitling them to enforce the trust against the State by proceedings.

In a number of English decisions, it has been held that in equivalent circumstances the Crown was not a trustee and could not be sued. In *Kinloch v Secretary of State for India*,[2] where Queen Victoria had by her warrant granted 'booty of war' to the Defendant to distribute amongst those declared entitled to it by the Admiralty Court, it was held that no trust was created: the Secretary of State merely held the booty as agent for the Crown for the purposes of distribution. Similarly, in *Civilian War Claimants' Association v R*,[3] the House of Lords held that the Crown was not a trustee in respect of money forming part of the reparations paid by Germany after the First World War which was claimed to represent compensation to civilian victims of aggression. And in *Tito v Waddell (No 2)*,[4] Megarry V-C reached a similar conclusion in relation to funds and royalties alleged to be payable by the Crown under certain agreements to a number of Banabans, inhabitants of Ocean Island in the Indian Ocean. In all these cases, it was held that the Crown was discharging a sovereign function and could not be sued as a trustee.

It is thought that, depending on the circumstances of the particular transaction, these legal principles are also applicable in Ireland, although the constitutional structure is entirely different. Megarry V-C draws a distinction between what he calls 'true trusts'—the type of trust which can be enforced in a court of equity — and 'higher trusts', by which he means the obligation of the State to do justice to its citizens. This distinction in no sense depends on any survival of the royal prerogative, which has for long ceased to play any part in Irish constitutional theory. It is based on the entirely different concept that the entrusting to the executive of property to be applied for the benefit of a defined section does not create a trust in the equitable sense which can be enforced in a court of law. (There are also indications of a similar approach in decisions in the USA.[5]) There seems no reason why in an appropriate case the same considerations should not apply *mutatis mutandis* in Ireland. The point, however, has yet to be judicially considered.

1 [1950] IR 142.
2 (1882) 7 App Cas 619.
3 [1932] AC 14, HL.
4 [1977] Ch 106.
5 Eg *Chippewa Indians of Minnesota v US No 2* 307 US 1 (1939).

Personal representatives and trustees

9.04 The distinction between personal representatives, whether they be executors or administrators and whether the deceased died testate or intestate, and trustees must be fully appreciated. No difficulty arises if, as frequently happens, an executor is also appointed by the will to be a trustee of the estate bequeathed by the will. Sometimes an appointment may be made for a specified purpose, as where a testator appoints trustees for the purposes of the Settled Land Acts 1882 to 1890. This will arise where the will creates a 'settlement' of real or leasehold estate—broadly speaking, where property is limited to more than one person in succession, most commonly to A for life with remainder to B. In such a case, it will be necesary to have at least two trustees appointed for the purposes of the Acts, since in the event of the tenant for life exercising his statutory power of sale, two trustees are required to give a receipt for the capital money.[1]

If the executor is not expressly appointed a trustee, the position is not the same. Under s 10(3) of the Succession Act 1965 a personal representative when a grant of probate or administration issues to him holds the estate of the deceased in trust for the person entitled to it by law. But as we have seen,[2] it does not necessarily mean that the personal representative is a trustee for those entitled under the will or an intestacy as beneficiaries. They will be entitled only to the residue of the estate after the debts have been paid, and, in the case of an insolvent estate, they will be entitled to nothing at all and the creditors to everything.[3]

1 Settled Land Act 1882, s 39(1).
2 See para 4.05, above. It was for some years thought that a personal representative was an express trustee for the purposes of the statutes of limitations so that time did not run in his favour when he was in possession of land: *Re Loughlin* [1942] IR 15. That heresy was finally laid to rest by the Supreme Court in *Vaughan v Cottingham* [1961] IR 184, a decision which was given statutory effect by s 123 of the Succession Act 1965.
3 See para 4.05, above.

Number of trustees

9.05 There is no limit to the number of persons who may be trustees, although it may be administratively unwieldy to have more than a certain number. Save in one instance, it is sufficient to have a single trustee. The exception has already been noted: there must be at least two trustees for the purposes of the Settled Land Acts in order to give a receipt for capital money on a sale by the tenant for life. It should be observed that there is no provision, as there is in England, entitling a trust corporation to give a receipt in such circumstances.

No provision for public trustee, judicial trustee or custodian trustee

9.06 There is no public trustee in the normal sense in Ireland.[1] In this respect, our law differs from English law under which, since 1906, there has been a public official so designated to whom property may be given upon specified trusts. There is also no provision in Ireland for the appointment by the Court of a 'judicial trustee' upon whom the administration of an estate or a trust fund may be conferred when particular circumstances warrant the appointment, as in England. The institution of the 'custodian trustee' is also unknown in our law: in England, it is possible to appoint such trustees in whom the legal ownership of relevant property is vested, while the actual administration of the affairs of the trust is carried on by 'management trustees.'

1 There is a Public Trustee whose functions are confined to matters arising under the Land Purchase Acts. He cannot undertake other work: *Re Leeson's Goods* [1928] IR 168.

Appointment of trustees

9.07 The first trustees are usually appointed by name in the document creating the trust. No particular formalities are required, but it will be remembered that an express trust of land must be in writing[1] and that a trust of any property created by will must also be in writing and comply with the requirements of the Succession Act 1965.[2]

Where a trustee dies, or for some reason it is necessary to replace him, the power to appoint a person in his stead may be exercised by a person nominated for that purpose by the instrument creating the trust. There is, however, a statutory power vested in certain persons in defined circumstances to appoint new trustees and since the power in question is reasonably comprehensive, it is usual to rely on the statutory power and not to confer an express power of appointment in the document creating the trust.

The statutory power is to be found in s 10 of the Trustee Act 1893 and is in the following terms:

'Where a trustee, either original or substituted, and whether appointed by a court or otherwise, is dead, or remains out of *Ireland* for more than twelve months or desires to be discharged from all or any of the trusts or powers reposed in or conferred on him, or refuses or is unfit to act therein, then the person or persons nominated for the purpose of appointing new trustees by the instrument, if any, creating the trust, or if there is no such person, or no such person able and willing to act, then the surviving or continuing trustees or trustee for the time being, or the personal representative of the last surviving or continuing trustee, may by writing appoint another person or persons to be a trustee or trustees in the place of the trustee dead, remaining out of *Ireland*, desiring to be discharged, refusing or being unfit or being incapable, as aforesaid.'

The section goes on to provide that, on any such appointment, the number of trustees may be increased, and for the appointment of a separate set of trustees for any part of the trust property held on distinct trusts.[3] It is not necessary to appoint more than one trustee where only one was originally appointed, or to fill up the original number of trustees where more than two were appointed. Except, however, where only one trustee was originally appointed, a trustee cannot be discharged, unless there are at least two trustees to perform the trust.[4]

A number of features of this power should be noted. First, while the power to appoint new trustees (in the absence of any provision in the instrument to the contrary) is primarily vested in the surviving trustees or trustee, the fact that all the trustees are dead or unable or unwilling to act, does not produce a deadlock: the power can then be exercised by the personal representative of the last surviving trustee. Second, the power is not confined to the replacement of the original trustees: it can be availed of in the case of substitited trustees. Third, while the number of trustees may be increased where a trustee is being replaced in exercise of this power, there is otherwise no power to appoint additional trustees. In this, the law differs significantly from the law in England and Northern Ireland.

Where a trustee dies and there are surviving trustees, both the office of trustee and the estate which he owned in the trust property devolve upon the survivors: trustees are invariably joint tenants of the property subject to the trust. When the last surviving trustee dies, the estate devolves upon his personal representative.[5]

1 See para 8.02, above.
2 Ibid.
3 This latter power may be exercised even though no new trustees are being appointed for any other part of the trust property.
4 1893 Act, s 11 (1).
5 Conveyancing Act 1881, s 30.

9.08   It will be seen that the appointment of a new trustee under the statutory power must be in writing, but need not be by deed. In practice, however, it is invariably made by deed. This is because where the deed contains a declaration by the appointor vesting the trust property in new trustees, that declaration operates to vest the estate in the property in the new trustees without the execution of any conveyance or assignment.[1] There are two major exceptions: first, where the land has been mortgaged and, secondly, where the trust property includes stocks or shares in a company. So far as this second exception is concerned, it should be borne in mind that under s 123 of the Companies Act 1963:

'no notice of any trust, express, implied or constructive, shall be entered on the register (of shareholders of a company) or be receivable by the Registrar (of Companies).

It would make the task of managers and secretaries of companies extremely difficult if on every appointment of a new trustee the legal ownership of the shares changed without any transfer of shares being executed and lodged for registration in the ordinary way.

1 Trustee Act 1893, s 12.

Appointment of new or additional trustees by the Court

9.09 It is a cardinal maxim of the law that 'a trust shall not fail for want of a trustee.' This is given statutory force by s 25 of the Trustee Act 1893 which gives the Court extensive powers to appoint new or additional trustees, including power to appoint a trustee where there is no trustee at all. The power is exercisable

> 'whenever it is expedient to appoint a new trustee or trustees and it is found inexpedient, difficult or impracticable so to do without the assistance of the Court.....'

The Court will not make an appointment where a valid appointment can be made, ie in exercise of a power in the instrument itself. The only exception is where a vesting order under the Act (as to which see para 9.12, below) is required. Similarly, the Court will not make an appointment if it can be validly made in exercise of the statutory power discussed in the preceding paragraph.

9.10 The circumstance in which the Court will make an appointment can be briefly summarised.

(1) Where the trustee is incapable of acting, because of mental or physical infirmity.
(2) Where the trustee is a minor
(3) Where the trustee is permanently residing abroad.
(4) Where the trustee has become bankrupt.
(5) Where the surviving trustee had died intestate and representation has not been raised to his estate.

The Court has also an inherent power to appoint a trustee where the original instrument has not appointed any trustee.

1 *Pollock v Ennis* [1921] 1 IR 181.

9.11 In appointing a new trustee, the Court will normally have regard to the wishes of the settlor, expressed in, or to be inferred from, the terms of the trust instrument. Generally speaking, a beneficiary will not be appointed. Nor will persons resident out of the jurisdiction be appointed, save in special circumstances. A sole trustee will also not be appointed, save in special circumstances.

If the application is made to the High Court, it must be brought by special summons grounded on an affidavit.[1] If it is made to the Circuit Court, it must be by petition grounded on an affidavit.[2] It should be noted that the Circuit Court now has an extensive jurisdiction in this area: as a result of the amendment effected by the Courts Act 1981, the jurisdiction of the Circuit Court is only excluded where the rateable valuation of any land subject to the trust exceeds £200.[3]

The application should be entitled in the matter of the trust and of the Act. The affidavit, in addition to setting out the circumstances which are relied on as justifying an appointment by the Court, should give details of the occupations of the proposed trustees and should show that they are fit persons to be appointed. A written consent to act from them should be exhibited and it is also desirable to have affidavits as to the fitness of the proposed trustees from persons acquainted with them.

1 Order 3 R 11, Rules of the Superior Courts.
2 Order 48, R 1, Rules of the Circuit Court 1950.
3 Courts (Supplemental Provisions) Act 1961, Third Schedule, reference 26, as amended by Courts Act 1981, s 2(1) (a) and (d).

9.12 The Court has also jurisdiction to make orders in relation to land, stocks, shares and choses in action generally, vesting the relevant property in any person as it may direct. The circumstances in which the Court will make the order are set out in ss 26 and 35 of the Act of 1893 and may be summarised as follows:

(1) Where the Court has appointed or appoints a new trustee;
(2) Where a trustee is a minor, is out of the jurisdiction or cannot be found;
(3) Where it is not certain whether the last surviving trustee is alive or dead;
(4) Where there is no personal representative of a trustee who has died intestate;
(5) Where a trustee has been required by a beneficiary who is entitled to land, shares or other choses in action to transfer the land etc to him and the trustee has wilfully refused or neglected to do so for twenty-eight days.

The vesting order in the case of land has the same effect as a conveyance or assignment of the land.[1]

1 1893 Act, s 32.

Retirement of trustees

9.13 Once a trustee has accepted his appointment—either expressly or implicitly, where he fails to disclaim the appointment within a reasonable time—he cannot retire save in limited circumstances. If the beneficiaries are all sui juris and absolutely entitled to the trust property, they can release the trustee from his office and effectively put an end to the trust themselves. And where there are more than two trustees, any one of them may declare by deed that he is desirous of being discharged from the trust.[1] If his co-trustees and anyone else who is empowered to appoint new trustees consent by deed to his discharge and the vesting of the property in the continuing trustees, then the trustee wishing to be discharged is deemed to have retired. The trustee may also apply himself to the Court for an order under s 25 of the 1893 Act appointing a new trustee in substitution for him, and as we have seen, the Court will make such an appointment where it is 'inexpedient, difficult or impracticable' not to do so.

1 Trustee Act 1893, s 11.

Removal of trustees

9.14 A trustee may be removed from his office under an express power in the instrument creating the trust. He may also be removed where the Court exercises the power conferred by s 23 of the 1893 Act to appoint a new trustee in place of an existing trustee.

In addition, the court has an inherent jurisdiction to remove a trustee without necessarily replacing him, where it appears necessary for the proper execution of the trusts. The leading Irish case which illustrates this principle is *Arnott v Arnott*.[1] In that case, the plaintiff, who was a member of a family with extensive business interests, sought to have the defendant, his stepmother, removed as trustee. His father had appointed him and another member of the family to be trustees of his will along with the defendant but had also made it clear that the family business was in effect to be managed by the plaintiff and that the formal assent only of the defendant would be required to any decisions. Murnaghan J found that the defendant had persistently refused to accept that this was the plain meaning of the will and had virtually rendered the trust unworkable. He accordingly removed her from office.[2]

1 58 ILTR 185.
2 Cf *O hUadhaigh v O Loinsigh* (1975) 109 ILTR 122.

Chapter 10

Powers and duties of trustees

10.01 The first duty of a trustee who has accepted office is to acquaint himself with the nature of his trust. He must, accordingly, without delay familiarise himself with the terms of the instrument creating the trust and find out what property is subject to the trust. Having satisfied himself on these matters, he must then find out whether the trust property is properly and safely invested.

Trustee's duty to collect or get in the trust property

10.02 The trustee's next duty is to ensure that all the trust property is in his possession or under his control. If any land subject to the trust has not been vested in him by deed of appointment, he must see that it is conveyed or assigned to him as soon as possible. Similarly, he must ensure that all stocks and shares are transferred into his name and that any title documents relating to the trust are given to him. An inventory should be made of any chattels which are the subject of the trust. Where the trust property includes cash in a bank or a building society, the new trustee should immediately inform the institution of his appointment so that the investment can be transferred into his name. If necessary, he should apply to the Court for directions as to whether proceedings should be instituted to recover any trust property.

Investment by the trustee generally

10.03 It is the trustee's duty to ensure that the trust property is invested in the manner which will prove most advantageous to all the beneficiaries. Where there are beneficiaries entitled to life interests only, as there frequently are, this will impose on the trustees a duty to balance the interests of the tenant for life and the remainderman so as to ensure that neither is unduly favoured. The interest of the tenant for life in receiving the highest possible income has to accommodate the interest of the remainderman in receiving the capital intact or preferably enhanced in value. The trustee may only pursue these objectives by investing in the manner authorised by law: if he makes an unauthorised investment then, however sensible it may have seemed at the time, he will be personally responsible for any loss which results. But he also has to bear in mind that the fact that a particular investment is authorised in law does not relieve the trustee of his obligation to use ordinary prudence before he makes such an investment. The duty is thus a twofold one: to invest in authorised securities only and to exercise ordinary prudence in doing so.

Authorised investments

10.04 In order to determine whether a particular investment is authorised, one must look first to the terms of the trust instrument and (depending on the terms of the instrument) then to the statute law regulating investments by trustees. Where the powers are not defined by the trust instrument, the trustee is confined to making the investments authorised by statute. Where there is a power of investment, but of a limited nature, the trustee will also be permitted to make the investments authorised by statute, unless the terms of the trust instrument preclude him either expressly or by implication from so doing. Where the power of investment is in sufficiently wide terms, recourse to the statutory powers may be unnecessary.

It is common in modern trust instruments to find an extremely wide power of investment being given. Thus, trustees may be authorised to invest money 'in or upon such investments as to them may seem fit'. It has been held in England that such a clause does not restrict the trustees to investments authorised by law: the only limitation is that it must be an *investment*, which was defined as a loan on security or the purchase of real or personal property producing income.[1] Or, to take a form of clause frequently employed to-day, it may provide that

'all moneys .... may be invested by the trustee in any manner in which he may in his absolute discretion think fit in all respects as if he were the sole beneficial owner of such moneys ....'

Again in the case of such a clause the trustee is not in any way confined to the statutory mode of investment. He, of course, remains subject to the paramount constraint of exercising ordinary prudence.

1 *Re Harari's Settlement Trusts* [1949] 1 All ER 430.

10.05 Where the powers of the trustee to invest are affected by the statutory controls, because there is no power of investment in the trust instrument or a limited power only, the relevant legislation is to be found in s 1 of the Trustee Act 1893, as substituted by s 1 of the Trustee (Authorised Investments) Act 1958. S 2 of the 1958 Act empowers the Minister for Finance to vary by order the list of authorised investments by addition, alteration or deletion.

Prior to the amendment effected by the 1958 Act, the investment powers were extremely confined and even as extended remain remarkably circumscribed, having regard to the economic realities of to-day. Incorporating the additions made by ministerial order,[1] they can be summarised as follows:

(1) Irish government securities;
(2) securities guaranteed as to capital and interest by the Minister for Finance;
(3) British government securities;
(4) real securities in Ireland;

(5) securities or mortgages of certain local authorities and similar bodies, eg harbour commissioners.
(6) Bank of Ireland stock;
(7) certain loan stock of the Bank of Ireland and Allied Irish Banks Limited;
(8) securities of the ESB, the Agricultural Credit Corporation Limited, and Bord na Mona;
(9) debentures or debenture stock of public quoted industrial and commercial companies registered in Ireland, provided that the total of such debentures and stock does not exceed the paid up share capital and that a dividend of at least five per cent has been paid on the ordinary shares in each of the preceding five years;
(10) interest bearing deposit accounts in specified banks, and credit institutions, including the Agricultural Credit Corporation Limited, the Industrial Credit Company Limited and the major building societies.

Conspicuously absent from this list are ordinary shares in publicly quoted companies either in Ireland or abroad, although in times of inflation investment in such 'equities' is the best method of protecting the beneficiary entitled to capital against inflation. Nor is there any power to avail of such new forms of investment as unit trusts, investment trusts and insurance bonds. This is in contrast to the situation in England and Northern Ireland where trustees have been empowered to invest in equities since 1961 and 1962 respectively. In the result, the conferring of a flexible power of investment on trustees is in many cases desirable. (In the case of charities, the Commissioners for Charitable Donations and Bequests for Ireland may invest, or on application by the trustees, may by order confer power to invest, the charity fund in any manner they think proper and whether the investment is authorised by the trust instrument or by law.[2] Section 9 of the Charities Act 1973 gives a similar power to the High Court.)

1 SRO Nos 285 of 1967, 241 of 1969, 377 of 1974, 41 and 344 of 1977 and 407 of 1979.
2 S 32 of the Charities Act as substituted by s 9 of the Charities Act 1973.

'Ordinary prudence' in investing

10.06 As has been emphasised, the fact that an investment is authorised, either by the terms of the trust instrument or any statute, does not absolve the trustee from responsibility, unless he exercises what has been called 'ordinary prudence' in making the investment. The leading case of *Learoyd v Whitely*[1] makes it clear, however, that the use of this phrase does not mean that the trustee is safe in exercising the same care as he would if he were investing his own money. Where his own money is concerned, a reasonably prudent person may be prepared to take some risks on the unanswerable ground that it is his to do as he likes with. Where it is other people's, the law does not permit such latitude: in the often quoted words of Lindley LJ in the Court of Appeal:

'The duty of the trustee is not to take such care only as a prudent man would take if he had only himself to consider: the duty rather is to take such care as an ordinary prudent man would take if he were minded to make an investment for the benefit of other people for whom he felt morally bound to provide.'[2]

As we have seen, a trust frequently comes into being because of the wish of the settlor that persons should enjoy his property in succession, the most common instance being the grant of a life estate to a spouse and the remainder to children. Accordingly, a trustee making an authorised investment not only has to consider whether it is unduly speculative or hazardous: he must also seek to balance fairly and impartially the sometimes conflicting interests of the persons entitled to successive interests in the property. On all such matters, obviously, the prudent trustee will take advice from those best qualified to give it, whether they be solicitors, stockbrokers, investment advisors, accountants or whatever.

The interests of the beneficiaries under a trust are almost invariably financial. It follows that the trustees must disregard any other considerations in investing the trust property. So it was held by Megarry V-C in *Cowan v Scargill* [3] that trustees were not entitled to take into account their own personal opinions when considering investments in South Africa, for example, or in industries of which they might disapprove because of personal convictions, such as armaments, alcohol, or tobacco. It may be, however, that the trustees of a charity might properly refrain from making an investment which would be inconsistent with the objects of the charity, eg an investment by trustees of a trust for cancer research in the tobacco industry.

1 (1886) 33 Ch D 347; on appeal, (1887) 12 App Cas 727.
2 33 Ch D 347 at 355.
3 [1984] 2 All ER 750.

Mortgages

10.07 The power to invest in 'real securities' is a power to invest in mortgages of land, not in purchases of land.[1] It is not, however, strictly confined to mortgages of freehold land: it extends (unless prohibited by the trust instrument) to a mortgage of leashold land held for an unexpired term of not less than 200 years at a rent not greater than 5p per annum.[2] A power to invest in company's mortgages extends to debenture stock and a power to invest in companies' shares, mortgages and debentures extends to mortgage debentures in the case of companies incorporated by or acting under the authority of Acts of Parliament.[3]

Trustees should exercise greater caution before they invest in a second mortgage of land.[4] They should also exercise prudence in accepting an equitable mortgage as security, since it may be postponed to a bona fide purchaser for value without notice.[5] However, it may be safe to do so when it is registered or (in the case of registered land) a caution or inhibition is entered on the folio.[6] It would also appear that they should not invest in a judgement mortgage.[7] Nor should the trustees ever join in a contributory mortgage, ie one where other people join in the loan.[8]

A trustee making an advance on the security of a mortgage was at common law required to satisfy himself as to the sufficiency in value of the security offered and the title of the borrower. The trustee was, however, given a degree of statutory protection when making such an investment by s 8(1) of the Trustee Act 1893. Under that provision, the trustee is relieved of liability arising from any disproportion between the amount of the loan and the value of the mortgaged property, if certain conditions are met. They are:

(1) that the trustee in making the loan was acting upon a valuation report

made by an able practical surveyor or valuer independently instructed by the trustee;

(2) that the amount of the loan does not exceed two-thirds of the value as stated in the report;

(3) that the loan was made under the advice of the surveyor expressed in the report.

If the loan is proper in all respects other than the amount advanced, the trustee's liability is confined to so much of the loan as exceeds the amount which he might properly have advanced, together with interest. The value of any business carried on in the mortgaged property should be disregarded in determining the amount which should be advanced.

1 *Robinson v Robinson*, (1877) IR 10 Eq 189.
2 Trustee Act 1893, s 5(1).
3 Ibid, s 5(2), (5).
4 *Smithwick v Smithwick*, (1861) 12 I Ch R 181 at 196.
5 See para 5.06, above.
6 See para 5.11, above.
7 *Johnston v Lloyd*, (1844) 7 Ir Eq R 252.
8 *Webb v Jonas* (1888) 39 Ch D 660.

Trustee's duty to convert the trust property: the rule in Howe v The Earl of Dartmouth

10.08 It has long been common for settlors and testators to provide that property is to be held under a *trust for sale*.[1] The object of such a trust is to ensure that the relevant property is sold as soon as practicable, although it is usual to give the trustees power to postpone the sale at their discretion. It became a particularly common form of trust from the last century onwards since it avoided the rigidity of the old fashioned strict settlement of land where there was no trust and the land was held inflexibly by members of the same family over the generations, usually in the form of an estate tail. Even where the land was held on trust and the tenant for life enjoyed the powers of sale and leasing conferred by the Settled Land Acts 1882 to 1890 there was not the same flexibility as the trust for sale afforded.

Apart from the requirement to convert the trust property into money which arises under a trust for sale, the trustees may be under a duty in law to convert the trust property into another form. This principally arises in the case of a residuary bequest under a will where property is settled for the benefit of persons in succession and any part of it is invested in wasting, hazardous or unauthorised securities. Under the rule in *Howe v The Earl of Dartmouth*,[2] the trustees are under a duty to convert such securities into authorised securities. Similarly, where the residuary bequest is of a reversionary interest they are obliged to convert the interest into an authorised interest in possession. In each case, the object is to ensure that the persons entitled enjoy the same thing in succession. But it only applies in the case of a residuary bequest: where there is an *inter vivos* settlement or a specific bequest, it is assumed that the intention was that the beneficiary was to enjoy the property *in specie*, ie in its actual state of investment.[3] Moreover, it will be excluded where the will shows that it was the intention of the testator that it should not apply.[4] Thus, the rule will not apply where the trustee is empowered to postpone conversion for a fixed period and properly exercises that power.[5]

It will be seen that the duty to convert is in theory for the benefit of the remainderman, when the property is invested in hazardous or unauthorised securities, and to the disadvantage of the tenant for life who may be assumed to be deriving a high income from the investments. In modern conditions, however, the reverse is frequently the case: investment in unauthorised investments, such as industrial equities, will generally provide the remainderman with an excellent prospect of capital appreciation but afford the tenant for life no more than a modest yield. Conversion into gilt edged securities or an investment in a merchant bank may by contrast give the tenant for life in such a situation a high interest rate but deprive the remainderman of capital growth.

1 On trusts for sale generally, see Wylie, *Land Law*, pp 415-416.
2 (1802) 7 Ves 137.
3 *Re Beaufoy's Estate* (1852) 1 Sm & G 20.
4 *Re Abbott, Grieve v Vaughan* [1934] IR 189, HC.
5 *Re Pitcairn* [1896] 2 Ch 199.

10.09 Either in the case of a trust for sale or where the rule in *Howe v The Earl of Dartmouth* applies, it may not be possible or desirable to effect an immediate conversion. In the case of a will, moreover, the trustee will in any event have his 'executor's year' during which he is entitled to retain the property in its present state of investment. Thereafter the onus rests on him of justifying the postponement of the conversion. It may, for example, be reasonable to delay in the hope that a recessionary period may come to an end. But where persons are entitled in succession, and whether the postponement of conversion was reasonable or not, it will be necessary for the trustees or the court to make an apportionment between the successive interests when the conversion is eventually effected.

In the case of wasting, hazardous or unauthorised securities, this is done, broadly speaking, by calculating the value of the property at the end of the executor's year and allowing the tenant for life interest at the rate of four per cent on that value from the date of death until the date of realisation. When the unauthorised investments are sold in the course of the year, he is entitled to the same rate on the net proceeds of sale. If there is a surplus of income after the payment of the four per cent, it must be invested in authorised securities.[1]

If the trustees are entitled to postpone conversion for a *definite* period, the rule in *Howe v The Earl of Dartmouth*, as we have seen does not apply and where the conversion is properly effected, the tenant for life is entitled to the full income prior to conversion. But if the trustees are entitled to postpone conversion for an *indefinite* period, the rule does apply. It has been held, however, that in this instance it is illogical to take the end of the executor's year as the appropriate date for valuation and the valuation is taken instead as of the testator's death.[2]

Where the conversion is of an interest or property which is *not* producing income, the tenant for life has to be compensated on an apportionment after a delayed conversion. This is done by calculating the sum which, if invested at four per cent on the day of the testator's death with compound interest payable at yearly rests, would have amounted after deduction of tax to the sum realised on conversion. This sum is the capital and the balance then is payable to the tenant for life. This is known as the rule in *Re Earl of Chesterfield's Trusts*.[3]

1 *Re Fawcett* [1940] Ch 402.
2 *Re Parry* [1947] Ch 23.
3 (1883) 24 Ch D 643.

10.10 While the rate of four per cent has been adhered to by the English courts for many years, there seems no reason why, if the matter came before the Irish courts to-day, the rate would not be fixed at whatever is the current rate payable on judgement debts.[1]

It should also be pointed out that while the rule in its traditional form applies only to personalty, this distinction can hardly have survived in our law following the enactment of the Succession Act 1965. S 12(1) provides that all rules of law relating to a number of matters are to apply, so far as applicable, to real estate as if it were personal estate. Among the matters so specified are

'the powers, rights, duties and liabilities of personal representatives in respect of personal estate.'

It would follow that where, for example, freehold property is not yielding income, to the detriment of the tenant for life, the trustees should be under a duty to sell and invest the proceeds of sale in authorised securities, unless of course the will manifested a contrary intention.[2]

1 Now 11 per cent under ss 19 and 20 of the Courts Act 1981.
2 This view has apparently been taken in Canada: see Sheridan and Keeton, *Law of Trusts* 11th edn, p 273.

10.11 Some other points as to apportionment by the trustee between successive interests may be briefly noted at this point. They arise principally, but not exclusively, in relation to shares and dividends.

(1) *No apportionment need be made by the trustee in the case of a sale 'ex-dividend' or 'cum-dividend'.* Where a sale of shares is effected shortly before the dividend is declared, the price will be increased to allow for the dividend about to be declared. Nevertheless there will be no apportionment and the remainderman will benefit accordingly, since he gets the benefit of the dividend which strictly forms part of the income. Conversely, where the sale is effected just after the dividend is declared, the price will be reduced accordingly and the remainderman will suffer, since his capital is reduced although he has not got the benefit of the dividend.[1] This is justified on the basis that the beneficiaries 'take the rough with the smooth' and over the whole spectrum of transactions a rough justice is achieved.[2] It has been accepted, however, that, in cases of glaring injustice, an exception might be allowed.[3]

(2) *Arrears of dividend on cumulative preference shares belong to the person entitled to the income at the time the dividend is declared.* Where preference shares are cumulative — ie where the shareholder is entitled to be paid arrears of dividend out of the profits of the current year — it is not the person entitled at the time the dividend fell into arrears who is entitled to the dividend, but the person entitled at the time the dividend is declared, since until that time there is no legal entitlement to the dividend.[4]

(3) *Where a company distributes as dividend a reserve fund, the dividend belongs to the tenant for life.* The effect of such a distribution may reduce the market value of the shares. But it remains income and not capital and accordingly belongs to the tenant for life and not the remainderman.[5]

(4) *Where the company distributes accumulated profits in the form of an*

issue of bonus shares, it is a capital distribution and the tenant for life is not entitled to it. This was decided by the House of Lords in *Bouch v Sproule*[6] and the principle has been applied in a number of Irish cases.[7] But where the profits are distributed other than as shares, eg as a cash bonus or in the form of a capital dividend, it is a distribution of income and the tenant for life is entitled.[8]

(5) *Where the debts of a testator are not paid immediately out of his estate, an appropriate reduction must be made in the income of the tenant for life.* If the debts are not paid immediately — and they usually are not — the tenant gets more income than he is entitled to until such time as they are paid. An adjustment must be made, accordingly, between capital and income, so as to provide that the tenant gets the income of the net estate only from the date of death. This is known as the rule in *Allhusen v Whittell*.[9] It may be excluded by the testator and frequently is.

(6) *The trustees are required to apportion the cost of repairs and maintenance between capital and income.* Where the work has the effect of permanently improving the property, it will be treated as a capital payment.[10] Normal current repairs and maintenance are, however, a proper charge on the income of the tenant for life.[11]

---

1 *Scholefield v Redfern* (1863) 2 Drew & Sm 173.
2 *Re McLaren's Settlement Trusts* [1951] 2 All ER 414.
3 Ibid, 420.
4 *Re Wakley* [1920] 2 Ch 205.
5 *Re Thomas* [1916] 2 Ch 331.
6 (1887) 12 App Case 385.
7 Eg *Re Carson* [1915] 1 IR 321.
8 *Re Meagher's Will Trusts* [1951] IR 100.
9 (1867)LR 4 Eq 295. See *Cooke v Lord Miltown* (1844) 7 Ir Eq R 391.
10 *Brereton v Day* [1895] 1 IR 518; *Bank of Ireland v Geoghegan* (1955–6) Ir Jur Rep 7.
11 *Kingham v Kingham* [1897] 1 IR 170; *Re Waldron and Bogue's Contract* [1904] 1 IR 240.

Trustee's duty to distribute the trust estate

10.12 We have seen that the paramount duty of the trustee is to administer the trust property in accordance with the directions of the settlor. In accordance with this principle, he must distribute the property to those entitled to it.

The trustees must, accordingly, ascertain from the trust instrument who are those entitled and take the necessary steps to ensure that they receive whatever they are entitled to. In the case of a trust for sale, the trustees are usually entitled to postpone the sale if in their proper exercise of their discretion they think it appropriate so to do.

In the case of personal representatives, where there may be difficulty in ascertaining who are the persons beneficially entitled, whether as next-of-kin or otherwise, or who are the creditors, a personal representative can protect himself by publishing a statutory advertisement for beneficiaries or creditors. If a person entitled has not lodged a claim with the personal representative before the end of the period specified in the advertisement, he is entitled to proceed with the distribution and will not be liable personally if it should transpire that someone entitled has been omitted.[1] A similar protection was afforded to trustees *generally* in England by the Trustee Act 1925 but there has been no corresponding legislation in Ireland.

Where the trustee underpays a beneficiary, he is liable to pay him the correct amount, but can recoup himself from the beneficiary who has been overpaid in consequence. It is said on the authority of *Re Horne*[2] that where the trustee is himself the beneficiary who is underpaid he must suffer the consequences of his own mistake, but this decision has attracted some criticism and it must be at least doubtful whether it would be followed in Ireland to-day.[3]

A trustee is required to distribute the estate, not merely in accordance with the settlor's directions, but also in accordance with law. It is a breach of trust for the trustee to distribute the estate otherwise than in accordance with law, even though, in so doing, he has acted on counsel's advice.[4]There is in general no power to relieve the trustee from the consequences of such a mistake.[5]

Where a trustee is in any doubt as to the distribution of the estate, he can apply to the High Court for directions. This is a relatively simple procedure: the application is made by special summons grounded on an affidavit.[6] If the matter is one of extreme difficulty, he can pay the money representing the estate into court, but this practice is not encouraged and should only be availed of as a last resort. Where the problem is that a particular beneficiary has gone abroad and has not been heard of for some time, he can apply to the Court for a 'Benjamin Order' and if a period of seven years has elapsed since the beneficiary was heard of, the Court will normally act on the presumption that he is dead and permit the trustee to distribute the estate on that assumption.[7]

It is not only the trustee who can avail of the procedure by way of special summons. Any person who can show a sufficient *locus standi*, as, for example, one of the beneficiaries, is entitled to apply to the court in this manner. It cannot, however, be used where there is an allegation of wilful default or breach of trust against a trustee: in that case, there must be a plenary hearing.

1 Succession Act 1965, s 49(2).
2 [1905] 1 Ch 76.
3 Sheridan and Keeton, op cit p 292.
4 *National Trustee Co of Australasia v General Finance Co of Australasia* [1905] AC 373, PC.
5 See para 10.28, below.
6 Rules of the Superior Courts, Order 3, rr 1 and 2; Rules of the Circuit Court 1950, Order 48, r 1. In the Circuit Court, the application is by petition.
7 *Re Benjamin, Neville v Benjamin* [1902] 1 Ch 723.

Trustee's duty to keep accounts and provide information

10.13 A trustee is obliged to keep proper accounts of his trusteeship.[1] He is not, however, obliged to have them audited, although this may be desirable, depending on the size or complexity of the trusteeship. He is also obliged to give the beneficiaries all information they may reasonably require as to the affairs of the trust.[2] The beneficiaries are also entitled to inspect the accounts, but not, it would seem, to receive copies of them save at their own expense.[3] The trustee is, however, only obliged to give a beneficiary information relating to his interest in the property: thus, a remainderman is entitled to be fully informed of the position as to the capital but not as to the income of which the tenant for life is in receipt.

In the case of a discretionary trust, it was held by Kenny J in *Chaine-Nickson v Bank Of Ireland*[4] that a beneficiary is entitled to copies of trust accounts and to details of investments representing the trust fund. He rejected a submission that, since the beneficiaries under such a trust may never become entitled to any part of the trust fund, the trustees are under no duty to give them information relating to the trust. It would appear from the English decision of *Re Londonderry's Settlement*[5] that the duty of the trustees under such a trust does not extend to furnishing the beneficiaries with confidential information which relates to the exercise of their discretion. This case has, however, been criticised, it would seem with some force, on the ground that it effectively precludes the beneficiaries from making the trustees accountable for an improper exercise of their discretion.[6]

The trustee's duty is confined to beneficiaries: he is under no obligation to tell someone proposing to acquire the beneficiary's interest what the state of that interest is. To that extent, *Low v Bouverie*[7] is thought still to represent the law on this matter. But if the trustee elects to give such information and he negligently misstates the position, as a result of which the intending purchaser suffers damage, he would appear now to be liable on the basis of *Hedley Byrne & Co Ltd v Heller & Partners Ltd.*[8] The former law, as also stated in *Low v Bouverie,* that he would only be liable in such circumstances if he was guilty of fraud, must be seen in the light of the later House of Lords decision (which has been frequently applied in Ireland)[9] that a liability for negligent misstatement may arise in such a case.

1 *Crawford v Crawford* (1867) LR 1 Eq 436.
2 *Moore v McGlynn* [1894] 1 IR, 74, 86 per Chatterton V-C.
3 *O'Rourke v Darbishire* [1920] AC 581 at 626, per Lord Wrenbury. Cf *Chaine-Nickson v Bank of Ireland* (below).
4 [1976] IR 393.
5 [1965] Ch 918.
6 Samuels (1965) 28 MLR 220.
7 [1891] 3 Ch 82.
8 [1964] AC 465.
9 The first reported case is *Securities Trust Ltd v Hugh Moore and Alexander Ltd* [1964] IR 417 HC. It has been suggested that it was anticipated in Ireland by *Macken v Munster & Leinster Bank Ltd* (1961) 95 ILTR 17. See McGrath, 1983 DULJ 296.

Sales by trustees

10.14 A trustee as such has no power of sale. His obligation is to preserve the trust property *in specie*, ie as it is. He can only sell the trust property by virtue of
  (i) an express or implied power of sale contained in the trust instrument;
  (ii) a statutory power of sale; or
  (iii) an order of the court.
An express power of sale presents no problem. As we have seen, even where there is no express power, there may be an implied trust for sale under the rule in *Howe v The Earl of Dartmouth* which obliges the trustee to sell.[1] And a personal representative, whether he be a trustee or not, is always entitled to sell any part of the estate of the deceased in the course of

administration for the purpose of paying debts and legacies, disposing of any wasting or hazardous property and generally completing the administration of the estate in accordance with law.[2]

Where a trust for sale or power of sale is vested in a trustee, the manner in which it may be exercised is regulated by statute. The relevant provision in Ireland is s13 of the Trustee Act 1893 and it is worded so as to enable the trust or power to be exercised in as flexible and efficient a manner as possible. The trustee is entitled to sell the whole or part of the relevant property and to do so either by public auction or private contract. He can sell in lots, if he wishes, and impose such conditions as he thinks fit. He may buy in the property at the auction and can also rescind or vary any contract and re-sell without being answerable for any loss. There is no equivalent to the provision in the English Trustee Act 1925, however, entitling the trustee to dispose of minerals underneath the land separately from the land itself.

The 1893 Act also precludes a beneficiary from successfully challenging a sale by a trustee on the ground that it was made subject to conditions which were 'unnecessarily depreciatory', unless the condideration for the sale was rendered inadequate as a result.[3] There is similar protection for a purchaser, unless he is acting in collusion with the trustee at the time the sale is made.[4]

Where a personal representative is selling in the course of administration, it is expressly provided by s 51(1) of the Succession Act 1965 that a purchaser is not concerned to see to the application of the purchase money. This important protection has been extended by statute in England and Northern Ireland to all trustees, but not so far in Ireland. However, if the purchaser obtains a receipt from all the trustees, this is by statute a sufficient discharge for him and relieves him from seeing to the application of the proceeds.

1 Para 10.08, above.
2 Succession Act 1965, s 50(1). Note, however, that before selling he must give effect, as far as practicable, to the wishes of the beneficiaries who are *sui juris* or, if they are not in agreement, of a majority.
3 S 14(1).
4 S 14(2).

10.15 As we have just seen, trustees are given a statutory power of giving a receipt under s 20 of the Trustee Act 1893. It provides that

' the receipt in writing of any trustee for any money, securities, or other personal property or effects payable, transferable, or deliverable to him under any trust or power shall be a sufficient discharge for the same, and shall effectually exonerate the person paying, transferring or delivering the same from seeing to the application or being answerable for any loss or misapplication thereof.'

It should be remembered, however, that a sole trustee cannot give a valid receipt for the proceeds of sale or other capital money arising under a trust for sale of land or for capital money arising under the Settled Land Acts.[1] Nor is there any exception, as there is in England and Northern Ireland, where the sole trustee is a trust corporation.

Where there is more than one trustee, all the trustees must join in the receipt. The only exception is where the trust instrument expressly authorises one of them to give a good receipt and discharge.[2]

1 1882 Act, s 39(1).

2 *Lee v Sanky* (1873) Lr 15 Eq 204; *Re Flower and Metropolitan Board of Works* (1884) 27 Ch D 592.

Compromises etc

10.16 Trustees are expressly empowered by s 21 of the 1893 Act to

(a) accept any composition or any security, for any debt or property claimed;
(b) allow any time;
(c) compromise, compound, abandon, submit to arbitration or otherwise settle any debt, account, claim or thing whatever relating to the trust.

It is further provided that they may take any of these steps without being responsible for any loss which may result.[1] S 15 of the English Trustee Act 1925 adds the proviso that the step in qustion should have been taken 'in good faith.' But while this was not spelled out in the earlier section still operative in Ireland, it was held by Jessel MR *Re Owens, Jones v Owens*,[2] that this was the probable effect of s 21.

1 See *Graham v McCashin* [1901] 1 IR 404; *Re Boyle* [1947] IR 61 at 69.
2 (1882) 47 LT 61 at 63.

Maintenance of minors

10.17 Trustees are expressly empowered by s 43 of the Conveyancing Act 1881 to pay the whole or part of the income of any property to which an infant is entitled under the trust for or towards his maintenance, education or benefit. The power exists where the infant is entitled

(a) for life, or for a greater interest than life, absolutely; or
(b) for life, or for a greater interest than life, contingently on attaining 18 or on the occurrence of some event before attaining that age.

Accordingly, where the infant is entitled absolutely, no problem arises. But if the vesting of the interest in the infant is contingent on the happening of some event in the future, the power is more limited. It will then only be available if the contingency is the attaining by the infant of the age of 18 or the happening of some event prior thereto, e.g. his getting married. If, for example, the trust instrument provides, as it frequently does, that the property is not to vest until the infant reaches the age 25 (or even 21) or marries before that time, the trustees have no statutory power to pay money for the infant's maintenance. This unnecessarily restricted power was liberally extended in England by the 1925 Act, but there has been no corresponding legislation here. This is even more likely to cause hardship since the age of minority was lowered to 18.[1] It should be borne in mind that, of course, we are talking merely of the statutory power: there is nothing to prevent the settlor from expressly empowering his trustees to apply the income of the infant's property for his maintenance and this is invariably done in modern settlements.

A general restriction on the statutory power of maintenance should be noted: it will only be available where the property to which the infant is entitled carries the intermediate income, i.e. the income arising between the time the trust takes effect and the infant attains his majority or (in the case of a contingent gift) the contingency occurs. The property will not carry the intermediate income in this sense if it is payable to someone other than the infant or if there is an express direction by the settlor to the trustee to accumulate the income and add it to the corpus when it vests it in the infant.[2] It is clear that, in the absence of any declared intention of the settler to the contrary, a bequest of the residuary estate under a will carries the intermediate income.[3] (The distinction formerly drawn between real and personal estate in this context disappeared from our law with the enactment of the Succession Act 1965). But a general or specific legacy does not carry the intermediate income unless

(i)   the donor stood *in loco parentis* to the infant and had provided no other fund for maintenance;[4]
(ii) the income was expressly or impliedly to be applied for maintenance;[5] or
(iii) the gift was expressly or impliedly directed to be separated immediately from the rest of the estate.[6]

In England and Northern Ireland, the Court has power to make an order for the payment of maintenance out of an infant's capital under express statutory provisions to that effect. There is no such statutory power in Ireland, but it has been held that the Court has an inherent power to make such payments in appropriate cases.[7] There is no doubt as the power to do so in cases of destitution: in any other case, it is a jurisdiction 'not to be exercised lightly'.[8]

1 By the Age of Majority Act 1985.
2 *Re Turner's Will Trusts* [1937] Ch 15.
3 *Re Adams* [1893] 1 Ch 329. Cf *Re O'Connell's Estate* [1932] IR 298.
4 *Re Ferguson* (1915) 49 ILT 110.
5 *Re Churchill* [1909] 2 Ch 431.
6 *Johnston v O'Neill* (1879) 3 LR Ir 476, 480/1 per Chatterton VC.
7 *Re O'Neill* [1943] IR 562.
8 Ibid, at 564-565 per Maguire P.

Fiduciary restraints on trustees

10.18 Because a trustee, as the name itself denotes, is one in whom another reposes trust or confidence, the law has for long taken a strict view of any advantages he may derive from his position. In general terms, it may be said that a trustee is not allowed by the law to obtain any material benefit from his position except with the consent of all the beneficiaries. Such exceptions as there are to this overriding principle are limited in scope and carefully defined. The unbending attitude of the law in this area is not simply based on the principle that those in whom trust is placed by others should not profit financially from that trust: it is also based on the practical consideration that the efficient execution of the trust may be hindered if the trustee finds himself in a position where his personal interests are in conflict with those of the beneficiary.

While we are concerned only with trustees, it should be borne in mind that restraints of this nature are not confined to those whom the law recognises as trustees in the strict sense. They also apply to others who enjoy a relationship of confidence with others and who are generically called 'fiduciaries'. Thus, personal representatives, (whether or not they are express trustees as well), partners, company directors, solicitors, and employees who are entrusted with confidential information have all been treated as fiduciaries who are obliged to account for any material advantages they derive as a result of their position.[1] (This is not to say that they are not entitled in certain cases, such as company directors, employees and solicitors, to remuneration for the work they do: so indeed are trustees generally, as we shall see in a moment, provided the trust instrument expressly so provides.) The importance of other fiduciaries such as these for our subject is that where they in fact derive material benefits from their position, they become constructive trustees of those benefits for the persons to whom they owe the fiduciary duty.[2]

It is a cardinal feature of this legal principle that it is rigorously applied even where there has not been the slightest element of improper behaviour on the part of the trustee, let alone conduct amounting to fraud. The only concession of any significance which is allowed to an honest trustee who has by his diligence and without any help from his beneficiary earned a profit from his trust is that, while he is not permitted to retain the profit, he may be allowed reasonable remuneration for the effort he has expended in enhancing the value of the beneficiary's interest.[3]

While this is the general principle, there are two particular applications of it which require specific mention.

1 See para 13.05, below.
2 Ibid.
3 *Boardman v Phipps* [1967] 2 AC 46.

(i) *A trustee is not entitled to any remuneration for his work as trustee*

10.19 Since he cannot derive any financial benefit from his trusteeship, a trustee is not entitled to charge for his work as trustee, no matter how onerous and time-consuming it may be.[1] To this rule there are four exceptions.

(*a*) **Where the trust instrument expressly provides that the trustee is to be entitled to remuneration for his services.** Thus, it is frequently provided in a will or other instrument creating a trust that a solicitor trustee is to be entitled to charge his usual professional fees in respect of any work done by him as a solicitor in connection with the trust. Such a charging clause is always strictly construed by the court and it does not, for example, entitle the solicitor to charge for work done in connection with the trust which is not legal in character,[2] unless it is expressly so worded, as it frequently is.

(*b*) **Where all the beneficiaries are of full age and sui juris and consent to the trustee's being paid remuneration**. But such arrangements will be carefully scrutinised and are not to be encouraged.[3]

(*c*) **Where the court in special circumstances allows the trustee remuneration**. An obvious example is where a trustee is allowed remuneration in respect of work which has generated a profit for the beneficiary and which the trustee is not allowed to retain.[4]

(*d*) **Where a solicitor trustee is a party to litigation affecting the trust to which a co-trustee is also a party and acts for himself and the co-trustee**

without any additional costs being incurred as a result. This, the so-called rule in *Cradock v Piper*,[5] seems anomalous and difficult to justify but it has been applied in Ireland.

(ii) *A trustee is not allowed to deal in or purchase the trust property*

A trustee may not under any circumstances whatever buy the trust property or any part of it from himself or his co-trustees.[6] Such a transaction, however, is not void, but only voidable and will stand unless challenged by the beneficiary within a reasonable time.[7] The rule is less stringent where the trustee purchases the trust property from the beneficiary. The transaction will not be set aside, provided the trustee satisfies the court that it should stand, but the onus is on him to do so. Such a purchase will be scrutinised with great care and in particular it will normally be necessary to meet the following conditions[8] if it is to be upheld:

(1) The relationship of trustee and beneficiary must have been dissolved or virtually dissolved, ie they must meet at 'arm's length'.
(2) The trustee must not take any unfair advantage of the beneficiary.
(3) The trustee must pay the full value for the interest, unless it is proved that the beneficiary intended a gift to him, in which case it must be shown that the beneficiary knew the value of the intended gift.
(4) The trustee must furnish the beneficiary with all the information he has which might affect the beneficiary's judgement before he sells.
(5) If the trustee is in a position where the beneficiary reposes confidence in his judgement, he must give the beneficiary the benefit of that judgement.

If the beneficiary has received independent legal advice before he enters into the transaction, it will usually be upheld, but the absence of such advice is not fatal.

These principles are illustrated by the decision of Costello J in *Smyth v Smyth*.[9] In that case, the plaintiff was a young man who had been left a plot of land under his father's will. Under the will, the defendant (the plaintiff's uncle) had a life interest in the land. He was also one of the trustees under the will. The plaintiff suggested to the defendant that the latter should buy out his (the plaintiff's) interest in the land for £3,000. The defendant said that he was not interested, but ultimately said that he would pay £1,500. The plaintiff agreed to accept this and the land was duly transferred to the defendant. The plaintiff subsequently sought to have the transfer set aside on a number of grounds, including the fact that it was a sale by a beneficiary to a trustee. While the evidence established that the plaintiff was an alcoholic, Costello J found that his condition had not reached that stage when the bargain was concluded.

The learned judge found that the land had not been sold at an undervalue. He also found that the defendant had not taken any unfair advantage of the plaintiff and, although the plaintiff had not been independently advised (the same solicitor acted for both parties) this was not a sufficient reason for setting aside the sale.

(iii) *A trustee may not delegate his office*

Since the essence of trusteeship is the placing of confidence by one person in another, it follows logically that the office of trustee and the duties and powers which we have been discussing are strictly personal in their nature and their performance cannot be delegated by the trustee to another.[10] Equally obviously, if the trustee is in a position where the proper exercise of his office demands the obtaining of expert advice, be it from a solicitor, stockbroker or valuer or anyone else, he is not merely entitled to take such advice but also to act on it and this will not constitute a wrongful delegation by him of the trust office.[11] Moreover, there are many circumstances in which it is clearly sensible for the trustee to employ agents, eg a solicitor in the sale of a house. More generally, it can be said that wherever a reasonable person in the conduct of business would employ an agent, it is legitimate for the trustee to do the same. The law was thus stated by Kay J in *Fry v Tapson*:[12]

> 'Trustees acting according to the ordinary course of business and employing agents, as a prudent man of business would do on his own behalf, are not liable for the default of an agent so employed.'

But the agent so employed must be acting within the scope of his usual business if the trustee is to avoid liability for his defaults. Thus, it would not be within the usual scope of a solicitor's or accountant's professional activity to invest money on behalf of a client.[13] A solicitor is, however, expressly authorised by statute to receive the purchase money on a sale of property on behalf of a trustee and solicitors and bankers are also expressly authorised to receive insurance moneys.[14] The solicitor or banker must be expressly empowered to give a receipt for the money, however: a general power of attorney will not be sufficient.[15] It is also essential that the solicitor have custody of a deed (in the case of property) containing a receipt for the money and (in the case of insurance moneys) a policy of insurance with a receipt endorsed on it by the trustees.[16]

The powers of a trustee to delegate the exercise of his functions to agents have been considerably extended by statute in England and Northern Ireland, but there has been no equivalent legislation in this country.

1 *Re Ormsby* (1809) 1 Ball & B 189.
2 *Re Chalinder and Herington* [1907] 1 Ch 58 at 62 per Warrington J.
3 *Ayliffe v Murray* (1740) 2 Atk 58.
4 *Boardman v Phipps*, above. Cf *Re Duke of Norfolk's Settlement Trusts* [1981] 3 ALL ER 220.
5 (1850) 1 Mac & G 664; *Re Smith's Estate* [1894] 1 IR 60.
6 *Nesbitt v Tredennick* (1808) 1 Ball & B 29; *Smith v Kay* (1859) 7 HL Cas 750 at 779 per Lord Kingsdown; *King v Anderson* [1874] IR 8 Eq 625 at 628 per Napier C.
7 *Webb v Rorke* (1806) 2 Sch & Lef 661 at 672 per Lord Redesdale.
8 See the discussion in Jacob's *Law of Trusts*, 4th edn, pp 1733-1734. See also *Kilbee v Sneyd* (1828) 2 Moll 186; *De Montmorency v Devereux* (1846) 2 Dr & Wal 410.
9 Unreported, judgement delivered 22 November 1978; Wylie Casebook 410.
10 *Turner v Corney* (1841) 5 Beav 515, 517; Re *O'Flanagan's and Ryan's Contract* [1905] 1 IR 280.
11 *Joy v Campbell* (1804) 1 Sch & Lef 328 at 344 per Lord Redesdale. The trustee may also delegate under an express power to that effect: *Doyle v Blake* (1804) Sch & Lef 231.
12 (1884) 28 Ch D 268 at 270.
13 *Royland v Witherdan* (1851) 3 Mac & G 568.
14 Trustee Act 1893, s 17.
15 *Re Hetling and Merton's Contract* [1893] 3 Ch 269.
16 Trustee Act 1893, s 17.

Liability of trustee for the default of his agent

10.20 It follows from the principles mentioned in the preceding paragraphs that a trustee who employs an agent in the ordinary course of business is not liable for his default. Provided that the appointment is proper and that there is no misconduct or other default on the part of the trustee himself, he will not be held answerable for the default of his agent.

If the employment of the agent is not justified or if there is some default on the part of the trustee, such as inadequate supervision on his part of the agent's activities, then at common law the trustee is liable. He is, however, given some added degree of protection by s 24 of the Trustee Act 1893 which provides that

'A trustee shall be chargeable only for money and securities actually received by him notwithstanding his signing any receipt for the sake of conformity and shall be answerable and accountable only for his own acts, receipts, neglects or defaults and not for those of any trustee, nor for any banker, broker or other person with whom any trust money or securities may be deposited, nor for any other loss, unless the same happens through his own wilful default....'

The first consequence of this provision is that a trustee who signs documents, such as receipts, which have already been signed by his co-trustees for the sake of conformity, is not liable for any default of his co-trustees except where he is guilty of wilful default. The second consequence is that he may safely deposit money with persons to whom it is usual to entrust money for deposit, such as bankers, without incurring any responsibility, again unless he is guilty of wilful default.

The phrase 'wilful default' was originally construed as rendering the trustee liable where he failed to show ordinary prudence. In the English decision of *Re Vickery*,[1] however, Maugham J gave it a more restricted meaning and said that the trustee would only be liable where there was 'either a consciousness of negligence or breach of duty or a recklessness in the performance of a duty.' It would seem that provided the trustee acted honestly in selecting the person with whom to deposit the money, he would thus be protected even if his action could be described as imprudent. It would also seem to follow from Maugham J's formulation that he would be protected where he had left the money on deposit for a longer time than was prudent, unless his action could be said to have been consciously negligent or reckless.[2]

1 [1931] 1 Ch 572.
2 This in turn was the formula used by Johnson J in *Graham v Belfast and Northern Counties Ltd* [1901] 2 IR 13, 19 to define 'wilful default' in another context. But doubts have been expressed as to whether Maugham J's formula is too relaxed: see Sheridan and Keeton, op cit, pp 246-7

Liability of trustees for breach of trust

10.21 A trustee is liable to the beneficiary for any breach of trust. This is so whether it takes a positive form (e.g. making an unauthorised investment) or is simply a failure to act (e.g. permitting the trust property to remain invested in an unauthorised manner.) The motives of the trustee are immaterial: he may have acted in what he genuinely believed to be the interests of the beneficiary, without any trace of fraud and without profiting himself. Provided the beneficiary can establish that he has suffered a loss and that it is the result of the breach of trust, he is entitled to damages. Even where he cannot establish that he has suffered any loss as a result of the breach of trust, he can compel the trustee to account to him for any profit which the latter has made as a result of the breach of trust, and logically so, since the same result would follow, as we have seen, without any breach of trust.

The trustee who has been in breach of trust is obliged to make full restitution to the beneficiary. Where the breach consists of an unauthorised investment, the measure of damage will be the loss incurred by the beneficiary in selling it, if that is what the beneficiary elects to do.[1] (The beneficiaries, if all sui juris, may elect to retain an unauthorised investment, but until they make their decision they have a lien on the investment and the trustee accordingly cannot dispose of it without their consent.[2]) Where the breach consists in retaining an unauthorised investment for an excessive period—or retaining wasting personalty in breach of the rule in *Howe v The Earl of Dartmouth* for a similarly excessive period — the measure of damage will be the difference between the price which it would have fetched if sold at the proper time and the actual price, assuming of course that the beneficiary is at a loss.[3] Where the breach is the sale of an investment at a time when it should not have been sold, the damages are the difference between the price actually realised and that which would have been got had the property been sold at the date of judgement in the action.[4]

1 *Knott v Cottee* (1852) 16 Beav 77.
2 *Wright v Morgan* [1926] AC 788 at 799, PC.
3 *Grayburn v Clarkson* (1868) 3 Ch App 605.
4 *Re Bell's Indenture* [1980] 3 All ER 425. In an earlier case, *Re Massingberd's Settlement* (1890) 63 LT 296, the date of commencement of the proceedings had been taken as the appropriate date, but the preference of Vinalott J in the later case for the date of the hearing seems logical. Cf Pettit p 426.

10.22 At common law the beneficiary was entitled to interest at the rate of four per cent on any damages recoverable by him from the trustee in respect of a breach of trust.[1] If he had actually received more interest, it was held that he had to pay the beneficiary whatever he received.[2] Moreover, if the breach of duty consisted in the failure to invest in a specified security which would have brought in more than the four per cent he was required to pay the increased rate.[3] The minimum rate now payable is that fixed for all damages by s 19 of the Courts Act 1981, ie 11 per cent, but it is submitted that a beneficiary who can prove that the trustee has received more than this or would have had he invested in a specified security as required is not confined to the statutory rate. It has also been held in England that, at least in cases of fraud or wilful misconduct, the beneficiary is entitled to compound interest.[4]

1 *Re Beech* [1920] 1 Ch 40.
2 *Jones v Foxall* [1852] 15 Beav 388.
3 Ibid.
4 *A-G v Alford* (1855) 4 De G M & G 843, 852.

10.23 It has been held in England that in assessing the damages payable by a trustee for a breach of trust, no adjustment in his favour is to be made in respect of any tax or duty that would have been payable by the beneficiary had the trust fund been preserved in accordance with his duty.[1] The rule is thus different from the rule applicable to the assessment of damages for breach of contract: the decision in *Glover v BLN Ltd and Another (No 2)*[2] requires the damages recoverable by a person who has suffered a breach of contract to be reduced by the amount of tax he would have had to pay on any profits or income which the damages are intended to replace. But the damages for breach of trust are intended to restore the trust fund to the state it would have been in had no breach of trust taken place and hence any tax payable by the beneficiary at the time of distribution is not material.

The liability of the trustees is joint and several. The beneficiary may sue them all or one or more of them.[3] But if any trustee is required to pay more than his share of the liability, he may recover an appropriate contribution from his co-trustees under the Civil Liability Act 1961.[4]

A trustee who has retired is not liable for any breaches of trust committed after his retirement, provided he has lawfully retired and that he has not given up his trusteeship with a view to facilitating the very breach of trust in question. If it is clearly shown that at the time he resigned, he had the actual breach in contemplation — in the words of Kekewich J, in *Head v Gould*[5] if he has been an accessory before the fact— he will be liable. Similarly, the estate of a deceased trustee is liable only for breaches of trust which took place during his lifetime.[6] A new trustee is not liable for any breaches of trust committed by those whom he replaces,[7] but he must be careful to take the necessary steps as soon as practicable to remedy the consequences of any breach of trust of which he becomes aware.

1 *Bartlett v Barclay's Bank Trust Co Ltd* [1980] Ch 515.
2 [1973] IR 432.
3 *Alleyne v Darcy* (1854) 4 Ir Ch R 199 at 206, per Brady LC.
4 *Collings v Wade* [1903] 1 IR 89.
5 [1898] 2 Ch 250 at 273–274.
6 *Re Palk* (1892) 41 WR 28.
7 *Re Strahan* (1856) 8 De G M & G 291.

10.24 We next consider the possible defences by a trustee in an action for breach of trust. They can be divided into four broad headings:

   (1) that the breach of trust was instigated or requested by the beneficiary;
   (2) that the beneficiary agreed to or acquiesced in the breach of trust;
   (3) that the action is barred by the Statute of Limitations 1957;
   (4) that the action is not maintainable because of laches on the part of the beneficiary.

Where the breach of trust has been committed by the trustee at the instigation or request or with the consent in writing of the beneficiary, this will not merely provide the trustee as a general rule with a defence to an action against him by that beneficiary. The court may also, at its discretion, order the interest of that beneficiary to be impounded with a view to indemnifying the trustee against any loss he has suffered, or will suffer, as a result of carrying out the beneficiary's wishes.[1] Thus, if there is more than one beneficiary, the trustee will in such circumstances, be entitled to be indemnified out of the impounded interest against any claim by the others. The power to order the impounding of the beneficiary's interest was conferred by s 45 of the Trustee Act 1893, but existed at common law prior to that statute.[2] In its statutory form, the power is in wider terms, but is an essentially discretionary one.[3] It will not normally be exercised in the trustee's favour except upon proof that the beneficiary was aware that the facts amounted to a breach at the time he requested, instigated or consented to the breach.[4]

1 Trustee Act 1893, s 45.
2 *Brown v Maunsell* (1856) 5 Ir Ch R 351 at 354; *Raby v Ridehalgh* (1855) 7 De GM & G 104.
3 *Anketell Jones v Fitzgerald* (1931) 65 ILT 185.
4 *Re Somerset* [1894] 1 Ch 231 at 270 CA; *Mara v Browne* [1895] 2 Ch 69 at 93.

10.25 Where the beneficiary has agreed to the breach or acquiesced in it subsequently, this will provide a defence to an action for breach of trust.[1] Where there is more than one beneficiary, of course, the fact that one consented to it will not preclude the other from instituting proceedings in respect of the breach. Moreover, all the beneficiaries who are alleged to have acquiesced must have been of full age and *sui juris* at the time of the acquiescence.[2] They must also have given their consent freely — ie without any undue influence being brought to bear on them — and with full knowledge of all the relevant circumstances, including not merely the facts of the particular transaction but also their own legal rights.[3] It has, however, been held in England that they need not know that a breach of trust is involved.[4]

What amounts to acquiescence is a question of fact to be decided in each case, but it is clear that it may be by conduct as well as by words.[5] There is some uncertainty as to whether the passage of time without objection on the part of the beneficiary can amount to acquiescence. Clearly, the longer the time that has elapsed, the slighter the acts that may be relied on as establishing acquiescence and in one case Campbell LC suggested that a sufficiently lengthy lapse of time might be evidence in itself.[6]

1 *Farrant v Blanchford* (1863) 1 De G J & Sm 107.
2 *Brice v Stokes* (1805) 11 Ves 319.
3 *Roche v O'Brien* (1810) I Ball & B 330 at 339 per Manners LC.
4 *Re Pauling's Settlement* [1961] 3 All ER 713 at 730; *Holder v Holder* [1968] Ch 353.
5 *Egg v Devey* (1847) 10 Beav 444.
6 *Life Association of Scotland v Siddal* (1861) 3 De G F & J 58 at 77.

10.26 Section 2(2) of the Statute of Limitations 1957 provides that no action may be brought against a trustee after the expiration of a period of six years from the date on which the cause of action accrues. The trustee cannot, however, rely on the limitation period in two circumstances specified in s 44, ie where the action is

'(a) in respect of any fraud or fraudulent breach of trust to which the trustee was a party or a privy; or

(b) to recover from the trustee trust property or the proceeds of trust property in the possession of the trustee or previously received by the trustee and converted to his own use.'

The Irish Court of Appeal said in *Collings v Wade*[1] that fraud in the corresponding section of the 1888 Trustee Act meant actual dishonesty. A different view was taken in England, where it was said that fraud need not amount to any form of moral obliquity to enable the beneficiary to rely on the section.[2]

The second circumstance specified prevents the trustee from relying on the statute to defeat a claim by a beneficiary where he actually has the trust property in his possession. But if he no longer has it — if, for example, it has been used to maintain an infant beneficiary[3] or has been lost[4] — the exception will no longer apply.

A personal representative, as we have seen, holds the estate of the deceased on trust for those entitled to it by law, whether as next-of-kin under an intestacy, beneficiaries under a will, persons entitled as of legal right under the Succession Act 1965 or creditors.[5] The 1957 Act, as amended, provides for a limitation period of six years in the case of actions in respect of any claim to the estate of a deceased person, ie the same as is applicable to trustees. It is also clear, however, that personal representatives are not trustees for the purposes of s 44 of the 1957 Act so that time runs in favour of a personal representative who retains possession of the estate: the decision to that effect in *Vaughan v Cottingham*[6] putting an end to a long period of uncertainty was given the force of statute by s 123 of the Succession Act 1965.

1 [1896] 1 IR 340.
2 *Re Sale Hotel and Botanical Gardens Ltd* (1897) 77 LT 681.
3 *Re Page* [1893] 1 Ch 304.
4 *Re Tufnell* (1902) 18 TLR 705.
5 See para 9.04, above.
6 [1961] IR 184.

10.27 Laches may also defeat the claim of the beneficiary. We have already seen that acquiescence by the beneficiary in the breach of trust may defeat his claim and that comparatively slight evidence only of acquiescence is required where the delay in bringing the proceedings is considerable. There is also some judicial authority for the proposition that extreme delay of itself and without evidence of acquiescence may also defeat the claim, apart from any question of the Statute of Limitations, because of the law's dislike of stale claims;[1] and it would seem that where the rights of other persons have been affected to their detriment by the delay in bringing the proceedings, this may be a ground for resisting the claim.[2]

1 *Re Sharpe* [1892] 1 Ch 154 at 168 per Lindley LJ.
2 See para 3.12, above.

10.28 In England since 1925 and in Northern Ireland since 1958, the court has also power to relieve the trustee from liability where he has acted 'honestly and reasonably and ought fairly to be excused for the breach of trust.' There is no such provision in Ireland, except in the extremely limited (and now practically non-existent) context of a sale under the Land Purchase Acts.[1] (The Government announced in 1984 that the Irish Land Commission was being wound up but so far there has been no legislation to that effect).

1 Irish Land Act 1906, s 51(4).

10.29 A breach of trust may also mean that the trustee is exposed to criminal liability. Under s 21 of the Larceny Act 1916, a trustee who appropriates the trust property with intent to defraud to his own use or benefit or for any illegitimate purpose is guilty of a misdemeanour and liable on indictment to seven years' penal servitude or two years' imprisonment and/or a fine not exceeding £100. The law has not been amended as it has in England and Northern Ireland, to enable a prosecution to be brought where a trustee 'dishonestly appropriates property belonging to another with the intention of permanently depriving the other of it'.

10.30 The remedy of a beneficiary who is the victim of a breach of trust is twofold: he can bring proceedings either *in personam* or *in rem*. In other words, he can either sue the trustee personally for the amount of the loss which he has sustained or he may seek to recover the trust property itself into whoever's hands it has come. The second of these remedies, which may require a 'tracing order' has been the subject of much discussion and litigation both in England and Ireland. It is dealt with in detail in Chapter 20.

Variation of trusts

10.31 It has been emphasised already that the paramount duty of the trustee is to administer the trust in accordance with the terms of the trust instrument. He is not entitled to deviate from its terms in any way, although it may seem impractical or even irrational to carry out the settlor's intentions literally. Obviously if all the beneficiaries are of full age and *sui juris*, they may put an end to the trust by requiring the trust property to be distributed amongst them and equally they may agree to the continuance of the trust on different terms. But that situation apart, and subject to four clearly defined exceptions, the trustee cannot vary the terms of the trust.

With the growth of the use of trusts as a means of easing the tax burden on those concerned, this has often proved a source of frustration for all except the revenue: a variation of the trusts may be manifestly in the interests of all the beneficiaries, the settlor may be perfectly happy with the alterations and yet it may not be possible to effect them, because, for example, there are minor or unborn beneficiaries who cannot consent. The Court of Appeal and the House of Lords made it clear in *Chapman v Chapman*[1] that the courts had no power to sanction an alteration of the beneficial interests under a trust in such circumstances and it is thought that this is still the law in Ireland. The law in England and Northern Ireland has since been changed so as to enable the courts in defined circumstances to permit the variation of trusts.

It is clear from *Chapman v Chapman* and the earlier authorities there referred to that the court has an inherent jurisdiction, apart from statute, to permit a departure from the terms of the trust instrument in four cases. In the absence of any equivalent to the English Variation of Trusts Act 1958, these, so far as authority goes, are the only cases in which an alteration of trusts is permitted by the court in Ireland.

1 [1954] AC 429; on appeal from *Re Chapman's Settled Estates* [1953] Ch 218.

10.32 (i) Where the trustees of settled property are allowed to enter into a business transaction which was not authorised by the trust instrument. There was a series of cases, known as 'salvage cases', where the court permitted the sale or mortgage of an infant's property, to effect essential repairs or for some similar purpose. The ambit of these was extended by the Court of Appeal in *Re New*[1] where it was said that peculiar circumstances might arise for which provision had not been made by the settlor which rendered it desirable or even essential for the benefit of the estate and all the beneficiaries to empower the trustees to do certain things not authorised by the trust instrument. It was said by Romer LJ that the jurisdiction was only to be exercised with 'great caution' but its limitations have not been further defined.[2]

(ii) Where maintenance is permitted out of income directed to be accumu-

lated. It will be possible to do this without recourse to the court where the trust instrument so permits. In some cases, it will be possible to rely on the statutory power under s 43 of the Conveyancing Act 1881.[3] Where this is not possible, the court may permit it on the assumption that the settlor who creates a trust for the benefit of his family does not intend them to go unprovided for or without reasonable means.[4] It should be noted that this exception is not confined to beneficiaries during their minority.

(iii) Where the court directs changes in the nature of a minor's property, eg by ordering personalty to be converted into realty. This is of largely historic interest: at one stage trustees could not effect such a conversion, since it could affect the minor's power of testamentary disposition, which differed according as to whether the property was real or personal, and could also affect rights of succession to his estate. They could, however, effect such a conversion with the sanction of the court where it was shown to be for the infant's benefit. With the abolition of the relevant rules differentiating between realty and personalty which was completed by the Succession Act 1965, the basis for the exception would seem to have disappeared.

(iv) Where the trustees are allowed to enter into a compromise on behalf of infants and unborn beneficiaries. This may be done where there is a dispute as to the rights of such persons and the court is asked to sanction a compromise on their behalf.[5] It has been pointed out, however, that since the rights by definition are in dispute, this is hardly an example of altering the trusts.

It should be observed that there were two dissentients from the decision of the Court of Appeal and House of Lords in *Chapman v Chapman*, Denning LJ and Lord Cohen. Denning LJ's judgement is a comparatively early example of his willingness to extend the frontiers of the equitable jurisdiction, in this case by a radical extension of the jurisdiction traditionally exercised in ease of minors and others under disability. Such an approach has not been the subject of any recorded Irish decision and, while it cannot be said that it would necessarily be rejected, it should be pointed out that, apart from any other difficulties, it is most likely to arise in cases where the effect of the alterations will be to ease the tax burden on the beneficiaries. It remains to be seen whether the courts would consider it appropriate to facilitate such an objective.

1 [1901] 2 Ch 534.
2 For a modern Irish example, see *Bank of Ireland v Geoghegan* (1955-6) Ir Jur Rep 7.
3 See para 10.17, above.
4 *Re Collins* (1886) 32 Ch D 229.
5 *Chapman v Chapman*, above.

Chapter 11

Charitable trusts

11.01 As we have seen, trusts for purposes rather than human beings are rarely valid. They are regarded as difficult, perhaps impossible, to enforce, uncertain in their ambit and generally beyond the capacity of the court to control. In additon, they will very often contravene legal rules against creating perpetuities and inalienability.[1]

To this general doctrine the great exception is *charitable trusts*. The trusts with which we have so far been dealing are sometimes called 'private trusts' to distinguish them from charitable trusts and with good reason, because the distinctive feature of the charitable trust is that it is *for the public benefit*.

Charitable trusts are of great importance in our law and not simply because they enable donors and testators to advance charitable causes without running the risk that their gifts will be treated as invalid. They are also exempt in significant respects from various taxes and this again has meant that it is increasingly important for the modern lawyer to understand when a trust is properly regarded as charitable.

1. See para 7.06, above.

The four classes of charitable trusts

11.02 The trusts which our law recognises as 'charitable' have been divided on high authority into four broad classes, i e

  (*a*) trusts for the relief of poverty;
  (*b*) trusts for the advancement of education;
  (*c*) trusts for the advancement of religion; and
  (*d*) trusts for other purposes beneficial to the community, not falling under any of the three preceding headings.

This was the classification provided by Lord Macnaghten in *Commissioners for Special Purposes of Income Tax v Pemsel*.[1] It has been adopted in numerous cases in all the common law jurisdictions since it was first articulated in 1891 and it still represents the law in Ireland. Yet neither the student nor the lawyer should suppose for a moment that it means that a charitable trust is always easy to identify. On the contrary, there are few areas of the law which bristle with so many confusing and apparently irreconcilable decisions. Frustration at this state of affairs has not been confined to those who have to study the law or advise their clients; judicial comments on the topic have been notably acerbic. Gavan Duffy J lamented that

' "charity" is in law an artificial conception which during some 300 years under the guidance of pedantic technicians seems to have strayed rather far from the intelligent realms of plain common sense ....'[2]

In England, Viscount Simonds allowed that

'it is a trite saying that the law is life, not logic. But it is I think conspicuously true of the law of charity that it has been built up, not logically, but empirically.'[3]

Thus, to take some of the more astonishing distinctions which the courts have solemnly countenanced, a gift for the suppression of cruelty to animals is charitable[4] but a gift for philanthropic purposes is not;[5] a gift to the Archbishop of Wales to help carry on the work of the Church of Wales is not charitable[6] but a gift to the Bishop of the Windward Isles to use as he thinks fit in his diocese is;[7] a gift for the propagation of the views of Joanna Southcott ('a demented visionary') is charitable,[8] but Bernard Shaw's gift for the rationalisation of the English alphabet is not.[9] The historical background throws some light on why the law has become such a morass of conflicting decisions.

1 [1891] AC 531 at 583.
2 *Re Howley* [1940] IR 109 at 114.
3 *Gilmour v Coats* [1949] AC 426 at 448-449, HL.
4 *Re Wedgwood* [1915] 1 Ch 113.
5 *Re Macduff* [1896] 2 Ch 451.
6 *Re Jackson* [1930] 2 Ch 389.
7 *Re Rumball* [1956] Ch 105.
8 *Thornton v Howe* (1862) 31 Beav 14 at 19. The description of her is by Gavan Duffy J in *Maguire v A-G* [1943] IR 238 at 245.
9 *Re Shaw* [1957] 1 All ER 745, compromised on appeal [1958] 1 All ER 245.

11.03 The law of charitable donations and bequests is described by one leading Irish authority on the subject as 'extemely obscure in origin.'[1] In medieval times, gifts for what we would recognise as charitable purposes — and which, of course, frequently involved gifts to religious bodies — were affected by the law of 'mortmain'. The law of mortmain — which literally means 'dead hand' — rendered unlawful the alienation of land in such a way that the feudal lord was deprived of his service.[2] Hence gifts to corporations, whether they were monasteries, hospitals, schools, or whatever, were likely to prove unlawful. Despite this, such pious or spiritual uses, as they were called, gradually achieved legal recognition. In particular, the tenures of frankalmoign and divine service enabled land to be held by religious bodies without the necessity for any service other than the spiritual.

The Reformation, in Ireland as in England, had profound consequences for the development of the law of charities. Before that event, charity in both countries was virtually the exclusive province of the church. Recent research has cast doubt on the formerly held view that the dissolution of the monasteries at that time was responsible for bringing to an end a great range of charitable activities carried on by monastic orders. It would seem that the monastic institutions as a source of charity had been decaying for some time before the Reformation.[3] But it remains true that the dissolution of the monasteries in England and Ireland in the sixteenth century had major consequences: not merely did it mean the end of the schools, hospitals etc which the religious orders had provided, it also resulted in the rise of new secular institutions fulfilling such purposes in their place. It was to bring such charities under some form of control and correct abuses which had crept into their administration that the two statutes were passed in England and Ireland in the reigns of Elizabeth I[4] and Charles I[5] respectively which still provide the genesis of the legal definition of charity applicable in both jurisdictions to-day.

Each statute has been long since repealed but the enumeration of charitable objects which they contain has been regarded as providing an 'index' to charities recognised by the law. In addition, the law identified new purposes as charitable as they arose for consideration. The list of charitable purposes in the relevant statute is accordingly not exhaustive: a trust may still be charitable if it is within 'its spirit and intendment'.[6]

There was considerable judicial debate at one stage as to whether the two Acts were identical in effect, despite their different wording. It was held by Sir Edward Sugden LC in *Incorporated Society v Richards*[7] that the Irish Act was an 'exact pattern' of the English Act and intended to effect the same results. In *A-G v Delaney*,[8] Palles CB said that a charitable purpose in Ireland was identical with what would be a charitable purpose in England under the statute of Elizabeth, save to the extent that the law as to 'superstitious uses' differed in the two countries.[9]

It is also clear that, while the two Acts provided new machinery for the control of charities, the court of chancery exercised an inherent jurisdiction in relation to charities which preceded the two statutes. Both before and after the Acts, charitable trusts could be, and were, enforced by the Attorney-General in the Court of Chancery.[10]

1 Delaney, *Law Relating to Charities in Ireland*, p 1.
2 See para 2.05, above.
3 See Jordan, *Philanthropy in England*; Sheridan and Keeton, *The Modern Law of Charities*, 3rd edn, p 4.
4 43 Eliz 1, c 4.
5 10 Car 1, sess 3, c 1 (Ir).
6 *Morice v Bishop of Durham* (1804) 9 Ves 399.
7 (1841) 4 I Eq Rep 177.
8 (1875) IR 10 CL 104.
9 See para 11.15, below.
10 He originally represented the Crown as *Parens Patriae*, 'father of his country'.

11.04 The charitable purposes set out in the English preamble are

'The relief of aged, impotent and poor people, the maintenance of sick and maimed soldiers and mariners, schools of learning, free schools and scholars in universities; the repair of bridges, ports, havens, causeways, *churches*, sea banks and highways, the education and preferment of orphans, the relief, stock or maintenance for houses of correction, the marriages of poor maids, the supportation, aid and help of young tradesmen, handicraftmen and persons decayed, the relief and redemption of prisoners or captives, the aid or ease of any poor inhabitants concerning payment of ... taxes.'

Those in the Irish statute are:

'the erection, maintenance or suppport of any college, school, *lecturer in divinity*, or in any of the liberal arts or sciences, or for the relief of any manner of poor, succourless, distressed or impotent persons, or for the building, re-edifying or maintaining in repair of any *church*, college, school or hospital, or for the maintenance of any *minister and preacher of the holy word of God*, or for the erection, building, maintenance or repair of any bridges, causeyes, cashes, paces and highways within this realm, or for any other like lawful and charitable use and uses, warranted by the laws of this realm now established and in force .....'[1]

With the exception of the reference to the repair of churches, the English preamble is notably silent as to religious purposes and this no doubt reflects the new secularism of the Tudor age which, as applied to charity, was to mean the replacement of the Church as the main vehicle of social concern by private charity until the rise of modern welfare legislation. There is some support for the view that the greater number of references to religious purposes in the Irish statute reflects a difference in the law as to charitable trusts for the advancement of religion in the two countries.[2] It has to be remembered, of course, that the words to which emphasis has been added did not indicate any concern on the part of those responsible for the enactment with the preservation of the majority religion (rather the reverse). But it was undoubtedly in this area that the most significant differences in the law of charities in the two jurisdictions emerged in the nineteenth and twentieth centuries, a topic to which we shall return when we come to consider in more detail the third of Lord Macnaghten's classes, 'trusts for the advancement of religion.'

1 The wording and spelling are slightly modernised in both excerpts.
2 As to the historical background, see Brady, *Religion and the Law of Charities in Ireland*, Chapter III.

The legal definition of charity

11.05 It is to the Statute of Charles 1, accordingly, that we must return, if we want to ascertain whether an object is charitable in law. Yet, as we have seen, that merely provides a list of charitable objects and does not attempt any definition as such of a charity. It is to the 'spirit and intendment' of the statute that the courts are required to look in deciding whether a particular purpose not specified in it is charitable. Exceptionally, it may be possible to identify a purpose as charitable by analogy with one of the specified objects: thus, it is an easy progression from the repair of churches, via churchyards and burial grounds, to crematoria. In other cases, the courts have preferred to adhere to the admittedly vague and undefined approach based on the 'spirit and intendment' or the 'equity' or 'mischief' of the Statute as affording less restrictive criteria.[1] Two general principles emerge from the many decisions.

(1) **A trust to be charitable must be for the benefit of the community.** It has been repeatedly stated that there can be no charitable gift without public benefit.[2] It need not benefit the entire community directly and is very rarely intended so to do (though it may frequently have that effect indirectly). But where it benefits a section of the community only, there are two requirements:

(a) the section must not be numerically negligible, and
(b) the quality which distinguishes the section from the rest of the community must not be one which depends on the members' relationship to a particular individual.

These requirements were emphasised by the House of Lords in *Oppenheim v Tobacco Securities Trust Co Ltd*,[3] where a trust for the education of children of employees, or former employees, of a group of companies was held not charitable, although the number of employees exceeded 110,000. Similarly, it has been held in Ireland and England that the relations of the donor do not constitute a section of the community sufficient to render a gift to them charitable. Thus, Gavan Duffy J in *Re McEnery; O'Connell v A-G*[4] declined to hold as charitable the establishment of a trust fund for enabling the children and male descendants of the testator's brother to obtain professions. This was undoubtedly for the advancement of education within the second category, but was 'too narrow to be charitable'. A similar view was taken later by the Court of Appeal in England in *Re Compton, Powell v Compton.*[5] As we shall see, however, exceptions have been permitted to this rule where the gift is for the benefit of 'poor relations' or 'poor employees' of a particular person or firm.[6]

A gift for the benefit of the inhabitants of a particular locality is, however, generally treated as charitable since the decision of the House of Lords in *Goodman v Saltash Corporation.*[7] So in *Duffy v Doyle*[8] McWilliam J upheld as charitable a gift to the 'parish of Bray, Co. Wicklow.' Here, again, the gift is to a sufficiently large section of the public and is not rendered private in character by being confined to members of a particular family or association. But caution should be observed: if the gift is for specified purposes in a locality, it will not be charitable, unless those purposes are charitable.[9]

In general, then, a gift must be for the benefit of the community if it is to be charitable. If it falls within one of the recognised categories of charity, it will be assumed to be for the public benefit and therefore charitable, unless the contrary is shown.[10] In one important instance in Ireland, it is conclusively presumed from the nature of the gift that it is for the public benefit, i e where it is for the advancement of religion. This change in the law was introduced by the Charities Act 1961 and is considered in more detail in para 11.16 below.

(2) A trust is not charitable simply because it is for the benefit of the community. It must also be for what the law recognises as a charitable purpose. That purpose can be the relief of poverty or the advancement of education or religion; but if it is sought to bring it within the fourth of Lord Macnaghten's categories, it must still be for some purpose which the law recognises as charitable. It is not sufficient that it is for the public benefit.[11] The fourth category is a compendious description, in other words, of all the categories of charitable trust other than the first three.

1 See particularly the observations of Russell LJ in *Incorporated Council of Law Reporting for England and Wales v A-G* [1972] Ch 73 at 88.
2 *Pemsel's Case*, (above); *Re McEnery, O'Connell v A-G* [1941] IR 323.
3 [1951] AC 297, HL.
4 Above.
5 [1945] Ch 123.
6 See para 11.08, below.
7 (1882) 7 App Cas 633.
8 Unreported; judgement delivered 9 May 1979.
9 *Houston v Burns* [1918] AC 337.
10 *National Anti-Vivisection Society v IRC* [1948] AC 31 at 65, per Lord Simonds.
11 *A-G v National Provincial Bank* [1924] AC 262 at 265 per Viscount Cave.

Gifts for mixed charitable and non-charitable purposes

11.06 It is one of the advantages of a charitable gift that the testator or donor may leave the choice of charitable objects to be benefited to his executor or trustee. In the case of wills, the law has always insisted that a testator cannot leave it to his executor to make his will for him: to this, the great exception is charitable gifts. Thus in the leading case of *Moggridge v Thackwell*,[1] Lord Eldon upheld as a valid charitable gift a bequest to a named person 'desiring him to dispose of the same in such charities as he may think fit....' If necessary, the Court will direct a scheme to be drawn up for effectuating the charitable intention and submitted for approval.

But in such cases, although a discretion is left to the trustees, there is no question of any part of the fund being applied for non-charitable objects.

The instrument creating the trust may also empower the trustees to apportion the trust fund between charitable and non-charitable objects and if the latter are valid, the whole trust will be upheld.[2] But if the non-charitable objects are invalid — e g for uncertainty or for creating a perpetuity, — only the charitable gifts will be upheld. It is also clear that where a charitable object cannot be carried without incidentally effecting a non-charitable object, the gift will still be treated as charitable.[3]

1 (1803) 7 Ves 36; affd (1807) 13 Ves 416.
2 *Salusbury v Denton* (1858) 3 K & J 529; *Hunter v A-G* [1899] AC 309 at 324 per Lord Davey; *Re Gavacan* [1913] 1 IR 276.
3 *Re Eighmie* [1935] Ch 524.

11.07 The fact that charity has a technical meaning in law, which is not the same as its popular meaning, has caused considerable problems in cases where the testator has used language which would permit the executor or trustee to apply the fund to both charitable and non-charitable objects. The leading case of *Morice v Bishop of Durham*[1] made it clear that where this was the case, the entire gift was in law non-charitable and could accordingly fail as being an unenforceable purpose trust. These difficulties have been largely removed in this country by s 49 of the Charities Act 1961. To understand its significance, however, it is necessary to appreciate the law as it stood before the enactment.

The use by testators of expressions such as 'benevolent' in conjunction with the word 'charitable' led the courts to conclude, in some English cases, that the gift was capable of being applied for both charitable and non-charitable purposes. Although to the layman, the words 'charitable' and 'benevolent' might be treated as synonymous, this was not so in law, having regard to the technical definition of 'charities'. It was only where the courts could discern from all the language used in the will an intention on the part of the testator to benefit charitable objects *exclusively* that the gift would be upheld as charitable.

The most spectacular example of the unforeseen results of such an injudicious use of language was *Chichester Diocesan Fund v Simpson*.[2] The testator, Caleb Diplock left what was in those days the very considerable sum of approximately £250,000 'for such charitable institution or institutions or other *charitable or benevolent* object or objects as my executors.-...may...select....' It was the 'or' between 'charitable' and 'benevolent' that proved fateful. Although the money had all been distributed by the executors — principally to hospitals in England — a distant relative in Australia was alerted to the possible frailty in the will and brought proceedings. (The testator had left no close relatives.) The House of Lords upheld the Court of Appeal's decision that the fund was capable of being applied for non-charitable as well as charitable objects and was consequently invalid. An object could be 'benevolent' without necessarily being charitable and the argument that the word was used by the testator simply in an explanatory fashion — as one might refer to a person as being 'dishonest or untrustworthy' — was rejected. Since the particle 'or' was disjunctive, i e it was primarily used to signify an alternative, the only inference which could be drawn from the language used was that the testator envisaged his bounty being spent on objects which were 'benevolent' without necessarily being charitable. (As we shall see in Chapter 20, the subsequent disentangling of the legal problems caused by the testator's unlucky use of 'or' rather than 'and' led to some important developments in the equitable remedy of 'tracing'.)

It was to deal with this kind of situation that section 49 of the Charities Act 1961 was enacted. Sub-s (1) provides that

'Where any of the purposes of a gift include, or could be deemed to include, both charitable and non-charitable objects, its terms shall be so construed or given effect as to exclude the non-charitable objects and the purpose shall, accordingly, be treated as charitable.'

This provision is modelled on sections appearing in Australian legislation. It was held by the judicial committee of the Privy Council in *Leahy v A-G for New South Wales*[3] that the corresponding section in the New South Wales Act was not confined to cases where alternative purposes, some charitable and some not, had been specified in the trust instrument. It was sufficient that the testator had used language which allowed the property to be applied for both charitable and non-charitable purposes. In that case, he had bequeathed property in trust for 'such order of nuns..... as my executors and trustees may select......' Were it not for the section, this would have empowered the trustees to select a contemplative order which, under English law, would not have been a charitable object, but the gift was saved by the section. It was immaterial that the testator had not specified the selection of 'orders of nuns, contemplative or active.' But it is also essential that — as in that case — the language used should at least indicate a general charitable intention. Presumably the reasoning adopted in this case would be applied to the Irish section, on which there have so far been no decisions.

It is still possible for the instrument creating the trust to provide for an apportionment between charitable and non-charitable objects and where this is done the charitable objects only will be upheld, where the non-charitable objects are invalid. This is made clear by sub-s (2) which provides that sub-s (1) is not to apply where

'(b) (i) the terms of the gift make, or provide for the making of, an apportionment between the charitable and non-charitable objects and
    (ii) the non-charitable objects are identifiable from an express or implied description.'

1 Above.
2 [1944] AC 341.
3 [1959] AC 457.

Trusts for the relief of poverty

11.08 Such trusts can obviously take many forms. They may be for the relief of the poor generally or in a particular neighbourhood. Poverty is, moreover, a relative term and a gift can be charitable under this heading even though the recipients are not destitute. The relief of what might be called 'genteel poverty' will qualify.[1]

A gift to the poor relations of a named person might appear to be vulnerable to the rule that charitable gifts must be for the public benefit. It is clear, however, that a gift to relations who are poor will be upheld as a valid charitable gift for the relief of poverty. The decisions to that effect— of which an early example is the Irish case of *Mahon v Savage*[2] — have been generally regarded as somewhat anomalous exceptions to the requirement of public benefit, which are too firmly rooted in the law to be displaced. They were eventually given an unequivocal blessing by the English Court of Appeal in *Re Scarisbrick*,[3] and while Budd J left open the question in *Re Parker's Will, Parker v Kilroy*,[4] where the gift was to 'such of my necessitous nieces and nephews' as might be selected, there seems no reason to suppose that *Re Scarsibrook* would not be applied in Ireland. It was also thought at one time that such a gift had to be one in perpetuity to qualify as charitable: if it was of such a nature as to require immediate distribution or distribution within the perpetuity period, it was said to lack an essential feature of a charitable gift. This view was, however, rejected in *Re Scarsibick*. But the gift must not be confined to the next-of-kin of the settlor who would be entitled to succeed to his estate under the Succession Act 1965, if it is to qualify as charitable.[5]

It has also been held by the House of Lord in *Dingle v Turner*[6] that the same principle applies to a gift to poor employees of a particular firm. It would follow that gifts to relieve poverty among other limited groups, such as trades and professions and social clubs, are also charitable and there are decisions to that effect.[7]

1 Eg *Re Young* [1951] Ch 344.
2 (1803) 1 Sch & Lef 111.
3 [1951] Ch 622.
4 [1966] IR 309.
5 *Re Scarisbrick* (above).
6 [1972] AC 601.
7 Summarised in Sheridan and Keeton, op cit, p 132.

Trusts for the advancement of education

11.09 These have been held to be charitable since the earliest days of our charity law. Gifts for the establishment of schools and universities present no problem, although they are unusual today when such institutions are more often endowed from public resources. A gift for educational purposes generally is also a valid charitable gift.[1]

Trusts for the advancement of education do not, however, have to be for conventional educational purposes in order to rank as charitable. They are certainly not confined to 'teaching' as that expression is normally used. A leading example is the trust established by the will of Mrs Bernard Shaw for (among other things)

'the teaching, promotion and encouragement in Ireland of self-control, elocution, oratory, deportment, the arts of personal contact, of social intercourse and the other arts of public, private, professional and social life.'

This was held to be a valid charitable gift[2] as have trusts for various cultural purposes, such as the establishment of theatres,[3] art galleries and museums[4] and the promotion of literature[5] and music.[6] In the case of artistic charities, however, it has been held in England that whether such a gift is for the public benefit and accordingly charitable is a matter of fact for the court to determine, even though this may involve it in passing judgement on works of art.[7] (In Ireland, in recent times, the courts have assumed a similar role in determining whether particular publications are 'creative' and hence eligible for tax exemption.)[8] Zoos have also been held to be educational charities.[9]

Education in this context extends to education for a profession. But a gift for the benefit of a professional body is not charitable, since the gift is regarded as advancing the interests of the members of the particular profession rather than the public interest generally. The leading Irish case on the topic is *Miley v A-G for Ireland and Rooney*,[10] where a gift for the benefit of the College was held to be applicable in part to non-charitable purposes and failed. It was charitable insofar as it could be applied to medical education and non-charitable insofar as it could be applied to advancing or protecting the interests of surgeons as a profession.

Gifts for the endowment of university chairs and scholarships are charitable. Problems have arisen, however, with what are called 'founder's kin' provisions, where the terms of the gift indicate a preference for the award being made to a relative of the donor or even make that a condition of the gift. It would seem from the leading case of *Caffoor v Commissioner of Income Tax Colombo*[11] that if the gift is made with a view to establishing a family trust for the purpose of educating the donor's relatives, it will fail as lacking the element of public benefit. A mere indication that the relatives are to be given some form of preference in the selection of the persons to be benefited, however, is not of itself sufficient to prevent it from being charitable.

1 *Whicker v Hume* (1858) 7 HL Cas 124.
2 *Re Shaw's Wills Trusts, National Provincial Bank Ltd v National City Bank Ltd* [1952] Ch 163. Vaisey J described the clause as 'providing excellent material for the allocution of a somewhat pragmatical headmistress at an annual speech day or other ceremonial occurrence with its judicious admixture of criticism of awkward manners, vulgarities of speech and so on.....'
3 *Re Shakespeare Memorial Trust, Earl Lytton v A-G* [1923] 2 Ch 398.
4 *Re Town and Country Planning Act 1947, Crystal Palace Trustees v Minister of Town and Country Planning* [1951] Ch 132.
5 *Re Hopkins' Will Trusts* [1965] Ch 669.
6 *IRC v Glasgow Musical Festival Association* [1926] SC 920; *Shillington v Portadown Urban Council* [1911] 1 IR 247. Not does it matter that the gift is to encourage interest in the music of one composer: *Re Delius, Emmanuel v Rosen* [1957] Ch 299.
7 *Re Pinion*, [1965] Ch 85.
8 Under the Finance Act 1969, s 2. Cf *Healy v Revenue Comrs*, High Court, (Barrington J); unreported; judgement delivered 12 March 1986.
9 *Re Lopes, Bence–Jones v Zoological Society of London* [1931] 2 Ch 130.
10 [1918] 1 IR 455.
11 [1961] AC 584.

Trusts for the advancement of religion

11.10 This branch of the law of charities has since the Reformation been the subject of much controversy and in no other area is the divergence between English and Irish law so marked. The fundamental difference between the two jurisdictions at common law was that in Ireland the test as to whether a particular religious purpose was for the public benefit, and hence charitable, was held to be a subjective one: if the donor made a gift for a religious object which he believed to be for the public benefit, the gift was upheld, provided his belief was rational, moral and legal.[1] In England, the test was an objective one: the court had to be satisfied by legal proof that the gift was in fact for the public benefit.[2] In Ireland, the 'subjective' test has now to an extent been given statutory form in s 45 of the Charities Act 1961, to which we shall return. This difference between English and Irish law has been of great importance in the case of bequests—very common in Ireland—for the celebration of masses and to contemplative religious orders.

Apart altogether from these considerations, the law as to such charitable trusts is properly summed up by Sheridan and Keeton as being in 'an unholy mess'.[3] Gifts for the advancement of religion generally have been upheld,[4] as have gifts in aid of particular religions. Here the law has drawn no distinction between different varieties of religious belief: as we have seen, a gift for the propagation of Joanna Southcott's writings was upheld as charitable.[5] Nor is charity confined in law to the Christian religion. Professor Newark in an influential article[6] proposed a definition of 'religion' for the purposes of Lord Macnaghten's third category as—inter alia—'a doctrine recognising the spiritual sovereignty of a Superior Being and which usually enjoins acts which honour or supplicate this being....' This would clearly embrace other monotheistic religions such as Judaism and Islam. There seems no reason, however, why gifts for polytheistic religions, such as Hinduism, should not be recognised as charitable.[7] Although the preamble to the Constitution has led to judicial descriptions of the State as 'Christian' in its nature,[8] it would seem that this is not a sufficient reason for confining charitable protection in law to monotheistic religions, still less to the Christian religion.

1 See para 11.15 below.
2 Ibid.
3 p 66.
4 *Arnott v Arnott* [1906] 1 IR 127.
5 See para 11.07 above.
6 'Public Benefit and Religious Trusts', (1946) 62 LQR 234.
7 Halsbury, Laws of England, 4th edn, Vol 5, para 530, n 3. But not it would seem, spiritualism: see *Re Hummeltenberg* [1923] 1 Ch 237.
8 E.g. *Norris v A-G* [1984] IR 36 per O'Higgins CJ.

11.11 Gifts to the holders of specified ecclesiastical offices have provoked an extraordinary diversity of judicial decisions. At the outset, one has to distinguish between a gift to a clergyman or minister by name — 'the Very Reverend John Murphy' — and by reference to his office—'the Very Reverend John Murphy or the parish priest of X for the time being'. In the former case, it will be construed as a beneficial gift and in the latter as a gift in trust. If the duties of the office are charitable in nature, the trust will be charitable. Thus a gift to a bishop, parish priest, vicar or minister which is not a beneficial gift but a gift in trust *virtute oficii* will normally be charitable.[1]

If, however, other words are added to the gift in trust — e.g. to 'the most reverend Dr X or his successor for such purposes in the diocese as he wishes'[2]—an extremely refined distinction is insisted on by the authorities. If the words are simply intended to indicate that within the scope of the trust defined by the nature of the office the donee is to exercise his own discretion, the gift will remain charitable. But if the words are intended to indicate the trusts on which the donee is to hold the property, the gift at common law will fail if they are not exclusively charitable. Thus in the example given, the gift was upheld as charitable. But where the gift was to 'the Archbishop of Westminster....to be distributed at his absolute discretion between such charitable religious or other societies institutions persons or objects in connection with the Roman Catholic faith in England as he shall in his absolute discretion think fit' it was held not to be charitable: the words were indicative of the trusts and they could extend to non-charitable objects.[3] This distinction may be of no more than historic interest in Ireland, however: it is assumed that in all such cases the gift will now be treated under s 49 of the Charities Act 1961 as being for charitable purposes only.[4]

It should finally be noted in this connection that in Ireland because of the effect of s 16 of the Charitable Donations and Bequests Act 1844 (which rendered void charitable bequests of land made within three months of the testator's death), it was common to insert in wills what was called the 'O'Hagan Clause'. This provided that in the event of the testator dying within the three months period the property was to go to the bishop, or whoever the appropriate person might be, for his own benefit. This substituted gift, being a beneficial gift to the bishop, would not be charitable and hence unaffected by s 16. In *Re Meehan, Tobin and Another v Meehan*,[5] Budd J held that such a substitutional gift to the Bishop of Waterford and Lismore 'absolutely' was a beneficial gift and hence not charitable. Section 16 was, however, repealed by the Charities Act 1961 so that the O'Hagan clause is no longer necessary in Irish wills.

1 *A-G v Molland* (1832) 1 You 562; *Thornber v Wilson* (1855) 3 Drew 245; *Gibson v Representative Church Body* (1881) 9 LR Ir 1.
2 *Re Hogan's Estate, Halpin v Hannon* (1948) 82 ILT 74. Cf *Re Deighton, Reddy v Fitzmaurice* (1952) 86 ILT 127.
3 *Re Davidson, Minty v Bourne* [1909] 1 Ch 567. distinguished in *Re Flinn, Public Trustee v Flinn* [1948] Ch 241, where the gift was to 'the Archbishop of Westminister ..... for the time being ..... to be used by him for such purposes as he shall in his absolute discretion think fit' and was upheld as a valid charitable gift.
4 See para 10.07 above.
5 [1960] IR 82.

11.12 We have already seen that gifts for particular graves, tombs, etc were treated as valid purpose trusts, even though clearly not charitable, and that by virtue of s 50 of the 1961 Act they are now charitable within specified levels.[1] A gift for the repair of the whole churchyard is also charitable and this was extended by Budd J to a non-denominational cemetery maintained by Galway County Council in *Re Quinn's Will Trusts*.[2] While holding that it was a valid charitable bequest for the advancement of religion, he said that he would also have been prepared to hold that it was a charitable purpose beneficial to the community within Lord Macnaghten's fourth class. (This view was also taken in Scotland and England in *Scottish Burial Reform and Cremation Society Ltd v Glasgow City Corporation*.)[3]

1 See para 7.08 above.
2 (1953) 88 ILT 161.
3 [1968] AC 138.

11.13 Gifts for the support of clergymen have been upheld as being charitable.[1] Gifts for *residences* for clergymen have been held not to be charitable in a number of Irish rating cases. It is thought, however, that these cases turn on the narrower construction given to the words 'charitable purposes' in the Poor Relief (Ir) Act 1838 which under Irish law determines whether properties are exempt from rating.[2] It is clear from a number of Irish decisions that properties used for the advancement of religion are not exempt from rating: they must, in the words of the proviso be 'exclusively dedicated to religious worship.' Hence Maynooth College failed to win exemption from rating[3] and for the same reason Henchy J held that a Nun's residence attached to primary and post-primary schools conducted by The Sisters for Mercy was not exempt as being used for charitable purposes.[4] It is submitted that the same considerations would not apply if the question for determination was whether a gift for such purposes was charitable and on principle there would seem to be no reason why it should not be charitable.

1 *A-G v Brereton* (1752) 2 Ves Sen 425; *A-G v Sparks* (1753) Amb 201.
2 *Heron v Monaghan* (1856) 1 Ir Jur NS 270; *O'Connell v Valuation Comr* [1906] 2 IR 479; *Brendan v Valuation Comr* [1969] IR 202. See Brady, 'Charitable Purposes and Rating Exemption in Ireland' (1968) 3 Ir Jur NS 215; Keane, *Law of Local Government in the Republic of Ireland*, pp 291-293.
3 *Barrington's Hospital v Valuation Comr* [1957] IR 299.
4 *Brendan v Comr of Valuation* (above).

11.14 Once it is accepted that in identifying charities the law does not distinguish between varieties of religious belief, it would seem a logical consequence that the encouragement of any doctrine or ritual which, according to the tenets of a particular religion, was for the benefit of the community should also be a charitable purpose. Any other criterion would seem to require the court to conduct an inquiry as to whether a particular religious doctrine or ritual was for the benefit of mankind and thus to subject matters which of their nature are incapable of proof to the seemingly inappropriate requirements of the law of evidence. The only necessary qualification, on this view, would be that the purpose should be neither illegal nor immoral. This has been the view of the law taken in Ireland in the case of trusts for the advancement of religion since the celebrated decision of the Court of Appeal in *O'Hanlon v Logue*,[1] but in England the courts have adhered unyieldingly to the principle that the element of public benefit must be capable of proof in a gift for religious purposes as much as any other gift, if it is to qualify as charitable.[2] It would appear that the approach of the Irish courts has been given statutory form in Ireland in the Charities Act 1961. The question has given rise in the past to acute judicial controversy in two areas in particular, gifts for the celebration of masses and for the benefit of contemplative orders.

1 [1906] 1 IR 247.
2 See para 11.15, below.

11.15 Gifts for the celebration of masses, an extremely common form of bequest in Ireland, have a long and tangled legal history. Before the Reformation such gifts were clearly lawful and in Ireland their legality remained unaffected by the Statute of Chantries which did not extend to this country. (In England it was thought for centuries that the statute had the effect of rendering unlawful as 'superstitious uses' gifts for the celebration of masses: the cases which so decided were, however, overruled by the House of Lords led by Lord Birkenhead in the famous decision of *Bourne v Keane*.)[1] Accordingly when the penal laws came to an end, there was no question of a gift for masses being unlawful, as it was believed to be in England. But in *A-G v Delaney*[2] the Irish Court of Exchequer, presided over by Palles CB (himself a Roman Catholic) held that while not illegal , a gift for the celebration of masses was not charitable where there was no stipulation that the masses were to be said in public. (It was, of course, frequently the case that a testator simply bequeathed money for the celebration of masses for the repose of his soul without any requirement that they be said in public.) Palles CB was of the view that masses said in private lacked the essential element of public benefit which might attach to masses celebrated in public where the edification of the congregation could be regarded as supplying the necessary element of public benefit. His two colleagues expressed reservations as to whether even masses celebrated in public were a charitable object. However, in a later case of *A-G v Hall*[3] a contrary view was taken and ultimately all doubts were laid to rest by the decision of the Irish Court of Appeal in *O'Hanlon v Logue*.[4] In a remarkable judicial *volte face*, Palles CB reversed his decision of some forty years earlier and concluded that such gifts were charitable: they were properly regarded, when their history in pre-Reformation days was traced, as 'gifts to God' and this supplied the element of public benefit which he had earlier found missing. He also considered — and it was on this ground that his colleagues, Fitzgibbon and Holmes LJJ, preferred to rest their judgements — that where a donor believed that in accordance with the tenets of his religious faith a particular observance or ceremony would be for the spiritual welfare of the community this could be treated as a valid charitable gift for the advancement of religion. The courts, in other words, should not require proof in such circumstances that a gift, objectively viewed, was for the public benefit, since in matters which depended on religious beliefs proof in accordance with legal principles was neither possible nor appropriate. Provided the observance in question was not immoral, irrational or illegal, it should be upheld as charitable.[5]

1 [1919] AC 815.
2 (1875) IR 10 CL 104.
3 [1897] 2 IR 426.
4 Above.
5 In England, the validity of a gift for masses even when said in private was subsequently upheld as a valid charitable gift at first instance: *Re Caus* [1934] Ch 162. But the decision is regarded in that jurisdiction as of doubtful authority: see the observations of Lord Reid in *Gilmour v Coats* at p 460 and *Tudor on Charities*, 6th edn, pp 64-68. It would appear that the same is true in Northern Ireland: see Brady, *Religion and the Law of Charities in Ireland*, Chapter Four, 'O'Hanlon v Logue in Northern Ireland.'

11.16 Gifts to contemplative religious orders have also created difficulties. There was no problem with communities of nuns and monks which were engaged in teaching, nursing or looking after the poor, since such activities were in the eyes of the law charitable in themselves. It is true that in post-Reformation times, certain catholic orders, notably the Society of Jesus, were illegal, but these disabilities were removed by the Government of Ireland Act 1920[1] and in any event could not have survived the enactment of the Constitution in 1937.

Gifts to contemplative orders were regarded as being in a different category in England since the decision in *Cocks v Manners*.[2] Sir John Wigrams V-C there held that a voluntary association of women for the purpose of working out their own salvation by religious exercises (in that case Dominican nuns) was not a charitable institution in either the popular or the legal sense. The question came before the Irish High Court in *Maguire v A-G*[3] where the gift was for the founding of a convent for the perpetual adoration of the Blessed Sacrament. Gavan Duffy J treated the judgement in *Cocks v Manners* as involving a finding of fact that there was no element of public benefit in a gift to a contemplative order and vigorously rejected its relevance to Irish conditions, saying

'there is not now and never has been the flimsiest warrant for attributing the same outlook to public opinion here. I shall waste no time in establishing the proposition of fact that the cloister is a powerful source of general edification in this country.'

The learned judge also founded himself on the first ground relied on by Palle CB in *O'Hanlon v Logue*, ie that such a gift was a pious or charitable use dating from pre-Reformation times which had not been expelled from the common law by that event. This conclusion he considered to be reinforced by the language of the preamble to the Constitution. In the result he did not appear to think it necessary to rely on the subjective approach to the validity of such gifts unanimously favoured by the Court of Appeal in *O'Hanlon v Logue*.

The whole question was reopened in 1948 in England in *Gilmour v Coats*[4] when it was argued that such gifts were charitable on three grounds:

(i) that under the Roman Catholic doctrine of intercessory prayer, such gifts were for the benefit of all the faithful and hence could properly be regarded as being for the public benefit;

(ii) that in any event the activities of the community were a source of public edification by example;

(iii) that a gift which facilitated the entry of people into religious communities was a gift for the advancement of religion and hence charitable.

The first argument failed because of the application of the objective test, which had been rejected in *O'Hanlon v Logue*. Since the truth of the doctrine of intercessory prayer was incapable of being tested in a court of law, it could not be shown that the trust was for the public benefit. The second argument — that based on 'example'—was rejected, as being 'too vague and intangible' to satisfy the test of public benefit. The third argument also failed because, as it was said, it assumed that a gift for the advancement of religion was for the public benefit, whereas the view of the Court of Appeal and the House of Lords was that in English law not all religious purposes were regarded as being for the public benefit.

When the question came before the Irish courts again, however, in *Re Sheridan, Bank of Ireland Trustee Co Ltd v A-G*[5] Dixon J refused to follow *Gilmour v Coats*, holding that the subjective test was well established in our law by *O'Hanlon v Logue* and was in any event preferable to the objective test favoured in England. He considered the law to have been correctly stated by Gavan Duffy J in the earlier decision. In *Munster and Leinster Bank Ltd v A-G*[6] Black J had treated *Cocks v Manners* as correctly stating the law, but, as Dixon J pointed out, his remarks to that effect were *obiter* and another Irish decision — of Overend J in *Re Keogh McNamee v Mansfield*[7] — which also appeared to favour *Cocks v Manners* was distinguished by Dixon J, since the gift in that case was in its terms applicable to unarguably non-charitable purposes.

Despite this powerful current of Irish judicial authority in favour of upholding such bequests as charitable, there seems to have been some uncertainty as to whether in the event the Supreme Court might not have adopted the approach of the House of Lords in *Gilmour v Coats*, and this may have prompted s 45 of the Charities Act 1961[8] which provides that

'(1) In determining whether or not a gift for the purpose of the advancement of religion is a valid charitable gift it shall be conclusively presumed that the purpose includes and will occasion public benefit.

'(2) For the avoidance of the difficulties which arise in giving effect to the intentions of donors of certain gifts for the purpose of the advancement of religion and in order not to frustrate those intentions and notwithstanding that certain gifts for the purpose aforesaid, including gifts for the celebration of masses, whether in public or in private, are valid charitable gifts, it is hereby enacted that a valid charitable gift for the purpose of the advancement of religion shall have effect and , as respects its having effect, shall be construed in accordance with the laws, canons, ordinances and tenets of the religion concerned.'

It would seem that sub-s (1) puts it beyond doubt that gifts to contemplative orders are valid charitable gifts. Such gifts must surely be regarded on any view as for the advancement of religion, if only on the basis of the third argument advanced in *Gilmour v Coats*, i e that they facilitate the entry of people into religious communities.[9] That argument was rejected by the House of Lords, but on the ground that gifts for the advancement of religion were not necessarily for the public benefit. Once it is conclusively presumed that they are, the last argument for treating them as other than charitable seems to disappear. It is true that the draughtsman has refrained from defining the expression 'a gift for the purpose of the advancement of religion' but it would seem perverse to exclude a gift to a contemplative order from that description. Sub-section (2) seems also intended to put the charitable nature of such gifts beyond controversy by embodying in law the subjective test that such gifts are to be construed in accordance with the tenets of the religion concerned.[10]

1 *Shaw v A-G* [1935] IR 782.
2 (1871) LR 12 Eq 574.
3 [1943] IR 238.
4 [1949] AC 426.
5 [1957] IR 257.
6 [1940] IR 19.
7 [1945] IR 13.
8 Brady, op cit. See Dail Debates, *Official Report*, vol 184, cols 577/8.
9 Above.
10 The wording, however, appears curiously maladroit. In its terms, the sub-s would seem to be confined to 'valid charitable gifts', although by definition such gifts do not require validation.

11.17 Gifts for missionary and evangelical purposes have been upheld as charitable, including trusts intended to convert persons from one variety of Christianity to another. Lord O'Brien CJ in *A-G v Becher*[1] upheld as charitable a gift to promote the glory of God by saving the souls of Roman Catholic Irishmen through the instrumentality of the Church of Ireland. It is also thought that gifts for the religious instruction and training of clergy would be held to be charitable in Ireland. There are English decisions to that effect[2] and it would not seem that *Trustees of Maynooth College v Commissioner of Valuation*[3] is an authority to the contrary. That was a rating case and, as we have seen, such cases are determined in Ireland by reference to the proviso to s 63 of the Poor Relief (Ir) Act 1838.[4] Since the college was not 'used exclusively for charitable purposes' within the restricted meaning given to those words in Irish law, it was not exempted from rating. But a gift to the College or any similar body would, it is thought, be clearly a gift 'for the advancement of religion' within the Pemsel classification and accordingly a valid charitable gift.

A gift to pay for invalids to go to Lourdes was also held to be a valid charitable gift by Budd J in *Re McCarthy's Wills' Trusts*[5] on the ground that such pilgrimages, at least when they take an organised form, can be a source of edification to the public and hence of public benefit.

1 [1910] 2 IR 251.
2 *Re Williams, Public Trustee v Williams* [1927] 2 Ch 283.
3 [1958] IR 189.
4 See para 11.13, above.
5 [1958] IR 311.

The fourth class

11.18 The fourth Macnaghten class of charitable trusts is 'trusts for other purposes beneficial to the community'. They have also been categorised — in the language of Sir Samuel Romilly speaking as counsel in *Morice v The Bishop of Durham*[1] — as trusts for 'objects of general public utility.' As we have seen, however, not every trust which is beneficial to the community or of public utility qualifies as charitable. It must be for a purpose that the law is prepared to recognise as charitable.

We have also seen that trusts for the well recognised objects of the relief of poverty or the advancement of education and religion are presumed to be for the public benefit, the last named in Ireland conclusively so.[2] Trusts in the fourth class, enjoy no such presumption: they must be shown to be for the public benefit. It has been said in England, however, that once established as such, they will at least enjoy a *prima facie* presumption that they are also charitable. The law was thus stated by Russell LJ in *Incorporated Council of Law Reporting for England and Wales v A-G:*[3]

'The courts in consistently saying that not all such (trusts) are necessarily charitable in law are in substance accepting that if a purpose is shown to be so beneficial or of such utility, it is prima facie charitable in law, but have left open a line of retreat based on the equity of the Statute (of Elizabeth) in case they are faced with a purpose (e.g. a political purpose) which could not have been within the contemplation of the Statute even if the then legislature had been endowed with the gift of foresight into the circumstances of later centuries.'

1 Above.
2 See para 11.05, above.
3 [1971] Ch 626.

11.19 A divergence of view between Irish and English judges has also emerged in relation to the fourth category as to whether charitable trusts within it are to be ascertained by reference to a subjective or an objective test. On closer examination, however, it would seem that the difference of approach is by no means as marked as in the case of religious trusts. The question has arisen mainly in connection with trusts which seek in one form or another to alleviate suffering in animals.

In the first of the major cases, *Re Foveaux*[1] it was held in England that an anti-vivisection trust was charitable, Chitty J taking the view that where there was controversy as to whether a particular purpose was beneficial to the public but the testator clearly thought that his gift would be beneficial, the court should adopt a neutral posture. As a result in that case he upheld the gift as a valid charitable gift. A similar approach was adopted by the Irish Court of Appeal in *Re Cranston, Webb v Oldfield*,[2] where the gift was to a vegetarian society, Fitzgibbon LJ posing and answering the basic question thus:

'What is the tribunal which is to decide whether the object is a beneficient one? It cannot be the individual mind of the judge for he may disagree *toto coelo* from (*sic*) the testator as to what is or is not beneficial. On the other hand, it cannot be the *vox populi*, for charities have been upheld for the benefit of insignificant sects and of peculiar people. It occurs to me that the answer must be — that the benefit must be one which *the founder* believes to be of public advantage and his belief must be at least rational and not contrary either to the general law of the land or to the principals of morality. A gift of such a character, dictated by benevolence, believed to be beneficient, devoted to an appreciably important subject and neither *contra bonos mores* nor *contra legem* will, in my opinion, be charitable in the eye of the law as settled by decisions which bind us. It is not for us to say that these have gone too far.'

But in *Re Hummeltenberg*,[3] Russell J took the view that the opinion of the testator as to whether the trust was charitable was irrelevant: this, he said, could lead to the upholding of trusts for fantastic objects such as 'training poodles to dance.' And in *National Anti-Vivisection Society v IRC*[4] the Court of Appeal and the House of Lords overruled *Re Foveaux*, holding that an anti-vivisection trust was not charitable. It is an important feature of the latter decision, however, that the appeal was from a decision of the Special Commissioners for Income Tax who having heard evidence concluded that the benefits to humanity from experiments on animals were far greater in scale and importance than the incidental suffering caused to some animals. This was treated as a finding of fact which could not be disturbed in the appellate courts so that the net issue was whether a trust so found to be detrimental in its effects to society at large had to be regarded as charitable because of the testator's view to the contrary. Lord Simonds, although expressing his preference for the dissenting judgement of Holmes LJ in *Re Cranston*, was careful to say that he was not holding that case to have been wrongly decided. There was no question in the latter case of any finding that the aims of the vegetarian society were positively detrimental so that, in his view, it lent no support to the case advanced for the anti-vivisectionists.

It would seem that, on any view, the subjective approach must be more significantly modified in the case of trusts in the fourth category than in the case of religious trusts. Fitzgibbon LJ would have been at one with Russell J on the elimination of the 'dancing poodle' trust, since he refers to the need for the trust to be devoted to an 'appreciably important subject'. Whether the subject is of that importance must presumably be determined objectively by the court, as must the question whether it is dictated by 'benevolence'. It must also fulfill the requirements of not being irrational or contrary to immorality and again this necessarily implies an objective determination by the court. Nor would it be out of harmony with this approach for an Irish court to decline to treat as charitable a trust positively established as harmful in its effects, however well intentioned the testator may have been. (It may also be remarked in passing that the vivisection controversy illustrates another aspect of the law of charities which is of particular relevance in the fourth class: the law cannot remain static in relation to such charities and the increase in knowledge in a particular area can demonstrate—as it did in the vivisection cases — that a trust once regarded as charitable may lose that status.)

1 [1895] 2 Ch 501.
2 [1898] 1 IR 431.
3 Above.
4 [1948] AC 31.

11.20 Gifts in the fourth class have also foundered because of the vagueness of the community intended to be benefited. So in *Keren Kayemeth Le Jisroel v IRC*,[1] a gift intended to provide financial assistance for the resettlement of Jews in the Middle East in the 1930's was held not to be a valid charitable gift. Whether the Jews intended to be resettled were those already living in the area or the Jewish community throughout the world, they did not constitute a sufficiently defined community to be the object of a charitable trust. Similarly, a gift for the benefit of Welsh people living in or near or visiting London was not charitable.[2] And in *Re ni*

Bruadair deceased, O hUadhaigh and Another v A-G and Others,[3] Gannon
J held to be not charitable a bequest for 'the benefit of the Republicans of
the time according to the objects of the Republicans as they were in the
years 1919 to 1921,' saying

> 'there appears to be no binding factor or limitation by organisation, by conduct
> or activity, by location, by regulation or by any unifying factor as a class of the
> public other than the adoption of political thoughts and ideas....'

1 [1932] AC 650.
2 *Williams' Trustees v IRC* [1947] AC 447.
3 Unreported; judgement delivered 5 February 1979; Wylie Casebook 462.

11.21 As can be seen, the variety of trusts which has arisen for consideration in the 'unchartered hinterland' of Lord Macnaghten's fourth class is
remarkable. Here we can only deal briefly with some of the more
important headings.

(a) The old and the disabled. The Irish statute refers to the 'relief or
maintenance of poor, succourless, distressed or impotent persons.' It is
clear that trusts intended to reliev the burdens of old age are charitable,
whether the old people concerned are poor or not. In *Re McCarthy's Will
Trusts*,[1] Budd J held charitable a gift to a benevolent fund for 'elderly or
infirm' nurses. Similarly, trusts for the disabled are charitable, whether the
recipients are poor or not.[2] Conversely, a trust for young people, without
any further qualification, is not charitable.[3]

(b) Health. The repair of hospitals is specifically referred to in the
preamble, but a gift for a hospital generally is also charitable as being for
the relief of 'impotent persons'. The fact that the hospital may admit fee
paying patients in addition to those treated without charge was held not to
affect its charitable status by the Supreme Court in *Barrington's Hospital v
Valuation Com.*[4] Even where the hospital — or nursing home — is
confined to paying patients, it may still be charitable. In *Re Resch's Will
Trusts*[5] Lord Wilberforce, giving the advice of the Judicial Committee of
the Privy Council, said that the provision of medical care for the sick in
modern times is accepted as a public benefit suitable to attract the
privileges of a charity. Consequently a nursing home run on a fee paying
basis but the profits of which were devoted to a general hospital run in
conjunction therewith was charitable. The same reasoning was applied by
Kenny J to St Vincent's Private Nursing Home in Dubin in *Gleeson & Ors
v A-G.*[6]

Trusts encouraging total abstinence from alcohol have been held
charitable in England and Scotland,[7] but these decisions have been
criticised on the ground that no clear public benefit is involved, in contrast
to trusts encouraging 'temperance' where the object can be taken to be the
discouragement of excessive drinking.[8] It seems clear that, contrary to
Canadian authority,[9] a trust designed to secure prohibition in legislative
form is not charitable. This would be generally regarded as a political
objective and thus not charitable.[10] (This was a further ground on which
anti-vivisection trusts were held not charitable in England: the only
effective method of securing the trust's objectives was by legislation.)

Trusts for the benefit of medical science generally are charitable, but
those intended for the benefit of professional medical or noursing associations are not.[11]

(c) Recreational. Recreational charities have not fared well at the hands of the law. This is because gifts which are intended to provide pleasure for people are not regarded as charitable. Those which have been upheld have usually been treated by the courts as coming within the second Pemsel class, the advancement of education, which as we have already seen, embraces sport, theatre, music, literature and the arts generally.

The leading Irish case on the topic is *Clancy v Commissioner of Valuation*.[12] Exemption from rating was sought for a hall built to promote temperance among the poor and labouring classes of the town of Sligo and the surrounding districts. Various recreational facilities were provided in the hall, but it was held that it was not devoted exclusively to charitable purposes, principally on the basis that the facilities were open to rich and poor alike. A similar result was arrived at in the Northern Ireland case of *Trustees of Londonderry Presbyterian Church House v Commissioners of Inland Revenue*.[13] If, however, such a gift can be construed as being for the benefit of a locality, it may be upheld as charitable as happened in *Shillington v Portadown UDC*.[14] Gifts of parks for the use of the public have also been upheld as charitable in a number of cases.[15]

There is no equivalent in Ireland to the English Recreational Charities Act 1958 which gives charitable status to the provision of facilities for recreation and leisure time occupations if they are provided 'in the interests of social welfare'.

(d) Animals. We have seen that trusts for the maintenance of particular animals ('my dog Rover') have been enforced by the court, despite the fact that they are trusts for non-charitable purposes, in what is generally admitted to be an anomalous series of cases.[16] But trusts for the welfare of animals generally have been held to be charitable. The reason normally given by judges is that such gifts by encouraging kindness to animals help to 'elevate the human race'.[17] As we have seen, however, it has been held in England that this does not apply to anti-vivisection trusts.[18] On the other side of the line, we have seen that the Irish courts upheld as charitable a gift for the encouragement of vegetarianism, although as much because it could be said that this would promote a healthier diet as on compassionate grounds.

(e) Political objects. In a number of cases, political purposes have been held not to be charitable. So in Ireland, the Fianna Fail party[19] and in England the Conservative and Labour parties,[20] have failed to qualify as charitable objects. The objects were more widely defined in the bequest already referred to in *Re ni Bruadair, O hUadhaigh and Another v the Attorney General and others*.[21] The deceased in that case was a remarkable lady who was a daughter of the Earl of Midleton and was originally named Albina Lucy Broderick. Coming to live in County Kerry in 1906, she espoused the cause of nationalism and with all the zeal of a convert adopted the Irish version of her name, Gobnait ni Bruadair, immersing herself in many local activities, including the establishment of a hospital and cooperative store. When she died aged over 90, her will, as translated from the Irish in which it was written, contained the bequest already quoted. Gannon J, as we have seen, found that it was too vague in its terms to constitute a valid charitable gift. But the learned judge also indicated that even if the will had specifically directed the trustees to use the fund for the purpose of implementing the Democratic Programme adopted by the First Dail in January 1919, it would not have constituted a valid charitable object, since that programme was essentially a statement of political objectives.

It has also been held in England that this principle is not confined to domestic political activities. As a result, the Amnesty International Trust was denied charitable status on the ground that it was seeking to procure the reversal of government decisions in other jurisdictions.[22] The English Charity Commissioners have also warned that organisations principally concerned with the relief of poverty or the advancement of education in Third World countries may lose their charitable status if they cross the boundary into political activity.[23]

1 Above. cf *Re Robinson* [1951] Ch 198.
2 *Sanderson's Trustee v Edinburgh Royal Blind Asylum* [1919] 1 SLT 39.
3 *Re Payne* (1968) Qd R 287; *A-G v Cahill* [1969] 1 NSWR 85.
4 [1957] IR 299.
5 [1969] 1 AC 514.
6 Unreported; judgement delivered May 1973.
7 *Re Hood*[1931] 1 Ch 240; *IRC v Falkirk Temperance Cafe Trust* 1927 SC 261.
8 Sheridan and Keeton, op cit p 148. See *Clancy v Valuation Comr* [1911] 2 IR 173.
9 *Farewell v Farewell* (1892) 22 OR 573.
10 See para (e), below.
11 *Mylie v A-G* [1918] 1 IR 453; *General Nursing Council for England And Wales v St Marylebone Corpn* [1959] AC 540.
12 Above.
13 [1946] NI 178.
14 Above.
15 *Re Hadden* [1932] 1 Ch 133. Cf *Valuation Comr for Northern Ireland v Lurgan Borough Council* [1968] NI 104 at 125, per Lord McDermott CJ.
16 See para 7.09, above.
17 *Re Wedgwood* [1915] 1 Ch 113 at 122 per Swinfen Eady LJ. In *Re Grove-Grady* [1929] 1 Ch 557, the Court of Appeal held that a bequest to establish a nature reserve was not charitable since protecting such an area from intrusion by man and leaving the animals to prey on one another did nothing to elevate mankind. With the increased awareness of the importance of preserving the environment, this decision would hardly be applied in Ireland to-day. It has not been followed in Australia: *A-G (NSW) v Sawtell* 1978 2 NSWLR 200.
18 Above.
19 *Goff v Gurhy*; unreported; Supreme Court; judgement delivered 24 April 1980.
20 *Bonar Law Memorial Trust v IRC* (1933) 49 TLR 20; *Re Hopkinson* [1949] 1 All ER 346.
21 Unreported; judgement delivered 5 February 1979; Wylie Casebook 462.
22 *McGovern v A-G* [1982] Ch 321. See Nobles (1982) 45 MLR 704.
23 Sheridan and Keeton, op cit p 46.

The cy-près jurisdiction

11.22 It is sometimes impossible to give effect to the intentions of a person who makes a gift to charity, or to give effect to them in the precise terms which he has prescribed. Even where it is possible, it may be impractical or inconvenient to do so. The institution to which he made a bequest may have ceased to exist or he may have imposed conditions which are not capable of fulfilment, to mention but two examples. To cope with such problems, the courts have for long exercised what is known as the *cy-près* jurisdiction.

'*Cy-près*' is a Norman French expression which has been generally interpreted by the courts as meaning 'as near as possible'. The courts in developing the *cy-près* jurisdiction have, accordingly, sought to carry out a donor's intentions in a manner which resembles as closely as possible the terms of his gift, where it is no longer possible or practicable to carry them out literally. While the origins of the jurisdiction need not detain us here, it may be noted that it has been generally thought to derive from the days when the administration of the estate of deceased persons was the province of the church—in the person of the ordinary of the dioceses—not, as in our times, of the courts. Because it was thought that those who died intestate would have wished to devote some at least of their estate to 'pious uses', the ordinary treated a given proportion of the property as dedicated to that purpose. In a more secular age, however, the jurisdiction developed into a means of ensuring that the charitable intentions of a donor were not frustrated by the altered circumstances existing when his gift took effect. In its modern form, its nature was thus defined by Budd J in *Re Royal Hospital Kilmainham*:[1]

'The law requires that if a charity can be administered according to the directions of its founder, it should be so administered. Where it is established that a gift has been made with a general intention of charity and a failure of purpose ensues, it is not allowed to fail but will be carried out cy-près....... The principle is applied where the method indicated by the donor of carrying out his charitable intentions becomes impracticable, or his intentions cannot be executed literally, most frequently owing to altered circumstances.'

Accordingly where the person making the charitable gift has shown a general charitable intention — and not simply an intention to benefit the particular charity and no other — the gift will not fail because it is no longer possible to carry out his intentions in the manner he has indicated. In such a case, the Court—or the Commissioners for Charitable Donations and Bequests where the gift is within certain financial limits — will order a scheme to be prepared for carrying out his intentions in a manner as close as possible to the terms of the gift. There are, as we shall see, certain exceptions to the rule requiring that a general charitable intention should have been shown.

1 [1966] IR 451 at 469, 471.

11.23 The decisions of the courts as to when the cy-pres jurisdiction can be invoked led to some very fine distinctions being drawn. Ultimately, however, the law was both clarified and liberalised by s 47(1) of the Charities Act 1961 which sets out the occasions on which the purposes of a charitable gift may be altered under the cy-pres jurisdiction. They may be summarised as follows:

(1) Where the original purposes have been fulfilled in whole or in part as far as may be.
(2) Where the original purposes cannot be carried out, or cannot be carried out according to the directions given and to the spirit of the gift.
(3) Where the original purposes have been adequately provided for in whole or in part by other means.
(4) Where the original purposes have ceased to be charitable as being useless or harmful to the community or for other reasons.
(5) Where the original purposes have ceased in any other way to provide a suitable and effective method of using the property available by virtue of the gift, regard being had to the spirit of the gift.
(6) Where the original purposes provide a use for part only of the property.

(7) Where the property and other property applicable for similar purposes can be more effectively used in conjunction.
(8) Where the original purposes were laid down by reference to an area which has ceased to be a unit or an area or class of persons which has ceased to be suitable or practical in administering the gift, regard being had to the spirit of the gift.

11.24 As we have seen, the cy-pres jurisdiction as a general rule may not be invoked unless the donor has shown a general charitable intention. In other words, if the donor intended to benefit the named object and no other and his intentions cannot be carried out, the gift will fail. To this general rule, there are, however, certain exceptions. It is not necessary that a general charitable intention should have been shown where the donor has made an absolute and perpetual (or 'out and out') gift of the property to the charity and the impossibility or impracticality of carrying out his intentions only arises after the gift has taken effect. Of this, the best Irish example is *Re Royal Kilmainham Hospital*[1] which is discussed in more detail below. But if a testator makes a bequest to a named institution which is no longer in existence when he dies, it will be necessary to show a general charitable intention on his part as distinct from an intention to benefit the named institution. If no such general intention is established, the property cannot be applied cy-près.[2] In determining whether a general charitable intention has been shown, where that is required, the court construes the document creating the charitable trust as a whole.

The legal principles which require that, subject to the exceptions noted, a general charitable intention must have been manifested by the donor before the gifts can be applied *cy-près* have been left untouched by the enactment of s 47(1) of the Charities Act 1961. As we have seen, that sub-section extends the range of cases in which the property may be applied *cy-près*, but sub-s(2) provides that sub-s (1) is not to

'affect the conditions which must be satisfied in order that property given for charitable purposes may be applied *cy-près* except in so far as those conditions require a failure of the original purposes.'

It follows that, subject to the specified exceptions, it is necessary to establish a general charitable intention before the gift can be applied cy-près.

1 Above.
2 *Clark v Taylor* (1853) 1 Drew 642; *McKeown v Ardagh* (1876) IR 10 Eq 445. See Sheridan and Delaney, *The Cy-près Doctrine* pp 108-112. Cf *Re Spence* [1979] Ch 483.

11.25 The leading modern Irish case on the *cy-près* jurisdiction is *Re Royal Hospital Kilmainham*. The hospital was founded under a charter granted by Charles II in 1684 for the support and maintenance of old soldiers of 'our army of Ireland'. It was endowed with a magnificent building (recently sumptuously restored) and extensive lands overlooking the Liffey near Dublin. It gradually ceased to function after 1921, the remaining pensioners being transferred to the Royal Hospital, Chelsea, and the building and lands vested in the Irish government. There were, however, funds in court representing compensation paid to the Hospital for some of the lands which had been compulsorily acquired for a railway in the nineteenth century. A question accordingly arose as to how these funds should be applied and ultimately the Royal Hospital Kilmainham Act 1961 was passed which provided that, on the application of the Attorney-General, the High Court might order certain payments to be made out of the income of the funds to the Royal Hospital Chelsea and settle a scheme in relation to the balance of the funds for some specified charitable purposes for the benefit of the Defence Forces.

When such an application was made to the High Court by the Attorney-General, it was conceded on his behalf that the funds did not have to be applied by the Court in the manner indicated by the Act, since the language of the Act was enabling rather that mandatory. (The draughts-man was presumably mindful of the fate that had overtaken the Sinn Fein Funds Act which had purported to deprive the High Court of any discretion in somewhat similar circumstances.)[1] It was submitted inter alia on his behalf, however, that the original gift was not charitable: it was simply the provision of the hospital by the crown as an executive act of accommodation for veterans. On this view, the property vested in the State along with other crown property in 1922. Alternatively, it was said that the defence forces as being 'the army of Ireland' were now the object of the trust. If, however, they were not the original object they should be treated as the proper object under the *cy-près* jurisdiction, since it was impractical to benefit the original objects in the manner intended by the founder. (It was accepted during the argument that there were a number of British army veterans who had served in the British army in Ireland before 1921, but obviously this was a diminishing class which in time would disappear completely.) Budd J rejected these submissions, holding that the original gift was charitable and that the defence forces were not now 'the army of Ireland' within the meaning of the charter. He also held that the original gift was an 'out and out gift' and that, in any event, it had been made with a general charitable intention. Accordingly, since it was not possible to carry out the founder's original intentions, he concluded that the property should be applied *cy-près* and that both the surviving British veterans and the present defence forces should be the beneficiaries.

The decision demonstrates interestingly how far the courts have travelled from implementing what might have been thought to be the donor's intentions when it comes to applying a gift *cy-près*. In an earlier decision Meredith J had frankly recognised this difficulty when in *Governors of Erasmus Smith School v A-G*,[2] he said:

'donors cannot be expected to provide expressly for more than the world and the time with which they are familiar.'

The 1961 Act seeks to preserve some degree of fidelity to the donor's wishes by the emphasis it places on 'the spirit of the gift.' Applying his charitable foundation for the benefit of the army of any republic—let alone an Irish republic — could hardly meet in any sense the wishes of even as affable a monarch as Charles II.

1 *Buckley (Sinn Fein) v A-G* [1950] IR 67.
2 (1932) 66 ILT 57.

The sign manual procedure

11.26 Where the donor has appointed a trustee and the charitable purposes can no longer be carried out, the appropriate procedure is, accordingly, a *cy-près* application. Where, however, no trustee is appointed but a general charitable intention can be discerned in the will or other instrument, the proper course is for the government to ensure the administration of the gift for charitable purposes under what is called the sign manual procedure. This situation arises very rarely in practice and there is only one recorded example of the invocation of the sign manual procedure in Ireland since 1922. In that case — *Merrins v A-G*[1] — the testatrix in a home made will left property for 'charity' but appointed no trustee. Black J ordered the surviving executor to submit a memorial to the government for the ascertainment of 'the government's will and pleasure' as to the application of the property.

1 [1945] 79 ILT 121.

The Commissioners for Charitable Donations and Bequests for Ireland

11.27 As we have seen the Attorney-General is the protector of charities in Ireland. Thus if it becomes necessary for the trustees to bring proceedings affecting the charity, he will normally be joined as a defendant to ensure that the interests of the charity are safeguarded. But the importance of charitable institutions in our society and the vast sums collected from the public or donated by individuals for them make it vital that their day-to-day activities should be subject to scrutiny by a body accountable to the public. This is not the role of the attorney whose involvement in the affairs of a charity may depend on the fortuitous circumstance of proceedings having been brought, but of the Commissioners for Charitable Donations and Bequests for Ireland.

This body has an interesting history. Before its establishment in 1844 charities in Ireland were accountable to a committee of fifty members. Since only one of them at any one time was a Roman Catholic, Catholic testators were reluctant to leave their money or land to the church: they were apprehensive that if their gift could not be applied as they directed, the committee (who like their successors enjoyed a limited *cy-près* jurisdiction) would apply it for the benefit of the protestant religion. It is a curious irony that it was a politician generally execrated in Ireland who was responsible for the major reform which ended this state of affairs. Sir Robert Peel—derisively christened 'Orange' Peel by O'Connell—initiated the legislation which established the Commissioners as part of a series of measures designed to remedy Irish grievances and reconcile the mass of the people to the Union.[1] The Commissioners were ten in number, of whom five had to be Roman Catholics.

1 By a further irony, his proposals were bitterly fought by a section of the hierarchy led by the redoubtable Archbishop McHale of Tuam. For a fascinating and authoritative account of the struggle, see Donal Kerr, *Peel, Priests and Politics*.

11.28 In 1961 the powers and duties of the Commissioners were modernised and clarified in the Charities Act of that year. They are now eleven in number, each commissioner being appointed by the government. The requirement as to a specified number being Catholic has dropped. As one would expect, a number of them are usually lawyers and it has been customary to appoint at least one High Court judge to be a commissioner. The Act also provides that the fact that a judge is a commissioner is not to preclude him from hearing any particular case.[1]

The powers of the Commissioners can be briefly summarised. They may, with the consent of the Attorney General institute proceedings to recover charitable funds that have been misapplied.[2] They also have general power to authorize or direct the taking of proceedings in any charitable matter or to certify to the Attorney-General their view that such proceedings should be brought.[3] They can give their opinion on any matter affecting a charity to the trustees and if the latter act on it they will be fully protected.[4] They can also authorise the trustees to compromise any proceedings brought by or against them.[5] Where there are not a sufficient number of trustees to administer a particular charity, they can appoint new ones.[6]

The Commissioners can also authorise the sale of any part of charity property and give directions as to the investment of the proceeds.[7] In the case of some charities, the instrument which established it may contain an express power for such a purpose and in that event an order of the commissioners will not be necessary. In the case of land held by religious bodies, it is not uncommon to find that the trusts have been kept off the title and from the purchasers' point of view it is not necessary in such cirucmstances to seek an authorisation from the Commissioners. But even where the trusts have been kept off the title, it is preferable from the point of view of the trustees to seek the authorisation.

The Commissioners enjoy the same jurisdiction as the High Court to frame a scheme for the application of a gift *cy-près* where the conditions already referred to have been met. The Commissioners' jurisdiction is confined, however, to cases where the charitable gift does not exceed £25,000 in value.[8]

The Commissioners are also empowered to frame *cy-près* schemes for the administration of a charity established or regulated by statutes or charter.[9] They are entitled to frame such schemes where they are satisfied that it would be for the benefit of the charity but is outside its powers because of some provision in the statute or charter.

The somewhat limited nature of the powers of the Commissioners as contrasted with their English counterparts should be noted. In England, there is provision for the registration of charities and charities so registered are conclusively presumed to be charities.

1 S 13.
2 S 23.
3 Ss 25-26.
4 S 21.
5 S 22.
6 S 43.
7 S 34.
8 S 29 as amended by s 8 of the Charities Act 1973.
9 Charities Act 1973, s 4.

Chapter 12

Resulting trusts

12.01 We have been dealing so far with trusts that come into being because of the declared intention of the party who creates the trust, ie the settlor or testator. Such trusts are the most common type of trust, but there are also trusts which arise, not because of the expressed intention of the settlor, but by operation of law. They arise either because the law presumes that it was the intention of the original owner of the property that it should be held in trust (in which case they are known as *resulting* or *implied trusts*) or because the law considers it inequitable that persons should retain property for their own benefit (in which case they are known as *constructive trusts*).

The following statement of the law by Underhill[1] was cited with approval by Lord Reid in *Vandervell v IRC*:[2]

> 'where it appears to have been the intention of the donor that the donee should not take beneficially, there will be a resulting trust in favour of the donor.'

Hence the label given by the law to such trusts: they are all instances where, because the law presumes that the donee was not intended to enjoy the property himself, it returns to the donor or his estate. By contrast, intention is not a necessary ingredient in the creation of a constructive trust: in this instance, the law imposes what it considers to be a just solution to the problem of ownership which necessitates a finding that it is held by one person in trust for another.

1 11th edn, 192.
2 [1967] 2 AC 291.

Where a resulting trust is presumed to arise

12.02 Resulting trusts have themselves been divided into two broad categories. In the first, a trust has in fact been declared but for some reason the entire beneficial interest in the property has not been disposed of. In such cases, the interest not disposed of will be held in trust for the settlor. Such a resulting trust will accordingly arise where a trust fails for uncertainty or illegality. Or it may arise where the property is conveyed by A to trustees to hold in trust for B during his lifetime but no trusts are declared of the remainder. In that event, the trustees upon the death of B will hold the property in trust for A or his successors. In the second, property is transferred by A to B voluntarily or A buys property in the name of B. In these cases, the law presumes that B was intended to hold the property in trust for A.

Trusts in the first category have been judicially described as 'automatic resulting trusts' and those in the second as 'presumed resulting trusts'.[1] This is on the basis that trusts in the first category, strictly speaking, do not depend on any presumption as to the owner's intentions but are the automatic consequence of the failure to dispose of the property. In a looser sense, however, they can be said to arise because the only intention which the law can reasonably attribute to the owner where he has for some reason failed effectively to dispose of his property is that it should revest in him or his successors (rather than escheat to the State as *bona vacantia*, for example).

1 *Re Vandervell's Trusts (No 2)* [1974] 1 All ER 47 per Megarry J.

12.03 In the case of presumed resulting trusts, the inference drawn by the law as to the intention of the owner, being no more than a presumption, may be rebutted by evidence that he intended a gift of the property. (No question of rebuttal arises in the case of automatic resulting trusts, since if there was evidence of his intention which could be given legal effect to, the resulting trust would not have arisen in the first place.) Moreover, depending on the relationship of the parties, the presumption of a resulting trust may be displaced by another presumption in favour of a gift, ie the presumption of *advancement*. Thus where property is transferred by a father into the name of his son, the presumption of a resulting trust in favour of the father is displaced by the presumption that the father intended a gift to his son.

In determining whether there is evidence to rebut the presumption of a resulting trust, the law distinguishes between acts and statements made before or at the time of the gift and those occuring subsequently. Acts and statements made by a person before or at the time of the transaction giving rise to the presumption are admissible *either* against him *or* in his favour. Thus a statement by a person that the property is to be held in trust for him and that a gift is *not* intended will be admissible in his favour if made before or at the time of the transaction.[1] Equally a statement by him that he intended a gift of the property will be admissible *against* him if made at the time. But where the statement is made *after* the transaction, the law is different: such statements will only be admissible *against* the person making them.[2] Thus a statement by the owner that he intended a gift will be admissible against him although it was made after the transaction. But a statement made after the transaction that no gift was intended will not be admitted in his favour.

1 *Williams v Williams* (1863) 32 Beav 370.
2 *Redington v Redington* [1794] 3 Ridg Parl Rep 106; *O'Brien v Shiel* (1873) IR 7 Eq 255; *R F v M F* unreported; Supreme Court; judgement delivered 24 October 1985.

The presumption of advancement

12.03A The presumption of a resulting trust may also be displaced, as we have seen, by the presumption of advancement. This arises where, because of the relationship between the parties, the law presumes that a gift was intended of property rather than that it should be held on a resulting trust for the owner. It undoubtedly arises in the case of a father and his child[1] and also extends to anyone to whom a person stands *in loco parentis*[2] (because they have assumed the responsibilities of parenthood for that person.) It was said in England in a number of cases that the presumption did not extend to the mother, because the duty of maintaining the children rested on the father and that there was no reason why the mother should be presumed to make a gift.[3] In the greatly changed circumstances of to-day, it may be doubted whether this would still be regarded as the law; and to the extent that it discriminates between parents on the basis of their sex, it would appear to be contrary to Article 42.1. of the Constitution. The distinction is difficult to reconcile with cases such as *Re Tilson*[4] in which the joint responsibilities and rights of parents in the education and upbringing of their children—as contrasted with the older common law rule of the *patria potestas* (or paternal power)—were stressed.

1 *Alleyne v Alleyne* (1845) 8 Ir Eq R 493; *Re Wall's Estate* [1922] 1 IR 59.
2 *Re Orme* (1883) 50 LT 51.
3 *Bennett v Bennett* (1879) 10 Ch D 474; *Gross v French* (1975) 238 Estates Gazette 39, CA. But note that the presumption will arise in the case of a widowed mother: *Gore-Grimes v Grimes* [1937] IR 470.
4 [1951] IR 1.

12.04 The presumption was also said to arise when a husband transferred property to his wife voluntarily or bought property in her name.[1] Because of the relationship between them, the husband was presumed to have made a gift of the property to his wife and this displaced the presumption of a resulting trust. But the reverse did not apply: where a wife transferred property to her husband voluntarily or bought it in his name, the presumption of a resulting trust in her favour was not displaced by a presumption that she was making a gift to her husband. The reason was largely historic: in the days before the Married Women's Property Act 1882, when the common law did not recognise that a married woman could dispose of property, the courts of equity took on a special role as the protector of their interests and hence the unequal treatment of husbands and wives in this context.[2]

While the distinction has never been formally abandoned either in Ireland or England, there has been a growing tendency in the latter jurisdiction to treat the doctrine of advancement as largely irrelevant to transactions between husbands and wives in contemporary society.[3] The question usually arises on the breakdown of marriage when the ownership of property, most notably the family home, has to be determined. In modern circumstances, the purchase money for the family home is rarely provided by either husband or wife, except to the extent of a relatively small deposit. The finance in the great majority of such cases is advanced on the security of a mortgage by a bank, building society or local authority and is repayable as to principal and interest by instalments over a period of anything from twenty to thirty years. In many cases, the wife is working herself and sometimes assists with the repayment of the instalments. To treat the husband as—in the absence of evidence to the contrary—making a gift of his interest to his wife because the purchase is made in her name but to refrain from drawing a similar inference in the case of the wife because of her supposedly helpless status as recognised by Victorian judges seems illogical and anomalous. In *Pettitt v Pettitt*,[4] Lord Diplock commented:

'It would, in my view, be an abuse of the legal technique for ascertaining or imputing intention to apply to transactions between the post-war generation of married couples "presumptions" which are based on inferences of fact which an earlier generation of judges drew as to the most likely intentions of earlier generations of spouses belonging to the propertied classes of a different social era.'

1 *Re Eykyn's Trust* (1877) 6 Ch D 115 at 118 per Malins V-C; *RF v MF*, above.
2 Cf *Pettitt v Pettitt* [1970] AC 777 at 824 per Lord Diplock.
3 *Ibid; Silver v Silver* [1958] 1 All ER 523 at 525 per Evershed MR.
4 Above.

12.05 There has been little discussion of the matter in reported Irish cases. In *W v W*,[1] the decision which contains the most comprehensive and generally accepted statement of the law in Ireland as to the ownership of the matrimonial home, Finlay P laid down a number of propositions, dealt with in more detail at a later stage, which expressly recognise the doctrine of advancement as applicable to transactions between husbands and wives. In *JC v JHC*,[2] where property had been purchased in the joint names of husband and wife, but all the purchase money had been contributed by the husband, Keane J referred to the already quoted remarks of Lord Diplock in *Pettitt v Pettitt* but found that in the particular case the evidence in any event pointed clearly to an intention on the part of the husband that the property should be beneficially owned by his wife and himself jointly.

In *F v F*,[3] the husband purchased a house in the joint names of his wife and himself at a stage when the marriage had already broken up but he was anxious to effect a reconciliation. The wife said that if the house were purchased in their joint names, she would resume living with him. She did not in fact do so and subsequently brought proceedings claiming to be beneficially entitled to a half share in the house. Her claim was rejected by D'Arcy J and the Supreme Court upheld his view. Having restated the doctrine of advancement in its traditional form, Henchy J went on:

'In construing conduct alleged to amount to advancement, the court's task is essentially a fact-finding one. It has to ascertain, from the admissible matters relied on by the parties, the true intention behind the transaction which has given the wife a paper title. If the relevant circumstances show that the paper result produced by the conveyance conceals the real intention of the husband in entering into the transaction, so that the benefit contended for by the wife was not intended, the court will hold that the presumption of advancement has been rebutted.'

He went on to hold that in the case being considered the presumption had been clearly rebutted, since it was plain that the husband would never have agreed to the transaction if the wife had not promised to live in the house. There is, however, no reference to the English authorities and the case accordingly affords no support to the proposititon that the presumption, in modern circumstances, is of limited relevance.

The question may also arise, however, at some stage as to whether the presumption of advancement as between husbands and wives survived the enactment of the Constitution. Since it derived from a legal system where married women had no right to dispose of property, it applied only to a transfer of property by a husband to his wife. With the removal of that disability, confining the doctrine in this manner has become increasingly anomalous and, as we have seen, the relevance of the doctrine in any form in modern conditions has been doubted in England.[4] It undoubtedly leads to an inequality of treatment which would seem to offend against Article 40.1 and is scarcely justifiable by the saving words of Article 40.1. which permit inequality of treatment arising from 'differences of capacity, physical and moral, and of social function'.

1 (1981) 1 ILRM 202, HC.
2 Unreported; judgement delivered 4 August 1982.
3 Above.
4 See Para 12.04, above.

Resulting trusts arising where the beneficial interest fails

12.06 We deal first with that category of resulting trust which arises because the entire beneficial interest in the property has not been disposed of. This may arise in a number of different ways.

(a) Trusts failing for uncertainty or lack of beneficiaries

As we have seen, a trust may fail because it is uncertain[1] and in that case there will be a resulting trust in favour of the settlor. Again, there may be simply no beneficiary, as where the property is left to someone for life and there is no remainder. Here also there will be a resulting trust in favour of the settlor.

(b) Trusts failing for illegality[2]

The general principle is the same: if the trust fails for illegality, the property will revert to the settlor. But there is one important qualification. Where a person has intentionally created an executed trust for an illegal purpose or consideration, the beneficiary is entitled to rely on the maxim *in pari delicto, potior est conditio possidentis* (ie where both parties are at fault, the person in possession is in the stronger position.) If he does, there will be no resulting trust.[3] This will not apply, however, where the illegal purpose is not carried into effect.[4] Nor will it apply where the effect of allowing the trustee to retain the property would be to effectuate an illegal object, defeat a legal prohibition or protect a fraud.[5]

Thus in *Ayerst* v *Jenkins*,[6] a man married his deceased wife's sister, which was then against the law. He transferred certain property to trustees as part of a marriage settlement and his personal representatives after his death sought to set it aside on the grounds of its illegality. The attempt was rejected by the House of Lords. The trust had been fully effectuated and refusing the claim did not implement any illegality, defeat any prohibition or protect a fraud.

(c) Surplus of funds voluntarily subscribed

A resulting trust may also arise where funds have been voluntarily donated or subscribed for a particular purpose and there is a surplus remaining after the purpose has been achieved. Here we must distinguish between three different sets of circumstances

(i) The fund may have been donated or subscribed for the benefit of named individuals. In such a case, where the purpose has been fulfilled, there will be a resulting trust in favour of the donors of any balance remaining, unless it is clear that the donors intended to part with the money absolutely or, as it is sometimes put, there was an 'out and out' gift.

Thus in the leading case of *Re Abbott's Fund Trusts*,[7] a fund had been subscribed for the maintenance of two distressed ladies. On the death of the survivor, there was a resulting trust in favour of the donors. In a later case,[8] the money had been subscribed solely for the education of the children of a deceased clergyman 'and not for equal division among them'. It was held, however, in this case that, although a balance remained after the children's education had been completed, it was not held on a resulting trust for the donors: the donors had clearly intended to part completely with their money, the education of the children being merely the motive of the gift.

(ii) The fund may have been contributed by so many donors, many of them anonymous, that it is impracticable to trace them. Thus money may have been collected by means of a flag day, a house to house collection, a bingo session or some other method involving small contributions from hundreds to anonymous donors. At one time, there was considerable doubt as to whether such a surplus had to be paid into court as being held on a resulting trust for the donors who would then have to be ascertained, or whether it was *bona vacantia*, ie property without a legal owner which vested in England in the Crown and in Ireland in the State.[9] It was only where the court was satisfied that the money had been contributed with a general charitable intention, that the obviously sensible and practicable course could be taken of applying it *cy-près*, ie to the next nearest purpose.[10]

These difficulties were removed in Ireland by s 48 of the Charities Act 1961. This provides that the High Court may apply property given for specific purposes which fail as if it were given for charitable purposes generally where it belongs

(a) to a donor who, after such advertisements and inquiries as are reasonable, cannot be identified or cannot be found, or
(b) to a donor who has executed a written disclaimer of his right to have the property returned.

In the case of cash collections through collecting boxes, lotteries, etc., it is to be conclusively presumed, without any advertisement or inquiry, that the property belongs to donors who cannot be identified and, in other cases, the court may order it to be treated as such where it would be unreasonable to incur expense, having regard to the amounts likely to be returned to the donors, or for the donors to expect the property to be returned, having regard to the nature, circumstances and amounts of the gifts.[11]

(iii) Funds of inactive or moribund clubs and societies. A club or society may have become permanently inactive or moribund because the purpose for which it was established no longer exists or circumstances have rendered the continued existence of the club meaningless. If the funds of the club are still in existence, there is authority for the proposition that they are held on a resulting trust for the members of the club,[12] but it is submitted that the better view is that in such circumstances the funds are owned by all the surviving members of the club collectively. The distinction is not entirely academic, because if the funds were held on a resulting trust, it would follow logically that the personal representatives of deceased members who had contributed to the funds should be entitled to a return pro rata of their contributions. It is clear, however, that a club consists of an association of persons whose rights as members are governed by contract. Consequently the assets of the club, unless the rules provide otherwise, are owned by all the members of the club, since that is the basis on which contributions were made in the form of subscriptions by the members. The members pay their subscriptions in return for enjoying the benefits of membership. It follows that the assets should be owned by them to the exclusion of the personal representatives of the deceased members.

The leading Irish authority is *Tierney v Tough*.[13] In that case, the plaintiffs were members of a society which was formed for the benefit of boatmen and workmen employed by the Grand Canal Company. The members' subscriptions were applicable in the main to the payment of benefit during sickness or upon death. These purposes became superfluous with the passing of the National Insurance Act 1911 and the plaintiffs took out a summons to determine to whom the remaining funds of the society belonged. The Attorney General claimed that they were vested in the Crown as *bona vacantia* or alternatively should be applied *cy-près* for charitable purposes. Both these claims were rejected by Sir Charles O' Connor MR. He also rejected the claim of the Canal company itself— which was a trustee of the society and entitled to nominate three members of the committee—to be entitled to the funds. He held that the funds were the property of the society, that the society consisted of the surviving individual members, that the property of the former was accordingly the property of the latter and that it should be divided among them in the proportions to the amounts contributed by them. He rejected the proposition which had found favour with Byrne J in *Re Printers and Transferred Amalgamated Trades Protection Society*[14] that the funds were held on a resulting trust.

It will be noted that in that case it was held that the members were entitled to the funds in the proportions contributed by them. Whether this result follows in any case will depend on the construction to be put on the rules. In the absence of any guide to the members' intentions in the rules, the funds will be divisible among the members in equal proportions.[15]

It was held in one case in England that these principles applied only to members' clubs funds. If contributions were made to a fund which was applicable solely for the benefit of persons *other* than members of the club—their wives or dependants, for example—there would not be the same basis for dividing the surplus among the members nor could it be held on a resulting trust since the contributions were made on a contractual basis. But the surviving members of the club would, on this analysis, be entitled to a surplus of funds on the ground that the contract of membership has been frustrated or there had been a failure of consideration. This was the view taken by Goff J in *Re West Sussex Constabulary Trust*[16] but disapproved of by Walton J in *Re Bucks Constabulary etc Fund Friendly Society*.[17] It appears that Goff J's view was based on the decision of the Court of Appeal in *Cunnack v Edwards*,[18] where the funds of a society intended to be applied solely to the widows of the members were declared to be bona vacantia, when there was only one member of the society left. It has been pointed out that *Cunnack v Edwards* is explicable by reference to the wording of the relevant statute governing friendly societies to which the society was subject and to the fact that the principle of dividing the property among the surviving members could not be applied where only one member survived.[19]

It is thought that the criticisms of the *West Sussex* case are well founded and that there should be no difference in principle between a case where the members' funds are intended to be used for their own benefit and one in which they are solely applicable to other persons, such as their wives or dependants: in either case, the members collectively are entitled to determine the destination of the funds and this should exclude any question of *bona vacantia* or a resulting trust benefiting the estates of deceased members.

(iv) Residue after satisfaction of express trust. Sometimes property is assigned to trustees with a specific object in mind, such as the payment of the assignor's debts. Clearly, any residue left after the property has been sold and the creditors paid belongs on a resulting trust to the assignor. If, however, it should appear that there was an intention to assign the property for better or worse in satisfaction of the debts—in other words, if the assignment of the property constituted an accord and satisfaction between the debtor and his creditors—this presumption of a resulting trust will be excluded and the surplus will belong to the creditors.[20]

1 See para 7.01, above.
2 As to such trusts, see Chapter 14, below.
3 *Re Great Berlin Steamboat Co* (1884) 26 Ch D 61.
4 *Birch v Blagrave* (1755) Amb 264.
5 *Ayerst v Jenkins*, (1873) LR 16 Eq 275.
6 Above.
7 [1900] 2 Ch 326.
8 *Re Andrew's Trust* [1905] 2 Ch 48.
9 In *Re Gillingham Bus Disaster Fund* [1958] Ch 300, Harman J held that a surplus should be paid into court despite manifest difficulty in ascertaining who the donors were, but a different view was taken by Goff J in *Re West Sussex Constabularly etc Trust* [1971] Ch 1.
10 See paras 11.22-11.23, above.
11 Note that in Ireland these provision are applicable whether the specific purposes which fail are charitable or non-charitable. The corresponding provisions in England and Northern Ireland apply only where the specific purposes which fail are charitable.
12 *Re Printers and Transferred Amalgamated Trades Protection Society* [1899] 2 Ch 184.
13 [1914] I IR 142.
14 Above.
15 Underhill, p 258.
16 Above,
17 [1979] 1 All ER 623.
18 [1896] 2 Ch 679
19 Underhill, p 259.
20 *King v Denison* (1813) 1 Ves & B 260; *Smith v Cooke* [1891] AC 297.

Resulting trusts arising from voluntary dispositions

12.07 A presumption of a resulting trust arises where A has conveyed or transferred property to B, or A and B jointly, there is no consideration for the conveyance or transfer and the document is silent as to the intention of the donor.[1] It must be stressed again, however, that it is no more than a presumption and may be easily rebutted.

The presumption applies to voluntary conveyances and transfers of both real and personal property. In the case of freehold land, however, the law in Ireland is somewhat different from that in England and it is therefore desirable to treat voluntary conveyances of freehold land separately.

(a) Freehold land

As we have already seen, the Statute of Uses (Ireland) 1634,[2] like its English counterpart, was intended to put an end to the practice of granting land to passive feoffees to uses, thereby depriving the crown of its feudal dues. After the statute, where land was conveyed to such a passive feoffee to uses, the use was automatically executed. Nor could this be circumvented by declaring a second use: in such a case the second limitation was simply ignored, upon the principle, laid down in *Tyrrel's Case*,[3] that there could not be a use upon a use. The courts of equity, however, by developing the concept of the trust compelled the owner of the legal estate to hold it in trust for the person beneficially entitled. But if a conveyance of land was made 'to A and his heirs' and no uses were declared, there was a resulting use to the grantor. In order to avoid such a resulting use arising, it was necessary to convey the property 'unto *and to the use of A* and his heirs.'[4] After the simplification of conveyancing by nineteenth century legislation, such a formula was strictly unnecessary in the case of a conveyance for value, but was still employed in order to eliminate the necessity for subsequently proving that consideration had been given. In the case of a voluntary conveyance, however, it remained essential to prevent a resulting use arising. But even where the proper conveyancing formula was used, there was still a presumption of a resulting *trust* in favour of the settlor, at least in the view of some eminent authorities, most notably Maitland.[5]

This is still the position in Ireland, where there is no equivalent to s 60 (3) of the Law of Property Act 1925 in England which provides that:

'In a voluntary conveyance, a resulting trust for the grantor shall not be implied merely by reason that the property is not expressed to be conveyed for the use or benefit of the grantee.'

Even in that jurisdiction, it is not clear whether the effect of the section is to put an end to the presumption of a resulting trust: in *Hodgson v Marks*, [6]Russell LJ described that proposition as 'debateable'. It is thought, however that there is no room for doubt in this jurisdiction and that here the presumption of a resulting trust still arises in the case of a voluntary conveyance of freehold land.

(b) Other property

In the case of other property, the law was thus stated by Lord Upjohn in *Vandervell v IRC*:[7]

'Where A transfers, or directs a trustee for him, to transfer the legal estate in property to B otherwise than for valuable consideration it is a question of the intention of A in making the transfer whether B is to take beneficially or on trust and, if the latter, on what trusts. If as a matter of construction of the document transferring the legal interest, it is possible to discern B's intentions, that is the end of the matter and no extraneous evidence is admissible to correct and qualify his intentions as ascertained. If, however, as in this case (a common form transfer of shares) the document is silent, then there is said to arise a resulting trust in favour of A; but this is only a presumption and is easily rebutted.'

Vandervell v IRC neatly illustrates the importance of the distinction between the resulting and constructive trusts. In that case, V, a wealthy businessman had transferred shares in a private company of which he was the principal shareholder to a trust company: some of those shares were held by the trust company in trust for his children. He also wished to make a gift of £150,000 to the Royal College of Surgeons in order to found a chair of medicine. This was done by transferring a further parcel of shares in the private company to the college and then declaring dividends on them to the required amount. At that stage, there was no reason why the college should go on owning the shares and this indeed was thought likely to create problems if the private company were subsequently floated. Accordingly, as part of the scheme the trust company were given the option of repurchasing the shares at £5000, a sum far below the real value of the shares. Unfortunately, no one seems to have adverted to the question of who was then to be entitled to the shares and they were left in a perilous limbo. It was essential from V's point of view that he should not retain any semblance of ownership to the shares, since that would involve him in calamitous tax consequences. The revenue claimed that since no trusts had been declared by V in respect of the shares, they could only be held by the trust company on a resulting trust in favour of V. It was argued on V's behalf that it was clearly his intention to part with all his beneficial interest in the shares and that they were held by the trust company either on the trusts of the children's settlement or beneficially. The argument that they were held on the trusts of the children's settlement does not appear to have been pressed very strongly and in the end V was driven to contend that they were held beneficially by the trust company on a form of 'gentleman's agreement' that the trust company would act in accordance with his wishes. By a majority, the House of Lords upheld the Revenue's contention. The evidence did not indicate any intention on the part of V that the trust company would own the shares in their own right and accordingly the presumption of a resulting trust had not been rebutted.

In Vandervell's case, all those interested in the property—the children, the college, the trust company and V himself—would surely not have wished to see V paying large sums to the revenue as a result of his generosity. If the principles associated with a constructive trust were being applied—arriving at an equitable conclusion as to the ownership of the property without being fettered by the known or assumed intentions of the parties—the trust company would have been held entitled to the shares beneficially. But this was not the issue in the case: the contest was not between competing interests in the property itself but between the revenue and the taxpayer. In such disputes, there is no room for broadly equitable solutions: either the tax is payable or it is not. And so the inexorable logic of the resulting trust, which is primarily designed to ascertain the ownership of property where the trusts have not been declared in full rather than imposing a solution in accordance with equitable principles, led to a conclusion that no one concerned in the property could have desired.

1 *Doyle v Byrne* (1922) 56 ILT 125.
2 Para 2.06, above.
3 (1557) 2 Dyer 155a.
4 See para 2.06, above.
5 Maitland, Equity, p 79.
6 [1971] Ch 892.
7 [1967] 2 AC 291.

12.08 A similar approach can be seen in cases concerned with money placed in a bank account in the joint names of the depositor and another person. Here the courts in Ireland have applied the doctrine of the resulting trust, where to do otherwise would conflict with another potent force in the law: the statute law governing testamentary succession.

Placing money on joint deposit receipt in the bank has been a traditional method in Ireland—particularly in rural areas—of seeing to the succession to one's cash on one's death without bringing down a claim by the revenue for duty by making a will. (It may also sometimes have been prompted by a desire to avoid the publication of the concealed bequest in a will.) In such a case, the depositor usually intends to have the interest paid to him during his lifetime, while ensuring that the capital goes to the person whom he wishes to benefit on his death. It may be that the form of the deposit receipt precludes either of the persons named in the receipt from dealing with the capital without the consent of the other. But whatever may be the position in such a case, there can be no doubt that in Ireland if the donor retains a power of disposing of the capital, a resulting trust arises in his favour, and upon his death the property goes to his next-of-kin, if there is an intestacy, or his residuary legatee, if there is a will.

This was so held by the Supreme Court in the leading case of *Owens v Greene*; *Freely v Greene*.[1] An old man, AF, kept large sums of money on deposit in the bank in the joint names of himself, and PF, a distant cousin. He asked the manager to make sure that the receipt was in such a form that he (AF) could draw the interest without going to PF. He withdrew and relodged the cash on several occasions and eventually deposited some of it in the joint names of himself and Father O, who was not related to him. He made it clear to the manager that PF and Father O were to be entitled to the money if anything happened to him. After his death, PF and Father O claimed the money, but it was held unanimously by the Supreme Court that they had failed to rebut the presumption of a resulting trust in favour of AF's executor. It was clear from the evidence that AF had not intended to part with the money during his lifetime and that in these circumstances he was attempting to make a testamentary disposition without complying with the relevant statutes: consequently there was no enforceable trust in favour of PF and Father O. The court applied earlier Irish decisions such as *O'Flaherty v Browne*,[2] and *Gason v Rich*[3] and disapproved of a decision to a contrary effect by Gibson J in *Diver v McCrea*.[4] It is also clear from the judgement of FitzGibbon J that he considered the same principle applicable where the form of the receipt made it impossible for the donor to deal with the capital without the concurrence of the donee: a resulting trust still arose in favour of the donor.[5] That also appears to have been the view of Kennedy CJ, although his judgement lays stress on the possibility of rebutting the presumption by appropriate evidence:

'If he had finally made up his mind .... as to how he would dispose of his monies, it was, in my opinion, competent for him to have placed his monies on joint deposit account as he did, with the intention of making then and there immediate complete gifts in trust for himself and (PF) in the one case and Father (O) in the other case as joint tenants with right of survivorship as regards the capital sums only, the interest to be paid to him (AF) during his life, such intention as regards the capital not to be capable of alteration .....'[6]

It was clear, however, that in that case the evidence did not support such a finding.

A different view has been taken in England: in *Young* v *Sealey*,[7] Romer J, while confessing that he was attracted by the reasoning of *Owens* v *Greene*, felt coerced by earlier English decisions not to follow it. It had been followed,however, in some Canadian decisions.[8] It remains, of course, the law in Ireland unless over-ruled by the Supreme Court, who are not fettered by *stare decisis*.[9] There seems no good reason why it should not continue to be applied: the English decisions such as *Young* v *Sealey* appear to permit the making of 'noncupative' wills, as they are sometimes called, without any logical justification.

1 [1932] IR 225, SC.
2 [1907] 2 IR 416.
3 (1887) 19 LR Ir 391.
4 (1908) 42 ILT 249.
5 At p 245.
6 At p 239.
7 [1949] Ch 278.
8 Underhill, p 274.
9 See para 2.22, above.

12.09 It is clear that the resulting trust which arises in such circumstances may be displaced by the presumption of advancement. (The beneficiaries in *Owens* v *Greene*[1] could not rely on such a presumption.) This has led to some problems, however, in the related area of bank accounts in the joint names of husband and wife. This is, of course, a common arrangement to-day: the problem arises if, on the death of the husband, the account is in credit as a result of money lodged by him. Does this belong to his estate? Or is the wife entitled to it, the presumption of a resulting trust being displaced by the presumption of advancement in her favour? In a number of English decisions, it has been held that the answer depends on whether the account was opened in joint names simply as a matter of convenience to enable both parties to the marriage to draw upon it when they wished, or whether it was intended to make provision for the wife out of it. This latter intention will be more readily inferred, it would appear, if the account was operated by the husband alone.

Another problem arises in the case of such a joint bank account, where husband and wife have both contributed to it and a dispute arises as to the ownership of a credit balance in the account or of investments made with the money in the account. The general rule is that the parties are entitled to share the funds in the account equally and not in proportion to their contributions, and in *Jones* v *Maynard*,[2] Vaisey J said that they were also entitled to share equally in any investments made with the funds. In that case, however, there was evidence that the parties intended investments made out of the funds in the account to represent 'our savings'. In *Re Bishop*,[3] Stamp J said that where both parties are entitled to draw on an account, an investment made by husband or wife with money so withdrawn will belong to the party in whose name the investment is made. Similarly, if the investment is made in the joint names of husband and wife, they will be entitled to it jointly and no question of a resulting trust or of the presumption of advancement will arise. (It should be remembered that we are here concerned with cases in which husband and wife have both been contributing to the joint account. Where the money has been contributed by the husband alone, the question as to whether an advancement to the wife should be presumed will depend, as we have seen, on whether the account being in the names of both is simply a matter of convenience or whether it was intended to make provision for the wife.)

1 Above.
2 [1951] Ch 572.
3 [1965] Ch 450.

12.10 The Irish decisions on joint deposit accounts such as *Owens v Greene*[1] have been criticised by some academic writers, at least so far as the reasoning on which they are based is concerned.[2] It has been pointed out that they proceed on the assumption that there is a resulting trust of the *money* in the bank and that this overlooks the fact that the customer does not *own* money in that sense: the bank is indebted to him to the extent that his account is in credit. The relationship of banker and customer is one of contract and unless the depositor, in placing the money in joint names, can be said to be acting as an agent of the other person, that person has no right to sue the bank for the money. (It will be recalled that in our law a person cannot enforce by action benefits conferred on by him by a contract to which he is not a party.)[3] Unless such an agency can be proved, there is nothing to be held in trust, not even the chose in action consisting of the customer's right to sue the bank. Consequently, there cannot be a resulting trust and it would also follow that the presumption of advancement cannot arise, since it only becomes relevant in rebuttal of the presumption of a resulting trust.

On this analysis, the decision in *Owens v Greene* can still be supported on the ground that that was a case of an incompletely constituted trust in favour of volunteers, which as we have already seen the law will not enforce.[4] There are indeed passages in the judgement of FitzGibbon J which would suggest that this was how he was regarding it.[5] If the chose in action consisting of the customer's right to sue the bank had been validly assigned either in law or equity, this would have been a completely constituted trust and no problem need have arisen. Similarly, if there was an express declaration of trust by the depositor. But this would not explain the cases in which a wife or other person entitled to the presumption of advancement succeeded where they were named in the deposit receipt. Here it is necessary to postulate the resulting trust in order to bring the doctrine of advancement into play and the theoretical basis of the decisions remains unclear. Less difficulty may be seen where the name of the person to be benefited is added *subsequently* by the depositor: here it may be possible to establish that the issue of the receipt in the new form constitutes the legal assignment of the chose of action. This was so held by Gavan Duffy J in *Murray v Murray and Another*[6] where he held that the depositor's action in signing a requisition for a new form of receipt satisfied the requirements of 'notice' and 'writing' of the relevant section of the Judicature (Ir) Act 1877.

Fortunately many of these difficulties are removed by s 8 of the Married Women's Status Act 1957 under which contracts for the benefit of spouses and children are enforceable by the spouses and children in their own name as though they were parties to the contract, provided that the contract is expressed to be for the benefit of, or by its express terms purports to confer a benefit upon, the spouse or child.

1 Above.
2 Sheridan, 'Reflections on Irish Deposit Receipts' (1950-2) 9 NILQ 101; V.T.H.D. 'Joint Deposit Accounts: Some Misconceptions' (1957) 23 Ir Jur 31.
3 See para 6.03, above.
4 See para 8.07, above.
5 At pp 246-247.
6 [1939] IR 317.

12.11 The general principle, as we have seen, is that property held on a resulting trust 'results' to the settlor. (The special considerations affecting surplus funds of clubs and societies and related problems have already been discussed.)[1] There is, however, one notable exception, sometimes referred to as the rule in *Lassance* v *Tierney*[2] and sometimes as the rule in *Hancock* v *Watson*.[3] Where property is given to a person absolutely in the first instance and then trusts are engrafted on that interest which fail for some reason, the resulting trust will be in favour of the person absolutely entitled. But it must be clear that an absolute interest was intended in the first instance.

Where neither the settlor nor his next of kin are ascertainable, the property vests in the Minister for Finance and the Public Service as *bona vacantia*.[4]

1 See para 12.06, above.
2 (1849) 1 Mac & G 551. It was applied by the Supreme Court in *Re D'Arcy, Russell* v *D'Arcy* [1938] IR 171.
3 (1902) AC 14.
4 State Property Act 1954, s 29.

Resulting trusts arising where the purchase money has been provided in whole or in part by a third party

12.12 Where A has provided the purchase money for property which has been conveyed or transferred to B, or A and B jointly, B will hold the property on a resulting trust for A. This has been the law since *Dyer v Dyer*,[1] but the application of the principle has given rise to much difficulty in modern times where the property purchased is a matrimonial home.

It is clear that where the property is purchased with money provided by the husband but is conveyed or transferred to the husband and wife jointly, they will be beneficially entitled to the property as joint tenants.[2] The presumption of a resulting trust which would normally arise is rebutted by the presumption of advancement, which has already been explained. Where however, the purchase money is provided by the wife and the property is conveyed to the husband and wife jointly, the presumption of advancement does not operate and accordingly, in the absence of rebutting evidence, the property will be held on a resulting trust for the wife.[3] Similarly, where the property is conveyed or transferred into the sole name of the wife, having been purchased with money provided by the husband, she will be presumed to be solely entitled beneficially under the presumption of advancement.[4] Where, however, it is purchased with money solely provided by the wife but conveyed or transferred into the name of the husband, he will hold it on a resulting trust for the wife, the presumption of advancement not applying in this case.[5] As we have seen, the Irish courts have not so far adopted the approach favoured in recent English decisions of treating the doctrine of advancement as of lesser importance in modern conditions and its constitutionality has yet to be tested.[6]

1 (1788) 2 Cox Eq Cas 92 at 93 per Eyre CB.
2 *Re Eykyn's Trusts*, above; *W v W* above.
3 *Rich v Cockell* (1804) 9 Ves 369; *W v W, above.*
4 *Re Eykyn's Trusts*, above; *W v W*, above.
5 *Mercier v Mercier* [1903] 2 Ch 98 CA; *W v W*,above.
6 See para 12.05, above.

12.13 It is more usual in modern conditions for the matrimonial home to be purchased with the assistance of a mortgage, usually repayable by instalments over a lengthy period. In such circumstances, both parties may effectively contribute to the purchase price, whether by paying some or all of the deposit or some or all of the instalments. Sometimes the contribution to the purchase price by either party may be indirect, as where the parties pool their earnings when they are both working and mortgage repayments are made out of the pool. It is clear beyond doubt that, where the property is in the husband's name and the wife makes reasonably significant contributions to the deposit or the repayment of the instalments or both, the husband will be a trustee for the wife of a share in the property roughly corresponding to the proportion of the purchase money represented by the wife's total contribution. This was so held by Kenny J in *C v C*[1] and the same view was taken by Finlay P in *W v W*[2] and by the Supreme Court in *McC v McC*.[3]

What is far less clear is the position when the contributions are indirect. Both parties may have contributed their income to a common pool from which the mortgage repayments are met. Or the wife may out of her earnings have paid for various household expenses which would normally have been the husband's responsibility and thereby made it easier for him to make the repayments while preserving the family's standard of living. In other cases, the contributions relied on have been in the form of work carried out by one of the parties to the house or improvements of one sort or another effected to it. And where no financial contributions, direct or indirect, have been made, it has been suggested that the wife's activities in looking after the children and performing household tasks is a contribution analogous to a financial contribution which should give her a beneficial interest in the house itself.[4]

As we have seen, a resulting trust comes into being because the law assumes from the circumstances that it was the intention of the owner of the property that it should be held in trust for him. In the case of a matrimonial home or other property acquired when people are married, the parties naturally do not contemplate the breakdown of the marriage and the law in presuming that a resulting trust has come into existence is not saying that the property was acquired by husband or wife with the intention that it should be held on trust for one or other of them. It is rather inferring from the circumstances of the case that, had they addressed their minds to the matter at the time the property was acquired, it would have been their intention that it should be so held. In the case of an instalment mortgage, the repayments relied on may have been made after the property was acquired and similarly with improvements effected to the property. It may be for this reason that the courts have wavered between treating the trust which may arise as a resulting trust and as a constructive trust.[5] The difficulty with treating it as a resulting trust is that one is imputing to the parties an intention to create a trust from their actions *after* the property was acquired. The same difficulty does not arise in treating it as a constructive trust, since in that instance, as we have seen, the trust is imposed as the just and equitable solution to the problem of ownership irrespective of the intentions of the parties, actual or imputed.

In the leading English case, *Gissing* v *Gissing*[6] the law lords were satisfied that the expenditure relied on by the husband as giving him an interest in the matrimonial home purchased in his wife's name and with her money was insufficient to justify the inference that she held the property to any extent in trust for him. They were not in agreement however, as to the nature of the contributions which would be sufficient to justify such an inference. Lord Diplock said:

'Where the wife has made no initial contribution to the cash deposit and legal charges and no direct contribution to the mortgage instalment nor any adjustment to her contribution to other expenses of the household which it can be inferred was referable to the acquisition of the house, there is, in the absence of evidence of an express agreement between the parties, no material to justify the court in inferring that it was the common intention of the parties that she should have any beneficial interest in a matrimonial home conveyed into the sole name of her husband, merely because she continued to contribute out of her own earnings or private income to other expenses of the household. For such conduct is no less consistent with a common intention to share the day-to-day expenses of the household, while each spouse retains a separate interest in capital assets acquired with their own monies or obtained by inheritance or gift.'[7]

Lord Reid, however, took a different view, saying that he saw no good reason for the distinction, which he thought in many cases would be 'unworkable'.[8] In a number of cases in the Court of Appeal, presided over by Lord Denning MR,[9] however, it was held that the inference of a trust may be drawn even in the case of an indirect contribution to the mortgage repayments taking the form of payments for household expenses. But when the issue came before the Court of Appeal in Northern Ireland in *McFarlane v McFarlane*,[10] the view of Lord Diplock in *Gissing v Gissing* was preferred. Lord McDermott LCJ said

'The conclusion I have reached on this important and difficult question is that there is a relevant distinction between the two types of contribution and that the indirect contribution if it is to earn a beneficial interest in the property acquired must be the subject of agreement or arrangement between the spouses. Here I do not refer to a contractual relationship solely, but would include any understanding between the spouses which shows a mutual intention that the indirect contributions of one or the other will go to create a beneficial proprietary interest in the contributor.'

1 [1976] IR 254.
2 Above.
3 (1986) 6 ILRM 1.
4 Shatter, *Family Law in the Republic of Ireland*, 3rd edn, p 511, n155.
5 See para 12.16, below.

6 [1971] AC 886.
7 At pp 909-910.
8 At p 896.
9 *Falconer v Falconer* [1970] 3 All ER 449; *Hargrave v Newton* [1971] 3 All ER 866; *Hazell v Hazell* [1972] 1 All ER 923; *Kowalczuk v Kowalczuk* [1973] 2 All ER 1042.
10 [1972] NI 59, CA.

12.14 The first Irish case in which the question was considered was *C v C*.[1] In that case, the wife paid the deposit on the house and also paid a number of mortgage instalments. It was not, accordingly, a case of indirect contributions. Kenny J, however, in the following passage hints that indirect contributions may have the same effect:

'When the matrimonial home is purchased in the name of the husband, either before or after a marriage, the wife does not become entitled as wife to any share in the ownership either because she occupies the status of wife, or because she carries out household duties. In many cases, however, the wife contributes to the purchase price or mortgage instalments. Her contributions may be either by payment to the husband of monies which she has inherited or earned *or by paying the expenses of the household so that he has the money which makes it possible for him to pay the mortgage instalments ..... '*[2]

In *McGill v S*,[3] Gannon J declined to treat this passage as authority for the proposition that the sharing of expenses without more could lead the court to infer the relationship of trustee and beneficiary, saying

'The Court will not impute a relationship of trustee and cestui que trust from the facts of a couple living together in (or seemingly in) the married state and sharing expenses without any more cogent evidence. I do not think that Mr Justice Kenny intended to indicate anything short of this in the two judgements from which extracts were quoted .....'[4]

That was a claim by the defendant in respect of expenditure by her on the house in which she was cohabiting with the plaintiff, but it is clear that the same principles would be applicable to spouses. Gannon J cited the passage already referred to from the speech of Lord Diplock in *Gissing v Gissing* and a passage from the judgement of Sir Robert Lowry in *McFarlane v McFarlane* (which was to the same effect as the passage from the judgement of Lord McDermott LCJ already referred.to) and clearly preferred these views to those of the English Court of Appeal.

A different view had been taken by MacMahon J in *R v R*[5] decided before *McGill v S* but not referred to in the latter case. In that case, the wife spent some of her earnings on providing food and other requisites for the household and some on herself for clothes and having her hair done. McMahon J held that where the wife's earnings are used for household expenses and as a result the husband has additional money with which to pay the mortgage instalments, this will be sufficient to give her a claim to a beneficial interest.

The decisions of Kenny J in *C v C* and Gannon J in *McGill v S* were considered by Finlay P in *W v W*.[6] In that case, the wife claimed a beneficial interest in a farm which was registered on a folio in the name of her husband. The evidence established that certain mortgages to which the farm was subject had been paid off by means in part of sums contributed by the wife and that her money had also been used in carrying out improvements to the farm and the buildings and stock on it. Having referred to the authorities, Finlay P laid down the following general principles:

'1. Where a wife contributes by money to the purchase of a property by her husband in his sole name, in the absence of some inconsistent agreement or arrangement, the Court will decide that the wife is entitled to an equitable interest in that property approximately proportionate to the extent of her contribution as against the total value of the property at the time the contribution was made.

'2. Where a husband makes a contribution to the purchase of property in his wife's sole name, he will be presumed by a rebuttable presumption to have intended to advance his wife and will have no claim to an equitable estate in the property unless that presumption is rebutted. If it is, he would have a claim similar to that indicated in respect of the wife with which I have already dealt.

'3. Where a wife contributes either directly towards the repayment of mortgage instalments or contributes to a general family fund thus releasing her husband from an obligation which he otherwise would have to discharge liabilities out of that fund and permitting him to repay mortgage instalments she will in the absence of proof of an inconsistent agreement or arrangement be entitled to an equitable share in the property which had been mortgaged and in respect of which the mortgage was redeemed approximately proportionate to her contribution to the mortgage repayments, to the value of the mortgage thus redeemed and to the total value of the property at the relevant time.

'4. Where a husband contributes either directly or indirectly in the manner which I have already outlined to the repayment of mortgage charges on property which is in the legal ownership of the wife, subject to the presumption of advancement and in the event of a rebuttal of that presumption, he would have a like claim to an equitable estate in the property.

'5. Where a wife expends monies or carries out work in the improvement of a property which has been originally acquired by and the legal ownership in which is solely vested in her husband, she will have no claim in respect of such contribution unless she establishes by evidence that from the circumstances surrounding the making of it she was led to believe (or of course that it was specifically agreed) that she would be recompensed for it. Even where such a right to recompense is established either by an expressed agreement or by circumstances in which the wife making the contribution was led to such belief, it is a right to recompense in monies only and does not constitute a right to claim an equitable share in the estate of the property concerned.

'6. A husband making contributions in like manner to property originally acquired by and solely owned as to the legal estate by his wife may again, subject to a rebuttal of presumption of advancement which would arise, have a like claim to compensation in similar circumstances but would not have a claim to any equitable estate in the property.'

Applying these principles, he directed an issue to be tried as to the extent to which the wife had contributed to the repayment of the mortgages. He rejected, however, the claim to an equitable interest to the extent that it was based on improvements carried out to the farm to which the wife had contributed.

Some important features of the principles laid down by Finlay P should be noted. In the first place, while he accepts that direct contributions to the repayment of a mortgage will always give the wife a proportionate share in the equitable estate—or, in other words, will create the presumption of a resulting trust—the same consequence will only follow in the case of indirect contributions if the contributions are made to a 'general family fund'. While *R v R* is not referred to, *McGill v S* is and it seems reasonable to conclude that Finlay P agreed with the view of Gannon J that the sharing of household expenses would not of itself support the inference of a resulting trust. In the second place, Finlay P rejects the suggestion that the carrying out of any work to the premises by either spouse *after* its acquisition can ever be sufficient, however substantial it may be, to enable an equitable interest to be a resulting trust to be created. The most it can give is a personal right to the spouse to recover the money which the spouse was led to believe that she would be repaid or where there was an express agreement to that effect.

The difficulty in establishing the borderline between contributions to the repayment of the mortgage which will give rise to a resulting trust and indirect contributions which will not is illustrated by two subsequent decisions. In *B v B*,[7] Barrington J accepted the wife's evidence that there was a 'kind of an agreement' under which the husband paid the mortgage repayments and the ESB bills and the wife bought virtually everything else that was needed for the house. This clearly approximates more closely to the 'general family fund' arrangement referred to by Finlay P and in the event the wife was found to have acquired an equitable interest. By contrast in *G v D*,[8] there was no agreement even of the loosest kind: the wife simply kept on paying her salary into her bank account as she had done before her marriage and regularly spent part of it on the housekeeping. Keane J rejected the wife's claim to a beneficial interest, declining to follow the decision of McMahon J in *R v R* and expressly adopting the approach of Lord Diplock in *Gissing v Gissing* and the Northern Ireland Court of Appeal in *McFarlane v McFarlane*.

The subject was considered for the first time by the Supreme Court in *McC v McC*.[9] In that case, the wife's contribution of £600 was utilised entirely in furnishing and fitting out a house, the purchase of which was wholly financed by an advance given by the husband's employers and secured by a mortgage. The Supreme Court upheld the conclusion of Costello J that the wife was entitled only to a one-third share in the furniture and fittings. Henchy J said that since the decision of Kenny J in *C v C*.

'it has been judicially accepted that where the matrimonial home has been purchased in the name of the husband, and the wife has, either directly or indirectly, made contributions towards the purchase price or mortgage instalments, the husband will be held to be a trustee for the wife of a share in the house roughly corresponding with the proportion of the purchase money represented by the wife's total contribution. Such a trust will be inferred when the wife's contribution is of such a size and kind as will justify the conclusion that the acquisition of the house was achieved by the joint efforts of the spouses.

'When the wife's contribution has been indirect (such as contributing, by means of her earnings, to a general family fund) the court will, in the absence of any express or implied agreement to the contrary, infer a trust in favour of the wife, on the ground that she has to that extent relieved the husband of the financial burden he incurred in purchasing the house.'

It would appear from this passage that Henchy J was adopting a similar approach to that of Finlay P in *W v W*, since he uses the same expression ' a general family fund' in dealing with the circumstances in which indirect contributions will give the wife an equitable interest. Since he treats this as merely an example, however, of the manner in which indirect contributions will support such an inference, it cannot be said that he is necessarily excluding indirect contributions of the type found sufficient by McMahon J in *R v R* and insufficient by Keane J in *G v D*.

1 Above.
2 At p 256.
3 [1979] IR 283.
4 At p 289.
5 Unreported; judgement delivered 12 January 1979.
6 Above.
7 (1980) ILRM 257.
8 Unreported; judgement delivered 24 April 1981.
9 (1986) 6 ILRM 1.

12.15 While there remain, accordingly, areas in which certainty is not possible, it would seem clear that the law in Ireland is as follows.

(a) The mere fact that a house is purchased as a matrimonial home does not give both spouses an interest in it. This is clear from the decisions of Kenny J in *C v C*[1] and Barrington J in *B v B*[2] and has not been questioned in subsequent decisions. The doctrine that the house, furniture and other property acquired as part of the process of building a matrimonial home are 'family assets' which should be divided between the spouses in such shares as the court considers just and equitable was developed in the Court of Appeal in England under the influence of Lord Denning MR but was rejected by the House of Lords in *Pettitt v Pettitt*[3] and our courts have taken a similar approach. The jurisdiction given to the courts by the Married Women's Status Act 1957 to determine questions arising between husband and wife as to the title to property does not empower the court to divide the property between husband and wife in such proportions as the court considers just and equitable.

(b) Where the matrimonial home is purchased in the joint names of the husband and wife, the inference will normally be drawn that they are entitled to the property jointly. This inference will follow even though the husband has contributed all the purchase money, because of the doctrine of advancement. Where, however, the purchase money is provided entirely by the wife, the property will be held on a resulting trust for her.[4]

(c) Where the matrimonial home is purchased in the name of the husband, but the wife has contributed significantly to the purchase price or the repayment of the mortgage, the property will be held on a resulting trust to the extent of her contributions. If, however, it is purchased in the name of the wife, the same result will not follow where the husband has made such contributions, unless he can rebut the presumption of advancement.[5]

(d) Where the wife's contribution has been indirect in the form of a contribution to a general family fund which is used in part to repay mortgage instalments, the property will be held on a resulting trust for her to the extent of her contributions. It is less clear whether the same result will follow if there is no 'family fund' or anything which could be said to constitute an 'arrangement' from which it could be inferred that there was an implied agreement that the property should be jointly owned. The judgement of Henchy J in *McC v McC*,[6] however, seems more in accord with the approach of Lord Reid in *Gissing v Gissing*[7] than that of Lord Diplock in the same case and the Northern Ireland Court of Appeal in *MacFarlane v MacFarlane*.[8] It accordingly seems more likely that indirect contributions, even where they take the form of payment of some household expenses without any further evidence of an agreement or arrangement will ultimately be held by the Supreme Court to be capable of giving rise to the inference of a resulting trust, provided they are significant in extent, contrary to the views expressed by Gannon J in *McGill v S*,[9] Keane J in *G v D*,[10] Murphy J in *SD v SD*[11] and Mackenzie J in *B v B*.[12]

(e) Money spent on improvements to the property after it has been acquired cannot give rise to a trust, although it may give a personal right to recovery of the money where the person spending it has been led to believe that it will be repaid. There need not be an express agreement to found such a right and it might be thought that where the expenditure is relatively substantial, the inference might be readily enough drawn. But in *D v D*,[13]Barron J declined to draw such an inference although the expenditure by the wife was relatively substantial and was on the building of a house on land already acquired in the husband's name.

(f) The carrying out by a wife of her normal household activities including the care of children will not normally entitle her to an equitable interest in the family home. This, as has been seen, was the view taken by Kenny J in *C v C* [14]and it was endorsed by Finlay P in *RK v MK*.[15] It has been suggested that this view of the law may be inconsistent with Article 41.2 of the Constitution which recognises that 'by her life within the home, woman gives to the State a support without which the common good cannot be achieved,' and requires the State 'to ensure that mothers shall not be obliged by economic necessity to engage in labour to the neglect of their duties in the home.' But there seem to be serious difficulties in the way of such an argument. If a working wife by contributing to the purchase from her earnings enables the family to live in a more attractive home, allowing her an equitable interest would seem to encourage other wives to do the same, in contravention of the philosophy enshrined in Article 41.2. Surviving as it does from a different era in Irish social history, Article 41.2 is probably of little practical assistance in developing sensible legal principles in this area.[16]

1 Above.
3 Above.
5 Ibid.
7 Above.
9 Above.

2 Above.
4 Above.
6 Above.
8 Above.
10 Above.

11 Unreported; judgement delivered 1974.
12 Unreported; judgement delivered April 1986. See further Shatter, op cit, pp 492-495; Cooney, 'Wives, Mistresses and Beneficial Ownership' (1979) 14 Ir Jur (ns) 1; Brady, 'Trusts, Law Reform and the Emancipation of Women', (1984) 6 DULJ 1; O'Connor, 'Indirect Contributions and the Acquisition of a Beneficial Interest in Property', (1984) 3 ILT (NS) 40. In England, the Court of Appeal have recently shown an inclination to return to a more orthodox approach: *Burns v Burns* [1984] Ch 317, [1984] 1 All ER 244.
13 Unreported; judgement delivered 10 May 1984.
14 Above.
15 Above.
16 The article does not say in so many words that 'woman's place is in the home' but it is difficult to know what else was intended by the emphasis placed on 'her life within the home' and 'her duties in the home'. One does not have to be a social historian to know that attitudes have changed in Ireland as elsewhere over the past half century. There has also been a suggestion that the article imposes on the State a duty to ensure that married women are paid from public funds for work of social value which they perform in the home. Whatever the merits of such a proposal, it is remarkably disingenuous to suggest that it was in the minds of the framers of the Constitution in 1937.

12.16 As we have noted, there is little agreement to be found in the authorities as to the basis in law of the spouse's beneficial interest in such circumstances. In *Gissing v Gissing*[1] Lord Diplock said it was immaterial whether the trust which arose in such circumstances was called a resulting, constructive or implied trust, and in *G v D*[2] Keane J used the terms 'resulting' and 'constructive' trusts as though they were interchangeable. It is noteworthy, however, that Lord Diplock treated the beneficial interest of a spouse who has contributed directly to the repayment of the mortgage as founded on the inequity of permitting a purchaser to accept contributions to the purchase price and at the same time deny the existence of any beneficial interest in the contributor, when it was the common if unexpressed intention of the parties that the contributor should have an interest. This emphasis on the element of intention, which as we have repeatedly stressed, need not exist in the case of a constructive trust, suggests that whether the trust comes into being as a result of direct of indirect contributions, it constitutes in all cases a development of the traditional concept of the resulting trust: it is true that in *D v D*,[3] Barron J treated the trust which arose in his view from the expenditure by one spouse of money on the property as a constructive trust, but this is because the expenditure was incurred *after* the property was acquired. In such circumstances, the expenditure is wholly dissimilar in its legal character from the repayment of mortgage instalments, since it is unrelated to the acquisition of any interest in the property. By contrast, the repayment of instalments effectively represents the provision of the purchase price of the property free from incumbrances.

1 Above.
2 Above.
3 Above.

12.17 In England, the problems affecting the ownership of the matrimonial home discussed in the preceding paragraphs have not troubled the courts so much since the enactment of the Matrimonial Causes Act 1973 which enables the court on a divorce to do what is just having regard to all the circumstances. The Irish courts have not been given any corresponding powers in the case of judicial separations.[1] Even if they were, the problem could still arise in the case of unmarried couples cohabiting, a state of affairs increasingly more common in the absence of a divorce jurisdiction.

1 Recommendations to that effect by the Law Reform Commission in their *First Report on Family Law*, (LRC/1—1981) pp 17–20 have not been implemented.

Chapter 13

Constructive trusts

13.01 The essential difference between the constructive trust and all other forms of trust is that it comes into being irrespective of the intention of any of the parties. An express trust only arises because of the declared intentions of the parties, and even a resulting trust carries into effect what the law presumes obligations are imposed on the trustee by the law itself and do not depend on anyone's intentions.

Constructive trusts themselves may be divided into two broad categories. In the first, the constructive trustee is already a trustee and the trust arises because he has derived some benefit or profit from his trustee ship to which he is not entitled. Unless the benefit forms one of the well recognized exceptions to the rule that a trustee may not benefit from his trust—as where a solicitor trustee is expressly authorised to charge for his services[1]—the trustee holds the benefit as an accreation or addition to the trust property. Nor is the principle confined to trustees in the strict sense—it has been extended to a number of categories where a person stands in a fiduciary relationship to another.[2]

In the second category, there is no existing relationship of trustee and beneficiary nor is there even a fiduciary duty owed: the constructive trust arises because of the particular circumstances in which a person holds property. The example most frequently encountered in practice is that of the vendor of land: between the contract for sale and its completion, he remains the legal owner of the land but holds it in trust for the purchaser.[3]

1 See para 10.19, above.
2 See para 13.05, below.
3 See para 13.08, below.

13.02 This last mentioned case is just one of the wide variety of instances in which the law has been prepared to draw the interference of a constructive trust. Like the conventional express trust, its origins in a jurisdiction based on the requirements of conscience are clear. Equity will not permit the legal owner of the property to retain it where that would amount to a fraud. Again the special meaning of that expression in our subject must be stressed.: it does not necessarily connote any wrongdoing on the part of the constructive trustee who may have acted perfectly honourably and from the best of motives.

The constructive trust has thus proved a remarkably elastic concept but, as we shall see, the readiness of some judge in various jurisdictions to fall back on it as providing a 'fair' solution to a wide range of different legal

CORRIGENDA

Keane: Equity and the Law of Trusts in the Republic of Ireland

The reader's attention is drawn to the following text corrections. The Publishers apologise for the inconvenience caused by these printing errors.

Paragraph 13.01, page 178, lines 5, 6: Should now read 'the law presumes to have been their intention. But in a constructive trust, the equitable obligations are imposed on the trustee by the law itself and do not depend on anyone's intentions'.

Paragraph 13.05, page 181, line 2: Should now read 'estate of a deceased person. There were three trustees, one of whom was active in the affairs of the trust. A second, the daughter of the deceased, was not and the'

Paragraph 13.08-09, page 183, line 13: Should now read 'Since the vendor is obliged as a constructive trustee of the property to take'

Paragraph 13.13, page 189, line 21: Should now read 'suggestion of an error on the part of Citibank NA. It seems unsatisfactory that the bank's position – or that of anyone receiving trust money'

BUTTERWORTH & CO (PUBLISHERS) LTD

problems has caused misgivings among those who would prefer to see the law move forward in a less haphazard fashion.[1]

1 See paras 13.10-13.14, below.

Benefits obtained by trustees and other fiduciaries

13.03 The classical and well recognised case in which a constructive trust arises because a trustee—or some other person in a fiduciary position—derives a benefit from his trust is that of the lessee who obtains a renewal of his lease. If he held the lease or tenancy as trustee for another, the law will not permit him to obtain a renewal of it for himself.

Thus in the leading case of *Keech v Sandford*[1] (also known as the *Romford Market case*) the trustee held a leasehold interest in the profits of a market on behalf of an infant. When the lease expired, the owner of the market refused to renew the lease in favor of the infant, but was willing to grant one to the trustee personally. The trustee accepted the lease, but it was held that he was obliged to pay to the infant the profits he received. The trustee was not permitted to derive any advantage from his office and accordingly any profit he obtained and which he would not have received were it not for his office was impressed with a trust in favour of the infant. It was immaterial that the settlor would probably have been perfectly happy for the trustee to have the lease if the object of his benevolence could not. It was equally immaterial that the trustee's conduct was not in any way dishonest or fraudulent.

This principle has acquired in Ireland the horticultural description of *grant*, the idea being that the renewal lease derives its sap from the old lease which was held in trust, and consequently cannot be treated as though it had an independent life of its own capable of being enjoyed by the trustee without regard to the stock whence it sprang. It will apply where the tenant is entitled to a renewal of the old lease by statute (such as the Landlord and Tenant Acts 1967 to 1984) or because of a covenant in the lease; or where the lessor has customarily renewed the lease in the past; or even where there is no right or custom of renewal. But 'there must still be life in the old stock'[2] if the old lease has been surrendered or (as in *Dempsey v Ward*)[3] the lessee has been ejected and he (or his assignee) makes a new bargain with the lessor, the new lease will not be treated as a grant on the old.

1 (1726) Sel Cas Ch 61.
2 *Dempsey v Ward* [1899] I IR 463 at 474-475 per Fitzgibbon LJ.
3 Above.

13.04 The principle has also been applied where the lessee/trustee has bought the reversion. But the limitations on this application of the doctrine in *Keech v Sandford* should be noted. The acquisition of the superior interest by the lessee may not deprive the lessee of any benefit: if, for example, he is legally entitled to have his lease renewed, whether by statute or otherwise, he is probably not prejudiced in any way.[1] *Keech v Sandford* was admittedly applied in a rigorous manner by the Irish Court of Appeal in *Gabbet v Lawder*,[2] where the lessee had a right of renewal under the Irish Church Act 1869. The Church Commissioners offered the lessee—who was a trustee—the ground rent, as they were statutorily obliged to do, before putting it up for auction. Thinking the price too high, he refused, but bought it at the auction for a lower sum. His personal representative subsequently claimed that his estate was beneficially entitled to the rent, but a constructive trust was held to have arisen. In a number of English cases, however, it has been said the rule in *Keech v Sandford* will not apply to a purchase of the reversion unless the interests of the beneficiary are prejudiced by the purchase.[3] In a more recent English case—*Protheroe v Protheroe*[4] — it has been held that the constructive trust arises *whenever* the lessee/trustee buys the reversion, but none of the authorities were referred to and it is thought that the decision will not be applied in Ireland.[5]

1 *Griffith v Owen* L1907R 1 Ch 195 at 205 per Parker J.
2 (1883) 11 LR Ir 295.
3 *Randall v Russell* (1817) 3 Mer 190; *Griffith v Owen*, above.
4 [1968] 1 All ER 1111.
5 For a criticism of the decision, see Megarry 84 LQR 309.

13.05 As we have seen, the rule that the trustee holds any benefits he derives in trust for his beneficiary applies not merely to trustees as such but to others in fiduciary positions. Thus, it has been held to apply to personal representatives,[1] partners,[3] company directors[3] (in relation to the company), joint owners of property,[4] bankers,[5] solicitors[6] and agents.[7] It has been doubted (largely on the authority of *Lister & Co v Stubbs*)[8] whether it applies to all agents (as distinct from 'fiduciary' agents) but there are sound reasons for supposing it does.[9]

An important distinction should be observed, however, between trustees and those who are occupying other fiduciary positions. In the case of trustees (with whom, for this purpose, personal representatives may be equated) the presumption that they hold any such benefits in trust is absolute and may not be rebutted.[10] In other cases, it is no more than a *prima facie* presumption which the fiduciary may rebut by satisfying the court that it is reasonable in the circumstances that he should retain the benefit.[11] Moreover, where the benefit claimed is the renewal of a lease, a person who at first sight occupies a fiduciary position may be held to be under no such duty. In the leading case of *Re Biss*,[12] a shopkeeper holding under a yearly tenancy died intestate, leaving a widow and three children. The widow, who was the administratix continued to run the business with the help of one of the sons. She applied for, but was refused, a renewal of the tenancy. The son then obtained a renewal in his own right. It was held, although he was a tenant in common, he did not stand in any fiduciary relationship to the next of kin and was accordingly entitled to obtain a renewal of the tenancy in his own right.

While that again was a case of a lease being renewed, it must not be supposed that the principle is in any sense confined to such a case. In the case of 'fiduciary agents' for example—bankers, solicitors, agents dealing with land, to take the most usual instances—the agent is obliged to account to his principal for any material advantages which he derives from his position, whether it takes the form of secret profits, commission, straightforward bribes or whatever.[13] And as has been mentioned it is by no means clear that the principle is confined to such 'fiduciary' agents: it may well extend to every form of agency.

The lengths to which the law may be prepared to go to ensure that fiduciary agents account for benefits derived from their position were illustrated by the remarkable decision of the House of Lords in *Boardman v Phipps.*[14] In that case, Boardman was the solicitor for the trustees of an estate of a deceased person. There were three trustees, was not and the third, the widow, was senile. With the approval of the active trustee and the daughter, Boardman and one of the beneficiaries set about attempting to purchase shares in a company in which the trust had a minority shareholding with a view to acquiring control and improving its profitability. They did not succeed in acquiring the necessary shares and they then sought to negotiate a distribution of the assets between the trust and the majority shareholders. These negotiations were conducted by Boardman, purportedly on behalf of the trust, but in fact without their authority. The negotiations failed, but in the course of them, Boardman obtained much useful information which he would not have acquired and he not represented to the directors that he was acting for the trustees. Armed with this information, Boardman and the beneficiary acquired the outstanding shares in the company with the consent of the active trustee and the daughter. When the assets of the company were distributed, Boardman and Phipps made a substantial profit on their shares and so also did the trust in respect of their shares. It was held by a majority of the House of Lords that Boardman and Phipps could not retain the profits they had made and musthand them over to the trustees. They had done nothing wrong and the trust indeed had benefited by all their hard work. Two of the trustees, moreover, had expressly consented to their acquiring the shares. But Boardman and Phipps would not have made the profits without the information which had come to them because Boardman had held himself out as being the agent of the trustees and hence had acquired that information in a fiduciary capacity. The trustees were not given all the information in Boardman's possession at the time they gave their consent and it was only an informed consent which would have protected the fiduciary. (The widow had in any event not consented.) As some compensation, Boardman and Phipps were allowed remuneration on a liberal scale for the work they had done.

1 *Gabett v Lauder*, above; *McCracken v McClelland* (1877) IR 11 Eq 172.
2 *Aas v Benham* [1891] 2 Ch 244, CA.
3 *Regal (Hastings) Ltd v Gulliver*, [1942] 1 All ER 378.
4 *Hunter v Allen* [1907] 1 IR 212.
5 *Selangor United Rubber Estates Ltd v Cradock (No 3)* [1968] 2 All ER 1073.
6 *Lawless v Mansfield* (1841) 1 Dr & War 557; *Brown v IRC* [1964] 3 All ER 119, HL.
7 *Patten v Hamilton*, [1911] IR 46, CA.
8 (1890) 45 Ch D 1.
9 See the criticism of the decision in Jacobs, *Law of Trusts in Australia*, 4th edn, pp 239-242.
10 *Re Biss*, [1903] 2 Ch 40, CA. It has been said that the presumption is also absolute in the case of agents and tenants for life: see Pettit, p 140.
11 *Re Biss*, above, at 56 per Collins MR.
12 Above.
13 *Williams v Barton* [1927] 2 Ch 9; *Boardman v Phipps* [1967] 2 AC 46.
14 Above.

13.06 There has also been an interesting extension of the law in this area to situations where employees of firms seek to benefit from business opportunities which arise during their work for the firm in question. The leading case on the topic in *Industrial Development Consultants Ltd v Cooley*.[1] The defendant was the managing director of the plaintiff firm which offered to its customers a range of construction services, including those of architects, engineers and project managers. The plaintiffs had discussions with a potential customer about the possibility of their designing buildings for it.

Their proposals were rejected, but at the suggestion of the customer, the defendant, who was himself an architect, obtained his release from his contract of employment with the plaintiffs on the pretext of being ill and then entered into a lucrative contract for precisely the same work. He was held to be a constructive trustee of the profits for the firm.

In that case, the employee happened to be the managing director, but a subsequent Canadian decision is authority for the proposition that the principle is not confined to directors of companies, but applies to other executives. In *Canadian Aero Services Ltd v O'Malley*,[2] Laskin J said that the principle prohibits an executive, whether he be a director or hold some other office,

> 'from appropriating to himself a business opportunity which in fairness should belong to the company.'

There have so far been no reported Irish cases in this area. However, the principle of ensuring that employees do not reap a profit from business opportunities which they owe to their employers, where standards of loyalty and good faith require that the profit should go to the company, is clearly a healthy one and there seems no reason to suppose that the Irish courts will not enforce it. As to the general accountability of fiduciaries, it may be safely said that the outer limits of the doctrine have been set by *Boardman v Phipps*[3] and it may indeed be doubted whether the Irish courts would find it necessary to go as far as the House of Lords did in that case.

1 [1972] 2 All ER 162.
2 (1974) 40 DLR (3d) 371.
3 Above.

Constructive trusts where there is no fiduciary relationship

13.07 The second category of constructive trusts arises where there is no fiduciary relationship between the parties, but the circumstances render it indequitable for the legal owner of the property to deny the title of another. We shall deal with the principal categories in turn.

(i) The vendor of property

13.08–09 Where there is a contract for the sale of any property of which the court will order specific performance, the vendor of the property is usually regarded as holding the property on a constructive trust for the purchaser.[1] Although this most frequently arises in the case of contracts for the sale of land, the rule applies to contracts for the sale of any property. Its practical consequence is that the vendor is under a duty to take a reasonable care of the property until the contract is completed and the property transferred to the purchaser.[2] Moreover, since the purchaser is entitled (subject to payment of the purchase money) to the beneficial interest in the property, it is at his risk and thus in the case of land he will have to bear the loss if the property is destroyed or damaged by fire between the signing of the contract and the conveyance to him.[3] It follows that the prudent purchaser should insure the property as soon as the contract is signed and this is the usual practice. If the vendor insures the property, and it is destroyed before completion, he and not the purchaser will be entitled to the proceeds of the policy, unless it has been expressly agreed that the policy is to be held in trust for the purchaser.[4]

Normally in the case of a trust the beneficiary is entitled to any benefits which derive from the property, but as we have just seen this is not always so where the trust arises from a contract of sale. The vendor is entitled to any rents or profits derived from the property before completion.[5] These unusual features have led to some doubts being expressed as to whether the relationship of trustee and beneficiary exists at all and in *Rayner v Preston*,[6] Brett LJ was unequivocally of the view that it did not. However, the weight of judicial opinion is firmly in favour of treating it as creating a trust.

Since the vendor is obliged as a constructive of the property to take reasonable care of the property until the sale is completed, he must in the case of a business carry it on to prevent the goodwill being lost.[7] The purchaser will, however, have to bear any losses that the vendor incurs in so doing, provided the vendor notifies him of the losses being incurred and gives him the option of discontinuing the business.[8] This again is in harmony with the general principle that the property is at the purchaser's risk from the time of the contract.

The vendor is entitled to remain in possession of the property until completion unless the contract provides otherwise. He is also entitled to a *lien* on the property for the balance of the purchse money until it has been paid and this lien will continue in existence after completion, if any of the purchase money remains outstanding.[9] The lien means that the vendor is entitled if necessary to have the property sold in order to have this price paid in full. In the case of registered land, the lien can be registered as a burden under s 69(1) of the Registration of Title 1964 and this should always be done, as it is not one of the burdens which affect registered land without being registered. But in the case of unregistered land, it would appear that the lien cannot be registered in the Registry of Deeds and, it would seem that a purchaser for value without notice of the lien will not be affected by it. Hence a vendor who leaves any part of the purchase money outstanding must protect himself by requiring the purchaser to execute a mortgage which can then be registered in the Registry of Deeds. The purchaser similarly has a lien on the property until completion in respect of any part of the purchase price which he has paid before completion.[10]

(ii) Mortgages

A mortgage is a constructive trustee of any surplus arising from the proceeds of sale of the mortgaged property after the payment of his debt. He holds the surplus on trust for the next incumbrancer or if there be none for the person entitled to the equity of redemption. This equitable doctrine was given statutory force by s 21(3) of the Conveyancing Act 1881.

It has also been held that a mortgagee is a constructive trustee of any income he receives, if he takes possession of the mortgaged property, which exceeds the amount due to him.[11] He is also under an obligation to the mortgagor when selling the mortgage property to take reasonable steps to obtain the best price.[12]

(iii) Mutual wills

It is quite common for husband and wife to make mutual wills under which each leaves all his or her property to the other and their children. The arrangements may take different forms, but it is clear that where such wills are made in pursuance of an agreement to that effect and the survivor alters his will, his estate will be held by his personal representatives on a constructive trust for the benefit of the persons entitled under the will made by him in pursuance of the agreement.[13] While the making of such mutual wills is most frequently encountered in the case of husbands and wives it is not necessary for the parties to be so related for the constructive trust to arise.[14]

It is essential that there be evidence of an agreement: the mere making of the mutual wills is not of itself sufficient to give rise to the constructive trust.[15] It is only where one party has made a will in particular terms on the faith of a promise by the other to make a will in particular terms and not to alter or revoke it that the court will deem it inequitable for the survivor, having benefited under the agreement, to depart from his obligation under that agreement. The evidence of the agreement may be found in the wills themselves as in *Re Hagger*.[16]

(iv) Strangers receiving or dealing with trust property

A person who is not a trustee may nonetheless find himself in the position of a trustee because of his own actions in relation to the trust property. Here we must distinguish three situations.

(a) A person who is not a trustee may interfere in the affairs of the trust—intermeddle with them, it use the legal phrase—as, for example, by doing acts which it is the business of the trustee to do. He then becomes a trustee *de son tort*, ie 'by reason of his wrong', and is liable to account to the beneficiary as a constructive trustee in respect of any property he holds.[17]

(b) A person who is not a trustee may receive trust property with knowledge, actual, constructive or imputed, that it is trust property which is being transferred in breach of trust. In such circumstances, he becomes a constructive trustee of the property.[18] The same result follows where someone (other than a bona fide purchaser for value without notice) acquires the trust property innocently and subsequently becomes aware that it is trust property.[19]

(c) Persons who do not actually receive the trust property may become liable as constructive trustees if 'they assist with knowledge in a dishonest and fraudulent design on the part of the trustees.'[20]Thus, solicitors, bankers and others who knowingly assist in the dishonest or fraudulent diversion of monies impressed with a trust will themselves be liable as constructive trustees to account to the injured beneficiary.[21] But illegality in the transaction is not enough (e.g. the giving of financial assistance to a company to purchase its own shares): it must be trained with dishonesty in some way.[22]

It has also been held in a number of English cases that constructive knowledge is sufficient to bring the category into operation. The person need not be actually aware of the fraudulent or dishonest design: if he wilfully shuts his eyes to the obvious, that will suffice.[23] In *Baden Delvaux and Lecuit v Societe Générale pour Favorizer le Development du Commerce et de l'Industrie en France SA*,[24] five categories of knowledge were defined as sufficient:

'(i) actual knowledge,

(ii) wilfully shutting one's eyes to the obvious,

(iii) wilfully and recklessly failing to make such inquiries as an honest and reasonable man would make,

(iv) knowledge of circumstances which would indicate the facts to an honest and reasonable man,

(v) knowledge of circumstances which would put an honest and reasonable man on enquiry.'

But doubts have been expressed (eg by Megarry V-C in *Re Montague's Settlement-*)[25] as to whether the last two categories are properly included, since they would seem to make the person liable as a constructive trustee simply because he had been negligent. It would seem safer to say that there must have been some 'lack of probity' on the part of the illegal constructive trustee.[26]

A recent example where the authorities are reviewed in detail) is *Lipkin Gorman v Karpnale Ltd & Another*[27] which arose out of the activities of C, a partner in the plaintiff firm of solicitors who gambled and lost in the Playboy Club in London sums amounting to over £200,000, most of them from the clients' account. One of the defendants was Lloyds Bank plc, it being alleged against them that their branch manager, F, had allowed C to continue making withdrawals from the account at a time when he was aware that C was gambling heavily. It was held by Alliott J that F had either shut his eyes to the obvious source of C's funds for gambling or had recklessly failed to make the enquiries a reasonable man ought to have made. Hence the bank were liable as constructive trustees.

1 Lysaght v Edwards (1876) 2Ch D 499; *Tempany v Hynes* [1976] IR 101.

2 *Tempany v Hynes*, above. As already noted, (para 5.16, above) in that case a majority of the Supreme Court, applying the decision in *Rose v Watson* (1864) 10 HL Cas 672, were of the view that this was the only extent to which the vendor became a trustee: the beneficial estate did not pass until the purchase money, or at least part of it, was paid.

3 *White v Nutts* (1702) 1 P Wms 61.

4 *Rayner v Preston* (1881) 18 Ch D 1, CA. There is no equivalent in Ireland to s47 of the English Law of Property Act 1925 which provides that where, after a contract of sale, money becomes payable under a policy of insurance maintained by the vendor in respect of the property, such money on completion is to be paid by the vendor to the purchaser.

5 *Cudden v Tite* (1858) 1 G.tt 395.

6 Above.

7 *Golden Bread Co Ltd v Hemmings* [1922] 1 Ch 162 at 172.

8 Ibid.

9 *Mackreth v Symons* (1808) 15 Ves 329.

10 *Whitbread & Co v Watt* [1902] 1 Ch 835. Note the contrast where there is no contract, but the prospective purchaser has paid a 'booking deposit': in this case, he has no lien and ranks as an unsecured creditor in the event of the vendor's insolvency. *Re Barrett Apartments Ltd* (1985) ILRM 679 SC.

11 *Thompson v Hudson* (1870) LR 10 Eq 497.

12 *Casey v Irish Intercontinental Bank* [1979] IR 364.

13 There are no reported Irish cases to this effect, but there are English authorities eg *Dufour v Pereira* (1769) 1 Dick 419; *Stone v Hoskins* [1905] P 194.

14 *Walpole v Lord Orford* (1797) 3 Ves 402.

15 *Re Oldham* [1925] Ch 75.

16 [1930] 2 Ch 190. Or it may be inferred from the conduct of the parties or the circumstances generally: *Dufour v Pereira*, above; *Stone v Hoskins*, above.

17 *Mara v Browne* [1896] 1 Ch 199 at, 209 *per* AL Smith LJ.

18 *Karak Rubber Co Ltd v Burden (No 2)* [1972] 1 All ER 1210 at 1234.

19 Ibid. Cf *Thompson v Simpson* (1841) 1 Dr & War 459; *Sheridan v Joyce* (1844) 7 I Eq R 115; *McArdle v Gaughran* [1903] 1 IR 106; *Carey v Ryan* [1982] IR 179 at 185 per Henchy J.

20 *Barnes v Addy* (1874) LR 9 Ch App 244 at 251-2 *per* Lord Selborne LC.

21 *Selangor United Rubber Co Ltd v Cradock (No 3)* [1968] 2 All ER 1073; *Karak Rubber Co*

Ltd v Burden (No 2) above. Cp *Shield v Bank of Ireland* [1901] 1 IR 222, MR where it was held that the bank were not on notice of the fact that trust monies in a bank account were being applied by the customer in breach of trust and hence were not constructive trustees.
22 *Belmont Finance Corpn Ltd v Williams Furniture Ltd* [1979] 1 All ER 118.
23 Underhill, p333.
24 [1983] BCLC 325, Ch D.
25 unreported; judgement delivered 29 March 1985.
26 *Carl-Zeiss-Stiftung v Herbert Smith & Co* [1969] 2 Ch 276 at 300-301, CA per Edmund Davies LJ.
27 [1987] BCLC 159, Ch D.

'New model' constructive trusts

13.10 In recent years, there has been much discussion in other jurisdictions as to whether a constructive trust can be said to arise in any circumstances where permitting the defendant to retain the property would result in his being 'unjustly enriched'.[1] This, it has been said, effectively means treating the constructive trust as a form of remedy intended to restore property to a person to whom in justice it should belong rather than as an institution analogous to the express or resulting trust. The constructive trust, in its traditional form, arises because of equity's refusal to countenance any form of fraud: in this wider modern guise it is imposed by law 'whenever justice and good conscience require it'.[2]

1 See generally Hanbury, pp 328-334; Pettit, pp 155-157; Waters, *The Constructive Trust*, pp 41-173 and *The Law of Trusts* (Can), pp 384-394.
2 *Hussey v Palmer* [1972] 3 All ER 744 at 747 per Lord Denning MR.

13.11 As we have seen, the courts in England and Ireland have sometimes used the language of the constructive trust in dealing with the problems associated with ownership of the matrimonial home.[1] Yet it would seem that the stress laid in some of the decisions—notable *Gissing v Gissing*[2]—on the necessity of being able to infer an intention to create a trust is not consistent with the existence of a constructive trust. If a husband or wife is declared to have an interest in the matrimonial home, it is because his or her direct contributions to the purchase price—or more doubtfully indirect contributions[3]—enable the court to infer that it was the common intention that he or she should have such an interest.

There have also been cases in England, however, in which it has been held that a constructive trust has arisen as a result of informal arrangements, frequently in a family context. Where—as in *Cullen v Cullen*[4]—one person is in possession of property as a result of such an arrangement and has acted to his own disadvantage in reliance upon the arrangement, the courts in both Ireland and England were able to infer the existence of a licence which could not be terminated during the lifetime of the licensee. But although the person could not be disturbed during his life, the courts stopped short of holding him entitld to any *interest* in the property of which he could dispose or which would be binding upon a third party.[5]

In England, however, Lord Denning MR was prepared to take that hurdle. In *Binions v Evans*,[6] the defendant's husband was employed by an estate and lived in a cottage owned by them for which he paid no rent. When he died, his 73 year old widow was permitted by the estate to continue living in the cottage as a 'tenant at will..... for the remainder of her life or until determined as hereinafter provided.' There was no provision for determination of the tenancy by the estate. They sold the

186

property to the plaintiffs, who paid a reduced price because of the defendant's tenancy. Nevertheless, the plaintiffs purported to determine the tenancy. The Court of Appeal unanimously denied their right to do so. But while Megaw and Stephenson LJJ were content to treat the instrument as creating a tenancy for life, Lord Denning took a different stance: the defendant was no more than a licensee, but the court could and should impose a constructive trust in her favour which would prevent the plaintiffs turning her out.

In *Hussey v Palmer*,[7] the learned Master of the Rolls went even further. In that case, the plaintiff had been living with her daughter and son-in-law. She had paid £607 to a contractor to build on another room in the expectation that she could live there for the rest of her life. When disputes later arose and she left, she sought the return of the £607. She was in obvious difficulties in the informal arrangement of this sort in establishing that it was a loan rather than a gift, but Lord Denning did not consider them insuperable. Having observed in passing that it did not matter whether one proceeded by way a resulting trust of a constructive trust, he went on

'By whatever means it is described, it is a trust imposed by law wherever justice an good conscience require it. It is a liberal process, founded upon large principles of equity, to be applied in cases where a defendant cannot conscientiously keep the property for himself alone, but ought to allow another to have the property or a share in it..... It is an equitable remedy by which the court can enable an aggrieved party to obtain restitution.'[8]

Hence, the plaintiff was entitled to a share in the house proportionate to her contribution.[9]

1 See para 12.16, above.
2 [1971] AC 886.
3 Para 12.15, above.
4 [1962] IR 268.
5 Ibid, at 292 per Kenny J.
6 [1972] Ch 359.
7 Above.
8 At 747.
9 See also *Eves v Eves* [1975] 3 All ER 768; *DHN Food Distributors Ltd v Tower Hamlets London Borough Council* [1976] 1 WLR 852.

13.12 The emergence of these 'new model' constructive trusts, as they have been called, has not been greeted with universal enthusiasm.[1] But they do reflect a judicial trend which has been making substantial advances in the United States and Canada. In those jurisdictions, the concept of 'unjust enrichment' has gained a securer juristic footing than in England or (so far at any rate) Ireland. Broadly speaking, it may be said that the application of the principle of unjust enrichment requires the restoration by the defendant to the plaintiff of a benefit which it would be unjust for him to retain.[2]

Sometimes this can be done by a simple award of money, eg the refund of money paid under a mistake of fact. But sometimes the restoration of the benefit can only be achieved by giving the plaintiff an interest in property. Thus, the constructive trust is imposed by the court as an equitable remedy intended to restore to the plaintiff the benefit of which he has been deprived. In the words of Cardozo 4, 'a constructive trust is the formula through which the conscience of equity finds expression.'[3]

The doctrine of 'unjust enrichment' seeks to remedy cases of apparent injustice which cannot be accommodated within any of the recognized compartments of English civil law, ie contract, quasi-contract, tort or equity. Its acceptance in the United States was powerfully confirmed by the publication in 1937 of the *Restatement of Restitution*.[4] And the constructive trust has been eagerly utilised as a method of remedying 'unjust enrichment'. So in *Pettkus v Becker*[5] the Canadian Supreme Court by a majority held that a common law wife was entitled to a proprietary interest in the assets of a bee-keeping business by virtue of a constructive trust. Dickson J, speaking for the majority, held that there was no evidence from which a common intention to hold the assets jointly could be inferred, and hence no room for the presumption of a resulting trust.[6] But this did not prevent the court from imposing a constructive trust on the ownership of the assets, if the defendant had in truth been unjustly enriched. The learned judge, applying the criteria which he had laid down in *Rathwell v Rathwell*,[7] said that this was such a case: there had been 'an enrichment, corresponding deprivation and absence of any juristic reason for the enrichment.' Hence, a constructive trust should be imposed: 'the principle of unjust enrichment lies at the heart of the constructive trust.'

1 Underhill, P 321; Jacobs, *Law of Trusts in Australia*, 4th edn, pp 252-257.
2 See Goff and Jones, *The Law of Restitution*, 3rd edn, particularly pp 60-81.
3 *Beatly v Guggenheim Exploration Co* 225 NY 380, 386 (1919). Cf Scott, *'Constructive Trusts'*, 71 LQR 39.
4 See especially $160
5 [1980] 2 SCR 834.
6 See para 12.13, above.
7 (1978) 2 SCR 423.

13.13 The viability of constructive trusts framed as a remedy for unjust enrichment—or, to use Lord Denning's even more Olympian formula 'justice and good conscience'[1]—is most searchingly tested at the stage of insolvency. If the trust thus called into being is in any real sense a trust—if it confers rights *in rem* on the plaintiff and not merely a right *in personam* against the defendant—then it must prevail not merely over the rights of third parties who acquire the property, but also over those of the general body of unsecured creditors of the defendant. To assume that such rights *in rem* have come into existence solely in order to do what seems to be justice in a given case may be perilous, especially in a system of ownership of land where registration and notice play a large part.[2] But the difficulties are not confined to cases where land is the subject of the claimed trust: they also arise where the plaintiff seeks to impose a trust on money paid to the defendant.

As we shall see in more detail in Chapter 20, English law has since *Re Hallett's Estate*[3] permitted a person whose money has been mixed with another's to 'trace' his money into the account, but only where a fiduciary relationship exists, e.g. where a trstee mixes a beneficiary's money with his own in a bank account. In *Chase Manhattan Bank NA v Israel-British Bank (London) Ltd*[4] where the plaintiffs paid some £2 million into the defendant's bank by mistake, Goulding J held that the latter were constructive trustees of the money. He surmounted the difficulty of there being no fiduciary relationship between the banks by holding that such a 'fiduciary' duty to report arose whenever a person retained money which had been paid to him by mistake.[5]

A similar view was taken by Carroll J in *Re Irish Shipping Ltd*.[6] In that case, a Korean bank made a duplicate payment in error to the bank account of a company which subsequently went into liquidation. The bank to whom the money was paid (Citibank NA) claimed to set off debts due by the company to them against the mistaken payment, but it was held that they were not entitled to do so. Carroll J treated the money as being subject to a constructive trust when paid in error to Citibank NA and concluded that the Korean bank were entitled to trace the money into the company's account. It was argued on behalf of Citibank NA that as they had no notice of the trust, they could not be affected by it and were entitled to treat the money as belonging to the company and hence available for set off. The learned judge, however, was of the view that the bank's lack of knowledge was immaterial. While she accepted that Citibank NA would not have been affected by an express trust of which they had no notice, she thought that different consideration arose where the money was subject to a costructive trust.

> If the concept of a constructive trust is an equitable device for achieving justice, it should not work an injustice. If these funds are treated as ordinary trust moneys..... Citibank would succeed. But this a case of money coming into (the company's) bank account in error.

In that case, the mistake was made by the Korean Bank. There was no suggestion of an error on the part of anyone receiving trust money innocently—should differ depending on whether the monies in question are impressed with a constructive trust or an express trust, since *ex hypothesi* the bank does not know which it is. We shall return to this topic when we come to consider the remedy of tracing in Chapter 20; for the moment it is sufficient to note that Carroll J, in common with Goulding J, accepted that a 'fiduciary' relationship in the conventional sense was not essential to give rise to the constructive trust.

The Irish Shipping Ltd was a case of set-off and the successful invocation of the constructive trust was thus fatal to the claim of a specific creditor. In other cases, such as *Chase Manhattan Bank Na v Israel-British Bank (London) Ltd*, the general body of unsecured creditors will be the potential victims. There may seem to be no good reason in such cases why the general body of unsecured creditors should benefit from a windfall at the expense of the person who mistakenly made the payment. Yet the difficulties remain of drawing the line between transactions which are capable of attracting the protection of a constructive trust and those which are not. Is not every trader who sells goods on credit the victim of an injustice when his debtor becomes insolvent? But the law has always distinguished between the secured creditor, who has an interest, be it by way of mortgage, change, lien or trust in this debtor's property, and the unsecured creditor who has not.[7] If the constructive trust as a remedy, uncoupled from any fiduciary relationship, has become established in our jurisprudence that basic distinction has been significantly eroded by the process of judge made law.

1 Above.
2 See Chapter Five.
3 (1880) 13 Ch D 696.
4 [1981] Ch 105.
5 A process of reasoning described as 'tortuous' by Hanbury (p 639), although the editor approves of the result.

6 (1986) ILRM 518.
7 *Re Barrett Apartments Ltd* (1985) ILRM 679 per Henchy J.

13.14 English law has been generally cautious in its approach to the concept of 'unjust enrichment': it has been regarded as too nebulous a concept to be of any practical value. In the leading case of *Moses v Macferlane*[1] Lord Mansfield spoke of the defendant being 'under obligation, from the ties of natural justice, to refund', but later decisions have not lent support to the school of thought which saw in this the germ of an English law of unjust enrichment.[2]In *Reading v A-G*[3] Lord Porter said

> I am content for the purposes of this case to accept the view that (the doctrine of unjust enrichment) forms no part of the law of England and that a right to

restitution so described would be too widely stated.' Nor has Lord Denning's more recent 'justice and good conscience' rubric gained widespread acceptance. Browne-Wilkinson J in *Re Sharpe*,[4] although obliged to follow such decisions as *Binions v Evans*[5] expressed his misgivings thus:

> doing justice to the litigant who actually appears in the court by the invention of new principles of law ought not to involve injustice to the other persons who are not litigants before the court but whose rights are fundamentally affected by the new principles.'

Even in Canada where the concept of 'unjust enrichment' with the constructive trust as its corresponding remedy has been embraced by the Supreme Court, dissenting voices have been raised; Martland J referred[6] to *Hussey v Palmer*—the highwater mark of this 'new model' in England—as of questionable validity.

It remains to be seen how far such 'new model' trusts will win recognition in Ireland. It may be observed, however, that Finlay P in *W v W* rejected the suggestion that expenditure on the matrimonial home after its acquisition could enable the paying spouse to assert an equitable interest. The claims in such circumstances—if justifiable at all—would be a purely monetary one. This seems difficult to reconcile with the approach of Lord Denning in *Hussey v Palmer*. Another indication of a more orthodox approach is to be found in the judgements of the Supreme Court in *Re Barrett Apartments Ltd*.[7] In that case, a number of prospective purchasers of flats had paid 'booking deposits' to a building firm which subsequently went into liquidation. Keane J held that they were entitled to a lien on the block of flats for the amount of the deposit, but the Supreme Court held unanimously that they ranked as unsecured creditors only. The deposits were presumably held by the builders or their agents in a fiduciary capacity and hence the position of the prospective purchasers closely resembled that of the ultra vires depositors in *Sinclair v Brougham*[8] or the stamp investors in *Shanahan's Stamp Auctions Ltd v Farrelly and another*.[9] While the existence of a constructive trust does not appear to have been relied on at any stage, the decision is another indication that the Irish courts will continue to tread cautiously in this area.

1 (1760) 2 Burr 1005.
2 *Sinclair v Brougham* [1914] AC 398 at 452 per Lord Sumner; *Holt v Markham*, [1923] 1 KB 504 at 513 per Scrutton LJ. For a warmer response, see the dicta of Lord Wright in *Fibrosa Spolka Akcyjna v Fairbairn Lawson Combe Barbour Ltd* [1943] AC 32 at 64.
3 [1951] AC 507 at 513. Nor can one detect much enthusiasm for the doctrine on the part of

Kingsmill Moore J, speaking for the Supreme Court, in *A-G v Ryan's Car Hire Ltd* (1965) IR 642 at 664, when he referred to 'the somewhat vague brocards of unjust benefit or restitution or quasi contract.' But Henchy J was prepared to acknowldge the concept of 'unjust enrichment' in the context of money paid under compulsion in *Murphy v A-G* [1982] IR 241 at 316-317, SC.

4 [1980] 1 All ER 198.
5 Above.
6 In *Pettkus v Becker*, above.
7 (1985) ILRM 679.
8 [1914] AC 398.
9 (1962) IR 386. See para 20.10 below. In *Sinclair v Brougham*, the ordinary creditors had been paid off so that the question of their rights did not arise. In *Shanahan's Stamp Auctions Ltd*, however, Budd J held that the right of the stamp investors to trace their money into the stamps had priority over the rights of the unsecured creditors.

Chapter 14

Void and voidable trusts

14.01 Trusts may be void, ie of no legal effect, because they are illegal or because their enforcement would be contrary to public policy. There are also trusts which are voidable, ie they are not void *ab initio* (from their creation) but only if and when their validity is successfully challenged. The significance of the distinction is that void trusts can in general give rise to no enforceable legal rights while voidable trusts may.

Clearly a trust for illegal purposes, such as the encouragement of terrorism, would be void. But there are few examples in practice of trusts being treated as void for this reason alone since, as we saw in chapter 7, purpose trusts are usually unenforceable anyway unless they are charitable. But a trust may be void on the ground of illegality because its enforcement would violate some statutory or common law prohibition. Of these the most important in practice are the rules against perpetuities and inalienability.[1]

1 See para 7.06, above.

14.02 A trust in favour of *individuals* may also be void because its enforcement would offend public policy. At common law, one important example was a trust to provide for future illegitimate children. But there is also a range of trusts in favour of individuals which are void because they are subject to *conditions* which the law refuses to enforce as being illegal or contrary to public policy. Examples of the latter are conditions relating to the marriage or education of the beneficiary.

14.03 Trusts in favour of *future* illegitimate children were void at common law because it was regarded as contrary to public policy to encourage extra-marital sexual relations.[1] This has not been the law in England or Northern Ireland since 1970 and 1977 respectively. There has been no similar legislation in the Republic but it must be at least doubtful whether this rule of the common law survived the enactment of the Constitution. It has been emphasised in a number of cases that the constitutional guarantees of marriage and the family do not reflect any inferior status of illegitimate children.[2] Although as a matter of statutory construction the Supreme Court have held that the rights of the issue of a person on his intestacy to a share in his estate are confined to children born within wedlock,[3] it does not follow that a trust to provide for future children of an extra-marital union would be contrary to public policy. To penalise the children of such a union would seem to subject them to an inequality of treatment which would offend Article 40.1 of the Constitution. (It should, of course, be remembered that the rights of such children under a trust of this nature would be subject in an appropriate case to the statutory rights of a spouse and legitimate children.)

1 *Thomson v Thomas* (1891) 27 LR Ir 457. The child in any event must be already born or *en ventre sa mere* when the trust takes effect, to avoid offending the rule against perpetuities.
2 *Re M* [1946] IR 334, 344 per Gavan Duffy P; *G v An Bord Uchtala* [1980] IR 32 at 55-56, per O'Higgins CJ.
3 *O'B v S* [1984] IR 316; sub nom *Re William Walker's Goods* (1985) 5 ILRM 86.

Trusts subject to unenforceable conditions

14.04 In this area, it is important to distinguish between *conditions precedent* (which must be complied with before the trust takes effect) and *conditions subsequent* (which cannot or need not be complied with before the trust takes effect, but non-compliance with which brings the trust to an end and divests the beneficiary of the property). An example of the first category is a gift or bequest of property on condition that the donee marries a particular person. An example of the second category is a gift on condition that the donee never marries.

14.05 Conditions which are illegal in their nature do not present any great problem: clearly, the law will not enforce a trust which is intended to encourage or facilitate the commission of a crime or an unlawful act. In the case of a condition subsequent, the law will simply disregard such a condition so that the trust will continue and the beneficiary will not be divested of the trust property for failing to comply with it.[1] In the case of a condition precedent, the common law drew a distinction between conditions which were illegal because *malum prohibitum* and those which were illegal because *malum in se*. The first category consisted of conditions which were illegal as being contrary to some statute or law and the second category of those which were evil in themselves, eg a condition requiring a man to be killed. It was said that conditions in the first category would simply be disregarded by the court and that accordingly the trust would take effect in such a case; but that conditions in the second category would prevent the trust from taking effect.[2] This was said to be giving effect to the presumed intention of the settlor, but doubts as to the correctness of the decisions were expressed by Dixon J in *Re Blake*[3] and it is submitted that his reservations were well founded. As he remarked, it seems strangely unreal to attribute to testators an appreciation of a distinction of this rarefied nature. Whether the condition is *malum prohibitum* or *malum in se*, the trust should be void.

1 *Egerton v Earl Brownlow* (1853) 4 HL Cas 1.
2 *Re Piper* [1946] 2 All ER 503 at 505 citing Jarman on Wills, 7th edn, Vol 2, p 1443.
3 [1955] IR 89 at 100.

14.06 Conditions which are vulnerable on grounds of public policy present more of a problem. Concepts of public policy do not remain static and in Ireland, moreover, they are frequently affected by constitutional considerations which do not arise in England. A type of condition which has given rise to particular difficulties is one relating to *marriage*.

Conditions imposed on a gift which fettered the donee's freedom to marry offended a principle of public policy which was said to be based on Roman law and to have found its way thence into the law of England via the ecclesiastical courts. Its place in that law has been described as 'ambiguous and rather restricted.'[1]

Conditions intended to be in general restraint of marriage, ie which required the donee to remain a bachelor or spinster for the rest of his or her days, were undoubtedly void. Accordingly, since they were of necessity conditions subsequent, the breach by the donee of such a condition did not lead to a forfeiture of the property.[2] But one must distinguish between conditions which are imposed to prevent marriage and those which simply ensure that a person is supported until marriage: a trust to pay an annual sum to a woman, so long as she remains unmarried, would certainly be treated as valid, since she may require maintenance until she has a husband to support her.[3]

A condition in *partial* restraint of marriage was treated by the Irish and English courts as in general enforceable, eg a condition that a gift was to be forfeited in the event of a second or subsequent marriage,[4] or the marriage of the donee without the consent of trustees, or the marriage of the donee to a particular person or below a certain age.[5]

Since the Constitution includes an undertaking by the State to uphold the institution of marriage,[6] the pre-1937 law as to conditions in general restraint of marriage presumably remains the law. What is more doubtful is the effect of the Constitution on conditions in partial restraint of marriage. It has been held that the right to marry is one of the unspecified 'personal rights' guaranteed by Article 41 of the Constitution[7] and it is clear that the courts must recognise and protect such rights in the construction of wills and settlements. In *Re McKenna*,[8] where the testator left property to his son on condition that he did not marry a Roman Catholic, Gavan Duffy P hinted at doubts as to the constitutional propriety of such a bequest, but did not elaborate as the point was not relied on. However, he presumably had in mind the articles expressly guaranteeing freedom of conscience and protecting marriage, since this was many years before the doctrine of unspecified personal rights was enunciated. It would seem strongly arguable that such a condition should now be treated as a restraint on the constitutional right of a donee to marry and hence void.

A more difficult question is as to the *effect* of such a condition being regarded as void. In the case of a condition subsequent, English law draws a remarkable distinction which, even apart from constitutional considerations, would probably not be recognised by the Irish courts to-day. In the case of real estate, a condition subsequent in partial restraint of marriage is always enforced. So if a testator leaves freehold land to his wife on condition that she does not remarry, the condition will be enforced and she will forfeit the estate in the event of her remarriage. But if the condition subsequent relates to personalty, it will only be enforced if there is a gift over of the property in default of compliance with the condition. So if leasehold property is left to her subject to a condition that in the event of her remarriage it is to go to her children, it will be enforced. But if there is no gift over, the condition will be treated as having been imposed *in terrorem* only and will not be enforced.[9]

This distinction entered English law because bequests of personalty were at one time the exclusive province of the ecclesiastical courts. The influence of Roman law in those courts already mentioned meant that conditions in restraint of marriage were looked on with disfavour and were only enforced if the testator had shown his clear intention that they should be by providing for a gift over.[10] It has been conceded by the Privy Council that the origin of the rule is not 'wholly logical'[11] but it remains part of English law. Were the matter to come before the Irish courts, however, it seems likely that the approach adopted would be that of Gavan Duffy J in *Exham v Beamish*[12] and that the courts would decline to enforce a rule of law dating from before 1921 which appears repugnant to commonsense. It may be observed indeed that in *Re Blake*[13] Dixon J expressed doubts as to whether the law administered by the English ecclesiastical courts continued to form part of our law after the Reformation. Assuming that the distinction does not exist in our law, it would seem reasonable to conclude that such conditions would simply be disregarded in all cases as unconstitutional fetters on the right to marry; but that question also remains unresolved.

1 *Leong v Lim Beng Chye* [1955] AC 648 at 665.
2 *Morley v Rennoldson, Morley v Linkson* (1843) 2 Hare 570.
3 The words used in such a case may be construed as words of limitation of the particular estate: *Page v Hayward* (1705) 2 Salk 570.
4 *Duddy v Gresham* (1878) 2 LR Ir 442.
5 *Jarvis v Duke* (1681) 1 Vern 19. The condition forbade the marriage of the beneficiary to one Bacon and her attempt to contest it attracted the sadly unromantic censure of the lord chancellor (Nottingham): 'nothing in the whole fair garden of Eden would serve her turn but this forbidden fruit.' For conditions forbidding marriage below a certain age, see *Stackpole v Beaumont* (1796) 3 Ves 89 at 97. It would appear, however, that the age must be reasonable. Note that a provision making the legacy conditional on the marriage of the legatee to a specified named person has also been treated as valid: *Viscount Falkland v Bertie* (1698) 2 Vern 333; *Kiersey v Flahavan* [1905] I IR 45.
6 Article 41.3.1.
7 *Ryan v A-G* [1965] IR 294 at 313 per Kenny J; *McGee v A-G* [1974] IR 284 at 301 per Fitzgerald, CJ.
8 [1947] IR 277.
9 *Duddy v Gresham*, above and *Leong v Lim Beng Chye*, above. See also *Kiely v Monck* (1795) 3 Ridg Parl Rep 205, a case decided under the revived appellate jurisdiction of the Irish House of Lords where the origin of the rule is explained by Fitzgibbon, LC.
10 *Duddy v Gresham*, above at 464 per Christian LJ.
11 *Leong v Lim Beng Chye*, above at 662.
12 [1939] IR 336. See para 2.22, above.
13 Above.

14.07 Conditions attached to gifts or bequests which are intended to facilitate or encourage separation or divorce have been treated as void on grounds of public policy in a number of cases[1] and again the Constitution would reinforce such an approach. A trust, however, to take effect upon the coming into legal operation of a separation which has already been decided upon and is irretrievable will be upheld.[2]

1 *Westmeath v Westmeath* (1830) I Dow & Cl 519; *Re Caborne* [1943] Ch 224.
2 *Wilson v Wilson* (1848) 1 HL Cas 538.

14.08 Conditions which weaken the ties between parent and child were held in England to be void.[1] This principle was applied by Gavan Duffy P in *Re Burke's Estate, Burke v Burke*[2] where he declined to enforce a condition that the testator's nephew was to be educated in a Roman Catholic school to be selected by the trustees. He took higher constitutional ground for his decision, however, holding that the condition was invalidated by Article 42.1 of the Constitution which provides that 'the State acknowledges that the primary and natural educator of the child is the Family and guarantees to respect the inalienable right and duty of parents to provide, according to their means, for the religious and moral, intellectual, physical and social education of their children.'

Conditions which require the beneficiary to be brought up in a particular religion will also be treated as void on the ground that it is against public policy for parents to be inhibited or influenced by extraneous factors in bringing up their children and that they are an unconstitutional interference with the parental rights and duties recognised by Article 42.1. In *Re Blake*,[3] Dixon J held to be void on this ground a condition requiring the grandchildren of the testator to be brought up in the Roman Catholic faith. In that case, while the grandchildren were entitled to the income of the property during their minority, the capital did not vest until they came of age. The offending condition was accordingly a condition precedent. Dixon J, while expressing the doubts already mentioned as to the validity of the distinction between conditions *malum prohibitum* and *malum in se*, held that it fell into neither character. He concluded that, in the case of a condition void on grounds of public policy, the intention of the testator should be effected by treating both gift and condition as void. However, doubts have been expressed as to whether the learned judge was correct in holding that this principle applied to conditions which were contrary to the Constitution. Wylie comments as follows:

'This case was, however, not followed by Kenny J in *Re Doyle*[4] in which he held that when a condition precedent attached to a gift is a violation of the donee's constitutional rights in the Republic, the donee takes the benefit of the gift without complying with the condition.'[5]

No written judgement appears to have survived in *Re Doyle* and it is only possible to glean the *ratio* of the decision from the form of the order actually made. However, since the late Mr Justice Kenny was the consulting editor for the Republic of Ireland of Wylie at the time this comment appeared, it must carry considerable weight.

In *Re Doyle*, the testator made a bequest in an unusual form: he left property to his daughter on condition that she was a Roman Catholic at the date of his death and had given an undertaking to her parish priest that she would continue to adhere to that faith. The testator's solicitor said that he had enquired from him whether he (the solicitor) should inform the daughter of the condition so that she could comply with it and that the testator had told him that he would tell her himself. In fact the daughter said that she did not become aware of the condition until after her father's death. Kenny J, answering questions raised by the executor on a construction summons, held that this condition was void as being impossible to perform. He also held, however, that the condition was void as being contrary to Article 44.2.1. of the Constitution which provides that

'freedom of conscience and the free profession and practice of religion are, subject to public order and morality, guaranteed to every citizen.'

Kenny J further held that the donee took the gift free from the condition. To the extent that the condition failed because it was impossible to perform, this accorded with earlier English decisions: the condition was undoubtedly a condition precedent, but it was clear that a condition precedent which to the knowledge of the testator could not be performed did not prevent the trust from taking effect.[6] Since the donee was a Roman

Catholic (and said on oath that she had not the slightest intention of ever ceasing to be one,) non-compliance with the remainder of the condition did not appear to arise. To that extent, anything Kenny J said on this aspect may have been *obiter* (and, as has been pointed out, no written judgement in any event is available). It may be that Kenny J intended to confine his finding as to the unconstitutionality of the condition to that part of it which required the giving of the undertaking. Since the donee would have taken the gift free from that condition on the impossibility ground, altogether apart from the constitutional ground, there is no necessary conflict here between *Re Blake* and *Re Doyle*.

A somewhat similar problem arose in England in *Blathwayt v Baron Cawley*.[7] In that case the settlement creating the trust provided that, if a beneficiary should be or become a Roman Catholic, his interest should be forfeited. The House of Lords held that this clause was valid as regards adult beneficiaries, but also expressed *obiter* opinions as to whether it was binding on minors. It was held that it was so binding because, in accordance with earlier decisions, the minor would not have to elect whether to comply with the condition until a reasonable period had elapsed after he came of age. In the result, public policy would not be offended, since the parents could bring up the infant in whatever religion they thought right, in the knowledge that his material interests would not be damaged by their conscientious decision. They were also of the view, however, that conditions of this nature, whether applicable to adult or infant beneficiaries, were not contrary to public policy: a testator was perfectly entitled, in their opinion, to make his bounty conditional on a person's being of a particular religion. The wider concept of religious discrimination which (in common with racial discrimination) was clearly contrary to public policy did not arise, since what was involved was a matter of personal choice and testamentary freedom.

Dixon J in *Re Blake* also referred without apparent disapproval to the earlier English decisions which had said that where a gift was conditional on the donee being of a certain religion when he came of age, the condition was valid but the minor was entitled to a reasonable time within which to decide whether he would comply with it. The learned judge was also prepared to give effect to the clearly expressed intention of the testator that his property should only be enjoyed by people of a particular religious faith. But it should be emphasised that Article 44.2.1. does not appear to have been relied on in that case: the condition was held to be invalid by reference only to the Article recognising parental rights and duties.

While *Re Doyle* is, in the absence of a written judgement, a somewhat unsatisfactory basis for doubting the authority of *Re Blake*, it would be obviously unsafe to regard the question as definitively governed by the earlier decision. On one view it might be said that the spirit of Article 44 is more respected by permitting testators to give effect to their conscientiously held religious beliefs. On another view, it could be urged that for the law to recognise trusts, which may depend for their efficacy on the overbearing of religious convictions by cupidity is contrary to that Article. Ultimately, only the Supreme Court can resolve this difficult question, but it is thought that the former view is preferable.

1 *Re Boulter, Capital and Counties Bank v Boulter* [1922] 1 Ch 75.
2 [1951] IR 216.
3 Above.
4 (1972), Unreported No 143 Sp.

5 Wylie, *Land Law*, p 498.
6 *Jarman on Wills*, 8th edn, pp 1457-1458.
7 [1976] AC 397.

Voidable trusts

14.09 Trusts may be voidable and hence liable to be set aside by the courts for a variety of reasons. They will, however, remain lawful, unlike void trusts, until successfully challenged. Thus they may be voidable because they came into being as a result of fraud, misrepresentation, mistake, duress or undue influence. The more important of these topics are dealt with elsewhere in this book.[1] At this stage, the discussion is confined to three cases in which the trust may be voidable as a result of certain statutes.

1 Chapter 17 (fraud, misrepresentation, mistake) and chapter 2 (undue influence).

14.10 The first category is of *settlements made with intent to defraud creditors*. People who fear that they may become insolvent occasionally succumb to the temptation of putting their property beyond the reach of their creditors. Such transactions have frequently taken the form of settlements of property for the benefit of the debtors' wives and families. The law has for centuries sought to protect creditors against such transactions, and the relevant Irish statute dates from the reign of Charles I.[1] (It in turn was modelled on an English statute on Elizabeth I[2] which has been said to be declaratory of the common law.)[3] The relevant provisions are verbose and unclear, but their principal effect can be briefly summarised. Conveyances made with intent to defraud creditors are voidable as against such creditors unless they are made in good faith for valuable consideration to a person who has no notice of the fraudulent intent.

Although the section itself uses the word 'void', it is clear that transactions affected by the section are voidable only.[4] The actual language of the section also indicates that it was intended to apply to every form of disposition of property (including, it would appear, oral agreements)[5] and not merely conveyances *strictu sensu*. While the provision preserving bona fide conveyances to persons without notice speaks of 'good consideration', it is settled that only transactions for valuable consideration—money, money's worth or marriage—are in fact preserved.

The onus of proving that the transaction was intended to defraud creditors is on the person who makes that claim.[6] This onus is far more difficult to discharge where the transaction is for valuable consideration.[7] The mere fact that the property is being sold rather than given away indicates that there may be motives for the transaction other than an intention to defraud creditors, such as the hope of raising money to meet their claims. Where there is such a sale, the onus is also on the person impeaching it to prove that the purchaser had notice of the fraudulent intent.[8] It is not, however, clear what is meant by the requirement that such sale is made bona fide. By definition the transferor cannot be acting in good faith if his intent is fraudulent. Similarly, a transferee who takes without notice would seem to be acting in good faith in any event. There are suggestions in some cases that it is designed to exclude from the saving provision transactions which are not genuine sales and where the transferor really intends to keep the property for himself.[9] It is difficult to imagine, however, that in the case of such a bogus sale, the transferee would not be in any event aware of the fraudulent intent.

1 10 Car I, sess 2, c 3.
2 13 Eliz I c 5.
3 *Cadogan v Kennett* (1776) 2 Cowp 432 at 434.
4 *Re Eichholz* [1959] Ch 708.
5 Ibid; *Rye v Rye* [1960] 3 All ER 810. Doubts have been expressed as to whether this is so in England (cf Pettit, pp 181-182), but there the single word 'conveyance' has been used in s 172 of the Law Property Act which replaces the more elaborately worded Elizabethan enactment.
6 *Llyods Bank Ltd v Marcan* [1973] 1 WLR 339 at 387.
7 *Harman v Richards* (1842) 10 Hare 81; *Bryce v Fleming* [1930] IR 376.
8 *Bryce v Fleming*, above.
9 *Rose v Greer* [1945] IR 503 at 510 per Overend J.

14.11 Since the Act of Charles I speaks of 'fraudulent and covenous conveyances..... of purpose and intent to deceive.....', it would seem to suggest that only transactions tainted in some way by dishonesty are captured. But in *Lloyd Bank Ltd v Marcan*,[1] Pennycuick V-C said that since the section aimed at transactions which were intended to 'hinder, delay or defraud' creditors, actual deceit or dishonesty was not a necessary ingredient. It was sufficient if the effect was to deprive creditors of 'timely recourse' to property otherwise available to them. In the Court of Appeal, Russell LJ said that a debtor who intended to put his property out of his creditors' reach was *ex hypothesi* behaving in a dishonest fashion, but Cairns LJ considered that a dishonest intention was necessary, at least in the case of a transaction for consideration. In *Rose v Greer*,[2] Overend J said that the statute was directed against 'bogus or colourable transactions under which the debtor retains a benefit for himself.' But this appears to be too narrow a definition.

Proof of intention to defraud is, as already indicated, much easier in the case of a voluntary transaction. The law may presume from the circumstances such an intention, placing the onus on the defendant to establish that the voluntary conveyance was not intended to defraud. Such an inference may be drawn where the disposition was of all the transferor's property;[3] or where he retained possession of it;[4] or where he reserved benefits to himself;[5] or where there was a power of revocation.[6] It would seem that it could also be drawn where the transferor was about to engage in a hazardous trade.[7] While it is obviously a relevant consideration in such cases, it is not necessary that the transferor should have been insolvent at the time to give rise to the presumption.[8]

There is a line of authority for the proposition that in certain circumstances an *irrebuttable* presumption of fraudulent intention may be drawn, even though on the evidence the court is satisfied that such was not the real intention. The passage usually relied on is the following from the judgement of Lord Hatherly in *Freeman v Pope*:[9]

'It is established by the authorities that in the absence of any such direct intention, if a person owing debts makes a settlement which subtracts from the property, which is the proper fund for the payment of those debts, an amount without which the debts cannot be paid, then, since it is the necessary consequence of the settlement..... that some creditors must remain unpaid, it would be the duty of the judge to direct the jury that they must infer the intent of the settlor to have been to defeat or delay his creditors, and that the case is within the section..'

Although this view of the law was subsequently denounced by Lord Esher

MR as 'monstrous'[10] it seems to receive support from this passage in the judgement of Palles CB in *Re Moroney*:[11]

'In other cases, *no such intention actually exists* in the mind of the grantor, but the necessary or probable result of his so denuding himself of the property included in the conveyance, for the consideration, and under the circumstances actually existing is to defeat or delay creditors, and in such cases..... *the intent is, as a matter of law, assumed from the necessary or probable consequences of the act done.*'

Although the section is usually regarded as being primarily intended to protect creditors, the section refers to 'creditors and others.' In England, where the corresponding section of the Law of Property Act 1925 enables the transaction to be invalidated by 'any person prejudiced'; the Court of Appeal left open the question as to whether it could be availed of by a wife whose claim for maintenance against her husband had been abated by the latter's death and who sought to set aside a voluntary settlement he had made upon their son.[12]

1 Above.
2 Above.
3 *Twyne's Case* (1602) 3 Co Rep 80b.
4 *Edwards v Harben* (1788) 2 Term Rep 587 at 596 per Buller J.
5 *Maskeleyne & Cooke v Smith* [1903] 1 KB 671 at 676-677.
6 *Twyne's Case*, above.
7 *Mackay v Douglas* (1872) LR 14 Eq 106.
8 *Townsend v Westacott* (1840) 2 Beav 340.
9 (1870) 5 Ch App 538 at 541.
10 *Re Wise, Ex p Mercer* (1886) 17 QBD 290 at 298.
11 (1887) 21 LR Ir 27, 61-62.
12 *Cadogan v Cadogan* [1977] 3 All ER 831.

14.12 The second category is of *voluntary conveyances*. The Conveyancing (Ireland) Act 1634[1] rendered void any conveyance of land made with intent to defraud subsequent purchasers, only bona fide conveyances for good consideration being excluded. An artificial construction was given to the corresponding English enactment which meant that where a voluntary conveyance was followed by a conveyance for value, it was conclusively presumed that the voluntary conveyance was fraudulent.[2]

However, the Voluntary Conveyances Act 1893 appeared to put an end to this strained construction by providing that no voluntary conveyance made bona fide and without fraudulent intent was to be deemed void by reason of the 1634 Act. Although it was held in *National Bank Ltd v Behan*[3] that the onus remained on the person seeking to uphold such a voluntary conveyance to prove that it was made *bona fide* and without intent to defraud, this decision appears irreconcilable with the later decision of the Irish Court of Appeal in *Re Moore*[4] and it would seem that the better view is that since the 1893 Act the onus of proving bad faith is on the party alleging it.

1 10 Car I, sess 2, c 3.
2 *Doe d Otley v Manning* (1809) 9 East 59; *Gardiner v Gardiner* (1961) 121 CLR 565.
3 [1913] I IR 512.
4 [1918] I IR 169.

14.13 The third category is of *settlements rendered voidable by the subsequent bankruptcy of the settlor*. Under s 52 of the Bankruptcy (Ireland) Amendment Act 1872 a settlement of property is void as against the official assignee if the settlor becomes bankrupt within *two years* after its date. Furthermore, unless the persons claiming under the settlement can prove that at its date the settlor could pay all his debts without recourse to the property comprised in the settlement, it will be void as against the official assignee if the settlor becomes bankrupt within *ten years* of its date. The section does not apply to

(i) settlements made before and in consideration of marriage;

(ii) settlements made in favour of a purchaser or incumbrancer in good faith and for valuable consideration;

(iii) settlements made on or for the wife or the children of the settlor of property which has accrued to the settlor after the marriage in right of his wife.

A number of points should be observed about this provision. As in the case of conveyances affected by the Statute of Charles I, although the Act uses the expression 'void', the settlements are voidable only and remain in effect unless and until the official assignee takes steps to set them aside.[1] When the settlement is set aside, the property vests in the assignee subject to any charges created subsequent to its date by the settlor.[2] No fraudulent intent on the part of the settlor need be shown: the settlement is rendered voidable by the mere fact of the bankruptcy within the specified period. The crucial date for determining whether the settlement is captured is that of the act of bankruptcy and not the adjudication.[3]

The exception in favour of marriage settlements applies to settlements on the marriages of any persons and not simply the settlor himself.[4] The reference to 'purchasers' is not to purchasers in the conveyancing sense: any person who has furnished a quid pro quo will be treated as a purchaser.[5] And 'valuable consideration' is not confined to money: it extends to the release of a right or the compromise of a claim.[6] But it must be more than merely nominal or colourable consideration.[7]

Finally, it should be noted that the section is confined in its operation to traders, although it has been recommended by the Budd Committee on Bankruptcy Law that it should be extended to non-traders.

1 Kiely *Principles of Equity* pp 70/1 citing an unreported decision to that effect of Palles CB in *Re Doyle* (1891).
2 *Sanguinetti v Stuckey's Banking Co* [1895] 1 Ch 176.
3 *Re Mackay* (1915) 2 IR 347.
4 *Re Downes* (1898) 2 IR 635.
5 *Re Windle* [1975] 3 All ER 987.
6 *Re Pope* [1908] 2 KB 169.
7 *Re Abbott* [1982] 3 All ER 181.

Part three

The equitable remedies

Chapter 15

The injunction

15.01 An injunction has been defined as an order of the court requiring a person to refrain from doing, or to do, a particular act. Thus, it may restrain the defendant from trespassing on the plaintiff's land or it may require him to pull down a building which obstructs the plaintiff's light. It has been observed, however, that this and analogous definitions are in truth more in the nature of descriptions of an injunction. An award of damages in a personal injuries action is in form an order of the court requiring the defendant to pay the plaintiff money and yet no lawyer would dream of describing it as an injunction. Indeed one of the outstanding characteristics of an injunction is that it provides the plaintiff with relief in circumstances where his grievance could not be met by the payment of money. However, provided we remember that it is too comprehensive to constitute a true definition of an injunction, it will serve for our purposes.

While the other equitable remedies are still of importance—and the declaration has in particular assumed a new significance in the developing area of constitutional and administrative law [1]—there can be no doubt that for the practising lawyer the injunction has become in modern times the most potent. Not only does it achieve what money frequently cannot do— the assertion or protection of a valuable right—but it can do so with a speed and efficiency not normally associated with the legal process. The increasing resort to the interlocutory injunction—the order which can be obtained on four days' notice and preserves the *status quo* until the trial— and the interim injunction (granted without any notice at all to the defendant) is understandable from the plaintiff's point of view. Not merely does it give him instant relief: it frequently resolves the dispute between plaintiff and defendant in its entirety. This has perhaps been most noticeable in the field of labour law: the strangling at birth, so to speak, of the picket by means of an injunction has also frequently put an end to the dispute which provoked the picket and rendered any further litigation pointless. But this effect is not confined to the field of labour relations, although it is in that area that it has caused most controversy.

The popularity of the remedy has in recent years spawned a whole new breed of injunctions, known as *Mareva*[2] and *Anton Piller*[3] orders, which seek to ensure that, in advance of the litigation proper, the defendant does not deprive the proceedings of their efficacy by removing assets from the jurisdiction of the court, or even dissipating them within the jurisdiction, or by destroying or concealing the evidence on which the plaintiff hopes to rely.

1 See Chapter 19.
2 See para 15.34, below.
3 See para 15.42, below.

15.02 Injunctions can be either *prohibitory*—ie ordering the defendant to refrain from committing a particular act such as trepass on property—or *mandatory*, ie ordering the defendant to do something such as pulling down a building. The latter type was traditionally more difficult to obtain, not least because it might require the supervision by the court of the plaintiff's compliance (as where building works were ordered to be done) to an extent which was considered impractical. These difficulties were obviously much greater at the interlocutory stage and practically insuperable in the case of an *ex parte* application for interim relief. The courts, however, receded from their original reluctance to grant mandatory injunctive relief,[1] and one fiction which has been decisively expelled from the law is the granting of what was effectively a mandatory injunction in prohibitory form—forbidding the plaintiff *not* to do an act, such as pulling down a building—in order to preserve the pretence that a mandatory injunction is not being granted.[2]

We have already seen the distinction between interlocutory injunctions and perpetual injunctions granted at the trial, a distinction of the first importance in practical terms, since the principles on which the court acts in granting or withholding interlocutory relief are significantly different from those being applied when an injunction is being sought at the trial. Two further distinctions remain to be mentioned.

In the first place, we must distinguish between *quia timet* injunctions as they are called and others. A *quia timet* injunction is granted to restrain the commission of an act which the plaintiff fears the defendant is about to commit but which he has not yet commited. As we shall see, the courts adopt a wary approach to the granting of such injunctions resting as they do solely on the apprehension of the plaintiff which may turn out to be groundless.[3] In the second place, there is a distinction, now to some extent theoretical, between equitable injunctions and legal injunctions.

1 *Smith v Smith* (1875) LR 20 Eq 500.
2 *Jackson v Normanby* [1899] 1 Ch 438, CA.
3 See para 15.32, below.

15.03 Much of the old learning as to injunctions and their evolution in the law has ceased to be of everyday importance. But some knowledge of the development in the legal system which we have inherited of this most striking of equitable remedies is essential to both the student and the practitioner, and to that we now turn.

The development of the injunction

15.04 Equity, we know, acted upon the conscience of a party. One consequence of this was that the chancellor was prepared to restrain a plaintiff who had obtained a common law judgement from executing it, if he thought that it was unconscionable of the plaintiff to rely on his common law rights. This early use of the injunction, as we have seen,[1] led to the historic breach between the common law courts led by Coke as chief justice and the chancery led by Ellesmere, in which the latter eventually triumphed following the *Earl of Oxford's Case*[2] and the decisive intervention of James I in favour of the chancery. This form of injunction—sometimes called a 'common injunction'—no longer plays a prominent part in our law, but cannot be said to have completely disappeared. Thus, as we have seen, the courts may restrain a person by an analogous procedure from suing in another jurisdiction if this would be a breach of his obligations to the defendant.[3] And in England it has been held that the court will restrain by injunction the use of an affidavit filed in family law proceedings by a husband and setting out his assets in other unrelated proceedings.[4]

The jurisdiction of the courts of equity to grant injunctions in the more conventional form was clearly established at a relatively early stage. Equity would come to the aid of a plaintiff who was asserting an *equitable* right—eg under a trust—by ordering the defendant to refrain from infringing the right, e.g. in the case of a trustee by committing a breach of the trust. The chancellor, in addition, however, protected the *legal* rights of plaintiffs, so that, for example, he would grant an injunction to restrain the defendant from trespassing on the plaintiff's property. But since that was a right capable of being vindicated in a common law court by an award of damages, the chancellor would usually only intervene where damages were an inadequate remedy. Injunctions of the first type were called 'equitable injunctions in the exclusive jurisdiction' and those of the second type 'equitable injunctions in the auxiliary injunction.'

In practice, as the law of tort developed and the law recognised many legal rights of the plaintiff interference with which could not be adequately compensated by an award of damages, the second category began to outstrip the first in importance. Ultimately by the Common Law Procedure (Ireland) Act 1856, common law courts were given jurisdiction to grant injunctions to restrain the repetition or continuance of wrongful acts which could be the subject of common law proceedings. Thus, the common law courts could now grant injunctions themselves and plaintiffs did not have to resort to the auxiliary jurisdiction in equity, save in special circumstances.[5]

The next development of significance was the granting to the chancery court of the right to award damages in addition to or in substitution for an injunction. This provision in Lord Cairns' Act[6] was of considerable importance where the plaintiff could establish that his legal or equitable rights had been infringed but was denied relief by way of an injunction. The court might consider that damages were an adequate remedy. Moreover, the injunction, being a quintessentially equitable institution was a discretionary remedy: the court might decline to grant the relief if, for example, it would be unduly oppressive to the defendant to do so. In all such cases, the court could now substitute an award of damages.

1 See para 2.08, above.
2 (1615) 1 Rep Ch 1.
3 See para 3.06, above.
4 *Medway v Doublelock Ltd*, [1978] 1 All ER 1261, [1978] 1 WLR 710. For a rare Irish example of something approaching a common injunction, see *Dublin Co Council v Baily Holdings Ltd* (unreported; judgement delivered 10 November 1978) where the Supreme Court prohibited the owners of property from executing a decree for possession obtained by them in the District Court.
5 As in the case of a *quia timet* injunction, where no wrong had been committed.
6 Chancery Amendment Act 1858 (21 and 22 Vict c 27).

15.05 The enactment of the Judicature (Ireland) Act 1877 meant, as we have seen,[1] the disappearance from our law of the procedural differences which had characterised the system under which courts of common law and equity flourished side by side. It was still necessary for the plaintiff to commence his proceedings in the chancery division where the primary relief sought was an injunction, but even that difference was abolished with the establishment of the courts of the new state in 1924, including a unified High Court. It is, however, important to bear in mind that the Judicature Acts did not effect, and were not intended to effect, any change in the substantive law.

Thus a plaintiff could not now obtain an injunction in circumstances where he could not obtain one before the Acts were passed. The fact that the Court was now empowered to grant *interlocutory* relief in any case where it was 'just and convenient'[2] to do so seems to have misled judges of such eminence as Jessel MR into thinking that the equivalent English Act had enlarged the jurisdiction of the court to such an extent that it could now protect rights by the granting of injunctive relief which could not have been so protected before the Acts.[3] There were even dicta to the effect that the Court could simply grant an injunction where it was convenient to do so, although there was no trace of a legal or equitable right which could be said to have been infringed.[4] The view that the Act was purely procedural in its effect and did not enlarge the jurisdiction of the Courts to grant injunctions was firmly reasserted, however, in such cases as *Day v Brownrigg*,[5] where the plaintiff failed to get an injunction to restrain his neighbour from altering the name of his house from 'Ashford Villa' to 'Ashford Lodge', the same as that of the plaintiff's. Although the plaintiff had suffered manifest inconvenience, he had no proprietary interest in the name of his house and consequently no right known to the law which was capable of being protected by the grant of an injunction. This principle was reasserted by the House of Lords in later cases such *Siskina (Cargo Owners) v Distos SA*[6] and *Bremer Vulkan SchifBbau und Maschinenfabrik v South India Shipping Corpn Ltd*.[7]

1 See para 2.19, above.
2 Judicature (Ir) Act 1877, s 28(8).
3 *Aslatt v Southampton Corpn* (1880) 16 Ch D 143.
4 *Beddow v Beddow* (1878) 9 Ch D 89 at 92.
5 (1878) 10 Ch D 294.
6 [1979] AC 210.
7 [1981] 1 All ER 289.

15.06 In Ireland with the enactment of the Constitution of Saorstat Eireann and the present Constitution in 1937 all the pre-existing law was adopted as part of the law of the new State in each case, except to the extent that it was inconsistent with the Constitution. In addition, the Courts of Justice Act 1924 and the Courts (Supplemental Provisions) Act 1961, which established the courts provided for in each constitution, vested in the High Court in each case the originating common law and equitable jurisdiction vested in its predecessor. In the result, the jurisdiction of the High Court to grant injunctions—and this is also true of the Circuit Court—is a statutory jurisdiction exercised in accordance with the same principles of law and equity which governed its predecessors before 1924 except to the extent that those principles are inconsistent with the Constitution. It would seem that, as in England, the Judicature Acts effected no change in the substantive law affecting the granting of such injunctions: they cannot be granted save to protect rights known to the law. It is true that in *Moore and Others v A-G*,[1] Murnaghan J said in the

Supreme Court that the relevant section 'extended the principles upon which jurisdiction was formerly exercised by the Court of Chancery', but this does not seem to be consistent with the generally accepted view of the effect of the section.

There is one highly important rider to be added: while it is still only rights known to the law which can be protected by injunction, the range of such rights now includes rights guaranteed by the Constitution which may not have been previously recognised by the common law or equity. This topic is dealt with in more detail below.[2]

1 [1927] IR 569.
2 See para 15.16, below.

15.07 Finally, it should be noted that in two important areas of the law, the Oireachtas has supplemented the equitable jurisdiction of the Courts by enabling orders in the nature of injunctions to be granted where they could not be obtained before, or where it was at least doubtful whether they could be obtained. Under the Local Government (Planning and Development Amendment) Act 1977 the High Court may make an order restraining a person from carrying out an unauthorised development on land on the application of a planning authority or any person.[1] And under s 2 of the Family Law (Protection of Spouses and Children) Act 1981 the court (now the District Court and Circuit Court) may make an order (the so-called 'barring order') restraining a spouse from remaining in or re-entering the matrimonial home.[2]

1 S 27.
2 See Shatter, *Family Law in the Republic of Ireland*, 3rd edn, p576 et seq.

Principles on which the court acts in granting perpetual injunctions

15.08 There are three requirements which must normally be met before the court will grant a perpetual injunction. (This is the injunction granted at the trial of the action as distinct from an interlocutory injunction granted before the action comes to trial.)

(i) The injunction must be granted to protect a legal right of the plaintiff

It does not matter whether the right sought to be protected is a legal right deriving from common law (such as the right to the peaceful enjoyment of one's property) or from equity (such as the right of a beneficiary under a trust) or from the Constitution itself (in which case it can be either one of the specified constitutional rights, such as freedom of expression[1] or one of those unspecified, but recognised by the courts, such as the right of privacy[2]). But it must be a right recognised by the law: as we have seen, inconvenience suffered by the plaintiff is not sufficient to justify the granting of an injunction.[3]

It was at one time the law that where the injunction sought was in protection of a common law right, it would only be granted where the right was of a proprietary nature.[4] The same rule did not apply in the exclusive equitable jurisdiction where, for example, an injunction could be obtained to restrain the defendant from committing a breach of confidence, even though no proprietary right of the plaintiff was threatened.[5] While it is generally acknowledged that the rule survives if at all in only the most attenuated form, it is sometimes claimed that it still, for example, precludes an injunction being granted to restrain defamation of a purely personal nature.[6] It is also said to provide the basis of the principle that a mere licensee cannot claim an injunction in respect of nuisance.[7] Whatever may be the position in other common law jurisdictions, however, it is thought that the rule cannot have survived in Ireland. The courts have made it abundantly clear that constitutionally guaranteed rights will be protected by the courts by whatever is the remedy appropriate to the particular case,[8] and it is thought that, where the proper remedy is an injunction, the plaintiff will not be deprived of it by the absence of a proprietary interest. In cases of defamation, while an award of damages is the generally appropriate remedy, there seems no reason why the courts should not grant a perpetual injunction in a proper case, even where the defamation is purely personal and does not amount to a trade libel or injurious falsehood. To deprive the plaintiff of that remedy because of the rule under consideration and for no other reason would seem to amount to a failure by the court to vindicate the good name of the plaintiff, one of the rights expressly protected by Article 40.3.2.

(ii) The legal right must have been infringed or there must at least be a probability that it will be infringed

This principle is obvious and does not require elaboration.

(iii) The injunction will only be granted where there is no other adequate remedy

In particular, if damages are an adequate remedy, an injunction will not be granted. It should also be remembered in this context that since the injunction is a discretionary remedy it may still be refused where, for example, it would be oppressive to the defendant to grant it or where the plaintiff's conduct may disentitle him to the relief, even though damages are not an adequate remedy.

Some cases are more readily identifiable as appropriate to the granting of an injunction than others. Thus, any invasion of proprietary rights, such as trespass or nusiance, is a wrong peculiarly adapted to injunctive relief. In each case, the court has to balance the other remedies available to the plaintiff, the rights and interests of both parties and the consequences of granting the injunction. In general, however, it can be said that

'where the plaintiff has established the invasion of a common law right and there is ground for believing that, without an injunction, there is likely to be a repetition of the wrong, he is, in the absence of special circumstances, entitled to an injunction against such repetition.'[9]

The circumstances in which the court should exercise its jurisdiction under Lord Cairns' Act to award damages in lieu of an injunction were summarised as follows in a frequently quoted passage by AL Smith LJ in *Shelfer v City of London Electric Lighting Co:*[10]

(1) if the injury to the plaintiff's rights is small; and
(2) is one which is capable of being estimated in money; and
(3) is one which can be adequately compensated by a small money payment; and

(4) the case is one in which it would be oppressive to the defendant to grant an injunction.

In the same case, however, Lindley LJ rejected the notion that the effect of Lord Cairns' Act had been that the Court ought to allow a wrong to continue, simply because the wrongdoer was able and willing to pay for the injury he might inflict.[11] And in *Leeds Industrial Co-operative Society v Slack*,[12] Lord Sumner doubted

'whether it is complete justice to allow the big man with his big building and his enhanced rateable value and his improvement of the neighbourhood, to have his way, and to solace the little man for his darkened and stuffy room in his little house by giving him a cheque he does not ask for.'

These principles were applied by Costello J in *Patterson v Murphy*[13] where he granted an injunction restraining the defendants from quarrying activities by means of blasting which he found had actually damaged the plaintiffs' house and interfered with the plaintiff's comfort to an unreasonable extent.

A decision which is less easy to reconcile with the other authorities is *Halpin v Tara Mines Ltd*.[14] In that case, it was found that the defendants had by their mining activities 'sensibly diminished the reasonable comfort and peace of living' of the plaintiffs. But Gannon J also pointed out that, since the case had first come before him, the defendants had improved their working standards to a degree which made it unnecessary to continue the interim injunction originally granted. He went on:

'In a case such as this where the day to day working conditions of the defendants and the living conditions of the plaintiffs necessarily are subject to variable changes of circumstances, I do not think that it would be appropriate for the Court to prescribe definitive standards of tolerance by specified limitations similar to or on the lines of those to which the parties had agreed. If I were to make an order of injunction it would have to be of that imprecise nature indicated by Romilly MR in *Crump v Lambert*[15] with the consequences which he indicated, namely that the defendants might continue their work at the risk of severe penalty and the complete close down of their business if in later proceedings it might be shown that they caused or repeated the nuisances prohibited.'

He accordingly awarded damages in lieu of an injunction to each of the plaintiffs. The case is not reported and it is accordingly not possible to say what authorities were cited or what concessions made in the course of argument. It is respectfully submitted, however, that difficulty in complying with an injunction is not of itself a ground for withholding an injunction: the other requirements specified in *Shelfer's case* and *Patterson v Murphy* should be met. It may be noted that in the case cited in the passage just quoted (*Crump v Lambert*), an injunction was in fact granted, and that in *Patterson v Murphy*, Costello J treated *Halpin v Tara Mines* as distinguishable on its facts.

It is possible to discern a more indulgent approach in cases of interference with light. While rights of light are an undoubted proprietary right which the law has for long striven to protect, it has had to balance the degree of inconvenience caused to the plaintiff against the natural reluctance to order the removal of a building upon which money and labour have been expended and which may be in an urban area where new building is sometimes virtually impossible without causing some diminution in another person's light. In *Colls v Home and Colonial Stores*,[16] Lord Macnaghten said

> 'In some cases, of course, an injunction is necessary—if for instance the injury cannot fairly be compensated by money—if the defendant has acted in a high handed manner—if he has endeavoured to steal a march upon the plaintiff or to evade the jurisdiction of the court. In all these cases an injunction is necessary, in order to do justice to the plaintiff and as a warning to others. But if there is really a question to be tried as to whether the obstruction is legal or not and if the defendant has acted fairly and not in an unneighbourly spirit, I am disposed to think that the Court ought to incline to damages rather than to an injunction.'

This passage was adopted by Dixon J in *McGrath v Munster and Leinster Bank Ltd*[17] in which a solicitor claimed that a new building erected by the defendants in Dame Street had materially reduced the natural lighting in her office. While holding that she had established her claim, the learned judge, applying the principles stated by Lord Macnaghten, awarded damages in lieu of an injunction.

1 Article 40.6.1.
2 *McGee v A-G*, [1974] IR 284 SC; *Kennedy and others v Ireland and another*, unreported, High Court (Hamilton P), judgement delivered 12 January 1987.
3 Para 15.05, above.
4 Meagher, Gummow & Lehane, pp 560-562.
5 See para 30.01, below.
6 *Prudential Assurance Co v Knott* (1875) 10 Ch App 142.
7 *Malone v Laskey* [1907] 2 KB 141; overruled but not on this point by *A C Billings & Sons Ltd v Riden* [1958] AC 240. See para 15.10, below.
8 See para 15.16, below.
9 Spry, *Equitable Remedies*, 3rd edn, p 368.
10 [1895] 1 Ch 287.
11 Pp 315-316.
12 [1924] AC 851.
13 Unreported; judgement delivered 4 May 1978.
14 Unreported; judgement delivered 1976.
15 (1867) LR 3 Eq 409.
16 [1904] AC 179 at 193.
17 [1959] IR 313.

15.09 Other general principles affecting the granting of perpetual injunctions must next be considered. It should be emphasised at the outset, however, that while they are considered here in the context of perpetual injunctions, they are common to all forms of injunction. In the first place, as we have seen, an injunction is a discretionary remedy. The fact that the plaintiff has proved the violation of a common law right will automatically entitle him to damages *ex debito justitiae*, ie as a matter of right. But it will not entitle him automatically to an injunction. In deciding whether or not to grant an injunction, the court will take into account a number of matters, such as the question dealt with in the last paragraph as to whether damages is an adequate remedy. The conduct of the plaintiff will also be a relevant consideration, since in accordance with the maxim 'he who seeks equity must do equity'[1] and 'he who comes into equity must come with clean hands'[2] the court will not grant an injunction where the conduct of the plaintiff has been in some material respect inequitable. The injunction may also be refused where to grant it would be unduly oppressive or a hardship on the defendant.[3] If the plaintiff has acquiesced in the wrong complained of, this also may be a ground for refusing him relief;[4] and similarly if he has been guilty of *laches*, or undue delay in pursuing his remedy.[5] It should be pointed out, however, that an injunction will be more readily refused on the ground of laches at the interlocutory stage than at the trial of the action. Indeed, as we have seen, it may be doubted whether laches is *ever* a ground for withholding a perpetual injunction in respect of the breach of a *legal* right.[6]

It has also been said that the court cannot take into account the effect of the injunction on third parties or on the public generally in deciding how its discretion should be exercised in a particular case. In *Bellew v Irish Cement Ltd*,[7] the Supreme Court rejected an argument on behalf of the defendants that an interlocutory injunction should not be granted to restrain manufacturing operations allegedly causing nuisance in the form of dust when compliance with it might mean the closure of the factory throughout the long vacation with a consequently damaging effect on the entire building industry. Black J, however, dissented, taking the view that this was one of the matters which a court should be entitled to consider in exercising a discretion.[8] In England, a majority of the Court of Appeal somewhat surprisingly held in *Miller v Jackson*[9] that the plaintiff, whose house adjoined a cricket field and who suffered intermittent bombardment of his property from boundary hits, had to be content with damages instead of an injunction. Lord Denning MR, having waxed lyrical on the beauties of cricket on the village green, opined that the public interest in maintaining this essential feature of the English way of life had to outweigh the private discomfort of the plaintiff.[10] In a later case of *Kennaway v Thompson*,[11] however, a differently constituted Court of Appeal rejected this view as going too far and granted an injunction restraining motor boat racing, which was a source of noise, except at reasonable hours. Lawton LJ cited the following passage from *Shelfer's Case:*

'The court has always protested against the notion that it ought to allow a wrong to continue simply because the wrongdoer is able and willing to pay for the injury he may inflict. Neither has the circumstance that the wrongdoer is in some sense a public benefactor (e.g. a gas or water company or a sewer authority) ever been considered a sufficient reason for refusing to protect by injunction an individual whose rights are being persistently infringed.'[12]

These two were cases of perpetual injunctions. It may be that, at the interlocutory stage, it would be reasonable to take the effect on the public or third parties into account as at least one of the relevant factors, as suggested by Black J in *Bellew v Irish Cement Ltd.*

Reference has already been made to the statutory orders in the nature of injunctions which can now be obtained under planning and family law legislation. It should be noted that in such cases also the granting or withholding of the injunction is a matter within the discretion of the court. Thus in the case of orders under s 27 of Local Government (Planning and Development Amendment) Act 1977 an order requiring a use to be discontinued or a building to be demolished may be refused where the offending development has been acquiesced in by the parties most affected and the planning authority for a sufficiently lengthy period[13] or where an order under the section would cause 'gross and disproportionate hardship.'[14]

It was also held by Kenny J in *Cullen v Cullen*,[15] after he had reviewed a number of authorities, that the court's equitable jurisdiction to grant injunctions should not normally be invoked in cases involving family disputes.

Finally, it may be remarked that while difficulty in complying with the injunction is not normally a good ground for refusing the relief, it may unquestionably be refused on the ground that compliance with it is impossible,[16] or will involve the defendant in an illegality.[17] Moreover, if it is clearly established that the granting of an injunction would be futile, this will also be a ground for refusing relief.[18] While this last principle is clearly established, its application to cases where governments have sought to restrain breaches of confidence by former employees has given rise to furious controversy in recent times.[19] This subject is considered in more detail in Chapter 30.[20]

1 See para 3.07, above.
2 See para 3.08, above.
3 *St Mary, Islington, Vestry v Hornsey UDC* [1900] 1 Ch 695, CA.
4 *Birmingham Canal Co v Lloyd* (1812) 18 Ves 515.
5 *Archbold v Scully* (1861) 9 HL Cas 360.
6 See para 3.11, above.
7 [1948] IR 61.
8 P 76.
9 [1977] QB 966, [1977] 3 All ER 338.
10 P 981.
11 [1981] QB 88, [1980] 3 All ER 329, CA.
12 At 315-316 per Lindley LJ.
13 *Dublin Corpn v Mulligan*, unreported (Finlay P), judgement delivered 6 May 1980.
14 *Morris v Garvey* [1983] IR 319, SC.
15 [1962] IR 268. It should be noted, however, that, as between husbands and wives, a jurisdiction to grant injunctions has been successfully invoked on some occasions recently in the High Court since the 'barring order' jurisdiction was transferred to the Circuit Court and District Court. See Shatter, op cit, 588 et seq.
16 *Pride of Derby and Derbyshire Angling Association Ltd v British Celanese Ltd* [1953] Ch 149 at 181.
17 Ibid.
18 Spry, op cit, pp 388-389.
19 *A-G v Guardian Newspapers Ltd* [1987] NLJ Rep 785, HL.
20 See para 30.09, below.

Injunctions in specific cases

15.10 Nuisance. This is a wrong which is peculiarly susceptible to being remedied by an injunction. Of its nature, it is continuous rather than confined to a single act or omission or *fasciculus* of acts or omissions, the essential feature of the wrong of negligence which is at the other end of the spectrum and where the injunction is rarely employed.

Nuisances are divided into two categories, public and private. A private nuisance arises where there is an unreasonable interference with the right of a person to the quiet and peaceful enjoyment of his property.[1] The action can only be maintained by a person with an interest in the property: thus, a person who is simply permitted to use the property by the owner but has no proprietary interest is not entitled to an injunction (or for that matter, damages).[2] The position of such a person, known in law as a bare licensee, should be contrasted with someone having an interest, however small, such as a weekly tenant. Even though the latter can be put out at a week's notice, he is still entitled to maintain proceedings for nuisance and in an appropriate case can be granted an injunction.[3]

A public nuisance is an interference with the rights of the public generally. Thus, anyone who uses the public highway for any purpose other than that for which it is intended, ie passing and re-passing, commits a public nuisance.[4] But the only person who may bring proceedings in respect of such a nuisance is the Attorney General acting on behalf of the public. The individual citizen has no right to bring such an action, unless he can prove that his private rights have been infringed or that he has suffered some damage peculiar to himself and not sustained by the public at large.[5] So, to continue our example of the highway, it is clear that a person whose access to the highway has been obstructed may normally bring proceedings against the person creating the obstruction.[6] But if one or more private citizens wish to bring proceedings in respect of what they allege is a public nuisance which has not caused any of them damage peculiar to himself or infringed any of their private rights, they can only do so in the form of a *relator* action. In such cases, where the Attorney General consents, the action is brought in his name 'at the relation of' the real plaintiffs. This topic is considered further below.[7]

1 3 Blackstone's *Commentaries*, 14th edn, p 216.
2 *Malone v Laskey* [1907] 2 KB 401; overruled, but not on this point, by *A C Billings & Son's Ltd v Riden* [1958] AC 240, [1957] 3 All ER 1.
3 *Simper v Foley* (1862) 2 John & H 555. But he will not be granted a *perpetual* injunction.
4 *Harrison v Duke of Rutland* [1893] 1 QB 142. Clearly there are some incidental uses which are now sanctioned by law other than passing and repassing, eg parking a car where it does not cause an obstruction and the parking is not otherwise unlawful. See Keane, *Law of Local Government in the Republic of Ireland*, p 70.
5 *Boyce v Paddington Corpn* [1903] 1 Ch 109.
6 *Holland v Dublin County Council* (1979) 113 ILT 1.
7 See para 15.17, below.

15.11 Trespass to land is another wrong which readily attracts the remedy of the injunction. To-day it may take a different form than in former times, with the prevalence of 'sit ins' and other demonstrations which frequently take the form of trespassing on other people's property. In such a case, the relief granted is generally mandatory in substance, since the trespassers are effectively required to vacate the premises. But the injunction will nevertheless be granted, provided all the usual conditions are met, including the requirement that damages will not be an adequate remedy. In the case of a trespass which has as its consequence the serious disruption of a business activity, it is usually possible to meet this condition. *Trespass to the person*, while much less frequently the subject of an injunction, has been so restrained in England. In *Egan v Egan*,[1] a son was restrained from committing assaults on his mother.

1 [1975] Ch 218. It can, of course, give rise to a 'barring order' in the case of husband and wife: see para 15.07, above.

15.12 Picketing of premises is a wrongful act unless it is carried on peaceably and in contemplation or in furtherance of a trade dispute.[1] The precise legal nature of the wrong has been the subject of some dispute. On one view, 'watching and besetting' premises without legal justification is a tortious act. On another picketing of premises as such is not unlawful: it is only unlawful where it is carried on on the public highway and amounts to an abuse of the right to use the highway which can be restrained where the owner of the property suffers special damage.[2] Picketing which is not being carried on in a peaceable manner or which is not in contemplation or furtherance of a trade dispute is one of the wrongs most frequently restrained by an injunction to-day.

Injury to *industrial, commercial and intellectual property* is also commonly restrained by injunction. Patents, trade marks and copyrights are all protected in this way where appropriate by the grant of injunctions.

Injunctions will also be granted to restrain the tort of *passing off*, ie representing goods sold by the defendant as being those of the plaintiff.

Defamation may also be restrained by injunction. It was at one time thought that this was not possible, but this was based on the view that an injunction could only be granted where the plaintiff could establish a proprietary right. As we have seen,[3] this is probably no longer the case in Ireland. Similarly an injunction may also be granted in the case of an injurious falsehood, ie the malicious publication of a falsehood causing damage to the plaintiff, or a statement disparaging the plaintiff's title to land or goods or the quality of the goods.

1 Trade Disputes Act 1906.
2 Clerk and Lindsell on *Torts*, 15th edn, p 805.
3 See para 15.08, above.

15.13 Breaches of contract. In general terms, it may be said that the court will normally restrain the breach of a negative stipulation in a contract, even where the plaintiff has not suffered and will not suffer damage. Where a person agrees for valuable consideration that he will not do something, the court will give effect to what the parties themselves have agreed. This is known as the rule in *Doherty v Allman*[1] and although stated in remarkably wide terms in that case, to the extent that it has been suggested that the court has no discretion to withhold the injunction, it is in fact clear that the court is entitled to take into account all the circumstances of the case before deciding whether the injunction should issue. In particular, it may be refused like any other injunction on the grounds of delay, acquiescence or laches.[2]

The principle has been extended to implied negative stipulations in accordance with the maxim that 'equity looks to the intent rather than the form.'[3] An agreement to do something may be in effect an agreement not to do something else: for example, a contract to purchase all one's supplies of a commodity from a particular supplier is, by implication, an agreement not to purchase the supplies from someone else. For this reason, the court restrained a customer from taking electricity from another supplier where he had contracted to take all his supplies from the plaintiff: *Metropolitan Electric Supply Co v Ginder*.[4]

Moreover, every contract must be read subject to an implied agreement not to prevent performance of the contract. Thus in *Manchester Ship Canal Co v Manchester Racecourse Co*,[5] a contract to give a person the right to purchase the premises before anyone else—a right of 'first refusal'—was held to be subject to an implied agreement enforceable by injunction not to sell the premises to anyone else.[6]

Even where the stipulation is affirmative in form, it may be enforced, at least where the stipulation would be capable of being enforced if it stood on its own and where the court is satisfied that it is just that it should be so enforced.[7]

1 (1878) 3 App Cas 709.
2 *Sharp v Harrison* [1922] 1 Ch 502; *Wrotham Park Estate Co v Parkside Homes Ltd* [1974] 2 A11 ER 321.
3 Para 3.16, above.
4 [1901] 2 Ch 799.
5 [1901] 2 Ch 37.
6 See *Re Massarella*, unreported, High Court (Keane J), judgement delivered 10 July 1980.

7 Meagher, Gummow & Lehane, pp 582-583; *Dowty Boulton Paul Ltd v Wolverhampton Corpn* [1971] 2 All ER 277, [1971] 1 WLR 204.

15.14 As this last instance shows, enforcing one or more terms of a contract by injunction represents a form of *specific performance* of the contract. Since there are circumstances in which the court will not grant specific performance of a contract,[1] it follows that the court will not permit that remedy to be obtained in a different guise by the grant of an injunction. This is of particular importance in the case of contracts of personal service: it has always been the law that the court will refuse to order the specific performance of such a contract since it would be wrong to require people to continue in the employer-employee relationship when one or other wishes to terminate it. (One of the parties may, of course, be entitled to damages in respect of the wrongful termination.)

But even in cases of contracts of personal service, the courts have granted injunctions which have come remarkably close to decrees of specific performance, while not crossing that perilous dividing line. The leading case is *Lumley v Wagner*[2] in which an impresario sought to restrain an opera singer who had agreed to sing for him at Covent Garden, and not to sing at any other theatre during the currency of the agreement, from singing at Her Majesty's Theatre in breach of the agreement. It was urged on her behalf that giving effect to this stipulation effectively required the plaintiff to sing at Covent Garden and hence amounted to specific performance of a contract of personal service. Lord St Leonards LC rejected this argument, holding that the injunction sought would not compel the plaintiff to perform her contract. She could still refuse to sing at Covent Garden leaving the plaintiff to his remedy in damages, and there was nothing to prevent her from earning money in other ways provided she did not sing in theatres.

The decision has been a perennial source of controversy. Judges have refused to extend it, treating it as an anomalous encroachment on the fundamental maxim that the court should not require specific performance of a contract of personal service.[3] Its implications were remarkably underlined in *Warner Bros Ltd v Nelson*[4] where the plaintiffs, the great Hollywood studio, sought to restrain the defendant, Bette Davis, from acting with any other studio during the currency of her five year contract. Its terms prohibited her from rendering any services 'in that capacity' (ie as a film actress) during that period and the court granted an injunction prohibiting her from acting for other studios. It was held that, since the term in question did not prevent her from accepting other work, restraining her from breaking the term did not amount to an indirect form of specific performance. It was, of course, somewhat disingenuous to suppose that a star of her earning power would turn to stage or other work in those pre-television days and the decision was widely seen in the film industry as confirming the dominance of the studios and the relative ineffectiveness of the artists which lasted for another 25 years. On the other side of the line, in *Page One Records Ltd v Britton*,[5] Stamp J refused to enforce by injunction a term which restrained a group of musicians rejoicing in the name 'The Troggs' from employing as their manager any person other than the plaintiffs. He distinguished *Lumley v Wagner*, holding that, unlike the impresario in that case, the manager had duties of a personal and fiduciary nature to perform which rendered the relationship more of a partnership. Granting the injunction would effectively require the group to continue employing the plaintiffs since they had no business experience or aptitudes themselves. The court could not compel the performance of a contract so personal in its nature and dependent on mutual trust.

As *Page One Records Ltd v Britton* demonstrates, the principle that the court will not grant specific performance of contracts of personal service by the indirect method of an injunction applies to the employer's obligations as well as the employees. But there are also decisions in this area which are difficult to reconcile with that general principle, most notably, *Hill v C & A Parsons*.[6] The Court of Appeal in England there upheld an interlocutory injunction restraining the defendants from terminating the plaintiff's employment in breach of his contract. The decision, has, however, been distinguished in a number of subsequent cases and has been somewhat severely handled by academic critics.[7]

There are no reported modern Irish decisions in what might be called the *Lumley v Wagner* area and it remains to be seen how it would fare in to-day's conditions. The criticism of the line of English authority—that such cases subvert the general principle that there should not be specific performance of such contracts of personal service based in turn on the reluctance to turn contracts of service into 'contracts of slavery' to use Fry LJ's colourful phrase[8]—could be reinforced by constitutional arguments in this country. As we shall see,[9] one of the rights not expressly guaranteed by the Constitution but which has been recognised by the courts as one of the unenumerated personal rights guaranteed by Article 40 is the right to earn one's livelihood. It could be said that an agreement which compels a person to choose between working exclusively for a particular employer and not working at all (or working in a way other than that for which his talents best equip him) does not honour that guarantee and should not be enforced by the courts. But perhaps it could be more strongly argued on the other side that the law which frowns on enforcing contracts of personal service is itself based on rhetorical denunciations of 'contracts of slavery' which have little relevance to-day. In modern conditions, contracts of this nature tend to be negotiated by large impersonal organisations, such as commercial firms, trade unions and professional associations, which renders the case law dating from a different era somewhat irrelevant.

It is certainly the case that judicial reluctance to enforce contracts of personal service has waned more notably in cases where the employee is the party seeking the remedy. There has been a similar tendency on the part of the legislature as exemplified by the Unfair Dismissals Act 1977 which empowers the relevant tribunal to reinstate an employee who has been unfairly dismissed.[10]

1 See para 16.02, below.
2 (1852) 1 De G M & G 604.
3 *Whitwood Chemical Co Ltd v Hardman* [1891] 2 Ch 416, CA.
4 [1937] 1 KB 209.
5 [1967] 3 All ER 822.
6 [1972] Ch 305, [1971] 3 All ER 1345, CA.
7 Eg Meagher, Gummow & Lehane, p 545. See also *Chappell v Times Newspapers Ltd* [1975] 2 All ER 233, [1975] 1 WLR 482.
8 *De Francesco v Barnum* (1890) 45 Ch D 430 at 438.
9 See para 15.16, below.
10 Redmond, *Dismissal Law in the Republic of Ireland*, pp 116 et seq.

15.15 Wrongful removal from office. This must be carefully distinguished from the wrongful termination of a contract of employment referred to in the preceding paragraph. In the case of an office of any sort, whether it be in the public area such as the civil service or the Gardai, or in the private area, such as an officer of a company registered under the Companies Acts 1963 to 1986, the court may always prevent by injunction the wrongful removal of an office-holder from his office. In the typical case, the plaintiff will be relying on a failure to comply with requirements imposed by statute or by the constitution of the body concerned rather than the breach of a purely contractual right. If such provisions have not been complied with in some material respect, the court will restrain the defendants from preventing the plaintiff from exercising the office.[1] Moreover, even in the case of a private body, such as a company established in pursuance of statutory powers, it has been said that the constitution of the body must be read in the light of the constitutional guarantees as to fair procedures. This may require, for example, in the case of a managing director of a company, the observance of the maxim *audi alteram partem*, ie the obligation to give the office-holder a fair opportunity of answering any charges against him.[2]

It is, however, the case that it is frequently impractical for an office-holder to continue in an office where the persons exercising the power of removal have lost confidence in him. In such a case, an injunction may be somewhat futile since there is nothing to prevent the body concerned from repeating the procedure of removal while taking care to avoid any appearance of illegality. It may be more sensible in such circumstances for the aggrieved person to seek a *declaration*[3] that his removal from office has been unlawful, thus laying the ground for an award of damages should the court grant him such a declaration. This was the course adopted in *Garvey v Ireland*[4] where the government of the day removed from office the Commissioner of the Gardai without giving him an opportunity of speaking in his own defence. It was stated on behalf of the defendants that the government had lost confidence in the plaintiff, but he was granted a declaration that his removal from office had been unlawful and in due course was awarded damages.

1 *Malloch v Aberdeen Corpn* [1971] 2 All ER 1278, [1971] 1 WLR 1578, 1596; *Glover v BLN Ltd* [1973] IR 388.
2 *Glover v BLN Ltd*, above.
3 See Chapter 19.
4 [1981] IR 76.

Constitutional rights

15.16 Apart from rights at common law or equitable rights, injunctions will be granted also to protect or vindicate rights guaranteed by the Constitution. In *Byrne v Ireland*,[1] Walsh J said

'Where the people by the Constitution create rights against the State or impose duties upon the State, a remedy to enforce these must be deemed to be also available.'

The same learned judge elaborated this view in *Meskell v CIE*[2] in the following terms:

'It has been said on a number of occasions in this Court.... that a right guaranteed by the Constitution can be protected by action or enforced by action even though such an action may not fit into any of the ordinary forms of action in either common law or equity and that the constitutional right carries within it its own right to a remedy for the enforcement of it. Therefore, if a person has suffered damage by virtue of a breach of a constitutional right or the infringement

of a constitutional right, that person is entitled to seek redress against the person
or persons who have infringed that right.'

In that case, the plaintiff's employment with the defendants had been
terminated by them and he had been offered his job back on exactly the
same terms, provided he joined the Irish Transport and General Workers'
Union. He brought proceedings against CIE claiming damages for the
breach of his constitutional rights and for conspiracy. His action failed in
the High Court but an appeal was allowed by the Supreme Court who held
unanimously that two constitutional rights of the plaintiff had been
violated: that deriving from Article 40.6.1.iii guaranteeing freedom of
association which, the court held, carried a corresponding right of
dissociation[3] and the right to earn his livelihood which is one of the
unenumerated rights. (It should be noted that the plaintiff in that case
made no claim for re-instatement, perhaps because his legal advisers took
the view that the court would, in the then state of the law, decline to
enforce a contract of personal service. For the reasons suggested above, it
cannot be assumed that this approach would necessarily be adopted
to-day.)

It is clear therefore that, where it is appropriate to do so, the court will
grant an injunction to protect constitutional rights on the same basis as it
would give this form of relief in protection of other legal rights and that this
applies as much in the field of private law as in public law. The courts, in
other words, will treat it as a discretionary remedy which will only be
available where damages are not an adequate remedy. In practice, as we
shall see in Chapter 19 below, constitutional relief is generally sought by
way of a declaratory action and the instances in which injunctive relief have
been granted are rare. It would be available, for example, to protect the
right of personal liberty by restraining an unlawful arrest. This happened in
O'Boyle & another v A-G and Another[4] where Meredith J granted an
injunction restraining the Commissioner of the Gardai from executing an
arrest warrant issued in Northern Ireland in the Irish Free State without
legal justification, although the learned judge did not found his jurisdiction
to do so on the equivalent articles in the then constitution.

The most remarkable example of the use of the injunction in protecting
or vindicating constitutional rights, however, is the recent decision of
Hamilton P in *Attorney General (Society for the Protection of Unborn
Children Ireland Ltd) v Open Door Counselling Ltd and Another*.[5] That
case followed the enactment by the people of the Eighth Amendment to
the Constitution which provides (in Article 40.3.3.) that

'the State acknowledges the right to life of the unborn and, with due regard to
the equal right to life of the mother, guarantees in its law to respect, and as far as
practicable, by its laws to defend and vindicate that right.'

The defendants advised pregnant women resident in Ireland as to the
availability of abortion facilities in England and, in the event of any of
them wishing to consider further the option of having an abortion,
arranged to refer them to medical clinics in England. The proceedings were
brought by the Attorney General at the relation of the Society for the
Protection of Unborn Children Ireland Ltd, a voluntary body, and sought
declarations that the activities of the defendants were unlawful having
regard to the provisions of Article 40.3.3. and an injunction prohibiting the
defendants from carrying them on.

The learned President was satisfied that the activities in question were unlawful and granted the injunction sought. The abortions would, of course, take place only outside the jurisdiction and in a country where they were lawful, so that it was effectively the dissemination of information as to the availability of such facilities in other countries which was prohibited and not the abortions themselves. Article 40.6.1. of the Constitution which guarantees freedom of expression could not, in the view of the learned President protect such activities since they tended to interfere with a 'fundamental right', ie the right to life of the unborn.[6] The implications of the decision are obviously far reaching, since it would appear that the right of freedom of expression, already heavily qualified by the terms of Article 40.6.1. itself, must now be regarded as diluted further as a result of the Eighth Amendment.[7]

1 [1972] IR 241.
2 [1973] IR 121.
3 Cf *Educational Co of Ireland Ltd v Fitzpatrick (No 2)* [1961] IR 345.
4 [1929] IR 558.
5 (1987) ILRM 477.
6 It cannot, of course, have been intended to imply that freedom of expression is not itself a 'fundamental right' since it is expressly so described in the Constitution.
7 It had already been held by the Supreme Court in *The State (Lynch) v Cooney* [1982] IR 337, that the Article did not invalidate the use of s 31 of the Broadcasting Act 1960 (as amended) for the purpose of prohibiting election broadcasts by Sinn Fein.

Public and statutory rights

15.17 Where a public right is infringed, an injunction may be granted to restrain its further infringement on the application of the Attorney General. This role of the Attorney-General in the protection of rights of the public had been recognised before 1921 in a series of English decisions[1] and in *Moore v A-G*,[2] Kennedy CJ, speaking with the authority of having been the first person to hold the office in the new state and been closely involved in the drafting of the relevant constitutional provisions, said that the Attorney General of the Irish Free State remained the guardian of such public rights. (We have already seen that in cases affecting charities, it is usual to join him as the protector of charities.)[3]

Thus, the Attorney-General may apply for an injunction to restrain a public nuisance such as the obstruction of a highway. We have already seen[4] that the private citizen has no such right: he may only obtain an injunction in respect of a public nuisance where he can show that his private rights have been infringed or that he has suffered some damage peculiar to himself. If he or a number of citizens wish to take proceedings in respect of a public nuisance, or any public right which they claim has been violated, they may only do so in the form of a relator action. This is an action brought by one or more private citizens in the name of the Attorney-General or, in the technical language, by the Attorney-General at the relation of the real plaintiff. The consent of the attorney must be obtained to the proceedings being brought[5] and such consent will normally be forthcoming only where he is satisfied that there is an arguable case and that it is in the public interest that it should be litigated. He will usually require in addition an indemnity in relation to any possible liability for costs[6] and he remains in control of the proceedings to the extent that if he wishes he may at any stage discontinue them.[7] The undertaking as to damages, which as will be seen,[8] is an invariable condition for the obtaining of an interlocutory injunction must be given by the real plaintiff;

and the fact that the attorney gives his consent in no sense implies an undertaking on his part to compensate the defendant in the event of the action being dismissed.

This was made clear in the *A-G (Martin) v Dublin Corporation*[9] which arose out of the controversial decision of the defendants to proceed with the erection of new civic offices at Wood Quay, a site of archaeological significance. The plaintiff was Father Frank Martin, a well known historian, and in the proceedings he claimed an injunction restraining the defendants from proceeding with their building plans on the ground that the site was a national monument which could not be interfered with except with the consent of the Commissioners for Public Works in Ireland. This was clearly an action arising out of the alleged violation of a public right and it was accordingly brought in the Attorney General's name and with his consent. When an interlocutory injunction was granted temporarily halting the building, Father Martin gave the usual undertaking to compensate the defendants in the event of the action being unsuccessful. The action itself was ultimately dismissed by the Supreme Court and the defendants thereupon claimed that the attorney in authorising the proceedings had impliedly undertaken to compensate the defendants in the event of their being dismissed. But this submission was rejected by the Supreme Court.

1 *Eg, A-G v Brown* (1818) 1 Swan 265 at 294 per Lord Eldon.
2 [1930] IR 471.
3 See para 11.03, above.
4 See para 15.10, above.
5 *Weir v Fermanagh County Council* [1913] 1 IR 193 at 198-199.
6 *A-G (Humphreys) v Governors of Erasmus Smith's Schools* [1910] 1 IR 325.
7 Ibid.
8 See para 15.26, below.
9 (1980) ILRM 254.

15.18 The statute which confers the public right sought to be protected may itself provide a remedy. The question has accordingly arisen as to whether in such a case the only remedy is that provided by the statute, thus precluding the granting of an injunction to the Attorney General. In particular, it has been urged that where the statute provides a criminal sanction, the granting of an injunction would effectively mean that the defendant had been punished for a criminal offence without the protection of a criminal trial, contrary to Article 38.1. of the Constitution which provides that no person shall be tried on any criminal charge save in due course of law. Since the standard of proof required in an application for an injunction is that applicable in all civil proceedings, ie to establish the case on the balance of probabilities, granting an injunction in such cases, it was said, would wrongfully relieve the state from the requirement applicable in criminal cases, ie that the case should be proved beyond any reasonable doubt.

These arguments were, however, rejected by Costello J in *A-G v Paperlink Ltd and Others*.[1] In that case, the attorney sought an injunction restraining the defendant from carrying on a courier service which, it was alleged, infringed the statutory monopoly conferred on the Minister for Posts and Telegraphs (now An Post) by the Post Office Act 1908. The defendants argued that the statute offended the constitutional guarantees as to freedom of communication and the right to earn one's livelihood. But in addition it was submitted that the attorney could not maintain the proceedings, since the infringement of the statutory monopoly was a criminal offence under the statute. Costello J, however, held that it was possible for the attorney to obtain an injunction to restrain someone from acting in breach of a statutory provision even where his action constitutes an offence. This view of the law had been taken, the learned judge pointed out, by Porter MR in *Attorney General (O'Duffy) v Appleton Surgeon Dentist Ltd*[2] and by Lord Denning MR in *Attorney General v Chaudry*.[3] He emphasised, however, that the jurisdiction should only be exercised in exceptional cases. In addition, the court should consider the adequacy of the alternative remedy. In the instant case, he was satisfied that the circumstances were exceptional, that the deterrent effect of the fine imposed by the 1908 Act was negligible and that, accordingly, the injunction should be granted.

1 (1984) ILRM 373.
2 [1907] 1 IR 252.
3 [1971] 1 WLR 1614 at 1624.

15.19 The Attorney General may accordingly be granted an injunction to restrain the infringement of a public right and (within the limitations explained by Costello J) this is so even where there is a statutory remedy. It is submitted, however, that a member of the public will not be granted such an injunction, save in four exceptional cases. This general principle was uncompromisingly reasserted by the House of Lords in *Gouriet v Union of Post Office Workers*[1] after a successful attempt had been made to dislodge it in the Court of Appeal.

The plaintiff, a member of the public, had sought an injunction restraining the defendant union from instructing its member to 'black' mail coming from South Africa in breach, as it was alleged, of an ancient statute dating from the reign of Queen Ann. It was urged on his behalf that the requirement that such an action be brought only in the form of a relator action with the Attorney General as the nominal plaintiff was obsolete and should be discarded by the courts. The law lords were unanimously of the view, however, that not merely would such a step be 'straining judicial innovation to its limits':[2] it was also undesirable in principle. There had to be some safeguard, in their view, against the bringing of a multiplicity of actions by private citizens or of vexatious and frivolous proceedings. The appropriate officer to determine whether the public interest would be served by permitting a particular action to proceed was the Attorney General: it was not a function which could be efficiently or satisfactorily discharged by the courts.

It is thought that the same considerations would apply in Ireland, although the question has not arisen in the same form as in *Gouriet's case*. Even in the context of a challenge to the constitutional validity of statutes, where a broader approach to the question of *locus standi* is taken,[3] Henchy J has warned in *Cahill v Sutton*[4] against the danger of giving a charter to the meddlesome and the crank 'to litigate the constitutionality of a law rather than to observe it.' The right of the citizen guaranteed by the Constitution to access to the courts must yield, on this view, in some areas to the overriding public interest in the proper administration of justice.

1 [1978] AC 435.
2 At 586.

3 See para 15.21, below.
4 [1980] IR 269 at 284.

15.20 The exceptions to this general principle must now be considered. First, as we have seen,[1] a member of the public may obtain an injunction in respect of the infringement of a public right where he obtains the consent of the Attorney General to the bringing of a relator action in his name. Second, where a statute confers rights on *a defined class of citizens,* one of their number may enforce such rights, in an appropriate case, by an injunction. Thus, a shareholder in a company registered under the Companies Acts 1963 to 1986 is entitled under the Acts to inspect the balance sheet and profit and loss account. He cannot be deprived of such a right by the Memorandum and Articles of Association of the Company and any attempt by the company to deprive him of this right would be restrained by injunction.[2] Third, where a private citizen can show that the acts he complains of not merely infringe a public right but in addition affect a private right peculiar to him, he may obtain an injunction.[3] Thus, if a private right which he alone enjoys—such as his right of access to the highway from his property—is also violated by such an obstruction, the fact that it is a public nuisance will be no bar to the proceeding.[4]

A fourth exception emerged with the decision of Buckley J in *Boyce v Paddington Corporation.*[5] In that case, he said that a private citizen could sue in his own name in respect of a public nuisance in two cases: (a) where the defendant has infringed a private right of the plaintiff, the category of cases just referred to and (b) where no private right of the plaintiff had been violated, but the interference with a public right has in fact caused 'special damage peculiar to the plaintiff.'

While it is reasonably clear that this last exception is not confined to cases of public nuisance, the ambit of the principle is difficult to define and the cases are hard to reconcile. Two problems arise:

(i) what is meant by a 'public right'?
(ii) what is meant by 'special damage'?

In England, the approach to the first question has been to deny standing to the plaintiff unless he can show that a right has been violated which can be enjoyed by any member of the public who wishes to avail of it. On this view, it is not sufficient that the legislature has simply declared certain conduct to be unlawful. So in *Gouriet's case,*[6] it was held that the plaintiff had no right to sue except in the form of a relator action. Similarly, in *Lonrho Ltd v Shell Petroleum Co Ltd*[7] the rule in *Boyce's Case* was again unsuccessfully invoked. The plaintiffs complained that the defendants had broken various Orders in Council which gave effect to the policy of sanctions against Rhodesia, as it was then called, by importing oil into that country. As a result, the pipeline which the plaintiffs had constructed from the port of Beira was not used and they were thus deprived of revenue. The House of Lords said that the case fell within neither limb of Boyce's case: no private right of the plaintiff had been infringed and no rights available to the public at large had been violated.

A different approach was adopted in Ireland in *Irish Permanent Building Society v Cauldwell and Others,*[8] where it was held that the plaintiff had sufficient *locus standi* to challenge the allegedly unlawful registration of another building society. Again it would seem that no public right within the restricted meaning adopted in England would have been violated, were it to be held that the registration was unlawful. Admittedly, the case was one in which the primary relief sought was a declaration that the registration was unlawful but it would not appear that any different considerations should apply to the granting of such relief.

The latter case also adopts a broader approach to the second problem. It had been held in some English and Australian cases that mere financial loss or the possibility of it was not sufficient to afford the plaintiff *locus standi*.[9] In *Irish Permanent Building Society v Cauldwell and Others*, however, Barrington J held that it was sufficient that the plaintiffs were aggrieved persons with a substantial interest in the outcome of the case. It would seem that this less restrictive approach to the question of *locus standi* in such cases is preferable.

1 See para 15.17, above.
2 See Keane, *Company Law in the Republic of Ireland*, p220.
3 *Boyce v Paddington Borough Council* [1903] 1 Ch 109.
4 See para 15.10, above.
5 Above.
6 Above.
7 [1982] AC 173.
8 (1981) ILRM 242.
9 *Pudsey Coal Gas Co v Bradford Corpn* (1873) LR 15 Eq 167; *California Theatre Pty Co v Hoyts Country Theatres Ltd* (1959) 59 SR NSW 188.

15.21 One final comment should be made. The Irish courts have considered on a number of occasions in recent times the *locus standi* of persons seeking to challenge the constitutional validity of legislation. They have, however, tended to adopt a liberal approach to this question for two reasons. In the first place, the Attorney General is necessarily a defendant where the constitutionality of a statute is an issue and hence the proceedings cannot be brought in the form of a relator action. In the second place, it would be obviously undesirable that legislation of dubious constitutionality should remain in force because of purely procedural considerations. Thus, where the legislation in issue was that which determined the boundaries of constituencies for electoral purposes, the plaintiff's status as a voter was sufficient to afford him *locus standi*.[1] Even more spectacularly, plaintiffs on two occasions have been allowed standing to claim injunctions restraining the government from entering into international treaties, as in *Boland v An Taoiseach and Others*[2] where the treaty in issue was the Sunningdale Agreement and in *Crotty v An Taoiseach and Others*,[3] where it was the Single European Act adopted by the other member states of the EEC. (In the latter case, the claim failed in the High Court but succeeded in the Supreme Court. In the former case, it was unsuccessful in both courts.)

The major limitation in such cases is that the plaintiff must have been aggrieved or be capable of being aggrieved by the legislation in question, even if his grievance (as in *Crotty v An Taoiseach and others*) is simply in his capacity as a citizen. He cannot pray in aid a purely hypothetical injury which might be sustained by another where his own interests are unaffected.[4] It is clear, moreover, as remarked by Barrington J in *Irish Permanent Building Society v Cauldwell and Others*[5] that this approach is peculiar to constitutional cases and does not necessarily afford guidance as to what may happen in other cases.

1 *O'Donovan v A-G* [1961] IR 114.
2 [1974] IR 338.
3 (1987) ILRM 400.

4 *Cahill v Sutton*, above.
5 Above.

Interlocutory and interim injunctions

15.22 An interlocutory injunction is granted by the court to preserve the status quo until the plaintiff's claim for a perpetual injunction has been determined. While the jurisdiction to grant such injunctions was first conferred by the Judicature (Ireland) Act 1877, its exercise is now regulated by Order 50 Rule 6 of the Rules of the Superior Courts as follows:

> The Court may grant.... an injunction.... by an interlocutory order in all cases in which it appears to the Court to be just or convenient so to do.'

The granting or withholding of interlocutory injunctions is governed by certain well established principles which are now considered in detail.

15.23 In order to obtain an interlocutory injunction, the plaintiff does not have to prove as a matter of probability that a legal right of his has been infringed or will be infringed unless the court intervenes. That is the burden which rests upon the plaintiff at the trial when he seeks a perpetual injunction. In order to discharge that onus of proof, it is frequently necessary to adduce oral evidence and to invite the court to resolve a conflict of evidence between the plaintiff and the defendant. This is clearly impractical in the case of an interlocutory injunction where the issue between the plaintiff and the defendant is resolved, not in the course of a plenary hearing with oral evidence adduced on both sides but on the hearing of a motion brought by the plaintiff on fours days' notice to the defendant and in which the evidence is given on affidavit. It is not necessary, therefore, for a plaintiff to satisfy the court to the same extent on the hearing of an interlocutory application for an injunction of his right to an injunction as it would be at the trial. All that is required is that the plaintiff shows that there is a serious question to be tried.

It was at one time thought that it was essential for the plaintiff to demonstrate on an interlocutory application that he would probably succeed at the trial of the action. There were English decisions to that effect and in *Educational Co of Ireland Ltd v Fitzpatrick and others*[1] Lavery J, with whom the rest of the Supreme Court agreed, cited with approval a passage in Kerr on Injunctions which also stated this to be the test. But in the course of the same judgement, the learned judge also indicated that it was sufficient if the plaintiff showed that there was 'a fair question' to be decided.[2] In *Esso Petroleum Co Ltd v Fogarty*[3] the Supreme Court again seemed to favour the proposition that the plaintiff had to prove that the probability was that the defendant would fail at the trial, although Walsh J in the same case referred to a 'substantial question' test with apparent approval.[4] Other authorities in England and some commonwealth jurisdictions supported the view that the test was whether the plaintiff had a *prima facie* case[5] and this again appeared to place a greater burden on the plaintiff than was reflected in the 'serious question' test.

In *American Cynamid Co v Ethicon Ltd*,[6] however, the House of Lords unanimously rejected the more stringent tests and said (in the words of Lord Diplock) that it was sufficient for the plaintiff to establish that there

was a 'serious question' to be argued: it was not necessary for him to show
that he had a *prima facie* case or that he would probably succeed in the
ultimate trial. This view was based on the necessarily abbreviated and
inconclusive trial of the issue at the interlocutory stage and the inability of
the court to resolve issues of credibility (on which the ultimate outcome of
the case so often depends) on affidavit.

The same view was taken by the Supreme Court in *Campus Oil Ltd v
Minister for Industry and Energy and Others (No 2)*.[7] In that case, the
plaintiffs were a number of independent oil producers who were obliged by
regulation to purchase their supplies from the state owned oil refinery at
Whitegate. As a matter of policy, the government had determined to keep
the refinery in being and since the oil could be purchased more cheaply
elsewhere, this regulation was considered essential to its survival. The
companies issued proceedings claiming that this regulation was contrary to
the Treaty of Rome and Murphy J at the request of the defendants referred
the question to the Court of Justice of the EEC. This is turn led to delays
(exacerbated by an appeal to the Supreme Court from Murphy J's decision
by the defendants who had themselves sought the reference) and the
companies eventually ceased to comply with the regulation. The major
international oil producers thereupon threatened to halt compliance with
the mandatory regime, as it was called, and, since this would have led to
the closure of the refinery, the state authorities applied for an interlocutory
injunction requiring the companies to comply with the regulation, it being
urged on behalf of the state that if the status quo was not preserved, the
refinery would have to close down before the question could be determined
by the EEC Court.

Keane J granted the interlocutory injunction and applied the test
propounded by Lord Diplock in the *American Cynamid* case. He rejected
the submission on behalf of the defendants that this test was inconsistent
with the criteria laid down in *Educational Co of Ireland Ltd v Fitzpatrick
and others*, pointing out, as had also been remarked by Murphy J in the
earlier stages of the proceedings, that the test of a 'fair question' to be tried
referred to by Lavery J appeared to be no different in essence from that
adopted by Lord Diplock. On appeal, the Supreme Court took the same
view.

1 [1961] IR 323.
2 At 337-338.
3 [1965] IR 531.
4 P 541.
5 *Beecham Group Ltd v Bristol Laboratories Pty Ltd* (1968) 118 CLR 618.
6 [1975] AC 396.
7 [1983] IR 88.

15.24 The 'serious question' test can accordingly be safely regarded as
firmly embedded in Irish law in place of the *prima facie* case or 'balance of
probability' tests. It should be said, however, that the *American Cynamid*
case has not met with universal approval in all common law jurisdictions:
some Australian judges have preferred to apply earlier decisions adopting
the *prima facie* test, although others have seen no necessary conflict
between the *American Cynamid* case and the leading Australian case
Beecham Group Ltd v Bristol Laboratories Property Ltd.[1] Moreover, even
in England the Court of Appeal have followed the *American Cynamid* case
with some reluctance[2] (Lord Denning in fact dissenting), pointing out that
it is inconsistent with an earlier House of Lords decision in *Stratford and*

Sons v Linley.[3] It is submitted, however, that there is little likelihood of a different view being taken in Ireland: the test adopted in the *Campus Oil* case is a more practical and workable one than that which requires the plaintiff to prove in the necessarily truncated and inconclusive interlocutory proceedings that he is more likely to win than lose.

1 Above.
2 *Fellowes & Son v Fisher* [1976] QB 122; *Hubbard v Pitt* [1976] QB 142.
3 [1965] AC 269.

15.24A A If the Court is satisfied that there is a serious issue to be determined in the proceedings, it should at once, accordingly, proceed to consider the next criterion: whether the *balance of convenience* is in favour of granting rather than withholding the injunction.[1] The phrase 'balance of convenience' has been criticised with some force on the ground that the court should be concerned with justice rather than the convenience of either of the parties. However, provided that it is borne in mind that it is simply a useful shorthand expression, no great harm is done by its use. The court will not grant an injunction where it would be *unjust* to do so, no matter what the convenience of the parties may suggest. But there are a number of factors which should be taken into account when it has to be decided whether an interlocutory injunction should be granted and these are usefully embraced under the general rubric 'the balance of convenience'.

In the first place, the court will consider whether there is any real necessity to grant an injunction at all: whether, in other words, damage assessed at the trial will prove an adequate remedy. The plaintiff must, in the phrase usually employed, satisfy the court that in the event of the injunction not being granted, he will suffer *irreparable loss*.[2] This can be more readily demonstrated in some categories of cases than others: thus, in cases where the plaintiffs' business is being seriously interfered with by an act which is at least arguably wrongful, be it picketing of his premises or interference with his contractual relationships with third parties, the plaintiff usually can succeed in establishing at the interlocutory stage that irreparable damage will be caused if the allegedly wrongful acts are continued pending the hearing.

In the second place, the court must consider whether in the event of the plaintiff failing at the trial of the action, the undertaking as to damages which he is normally required to give[3] will adequately compensate the defendant for the damage caused to him by the granting of the injunction. Again this may be an important factor in cases where the effect of the injunction is to seriously interfere with a business carried on by the defendant. The position is even stronger if there is any serious doubt as to the ability of the plaintiff to compensate the defendant.

Where neither of these considerations is decisive, the court will take other factors into account. In the first place, it will in general 'as a counsel of prudence' seek to preserve the status quo pending the trial.[4] The status quo normally means the situation which existed at the time the proceedings were commenced: if, however, there has been unusual delay by the plaintiff in applying for the interlocutory injunction, it will be the status quo at the time of the application which will be relevant.[5] In the second place, where the damage likely to be suffered by either side as a result of the granting or withholding of the relief is not determinative, the court may take into account the comparative strength of the parties' respective cases.[6]

In other words, while it is sufficient for the plaintiff at the outset to show that there is a serious question to be tried to enable the court to proceed to consider the whole question of the balance of convenience, the court may return to the comparative strengths of the parties' positions where the damages aspect does not point clearly in favour of either party.

What were called in *American Cynamid* 'special factors' may also be taken into account in determining where the balance of convenience lies.[7] These are factors which will vary depending on the type of case involved. In some cases, there may be no conflict of fact disclosed by the affidavits and the only issue between the parties may be a legal issue which the Court is in a position to resolve on affidavit. If the legal problems are complex, it may still not be possible to resolve them on an interlocutory hearing: they may require the more mature and unhurried consideration of a plenary hearing. Where however there is no conflict of fact and the court can accordingly infer from the affidavits that the defendant has violated a legal right of the plaintiff—eg where the defendant is in breach of a term of a contract—the injunction may be granted without taking the balance of convenience into account. This was so decided in *Doherty v Allman*[8] and the same principle was applied by the Supreme Court in *Dublin Port and Docks Board v Brittania Dredging Co Ltd*.[9] If, however, the court is not satisfied as a matter of probability that the construction of the contract intended for by the plaintiff is correct, the ordinary principles will apply and the Court will take into account the balance of convenience. This was so held by Keane J in *TMG Group v Al Babtain*[10] and by the Supreme Court in *Irish Shell Ltd v Elm Motors Ltd*.[11]

'Special factors' also arise in cases of libel. It has been held that an interlocutory injunction should not be granted in the case of an alleged libel, where the defendant proposes to plead justification,[12] ie that the words complained of were true in substance and in fact, or that they constituted fair comment on a matter of public interest or that they were published by the defendant without malice on a privileged occasion.[13] Even where none of these defences arise, the court will still be slower to grant an interlocutory injunction in such cases.[14] The reason is that it involves the court in each case in a consideration of whether the words are or are not libellous and this is regarded as so pre-eminently a matter for the jury in the ultimate trial that the court is reluctant to pre-empt their decision in any way. The issue of 'libel or no libel' has since Fox's Act been regarded as peculiarly a matter for juries to determine and the underlying philosophy—that sensitive areas of freedom of speech should remain their exclusive province—has on the whole been adhered to in subsequent decisions. Most recently, the Supreme Court by a majority in *Barrett v Independent Newspapers Ltd*[15] has reasserted the principle that under no circumstances may the issue of 'libel or no libel' be determined other than by a jury. It would seem to follow that the approach to the granting of interlocutory injunctions to restrain alleged libels will be the same.

1 *American Cynamid Co v Ethicon Ltd*, above, at 408 per Lord Diplock.
2 *Johnson v Shrewsbury and Birmingham Rly Co* (1853) 3 De G M & G 914 at 931; *Moore v A-G* (1927) IR 569 at 575 per Kennedy CJ.
3 See para 15.26, below.
4 *American Cynamid Co v Ethicon Ltd*, above at 408, per Lord Diplock.
5 *Garden Cottage Foods Ltd v Milk Marketing Board* [1983] 2 All ER 770 at 775, HL.
6 *American Cynamid Co v Ethicon Ltd*, above, at 408, per Lord Diplock.
7 At 408 per Lord Diplock.
8 (1878) 3 App Cas 709.
9 [1968] IR 136.

10 (1982) ILRM 349.
11 [1984] IR 200.
12 *Bonnard v Perryman* [1891] 2 Ch 269; *Gallagher v Tuohy* (1924) 58 ILT 134; Cf *Cullen v Stanley & Co* [1926] IR 73, SC.
13 *Fraser v Evans* [1969] 1 QB 349; *A-G v BBC* [1980] 3 All ER 161 at 168 per Lord Salmon. *Bryanston Finance Ltd v de Vries* [1975] QB 703 at 724 per Lord Denning MR.
14 *Coulson v Coulson* (1887) 3 TLR 846; *Sinclair v Gogarty* [1937] IR 377 at 384 per Sullivan CJ.
15 (1986) ILRM 601.

15.25 Where pleadings and discovery are not required and it is practical to have the hearing at a relatively early date, the hearing of the motion is sometimes treated as the trial of the action. If there is an issue of fact, this will normally mean that oral evidence will be adduced at the hearing of the motion. In any other case, the court either grants or refuses the injunction on the hearing of the motion and, if the injunction is granted, it continues until the trial of the action. The Court may, instead of granting the injunction, accept an undertaking from the defendant not to commit or repeat the acts complained of.

15.26 An interlocutory injunction will not normally be granted unless the plaintiff gives an undertaking to abide by any order the court may make as to damages in the event of it being held at the trial that the injunction should not have been obtained.[1] This undertaking, known as 'the usual undertaking as to damages', is extracted from the plaintiff for the benefit of the defendant, but it is given to the court and not to the defendant. In consequence, the plaintiff can be punished for contempt in the event of his not complying with the undertaking. Where he is called upon to honour the undertaking, the court orders an inquiry as to the damages. These are assessed in the same way as damages for breach of contract: ie the plaintiff is entitled to the damages which are the natural consequence of the injunction having been granted.

It was at one time thought that there was one exception to the requirement that an undertaking be given, ie where the Attorney General obtains an injunction in protection of the rights of the public. In *Hoffman La Roche and Co and A-G v Secretary of State for Trade and Industry*,[2] however, the House of Lords held that the attorney was in no different a position from any other litigant in this context and it is thought that a similar approach would be adopted in Ireland. As we have seen, however, where no such undertaking is given by him in a relator action, he will not be liable.[3]

1 *Keenan Bros Ltd v CIE* (1963) 97 ILT 54.
2 [1975] AC 295, HL.
3 See para 15.17, above.

15.27 Where the matter is sufficiently urgent the court will grant an injunction on an *ex parte* application, ie without notice to the defendant. In such a case it is called an interim injunction and continues for a relatively short period until the hearing of a motion for an interlocutory injunction. Normally, the court will only allow such an injunction to continue in force until the next motion day and if necessary will abridge the time in order to allow the plaintiff to bring a motion for that day. As in the case of an interlocutory injunction, such an injunction will not be granted except on an undertaking as to damages and it is of the utmost importance that all the relevant facts are disclosed to the Court on the application, whether or not they support the granting of the injunction. Such applications should always be made grounded on an affidavit and preferably when there are already proceedings in being, although injunctions can be, and not infrequently are, granted before the proceedings have actually commenced. It is also possible for the application for an injunction to be made on oral evidence, but this practice is strongly discouraged by the courts and should only be availed of if there is clearly no alternative.

15.28 An interlocutory or interim injunction may be granted to restrain the performance of an act by a state authority pending the trial of an issue as to whether the particular act is constitutional or otherwise. In *Pesca Valenia Ltd v Minister for Fisheries and Others*[1] where the plaintiffs claimed that a statutory instrument made under fisheries legislation requiring them to employ a specified percentage of EEC nationals on their trawlers was unconstitutional and inconsistent with the Treaty of Rome, Lardner J granted an interlocutory injuncton restraining the first named defendant from prosecuting the plaintiffs pending the determination by the court of their claim. Although the legislation was presumed to be constitutional until the contrary was shown, once the plaintiffs had established that a serious question arose satisfying the *Campus Oil* test, they were entitled to the relief sought. This view was upheld by the Supreme Court.

That decision may render of doubtful authority an earlier decision of the High Court in *Nova Media Services Ltd and Another v Minister for Posts and Telegraphs and Others,*[2] in which the plaintiffs, who were operating a 'pirate' radio station without a licence under the Wireless Telegraphy Act 1926 claimed that the relevant provisions of the Act were unconstitutional and inconsistent with the Treaty of Rome. The first named defendant had seized the plaintiffs' broadcasting equipment under their statutory powers and the plaintiffs applied for an interlocutory injunction directing the return of the equipment pending the trial. Murphy J refused the application, holding that it was only in 'most extraordinary circumstances' that the courts would seek to restrain a Minister or other state agency from performing its statutory duty.

1 (1986) ILRM 68.
2 (1984) ILRM 161.

Mandatory injunction

15.29 A mandatory injunction is one which commands the defendant to do a specific act: it is to be distinguished from a prohibitory injunction, which simply restrains him from doing something. As we have seen[1] the traditional reluctance of the courts to grant mandatory injunctions has dwindled: to-day they are generally granted on the same principles as prohibitory injunctions. It is true that in *Redland Bricks Ltd v Morris,*[2] Lord Upjohn said that in the case of a mandatory injunction the plaintiff had to show upon the facts a 'very strong probability' that grave damage would occur to him in the future. The decision has, however, been strongly criticised.[3] On the facts, it is easy to sustain: a market garden firm sought a mandatory injunction requiring the defendant to restore land which was used in the past for quarrying, causing the plaintiff's land to subside, to its previous state. It was proved at the hearing that this would cost £3,000, but that the damage the plaintiff would sustain if the mandatory injunction was *not* granted, was at most £1,500 (The plaintiff's entitlement to a prohibitory injunction was not disputed.) A mandatory injunction in such circumstances would clearly have been an undue hardship on the defendant and was refused, but, as we have seen, that can also be a ground for refusing relief in the case of a prohibitory injunction.[4] It is submitted that there is no difference between prohibitory and mandatory injunctions so far as the burden of proof is concerned.

1 See para 15.02, above.
2 [1970] AC 652, HL.
3 Meagher, Gummow & Lehane describe Lord Upjohn's speech as an 'example of judicial atavism' and say that it 'scintillates with dubious propositions.'
4 See para 15.09, above.

15.30 The position is undoubtedly different at the interlocutory stage. Since there is no final adjudication on the respective rights of the parties at that stage, the defendant in general should not be required to carry out works which may involve him in expense and inconvenience if the plaintiff's claim should ultimately prove unfounded and he wishes to undo them. Moreover, as pointed out by Megarry J in *Shepherd Homes Ltd v Sandham*,[1] an interlocutory injunction normally seeks to regulate the conduct of the defendant by requiring him to continue to act as he had done in the past whereas a mandatory injunction generally looks to the future. However, the injunction may still be granted in special circumstances: thus, where the defendant has deliberately hurried on work with a view to stealing a march on the defendant, a mandatory injunction may be granted requiring him to undo work which he had already done.[2] And in the *Campus Oil*[3] case already referred to, Keane J granted a mandatory interlocutory injunction requiring the defendants to continue purchasing their supplies of oil from the plaintiff on the ground that this was an instance in which the order was designed to secure the effect normally aimed at by a prohibitory interlocutory injunction, ensuring that, pending the trial of the action, the defendants acted as they had done in the past. A similar view was taken by Costello J in *Irish Shell Ltd v Elm Motors Ltd*.[4]

1 [1971] Ch 340.
2 Ibid.
3 Above.
4 [1984] IR 200.

15.31 Mandatory injunctions are sometimes divided into two categories, those which are *restorative* and those which are *enforcing*. The first require the defendant to perform some act for the purpose of undoing the breach he has commited of the plaintiff's rights, eg pulling down a building which interferes with the plaintiff's right to light. The second requires the defendant to perform an act which is necessary if he is to fulfil his obligations to the plaintiff, e.g. complying with a particular term of contract. The distinction, it is thought, is of importance in one context only. An enforcing mandatory injunction is in many respects similar to a decree for specific performance, with one notable difference: the court may be asked to enforce a single term of a contract. The court will, accordingly, have to consider whether the term would be capable of being specifically performed if it stood alone and whether in all the circumstances it should be enforced on its own.[1]

1 *Dowty Boulton Paul Ltd v Wolverhampton Corpn* [1971] 2 All ER 277.

Quia timet injunctions

15.32 A *quia timet* injunction is one granted where the plaintiff fears that his rights are going to be infringed, but no actual injury has occurred at the time of the application. While the jurisdiction to grant an injunction in respect of threatened or apprehended wrongs is undoubted and of long standing, it is one which the courts have exercised with caution. In Lord Dunedin's words, 'no one can obtain a *quia timet* order by merely saying "timeo" ';[1] on the contrary, the courts have emphasised that particularly strong evidence of the apprehended injury is required before the relief can be given. Thus, Fitzgibbon LJ in *A-G v Rathmines and Pembroke Joint Hospital Board*[2] said:

'To sustain the injunction, the law requires proof by the plaintiff of a well-grounded apprehension of injury—proof of actual and real danger—a strong probability, almost amounting to a moral certainty.'[3]

In *'Independent Newspapers' v 'Irish Press'*,[4] Meredith J said

'This is a typical example of a quia timet action in which the Court does not grant an injunction unless it is satisfied that there is a reasonable probability that what is threatened to be done is calculated in the ordinary course of events, or according to the ordinary course of business, to cause damage to the plaintiff.'

Those tests were held by Finlay P to have been satisfied in *C & A Modes v C & A (Waterford) Ltd*[5] where the plaintiffs, the well known English shopping chain, sought to restrain a firm in Waterford from describing themselves as 'C & A Modes (Waterford) Ltd'. It was argued on behalf of the defendants that since the plaintiffs had not at that time established any shop in Ireland they had not suffered any damage and were not entitled to an injunction. The learned President was, however, satisfied that they had established a sufficiently strong case of threatened loss to justify the granting of a *quia timet* injunction, even if the action was properly so described. This decision was affirmed by the Supreme Court.

1 *A-G for Dominion of Canada v Ritchie Contracting and Supply Co Ltd* [1919] AC 999, PC at 1005.
2 [1904] 1 IR 161.
3 Cited with approval by Farwell J in *A-G v Nottingham Corpn* [1904] 1 Ch 673.
4 [1932] IR 615.
5 [1976] IR 148.

Damages in lieu of an injunction

15.33 The circumstances in which the court exercises its jurisdiction dating from Lord Cairns' Act[1] to award damages in lieu of an injunction have already been considered.[2] Since such damages could be awarded where a purely equitable right was being infringed, the result was that the court could now award damages where they would not have been recoverable at common law. Thus, for example, the vendor of land who imposed on the purchaser a restrictive covenant for the benefit of land retained by him was entitled under the rule in *Tulk v Moxhay*[3] to enforce that covenant against subsequent purchasers, subject to the important proviso that it was negative in character, ie that it simply restrained the owner from using the land in a particular way rather than requiring him to carry out works. He could enforce the covenant against the subsequent purchaser because the court of equity would restrain the latter from committing a breach of covenant. The vendor, however, prior to Lord Cairns' Act would have been unable to recover damages for such a breach unless he could show that he had actually suffered damage, eg where the value of the land which he had retained was reduced. Now, however, the court is entitled to award damages in such a case where it is for any reason inappropriate to grant an injunction.

A modern English example is *Wrotham Parks Ltd v Parkside Homes Ltd*[4] where the court refused to grant a mandatory injunction requiring the demolition of houses built in breach of convenant, but awarded damages, even though the plaintiff was unable to establish that the land retained by him would be reduced in value as a result of the breach.

Another example of the power of the court to award damages in the exercise of its equitable jurisdiction, where they would not have been recoverable at common law, is in the case of a *quia timet* injunction.[5] Such an injunction is of its nature normally granted in a case where the plaintiff is unable to recover damages at common law because no breach of his rights has been committed. But the House of Lords held (admittedly by a bare majority) in *Leeds Industrial Co-operative Society Ltd v Slack*[6] that damages could be awarded in such a case where it was not appropriate to grant an injunction. Moreover, since under the Act damages can be awarded in addition to an injunction, it would seem that the fact that a *quia timet* injunction has already been granted will not prevent an award of damages in the same case. So in *Rabbette v. Mayo Co Council*[7] where the plaintiff was granted an injunction restraining the defendant from beginning blasting operations which he claimed would damage the foundations of houses which he was building, O'Hanlon J awarded damages to the plaintiff in respect of the business losses which the plaintiff proved he had suffered because of the defendant's threatened activities.

1 Chancery Amendment Act 1858.
2 See para 15.08, above.
3 (1848) 2 Ph 774.
4 [1974] 2 All ER 321.
5 See para 15.32, above.
6 [1924] AC 851, HL.
7 (1984) ILRM 156.

The Mareva Injunction

15.34 Until 1975, the law in Ireland and England was as stated by the Court of Appeal in *Lister v Stubbs*:[1] 'you cannot get an injunction to restrain a man who is alleged to be a debtor from parting with his property.' The reason was stated graphically by Lord Hatherly LC in *Mills v Northern Railway of Buenos Aires Co*:[2]

> 'The only remedy (for an unsecured creditor) is to obtain his judgement and take out execution. It would be a fearful authority for this court to assume (restraining the defendant from dealing with his assets) for it would be called on to interfere with the concerns of almost every company in the Kingdom against which a creditor might suppose he has demands, which he had not established in a court of justice, but which he was about to proceed to establish.'

The law simply did not permit the plaintiff to freeze the defendant's assets before there had been any judicial determination in the plaintiff's favour. In 1975, however, two historic judgements in England decisively altered the whole current of the law. In the first, *Nippon Yusen Kaisha v Karageorgis*,[3] the plaintiffs were ship-owners who were owed large sums by the defendants under charterparties. The latter were out of the jurisdiction but there were funds standing to their credit in a London bank. The plaintiffs, concerned that the defendants would transfer the money abroad before judgement could be recovered against them, applied for and obtained on an ex parte application an injunction restraining them from reducing the fund below the amount of the claimed debt. In the subsequent case in the same year which gave the novel remedy its now familiar name— *Mareva Compania Naviera SA v International Bulk Carriers SA*[4]—a similar order was made. The court—presided over on each occasion by Lord Denning MR—pointed out that modern banking technology rendered it possible to switch funds around the world in seconds and that the law should not allow the injustice of a claim to which there was patently no answer being defeated in that manner. Since the banks could be given notice of the making of the order and would prudently notify the defendants that they could not permit drawings on the account which brought it below the prescribed level the account would be effectively frozen. No serious injustice was done to the defendants, it was said; the interim injunction would only last until the next motion day and it was open to them to come in and apply for a discharge or variation of the order in the meantime.

In a later case,[5] where the granting of the injunction was challenged and the matter was therefore more fully argued, Lord Denning rejected the submission that the Mareva injunction represented an entirely novel departure in English law. He compared it with the writ of foreign attachment which had at one time been available in the City of London and other parts of England and enabled a creditor to seize the goods of an absconding foreign debtor before he had obtained any judgement. He also conceded, however, that the Mareva injunction represented a major judicial innovation and had been developed by the Courts because it was not right to allow injustice to flourish while the rule making authorities or indeed parliament itself debated the correct procedures to be provided for in the changed circumstances of modern commerce.

1 (1890) 45 Ch D 1, CA.
2 (1870) 5 Ch App 621, HL.
3 [1975] 3 All ER 282, CA.
4 [1980] 1 All ER 213n.
5 *Rasu Maritima v Pertambangan* [1977] 3 All ER 324.

15.35 These early decisions suggested certain important limitations on the jurisdiction. It seemed to be applicable only to cases of foreign defendants where there was a serious reason to apprehend that the assets might be removed from the jurisdiction with a view to avoiding judgement.[1] It also appeared likely that the injunction would be granted only in exceptional circumstances and that the plaintiff would be required to establish a particularly strong case.[2] Yet these limitations were rapidly eroded: in *Siskina (Cargo Owners) v Distos SA*,[3] the only reported case in which a Mareva injunction was considered in the House of Lords, Lord Hailsham LC said that it seemed wrong that English defendants should enjoy immunity denied to others. (It should be noted, however, that the House of Lords were not invited in that case by the defendants to strike down the new practice and did not, of course, do so.) Megarry V-C, in *Barclay-Johnson v Yuill*,[4] made it clear that in his view the Mareva doctrine had shed 'all the possible limitations of its origin.' It applied to English people as much as foreigners and was not confined to commercial cases. (The view that it was not confined to foreign defendants was embodied in legislation in England in 1981,[5] but there has been no corresponding legislation in Ireland.) Megarry VC did appear in that case to treat the remedy as lying only to prevent the removal of assets out of the jurisdiction. But Lord Denning in another case said[6] that it also lay to prevent the defendant from dissipating his assets within the jurisdiction and many injunctions have been granted on a similar basis in Ireland. The requirement that the plaintiffs have a very strong—almost unanswerable—case, as they clearly had in the two seminal decisions, seems to have disappeared and to have been replaced by the criterion of a 'good arguable case.'[7] But it has also been said that this is simply a minimum requirement: it remains a matter of judicial discretion as to whether the order should be granted in any particular case.

1 Ibid.
2 Ibid.
3 [1979] AC 210 at 261.
4 [1980] 3 All ER 190.
5 Supreme Court Act 1981, s 37(3).
6 *Rahman (Prince Abdul) bin Turki al Sudairy v Abu Taha* [1980] 3 All ER 409. See para 15.36, below.
7 *Rasu Maritima v Pertambangan*, above.

15.36 The following guidelines were proposed by Lord Denning MR[1] as appropriate in determining whether the relief should be granted:

(1) the plaintiff should make full and frank disclosure of all matters in his knowledge which it is material for the judge to know.

(2) the plaintiff should give particulars of his claim against the defendant, stating the ground of his claim and the amount and fairly stating the points made against it by the defendant.

(3) the plaintiff should give some grounds for believing that the defendant has assets within the jurisdiction. The existence of a bank account is normally sufficient.

(4) the plaintiff should give some grounds for believing that there is a risk of the assets being removed or dissipated.

(5) the plaintiff must give an undertaking in damages, in case he fails.

In Fleming and others v Ranks (Ireland) Ltd and another [2] McWilliam J adopted the same approach as that of Megarry VC in *Barclay-Johnson v Yuill*[3] and granted an injunction against defendants who were Irish citizens and both resident and domiciled in the jurisdiction. Since that decision, Mareva injunctions have been granted at the interim and interlocutory stages in a vast number of cases in which the defendants were Irish citizens and resident within the jurisdiction. As we shall see, the new doctrine has been considered by the Supreme Court in only one recorded instance[4] and since in that case the defendants were foreign and not within the jurisdiction, the question as to whether such an injunction could be granted against Irish citizens resident within the jurisdiction did not arise.

1 *Third Chandris Shipping Corpn v Unimarine SA* [1979] 2 All ER 972.
2 (1983) ILRM 541. Cf *Powerscourt Estates Ltd v Gallagher* (1984) ILRM 123.
3 Above.
4 See para 15.40, below.

15.37 In its classic form, the Mareva injunction prohibits the debtor from reducing funds standing to his credit in a bank account below a figure equivalent to the debt and interest. Notice is given immediately to the bank by the creditor's solicitors and the bank are thereupon protected if they decline to allow any further drawings on the account bringing it below the permitted figure. Indeed, if the banks permit such drawings with knowledge of the making of the order they run the risk of being attached for contempt of court. It has been suggested, however, that they should exercise care in their choice of words when returning cheques by the debtor in favour of third parties. Customary phrases such as 'refer to drawer' may be held to be defamatory if there were in fact sufficient funds to meet the account and the injunction is subsequently discharged.[1] It would seem more desirable to use some formula such as 'funds sufficient but injunction granted against the account'.[2]

The essence of the relief is to prevent the debtor from removing or dissipating the assets with a view to avoiding payment of the debt. Hence it is usual to permit drawings on the account which are sufficient to meet normal day to day living expenses and also the payment of debts in the ordinary course of business.[3] In one instance,[4] the court in England permitted the payment out of the frozen fund of a debt which was technically irrecoverable because of a non-compliance with the relevant moneylending legislation, on the ground that an honourable businessman would pay such a debt in the ordinary course of business without relying on technicalities.

1 *Pyke v Hibernian Bank Ltd* [1950] IR 195.
2 Doyle, *The Mareva Injunction and Related Orders* (London).
3 As in *Powerscourt Estates Ltd v Gallagher*, above.
4 *Iraq Ministry of Defence v Arcepey Shipping Co* [1980] 1 All ER 480.

15.38 The position of banks and similar bodies, such as building socieities, was exhaustively considered by the Court of Appeal in *Z Ltd v AZ and Others*.[1] It was in fact strictly not necessary for the court to give the elaborate series of rulings which it did in that case, since in the court of first instance the substantive action in the course of which the Mareva injunction had been granted was settled and the Mareva injunction discharged by agreement between the plaintiff and the numerous defendants. (The case concerned what was alleged to be a gigantic international fraud and the parties, for some reason, were held entitled to remain anonymous. Lord Denning MR shrouded the facts even further in mystery by referring to the country from which the fraud was alleged to have emanated as 'Ruritania'.) The various banks in which funds captured by the injunction were lodged were notice parties to the proceedings and, notwithstanding the settlement of the proceedings and the discharge of the injunction, appealed, although against what it is by no means clear. They did so professedly with a view to obtaining what were called 'guidelines' on the operation of Mareva injunction and the invitation to lay them down was accepted with alacrity by the Court of Appeal. The matters dealt with in the judgements ranged far beyond the confines of a practice direction into areas of substantive law and, despite the eminence of the court, the weight to be attached in this jurisdiction to judgements which were effectively dealing with points that were entirely moot must be doubtful. However, since they appear to have been accepted as representing the law in the neighbouring jurisdiction, they should be summarised.

It was made clear that the banks would be liable to attachment for contempt if they permitted drawings on the account contrary to the order at a time when they knew the order had been made and this even though the defendant at the relevant time had not been served with the order or given notice of it. The court rejected the argument that in such circumstances the bank could not be guilty of contempt, since the defendant was not, holding that the bank itself would be in contempt by frustrating the course of justice. (Eveleigh LJ distinguished this form of contempt from the attachment which is used in aid of execution of the court's decrees.)[2]

The court also considered the difficulties that flowed from seeking to embody in the order the freedom of the defendant to continue operating the account, provided he did not thereby reduce the total of his assets below the amount of the plaintiffs claim. The difficulty, of course, was that the banks would not necessarily know what other assets the defendant had. But the court ruled that despite this consideration the order should specify a minimum figure to be retained in the account, leaving it to the defendant to come in and prove that he had other assets which rendered the fixed figure unnecessarily high.

It was also made clear by the court that the bank was entitled to be indemnified by plaintiff against the costs of complying with the order. These might be considerable: in the case of large clearing banks, where the branch or account number was not known to the plaintiff, compliance might involve the bank in 'trawling' through all the accounts at a number of branches and this could prove a costly business.

The position of the bank in relation to letters of credit, guarantees and performance bonds which they have issued to a customer was also considered. Such documents when issued by a bank are regarded in the international business community as virtually equivalent to cash.[3] Their effectiveness would be seriously undermined and the reputation of the bank gravely damaged if the person in whose favour they were issued could be told that they could not be honoured for so long as the account in question was frozen by a Mareva injunction. Accordingly, the court thought that their efficacy should remain unaffected by the grant of a Mareva injunction. Similar considerations, in their view, applied to cheque cards or credit cards issued by the bank. The bank should be permitted to honour cheques drawn in accordance with the bank card rules for which the customer had received cash or goods; and, when the bank's credit card had been used for the obtaining of cash or credit the third parties should be recouped out of the account despite the existence of the injunction.

1 [1982] 1 All ER 556.
2 See para 15.44, below.
3 *Hibernia Meats Ltd v Ministère de l'agriculture and others*, unreported; High Court (Keane J); judgement delivered 16 February 1984.

15.39 The Mareva injunction, like any other injunction operates *in personam* and not *in rem*, ie it restrains the defendant personally from dealing with the bank account or the particular asset to which it relates, but it does not give the plaintiff creditor any rights of a proprietary nature in the fund itself. Indeed if it should transpire that the assets have already in equity become vested in a third party, the injunction may be refused or, if already granted, discharged. Thus in *Cretanor Maritime Co Ltd v Irish Marine Management Ltd*,[1] a debenture holder appointed a receiver over all money due to the defendants. As a result funds standing to the credit of the defendants in a bank account became vested in equity in the debenture holder. The plaintiffs were owed money by the defendants under a compromise of arbitration proceedings and in advance of the settlement had obtained a Mareva injunction freezing the bank account. When they sought to implement the compromise, it transpired that there were not sufficient funds to meet both their claims and that of the debenture holder. It was held by the Court by Appeal that the injunction had been properly discharged in these circumstances by the judge of first instance: the funds were no longer the property of the defendant but of the debenture holder and could not be frozen so as to satisfy a judgement against the former.

The granting of the injunction may also prove unjust or inconvenient where third parties are concerned and if so should not be granted or, if granted, may be discharged on the intervention of the aggrieved third party. Thus in *Re Eleftherios*,[2] the owners of a vessel were given notice of the granting of an injunction freezing the defendants' assets, which included a consignment of coal forming part of the cargo. Compliance with the order would have meant the vessel's staying in port to the detriment of the owners' business. On their application, the Mareva injunction was discharged, the Court of Appeal holding that the court was obliged to take into account not merely the balance of convenience and justice as between the plaintiff and the defendant but also as between the plaintiff, defendant and third parties. In this case, the injunction represented an unjust interference with the freedom to trade of the third party and should be discharged. An earlier decision where a vessel had also been prevented from leaving port but the injunction was not discharged was distinguished on the ground that in that case the only inconvenience was to the port authority and this could be met by an undertaking to reimburse the authority and allowing limited movements of the vessel within the jurisdiction.

1 [1978] 3 All ER 164.
2 [1982] 1 All ER 796.

15.40 The Mareva injunction can only be granted where the plaintiff has a sustainable cause of action. The right to obtain an interlocutory injunction, whether in the Mareva or any other form, cannot provide a cause of action in itself: it is a form of ancillary and incidental relief which presupposes the existence of a cause of action. This has important consequences where it is sought to attach assets to satisfy a debt that would not be recoverable in this jurisdiction. It is now settled that this cannot be done and, curiously enough, it was attempts to do so which led to the only occasions on which the final courts of appeal in both Ireland and England considered the Mareva injunction. In *Caudron and Others v Air Zaire and Others*,[1] the plaintiffs were in the main ex-employees of the first named defendants and claimed to be entitled to substantial sums in respect of arrears of salary etc. They had in some instances recovered judgement in the courts in Belgium in respect of the sums said to be owed, although a question arose as to the jurisdiction of the Belgian courts to entertain the claim. It was clear that the contracts had been made outside the jurisdiction of the Irish courts and that the alleged breaches had also been committed outside that jurisdiction. The only free asset of the defendants was said to be a Boeing 737 aeroplane and on the application of the plaintiffs a Mareva injunction was granted in the High Court restraining the defendants from flying it out of the jurisdiction when it landed at Dublin Airport. The Supreme Court on appeal discharged the injunction: the plaintiffs in their plenary summons had claimed as the primary relief an interlocutory injunction in the Mareva form which would last only until the determination of the action and this could not be done under the Rules of the Superior Courts. Such relief could only be claimed *ex parte* or on notice of motion and not as the primary relief in the action itself. Finlay CJ rejected an alternative submission that the High Court should as a matter of policy extend its jurisdiction

(i) to enable it to adjudicate upon the merits of actions of any kind against a foreign defendant where the defendant had assets in Ireland; and

(ii) to enable the court to attach those assets so that they might be available to satisfy some future judgement of a foreign court which had jurisdiction to determine the dispute.

A similar submission had found favour with a majority of the Court of Appeal in *Siskina (Cargo Owners) v Distos SA*[2] but had been unanimously rejected by the House of Lords. The learned chief justice, while acknowledging that such a policy would be attractive and that there was much to be said for extending the concept of the admiralty action *in rem* to aircraft, went on:

'It seems to me, however, wholly inappropriate for this Court to seek to implement such a policy, which would appear to be a matter for international convention or agreement and for the introduction of substantive domestic legislation, by an interpretation which is not open on the Rule itself.'[3]

It is an interesting feature of both those decisions that in neither case did the court give any positive approval to the Mareva doctrine. That is now an academic matter in England where it has been given statutory form. In Ireland it would be imprudent to read too much into *Caudron v Air Zaire* which was concerned with a specific aspect only of this Mareva jurisdiction. But it is possible to detect a warning against judicial adventurousness in this area in Finlay CJ's comments.

1 (1986) ILRM 10.
2 Above.
3 P 23.

15.41 Even in the absence of legislation or rules of court giving effect to it, it is probably safe to say that the Mareva doctrine has become so entrenched in Irish law that there is little real danger of it being dislodged by the Supreme Court. It has moreover been accepted in many other common law jurisdictions, such as Canada and New Zealand and in the form of the *saisie conservatoire* has its equivalent in many civil codes. There is, however, one notable exception: the full Supreme Court of South Australia unequivocally denied that any such jurisdiction existed[1] and other Australian judges have also been sceptical.[2] One Australian commentator has gone so far as to compare the actions of the English judges in assuming the role of parliament to the excesses of the Stuart kings and has inquired:

'If the courts can restrain you from disposing of your assets, why cannot they equally restrain you from leaving the country? Or even your own home? Perhaps the day may come when an interlocutory mandatory injunction will be granted to compel the defendant to work harder or save more, so that he may generate sufficient assets to meet a future judgement....'[3]

On the credit side, the injunction has undoubtedly been a potent weapon in preventing blatant injustice. It had its origins, as we have seen, in the vast area of commercial litigation in the City of London and was specifically designed to meet the problem of foreign defendants who could remove assets at a moment's notice to defeat an unanswerable claim. Whether it was in the end prudent to extend it to all defendants must remain open to question. Lord Hailsham and Sir Robert Megarry both questioned the propriety of conferring such an immunity on English and Welsh litigants and the Lord Chancellor in addition asked rhetorically why it should only flourish in 'the Arcadia of the commercial law list.'[4] The invitation thus extended to judicial adventurousness was readily accepted and ultimately parliament was swept along in the general current of enthusiasm. In Ireland, as we have seen, McWilliam J also chose the bolder line in *Fleming v Rank (Ireland) Ltd and another*.[5]

It could be urged that there was indeed good reason for confining the injunction within its original limits to foreign defendants. There is surely a clear line of distinction to be drawn between citizens of a country who normally have assets within the jurisdiction which of their nature cannot be immediately and conveniently disposed of, such as a house, and foreign defendants who are not in that position. Sir Robert Megarry posed the question of the English citizen who appeared to have no defence to a claim and was blatantly removing his assets from the jurisdiction, asking whether the law could tolerate his being able to evade justice in a manner denied to foreign citizens.[6] But against this one has to balance the injustice of paralysing a business and possibly driving it into liquidation or bankruptcy because of an allegation which subsequently turns out to have been unfounded, and even more strikingly of affecting, perhaps irremediably, the rights of third parties who have nothing to do with the dispute which gave rise to the granting of the injunction in the first place.

1 *Pivoraroff v Chernabaeff* 16 SASR 329.
2 But it has been accepted by the Court of Appeal in New South Wales: *Riley McKay Ltd v McKay* [1982] 1 NSWLR 264.
3 Meagher, Gummow & Lehane, pp 576–577.
4 *Siskina (Cargo Owners) & Distos SA*, above.
5 Above.
6 *Barclay-Johnson v Yuill*, above.

The Anton Piller Order

15.42 We now come to another novel form of injunction also developed by the English courts in recent times and frequently invoked in the Irish courts as well. It arose first in cases of rights in intellectual property—eg patents, trade marks, copyright etc—and has proved particularly effective in the war being waged by the communications industry against video piracy in recent years. Essentially it takes the form of a mandatory injunction requiring the defendant to permit the plaintiff or his agents to enter his premises, inspect documents or other articles and remove any which belong to the plaintiff. It is normally granted *ex parte* without notice to the defendant. Its object is to prevent the defendant in such an action from removing or destroying pirated or stolen material before the action comes to trial. It is also usual to hear the application in camera so as to ensure again that the element of surprise which is vital to the efficacy of the remedy is preserved.

The Anton Piller order—it takes its name from one of the first cases in which the practice was upheld by the Court of Appeal[1]—has not been considered by the Supreme Court in any reported case, but its validity was upheld by the House of Lords in *Rank Film Distributors Ltd v Video Info Centre*.[2] Its grant or refusal is entirely a matter of judicial discretion, but certain preconditions to its successful invocation are clear. First, the plaintiff must have a very strong case. Second, there must be the possibility of very serious damage to the plaintiff. Third, there must be clear evidence that there are in fact such documents or other things on the defendant's premises and that there is a risk of their being removed or destroyed. Fourth, the inspection must not do any harm to the defendant or his case. Fifth, the plaintiff must not merely give the normal undertaking as to damages: the court must be satisfied that he will be a mark for the damages in the event of the claim being unfounded[3] and he must in addition undertake to preserve the property pending the trial and to notify the defendant at the time of the inspection of his right to apply to the court (normally on 24 hours' notice) to vary or discharge the order.

The order may also require the defendant to disclose to the plaintiff where any of the documents or things the subject of the application are and this, coupled with the requirement that he produce the documents or other things for inspection, has led to a finding in England[4] that the defendant may decline to comply with the order where to do so would involve self-incrimination. This point has never been taken in Ireland, but the same common law privilege against self-incrimination exists here also, and if it were successfully invoked the efficacy of the remedy would be seriously impaired. In England, the legislature has dealt with the situation in s 72 of the Supreme Court Act 1981 which provides that in proceedings relating to intellectual property, or passing off, the privilege is not to apply. The statements are still, however, inadmissible in criminal proceedings arising out of the same matters. It would seem desirable that similar legislation should be introduced in this country where video piracy is also widespread and the Anton Piller procedure is frequently invoked.

The jurisdiction of the court to hear the application in camera derives from s 45(1) of the Courts (Supplemental Provisions) Act 1961 which empowers the court to hear in private

'applications of an urgent nature for relief by way of..... injunction.'

That provision must be interpreted in the light of Article 34 of the Constitution which requires justice to be administered in public 'save in such special and limited cases as may be prescribed by law.' The power conferred by s 45(1) is clearly such a case, but it may only be exercised in a manner which is itself consistent with the Constitution. It is accordingly essential to satisfy the court on every application of this nature that it is of an urgent nature and that the efficacy of the remedy would be seriously affected by a hearing in open court.

1 *Anton Piller KG v Manufacturing Process Ltd* [1976] Ch 55.
2 [1982] AC 380.
3 *Vapormatic Co Ltd v Sparex Ltd* [1976] 1 WLR 939.
4 *Rank Film Distribution Ltd v Video Information Centre Ltd*, above.

Injunctions by way of judicial review

15.43 Obtaining a perpetual injunction in the High Court normally necessitates the institution of plenary proceedings with all the attendant delays associated with the delivery of pleadings, the service of notice of trial and the listing of the case for hearing. The Rules of the Superior Courts in the revised form which became operative in 1986 have, however, introduced an important change: a perpetual injunction can now be granted on a notice of motion brought under the 'judicial review' procedure.[1] This procedure can be invoked where the court considers it 'just and convenient' and it will clearly be appropriate where the injunction is sought in respect of some administrative act or omission and the facts giving rise to the application are of such a nature that any dispute can be resolved on affidavit.

The leave of the court must first be obtained before such an application can be made.[2] The application for leave is made ex parte, and must be made 'promptly' and in any event not later than three months from the date on which the grounds for the application arose.[3] If the court is of the opinion that the application should not be made by way of judicial review, it may order the proceedings to continue as if they were plenary proceedings.[4]

The court may also award damages to the applicant if he has included a claim for damages in his application.[5]

1 Order 84, r 18(2).
2 Order 84, r 20.
3 Order 84, r 21.
4 Order 84, r 26(5).
5 Order 84, r 24.

Enforcement of injunctions

15.44 Where the person bound by the injunction fails to comply with it or acts in contravention of it, he is guilty of contempt of court and liable to be punished accordingly. It should be noted that it is not simply the defendant in the proceedings who is so liable: any person who is aware of it and aids and abets in committing a breach is guilty of contempt.[1] The punishment may take the form of a fine, committal to prison or (in the case of a body corporate) the sequestration of its assets. It is to be noted that attachment is, however, a form of execution of the court's order and the court, accordingly, will not of its own motion punish a person for non-compliance with the court's order: the party who obtained the order must move the court. It must be distinguished from 'criminal contempt' where the court itself moves to punish persons who seek to frustrate the process of the court or to bring the court into disrepute or, in the traditional phrase, 'scandalise the court'.[2]

The court will not normally punish a person for an inadvertent or unintentional breach of the order. It will generally be required to be satisfied that there has been wilful disobedience of the order on the part of the person bound by it.[3] And while it is not sufficient for a person to plead that compliance was impractical or difficult, the nature of the disobedience will, of course, be a major factor in determining the penalty which should be imposed.

1 *Moore v A-G (No 3)* [1930] IR 471 at 486-487 per Kennedy CJ.
2 *Keegan v de Burca* [1973] IR 223.
3 O'Hanlon J has expressed the view that the court should be cautious in making committal orders where there is no likelihood that they will achieve compliance with the court's order, as where the defendant is seeking the publicity of imprisonment, at least where there is another course open: *Ross Co v Swan* (1981) ILRM 416.

Chapter 16

Specific performance

16.01 An order of specific performance is one requiring a party to a contract to carry out his legal obligations under that contract. The normal remedy available to a party in cases where the other party to a contract is in breach of the contract is damages, but the court of equity recognised at an early stage that damages were not always an adequate remedy and hence the remedy was evolved with which we are now concerned. It arises most characteristically in the case of agreements for the sale of land: the purchaser of a particular house will usually not be adequately compensated by an award of damages in the event of his vendor reneging on the deal and consequently the court in such a case orders the contract to be specifically performed by the vendor's executing an assurance of the property upon payment by the purchaser of the balance of the price. Indeed it has been said on high authority that this is the only true type of specific performance and that the remedy is strictly speaking confined to *executory contracts* where an antecedent agreement should be followed by the performance of a further act such as the execution of a deed or the payment of money.[1] But it is also commonly used to describe orders requiring a party to perform his part of a contract which has already been performed in part, ie *executed contracts*. The distinction is, perhaps, not of great practical importance, but it is true to say that specific performance of executed contracts is more akin to the injunctive relief discussed in the last chapter than true 'specific performance'. It is also the case that in Ireland at least the remedy is far more frequently invoked in its true form, since it is usually sought in actions for the specific performance of contracts for the sale of land.

---

1 *Wolverhampton and Walsall Rly Co v London and North Western Rly Co* (1873) LR 16 Eq 433 at 439 per Lord Selborne LC.

16.02 The remedy is, like the injunction, discretionary. The discretion as to whether to grant or refuse specific performance in any case is, however, exercised in accordance with settled principles which are discussed further below. It will not usually be granted where damages are an adequate remedy, and it may also be refused on grounds such as hardship, laches or inequitable conduct on the part of the plaintiff.

16.03 In order to obtain a decree of specific performance, it is necessary to establish that there is in existence a binding and valid contract. There must also have been consideration for the promise sought to be enforced: thus, a voluntary contract will not be specifically performed even where it is under seal, since equity will not come to the aid of a volunteer.[1]

1 See para 8.07, above.

Specific performance of different types of contract

16.04 Specific performance is most frequently sought in Ireland of contracts for the sale of land. Provided that the contract is for valuable consideration and that there is a note or memorandum of the contract sufficient to satisfy the requirements of the Statute of Frauds,[1] specific performance will be granted. Even where there is no such memorandum, the contract may still be enforced by such an order if there has been part performance sufficient to take the case out of the statute.[2]

Specific performance is not normally granted of a contract for the sale of pure personalty (ie personal property other than land).[3] Since it should be possible for equivalent goods to be purchased elsewhere, failure to perform the contract will normally be remediable by an award of damages. But where the subject matter is a unique or rare object, such as a particular painting or an heirloom,[4] specific performance may be granted. For the same reasons, specific performance will not be granted of a contract for the sale of shares, except where the shares cannot be purchased on the market at the time of the decree.[5]

Specific performance may be granted of building contracts or other contracts requiring the carrying out of particular works, such as repairs, provided three requirements are met:
  (i) the works to be carried out are specified precisely;
  (ii) damages are an inadequate remedy; and
  (iii) the defendant is in possession of the land on which the works are to be carried out.[6]
The reason for the first requirement is the reluctance of the courts to enforce contracts which will require constant supervision by the court, leading to numerous applications by the parties.[7] The second requirement is, of course, common to all cases in which specific performance is sought. The third requirement is imposed, because otherwise there would be no reason why the plaintiff should not carry out the work himself. It is sometimes said that the defendant must be in possession of the land *under the contract*,[8] but is clear from a later decision that this is not essential.[9]

1 (1695) 7 Will 3 c12.
2 See para 16.13, below.
3 *Cuddee v Rutter* (1720) 5 Vin Abr 538 pl 21.
4 *Falcke v Gray* (1859) Drew 651.
5 *Cuddee v Rutter*, above.
6 *Wolverhampton Corpn v Emmons* [1901] 1 KB 515 at 525 per Romer LJ; *Rushbrooke v O'Sullivan* [1908] 1 IR 232.
7 See para 16.06, below. Cf *Shiels v Clery* (1941) Ltd, unreported, High Court, judgement delivered 13 October 1979.
8 *Wolverhampton Corpn v Emmons*, above.
9 *Carpenters Estates Ltd v Davies* [1940] Ch 160.

Defences to actions for specific performance

16.05 We have already seen that the court will not grant a decree for specific performance of a contract which is personal in its nature, such as a contract of employment.[1] It is true that *Lumley v Wagner*[2] and the cases in which it was followed or applied have been described as amounting to decrees of specific performance of such contracts, but in such cases the courts have never gone further than restraining a person from breaking a term of his or her contract of service, such as an agreement not to perform services of a particular nature for anyone else during the currency of the agreement, and then only where the person injuncted can enforce the rest of the contract, eg by securing the payment of the money which he was to receive. The courts have refused to apply *Lumley v Wagner* where the person sought to be injuncted could not himself secure the performance of the other party's obligations, because they were personal in their nature.[3]

But this principle will not prevent the court from granting a decree in cases of 'true specific performance' where one of the terms of the contract sought to be enforced is that the parties will enter into a contract of personal service. Such a decree was granted by Megarry V-C in *Giles v Morris*.[4]

It has been said (by Megarry V-C, for example in *Giles v Morris*[5]) that there is no absolute rule against requiring the performance of contracts of personal service and that the tendency of the courts in this area is more a matter of 'strong reluctance' than a prohibition against such decrees. It remains the case, however, that there are virtually no examples of cases where such a decree has been given.

1 See para 15.14, above.
2 (1852) 1 De GM & G 604.
3 *Page One Records Ltd v Britton* [1967] 3 All ER 822.
4 [1972] 1 All ER 960.
5 At p 969.

16.06 The court will not grant a decree where its enforcement will require continual supervision by the court. We have seen that this will not necessarily prevent the specific performance of building contracts provided the three standard requirements are met.[1] But where the terms of the contract sought to be enforced are of such a nature that either (a) the officers of the court are going to be involved in supervising their being carried out or (b) continual applications to the court for rulings as to whether the contract is being complied with can reasonably be anticipated, specific performance will not be granted. Thus in the leading case of *Ryan v Mutual Tontine Chambers Association*,[2] a lease provided that a porter or a trustworthy assistant should be in constant attendance in a building. Specific performance of this term was refused on the ground that the execution of it would require 'constant superintendance'.

1 See para 16.04, above.
2 [1893] 1 Ch 116, CA.

16.07 'Want of mutuality' is also a defence to an action for specific performance. One of the most widely approved statements of this defence is as follows:

'Equity will not compel specific performance by a defendant if, after performance, the common law remedy of damages would be his sole security for the performance of the plaintiff's side of the contract.'[1]

The contract must, in other words, be specifically enforceable against both parties. Thus, a minor cannot obtain a decree of specific performance because the defendant having complied with the decree by, for example, paying the purchase price for a house, would have only a claim for damages in the event of the minor failing to execute the deed.[2] It should be noted, however, that in the case of a contract for the sale of land, the principle of mutuality does not require that *both* parties should have signed a note or memorandum sufficient to satisfy the Statute of Frauds. It might seem at first sight that if the defendant only has signed such a note, he will be unable to obtain a decree against the plaintiff. But this is not so, because the bringing of the action by the plaintiff necessarily involves the delivery of a pleading in which the existence of a concluded and enforceable contract is acknowledged and which is signed by his agent and it is settled that this in itself constitutes a sufficient note or memorandum.[3]

This last example illustrates another important point: the time for ascertaining whether there is want of mutuality is at the hearing of the claim and not the time at which the contract was entered into. The statement in Fry on Specific Performance[4] to the effect that it is the time of the contract is now generally thought to be wrong in the light of the decision of the Court of Appeal in *Price v Strange*.[5] In that case the defendant orally agreed to grant the plaintiff an underlease of a flat provided she carried out certain repairs. The plaintiff did some of the work, but was prevented from doing it all by the defendant's repudiating the agreement. It was claimed on behalf of the defendant that, since the plaintiff's agreement to carry out the repairs could not have been the subject of a decree for specific performance at the time it was given (because of the absence of writing) the plaintiff was precluded from obtaining a decree of specific performance by the absence of mutuality. Her claim for specific performance was, however, upheld by the Court of Appeal, the members of which expressly disapproved of the statement of the law in Fry.

1 Ames, *Lectures on Legal History*, p 370.
2 *Flight v Bollard* (1828) 4 Russ 298.
3 *Lord Ormond v Anderson* (1813) 2 Ba & B 363 at 370-371 per Lord Manners, LC; *Farr Smith & Co v Messers Ltd* [1928] 1 KB 397.
4 6th edn, p 222.
5 [1977] 3 All ER 371, CA.

16.08 Specific performance will not be granted where part only of the contract can be so enforced. In *Ogden v Fossick*,[1] the plaintiff agreed to grant the defendant a lease of coal wharf, provided the latter employed him throughout the currency of the lease and paid him a commission on the sale of the coal. The court refused to grant the plaintiff a decree of specific performance: although the agreement for a lease was clearly capable of being specifically enforced, the agreement to employ the plaintiff was not, for reasons which have already been explained.[2] This principle will not apply, however, where the agreement can be regarded as consisting in substance of two or more agreements: the court may then require the specific performance of such of the agreements as is so enforceable. Thus in the case of a sale of land in lots, where the vendor is unable to make title to one of the lots, specific performance may be granted of the agreement for sale of the remaining lots.[3] Moreover, the rule only applies in cases of executory contracts or 'true' specific performance. In the case of an *executed* contract, as we have already seen, the court may grant a mandatory injunction to compel performance of a term that remains unexecuted and this can be regarded as a form of specific performance in the broader sense.[4]

1 (1862) 4 De GF & J 426.
2 See para 16.05, above.
3 *Lewin v Guest* (1826) 1 Russ 325.
4 See para 16.01, above.

16.09 Specific performance may be refused on the ground that the contract was induced by *misrepresentation*[1] or *mistake*.[2] A misrepresentation may be a ground for the *rescission* of the contract, ie the setting aside of the contract, but the misrepresentation which will afford a defence to an action for specific performance need not be as grave in character.[3] In *Smelter Corporation v O'Driscoll,*[4] the agent for the purchasers honestly but mistakenly told the vendor that her land would be compulsorily acquired by the local authority if she did not sell to the purchasers. It was held by Butler J, whose decision was affirmed by the Supreme Court, that specific performance should not be ordered against the vendor,

Where the mistake relied on has been contributed to, however innocently, by the plaintiff, specific performance will normally be refused. Thus in *Denny v Hancock,*[5] the defendant purchased a property in the mistaken belief that some trees were within the boundary of the land being sold. The court found that the error had been caused in part by a map prepared by the plaintiff vendor and refused specific performance. But where the mistake is solely that of the defendant and has not been contributed to in any way by the plaintiff, specific performance will not be refused.[6] It is only where enforcing the contract would cause 'hardship amounting to injustice' that specific performance will be refused on the ground of a unilateral mistake of this nature.[7]

1 *Re Terry & White's Contract* (1886) 32 Ch D 14 at 29; *Peilow v O'Carroll* (1971) 105 ILT 21, SC; *Smelter Corpn of Ireland v O'Driscoll* [1977] IR 305, SC.
2 *Denny v Hancock* (1870) 6 Ch App 1. Mistake may also be a ground for rectification: see Chapter 18, below.
3 *Re Banister* (1879) 12 Ch D 131 at 142, CA.
4 Above.
5 Above.
6 *Tamplin v James* (1879) 15 Ch D 215.
7 Ibid, at 221 per James LJ.

16.10 The court will not grant specific performance where performance of the contract is *impossible*.[1] Thus if the consent of some body (such as the Irish Land Commission) is required to a sale of land, the court will not order specific performance of the contract where the consent has been withheld.[2] But where the defendant seeks to frustrate the contract by simply not applying for the consent, the court will grant the plaintiff relief which will effectively require the defendant at least to seek the necessary consent.[3]

Nor will the court grant specific performance of a contract where to do so would be *futile*. An agreement to enter into a partnership at will is not specifically enforced, for example, since the defendant could effectively frustrate the effect of the court's decree by terminating it immediately.[4] But it has recently been held in England that specific performance will be granted of a contractual licence of as brief a duration of two days[5] and it is thought that the same would apply to an agreement to grant a lease for even a very short term.

1 *Ferguson v Wilson* (1866) 2 Ch App 77.
2 *Wroth v Tyler* [1974] Ch 30 at 50.
3 *McGillicuddy v Joy* [1959] IR 189.
4 *Hercy v Birch* (1804) 9 Ves 357.
5 *Verrall v Great Yarmouth Borough Council* [1981] QB 202.

16.11 The relief may also be refused if it appears to the court that the plaintiff has been substantially in breach of his obligations under the contract[1] or is not ready and willing to perform his obligations thereunder.[2] But the law here looks to the substance of the agreement under consideration and not to its form.[3] In a contract for the sale of land, for example, the essential obligation of the vendor is to transfer the property on payment of the purchase price and of the purchaser in his turn to pay the purchase price on being tendered such a transfer. The fact that either party may be in breach of non-essential or trivial provisions of the contract will not prevent a decree being granted.[4] Similar considerations apply if the term in question is independent and collateral to the contract although contained in the same document.[5]

1 *Modlen v Snowball* (1861) 4 De GF & J 143.
2 *Dyster v Randall* [1926] Ch 932. Cf *United Yeast Co Ltd v Cameo Investments Ltd* (1977) 11 ILT 13.
3 See para 3.15, above.
4 *Dyster v Randall*, above.
5 *Green v Low* (1856) 22 Beav 625.

16.12 Finally, specific performance may be refused if to grant it would be unfair or a hardship on the defendant.[1] The mere fact that the consideration appears inadequate, however, is not of itself usually a ground, although it may be an important factor when other circumstances exist.[2]

Questions such as unfairness and hardship are to be judged at the time the contract is entered into. Changes of circumstances taking place later which make the contract less beneficial to one party are immaterial unless they are brought about by the action of the other party. In *Lavan v Walsh,*[3] Budd J said that the exceptions to this rule were 'very rare' and this was endorsed by the Supreme Court in *Roberts v O'Neill,*[4] where McCarthy J said that such exceptions would not ordinarily include cases of hardship resulting from inflation alone. (In the latter case, the owners of a licensed premises pleaded unsuccessfully that the rise in the value of such premises since the date of the contract would make it prohibitively expensive for them to buy another.)

1 *Conlon v Murray* [1958] NI 17; *Roberts v O'Neill* [1983] IR 47.
2 *Burrowes v Lock* (1805) 10 Ves 470.
3 [1964] IR 87.
4 Above.

Part performance

16.13 We mentioned at the outset that specific performance will not be granted where the contract is unenforceable because it is not in writing. This will most often arise in the case of contracts which under the provisions of the Statute of Frauds[1] cannot be enforced unless evidenced by a note or memorandum in writing signed by the party to be charged or his agent thereunto authorised in that behalf. Most commonly of all, it is pleaded as a defence to actions for the specific performance of agreements for the dispositions of interests in land.

16.13 *Specific performance*

There are two principal exceptions to the rule that specific performance will not be granted of contracts unenforceable for this reason. In the first place, the court will not allow the statute itself to be used as an instrument of fraud since that is what it is designed to prevent. Hence, if the defendant has been guilty of fraud (in its equitable sense) he will not be allowed to rely on the statute. In the second place, the contract may be enforceable where the plaintiff can prove acts of *part performance* of the contract which are sufficient to render compliance with the statute unnecessary.

1 (1695) 7 Will 3 c12 s2.

16.14 The doctrine of part performance was evolved by the courts of equity to mitigate the injustice which was thought to result from the operation of the statute. It affords a classic example of the delicate balance which the courts have sometimes had to maintain between not usurping the role of the legislature on the one hand and seeking to mitigate as far as possible the injustice capable of being wrought by adherence to a statute on the other. The leading exposition of the doctrine remains that of Lord Selborne LC in *Maddison v Alderson*[1] where a housekeeper sought to enforce an agreement by her employer to leave her by his will a life interest in certain land in consideration of her giving her services free. It was held that her performance of her obligations under the agreement as a housekeeper were not acts of part performance sufficient to take the case out of the statute. The learned lord chancellor said that the acts relied on had to be 'unequivocally and in their own nature referable to some such agreement as that alleged.'[2] Her continuance in the deceased's service without payment of wages was not such an act as to be in itself evidence of a contract, much less a contract concerning her employer's land. Lord Selborne made it clear that the basis of the doctrine of part performance was the prevention of fraud: the defendant was not 'charged' upon the contract itself, since that was what the statute expressly prohibited, but upon the 'equities' arising in the particular case. He posited the following example:

'Let the case be supposed of a parol contract to sell land, completely performed on both sides as to everything except conveyance, the whole purchase money paid, the purchaser put into possession, expenditure by him (say in costly buildings) upon the property; leases granted by him to tenants.'[3]

In such a case, he said, the matter had advanced beyond the stage of contract and the equities which arose at such a point could not be given effect to by the court without taking account of the contract.

The example suggested by Lord Selborne suggests that he was taking a relatively confined view of the circumstances in which part performance might validly be invoked. But there was considerable disagreement as to what was meant by his reference to the need for the acts relied on being unequivocally and of their nature related to 'some such agreement as that alleged'. In the case of a contract for the sale of land, by far the most common occasion for the invocation of the doctrine, was it enough that the acts related in the required manner to a contract for the sale of land? Or was it essential that they related to a contract for the sale of *the particular land?* The uncertainty was not removed by the fact that support for both points of view was to be found in the leading textbook on specific performance.[4] The current of modern authority would seem to favour the less strict view: it is thought that provided the acts are unequivocally

250

referable to a contract of the nature alleged and are at least not inconsistent with the existence of the particular contract, they will suffice.[5]

1 (1883) 8 App Cas 467, HL.
2 At 479.
3 At 475.
4 Fry on *Specific Performance*, 6th edn, p 278.
5 See para 16.15, below.

16.15 In general, the payment of money will not be regarded as a sufficient act of part performance. It is submitted that this is still the law, although in exceptional circumstances (such as arose in *Steadman v Steadman*[1] discussed in detail below) the payment of money may be sufficient of itself. One reason why the payment of money is usually not enough is that if the defendant denies the existence of the contract, the plaintiff can recover the money by action and hence no fraud arises. But this, of course, is not always so: where the vendor has become insolvent, the purchaser will be confined to proving in the bankruptcy or winding-up for whatever dividend the other unsecured creditors receive. On the other hand, it may be argued that in such circumstances the purchaser has a lien for the money upon the land the subject matter of the contract and that accordingly it is recoverable. There is clear authority for the proposition that the existence of such a lien does not depend on the existence of an enforceable contract.[2]

These problems were the subject of attention in *Steadman v Steadman*.[3] In that case, the parties were husband and wife. They compromised the differences between them at the door of the magistrate's court: the wife agreed to transfer her interest in the matrimonial home in consideration of the payment of £1500 by the husband. In addition, an existing maintenance order was to be discharged and a separate maintenance order was to be made, the husband agreeing to pay £100 in discharge of arrears of maintenance by a specified date. The husband paid the £100 but the wife changed her mind about transferring the home, since the property had risen in value. None of the terms had been reduced to writing and, when the husband sued for specific performance, the wife relied on the Statute of Frauds. In addition to the payment of the £100 the husband relied on the preparation of a draft deed of conveyance and its submission for approval to the wife's solicitors as sufficient acts of part performance. By a majority, the Court of Appeal upheld his claim and in the House of Lords an appeal from that decision was dismissed.

The most elaborate speech in the House of Lords was that of Lord Simon of Glaisdale. He was of the view that a tendency had developed—which he clearly thought should be halted—to treat the doctrine of part performance as a rule of evidence rather than as a principle of substantive law.[4] If it were treated as the latter, then the defendant could be held to his contract, where it would be inequitable to allow him to escape because the plaintiff had incurred expenditure or otherwise acted to his own detriment in reliance on the contract and the defendant had allowed him so to act. But if it were treated as a rule of evidence, then the plaintiff might have to show a nexus between the alleged acts of part performance and the actual contract which might not be easy to do. It was not necessary, in his view, for the plaintiff to do more than establish that he did acts of part performance of *some* contract to which the defendant was a party while the latter stood by, where it would be inequitable that the defendant would be allowed to plead that any such contract was unenforceable.

While the general principle that the payment of money is not of itself a sufficiently unequivocal act to constitute an act of part performance remains unaffected by the decision in *Steadman v Steadman,* it is also clear that by contrast taking possession of the land the subject of the contract is such an act.[5]

1 [1976] AC 536
2 *Re Barrett Apartments Ltd* (1985) ILRM 679, SC.
3 Above.
4 At 559.
5 *Wills v Stradling* (1797) 3 Ves 378 at 381.

16.16 It appears from some cases that a claim for specific performance may be dismissed on the ground that the *parties* to the suit are not the same as the parties to the contract. Thus, in the leading case of *Tasker v Small,*[1] a bill for specific performance was dismissed as against some defendants on the ground that the purchaser plaintiff had erroneously joined as defendants certain mortgagees and others in addition to the owner of the equity of redemption who was the actual vendor. It is thought that the rule in *Tasker v Small* would not be applied in Ireland to-day: in the case of a contract for the sale of land, if a number of parties interested in the land who are not parties to the contract are before the court, it would seem as much in their interest, as in the interest of the parties, that an order should be made determining the rights and liabilities of all concerned, subject of course, to provision being made for the costs of any parties who are before the court through no fault of theirs.

1 (1837) 3 My & Cr 63.

16.17 *Iura vigilantibus non domientibus subveniunt:* law comes to the aid of those who are vigilant and not those who slumber.[1] It follows that a claim for specific performance may be successfully resisted on the ground of *laches,* ie delay of such magnitude as would render it inequitable to enforce the contract. Whether the delay has been such as to render it inequitable to enforce the contract will depend on all the circumstances of the case.[2] Thus, while a delay of two years was not enough to defeat the plaintiff's claim in *Lazard Bros v Fairfield Properties,*[3] delay of less than two years was held to be fatal in *Stuart v London North Western Rly Co.*[4] But a delay between the issuing of the plenary summons and the action coming to trial will not be a bar to relief, unless the plaintiff by his dilatory prosecution of the proceedings has misled the defendant into thinking that he was relying on a claim for damages only.[5] Delay by the plaintiff in enforcing the decree for specific performance, although it may not preclude the ultimate enforcement of the decree, may mean the payment of compensation by the plaintiff to the defendant for any damage he has sustained as a pre-condition to such enforcement.[6]

Delays will not be material, however, where the plaintiff is already in possession of the land, has paid the purchase money, and merely seeks to have his title completed by the assurance to him of the legal estate.[7]

1 See para 3.10, above.
2 *Crofton v Ormsby* (1806) 2 Sch & Lef 583, 603/4 per Lord Redesdale. Cf *Guardian Builders Ltd v Kelly* (1981) ILRM 127.
3 (1977) 121 Sol Jo 793.
4 (1852) 1 De GM & G 721.
5 *Du Sautoy v Syms* [1967] Ch 1146.
6 *Easton v Brown* [1981] 3 All ER 278.
7 *Sharp v Milligan* (1856) 22 Beav 606.

Rights of the plaintiff where there has been a breach after the proceedings have commenced

16.18 It was at one time thought that, where a plaintiff began proceedings for specific performance of a contract and the defendant thereafter committed a breach which would in the absence of proceedings have entitled the plaintiff to repudiate the contract, the plaintiff was precluded by the existence of the proceedings from treating the contract as discharged: once he had committed himself to affirming the contract by issuing proceedings, he could not retreat. The same result followed where he had prosecuted the action to finality and obtained a decree. This doctrine, which seemed to have little to commend it in logic or commonsense, was largely demolished by the House of Lords in *Johnson v Agnew*.[1] It was held in that case that the court may in such circumstances in the exercise of its equitable jurisdiction permit the plaintiff to treat the contract as discharged. It has been suggested that the leave of the court should not even be necessary and that the invocation by the plaintiff of the equitable remedy of specific performance should not be treated as putting an end to the plaintiff's common law right to treat the contract as discharged.[2] There seems good sense in this view: it is difficult to see on what basis the court could withhold leave to the plaintiff if the circumstances were such as to justify him in treating the contract as at an end.

1 [1980] AC 367.
2 Meagher, Gummow & Lehane, pp 506-507.

Chapter 17

Rescission

17.01 The word 'rescission' is used in a number of different senses and these must be carefully distinguished.

In the first place, rescission may arise where one party to a contract has been in breach of a term which is essential or as is sometimes said 'goes to the root of the contract.' In that case, the innocent party has an option: he may elect to treat the contract as remaining in force and confine himself to a claim for damages or he may treat his obligations under the contract as at an end, in which case he is said to rescind the contract and his election so to do is properly called 'rescission'.[1] Rescission in this sense is a purely common law doctrine and is the act of the party himself.

In the second place, the contract itself may provide that in defined circumstances a party may put an end to the contract and again this is described as 'rescission.' Thus, contracts for the sale of land provide that the vendor may rescind the contract where, for example, the purchaser insists on a requisition with which the vendor is unable to comply.[2] Again rescission in this sense is the action of the party alone.

In the third place, there are a number of cases in which the courts themselves in the exercise of their equitable jurisdiction will set aside transactions, including not merely contracts, but deeds or other instruments. This may arise for a variety of reasons: the party may have been induced to enter into the transaction as a result of misrepresentation by the other or its execution may have been procured by undue influence, to mention but two examples. It is this form of rescission with which we are here concerned and it differs from the other two forms of rescission already mentioned in being the creation of equity and in being usually (but not invariably)[3] the result of the order of the court rather than the act of one of the parties. In general, however, the court will only set aside the transaction where it is possible to restore the parties to the same position as they would have been in had they not entered into the transaction in question. This is usually expressed by saying that the transaction will not be set aside unless *restitutio in integrum* is possible.[4] The courts of equity were more adapted to making such orders, because of the range of additional remedies open to them — such as the taking of accounts between the parties — in contrast to the common law courts. Even where *restitutio in integrum* was not possible, they were prepared to grant rescission, provided what was called 'practical justice' could be effected between the parties.[5]

As with cases of common law rescission, so also with those of equitable rescission, the contract or other transaction is voidable only and not void, ie it remains in being unless and until it is rescinded, either by the party himself in the case of common law rescission or by the court in the case of rescission in equity.[6] There is an important difference, however: where the contract is rescinded by the court, it is treated as voidable *ab initio*, ie as though it had been set aside from the beginning.[7] In cases of common law rescission, the parties are discharged or excused from performance *in futuro* only. It follows that any rights, including causes of action, which have already vested in a party at a time common law rescission is properly invoked, remain vested in that party.[8]

1 *Robb v James* (1881) 15 ILT 59.
2 Eg condition 18 of Law Society *Standard Conditions of Sale* (1986 edn).
3 See Meagher, Gummow & Lehane, pp 620-621.
4 *Northern Bank Ltd v Charlton* [1979] IR 149.
5 *Erlanger v New Sombrero Phosphate Co* (1878) 3 App Cas 1218.
6 Chitty on *Contract*, 25th edn, Vol I, p 375.
7 *Johnson v Agnew* [1980] AC 367 at 373; *Photo Production Ltd v Securicor Transport Ltd* [1980] AC 827 at 844.
8 *Photo Production Ltd v Securicor Transport Ltd*, above.

The equitable remedy of rescission

17.02 The cases in which the equitable remedy of rescission may be granted can be summarised as follows:

(1) Where a party has been induced to enter into a transaction by a misrepresentation, whether fraudulent or innocent, by the other party;
(2) Where one party has been silent in circumstances where the law requires him to make disclosure, ie contracts *uberrimae fidei*, where the 'utmost good faith' is required;
(3) Where an agreement has been entered into as a result of a mistake;
(4) Where one party has entered into a transaction as a result of what the law regards as the 'undue influence' of the other;
(5) Where the transaction is in the view of the court unconscionable and should not be allowed to stand.

The two last mentioned cases—of undue influence and unconscionable transactions—are usually referred to as examples of 'constructive fraud', ie cases in which the court takes the view that one party to a transaction has obtained advantages which a court of equity should not allow him to retain but has not necessarily been guilty of any morally culpable behaviour. They are dealt with more fully in Chapter 29. In this chapter we confine ourselves to rescission arising in the first three cases.

Fraudulent and innocent misrepresentation

17.03 A contract may be rescinded by the court where its execution has been procured by the misrepresentation of one of the parties. If the misresentation is fraudulent, ie if the party made the representation knowing it to be untrue or recklessly indifferent as to whether it was true or false, the innocent party will also be entitled to sue for damages.[1] Where the misrepresentation is innocent, however, his only remedy is in general rescission, unless he can prove that the representation was made negligently, in which case he may be entitled to damages.[2] (There is no equivalent in Ireland to the English Misrepresentation Act 1967 which entitles a party to damages for innocent misrepresentation in substitution for, or in addition to, rescission.)

The plaintiff must prove that he was induced to enter into the contract by the representation. But he will still be entitled to rescission although the representation in question may not have been his only reason for entering into the contract.[3] The better view would also appear to be that the representee does not lose his right of rescission because the representation is also a term of the contract itself. It had been thought on the authority of *Pennsylvania Shipping Co v Compagnie Nationale de Navigation*[4] that where it was so embodied in the contract itself, the representee would be entitled to rescind only where the term was a *condition* as distinct from a *warranty*. (As we have seen, at common law a party was entitled to rescind for breach of an essential term of the contract. Such a term was called a condition, in contrast to an inessential term which was called a warranty.) In the Australian case of *Academy of Health and Fitness v Power*,[5] however, Crockett J declined to follow the *Pennsylvania* case. He pointed out that whether a term was essential was determined by the court objectively and not by reference to what the parties may have thought. By contrast, whether a term constitutes a misrepresentation is determined subjectively, ie by reference to the effect it had on the mind of the representee. A term, objectively viewed, might be a mere warranty and yet have been one of the factors which induced the representee to enter into the contract. In such circumstances, it would be wrong to confine the injured party to a claim in damages which might be inadequate.

1 *Derry v Peek* (1889) 14 App Cas 337; *Northern Bank Ltd v Charlton*, above.
2 *Hedley Byrne & Co Ltd v Heller & Partners Ltd* (1964) AC 465; *Securities Trust Ltd v Hugh Moore & Alexander Ltd* [1964] IR 417.
3 *Edgington v FitzMaurice* (1885) 29 Ch D 459.
4 [1936] 2 All ER 1167 at 1171.
5 [1973] VR 254.

17.04 The traditional view of the law was that rescission was not available as a remedy for innocent misrepresentation where a contract had been executed. This was said to be so in the case of a conveyance of freeholds in *Wilde v Gibson*[1] and the rule was later reaffirmed in *Seddon v North Eastern Salt Co*.[2] It was applied to a lease in *Angel v Jay*[3] and has been followed in some later cases. In *Solle v Butcher*,[4] however, Denning LJ said that *Angel v Jay* had been incorrectly decided, although in the same case Jenkins LJ considered himself bound by it and Bucknill LJ expressed no view.

In the only reported Irish decision (in 1914),[5] the earlier English decisions were followed. In the leading modern Irish decision on rescission, *Northern Bank Ltd v Charlton*,[6] the point did not arise, since the misrepresentation in that case was held by the trial judge to be fraudulent. It is thought, however, that if the question did arise for consideration, it is unlikely that the earlier English decisions would be followed.[7] The only logical justification for the rule would appear to be the danger that in the case of some transactions innocent third parties who subsequently acquired an interest might be adversely affected. But, as we have seen, the right to set aside a deed because of misrepresentation is in any event better treated as a mere 'equity' which would not affect a third party purchasing for value without notice.[8]

1 (1848) 1 HL Cas 605.
2 [1905] 1 Ch 326.
3 [1911] 1 KB 666.
4 [1950] 1 KB 671.
5 *Lecky v Walter* [1914] 1 IR 378.
6 Above.
7 It has been abolished by statute in England: Misrepresentation Act 1967, s 1(6).
8 See para 4.03, above.

Contracts uberrimae fidei

17.05 For a transaction to be set aside for misrepresentation, the plaintiff must show that he has been misled by a statement made by the defendant. Generally speaking, mere silence as to a state of facts, however material, is not a misrepresentation which can ground a claim for rescission. To this, however, there is an important exception: in the case of contracts *uberrimae fidei*—those in which the law requires the utmost good faith from one or both parties—the mere non-disclosure of a material fact may entitle one of the parties to rescission. Three broad categories of cases have been identified by the law in this context as requiring *uberrima fides:*

(i) contracts of insurance;
(ii) contracts to take shares in a company;
(iii) family arrangements.

Of these the first is by far the most important in practice.

17.06 Contracts of insurance have for long been treated as giving rise to a duty on the person seeking insurance to make a full disclosure of all material facts which are known to him. This is because the insurer is taking on a form of risk which may involve him in substantial financial loss in circumstances where the insured is in a far better position to know the facts affecting the risk. In addition, proposal forms for insurance to-day contain stringent clauses binding on the insured and relieving the insurer from liability on grounds which go beyond the common law duty of disclosure.

The duty of the insured is to disclose every *material* circumstance which is known to him before the contract is concluded.[1] For this purpose he is deemed to know every circumstance, which, in the ordinary course of business, ought to be known by him.[2] A circumstance is material if it would influence the judgement of a prudent insurer in fixing the premium or determining whether he will take the risk.[3] Failure to disclose any such material circumstances will entitle the insurer to rescission. These criteria are laid down by s 18(2) of the Marine Insurance Act 1906, which codified the common law decisions relating to marine insurance, but it has been held in a number of cases that the same principles are applicable to other forms of insurance such as life, fire, accident, burglary or fidelity.[4]

The test laid down in the section is an objective one: in determining whether the circumstance is material, it is accordingly not relevant that the particular insurer would have accepted the risk at the same premium had he known of the circumstance. The leading Irish case on the topic is *Chariot Inns Ltd v Assicurazioni Gen & Another*[5] where the plaintiff company had taken out a policy of fire insurance on a licensed premises in Ranelagh with the first named defendants. The premises were destroyed by fire and the insurers suspected that the controlling shareholder in the plaintiff company had set fire to them himself because of financial difficulties. They repudiated liability on this ground, but also on the ground that the shareholder had not disclosed that another company controlled by him had made a successful claim against another insurer in respect of a fire on their premises not long before. The plaintiff company claimed that they had in fact disclosed this fire to their broker who had advised them that it was not necessary to disclose it. The insurers admitted that, had they been aware of the earlier fire, it would not have affected their acceptance of the risk. In the High Court, Keane J, applying the objective test, held that the circumstance was not material. On appeal, the Supreme Court applied the same test, but held that the particular non-disclosure was material. The brokers were, however, held liable in negligence for wrongly advising the plaintiff company that disclosure was not necessary.

It is only non-disclosure of material circumstances of which the insured is aware or of which he ought to be aware which will lead to rescission. If, for example, he says when applying for life insurance that he is not suffering from any disease whereas in fact unknown to himself he is suffering from cancer, this will not at common law or equity avoid the contract.[6] But, as we have seen, policies frequently make the accuracy of such statements in a proposal form a condition precedent to the insurers' liability, irrespective of the insured's knowledge or lack of it. Such clauses, although frequently criticised by the courts, are undoubtedly enforceable.[7]

It has also been recently held by the Supreme Court that the common law duty of disclosure will not necessarily apply to 'over the counter' insurance, eg policies taken out by intending airline passengers when booking a particular flight where full disclosure is so difficult or impractical that the insurer must be taken to have ruled it out as a requirement.[8]

1 *Chariot Inns Ltd v Assicurazioni Gen* [1981] IR 199.
2 Marine Insurance Act 1906, s 18(1).
3 *Chariot Inns Ltd v Assicurazioni Gen*, above.
4 *Joel v Law Union & Crown Insurance Co* [1908] 2 KB 863.
5 Above.
6 *Joel v Law Union and Crown Insce Co*, above.
7 *Joel v Law Union and Crown Insce Co*, above.
8 *Aro Road and Land Vehicles Ltd v Insurance Corpn of Ireland Ltd*; unreported, judgement delivered 22 July 1986.

17.07 Contracts to take shares in companies were also recognised at common law as requiring *uberrima fides* on the part of those responsible for the undertaking.[1] This common law duty was of particular relevance in the case of public companies, where people might well take shares in the company in the belief that anything material affecting its operations was to be found in the prospectus. Modern companies legislation now imposes stringent duties as to disclosure on those concerned with the flotation and the stock exchange requirements have grown increasingly rigorous. The latter have now been given the force of law in the European Communities (Stock Exchange) Regulations 1984, which implement in Ireland three EEC directives.[2]

1 *Central Rly Co of Venezuela (Directors etc) v Kisch* (1867) LR 2 HL 99 at 113.
2 See Keane, *Company Law in the Republic of Ireland*, Chapter 7.

17.08 The duty of disclosure has also been said to arise in a large number of family arrangements made between relatives and

'designed to preserve the harmony, to protect the property or to save the honour of the family.'[1]

In such cases, the courts have always insured that the parties must meet on an equal footing and hence that there must be a full disclosure of all material facts even though no inquiries have been made.[2]

1 Cheshire, Fifoot & Furmston on *The Law of Contract*, 11th edn, p 293.
2 *Gordon v Gordon* (1821) 3 Swan 400.

Mistake

17.09 In considering the attitude of equity to transactions affected by mistake, certain fundamental principles must always be borne in mind. If I buy a particular horse in the confident belief that it is sound and find the next day that it is unsound, I have undoubtedly entered into the contract under a serious misapprehension, but no court, whether it is applying legal or equitable principles, will release me from my bargain or give me damages on that ground alone. (It would be otherwise, of course, if I was expressly told that it was sound.)

There are two reasons for this. In the first place, it is all too easy for someone anxious to escape from a contractual obligation to say that he made a mistake. Confusion and uncertainty would reign in our law of contract if that were encouraged. In the second place, the effect at common law of an *operative* mistake was that the contract never existed in the first place, ie that it was void.[1] This could have damaging consequences for third parties: if an agreement for sale was void, the property in the goods remained in the vendor and a third party who bought them unaware of any mistake would find that he did not own them.[2]

1 *Cundy v Lindsay* (1878) 3 App Cas 459.
2 Ibid.

17.10 Whether the law will relieve a party from the consequences of a mistake depends in the first place on the nature of the mistake. In this context, the law has distinguished between three forms of mistake which may affect a contract in law or in equity or in both.

(1) Common mistake. A agrees to sell to B 'the Jack B. Yeats in my cottage in Wicklow.' There is a painting in the cottage purporting to be by the artist, but in fact, unknown to both A and B, it is a worthless imitation. The parties have contracted under a common mistake.

(2) Mutual mistake. A and B make the same agreement. The painting in the cottage is genuine but A has another, far more valuable, painting by Jack B. Yeats in his Dublin house. B mistakenly thinks A is referring to that painting, and A is unaware of his mistake. The parties are mutually mistaken as to each other's intentions.

(3) Unilateral mistake. B makes the same mistake as in (2) but this time A is aware of his error. Only one party is mistaken and hence the mistake is unilateral.

17.11 We consider first the effect of a common mistake. In this instance, no matter how fundamental the mistake may be, the contract will not be void.[1] The fact that the parties have contracted not merely under a misapprehension, but one that goes to the very root of their bargain, is not

259

a ground for treating them as never having entered into a contract in the first place. So, in our first example, the fact that both parties mistakenly believe the painting in the cottage to be a Yeats does not mean that there is no contract. If, however, the subject matter of the contract was simply not in existence—if the cottage with the picture in it had been destroyed by fire unknown to the parties—there would be in law no contract, not because there was no agreement, but because there was nothing about which to agree.[2]

This appears to be the effect of the much discussed decision by the House of Lords in *Bell v Lever Brothers*.[3] The defendant company had paid compensation for the termination of their contracts of employments to employees who, unknown to the company, had made profits for themselves from their positions which they had not disclosed to the company. It was agreed that the company would have been entitled to terminate the contracts had they been aware of the illegitimate profits. Yet the House of Lords by a majority of one, reversing the Court of Appeal and Wright J at first instance, held that the employees could retain the compensation. Lord Atkin, speaking for the majority, while conceding that there could be cases in which the parties must be treated as having contracted on the condition, implied if not stated, that a certain state of affairs existed, said that, such cases apart, a common mistake even as to a matter of fundamental importance was not of itself sufficient to avoid the contract. In the instant case, the parties had no doubt contracted on the assumption that the contracts were in existence, but it could not be said that they had contracted subject to an implied condition that the contracts would run for a fixed term as opposed to being immediately terminable for breach (the latter being the true position.)

It is unnecessary to consider all the ramifications of *Bell v Lever Brothers*, which belong strictly to the common law. But the case is also of great importance in the context of equity since it established that a common mistake would not render a contract void unless it related to the very existence of the subject matter of the contract itself, as in *Couturier v Hastie*,[4] where goods thought to be in transit had in fact become fermented and been sold to someone else. The view that *any* fundamental misapprehension is sufficient to render a contract void gains some support from passages in the speeches,[5] but cannot be treated as the *ratio* of the decision.[6]

1 *Bell v Lever Brothers Ltd* [1932] AC 161.
2 *Couturier v Hastie* (1856) 5 HL Cas 673.
3 Above.
4 Above.
5 Lord Warrington, at 206; Lord Atkin, at 235.
6 See the analysis of the decision in Cheshire, Fifoot & Furmston, op cit, pp 224-226. Cf *Leaf v International Galleries* [1950] 2 KB 86 at 89.

17.12 It would seem to follow from *Bell v Lever Brothers*[1] that, however inequitable the result might appear, a party could not be relieved from the consequences of a common mistake, no matter how fundamental, unless an equitable jurisdiction existed which for some reason could not be invoked in that case. It is not easy to understand how, if such a jurisdiction existed, the case managed to travel as far as the House of Lords fifty years after the Judicature Act without its being invoked. In some later English cases,[2] however, it was said that the courts did indeed possess such an equitable jurisdiction to set aside a contract where the parties contracted under a common mistake, provided

(a) the mistake was fundamental, and

(b) the party seeking to set aside the transaction was not himself at fault.

An older authority was relied on as confirming the existence of such a jurisdiction, ie *Cooper v Phibbs*,[3] which wound its way into the House of Lords from the wilder regions of County Sligo in 1867. In that case, a man rented his own fishery from his cousins under the mistaken belief, shared by them, that it belonged to them. The agreement was set aside on the ground of mistake (obviously a common mistake, although Lord Westbury referred to it as a mutual mistake.) His cousins were, however, entitled to be recouped for money they had spent on the fishery.

The most controversial modern invocation of the alleged jurisdiction was the decision of the Court of Appeal in *Solle v Butcher*.[4] In that case, a landlord and a tenant entered into a lease of a flat under the mistaken belief that it was not controlled by the Rent Acts. When the error came to light, the tenant sought to recover payments of rent made by him in excess of the statutory limit, while the landlord claimed to have the lease set aside. A majority of the court was in favour of setting aside the lease on terms: the tenant could remain in possession if he was prepared to accept a new lease at a higher rent.

1 Above.
2 *Solle v Butcher* [1950] 1 KB 671; *Grist v Bailey* [1967] Ch 532; *Magee v Pennine Insurance Co Ltd* [1969] 2 QB 507.
3 (1867) LR 2 HL 149.
4 Above.

17.13 *Solle v Butcher* has been strongly criticised[1] as being based on a misapplication of *Cooper v Phibbs*. The latter decision, it has been said, does not in truth assert the existence of an independent equitable jurisdiction to set aside a contract on the ground of common mistake. On this view, a contract is either void at common law because of a common mistake or it is not. If it is void, then there is no role for equity to play: the court cannot set aside a contract which does not exist and *a fortiori* it cannot do so on terms. In *Cooper v Phibbs*, the terms which the court imposed on the owner could have been so imposed in an action brought against him independently of the agreement for the lease. Hence the decision is consistent with the contract having been void at common law. It is true that the language both of the speech of Lord Westbury and the actual order of the House seem to point clearly to the court treating the agreement as voidable in equity, but, if so, this should be seen as an anomalous exception to the general rule that equity cannot set aside an agreement, on terms or otherwise, on the ground that it was entered into under a common mistake.

There is undoubtedly much force in this approach which has both logic and consistency with authority on its side. The mistake in *Bell v Lever Bros* was surely one that cried out for equitable intervention, and it is a little difficult to explain away a decision of the House of Lords in 1932 on the ground that their eyes were modestly averted from equitable considerations. Lord Blaneborough indeed suggested, somewhat complacently, that the outcome satisfied the requirements of equity.[2] If *Bell v Lever Brothers* introduced certainty into this branch of law (as Lord Atkin claimed) it could only be because it was established thereby beyond doubt in England that

(a) a contract was not void because it was entered into under a shared misapprehension, however fundamental. It was only where the parties contracted under a common mistaken belief that the subject matter was in existence that it could be regarded as so void.

(b) Where a contract was not void, it stood and could not be set aside by the court, however mistaken the parties may have been as to a fundamental matter.

This indeed was the basis of Winn LJ's dissenting judgement in the later Court of Appeal decision of *Magee v Pennine Insurance Co*.[3] In that case, the defendants settled a claim on foot of an insurance policy which they were in fact entitled to repudiate. Neither they nor their insured adverted to the fact that they were entitled to repudiate. The majority held that the agreement could be set aside under the court's equitable jurisdiction, but Winn LJ found the case indistinguishable from *Bell v Lever Brothers*.

Until the House of Lords pronounces again on the topic, the law in England accordingly remains unclear. Our courts will, of course, not be bound by *Bell v Lever Brothers, Solle v Butcher* or *Magee v Pennine Insurances*. Despite the reservations expressed as to the correctness of the last two decisions, it is thought that the courts should possess a jurisdiction in equity (even if it owes more to Lord Denning's penchant for innovation than strict precedent) to set aside a contract into which the parties have entered under a shared misapprehension as to a fundamental matters, provided three requirements are met:

(i) the party seeking relief has not been at fault;
(ii) third parties have not acquired rights in reliance on the contract;
(iii) the party seeking relief is prepared to submit to such terms as the court considers equitable.

1 ALG 66 LQR 169; Atiyah and Bannion, 24 MLR 421 at 440-442; Meagher, Gummow & Lehane, pp 362-5.
2 At 200. The plaintiffs had paid into court the amount of the profits from their illicit transactions. Nevertheless it must be doubtful whether the case would have been decided in the same way in the greatly altered judicial climate of to-day. It is also a remarkable example of the results of the English two tier system of appeal: six judges were in favour of the defendants (including Wright J, Scrutton LJ and Viscount Hailsham) and only three in favour of the plaintiffs, yet the latter succeeded.
3 Above.

17.14 Mutual mistake must next be considered. Here the court must first determine what the contract means in law as distinct from what the parties—or one of them—thought it meant. So, in our example, the court must first determine whether the agreement between A and B, properly construed, referred to the painting in the cottage or in the Dublin house. If, so construed, it referred to the painting in the cottage, B cannot escape from the agreement even though he is paying far more than he intended. What the contract objectively means is to be determined by the common law principles of construction, succinctly explained by Blackburn J in *Smith v Hughes*:[1]

'If, whatever a man's real intention may have been, he so conducts himself that a reasonable man would believe that he was assenting to the terms proposed by the other party and that other party upon that belief enters into a contract with him, the man thus conducting himself would be equally bound as if he had intended to agree to the other party's terms.'

Thus in *Tamplin v James*,[2] the defendant had been the successful bidder at an auction of a public house. He made his bid under the mistaken belief that a certain field was included in the lots offered for sale. There was no misdescription or ambiguity in the particulars and a decree of specific performance was granted against the defendant. More recently, in *Riverlate Properties Ltd v Paul*,[3] the Court of Appeal declined to order either rescission or rectification in a case where the terms of the lease executed by both parties imposed the burden of all repairs, internal and external on the lessors. The lessors had not intended to assume this obligation, but the lessee was unaware of their mistake.

Exceptionally, the court might decline to order specific performance in a case of mutual mistake, where to do so would cause hardship. This accords with the discretionary nature of that remedy, but is is clear that it will not be sufficient for the party resisting specific performance to say that he made a mistake: in the words of Bacon V-C, relief will only be granted where it would be 'against all reason and justice' to compel specific performance.[4]

While these principles are clearly established by the authorities, their application in practice has not been free from difficulty. A recent example is *Mespil Ltd and another v Capaldi and others*.[5] In that case, the landlord of premises brought proceedings against the tenant in respect of alleged breaches of certain provisions in the lease. The case was settled on the morning of the hearing on terms endorsed on counsels' briefs and signed by them. They provided for the payment to the landlord of certain sums in settlement of all his claims '*in these proceedings*'. The italicised words were inserted by counsel for the landlord because he was aware that his client had other claims against the tenant. Counsel for the tenant did not understand them to have this significance. When the mistake came to light, the tenant sought to have the settlement set aside on the ground that the parties were not *ad idem* and hence there was no agreement. This claim failed in the High Court: O'Hanlon J applied the test in *Smith v Hughes* and held that the words used in the settlement could only have been reasonably understood as preserving the landlord's rights in relation to other claims. The fact that the tenant's counsel understood them differently was, on this view, irrelevant. But this decision was unanimously reversed in the Supreme Court, where it was said that, since there was no *consensus ad idem*, there was no contract. It may be that the decision is capable of being distinguished on its facts: it is hardly an adequate basis for concluding that the well established principles already referred to have ceased to exist in Irish law.

1 (1871) LR 6 QB 597.
2 (1879) 15 Ch D 215.
3 [1975] Ch 133.
4 *Burrow v Scammell* (1881) 19 Ch D 175 at 182.
5 (1986) ILRM 373.

17.15 Finally, we come to unilateral mistake. Here, there is no difficulty: if one party is mistaken as to a fundamental matter and the other party is aware of his mistake, the court will in general grant equitable relief to the mistaken party.[1] This may take the form of rescission or a refusal to grant specific performance. There is some disagreement as to the theoretical basis of equity's intervention: on one view, the contract is in such circumstances a nullity and equity simply follows the law by treating it as such.[2] On another, which receives some support from the recent Australian decision in *Taylor v Johnson*,[3] the contract in such cases must be objectively construed and hence will stand at common law. Equity will, however, intervene to prevent what would in effect be fraudulent conduct (using the word of course, in its equitable sense) on the part of the person who is aware of the error. And where the mistake is not fundamental, but the other party seeks to take advantage of it in a manner which the court considers inequitable, the mistaken party may still be afforded relief. So, as we shall see in more detail in the next Chapter, where a particular term, not necessarily fundamental but conferring a benefit on one party, is omitted by him by mistake and the other party is aware of the mistake, equity will grant relief in respect of this form of unilateral mistake by ordering rectification.[4]

Where, however, the other party is not aware of the mistake, whether or not it is fundamental, equity in general gives no relief to the mistaken party. To this, as we have seen, *Mespil v Capaldi*[5] forms a somewhat problematical exception.

1 *Webster v Cecil* (1861) 30 Beav 62.
2 *Wilding v Sanderson* [1897] 2 Ch 534.
3 (1983) 45 ALR 265.
4 See para 18.06, below.
5 Above.

Laches, acquiescence and affirmation as bars to rescission

17.16 It has been repeatedly emphasised that those seeking equitable relief must do so with reasonable expedition: *vigilantibus non dormientibus iura subveniunt*.[1] Where a right of rescission arises it may be lost if the party entitled to relief does not move with what the law regards as sufficient speed.

This is not to say that delay of itself will necessarily be fatal. It will only deprive the plaintiff of relief

(a) if it gives rise to the inference that the plaintiff has acquiesced in the violation of his rights by the defendant or
(b) if it amounts to laches, ie delay which has resulted in some detriment to the defendant or third parties.[2]

Where a person knows that his rights have been violated and refrains from seeking relief for a significant period of time, he may be held to have acquiesced in the violation and to have waived his rights. Whether the period is long enough to give rise to such an inference must depend on the circumstances of the particular case.[3] It has, however, been held that the requirement that a person move with promptitude is particularly relevant in a case where the plaintiff seeks to have the register of members of a company rectified by deletion of his name.[4]

It is clear that where the delay has been significant and the defendant has acted to his own detriment in reliance on the validity of the transaction, this will amount to laches which will be a bar to rescission.[5] Equally, the law will not assist the plaintiff where he seeks to set aside a transaction involving the purchase of a hazardous or speculative enterprise unless he moves with reasonable speed. He will not be allowed to stand by and then make his move when it is clear that the business is in fact profitable.[6] Similarly, if he claims that the defendant is accountable to him for profits from running a business or managing a property, he cannot simply stand by while the defendant makes the profits for him and then step in and claim them.[7]

As we have seen,[8] the equitable remedy of rescission is, in theory at least, only available where a contract is voidable: if the contract is void, it never existed in the first place and cannot be rescinded. In the case of a contract which is voidable, third parties may have acquired rights under it before the claim for rescission is made and in such circumstances, delay on the part of the plaintiff will be treated as laches disentitling him to relief. Again such cases have arisen frequently in connection with contracts for the purchase of shares: the courts have declined to set aside such transactions where third parties have acquired the shares in good faith in reliance on the company's register.[9] If a party, with full knowledge of all the material facts, *affirms* a transaction, he will be held to have abandoned any right of rescission and will not subsequently be allowed to repudiate the transaction.[10]

1 See para 3.10, above.
2 Ibid.
3 *Lindsay Petroleum Co v Hurd* (1874) LR 5 PC 221 at 240; *Coey v Pascoe* [1899] 1 IR 125.
4 *Aaron's Reef v Twiss* [1896] AC 273 at 290, 294.
5 See para 3.10, above.
6 *Clegg v Edmondson* (1857) 8 De GM & G 787.
7 *Re Jarvis* [1958] 2 All ER 336.
8 Para 17.11, above.
9 *Aaron's Reef Ltd v Twiss*, above.
10 *Clough v London and North Western Rly Co* (1871) LR 7 Exch 26. Affirmation may be inferred from conduct as well as from words: ibid.

Chapter 18

Rectification

18.01 A court has no power to alter the terms of an agreement. It can interpret the agreement at which the parties have arrived and it can infer from the circumstances what they may have intended to agree if the agreement is silent on some matters. But it cannot alter the terms of the agreement because, for example, it operates harshly and unjustly against one of the parties. Both the common law and equity have always attached the greatest importance to upholding agreements freely arrived at and it has generally been left to the legislature to relieve against the consequences of unequal bargaining power as, for example, in hire purchase contracts[1] or, more recently, over the whole field of the supply of goods and services to the public.[2]

There are cases, however, where the agreement is executory in character: ie it requires the execution of a document in some form to give effect to the agreement of the parties. Thus, a contract for the sale of land is invariably followed by a conveyance assuring the land to the purchaser. It would be an absurdity if the parties were bound by such a deed where it was manifestly and unarguably at odds with the written contract by which it was preceded: if, for example, the agreement provided for the sale of a house and garden and the deed in error omitted the garden from the parcels of land conveyed. In such cases, the courts of equity assumed a jurisdiction to rectify the deed where it could be convincingly demonstrated that it did not reflect the antecedent agreement of the parties. The courts, however, for the reasons already given, proceeded cautiously in this area and it was for long supposed that the remedy was limited to such cases: ie where the document sought to be rectified because of a mistake common to both parties failed to carry into effect an antecedent concluded and enforceable agreement between the parties, generally in writing.

1 Hire Purchase Acts 1946 and 1960.
2 Sale of Goods and Supply of Services Act 1980.

18.02 The law has developed to some extent in this area: the balance of authority favours the view that it is no longer necessary to establish that there was a concluded and enforceable agreement between the parties, still less that it was in writing.[1] The remedy is, in other words, no longer confined to contracts which are executory in nature. All that is required is that the parties should have evinced in some manner a common intention which through a mutual mistake was not reflected in the actual agreement. But the care with which the law still moves in this whole field is underlined

266

by the heavy burden of proof which rests on the party who claims rectification of the written instrument.[2] Moreover, it is only in exceptional circumstances that the court will order rectification of a unilateral mistake, ie where the error in the instrument was due to a mistake by one party only.[3]

1 See para 18.04, below.
2 See para 18.08, below.
3 See para 18.06, below.

Rectification in cases of common mistake

18.03 It was, as we have seen, for long believed that in order to obtain rectification of an agreement on the ground of common mistake, it was necessary to prove that there had been a concluded and enforceable agreement between the parties which had not been reflected in the instrument sought to be rectified. It was made clear, however, in a number of later decisions that it was not essential that the previous agreement relied on should have been one that was enforceable in law. The leading Irish case is *Monaghan County Council v Vaughan*,[1] in which the tender of a contractor for the removal of materials from a derelict site was accepted by the defendant county council. The invitations for the tenders made it clear that the successful tenderer was to pay the council, and on this basis the plaintiff offered to take away the materials for the sum of £1200. In error, however, the document accepting his tender provided that the contractor was to be *paid* for taking away the materials. The plaintiff sought to rely on this mistake and claimed £1200 from the council. The county council counterclaimed for rectification of the acceptance document and payment by the contractor to them of the £1200. It was sought to resist the claim for rectification on the ground that there was no antecedent agreement between the parties which was capable of being enforced since any such agreement would have had to have been under the seal of the county council.[2] Dixon J rejected this argument, adopting a decision of Clauson J to the same effect in *Shipley UDC v Bradford Corpn*.[3]

1 [1948] IR 306.
2 Public Health (Ir) Act 1878, s 201(1).
3 [1936] Ch 375.

18.04 It was accordingly clear that the existence of an antecedent *enforceable* agreement was not a condition precedent to the granting of rectification. It remained unclear, whether it was still essential to prove a concluded agreement, whether enforceable or not. In the process of negotiations which lead up to the execution of a written contract it is common for parties to agree on various terms, but not to arrive at anything that could be described as a concluded agreement until the formal contract in writing is signed by both. If the parties have agreed on a specific term which they then by a mistake on both their parts omit from the written agreement, can the agreement be rectified? According to the decision of the Court of Appeal in *Lovell and Christmas Ltd v Wall*,[1] rectification could not be granted in such circumstances: a concluded agreement was essential. The decision was, however, of dubious authority since the point did not appear to have been argued and in *Shipley Urban District Council v Bradford Corpn*[2] Clauson J appeared to have taken a different view, as did

Dixon J in *Monaghan County Council v Vaughan*.[3] In both the latter decisions, however, the views expressed were *obiter*. In *Crane v Hegeman-Harris & Co Inc,*[4] Simonds J thought it unnecessary to have a concluded agreement, but that requirement seemed to have been revived by the judgement of Denning LJ in *Frederich E Rose (London) v William H. Pim Junr & Co Ltd*.[5] He did not have the support of his colleagues, however, on the Court of Appeal. But his view was shared in Ireland by Kenny J in *Lucy v Laurel Construction Ltd*.[6] The controversy was stilled in England by the decision of the Court of Appeal in *Joscelyne v Nissen*.[7] After a detailed review of the authorities, Russell LJ held that an antecedent concluded agreement was not necessary: what was required was a common *intention* to include or exclude a particular term which continued until the moment the contract was executed and which was manifested outwardly by the parties in some manner. The last mentioned requirement had not been insisted on by Simonds J, but is clearly important: it is not sufficient that the plaintiff should establish that it was his intention to include or exclude the term and that there was a probability—even a high degree of probability—that this was also the defendant's intention. He has to go further and show that this common intention had been expressed either in words or writing on some occasion prior to the contract. This test was adopted by the Court of Appeal in Northern Ireland in *Rooney & McParland v Carlin*,[8] in which case Lowry LCJ also commented that the existence of a concluded agreement was still relevant in determining whether the plaintiff had discharged the heavy burden of proof which rests on him in cases of rectification. The same tests were adopted by Keane J in the most recent Irish decision in this area, *Irish Life Assurance Co Ltd v Dublin Land Securities Ltd*,[9] the facts of which are stated in more detail below.

1 (1911) 104 LT 85.
2 Above.
3 Above.
4 [1939] 1 All ER 662.
5 [1953] 2 QB 450 at 461.
6 Unreported; judgement delivered 18 December 1970.
7 [1970] 2 QB 86.
8 [1981] NI 138.
9 Unreported; judgement delivered 2 May 1986. This case is under appeal.

Rectification in cases of unilateral mistake

18.05 If the mistake as to the inclusion or exclusion of the term is that of one party only, rectification will not in general be allowed. In other words, if there was no intention common to both parties which failed to find expression in the ultimate agreement, it will not be rectified simply because one of the parties executed that ultimate agreement in a mistaken belief as to what it contained.[1] Cases of unilateral mistake, as they are called, are distinguished from cases of common mistake of the type mentioned in the preceding paragraph.

1 *Fowler v Fowler* (1859) 4 De G & J 250; *Jameson v National Benefit Trust* 2 NIJR 19.

18.06 To this rule, two exceptions have been clearly established. In the first place, where the conduct of one of the parties amounts to fraud, rectification may be granted.[1] In the second place, even where the conduct falls short of what could be characterised as fraud, the document will still be rectified, if one party is aware that the other is executing it under a mistake and says nothing, at least in circumstances where such conduct on his part could be described as amounting to 'sharp practice'.[2] The test has also been expressed to be that the court will grant rectification in such cases of unilateral mistake, if it would be inequitable to allow the party seeking to rely on the mistake to do so.

The first exception hardly needs elaboration. The second has been established in a series of English decisions beginning with *Roberts v Leicestershire County Council.*[3] In that case, a building firm tendered for works which the defendants were proposing to carry out, specifying as the period within which the works would be completed in 18 months. Their tender was accepted, but in the contract documents as executed the period specified was 30 months. The defendant's officers were aware of the mistake but the builders were not. Had the period been that specified in the contract itself the builders' rates would have been higher. Pennycuick J held that, while this was clearly a case of unilateral mistake, the county council were not entitled to take advantage of a mistake of which their officers were aware and did nothing to prevent. While he expressed doubts as to the basis in law of this exception, he seems to have treated it as essentially a form of estoppel and made it clear that in his view there did not have to be actual fraud on the defendants' part to bring the exception into operation. In *Riverlate Properties Ltd v Paul*,[4] the Court of Appeal said that 'sharp practice' on the part of the defendant would be sufficient to bring the exception into operation, while in a differently constituted Court of Appeal in *Thomas Bates and Son Ltd v Wyndham's (Lingerie) Ltd*,[5] Buckley LJ, while seeming to have reservations about the necessity for showing 'sharp practice' said it was necessary to establish the following:

(i)   that one party wrongly thought the document included or excluded a particular term;

(ii) that the other party was aware of the mistake and did not draw attention to it;

(iii) that the inclusion or omission would have been to the mistaken party's benefit.

These authorities and others were considered by the High Court in *Irish Life Assurance Co Ltd v Dublin Land Securities Ltd.*[6] In that case, the plaintiff company negotiated with F. for the sale to him of a ground rents portfolio. There were over 9000 properties included in the portfolio and the formula for the price was agreed at a multiplier of the actual income which F would receive. It was accepted by both parties that included in the portfolio would be some sites which presented development opportunities. The plaintiff intended to exclude from the sale a particular site which had been the subject of a compulsory purchase order and in respect of which they were ultimately to receive £500,000—more than the actual price being paid for the portfolio. Due to a mistake on the part of the plaintiffs' solicitors, the lands were in fact included in the elaborate contract which was eventually executed by the plaintiffs and a company formed by F. Neither F nor his solicitors were aware of the mistake and knew nothing about the lands or their value. Keane J held that this was a case of unilateral mistake: it was not a case of an intention to exclude the land which by a mistake common to both parties was not reflected in the contract.[7] Applying the tests suggested in *Thomas Bates & Sons v*

Wyndham (Lingerie) Ltd[8] he concluded that there was nothing either inequitable or amounting to 'sharp practice' on the part of F. and accordingly the plaintiffs were not entitled to rectification.

A further exception was suggested in some earlier authorities: it was said that in a case of unilateral mistake, the party labouring under the error could offer the other a choice between treating the contract as rescinded or rectified so as to eliminate the mistake.[9] These authorities were disapproved of, however, by the Court of Appeal in *Riverlate Properties Ltd v Paul*:[10] if the defendant had not induced the contract by a misrepresentation, fraudulent or innocent, a mistake on the plaintiff's part as to its terms was no ground in equity for setting it aside.

1 *Clark v Girdwood* (1877) 7 Ch D 9, CA.
2 As in *Monaghan Co Council v Vaughan*, above. But Dixon J preferred to treat it as a case of common mistake.
3 [1961] Ch 555.
4 [1974] Ch 133.
5 [1981] 1 All ER 1077.
6 Above.
7 Keane J also found as a fact that an agent of the purchaser had been informed in general terms that a plot in the particular area which was subject to a CPO was excluded but held that imputed knowledge of this nature was not sufficient to found a case of common mistake.
8 Above.
9 *Garrard v Frankel* (1862) 30 Beav 445; *Paget v Marshall* (1884) 28 Ch D 255.
10 Above.

No rectification where parties mistaken as to meaning of contract

18.07 Rectification will not normally be granted where the document expresses what the parties have in fact agreed but results in consequences which the parties did not intend. Thus, the parties may have been mistaken as to the meaning of particular expressions in a document. The leading case on the topic is *Frederick E Rose (London) Ltd v Wm H Pim Junr & Co Ltd*,[1] where the plaintiffs agreed to sell 'horse beans' under the mistaken impression, shared by the defendants, that the expression was synonymous with 'feveroles' which was the commodity required by a customer. 'Horsebeans' were not the same in fact as 'feveroles', and the plaintiffs were under a potential liability because of this error. But even though it was a mistake common to both parties, the Court of Appeal held that the plaintiffs were not entitled to rectification.

The position should logically be no different where the document reflects the intentions of the parties but was executed by the parties under a mistake as to its consequences in law. It was held by the Irish High Court of Appeal in *Jackson v Stopford*[2] and by the Supreme Court in *Lowndes v de Courcy*[3] that this was not a ground for rectification. But there are some later English decisions which are not easy to reconcile with the general current of authority. Thus covenants to pay annuities or other sums 'free of tax' have been in effect reworded by the courts where the wording of the covenant as it stood would have left the covenantee with a less sum than was intended.[4] Similarly in *Re Butlin's Settlement Trusts*,[5] where the settlor's legal advisors had included a clause in a voluntary settlement which they thought allowed for majority decisions by the trustees in all matters, but as a matter of law did not, Brightman J granted rectification, to give effect to the settlor's real intentions. Whatever about the actual decision, it is clear that the language used by the learned judge went too far and is irreconcilable with the other authorities. Thus, he said at one point

'(Rectification) is .... available where the words of the document were purposely used but it was mistakenly considered that they bore a different meaning from their correct meaning as a matter of true construction.'[6]

1 Above.
2 [1923] 2 IR 7.
3 Unreported; judgement delivered 7 April 1960. Cf *Revenue Comrs v Moroney* [1972] IR 372 at 378 per Kenny J.
4 *Whiteside v Whiteside*, [1950] Ch 65.
5 [1976] Ch 251.
6 *Butlin's Case*, above.

Onus of proof in case of rectification

18.08 While different language has been used by judges to give effect to the concept, it is well settled that the onus of proof on a party claiming rectification of a written document is significantly greater than is normally the case in civil proceedings.[1] Thus Haugh J referred to it as a 'very heavy onus of proof'[2] and in an earlier case it was suggested that 'irrefragable' evidence was necessary.[3] (Sir Robert Megarry has suggested dropping the latter adjective from the legal vocabulary completely, if for no other reason than that no one can agree how it is pronounced.) More recently the Court of Appeal have suggested the phrase 'convincing proof'.[4] And in *Irish Life Assurance Co v Dublin Land Securities Ltd,*[5] Keane J held that even if a communication to an agent was sufficient to found a case of mutual mistake where the principal was unaware of the disputed term, the imprecision of the communication in that case was fatal, having regard to the high degree of proof required before the court would rectify the contract.

1 *McCormack v McCormack* (1877) 1 LR Ir 119 at 124 per Ball C.
2 *Nolan v Graves* [1946] IR 376.
3 *Countess of Shelburne v Earl of Inchiquin* (1784) 1 Bro CC 338 at 341 per Lord Thurlow LC.
4 *Josceleyne v Nissen*, above, at 98.
5 Above.

Rectification not always the appropriate remedy

18.09 Consideration may need to be given in some cases as to whether an action for rectification is the appropriate remedy. Such an action should only be brought where the document has failed to express the antecedent agreement or at least common intention of the parties and it is necessary to satisfy the court that this is so by adducing extrinsic evidence to that effect. But in many cases courts have declared that documents which are erroneous *on their face* should be read as though the error were corrected. Thus, words have been inserted, deleted or altered where it was necessary to make sense of a document and this can be done without bringing rectification proceedings.[1]

1 *Burchell v Clark* (1876) 2 CPD 88, CA.

Voluntary settlements and wills

18.10 Rectification may be granted of a voluntary settlement both at the instance of the settlor and the beneficiaries.[1] However, it will never be granted at the instance of the beneficiary where the settlor opposes rectification: if he does not wish to include or exclude a particular term in a voluntary settlement, there is no reason why the court should compel him to do so.[2] But where the settlor is dead, rectification may be granted against his personal representatives on proof that the settlement did not accord with the deceased's intentions, provided, of course, that these are convincingly established by reference to his written instructions or otherwise.[3] It has, indeed, been said that the heavy burden of proof required in rectification cases is even stronger in cases of voluntary settlements.[4]

There is no power to rectify mistakes in wills such as was conferred in England by the Administration of Justice Act 1982.[5]

1 *Fitzgerald v Fitzgerald* [1902] 1 IR 477, CA; *Re Butlin's Settlement Trusts*, above.
2 *Broun v Kennedy* (1863) 33 Beav 133 at 147 affd 4 de GJ & S 217.
3 *Van der Linde v Van der Linde* [1947] Ch 306.
4 Pettit, p 572.
5 S 20.

Chapter 19

Declarations

19.01 As its name suggests, an order taking the form of a declaration simply states what the rights of the parties are: it does not seek to compensate the plaintiff for a wrong done to him or to restrain the defendant from violating his rights. Nor does it compel the defendant to take any steps in relation to the plaintiff, as is the case with some forms of equitable relief, such as mandatory injunctions or specific performance. And while it may define in a binding and conclusive form the rights of parties to a contract or other transaction, it does not attempt to put an end to the existence of the contract as happens in cases of rescission, nor does it seek to alter the terms of a document so as to bring it into harmony with the intentions of the parties as is the case with rectification. The courts may, and frequently do, grant other forms of relief, such as injunctive relief, in cases in which the primary remedy sought is a declaration, but there is nothing to prevent a declaration being granted without any accompanying relief in an appropriate case.[1] A declaration may now, like an injunction, be obtained on an application for judicial review in an appropriate case, without the necessity for plenary proceedings.[2]

1 Rules of the Superior Courts, Order 19, rule 29.
2 See para 15.43, above.

General scope of the remedy

19.02 Manifestly then the declaration is an extremely useful form of relief since it enables a party to have his rights defined in circumstances where no other relief by way of damages or otherwise is available. Not suprisingly it is rivalled only by the injunction as a popular form of relief alternative to damages, but unlike that remedy it is comparatively modern in origin. Although it had existed for some time previously in Scotland in the form of the 'declarator' procedure, it was not available in England until the enactment of the Chancery Procedure Act 1852. The corresponding legislation in Ireland was s 155 of the Chancery (Ireland) Act 1867 which provided that

> 'no suit in the said (chancery) court shall be open to objection on the ground that a merely declaratory decree or order is sought thereby and it shall be lawful for the Court to make binding declarations of right without granting consequential relief.'

In its early days, the relief was most frequently sought in cases affecting private rights, such as disputes relating to property. In modern times, however, it has assumed a steadily growing importance in the area of public law and many of the major challenges to the constitutionality of statutes have been based primarily, and sometimes exclusively, on claims to declaratory relief.[1] In the areas of both private and public law, the courts are much more ready to entertain claims for such relief than in former times, as Walsh J pointed out in *Transport Salaried Staffs' Association v CIE*:[2]

'In modern times the virtues of the declaratory action are more fully recognised than they formerly were and English decisions and *dicta* in recent years have indicated a departure from the conservative approach to the question of judicial discretion in awarding declarations. A discretion which was formerly exercised "sparingly" and with "great care and jealousy" and "with extreme caution" can now, in the words of Lord Denning in the *Pyx Granite Co Ltd Case*[3] be exercised "if there is good reason for so doing", provided of course, that there is a substantial question which one party has a real interest to raise and the other to oppose. In *Vine v National Dock Labour Board*,[4] Viscount Kilmuir LC at p112 cites with approval the Scottish tests set out by Lord Dunedin in *Russian Commercial and Industrial Bank v British Bank for Foreign Trade*[5] who said at p448:- "The question must be a real and not a theoretical question; the person raising it must have a real interest to raise it; he must be able to secure a proper contradictor, that is, someone presently existing who has a true interest to oppose the declaration sought." It is also to be observed that the fact that the declaration is needed for a present interest has always been a consideration of great weight.'

But while this statement of the law recognises the wide ranging nature of declaratory relief in modern circumstances, it also lays stress on the law's insistence that the remedy should not be availed of to resolve purely hypothetical problems or points which lawyers like to describe as 'moot'.[6] This is not to say that the court has no jurisdiction to grant declaratory relief where the issue is theoretical: there have been cases in which the courts have granted the remedy in those circumstances. But it will undoubtedly be a highly material factor in considering whether the declaration sought should be granted: thus in *Draper v British Optical Association*[7] the plaintiff was refused a declaration that the defendants were not entitled to compel him to take certain steps, when all they had done was call a meeting to consider whether such action should be taken.

However, an attempt to make use of this ground to resist a challenge to the constitutionality of legislation failed in *Condon and Others v Minister for Labour and others*.[8] It was argued on behalf of the defendant in that case that since the impugned legislation (freezing the pay of bank officials) had been repealed, there was no subject matter on which the declaration could operate. Since the legislation in question had deprived the bank officials of remuneration which they would otherwise have earned, it could hardly be said that its constitutionality was moot, but O'Higgins CJ took higher ground in his judgement in the Supreme Court: he warned against the dangers involved in permitting governments and legislatures to place legislation on the statute book which violated constitutional rights and then to put it, and actions taken on foot of it, beyond challenge in the courts by the simple process of repeal. A claim that the proceedings in such circumstances were purely theoretical could not in his view be tolerated by the courts.

1 The history of the declaratory action is usefully summarised in the Law Reform

Commission's Working Paper No 8—1979: *Judicial Review of Administrative Acts: The Problem of Remedies*, pp 25-32.
2 [1965] IR 180 at 202-203.
3 [1958] 1 QB 554 at 571.
4 [1957] AC 488.
5 [1921] 2 AC 438.
6 Admirers of Mr Peter de Vries will recall the character whose country retreat was called 'Moot Point', 'because the lawyers say there's some kind of kink in the deed.'
7 [1938] 1 All ER 115.
8 [1981] IR 62.

Locus standi of the plaintiff

19.03 Although it is not necessary for the plaintiff to show that he has suffered or will suffer any damage in order to obtain a declaration, he must show that he has a sufficient interest in the subject matter of the proceedings to warrant the granting of a declaration at his instance. It is thought, however, that it is not necessary for him to show that his legal rights in the strict sense have been or may be affected and that the English decision to the contrary in *Gregory v London Borough of Camden*[1] is not the law in this jurisdiction. As we saw in Chapter Fifteen, when considering the *locus standi* of claimants for injunctions, Barrington J held in *Irish Permanent Building Society v Cauldwell and Others*[2] that the fact that the plaintiffs were aggrieved persons with a substantial interest in the outcome of the case was sufficient to give them *locus standi*. And as we also saw in that chapter, the courts have adopted a broader approach in cases where the constitutionality of legislation is in issue.[3]

1 [1966] 2 All ER 196.
2 (1981) ILRM 242.
3 See para 15.21, above.

Cases in which declaratory relief has been granted summarised

19.04 The cases in which the courts both here and abroad have granted declaratory relief are so many and various that one can only cite some of the more important categories. First, there are the many instances in which a declaration has been granted that a particular statute, whether enacted before or after the enactment of the Constitution, is invalid having regard to the provisions of the Constitution. The remedy may also be availed of to challenge the validity of subordinate legislation, as in *Cook v Walsh*[1] and *Cassidy v Minister for Industry and Commerce*.[2]

In the field of public law, the use of the declaration is by no means confined to attacks on the validity of legislation: it has been successfully invoked to strike down a wide range of administrative acts. Decisions of particular bodies, such as the Irish Land Commission,[3] the electoral Appeal Board,[4] Bord na Mona,[5] local authorities,[6] Ministers[7] and the government itself[8] have been declared to be invalid because the body acted without or in excess of jurisdiction or contrary to the requirements of natural or constitutional justice. The use of the declaration in this context is a product of the supervisory jurisdiction exercised by the High Court over the proceedings of inferior bodies and tribunals. The jurisdiction in question is inherent, ie it is not conferred by any statute. It was, however, well established before 1921 and its continued existence is documented in cases since then.[9]

1 (1985) ILRM 429.
2 Unreported; judgement delivered 13 May 1979.
3 *Foley v Irish Land Commission* [1952] IR 118, SC.
4 *Loftus v A-G* [1979] IR 221.
5 *O'Brien v Bord na Mona* [1983] IR 255.
6 *Finn v Bray UDC* [1969] IR 169.
7 *Latchford v Minister for Industry and Commerce* [1950] IR 33.
8 *Garvey v Ireland* [1981] IR 75.
9 *The State (Abenglen Properties Ltd) v Dublin Corpn* (1982) ILRM 590 at 596, per O'Higgins CJ.

Limitations on the granting of declaratory relief

19.05 In some cases, it will be impossible to obtain declaratory relief because the relevant statute excludes the courts, either expressly or by implication, from granting such relief. In the case of a compulsory acquisition of land, for example, effected under the Housing Act 1966, there is a procedure prescribed for challenging in the High Court the decision of the Minister for the Environment to confirm a compulsory purchase order made by a local authority.[1] Such proceedings must be brought, however, within six weeks from the date of the Minister's order and the section provides that his decision may not be challenged in any other form of proceedings, including actions for declaratory relief. It has been held in England that such 'preclusive' clauses, as they are called, do not oust the jurisdiction of the courts to grant relief in cases where the order impugned is a nullity. Thus, it was said, an order made without jurisdiction could be challenged in proceedings claiming declaratory relief even though the statutory time limit has expired. This principle might enable a belated challenge to be made where the Minister, or whatever body was involved, simply had no jurisdiction to make the order or even where the proceedings leading to the making of the impugned order were fatally flawed by a want of natural or constitutional justice or bad faith.[2] The English authorities on the point are, however, not altogether easy to reconcile and the matter has yet to be considered judicially in Ireland.[3]

Where the relevant statute does not expressly exclude the jurisdiction of the court, it may still be excluded by implication. The statute may provide its own remedy and a plaintiff may have to show that he has exhausted this remedy or indeed any other remedy that may be available. The leading Irish decision is *O'Doherty v A-G and O'Donnell*[4] where the plaintiff sought to challenge a decision by a judicial referee that he was not entitled to a military service pension. The statute required the referee to give the applicant an indication of his provisional view as to the latter's entitlement and to take into account any evidence or representations the applicant might wish to submit before giving a final decision. The referee purported to give his final decision without considering further evidence and submissions advanced by the applicant. The applicant claimed a declaration that the conclusion of the referee was wrong in law, but Gavan Duffy J refused to grant such relief. There was another remedy open to the applicant, viz. an order of mandamus compelling the referee to consider the additional submissions and evidence and to make a further and final decision. This was fatal to the plaintiff's claim, since

'it is decidedly not the practice to make a declaration where there is an appropriate remedy to which the plaintiff ought to have resorted.'[5]

A similar approach has been adopted by the courts in cases where the aggrieved party has sought the remedy of *certiorari*: thus for example in *The State (Abenglen) v Dublin Corporation*,[6] the Supreme Court declined to grant *certiorari* in a case where the respondent planning authority had refused to grant permission for development on grounds which arguably rendered their decision *ultra vires*. The majority said that the aggrieved applicants had another remedy, viz an appeal to An Bord Pleanala and hence *certiorari* could not issue.

1 S 78.
2 *Anisminic Ltd v Foreign Compensation Commission* [1969] 2 AC 147 distinguishing without expressly disapproving *Smith v East Elloe RDC* [1956] AC 736. In *R v Environment Secretary ex p Ostler* [1977] QB 122, however, *Anisminic* was in turn distinguished by the Court of Appeal which held that a challenge to the Order, even where based on lack of good faith, had to be brought within the statutory period.
3 See Keane, *Law of Local Government in the Republic of Ireland*, pp 237-243.
4 [1941] IR 569.
5 At 583.
6 Above.

19.06 Declaratory relief may also be refused because the order sought would effectively determine the guilt or innocence of a person charged with a criminal offence. In *A-G (Society for the Protection of Unborn Children Ireland Limited) v Open Door Counselling Ltd and Another*,[1] the facts of which have already been referred to,[2] one of the declarations claimed by the plaintiffs was that the defendants were engaged in a criminal conspiracy to corrupt public morals by advising pregnant women as to the availability of abortion facilities in England. While apparently satisfied that such a crime in the form of an indictible misdemeanour exists in Irish law,[3] Hamilton P declined to grant the declaration sought on the ground that this would usurp the function of the jury to whose verdict the defendants were entitled. It is thought that the same principle would apply in the case of a minor offence triable summarily or an offence tried by a Special Criminal Court established under the Offences Against the State Act 1939. The Constitution requires that no person should be tried on any criminal charge save in due course of law[4] and the lower standard of proof required in civil cases would seem to make a finding of criminal guilt or innocence in a civil case constitutionally suspect. There is, as we have seen, one important exception to this general principle: the Attorney General is not necessarily precluded from seeking the enforcement of a statute by injunction by the fact that the offending action constitutes a criminal offence.[5]

1 (1987) ILRM 477.
2 See para 15.16, above.
3 Applying the decision of the House of Lords in *Shaw v DPP* [1962] AC 220. It should be noted, however, that the learned President's approval of the decision was *obiter*. A question may arise as to whether it is reconcilable in Ireland with the constitutional policy against retroactive penal legislation which by analogy might render impermissible the declaration of conduct as criminal which had not previously been found to be such.
4 Article 38.
5 See para 15.18, above.

19.07 There have also been suggestions that declaratory relief should not be granted where it will leave unresolved other issues between the parties. Thus in *Neate (Epping) Property Ltd v Phillips*,[1] the Australian Supreme Court said that in cases where specific performance could be granted, it was undesirable that the court of first instance should confine itself to declaring the rights of the parties to the contract: it should also grant an order for specific performance or an inquiry as to damages if that is the appropriate consequence of its finding. But in a subsequent case,[2] it was pointed out that this should not be treated as requiring that the parties should in every case seek to deal with all aspects of their contractual relationship. So to hold would be to deprive the courts of their useful jurisdiction to dispose in a summary manner of specific disputes between parties as to particular issues arising under the contract. This is of particular significance in the Irish context where the procedure under the Vendor and Purchaser Act 1874 has frequently been found to provide a comparatively rapid and inexpensive method of dealing with such problems.

1 (1974) 131 CLR 286.
2 *Lohar Corpn Pty Ltd v Dibu Pty Ltd*, unreported; see Meagher, Gummow & Lehane, pp 460-461.

Equitable defences

19.08 It has sometimes been said that the remedy of the declaration cannot properly be categorised as an equitable remedy since unlike those remedies it is purely the creature of statute and that it follows from this that a claim to such relief cannot be successfully met by any of the equitable defences, eg that the plaintiff has come to court with unclean hands.[1] It is, in other words, no different in essence from a common law claim for damages which manifestly could not be successfully resisted on such a ground.

There is undoubtedly some logic in this approach which also has authority on its side: in *Chapman v Michaelson*,[2] the Court of Appeal declined to treat declaratory relief as a form of equitable relief. But it is not the law in Ireland, at least where the defence of laches (ie delay of such a nature as to render it inequitable to grant the relief) is raised. In *Loftus and Others v A-G*,[3] the plaintiffs sought a declaration that the refusal of the Appeal Board under the Electoral Act 1965 to register a political party formed by them under the title of the Christian Democratic Party was unlawful. The court refused to grant some of the declarations sought on the ground that the plaintiff had been guilty of 'inordinate and inexcusable delay' but granted others because it appeared that the rights of persons other than the plaintiffs might be affected by the rulings made. It is thought, however, that the High Court or the Supreme Court would be most unlikely to refuse declaratory relief on this ground alone where it was satisfied that legislation was repugnant to the Constitution.

1 See para 3.08, above.
2 [1908] 2 Ch 612; [1909] 1 Ch 238.
3 Above. See also *Murphy v A-G* [1982] IR 241.

Chapter 20

Tracing in equity

Tracing property at common law and in equity

20.01 At common law a person who was wrongfully deprived of his property was not confined to proceedings against the person who had taken it from him. He was entitled to follow the property into the hands of anyone else, but there was an important proviso: the property had to be still identifiable.[1] Thus, if A stole a box containing coins from B and handed the box complete with contents to C for safekeeping, B could sue C at common law for the return of the coins. But if C instead of keeping the coins in the box mixed them with money of his own, B had no remedy. B's position was better if the coins were used in the purchase of a property: provided that the property represented the proceeds of that money alone, B could recover. This was because he was entitled to ratify the unauthorised conversion of his own property into another form.[2] But where the property, either in its original or converted form, could no longer be identified or earmarked as his own the common law afforded him no remedy.

There was a further difficulty confronting the common law when it sought to trace property in this manner. If someone else became the *owner* of the property in law, that was the end of the matter in the view of the common law courts. Those courts did not recognise equitable interests in property, still less mere 'equities', and thus a person who became the owner of land which had been purchased with wrongfully applied trust monies might be able to resist the claim at common law of the beneficiary to 'trace' the funds into the land.

1 *Miller v Race* (1758) 1 Burr 452; *Banque Belge v Hambrouck* [1921] 1 KB 321, CA; *Re Diplock* [1948] Ch 465 CA; *Shanahan's Stamp Auctions Ltd v Farrelly* [1962] IR 386.
2 *Taylor v Plumer* (1815) 3 M & S 562.

20.02 This inability of the common law to trace property where it had become mixed with other property created particular problems in the case of bank accounts. If the trustee of property lodged monies belonging to the trust to his own bank account, it became mixed with his own in a manner as fatal to the beneficiary's claim as if it were coin mixed with other coin. In the case of running bank accounts, the law operated on the crude presumption laid down by *Clayton's Case:*[1] first in, first out. This meant that cheques drawn on the account were presumed to have been drawn against the earliest lodgment made. Thus if a trustee lodged £3000 of trust

279

money to his account, then lodged £2000 of his own and proceeded to draw cheques to the amount of £4000, the lodgment of trust funds would be presumed to have been drawn on the first. Of course, this would not matter if the trustee were solvent: he would be personally liable to repay the £3000 to the beneficiary. But if he became insolvent, the beneficiary would have no claim to the £1000 remaining in the account.

1 (1816) 1 Mer 572.

20.03 The common law, then, in the well known phrase of Atkin LJ, 'halted outside the banker's door'.[1] Whether this was because the approach of the common law was crude and simplistic, where that of equity was subtle and even metaphysical, need not detain us. By 1880, it was clear, to resume Atkin LJ's metaphor, that 'equity had the courage to lift the latch, walk in and examine the books.'[2] This major development of the law was the result of the decision in *Re Hallett's Case*,[3] where a solicitor trustee had lodged trust money and a client's money to his own account and made investments which left insufficient funds to meet the beneficiary's claim. The Court of Appeal rejected the argument that the drawings on the account were presumed to have exhausted the trust monies first. Instead, it was laid down that where a trustee mixed trust monies with money of his own in a bank account, the rule in *Clayton's Case* did not apply: the trustee was presumed to have drawn out his own money first. Moreover, the difficulty felt by the common law in permitting the owner to follow his money into a mixed account did not affect a court applying equitable principles: there was available in equity the remedy of a *declaration of charge* which enabled the court to say that the beneficiary was entitled in equity to so much of the fund as represented the amount of his money.

Similarly, in the case of property other than funds in a bank, the court could declare the beneficiary entitled to a charge on the property in respect of the money belonging to him which had been invested in its purchase, even where not all the purchase money was represented by his funds. In this case, the beneficiary had a choice: his charge entitled him to have the property sold to pay him off, but he could, if he wished, simply retain his interest in the property.

1 *Banque Belge v Hambrouck*, p 335.
2 Ibid.
3 (1880) 13 Ch D 696.

20.04 We have spoken of the right of the *beneficiary* to trace his property into other property, but it would be wrong to suppose that the remedy is confined to persons who are entitled to property under trusts. It has been established that it is available where the property is in the hands of a person who is in a fiduciary relationship with the owner, even though he is not a trustee in the strict sense.[1] And the right to trace remains available against third parties to whom the relevant property has been transferred or with whose property it has been mixed, except where it is transferred to a bona fide purchaser for value without notice of the trust or the fiduciary relationship.[2] However, in the case of such third parties, who themselves have not committed or been party to any breach of trust, competing equitable rights may arise and in the result there may have to be an adjustment between such claims.[3]

1 *Sinclair v Brougham* [1914] AC 398.

2 *Re Diplock,* above.
3 *Sinclair v Brougham,* above; *Re Diplock,* above.

20.05 Because the remedy which equity afforded the owner of the property was either a declaration of charge or the recognition that the owner enjoyed an equitable lien on the property for the money, it has sometimes been said that there is no such thing as a *distinct* remedy to which one can assign the name 'tracing'. This is certainly true to the extent that the proceedings will never seek an order to 'trace' as such but rather a declaration that the plaintiff is entitled to a charge or lien on the property or, in some cases, the transfer of funds in a bank to him. But the 'tracing' procedure has become so well established as a doctrine in its own right that it is probably more convenient to speak of it as an independent equitable remedy.

When the tracing remedy is available

20.06 A person, then, who is entitled to the equitable interest in any property, real or personal, will be entitled to trace that property, for so long as it continues to exist and even though it may have been mixed with other property, into the hands of anyone in a fiduciary relationship with him and into the hands of any third party, except a bona fide purchaser for value without notice of the fiduciary relationship. One should not be misled by the requirement that the property should continue to exist: as we have seen, it may have been converted into another form, as where money is used to purchase land, and the tracing remedy will still be available. But where the property is simply dissipated—as where the fiduciary spends it on his own living expenses—the remedy *in rem* cases ceases to exist and the owner is confined to his remedy *in personam.*

20.07 The remedy is only available to those who can be said to have a proprietary interest in the assets in question. Since it is essentially a remedy *in rem*—and this was its great advantage over the remedy *in personam* which was always available at common law—a merely *personal* right to recover the assets will not be sufficient. While we have, accordingly, stated the basis of the doctrine to be that the person invoking it must be entitled to the equitable interest in the property, it is questionable whether it necessarily follows from this that the absolute owner is not similarly entitled. The leading English textbooks have rightly remarked that it would be anomalous if a person was in a weaker position solely because he happened to be entitled to the legal estate as well as the beneficial estate.[1] It is submitted with some confidence that at least where there is a fiduciary relationship, the fact that the plaintiff is the absolute owner can make no difference. To hold otherwise would seem to be an acceptance of the view that once the legal and equitable interests are 'at home' in the same person the equitable interest no longer exists. The better view is that the equitable interest is recognised by the law whenever the exigencies of law or equity so require.[2]

Recent decisions in Ireland and England have gone further and cast doubt on the fundamental requirement that the claimant seeking to trace must have a proprietary interest in the fund. In *Chase Manhattan Bank NA v Israel-British Bank (London) Ltd,*[3] applied by Carroll J in *Re Irish Shipping Ltd,*[4] Goulding J held that money paid in error into an account was impressed with a constructive trust which rendered the invocation of the tracing remedy appropriate.[5] On one view, perhaps still the orthodox view, such a transaction is not different in kind from the debtor-creditor relationship and lacks the proprietary flavour essential to convert the claimant into a secured creditor in the event of an insolvency.[6]

1 See, for example, Goff and Jones, *Law of Restitution,* 3rd edn, pp 40-43.
2 See para 4.05, above.
3 [1981] Ch 105.
4 (1986) ILRM 518.
5 See para 13.13, above.
6 See para 13.14, above.

The position of volunteers and purchasers for value

20.08 As we have seen, the right to trace is available not merely against the person who has mixed money belonging in equity to another with his own money or invested it in property, but also against third parties into whose hands it may have come. The only exception is a purchaser for value who has no notice of the circumstances which have given rise to the right to trace. The remedy will thus be available against volunteers into whose hands it has come even though they are innocent in the sense of having no notice of such circumstances. These principles were established in a series of decisions which also determined the manner in which adjustments should be made as between such innocent volunteers and what should happen in the case of further dispositions by the innocent volunteers which might enhance or diminish the value of the property to be traced.

20.09 The principle that the remedy will be available against innocent volunteers was established beyond doubt in England by *Re Diplock.* It had been foreshadowed, however, by the decision of the House of Lords in *Sinclair v Brougham* and in particular the speech of Lord Parker in that case. It is with the latter decision, accordingly, that our account of how the law has developed in England and Ireland should begin.

Sinclair v Brougham, which must share with *Donoghue v Stevenson*[1] the distinction of being the most intensively raked over judicial decision of the century, arose out of the liquidation of a building society. The directors had invited the public to deposit money with the society, an activity which was in fact beyond its powers. When it went into liquidation, the ordinary creditors were paid off by agreement and there then remained enough in the form of assets to repay the shareholders in full the money which they had subscribed for their shares and leave a surplus. There were not enough assets, however, to meet *both* the claims of the shareholders *and* the depositors in full. The shareholders claimed to be entitled to be repaid in priority to the depositors. This claim succeeded in the Court of Appeal. The House of Lords, however, varied the order of the Court of Appeal and held that the shareholders and the depositors should share rateably in the assets in repayment of the moneys to which they were respectively entitled.

It will be noticed that the shareholders in that case were not in the strict sense 'volunteers': they had subscribed capital in the society and were entitled in return to an interest in the assets. But they were obliged to recognise the competing equitable claims of those who had entrusted their money to the society in the form of deposits. This could only be achieved by requiring the claims of both classes to abate rateably, since the assets left were not sufficient to pay both in full. It should be noted that, with the exception of Lord Dunedin, the law lords declined to treat the claim of the depositors to a return of their money as based on any form of unjust enrichment:[2] the directors of the society had received the deposits in a fiduciary capacity and when the money was placed in the name of the society it remained impressed with that character, thereby enabling the tracing remedy to be invoked.[3]

In analysing the respective rights of the innocent shareholders and the depositors, Lord Parker drew on the hypothetical situation that would arise if the 'mixing' were with the funds of an innocent volunteer and concluded that in such a case the volunteer could not claim priority over the person entitled: the innocent shareholders could be in no stronger position. In each case, the innocent party had to acknowledge in effect the right of the owner and the just solution, where the fund was insufficient, was to allow the parties to share rateably. It was an important link in the chain of reasoning that the owner of the property did not lose his 'ownership' as a result of the mixing: he became entitled to a charge, itself a proprietary right, on the fund, as a result of the wrongful mixing.

Lord Parker's illustration of the 'innocent volunteers' was the key to the next step in the development of the tracing remedy, the decision of the Court of Appeal in *Re Diplock*. We have already noticed the genesis of this astonishing legal marathon: the fateful use by the testator of the disjunctive 'or' and the consequent decision of the House of Lords that his attempted bequest for 'charitable or benevolent purposes' failed totally. The executors had paid the money to a wide range of charities, including a number of hospitals, before the challenge was launched by the next-of-kin. The charities were, of course, volunteers and in each case the cheque from the executors had been lodged to the charities' bank account, thereby effecting the mixing of the fund with the innocent volunteers' money. The Court of Appeal, reversing the decision of the trial judge, held that the necessary implication of the decision in *Sinclair v Brougham* was that the charities had to acknowledge the claim of the true owner, ie the next-of-kin, and to share the funds rateably. (The next-of-kin in that case also claimed to be entitled *in personam* against the executors who had misapplied the money. This claim was upheld by the Court of Appeal and also by the House of Lords on appeal. There was no appeal from the finding by the Court of Appeal that a remedy also lay *in rem*.)[4]

1 [1932] AC 562.
2 See para 13.12, above.
3 This produces the paradoxical result, pointed out by Goff and Jones, *The Law of Restitution* (above) that the depositors were in a better position than they would have been in, had the banking business been lawful. In that event, they should logically have been treated as no more than simple creditors, as all bank customers with money on deposit or current account are in law.
4 In the result, the executors were only personally liable for the balance remaining due to the next-of-kin when the appropriate sum was paid out of the charities' bank accounts.

20.10 It has been said by two leading academic commentators[1] that there is a divergence of authority in England and Ireland in this area: a number of Irish cases, notably *Re Ffrench's Estate*,[2] it is suggested, treat the right of the owner of the property to trace it as a mere 'equity' as distinct from an equitable interest in its own right and, as the English authorities proceed on the basis that the right to trace is itself a right of property, the consequences, it is said, may not be the same in the two jurisdictions.

The facts in *Re Ffrench's Estate* and the effect of the judgements have been summarised already.[3] It will be recalled that Porter MR was the only member of the court who decided the case on the basis that the right to trace was a mere 'equity'. Fitzgibbon and Barry LJJ preferred to rest their judgements on the ground that the subsequent equitable mortgagee could not be adversely affected by the breach of duty on the part of trustees in allowing the trust funds to be used in the purchase of land for the benefit of the tenant for life, when he had no notice of the trust. The majority, accordingly, were not basing their view on the rights of the beneficiaries being mere 'equities'. It is, of course, the case, as Barry LJ emphasised, that the importance of the registration system in Ireland enables even a purely equitable claimant to resist a previous equitable claim which is not registered and of which he had no actual notice. But the decision, it is thought, cannot be regarded as authority for the proposition that, in cases unaffected by questions of registration of title, the principles laid down in *Sinclair v Brougham* and *Re Diplock* are inapplicable in Ireland.

That this is not the case is clearly demonstrated by the decision of Budd J in *Shanahan's Stamps Ltd v Farrelly and another*. This case resulted from the dramatic collapse of an enterprise which produced a whole crop of causes celebres in the early 1960's. A firm of auctioneers advertised a scheme under which they promised large profits to people who were prepared to invest their money in the purchase and sale of stamps. The firm bought stamps and grouped the investors into syndicates. Specific stamps were allotted to the different syndicates and the theory was that when these were sold at auction, the investors would get the proceeds less the firm's commission and expenses. The investors were guaranteed that no matter what the stamps fetched, they would get their initial investment back as a minimum. It subsequently emerged that when the auctions were held, the amount to be paid to the investors was calculated as if all the lots of stamps had been sold whereas in fact many of them remained unsold. The investors were, of course, unaware that the auctions were being conducted on this bizarre basis, but apprehensions about the firm's financial stability mounted with an announcement that a large private collection which it was intended to auction had been stolen. The company went into voluntary and then compulsory liquidation and the unfortunate investors found that, to meet their claims for the return of £1.8 million there was £90,000 in cash and stamps with an estimated value of £280,000. The ordinary creditors were owed £34,000. No separate bank account had been opened in respect of the monies paid by the investors.

When the axe fell, the firm had already grouped some of the investors into syndicates to whom stamps had been allotted. Since it appeared possible that different legal considerations would apply to their claims as distinct from those who had been grouped into syndicates, the two classes of claims—described as the 'syndicated' and 'unsyndicated' investors— were separately represented when the liquidator sought directions from the court as to how he should proceed. He naturally advanced the claims of the ordinary creditors to be paid pari passu with the syndicated and unsyndicated investors. In support of this submission it was argued that both classes of investors were simply ordinary creditors and no more: it was never intended that they should have any interest in the stamps, their rights being confined to the net proceeds of sale of the auction of the particular lot allotted to the syndicate to which they belonged.

Budd J rejected this submission and held that the principles of *Sinclair v*

Brougham and *Diplock's case* were applicable: the company had received the investors' money on a fiduciary basis to invest on their behalf. Consequently, when the money was mixed with the company's own money, the investors were entitled to trace their money into the mixed fund. Moreover, in the case of the syndicated investors, although it was true that the investors never became the owners of the stamps allotted to them, the fact that they had been purchased with monies entrusted to the company on a fiduciary basis meant that the investors were entitled to trace their money into the proceeds of sale of these stamps and to have them sold for that purpose. The unsyndicated investors were, by the application of the same principles, entitled to trace their monies into the remaining stamps which had not been allotted to the syndicates.

1 Delaney, "Equitable Interests and 'Mere Equities' " (1957) 21 Conv 195; Wylie, *Land Law,* pp 117-118.
2 (1887) 21 LR Ir 283.
3 See para 5.05, above

Adjustments between competing claims to property

20.11 We have seen that the rule in *Clayton's Case*—first in, first out—does not apply in its full rigour to cases where the trustee makes payments from a bank account consisting partly of his own money and partly of the beneficiary's. Suppose, to revert to the illustration used already, the trustee lodges first £2000 of the beneficiary's, then £3000 of his own money and draws out £4000. The remaining £1000 belongs entirely to the beneficiary. But now suppose the trustee lodges a further £1000 of his own. In strict logic, since the trustee is presumed to be complying with the law, this money should be treated as being in repayment of the trust moneys wrongly spent and should also belong to the beneficiary. The law, however, has taken a different view: where this happens, the money will not be regarded as being lodged in repayment of the beneficiary's money. The rule is that the beneficiary's right to trace is exhausted once the drawings on the account have reached the stage at which all the trust moneys can be seen to have been spent: this is sometimes referred to as the rule of 'the lowest intermediate balance'.[1] It must yield, of course, to evidence from which the court can infer that the trustee did intend to replace the misapplied funds. So in *Re Hughes,*[2] Kenny J held that the rule did not apply where a solicitor withdrew funds from the clients' account for his own purposes and subsequently lodged money of his own to the account at a stage when the Law Society were investigating his affairs: the lodgment was clearly an attempt to replace the trust monies.

1 *Roscoe (James) (Bolton) Ltd v Winder* [1915] 1 Ch 62.
2 [1970] IR 237.

20.12 The money belonging to a beneficiary may have been dissipated by the trustee. If so, and there is nothing left in the account, the remedy *in rem* is, of course, gone. We have already seen, however, that where the money is not dissipated but invested in an asset, the beneficiary will be entitled to a charge on the asset *pro tanto*. Moreover, even where the trustee has paid money of his own into the account and there was enough at the time to enable the trustee to fund the investment with his own money, the beneficiary will be entitled to a charge on the asset in the event of the account being subsequently exhausted. It was held in *Re Oatway*[1] that the charge to which the beneficiary is entitled attaches to all the monies in the account and is not lost because at the time of the investment there was enough of the trustee's money in the account to fund it.

It might seem logical that the beneficiary should simply be entitled to a charge for the amount of his misapplied money and interest in the event of the trustee investing the money in an asset. It has been suggested, however, that where the investment yields a profit to the trustee, the beneficiary should be entitled to a proportionate part of the profit. This has been so held in the United States[2] and in *Re Tilley's Trusts*,[3] Ungoed-Thomas J expressed a similar view, although on the facts, he did not think the beneficiary was entitled.

1 [1903] 2 Ch 356.
2 Hanbury, p 647.
3 [1967] Ch 1179.

20.13 Where there is more than one person claiming to trace into the same property, and it is not sufficient to meet all their claims in full, because the assets have shrunk in some manner, they will share rateably in the property to the extent of the amounts which they are owed. But this will not apply in the case of a banking account: here *Clayton's Case* will apply, and the rights of the various beneficiaries will depend on when their monies were lodged to the account.[1] This is certainly rough justice: where one beneficiary's money is lodged one day and another the next, it seems inequitable that the first claim may be wiped out and the second survive. In *Shanahan's Stamp Auctions v Farrelly and Dawson,* where the syndicated investors' money had been converted into assets in the form of stamps, Budd J assumed for the sake of argument that *Clayton's case* continued to apply even where the money was no longer in the bank account, but found it impossible to apply in any event in that case, as it could not be established on what dates the relevant transactions took place. It would appear, however, that the rule in *Clayton's case* should not apply where the money is no longer in the bank account; and it may even be doubtful whether the courts would now continue to apply *Clayton's Case* (which has always been regarded as based on rather crude if convenient assumptions) to the case of competing claims of beneficiaries to money in a bank account.

1 *Re Hallett's Estate,* above at 743 per Baggalloy LJ; *Shanahan's Stamp Auctions Ltd v Farrelly,* above at 442.

Tracing remedy not confined to money and land

20.14 The tracing remedy is not confined to money and land: it can also be invoked where the money is converted into chattels, as in *Shanahans Stamp Auctions Ltd v Farrelly and another.* Moreover, where goods are sold subject to a 'reservation of title' clause, it may even be possible to trace the goods into other goods with which they have been mixed. Whether, however, the remedy remains when the goods have simply ceased to exist—as where they are used in the manufacture of other goods—has been doubted.[1]

1 *Borden (UK) Ltd v Scottish Timber Products Ltd* [1981] Ch 25. See Keane, *Company Law in the Republic of Ireland,* pp 170-175.

Chapter 21

Delivery up and cancellation of documents

21.01 Although it is rarely invoked to-day, there is a remedy available to a plaintiff who establishes that a particular document is void or voidable, in addition to a declaration to that effect and an order setting aside the document: the defendant may also be required to deliver up the actual document so that it may be cancelled. The object of obtaining the relief is to prevent a document which has been found to be of no lawful effect from continuing to exist: were it to remain in circulation, others might be misled and with the passage of time this could prove more difficult to undo.

21.02 It was at one time thought that the remedy was only applicable where the document was voidable, eg as having been obtained by fraud, duress or undue influence, in contrast to where it was void. In the latter case it was said that the illegality of the transaction being apparent on the face of the document, the remedy of cancellation or delivery up was superfluous. The contrary was held however by Lord Eldon LC in *Bromley v Holland*[1] and this has remained the law ever since.

1 (1802) 7 Ves 3.

21.03 As in the case of many other equitable remedies, the plaintiff will be deprived of relief if he is guilty of delay or acquiescence. Moreover, he may also lose his right to relief if he declines to submit to what the court considers equitable terms as a condition of granting him delivery up. Thus in *Lodge v National Union of Investment Co*,[1] the plaintiff had given securities to the defendant who was advancing him money. The transaction was illegal under s 2 of the Moneylenders' Act 1902 and the defendant was ordered to deliver up the securities for cancellation but only on terms that the plaintiff repaid the money already lent. It was suggested, however, in a later case that the case is not to be treated as a general authority for what happens in money-lending transactions: it was said that it might lead to the result that the court was indirectly enforcing an illegal transaction.[2]

1 [1907] 1 Ch 300.
2 *Kasumu v Baba-Egbe* [1956] AC 539, [1956] 3 All ER 266.

Chapter 22

Receivers

22.01 A receiver is a person appointed to take possession of property for the benefit of the persons who are legally entitled to it. The appointment of a receiver by the court is a long established equitable remedy and in this chapter we will be concerned with receivers so appointed: it is also extremely common for receivers to be appointed without recourse to the court by debenture holders and mortgagees but the functions and duties of such receivers are not the concern of a book on equity.[1]

It should be noted that the usual object of appointing a receiver is to ensure that property which is the subject matter of proceedings is preserved for the benefit of the persons ultimately found entitled to it. For that purpose, he is authorised to get in and recover possession of the relevant property. His appointment as a receiver does not, of itself, entitle him to carry on any business: if it is thought necessary for him to do so, he must be expressly appointed as a manager.[2] The jurisdiction to appoint a manager is of more recent origin: at one stage, the courts declined to become involved in the running of commercial enterprises.[3] Now it is common for the order to appoint the same person to be receiver and manager where a business is being carried on. It is sometimes said, in the case of a manager appointed by the court, that his appointment is simply intended to ensure that the business is carried on to the best advantage until it can be liquidated. However, while this is the usual position, it is not necessarily the case: there is authority for the proposition that the manager may be appointed in the case of an action for the rescission of a contract for the sale of a business so as to preserve the business until it is determined who is to carry it on.[4]

1 See Keane, *Company Law in the Republic of Ireland*, Chapter 23.
2 *Re Manchester and Milford Rly Co* (1880) 14 Ch D 645 at 651 Jessel MR.
3 *Re Newdigate Colliery Ltd* [1912] 1 Ch 468 at 472 per Cozens Hardy MR.
4 *Hannam v Lamney* (1926) 43 WN 68.

Circumstances in which a receiver is appointed by the court

22.02 Order 50, rule 6(1) of the Rules of the Superior Courts provides that

'the Court may ... appoint a receiver by an interlocutory order in all cases in which it appears to the Court to be just or convenient so to do.'

Receivers have been appointed in partnership actions and in actions for specific performance and rescission. They have also been appointed to take possession of a trust estate where it is not being properly managed.[1] They may be appointed over the estate of a deceased person until a grant of probate or letters of administration have been taken out.[2] Mortgagees, although already entitled to appoint under the terms of the mortgage deed, may apply to the court for an appointment.[3] Similarly, a debenture holder, although today invariably entitled to appoint a receiver of the undertaking and assets of the company in a wide range of circumstances, may obtain the appointment of a receiver by the court if he satisfies the court that his security is in jeopardy.[4]

1 *Evans v Coventry* (1854) 5 De GM & G 911; *Whitehead v Bennett* (1846) 6 LTOS 313.
2 *Re Oakes* [1917] 1 Ch 230.
3 *Tillett v Nixon* (1883) 25 Ch D 238.
4 *McMahon v North Kent Ironworks* [1891] 2 Ch 148.

Nature of the office of receiver appointed by the court

22.03 A receiver appointed by the court is an officer of the court and is not the agent of any of the parties.[1] His position is significantly different from that of a receiver appointed under a power in a mortgage or a debenture. In the latter case, the instrument under which he is appointed usually provides that he is to be deemed to be the agent of the mortgagor or the company. In the former case, as an officer of the court, he is not the agent of any of the parties. It follows that when he enters into a contract after his appointment, he can only do so as a principal and hence will be personally liable.[2] He will, however, be entitled to be indemnified out of the assets over which he has been appointed in respect of any such liability.[3] The fact that he is an officer of the court also means that anyone who interferes with his possession of the relevant property is guilty of contempt of court and punishable accordingly.[4] Since he is expected to act in the interests of all the parties to the action, he is usually required to be an impartial person. Hence, it is not usual to appoint one of the parties as receiver or anyone who has shown bias.

1 *Bacup Corpn v Smith* (1890) 44 Ch D 395 at 398 per Chitty J.
2 *Burt, Boulton and Hayaard v Bull* [1895] 1 QB 276, CA.
3 Ibid.
4 *Ames v Birkenhead Docks Trustees* (1855) 20 Beav 332.

Remuneration and security

22.04 A receiver is entitled to a proper salary or allowance.[1] This is payable out of any assets which come into his hands as receiver but he has no claim personally against the person who secured his appointment.[2] He is also usually required to give security for the due performance of his duties.[3]

1 Rules of the Superior Courts, Order 50, rule 16.
2 *Boehm v Goodall* [1911] 1 Ch 155.
3 Rules of the Superior Courts, Order 50 rule 16.

Receiver by way of equitable execution

22.05 This is a somewhat limited form of remedy which enables a judgement creditor to capture an equitable interest in property which cannot be reached by the ordinary processes of execution, eg an interest under a will. It must be shown, however, that it is not possible to execute the judgement.[1] It will accordingly only be granted where (a) the judgement debtor is entitled to an equitable interest in property which could have been seized in satisfaction of the judgement if the debtor had the legal estate and (b) execution cannot be had. Thus it has been granted in the case of debts to which the garnishee procedure does not for some reason apply.

1 *Re Shephard* (1889) 43 Ch D 131 at 137, CA, per Bowen LJ.

Chapter 23

Account

23.01 To the layman the word 'account' often suggests a bill. Its meaning for lawyers is somewhat different: it is usually taken as referring to a legal remedy which effectively compels one party to proceedings to produce information as to dealings which concern the other party. There was at one stage a common law action of account which, however, became so cumbersome and laden with technicalities that it fell into disuse in the mid-eighteenth century.[1] Litigants who wished to obtain an account were encouraged to resort to the court of equity which was thought to be more adapted to affording this kind of relief. In cases where the plaintiff was asserting an equitable right in those courts, he could always claim an account, eg a tenant for life could be required to account to the remainderman. But where the plaintiff was relying on a common law right, the circumstances in which he could obtain the relief were less clear. Ultimately, seven broad categories of cases emerged in which the court would order an account.[2]

1 *AG v Dublin Corpn* (1827) 1 Bli NS 312 at 337 per Lord Redesdale.
2 *London Chathan & Dover Rly Co v South Eastern Rly Co* [1892] 1 Ch 120.

Cases where an account will be ordered

23.02 While the courts have been reluctant to say that there is an exhaustive category of cases in which an account will be ordered, it is clear that the relief will normally be available in the following cases.

(a) Mutual accounts. Where there have been such accounts between the parties—ie where there have been receipts and payments between both parties—the court may order an account to be taken to find the actual balance due by one party to the other.[1] It will not be available where there have been receipts and payments on one side only: it is then a question of simply setting off the payments against the receipts and this does not justify the taking of an account by the court. Even in the case of mutual accounts, the remedy will not be available where they are extremely simple.[2]

(b) Fiduciary or quasi-fiduciary relationships. The most common example is the relationship of principal and agent. While there is some doubt as to whether the relationship is always properly described as a fiduciary one,[3] there is no doubt as to the general right of a principal to an account as against his agent or as to the similar right of any person who has reposed confidence in another person to such an account. Again, however, the account will only be ordered if the state of affairs is sufficiently complex to justify the intervention of the court.

(c) Partnerships. Clearly an account may be ordered as between partners where the court dissolves a partnership. Partners of course invariably stand in a fiduciary relationship to one another so that in a sense this is merely an example of the general category set out in (b). It seems sensible, however, to treat it as a category on its own, since it is classically the sort of case in which the taking of accounts is ordered in practice.

(d) Waste. An account was ordered where the plaintiff sought an injunction in respect of waste, in order to eliminate the necessity for two actions (he would otherwise have had to seek damages at law and an injunction at equity.)[4] Similarly, he would be entitled to an account in respect of the special category of waste called equitable waste (eg *permissive* waste where the defendant simply failed to do repairs.)[5] It must be doubtful whether an account would be ordered to-day solely on the ground that the plaintiff was seeking an injunction and the action was in respect of waste: since in Ireland he does not have to maintain an action in separate divisions of the court, he would presumably not be entitled to an account unless the case fell within one of the other categories being discussed.

(e) Industrial property. The remedy is undoubtedly available in cases of infringement of patents and trade marks and also in passing off cases.[6] There would also seem to be no reason why it should not be available in cases of copyright. In such cases, in contrast to the other categories, the object is not to ascertain the balance due from the defendant to the plaintiff, but rather to establish the profits earned by the defendant from his wrongful use of the plaintiff's property. There is a further distinction to be made between cases in which the defendant deliberately passes off his goods as those of the plaintiff and those in which he infringes the plaintiff's patent, trade mark or copyright: in the former he must account for the actual profits he has earned, whereas in the latter the obligation is restricted to accounting for so much of the profits as are attributable to the patent, trade mark or copyrighted article.[7]

(f) Where the plaintiff has been prevented from acquiring a legal right to be paid money by the defendant. While the cases where this has arisen have been ones where an employer has failed to settle a final account with a contractor,[8] it would also seem to be applicable where an agent is prevented from earning his commission by his principal.[9]

(g) Cases where the accounts are too entangled to be settled at law. This category of cases is one which undoubtedly exists[10] but has never been defined with precision.

(h) Wilful default. This usually arises where the defendant has been in possession of the plaintiff's property and could by prudent management have earned more money than he did. In this instance an account will be ordered to be taken of sums which would have been received by the defendant were it not for his wilful default.[11] Thus an account will be ordered against a trustee who has been guilty of a passive breach of trust, ie simply failing to carry out one or more of his duties. In order to obtain an order for an account, however, the plaintiff must prove that there has been at least one instance of wilful default on the part of the defendant.[12] The only exception is the case of a mortgagee in possession: as against him a mortgagor is entitled to an account as of course without having to prove any acts of wilful default.[13] Where it transpires for the first time during the course of the hearing that there has been wilful default, the plaintiff may be allowed to amend his pleadings so as to include a claim for an account.[14]

1 *O'Connor v Spaight* (1804) 1 Sch & Lef 305 at 309.
2 *Phillips v Phillips* (1852) 9 Hare 471.
3 See para 13.05, above.
4 *Jesus College v Bloom* (1745) 3 Atk 262.
5 *Duke of Leeds v Earl Amherst* (1846) 2 Ph 117.
6 *Smith v London & South Western Rly Co* (1854) Kay 408.
7 *Colbeam Palmer v Stock Affiliates Pty Ltd* (1968) 122 CLR 25.
8 *McIntosh v Great Western Rly Co* (1850) 2 Mac & G 74.
9 *London Chatham & Dover Rly Co v South Eastern Rly Co* [1892] 1 Ch 120 at 140.
10 *Taff Vale Rly Co v Nixon* (1847) 1 HL Cas 111.
11 *Bartlett v Barclay's Bank Trustee Co (No 2)* [1980] Ch 515.
12 *Sleight v Lawson* (1857) 3 K & J 292.
13 *Mayer v Murray* (1878) 8 Ch D 424.
14 Ibid.

Settled accounts

23.03 A plaintiff sometimes claims in a common law action that money is due by the defendant to him on 'an account stated and settled between the parties.' Similarly a defendant who is sued for a sum of money will sometimes seek to defend the action by pleading that there has been an account stated and settled between the parties. Where the plaintiff relies on an account stated and settled, he seeks to avoid having to give evidence of a whole series of transactions, involving mutual debits and credits, but instead hopes to prove that the parties had agreed the balance due. Similarly the defendant may say in answer to a money claim that such a balance was agreed between the parties.[1]

The phrase 'an account stated and settled' is a merger of the common law concept of an 'account stated' and the equitable concept of 'settled accounts'. Indeed while in modern pleading the habit has probably become ineradicable, the proper plea at common law is undoubtedly of an account stated *simpliciter*. The plea of 'settled accounts' is a defence to the equitable claim, with which we have been dealing in this chapter, to an account. Where the plaintiff claims the equitable remedy of an account, the defendant may successfully rely on this plea of there having been a 'settled account' between the parties. Such an account resembles closely the 'account stated' at common law: there must have been a series of mutual debits and credits and the striking of a balance which is, expressly or by implication, agreed between the parties.[2] It does not exist where there is simply an account due by one party to the other.[3]

A settled account may be reopened in cases of fraud[4] or mistake.[5] But except in case of fraud, the party re-opening the account will not be allowed to re-open the entire account. He may only challenge specific items by claiming that some items are wrongly omitted and that some have been wrongly included. The first procedure is called 'surcharging' and the second 'falsifying.'[6] Even in cases of fraud, the person seeking to re-open the accounts may be confined to surcharging or falsifying, if a lengthy period has elapsed or where to allow a general reopening might cause injustice.[7]

1 *Sequeira v Noronha* [1934] AC 332, PC.
2 *Anglo American Asphalt Co v Crowley Russell & Co* [1945] 2 All ER 324 at 331 per Romer J.

3 Ibid.
4 *Gething v Keighly* (1878) 9 Ch D 547.
5 *Gray v Minnethorpe* (1796) 3 Ves 103.
6 *Pitt v Cholmondely* (1754) 2 Ves Sen 565 at 566.
7 *Millar v Craig* (1843) 6 Beav 433.

Part four

The equitable doctrines

Chapter 24

Conversion and reconversion

24.01 Property under our law is either real or personal. The distinction is not as important as it was under the old rules for the descent of property which were abolished by the Administration of Estate Act 1959 and the Succession Act 1965. Prior to those enactments, real estate devolved on an intestacy to the heir-at-law and personal estate to the next-of-kin. The doctrine of conversion requires that in certain circumstances real estate is to be treated as if it were personal and vice versa, but since that distinction has been abolished, it has lost some of its importance. It remains significant where the testator makes separate dispositions of his real and personal estate and of course in establishing the devolution of title to property before 1967.[1]

The doctrine is based on the maxim that 'equity looks on that as done which ought to have been done'.[2] It follows from the maxim that where a person is under a duty to convert land into money or vice versa, the law will not allow the property to be treated as though it were still in its original form simply because the person concerned has failed to perform his duty. (In practice, although the doctrine has its origins in the different incidents of real and personal estate, it applies whenever a person is under a duty to convert land (whether real or leasehold) into money and vice versa.) This duty will normally arise where property is directed to be sold or purchased by will or deed of settlement. But the doctrine also applies where a person has agreed to sell land and, by a somewhat anomalous extension, where land is subject to an option to purchase. Conversion may also take place as the result of an order of the court requiring a sale and under the provisions of particular statutes. In the case of partnerships, real property is also treated as though it were converted into personalty unless the partners agree to the contrary.

1 The Succession Act 1965 came into force on 1 January 1967.
2 See para 3.18, above.

Conversion under a direction in a will or other instrument

24.02 Where an instrument, such as a will, contains a direction that real property is to be sold or that money is to be laid out in the purchase of real property, the realty or personalty will be treated as converted.[1] It must be clear, however, from the terms of the will or settlement that the executor or trustee is under a duty to sell: if he is given a discretion, the doctrine will not apply.[2] For conversion to take place, accordingly, the relevant terms of the will or settlement must be *imperative* rather than *discretionary*. A trust for sale will generally effect a conversion, even where the exercise of the trust can be postponed or where its exercise is dependent on the consent of the designated person.[3] But the trust for sale must be effectual: if it is void as offending the rule against perpetuities, there will be no conversion.[4] Conversion is deemed to take place in the case of a will on the death of the testator and in the case of a deed of settlement when it is executed.

1 *Batestte v Maunsell* (1976) IR 10 Eq 314.
2 *Smithwick v Smithwick* (1861) 12 Ir Ch R 181; *McGuire v McGuire* [1900] 1 IR 200; *Re Tyndall's Estate* [1941] Ir Jur Rep 51; *Re Wagstaff's Settled Estates* [1909] 2 Ch 201.
3 *Duke of Marlborough v A-G* [1945] Ch 78.
4 *Re Daveron* [1893] 3 Ch 421.

Conversion under a contract for the sale of land

24.03 Where land is sold, it will be treated as converted into money from the date of the contract. While there must be a valid contract for sale, it is not necessarily the case that the contract must be one of which specific performance would be decreed.[1]

Where a compulsory purchase of land is effected, the service of a notice to treat does not effect a conversion: it was held by the Supreme Court in *Re Greendale Building Co*[2] that where such a notice is served, the parties are not in the same position as a vendor and purchaser. That relationship does not arise between the acquiring authority and the landowner until the purchase price is agreed or determined by arbitration. At that point, however, the land will be deemed to be converted from land into money.

1 *Rose v Watson* (1864) 10 HL Cas 672, applied by the Supreme Court in *Tempany v Hynes* [1976] IR 101. This point was not, however, under discussion in the latter case. The view has been expressed that it is essential that specific performance be available if the conversion is to take place: see *Holroyd v Marshall* [1862] 10 HL Cas 191 at 209-210, per Lord Westbury LC. Cf Wylie, *Land Law*, p 126.
2 [1977] IR 256.

Conversion under an option to purchase

24.04 Where the owner of real estate grants an option to purchase and dies before it is exercised, the doctrine of conversion applies and the purchase money descends as personalty. So if he devises the land to A and leaves his personalty to B, it is B who is entitled to the purchase money when the option is exercised: A has no more than an estate which is defeasible on the exercise of the option.

This rule—which applies even where the option cannot under its terms be exercised until *after* the death of the grantor—is known as the rule in *Lawes v Bennett*[1] and has been frequently criticised as an anomalous extension of the doctrine of conversion. It will not be applied where an intention can be inferred to exclude it. In particular the courts have sought to confine its operation by holding that it does not apply where the grantor of the option *subsequently* makes a specific devise of the property. The law was thus stated by Page-Wood V-C in *Weeding v Weeding*[2] in a passage adopted by Palles CB in *Re Steele, Steele v Steele*[3]:

'When you find that in a will made *after* a contract giving an option to purchase, the testator, knowing of the existence of the contract, devises the specific property which is the subject of the contract without referring in any way to the contract he has entered into, there it is considered that there is sufficient indication of an intention to pass that property, to give to the devisee all the interest, whatever it may be, that the testator had in it.'

In *Lawes v Bennett,* by contrast, the device was general, not specific. The anxiety of the Courts to exclude the rule, where possible, is further illustrated by the decisions to the effect that where the will is republished by the execution of a codicil, the property will not be converted although the option was granted after the original will was made.[4] Moreover, the rule in *Lawes v Bennett* only applies as between persons claiming the real and personal estate of a deceased person. Thus, in *Edwards v West,*[5] a landlord was obliged to insure and the tenant had an option to purchase. The premises were burnt down and the landlord was paid the insurance money. The tenant then exercised the option to purchase, but it was held that he was not entitled to the insurance monies: the conversion did not take effect until he exercised the option.

In *Re Carrington,*[6] however, the Court of Appeal held that the rule applied where there was a specific legacy of shares over which an option to purchase was subsequently granted. It was held that when the option was exercised, the legacy had to be treated as ineffective (in legal language, *adeemed.*) The decision would seem to be irreconcilable with *Edwards v West.*

1 (1785) 1 Cox Eq 167. Cf *Re Lawless, Miley v Carty* [1927] IR 541.
2 (1861) 1 John & H 424 at 431.
3 [1913] 1 IR 292. See also *Duffield v McMaster* [1896] 1 IR 370.
4 *Re Pyle, Pyle v Pyle* [1895] 1 Ch 724.
5 (1878) 7 Ch D 858.
6 [1932] 1 Ch 1.

Conversion and the registration of title system

24.05 The relationship of the doctrine of conversion to the registration of title system should be noted. When freehold lands were purchased under the Land Purchase Acts and compulsorily registered under the Local Registration of Title (Ireland) Act 1891 (subsequently replaced by the Registration of Title Act 1964) the land devolved as personalty and not realty. It was held by Overend J in *Re Desmond, Creed v Kearney*[1] that where freehold land was vested in a tenant under the Land Purchase Acts but the title was not registered at the date of her death, the land devolved on intestacy to the heir-at-law. The provision that freehold land was to devolve as personalty was not applicable until registration was complete and the doctrine of conversion did not have the effect of making it so applicable in advance of registration.

1 [1943] IR 534.

Conversion under an order of the court

24.06 Where real property is ordered to be sold or money laid out in the purchase of real property, conversion takes place from the time of the order.[1] There is an exception, however, in the case of property owned by a person of unsound mind who is a ward of court. It has long been the practice in such wardship cases not to treat the doctrine of conversion as applicable, so as not to interfere with any rights of succession which may arise. To an extent this is provided for by s 67 of the Lunacy Regulation (Ir) Act 1871 which requires in effect that any surplus arising after the sale of the ward's property to pay debts or provide for his maintenance is not to be treated as converted. It would seem, however, that where the property is being sold or purchased simply in the course of managing the estate of the ward and not for such purposes as paying his debts or providing for his maintenance conversion will take place.[2]

1 *Re Beamish's Estate* (1891) 27 LR Ir 326.
2 *O'Connell v Harrison* [1927] IR 330 at 337-338 per Kennedy CJ; Re *Silva* [1929] 2 Ch 198.

Partnership property

24.07 Partnership assets consisting of real estate were treated in equity as personalty and in the result devolved as personalty and were also so treated for such purposes as the payment of debts.[1] Under s 22 of the Partnership Act 1890 this was given statutory effect: real estate is treated as personal estate, not only as between the partners and their personal representatives, but also as between the persons entitled to the real estate of the partners unless a contrary intention appears in the partnership agreement.

1 *A-G v Hubbuck* (1884) 13 QBD 275, CA.

Conversion when there is a partial failure of objects

24.08 There will be no conversion where there is a total failure of the objects of the conversion at or before the time at which the duty to convert arises. In such circumstances, the property remains in its unconverted form in the view of the law, even though it may have been in fact converted.[1] This principle applies whether the property has been settled by deed or will.

Where some only of the objects fail, the matter is more complex. If the settlement is by deed, the position is clear: the conversion is deemed to take place and the trustees hold the share of the failed objects on a resulting trust for the settlor as if it had been converted.[2] Thus in the case of realty held on a trust for sale, if the settlor died before 1967 and some of the objects failed, the next-of-kin would have been entitled. But where the settlement is by will, and the direction to the trustees was to convert realty into personalty, it is presumed that this no longer applies so far as any failed objects are concerned. In that case, under the rule in *Ackroyd v Smithson*[3] the property remains unconverted and prior to 1967 would have gone to the heir-at-law. This was on the theory that conversion was for the purposes of the will only and if those purposes failed the lapsed shares should be treated as unconverted. Similarly, if personalty was directed to be converted into realty, and the objects failed in part, the lapsed share remained in its unconverted form as personalty. Where realty is directed to be sold and there is such a partial failure, however, it is deemed to be realty solely for the purpose of determining *who is entitled*: for other purposes, it is deemed to be converted since the trustees are under a duty to convert the property in order to carry out the objects which have *not* failed.[4] Hence in the case of such a partial failure, the heir took it as personalty and if he died intestate it went to his next-of-kin. This was decided in *Re Richerson, Sayles v Heyhoe*,[5] which was followed by the Court of Appeal of Saorstat Eireann in *Re O'Connor deceased, McDermott v A-G*[6] It is also clear from these decisions that the same principle applies where money is directed to be invested in the purchase of real estate: in the event of a partial failure, the next-of-kin took it as real estate and on an intestacy it went to the heir.

1 *Donnellan v O'Neill* (1870) IR 5 Eq 523.
2 *Hewitt v Wright* (1780) 1 Bro CC 86.
3 (1780) 1 Bro CC 503.
4 *Re Richerson, Scales v Heyhoe* [1892] 1 Ch 379; *Re O'Connor, McDermott v A-G (No. 2)* [1923] 1 IR 142.
5 Above.
6 Above.

Reconversion

24.09 Property which has been deemed to have been converted according to the rules already explained may be deemed to be *reconverted* to its original form in certain circumstances. Thus in the case of a trust for sale where land has been notionally but not actually converted into money, all the beneficiaries may at a certain point be of full age and not under any disability. At that point, the money is reconverted into land on the principle that 'equity, like nature, does nothing in vain.'[1] For the law to insist that the property be still treated as money would be futile, since the beneficiaries can call on the trustees to transfer it to them in its unconverted form as land. Similarly where the legal and equitable estates are 'at home', ie vested in the same person, reconversion will take place.[2]

There will be no reconversion in the case of minors or persons of unsound mind.[3] In the case of a tenant in common, whether reconversion takes place of his undivided share of the trust fund depends on whether it is land directed to be converted into money or vice versa. In the first case, reconversion does not take place, since one tenant in common cannot insist on the land being divided into lots in opposition to his co-owners.[4] In the second case, where the tenant in common can simply call for his shares to be paid to him rather than invested in land, there is no such obstacle and reconversion is deemed to take place.[5] A remainderman, it would seem, may elect to take the property when it vests in its unconverted form and to that extent his interest will be reconverted. His election, however, cannot become operative until his interest vests in possession.[6] In the case of a contingent remainder—one which will only vest on the happening of a contingency rather than the determination of a previous interest—there is no reconversion unless the contingency happens during the life of the remainderman.[7] Thus, if R is entitled to the fee simple in lands held on trust for sale subject to the prior life interest of L, elects to take his interest as unsold and dies before L, his remainder prior to 1967 would have devolved on his heir-at-law. But if his remainder were only to vest in possession on another person dying without issue and he died before that happened, any election made by him during his lifetime — as by his will — would be ineffective and in that event the next-of-kin would be entitled.

1 *Harcourt v Seymour* (1851) 2 Sim NS 12, 45 at 46.
2 *Chichester v Bickerstaff* (1693) 2 Vern 295; *McDonagh v Nolan* (1882) 9–LR Ir 262 at 270 per Chatterton V-C.

3 *Orr v Alexander* [1925] NI 104.
4 Because the land may not be so advantageously sold. See *Holloway v Radcliffe* (1857) 23 Beav 163 at 172 per Romilly MR.
5 *Seeley v Jago* (1717) 1 P Wms 389.
6 *Meek v Devenish* (1877) 6 Ch D 566; *Hart v MacDougall* [1912] 1 IR 62.
7 *Re Sturt* [1922] 1 Ch 416.

Conversion under the Settled Land Acts

24.10 A form of statutory conversion is effected under s 22(5) of the Settled Land Act 1882. It provides as follows:

'capital money arising under this Act, while remaining uninvested or unapplied, and securities on which an investment of any such capital money is made shall, for all purposes of disposition, transmission and devolution, be considered as land, and the same shall be held for, and go to the same persons successively, in the same manner and for and on the same estates, interests and trusts as the land wherefrom the money arises would, if not disposed of, have been held and gone under the settlement.'

Chapter 25

Election

25.01 The doctrine of election arises in this way. A testator purports to leave property to A which belongs to B. The will also confers a benefit on B. Obviously B may refuse to hand over his property to A. But if he does decide to keep it together with the benefit given to him by the will, he must compensate A for the loss of what the will attempted to give him.[1]

An example makes this clear. T by his will leaves Bella Vista to A. It in fact belongs to B. But B is also given a legacy of £50,000. Bella Vista is worth £30,000. If B wishes to take *under* the will, he must give Bella Vista to A. If he wishes to take *against* the will by keeping Bella Vista, he must pay B £30,000 out of his £50,000 to compensate B for the loss of Bella Vista. B is thus required to elect between taking under the will and against the will. The doctrine is originally based on equity's reluctance to allow a person to take a benefit under a will or deed if he is not prepared to give effect to the intention of the testator or the settlor. And this in turn is an example of a more general principle that 'a person is not allowed to approbate and reprobate'.

It may seem an unlikely and eccentric thing for a testator to do. Why should he give someone else's property away and how often does this happen? It is a highly pertinent question, because in many cases where it arises the testator is happily unaware that he is doing anything of the sort. This is well illustrated in the case of powers of appointment, as again an example makes clear.

T is entitled to appoint by will certain shares settled by a deed of trust among his children A, B and C in such shares as he thinks fit. In default of appointment they are to go to A. In fact he has another child D, to whom he appoints the entire fund in the mistaken belief that he is also an object of the power. By his will he gives legacies to A, B and C. A is entitled in default of appointment to the shares, but if he wishes to keep them, he must compensate D out of his legacy.

Or it may happen that the testator purports to dispose of the entire interest in a property of which he is not the sole owner. Thus H and his wife, W, are entitled to Bella Vista are joint tenants. By his will H leaves Bella Vista to his son, S, and leaves the residue of his estate to W. W is in any event entitled to Bella Vista by survivorship but she must elect between retaining it and paying S compensation on the one hand and letting him have it and taking the residue without deduction on the other.

---

1 *Birmingham v Kirwan* (1805) 2 Sch & Lef 444 at 450; *Re Sullivan* [1917] 1 IR 38.

The essentials of election

25.02 It accordingly does not matter whether the testator is aware that he is disposing of someone else's property. Provided that it is clear that he intends to give that property away and at the same time benefit the true owner, the latter will be put to his election and the question as to whether the testator was aware of the actual ownership will be immaterial. The most acceptable modern statement of the doctrine is generally taken to be that of Jenkins LJ:

> 'The essentials of election are that there should be an intention on the part of the testator or testatrix to dispose of certain property; secondly that the property should not in fact be the testator's or testatrix's own property; and thirdly that a benefit should be given by the will to the true owner of the property.'[1]

It is also essential to distinguish cases of election in this sense from cases in which the testator makes it a *condition* of a particular devise or bequest that certain property should be given to another. In such a case, if the devisee or legatee does not comply with the condition, he simply forfeits the bequest and there is no question of election.

1 *Re Edwards* [1958] Ch 168 at 175.

25.03 It is accordingly clear that the essential first element of election is an intention by the testator to dispose of that particular property. Provided that was his intention and the other elements mentioned by Jenkins LJ are present, it will be a case for election. After much legal debate, it has generally been accepted that the doctrine does not rest on any *presumed intention* of the testator; except to this extent, that the court presumes that the testator wishes his whole will to be effective, including the bequest of someone else's property. When the doctrine first began to evolve in the eighteenth century, there was a tendency to treat the benefit under the will as forfeited if the true owner did not part with his property and this was a logical consequence of holding that the basis of the doctrine was the presumed intention of the testator that the owner should either carry out his wishes or lose his bequest. Such a view is, of course, difficult to apply to cases where the testator is wholly unaware of the real position as to ownership, which, as we have seen, frequently gives rise to cases of election. Towards the end of the eighteenth century the notion that the election arises because of the presumed intention of the testator began to wane and in 1818 Sir Thomas Plumer MR spoke of it as

> 'a universal rule of equity by which the court interferes to supply the defect arising from the circumstances of a double devise and..... lays hold of the estate for the purpose of making satisfaction to the disappointed devisee .....'[1]

It would obviously be imputing to the mistaken testator an intention he never had to suppose that he would have required the person benefited either to transfer the property given in mistake or compensate the disappointed beneficiary. Yet despite such weighty pronouncements as that of Plumer MR, the concept that the equity was based on the presumed intention of the testator continued to receive expressions of judicial approval, such as that of Lord St Leonards sitting as lord chancellor of Ireland.[2]

At this stage, however, it can be taken as settled law that the doctrine does not rest on presumed intention, but is, in Sir Thomas Plumer's words, an 'act of the Court' by which it endeavours to achieve equity by satisfying the disappointed beneficiary. In a modern English case,[3] Buckley LJ firmly rejected the view that the doctrine was based on the presumed intention of the testator.

'The cases in which the testator frames his will with the conscious intention of bringing the doctrine into play must be very rare. In a great majority of cases to which the doctrine is applicable it applies because the testator has made a mistake. His intention is not in doubt, but he has mistakenly assumed an ability to do something which, in fact, he cannot do of his volition.'

The doctrine of election is, therefore, an artificial concept which has little to do with what might have been thought to be the paramount concern of equity, i.e. that the testator's wishes should not be defeated. If Bella Vista is worth £60,000, B receives no benefit under the will, since he must either surrender the legacy of £50,000 or transfer his own property, which is worth more than that, to A. Yet the testator must have intended to benefit B by giving him the legacy.

1 *Gretton v Haward* (1819) 1 Swan 409 at 423.
2 *Hall v Hill* (1841) 4 Ir Eq R 27 at 37-38.
3 *Re Mengel's Wills Trusts* [1962] Ch 791, 796-797.

25.04 The courts in construing wills generally approach them on the assumption that a man intends only to dispose of his own property. Accordingly, the onus of proof is on those who assert that he has purported to dispose of someone else's and hence has created a case for election.[1] Moreover, since the court leans against supposing that he intended to dispose of another's property, it will usually treat general words of bequest or devise as confined to the testator's own property and, where he was not the full owner, will assume in the absence of evidence to the contrary, that he intended to dispose only of the interest to which he was entitled.[2] The court will also look to the whole will in determining whether the testator intended to dispose of the particular property.[3]

These principles of construction are well illustrated by one Irish and one English decision. In *Re Sullivan*,[4] the testator left his wife a legacy of £5000 which he directed to be paid out of securities standing in their joint names. He then went on to dispose of his residuary estate to other members of his family. The Irish Court of Appeal held that this raised a case of election: although the bequest of the residue was in general terms, it was quite plain from the terms of the legacy that the testator was treating the securities as his own absolute property which would pass with the residue. In fact, of course, they passed to his widow by survivorship and hence she was obliged to elect between taking under the will and letting the residuary legatees have the shares or taking against the will and compensating the residuary legatees out of her legacy. In *Re Mengel's Wills Trusts*,[5] the testator purported to dispose of 'all my personal and household goods and effects'. The succession to the property was, however, governed by Danish law under which the household goods etc were the joint property of husband and wife. It was held by Buckley J that these words nevertheless indicated a clear intention on the testator's part to dispose of the entire property in the goods and not simply of his own interest in them, and so the wife had to elect between keeping what she was entitled to under Danish law and retaining other benefits given to her by the will. The same will, however, contained a residuary clause and it was held that this being in general terms should be construed as confined to the testator's own property.

1 *Evans v Evans* (1863) 2 New Rep 408 at 410 per Turner LJ.
2 *Howells v Jenkins* (1863) 2 J & H 706, at 713 per Page Wood V-C: *Re Mengel's Will Trusts*, above.
3 *Wintour v Clifton* (1856) 8 De GM & G 641.
4 Above.
5 Above.

25.05 For election to arise, it is essential that the person called upon to elect must be given property under the will *and* be entitled to property apart altogether from the provisions of the will of which the testator has purported to dispose. If his claim to both properties derives under the will, there will be no case for election. The leading case is *Wollaston v King*,[1] in which A, B and C received bequests under a will out of the testatrix's own property. She also purported to by the same will to exercise a power of appointment in favour of X. That appointment was void as being contrary to the rule against perpetuities and A, B and C who were the residuary objects of the power hence became entitled to the share appointed to X. It was held by James V-C that A, B and C were not obliged to elect between the bequests given to them out of the testator's own property and that which came to them by virtue of the wrongful exercise of the power of appointment. Both benefits derived from the will and hence there was no case for election: there is no legal principle which requires one beneficiary under a will to compensate another who has been disappointed of a benefit which has failed and as a result gone to the first. The decision of Neville J in *Re McCartney*[2] which seemed to suggest the contrary, is generally regarded as wrongly decided.

1 (1869) LR 8 Eq 165.
2 [1918] 1 Ch 300. See Pettit, pp 627-628; Hanbury, p 306.

Gift under will must be available for compensation

25.06 Election does not arise unless the person whose property is purportedly disposed of by the testator can have recourse to the property left him by the will to compensate the person to whom his own property has been left. Thus in *Re Gordon*,[1] a mother directed a house to be sold and the proceeds to be treated as part of the residue. Her son was entitled to a protective life interest in one half of the residue. Under this form of protective trust the son could not dispose of his life interest. He was, however, entitled to the house as a joint tenant with his mother and hence it passed to him by survivorship. It was held by the Court of Appeal that no case for election arose, since there was no property of the testator to which recourse be had for compensation. It is thought that *Re Saul's Trusts*[2] which appears to suggest the contrary was wrongly decided.

1 [1978] Ch 145.
2 (1951) Ir Jur Reps 34.

True owner's property must be capable of alienation

25.07 Election will also not arise if the property which the testator has purported to dispose of and which belongs to another cannot be transferred by the true owner to the person to whom it has been left. The leading case on the topic is *Re Chesham*[1] where the property in question were heirlooms settled on a trust. They were given by will to someone who was not entitled to them. The person who was entitled to them was also given a benefit under the will but since he had only a life interest in the heirlooms it was held that no question of election arose.

1 (1886) 31 Ch D 466.

What constitutes election

25.08 In order to establish that a person has elected to take under or against the will, two ingredients are necessary: first, that he was aware of the nature and extent of his rights and second that he intended to elect. The law was thus stated by Chatterton V-C in *Sweetman v Sweetman*:[1]

'The requisites for holding a party bound by an election as concluded are, I think, these: first, he must have a knowledge of his rights, that is to say, he must know that the property, which the testator attempted to give to another person, was not the testator's property and that it would, upon the testator's decease, become, independently of the testator's will, the property of the party called upon to elect. It must be known by him as a matter of fact that the testator had not the power to give the property which he purported to devise and that it belongs, not by the will, but by an earlier title[2] to the person who is called upon to elect. Next, he must know the relative values of the properties between which he is called to elect; and further he must know as a matter of fact and not as a presumption of law that the rule of equity exists, that he cannot, under such circumstances, take both estates, but must make an election between the two. And, further, the court must be satisfied that he made a deliberate choice with the intention of making it.'

Provided these requirements are met, it is not necessary that there should have been an express election: an election may be inferred from the conduct of the party in question, as well as from an express election made orally or in writing.[3] A person under a disability, however, such as a minor or a person of unsound mind, cannot elect. In the case of a minor, any election which he is called upon to make will be deferred if possible until he is of age. If this cannot be done, an inquiry will be directed into what would be to his advantage and the court may elect on his behalf.[4] In a case of a person of unsound mind so found, his committee may elect on his behalf under the direction of the court.[5]

1 (1868) 2 IR Eq 141 at 152-153.
2 *Briscoe v Briscoe* (1844) 1 Jo & Lat 334.
3 *Moore v Butler* (1805) 2 Sch & Lef 249 at 266-267, per Lord Redesdale; *Morrison v Bell* (1843) 5 Ir Eq R 354.
4 *Wilder v Pigott* (1882) 22 Ch D 263.
5 *Cooper v Cooper* (1874) LR 7 HL 53.

Derivative interests

25.09 Where a person who could be required to elect dies without having done so, and both the properties pass to the same person, he in turn may be required to elect.[1] Thus, if Bella Vista which belongs to A is given by T to B and A is given £50,000, as we have seen A may be called upon to elect. If he dies, without having done so and both Bella Vista and the legacy pass to C, C may be required to elect. If, however, A by his will leaves Bella Vista to D while the legacy remains with C, the latter must still compensate B out of the legacy: the bequest by A of Bella Vista is itself an election which creates a right of compensation in B who was originally given it.[2]

Where upon the death of the person who could have been required to elect, the interest of that person in the property ceases, it would seem that there is no case for election. It is thought that *Re Saul*[3] which appears to suggest the contrary was wrongly decided. In that case, a testator bequeathed his residence to his wife for her life or until her re-marriage. He also purported to bequeath to one of his sons certain leashold premises of which he and his wife were joint tenants and to which she was accordingly entitled by survivorship. She retained possession of the residence and was in receipt of the rents from the other premises until her death and although called upon to elect did not do so. It was not suggested that the receipt of the rents constituted an election to take against the will. Dixon J held that her personal representatives could now be called upon to elect and that the compensation should be paid out of her estate since she had been in receipt of the rents for 18 years. Election in the true sense was, however, at that stage impossible: there was no property of the deceased left to her by the will to which recourse could be had since her interest ceased on her death. Her personal representatives were in no different position from the protected life tenant in *Re Gordon*[4] where, as we have seen, the Court of Appeal held that no case for election arose.

1 *Pickersgill v Rodger* (1876) 5 Ch D 163 at 174 per Jessel MR.
2 Ibid.
3 Above.
4 Above.

Election and the rule against perpetuities

25.10 Election does not arise where the donee of a power of appointment exercises it by his will in such a manner as to offend the rule against perpetuities[1] and at the same time confers a benefit on the persons entitled in default of appointment. Although in such a case the testator purportedly disposes of the property to which the persons in default are ultimately entitled and at the same time confers a benefit on them, they are not put to their election and can keep both sets of benefits. This was so held by the Irish Court of Appeal in *Re Handcock's Trusts*[2] on the ground that the court in requiring the persons to elect would be sanctioning a breach of the rule against perpetuities and that this would be contrary to public policy. This decision was followed in England in *Re Nash*[3] but has been strongly criticised, since at the time the election falls to be made it might well be possible to carry out the testator's intentions at least in part without violating the rule.[4]

1 See para 7.06, above.
2 (1889) 23 Lr Ir 34.
3 [1910] 1 Ch 1, CA.
4 Hanbury, p 818; Pettit, pp 626-627.

Chapter 26

Satisfaction and ademption

26.01 If a person owes money, or is under some other form of obligation, to another person and subsequently gives a benefit to that person, the law presumes that the giving of the benefit was intended to satisfy the debt or obligation in question and was not intended to be by way of additional bounty. This is known as the equitable doctrine of *satisfaction* and is the most important illustration of the maxim that 'equity imputes an intention to fulfill an obligation.'[1] It arises in different ways, as, for example, where A owes B £1000 and by his will leaves him a legacy of precisely £1000: the legacy is normally presumed to have been intended by A to satisfy his debt to B.

Closely related to the doctrine of satisfaction is that of ademption, which is a further illustration of the same maxim. The word 'ademption' is, however, used in two senses which must be carefully distinguished. First, it may refer to a case in which the subject matter of a bequest or devise is either alienated or ceases to exist during the testator's lifetime. So A may leave B a particular painting and afterwards may sell it or it may be destroyed during his lifetime. In either case, the bequest is said to be 'adeemed', ie taken out of the will. Secondly, it may refer to a case in which a bequest or devise is followed by a subsequent gift to the same person. In certain circumstances, this also has the effect of taking the bequest or devise out of the will so that again it is regarded as adeemed. It is this latter form of ademption which constitutes the equitable doctrine of ademption and with which we are here concerned.

There are six principal varieties of satisfaction and ademption, and they will be considered in turn:

(1) satisfaction of debts by legacies;
(2) satisfaction of 'portion debts' by legacies;
(3) ademption of legacies by 'portions' or 'portion debts';
(4) ademption of legacies by subsequent gifts;
(5) satisfaction of legacies by legacies;
(6) satisfaction of 'portion' and other debts by subsequent *inter vivos* payments.

1 See para 3.19, above.

Satisfaction of debts by legacies

26.02 Where A owes money to B and by his will leaves him a sum which equals or exceeds the amount of the debt, there is a presumption that the legacy is intended to satisfy the debt.[1] Thus if A owes B £150 and leaves him a legacy of £200, B cannot accept the legacy and successfully sue the estate for £150. Since, however, the rule is based on the presumed intention of the testator, it will not be applied where it appears that the intention was that B should enjoy a gift of the £200 in addition to being paid his debt of £150. The courts, indeed, have been notably ready to identify circumstances which will prevent the presumption from operating, since it has never been regarded with much enthusiasm. Kindersley V-C described it as a 'false principle'[2] and Stirling J in a later case[3] said that it was no sooner established than judges invented ways to get out of it.

Thus, the presumption will only operate where the legacy equals or exceeds the amount of the debt. A legacy of a lesser amount will not be treated as a *pro tanto* satisfaction of the debt.[4] It is also clear that if the legacy is of an uncertain, fluctuating or contingent character, it will not operate as a satisfaction of the debt.[5] Thus a gift of the residue will not normally be treated as a satisfaction, since its precise amount cannot be determined and may prove to be less than the debt.[6] Similarly, where the state of accounts between the testator and his creditor was fluctuating after the date of the will, the legacy will not be regarded as being in satisfaction.[7] And a legacy given subject to a condition or only to become operative on a contingency will not be presumed to be in satisfaction.[8]

If the legacy is given on terms—as to the time or mode of payment, for example—which are less advantageous to the creditor, the presumption will not arise.[9] But the mere fact that the legacy need not be paid for a year after the death of the testator—the so-called 'executor's year'—whereas the debt may be payable immediately will not be sufficient to prevent the presumption from arising. The decision by Stirling J in *Re Horlock*[10] that the presumption did not arise in such circumstances would reduce enormously the efficacy of the presumption, but in a subsequent case Swinfen Eady J took a different view. In *Re Rattenberry*[11] he held that since the legacy in these circumstances, although not payable for a year, carries interest as from the date of the death, it could properly be regarded as being satisfaction of a debt for a similar or lesser amount. It has been generally accepted that the latter view is preferable. If, however, the will *directs* payment of the legacy to be postponed and the debt is payable immediately, or before the expiration of the time for payment of the legacy, it will not be presumed to be in satisfaction: in such a case, interest will only be payable on the legacy as from the time fixed for payment.[12]

A bequest or devise of land will not normally be presumed to satisfy a pecuniary debt.[13]

1 *Garner v Holmes* (1858) 8 I Ch R 469 at 476.
2 *Hassell v Hawkins* (1859) 4 Drew 468 at 470.
3 *Re Horlock* [1895] 1 Ch 516 at 518.
4 *Coates v Coates* [1898] 1 IR 258.
5 *Crompton v Sale* (1729) 2 P Wms 553.
6 *Re Keogh's Estate* (1889) 23 LR Ir 257.
7 *Buckley v Buckley* (1888) 19 LR Ir 544 at 558.
8 *Mathews v Mathews* (1755) 2 Ves Sen 635.
9 *Haynes v Mico* (1781) 1 Bro CC 129.
10 Above.
11 [1906] 1 Ch 667.
12 *Haynes v Mico*, above.
13 *Eastwood v Vinke* (1731) 2 P Wms 613 at 616; *Coates v Coates*, above.

26.03 Two further extremely important limitations on the operation of the presumption should be noted. In the first place, it will not apply where the will under which the legacy is payable is executed before the debt is incurred. It cannot be presumed that a legacy is intended to satisfy an obligation which is not in existence at the time it is given.[1] In the second place, the terms of the will itself may make it clear that the legacy was not intended to be in satisfaction of the debt. Thus, a direction (commonplace in wills to-day) for the payment of the testator's debts will be sufficient to prevent the presumption arising.[2]

1 *Thomas v Bennet* (1725) 2 P Wms 341.
2 *Re Manners, Public Trustee v Manners* [1949] Ch 613 at 618 per Evershed MR.

Satisfaction of 'portion debts' by legacies

26.04 It is first necessary to understand what is meant by a 'portion debt'. Such a debt is incurred when a father or other person *in loco parentis* agrees to make a contribution to one of his children which is intended to be a permanent provision for the child. The most obvious example is a provision made on the occasion of the child's marriage, but it may also take the form of a gift intended to set the child up in a particular business or profession. Where the father incurs such an obligation and subsequently makes provision for the child in his will, there is a presumption that the portion debt is intended to be satisfied by the testamentary provision.[1] This is said to be an application of a maxim that 'equity leans against double portions'. It is sometimes said that this reflects the law's inclination to ensure that children are treated equally, but it has been pointed out that it should rather be seen as promoting consistency on the father's part as to the share which he intends each child to take and that, in any event, it also applies where there is only one child. It should also be noted that it only arises where the father agrees to make the provision, not where he has actually made it. In the latter case, since he has already made the advance, there is no reason to suppose that the benefit in the will was not intended as additional bounty to the particular child. But where he has merely agreed to make the provision,

> 'equity leans ... in favour of a provision by will being in satisfaction of (the agreement) ..., feeling the great improbability of a parent intending a double portion for one child, to the prejudice generally... of other children... '[2]

Like the doctrine of satisfaction of debts by legacies, this rule has been the subject of critical comment, not least from judges, although like the former doctrine it is a purely judge made rule. It can certainly produce remarkable results: if a testator agrees to set up a nephew or godson in business and subsequently leaves him money by his will, the beneficiary can take both. But a child of the testator, even where he is the only child, will be compelled to elect between taking the benefit under the will or that under the agreement. Lord Eldon LC spoke[3] of its harshness in the early days of its operation and Lindley LJ had this gloomy retort to counsel who argued that the doctrine should be confined as far as possible:

> 'we should not perhaps invent it in these days, but we have inherited it'.[4]

And Bowen LJ, remarking that in a particular case he thought that the application of the rule was leading the court away from the testator's intention but felt constrained by precedent to apply it, characterised his conclusion as 'a sacrifice on the altar of authority'.[5]

Despite these misgivings as to the desirability of the rule, it was expressly preserved in our law by s 63(9) of the Succession Act 1965. Under the section, advancements made to a child must be taken into account when determining the child's share on an intestacy and sub-s (9) provides that nothing in the section is to affect any rule of law as to satisfaction of portion debts by legacies.

1 *Thynne v Earl of Glengall* (1848) 2 HL Cas 131. *Re Bannon, Callanan v Ryan* (No 2) [1934] IR 701 at 730 per Murnaghan J.
2 *Thynne v Earl of Glengall*, at 153 per Lord Cottenham LC.
3 *Ex p Pye* (1811) 18 Ves 140 at 151.
4 *Re Lacon* [1891] 2 Ch 482 at 490.
5 *Montague v Earl of Sandwich* (1886) 32 Ch D 525 at 544, CA.

26.05 The first requirement for the presumption to arise is that the person making the provision is either the father or someone standing *in loco parentis* to the child.[1] It does not arise in the case of a mother,[2] grandfather, grandmother, uncle or with brothers and sisters or other relatives.[3] Nor does it arise as between father and illegitimate child. We have already seen that the presumption of advancement is similarly confined in its operation and a question may arise as to whether such judge made rules are consistent with the equal status of parents under the Constitution.[4] So far as any other person is concerned, whether they stand *in loco parentis* is a question which must be determined according to the circumstances of the particular case. It is obviously easier to establish where there is a close blood relationship and the fact that the person lived with the person concerned will clearly be an important, though not necessarily decisive, factor.[5] So will the extent to which a person regards himself as being *in loco parentis*.[6]

1 *Ex p Pye* (1811) 18 Ves 140. Cf *Re Bannon, Callanan v Ryan (No 2)*, above.
2 *Preston v Greene* [1909] 1 IR 172 at 177-178 per Meredith MR.
3 *Shudal v Jekyll* (1743) 2 Atk 516. Cf *Re Gleeson* [1911] 1 IR 113 at 119.
4 See para 12.03, above.
5 *Fowkes v Pascoe* (1875) 10 Ch App 343 at 350
6 *Powys v Mansfield* (1837) 3 My & Cr 359.

26.06 The second requirement is that both the provisions under consideration must be 'portions' in the legal sense. Merely casual payments of a relatively small nature will not be treated as portions.[1] On the other hand, the presumption will arise where a father agrees to give a large sum in one payment.[2] It is also clear that the gift must be substantial in itself to justify being treated as a portion, but, subject to that, the relative amount as compared to the size of the testator's estate is a factor which may be taken into account.[3] It has also been said that prima facie the gift must be made early in life.[4]

1 *Schofield v Heap* (1858) 27 Beav 93.
2 *Taylor v Taylor* (1875) LR 20 Eq 155.
3 *Re Hayward* [1957] Ch 528 at 542, CA, per Jenkins LJ.
4 *Taylor v Taylor*, above at 159 per Jessel MR.

26.07 The next requirement is that the provisions must be *ejusdem generis*, ie of the same kind. The rule as laid down by Lord Hardwicke LC is that 'the thing given in satisfaction must be of the same nature and attended with the same certainty as the thing in lieu of which it is given.'[1]

No problem arises then if a commitment to pay money is followed by a pecuniary legacy. But what if an agreement to purchase a child a share in a business is followed by such a legacy? Both portions are personalty, but would not seem to be 'attended with the same certainty'. In *Lawes v Lawes*,[2] Jessel MR said that the presumption of satisfaction only arose in such circumstances if the donor referred to the *value* of the portion which was not a pecuniary gift. This was approved by the Court of Appeal in *Re Jacques*.[3] In *Re George's Will's Trusts*,[4] Jenkins J, however, said that the necessity for a valuation only arose if the two portions were not *ejusdem generis*, but the difficulty remains as to when the two portions are to be so regarded. It would seem from the authorities that a pecuniary legacy and a share in partnership are not *ejusdem generis*[5] for this purpose and Lord Hardwicke specifically referred to the difference between land and money in this context.[6]

It also follows from this requirement that differences in the limitations subject to which the portions are given will prevent the presumption against double portions arising, provided the differences are more than slight. It is a question for the judge to decide in each case whether the differences are sufficiently slight to be disregarded and two leading cases illustrate the manner in which it has been approached. In *Lady Thynne v Earl of Glengall*,[7] the differences were that under a marriage settlement the settlor's daughter was to be given a sum of money for life with remainder to such of the children of the marriage as she and her husband should jointly appoint; whereas under the subsequent will of the settlor, the power of appointment was to the daughter alone and the objects were not confined to the children of that particular marriage. It was held that the differences were too slight to negative the presumption against double portions. On the other side of the line, in *Tussaud v Tussaud*,[8] the Court of Appeal held that the differences were more than slight where a wife under a marriage settlement had a general power of appointment not confined to her children, and in default of appointment there were successive life interests vested in the wife and husband in the same fund. By the will the wife alone had a life interest in the fund with the remainder to her children.

Again the manner in which the payment of the respective portions is secured may be sufficiently different to rebut the presumption against double portions. In *Re Gleeson*[9] it was held that a legacy which was hazardous and likely to fluctuate could not be regarded as in satisfaction of gift under a settlement which was well secured.

1 *Bellasis v Uthwatt*, (1737) 1 Atk 426 at 428.
2 (1881) 20 Ch D 81 at 88, CA.
3 (1903) 1 Ch 267, CA.
4 [1949] Ch 154 at 160.
5 *Holmes v Holmes* (1783) 1 Bro CC 555.
6 *Bellasis v Uthwatt*, above.
7 Above.
8 Above.
9 (1878) 9 Ch D 363 at 367.

26.08 It should also be noted that where the presumption does arise, the child is required to elect between taking the benefit which his father agreed to give him and taking the benefit under the will. The testator cannot, in other words, deprive the child of a legal right he already has by making provision for him under the will, but the child cannot take both portions. This form of *election in equity* should be carefully distinguished from the doctrine discussed in the previous chapter.

Where the amount of the legacy is less than the amount of the portion debt, it will not be regarded as completely satisfying the portion debt but only as satisfying it *pro tanto*.[1]

1 *Lord Chichester v Coventry* (1867) LR 2 HL 71.

Ademption of legacies by portions or portion debts

26.09 The presumption against double portions also means that, where the legacy is followed by the portion, the legacy will be adeemed by the portion: again the child is not allowed to take both gifts.[1] Unlike the case of satisfaction, however, there is in this instance no question of election: the child simply loses the bequest or devise. But under the decision in *Pim v Lockyer*,[2] the ademption only operates *pro tanto:* a child who is left £20,000 and is subsequently advanced £5000 to set him up in business can claim the balance of £15,000 under the will. As we have just seen, this was also subsequently applied to the satisfaction of portion debts by legacies.

The presumption of ademption, like the presumption of satisfaction, may be rebutted. But it is more difficult to rebut than that of satisfaction.[3] The reason is that in the case of satisfaction, the father is already under a legal obligation to advance the child in a particular manner and cannot without the child's consent substitute a different form of benefit. These factors make it relatively easier for the child to establish that the gift in the will was by way of additional bounty. But the same considerations do not apply where the will is followed by a second gift. The father is under no obligation to the child and can revoke his will. In such circumstances, it is more reasonable to suppose that he was simply anticipating the bounty given by the will and was not intending to benefit the child twice over. Thus, we have seen[4] that to raise a presumption of satisfaction the two provisions must be *ejusdem generis* and that, provided the differences between the two gifts are not 'slight' the presumption will be rebutted. In the case of ademption, on the other hand, such differences may be regarded as insufficient.

One further difference between ademption and satisfaction should be noted: as we have seen, the presumption of satisfaction only arises where there is an agreement or undertaking to make a gift as opposed to an actual gift. In the case of ademption, the presumption arises both where there is a subsequent gift and an agreement to make a gift.

Subject to these differences, the rules as to satisfaction and ademption are the same. Thus the same criteria are used to determine whether the testator stands *in loco parentis* to the child[5] and whether what has been given is a portion.[6]

1 *Curtin v Evans* (1875) IR 9 Eq 553.
2 *Pym v Lockyer* (1840) My 5 & Cr 39; Ct *Re Bannon, Callanan v Ryan (No 2)*, above.
3 Ibid at 38.
4 See para 26.07, above.
5 See para 26.05, above.
6 See para 26.06, above.

Benefits to strangers arising from presumption against double portions

26.10 Whether the presumption against double portions arises in a case of satisfaction or ademption, its application may lead to the conferring of a benefit on a stranger in blood to the testator at the expense of his children. Thus, if A leaves £20,000 by his will to his son, B, and subsequently advances him £25,000 on his marriage, the legacy is, as we have seen, adeemed because of the presumption against double portions. In the result, if A has left the residue of his estate to C, who is not a member of his family, C is enriched to the extent of £20,000 at the expense of B.

Doubts have been expressed from time to time as to whether the presumption can operate to benefit strangers at the expense of children in this manner, but the preponderance of authority is in favour of the view that it can. In *Meinertzagen v Walters*,[1] Mellish LJ indicated his view *obiter* that where a legacy was given to a child who was subsequently advanced, it followed inevitably that whoever got the residue benefited from the presumption at the expense of the child.

The question came before the High Court and the Supreme Court in *Re Bannon, Callanan v Ryan (No 2)*.[2] In that case, a testator left a legacy of £300 to his nephew JD and made another nephew his residuary legatee. A marriage was arranged between JD and a niece of the testator's wife and a business premises purchased for the couple. £225 of the purchase price of £700 was provided by the testator. It was held in the Circuit Court that the testator was *in loco parentis* to JD and that the legacy of £300 had been adeemed *pro tanto* by the provision of £225. On appeal to the High Court, Meredith J and Johnston J were divided. The former thought that both in principle and in the light of the authorities the presumption against double portions applied even though the benefiting nephew must be equated with a stranger in blood, in this context. Johnston J doubted whether this was the law, but in any event held that on the facts the presumption had been rebutted. The decision of the Circuit Court thus stood, but was reversed on appeal to the Supreme Court. The majority (Kennedy CJ and Fitzgibbon J) held that the facts proved did not support an inference that the testator was *in loco parentis* and did not find it necessary to consider whether the presumption would have applied if he had been. Murnaghan J, while reaching the same conclusion, took the same view as Meredith J, ie that the presumption applied in a case where a stranger benefited at the expense of the child.[3]

A greater complication arises if the child, instead of being given a legacy, is given a share of the residue. Even though the child's share of the residue may be of an uncertain amount until the administration of the estate is complete, it was held in *Montifiore v Guedella*[4] that the principle of ademption applied where the child thus entitled is subsequently advanced. But in *Meinertzagen v Walters*,[5] the view was taken that it was applicable in such circumstances only as between children: if the residue was divisible among the children of the testator and one of them was subsequently advanced, the child so advanced would have to account to his siblings for the amount of the advance when the shares to which they were entitled were being ascertained. But if a stranger was also entitled to a share of the residue – if, for example, as in that case, the widow, who for this purpose is a stranger, was also entitled – it was held that she was not entitled to benefit from the advance being taken into account. James LJ said that it

315

would be 'monstrous' if a person such as the widow, who would not herself be obliged to account for advances made to her, could gain an advantage from the obligation of a child to account for an advance.

In *Re Bannon,* however, Murnaghan J doubted whether this was correct: he considered that

'grave injustice might be done if advancements are not taken into account except as between children.'[6]

An example illustrates the different approaches. X dies leaving half his residuary estate to his wife, W, and half to their children, A, B, C and D. The residue is valued at £80,000. X during his lifetime has given £3,000 each to A and B, but nothing to C and D. Leaving the widow out of the reckoning, and adjusting the sums between the children, she has £40,000, A and B £8,500 each and C and D £11,500 each. Giving the widow the benefit of the advances, the apportionment is £41,000 to the widow, £8,500 each to A and B and £11,000 each to C and D.

1 (1872) 7 Ch App 670 at 674.
2 Above.
3 At 733-734.
4 (1859) 1 De G F & J 93.
5 Above.
6 Above, at 734.

Ademption of legacies by subsequent gifts

26.11 In one instance, a legacy given to a stranger may be adeemed by a subsequent gift. This is where the legacy is given for a particular purpose and there is a subsequent gift for the same purpose. The leading Irish case is *Griffith v Bourke*[1] where a legacy to a parish priest for the erection of a new church at Claremorris was held to be adeemed by a subsequent gift for the same purpose to the Archbishop of Tuam.

It appears from *Re Pollock*[2] that the requirement of a 'particular purpose' in this context may be met if the terms of both the legacy and the gift make it clear that they are being given by the same person with a view to fulfilling a particular moral obligation. In that case, the testatrix left £5000 to a niece of her deceased husband 'according to the will of my late beloved husband.' She subsequently made a gift of £300 to the niece and referred to it as 'a legacy from... Uncle John.' It was held that the legacy was adeemed *pro tanto*.

1 (1887) 21 LR Ir 92.
2 (1885) 28 Ch D 552.

Satisfaction of legacies by legacies

26.12 Where the same person is given a legacy of the same amount twice over in the same will, the second legacy is prima facie treated as merely a repetition of what has already been given and the legatee will not be entitled to be paid twice over.[1] Where, however, the two legacies are contained in different instruments, they are presumed to be cumulative.[2] But this presumption may be rebutted in a number of ways: thus, if the legacies are of the same amount and are given for the same motive they will be treated as substitutional.[3] And that is not an exhaustive statement of the circumstances in which the presumption may be rebutted: indeed it would appear preferable to treat this doctrine of 'satisfaction of legacies by legacies' as more akin to a principle of construction of wills, the primary concern in each case being to ascertain the intention of the testator.[4]

1 *Garth v Meyrick* (1779) 1 Bro CC 30.
2 *Foy v Foy* (1758) 1 Cox Eq Cas 163.
3 *Re Armstrong* (1893) 31 LR Ir 154; *Bell v Park* [1914] 1 IR 158.
4 *Le Cras v Perpetual Trustee Co Ltd* [1967] 3 All ER 915, PC.

Satisfaction of portion and other debts by subsequent inter vivos payments

26.13 It would appear that where a father incurs a portion debt in favour of a child and subsequently provides during his life a sum equal to or greater than the debt, it will be presumed that the later payment was in satisfaction of the debt.[1] But there will be no satisfaction *pro tanto*, where the subsequent payment is smaller.[2] Such cases are rare: even rarer are cases of ordinary debts, other than portion debts, where the presumption of satisfaction has been applied to a later payment.[3]

1 *Re Lawes, Lawes v Lawes* (1881) 20 Ch D 81.
2 *Crichton v Crichton* [1896] 1 Ch 870, CA.
3 *Drew v Bidgood* (1825) 2 Sim & St 424, a case of brother and sister where it was said that the presumption could arise, although it was held not to in the particular case.

Evidence rebutting presumption of satisfaction and ademption

26.14 The presumptions of satisfaction or ademption in any of the cases dealt with in this chapter may be rebutted by parol evidence as to the intention of the testator. Thus in a number of cases evidence as to the instructions given by the testator when his will was being drafted has been admitted. A note of caution was, however, sounded in one case as to the weight to be attached to such parol evidence: 'the Court ought to view and examine it with scrupulous care and great discrimination.'[1] It is also clear that evidence in rejoinder may be adduced by those relying on the presumption.[2]

Where the second instrument contains an expression of the testator's intention as to whether there is or is not to be satisfaction, parol evidence is not admissible to contradict it.[3] It is thought that this has not been changed by s 90 of the Succession Act 1965 which provides that

'extrinsic evidence shall be admissible to show the intention of the testator and to assist in the construction of, or to explain any contradictions in, a will.'

It was held by a majority of the Supreme Court in *Rowe v Law*[4] that this did not permit the introduction of extrinsic evidence in a case where the intention was clearly expressed and there were no contradictions in the will.

Where there is no such expression of intention and no presumption of satisfaction or ademption, extrinsic evidence will not be admitted, according to Lord St Leonards sitting as Lord Chancellor of Ireland in *Hall v Hill*,[5] to raise a plea of satisfaction or ademption.

The burden of rebutting the presumption rests in every case on the party asserting that it does not apply.[6]

The evidence most frequently relied on to rebut the presumption is that of statements made at the time of the second provision, but evidence of statements made before or thereafter also appears to be admissible.[7] Less weight should probably be attached to statements made *after* the second provision.

1 *Curtin v Evans,* above, at 558, per Sullivan MR.
2 *Powys v Mansfield,* above.
3 *Kirk v Eddowes* (1844) 3 Hare 509 at 516.
4 [1978] IR 55, O'Higgins CJ *dissentiente*. The case is also of interest, as being one of the few Irish cases in which attention was directed – in this instance by the learned chief justice – to the legislative history of the enactment.
5 (1841) 4 I Eq R 27. But it was held in an earlier Irish case – *Monck v Monck* (1810) 1 Ball & B 298 – that where the second instrument is not in writing such evidence is admissible.
6 *Papillon v Papillon* (1841) 11 Sim 642.
7 *Weall v Rice* (1831) 2 Russ & M 251.

26.15 It has been said that in the case of satisfaction of legacies by legacies different rules apply. Where the presumption was that the legacies were cumulative, parol evidence was not admissible to prove the contrary; where they were substitutional, it was. The rule in each case in other words favoured the legatee.

Chapter 27

Performance

27.01 Performance is an equitable doctrine which is closely related to satisfaction. Where a person is under an obligation to perform a particular act and subsequently does an act which can be regarded as a performance of his obligation, the law will presume that it was done in performance of his obligation.[1] Thus, like satisfaction, it is an illustration of the equitable maxim, 'equity imputes an intention to fulfil an obligation.'[2] It has usually arisen where a man has covenanted to purchase and settle land or convey and settle land or to pay money to trustees to be laid out by them in the purchase of land and has failed to fulfil his obligation in its entirety. If he subsequently purchases land, it will be presumed that this was in performance or part performance of his obligations. It differs from satisfaction in that in the case of that doctrine, the act performed—eg the payment of a legacy in presumed satisfaction of a debt—is not necessarily the same as the act contemplated.

The practical significance of the doctrine of performance in former times was that as a result of its operation realty might be treated as personalty and vice versa. It has ceased to be of such importance since the assimilation of the rules for the devolution of real and personal estate completed by the Succession Act 1965.

1 *Lechmere v Lady Lechmere* (1735) Cas *temp* Talbot 80; 2 White & Tudor's *Leading Cases in Equity*, 9th edn, p 349.
2 See para 3.19, above.

27.02 The doctrine of performance is also said to arise where a person covenants to leave a sum of money to another, or covenants that his executors will pay the money, and dies intestate. If as a result of his death intestate, the covenantee becomes entitled to a share in his estate, the doctrine of performance applies and the share on intestacy is taken to be a performance of the obligation in its entirety, if it equals or exceeds the sum covenanted to be paid, and *pro tanto* if it is less.[1] It has been doubted whether it applies where the covenantor has made a will and given the covenantee a legacy, but some academic writers take the view that it does.[2]

1 *Blandy v Widmore* (1715) 1 P Wms 324.
2 Pettit, p 618; Meagher, Gummow & Lehane, p 734.

Chapter 28

Estoppel in equity

28.01 'Estoppel' is a word used again and again by lawyers. But the diversity of circumstances in which the general concept of estoppel may become relevant—ranging all the way from the criminal law to equity—makes any systematic exposition of the subject difficult and likely to promote disagreement.

In the broadest terms, estoppel may be said to arise whenever a party to litigation is by a rule of evidence prevented from relying on particular facts in support of his case. Although he is in a position to prove the facts on which he seeks to rely, he is *estopped* from so doing and must suffer the consequences in the litigation.

At least three forms of estoppel were traditionally recognised at common law: estoppel by record, estoppel by deed and estoppel *in pais* or by representations. The first arises because a matter in issue between A and B has been determined in previous litigation between them (or their privies) and cannot be reopened. The second prevents a party from asserting a state of facts which contradicts a deed which he has executed. The third arises because of representations made by one party to another, whether by words or conduct, which have induced the other party, on the faith of the representation, to alter his position to his detriment: the maker of the representation is estopped from asserting a state of facts contrary to his earlier representation. In each of these categories of estoppel, it will be seen that the common law regarded a party as estopped or precluded from alleging a state of affairs at variance with what was determined by previous litigation or with a statement in a deed or with a representation.

It is the third category, estoppel by representation, with which we are concerned. One essential feature of this form of estoppel must be noted at once since it is of crucial importance in the discussion which follows. For an estoppel by representation to arise, the representation had to be a representation of an *existing fact* and not a mere expression of *intention*. If it were the latter, it was in essence a promise, and a promise could only give rise to legal consequences if it was contractual, ie if it was a promise made for consideration. Thus, if A told B that he owned a certain field, that was a representation of an existing fact which A might be estopped from denying in subsequent litigation between A and B. But if A told B that he would give him the same field at Christmas as a present, that was a promise and since B was offering nothing in return remained a mere promise and not a contract enforceable at common law. The practical importance of the distinction is illustrated by the decision in *Jorden v*

Money,[1] which for many years was regarded as having conclusively established the law on this topic.

The plaintiff in that case was indebted to a solicitor who entered judgement and also took a bond securing the amount involved. On the solicitor's death, his sister, Mrs Jorden, became entitled to the bond. When the plaintiff was contemplating matrimony and his financial affairs were being scrutinised by his future wife's family, Mrs Jorden assured him that the debt was gone and would never be enforced against him. In reliance on this statement, the plaintiff got married, but, contrary to her earlier protestations, Mrs Jorden and her husband attempted to execute the judgement some years later. The plaintiff brought proceedings claiming a declaration that the debt was abandoned, an order that the bond be cancelled and a common injunction restraining the defendants from seeking to enforce their judgement. He succeeded before Romilly MR, the Court of Appeal in Chancery was divided and the House of Lords ultimately held against him.[2] Romilly MR had held that Mrs Jorden was estopped by her previous representations—on the faith of which the plaintiff had altered his position to his financial detriment—from relying on her undoubted right at law to enforce the judgement and the bond. But the majority in the House of Lords held that estoppel did not arise where the representation was one of intention rather than fact. Mrs Jorden had not misled the plaintiff as to any particular state of facts: she had simply made a promise which, however binding in honour it should have been, was not capable of giving rise to legal obligations.

1 (1854) 5 HL Cas 185.
2 Another curious example of the English two tier system of appeals. The judge in the appeal court who disagreed with Romilly MR was Lord Cranworth. He sat again in the House of Lords and upheld his earlier judgement. Lord St Leonards disagreed and the majority was made up by Lord Brougham, presumably on a visit to London from Cannes, as Meagher, Gummow and Lehane suggest.

28.02 It appeared from two cases decided later in the nineteenth century that the doctrine thus laid down in *Jorden v Money* might not be unassailable. But these decisions seem to have attracted little attention until they were relied on to momentous effect by Denning J in *Central London Property Trust Ltd v High Trees House Ltd*[1] in 1947. He summarised the cases—*Hughes v Metropolitan Rly Co*[2] and *Birmingham and District Land Co v London and North Western Rly Co*[3] —thus:

'The law has not been standing still since *Jorden v Money*. There have been a series of decisions over the last fifty years, which, although they are said to be cases of estoppel, are not really such. They are cases in which a promise was made which was intended to create legal relationships which, to the knowledge of the person making the promise, was going to be acted on by the person to whom it was made, and which was in fact so acted on. In such cases, the courts have said that the promise must be honoured ..... They are not cases of estoppel in the strict sense. They are really promises—promises intended to be binding, intended to be acted on and in fact acted on .....'[4]

Denning J's reluctance to apply the term 'estoppel' to this type of case has not, however, deterred judges and text-book writers from subsequently elevating it into a new genus of estoppel, referred to sometimes as *quasi-estoppel* and more frequently as *promissory estoppel*.

Because this estoppel had its roots in a decision of the court of chancery in pre-Judicature Act days in which principles of equity were expressly invoked, it has also occasionally been referred to as 'equitable estoppel'. The aptness of this name has been disputed and it has been suggested that estoppel in equity is no different in any essential respect from equity at common law. Since, however, it had its origins in the equity jurisdiction it is thought that it is as much entitled to treatment as an equitable doctrine as any of the other doctrines dealt with in this part. But since it is the term by which it is most generally known, we will continue to refer to it as 'promissory estoppel'. Moreover, the expression 'promissory estoppel' serves to distinguish this form of estoppel from another which may also be regarded as a child of equity: 'proprietary estoppel.' This has arisen principally in cases where the owner of land has encouraged, or acquiesced in, the infringement of his title to the land by another in circumstances which, in the view of the law, render it inequitable for the owner to assert his legal title land in an unqualified manner.[5]

1 [1947] KB 130.
2 (1877) 2 App Cas 439.
3 (1888) 40 Ch D 268.
4 [1947] KB 130 at 134.
5 See para 28.12, below.

Promissory estoppel

28.03 The decision which is generally regarded as the fountainhead of promissory estoppel is *Hughes v Metropolitan Rly Co.*[1] This was a landlord and tenant case in which a lessor sought to forfeit a lease because certain specified repairs had not been carried out within a period of six months from the service of a notice on the lessee specifying repairs. The lessee's solicitors had replied to the notice indicating that their client was ready to begin the work of repair immediately, but suggesting that it be postponed until they heard whether the lessor was interested in purchasing his interest. Negotiations then began between the parties but ultimately broke down. The issue in the case was whether the time for completing the repairs ran from the date of the original letter or from the date on which the negotiations broke down. It was contended on behalf of the lessee that the negotiations between the parties precluded the lessor from asserting that the time for doing the work continued to run while they were in progress. This submission was accepted by the House of Lords, Lord Cairns LC stating that

'..... It is the first principle upon which all Courts of Equity proceed, that if parties who have entered into definite and distinct terms involving certain legal results—certain penalties and forfeitures—afterwards by their own act or with their own consent enter upon a course of negotiation which has the effect of leading one of the parties to suppose that the strict rights arising under the contract will not be enforced, or will be kept in suspense, or held in abeyance, the person who might otherwise have enforced those rights will not be allowed to enforce them where it would be inequitable having regard to the dealings which have thus taken place between the parties.'[2]

The language used by Lord Cairns in this passage made it clear that the court was simply concerned in that case with the question as to whether the court should grant relief against forfeiture of a lease where the lessor has acquiesced in the breach while the negotiations were continuing. The principle was, however, extended in the second of the two cases, the decision of the Court of Appeal in *Birmingham and District Land Co v London and N W Rly Co*[3]. Rejecting the suggestion that it was confined to forfeiture cases, Bowen LJ reformulated the principle thus:

> 'If persons who have contractual rights against others induce by their conduct those against whom they have such rights to believe that such rights will either not be enforced or will be kept in suspense or abeyance for some particular time, those persons will not be allowed by a Court of Equity to enforce the rights until such time has elapsed, without at all events placing the parties in the same position as they were before.'[4]

It would be over-simplifying the position to say that the principle thus enunciated remained completely dormant until given the kiss of life by Lord Denning in the *High Trees* decision, to give it the name by which it is now universally known. There were cases in both England and Australia, some of which were referred to in his judgement while others are collected in Spencer Bower and Turner on *Estoppel by Representation*[5], which could also be regarded as illustrations of the same principle. But it was undoubtedly *High Trees* which elevated the principle to its present significant but still uncertainly defined position in the law.

1 Above.
2 At 447.
3 Above.
4 At 286.
5 3rd edn, pp 372-374.

28.04 In *High Trees*, decided at a comparatively early stage in Lord Denning's long judicial career, a lessor sought to recover arrears of rent from his lessee. It was contended on behalf of the lessee that the lessor had agreed to accept a lower rent and that the lessor was estopped from making a claim which was at variance with that agreement. There was no consideration for the lessor's alleged promise to accept a lower rent and on the authority of *Jorden v Money* this would have seemed fatal to the lessor's claim. Denning J found as fact that there had been such an agreement but that it was only to operate for a period of financial stringency. Since that period had expired and the lessor's claim was confined to the rent from the end of the period, he was entitled to succeed. He said, however, that the lessor would have been estopped from claiming the arrears for the period in question under the principle laid down in *Hughes v Metropolitan Rly Co* and expanded in *Birmingham & District Land Co v London & NW Rly Co. Jorden v Money*, in his view, would not be a barrier to relying on such a promise, having regard to what those cases decided.

While Denning J suggested in *High Trees* that *Jorden v Money* was distinguishable, this seems difficult to justify: in Australia it has been held that the two cases are irreconcilable and that *Jorden v Money* must at this stage be regarded as wrongly decided.[1] In England, the House of Lords, while not expressly approving of *High Trees*, has equally not disapproved of it[2] and it has received positive sanction from the Privy Council.[3] It has also been accepted by courts of appeal in Canada,[4] New South Wales[5] and India.[6] As we shall see, however, the Supreme Court have not so far ruled on the validity of the doctrine in Irish law.

High Trees is probably rivalled only by *Hedley Byrne & Co Ltd v Heller & Partners Ltd*[7] among cases in the past fifty years for the amount of judicial and academic discussion it provoked. In most other respects, however, it differs strikingly from the latter decision: it was that of a judge of first instance, it was delivered extemporary and the crucial passages on which so much reliance was subsequently placed were strictly *obiter*.[8] But these are hardly important considerations at this stage: Lord Denning at many points in his subsequent career adopted and restated what he had said in *High Trees* and as we have seen the fundamental principle which it enshrines has been accepted at the final appellate level in a number of common law jurisdictions. In Ireland, it has twice been applied in decisions by the High Court and accordingly, while it has yet to be considered by the Supreme Court, it also represents the law in this jurisdiction. Moreover, it may be assumed with some confidence that, whatever other considerations may weigh with the Supreme Court if and when *High Trees* finally arises for consideration, declining to follow *Jorden v Money* will hardly be much of a problem.

1 *Legione v Hately* (1983) 46 ALR 1 at 20.
2 *Tool Manufacturing Co Ltd v Tungsten Electric Co Ltd* [1955] 2 All ER 657, HL.
3 *Emmanuel Ajayi v RT Briscoe (Nigeria) Ltd* [1964] 3 All ER 556.
4 *John Burrowes Ltd v Subsurface Surveys Ltd* (1968) 68 DLR (2d) 354.
5 *John Odlin & Co Ltd v Pillar* (1952) GLR 501.
6 *Union of India v MIS Indo Afgan Agencies* IR 1968 SC 718.
7 [1964] AC 465.
8 Only the last could be said of *Hedley v Byrne*.

28.05 The reverberations of *High Trees* throughout the common law world were due to what was seen by some commentators as its radical modification of a fundamental principle of the English law of contract, ie that a promise unsupported by consideration was not enforceable. There was clearly no consideration for the landlord's promise to accept a lower rent: how then could that promise be relied on even by way of a defence to the landlord's claim? If it could be so relied on, could it not equally and consistently provide a cause of action in itself? And what at that stage became of the whole doctrine of consideration?

The Court of Appeal were quick to respond to the suggestion that any such dramatic breach had been effected in the doctrine of consideration. In *Combe v Combe*,[1] they reversed a decision in favour of a wife who had claimed arrears of maintenance payments under an agreement in writing. It was held at first instance that the husband was estopped from disputing his liability, although it was conceded that the agreement itself was not supported by consideration. But Denning LJ, now himself a member of the Court of Appeal, was at pains to indicate an important limitation of the *High Trees* principle which the High Court judge had failed to appreciate: it did not afford a cause of action in itself. He said:

'(*High Trees*) does not create new causes of action where none existed before
..... Seeing that the principle never stands alone as giving a cause of action in
itself, it can never do away with the necessity of consideration when that is an
essential part of the cause of action. The doctrine of consideration is too firmly
fixed to be overthrown by a sidewind.'[2]

The most authoritative exposition of the *High Trees* principle in England is that of the Privy Council in *Emmanuel Ayodeji Ajayi v RT Briscoe (Nigeria) Ltd*, a case decided in 1964:

'The principle, which has been described as quasi estoppel and more aptly as
promissory estoppel, is that when one party to a contract in the absence of fresh

consideration agrees not to enforce his rights an equity will be raised in favour of the other party. The equity is, however, subject to the qualification: (*a*) that the other party has altered his position; (*b*) that the promisor can resile from his promise on giving reasonable notice, which need not be a formal notice, giving the promisee a reasonable opportunity of resuming his position; (*c*) the promise only becomes final and irrevocable if the promisee cannot resume his position.'[3]

1 [1951] 2 KB 215.
2 At 221.
3 At 559.

28.06 The first reported case in which *High Trees* came before the Irish courts was *Cullen v Cullen*[1] in 1962. The plaintiff in that case was the owner of a business and some land in County Wexford. He became mentally ill and went to another part of the country to avoid being committed to an institution. While there, he sent a message to his wife saying that in return for a signed statement from her and their three sons that they would not have him committed, he was prepared to transfer the business to the wife. The latter had won a portable house in a newspaper competition which she gave to her son, M, who in turn offered it to the plaintiff. He refused to accept it and the wife asked the plaintiff whether M could erect the house on the plaintiff's land. The plaintiff replied that, as he was making the land over to her, she could do as she wished. M then built the house on the land. Subsequently, the plaintiff instituted proceedings claiming injunctions restraining the defendants—M and his brother P—from interfering with the business and trespassing on the land. M counterclaimed for a declaration that he was entitled to the site and the house.

Kenny J dismissed the plaintiff's claim on the well established ground among others that an injunction should not normally be granted on a case arising out of disputes between members of a family. He also dismissed the son's counterclaim for reasons to which we shall return. But he awarded the plaintiff £50 damages on the ground that M had trespassed on the lands by erecting the house.

One of the additional grounds on which Kenny J thought the plaintiff should not be given an injunction was that he was estopped on the *High Trees* principle from asserting his ownership of the land against M, since he had expressly acquiesced in the building of the house on the land. It will be noted that there was no *contract* between the plaintiff and M: there was simply a proposal by the plaintiff to his wife that he should transfer the business and the land to her—not the sons—in return for a signed statement. It would seem indeed that this proposal was never either accepted or rejected by the wife. However that may be, there was clearly nothing even approaching a contractual arrangement between father and son and this is an important feature of the decision, having regard to the apparent limitation by the Privy Council in the *Emmanuel Ayodeji Ajayi Case* of the principle to promises relating to contractual rights.

Cullen v Cullen was, of course, decided before the Privy Council case, but Kenny J returned to the topic of promissory estoppel in the second of the two Irish decisions some years later, *Revenue Commissioners v Moroney*.[2] In that case, he unequivocally rejected the view of the Privy Council that the principle should be confined to cases where the promise relied on related to contractual rights.

In *Moroney's Case*, a father had decided to take his two sons into partnership with him in his business. In the partnership deed, the consideration for the transfer by the father to the two sons and himself of the business premises was stated to be £20,000 and the deed contained an acknowledgement by the father that the price had been paid. In fact, there was no arrangement between the father and the sons for the payment of any money: the sum of £20,000 (the actual value of the premises) was put into the deed as the consideration by the solicitor who prepared it for the practical reason that it would be more expeditiously dealt with in the Stamp Office. (If it were prepared as a voluntary deed in which the premises were tranferred for natural love and affection, thus reflecting the true position, the amount of the stamp duty would have required adjudication and hence there would have been delay in completing the transaction.) When the father died; the revenue asked for proof that the sum of £20,000 had been paid and when they were informed of the true position claimed that estate duty was payable on the sum of £20,000 as a debt due by the sons to the father's estate.

The revenue's claim was resisted in the High Court on the ground that there was in truth no debt: if the father had sued on the deed, he would have been met with the defence that the deed itself acknowledged the receipt and if he abandoned the deed and sued on the basis of the actual arrangement the claim would have been patently unsustainable since there had never been any agreement to pay money by the sons. Kenny J, however, invited counsel to invoke promissory estoppel as a ground on which the father's claim could have been resisted and, although this invitation was not greeted with any enthusiasm, the learned judge ultimately decided the case on this basis.

The evidence in the case, which was not in dispute, established that there was never any arrangement between the father and the sons for the payment of the £20,000. Kenny J, however, held that they had accepted a liability for the payment of the money when they executed the deed providing for a money consideration. But in his view, they could have resisted any claim by the father to the money on the ground that the father was estopped from pursuing the claim. Faced with the difficulty that there was no contract between the parties relating to the payment of £20,000, Kenny J said:

'In my view, there is no reason in principle why the doctrine of promissory estoppel should be confined to cases where the representation related to existing contractual rights. It includes cases where there is a representation by one person to another that rights which will come into existence under a contract to be entered into will not be enforced.'[3]

In the Supreme Court, the claim by the revenue also failed but this time on the ground that there was never any legal liability on the part of the sons to pay the money, either by virtue of the deed or otherwise. Hence it was not necessary to consider the applicability of the doctrine of promissory estoppel had there been such a liability.

1 [1962] IR 268.
2 [1972] IR 372.
3 At 381.

28.07 Judicial recognition of the *High Trees* doctrine, accordingly, does not rest on the surest of footings in Ireland, since in *Cullen v Cullen* the views of the High Court judge were strictly *obiter* and in *Moroney's Case*, the Supreme Court held that it did not arise at all. But, as we have seen, the observations of Denning J *in High Trees* were also *obiter*. The widespread acceptance of the doctrine throughout the common law world and the respect to be given to any considered utterance of Kenny J, whether obiter or not, suggest as a matter of commonsense that the doctrine should now be regarded as sufficiently established in our law and it was so treated by Griffin J in *Doran v Thompson Ltd.*[1] Its precise limitations however, remain to be authoritatively stated.

It is to those limitations that we now turn. Here there are four principal questions which must be addressed, ie:

(1) Is the doctrine confined to cases where the promise relied on related to the modification of existing contractual rights, contrary to the view of Kenny J in *Moroney's Case?*

(2) Can the estoppel itself constitute a cause of action, contrary to the view of the Court of Appeal in *Combe v Combe?*

(3) Must the party relying on the alleged estoppel prove that he has acted to his own detriment on the faith of the representation—as he would in the case of estoppel by representation *simpliciter*—or is it sufficient to prove that he has altered his position in reliance on the representation?

(4) Can the estoppel give rise to a permanent estoppel or does it simply prevent the person estopped from relying on his rights until the other party can be restored to his former position?

We shall consider each of these questions in turn.

1 [1978] IR 223 at 230. But on the facts in that case it was held by the Supreme Court that there was no estoppel.

28.08 The view that the estoppel is confined to cases where the promise relates to existing contractual rights again reflects the anxiety of the court not to allow the doctrine of consideration to be overturned, in Lord Denning's phrase, by a sidewind. If there is no contract in existence, then enforcing the promise even on a temporary basis begins to look suspiciously like enforcing a contract unsupported by consideration. By contrast, where there is a contract, restraining a party from enforcing his rights under it because it would be inequitable for him to do so in the particular circumstances can reasonably be regarded as not conferring recognition on any new contract but rather suspending the operation of an existing contract, whether temporarily or indefinitely.

The principle as stated by Lord Cairns and elaborated by Bowen LJ appears to be confined to cases where the parties were already under legal obligations to each other. Lord Cairns, as we have seen, was primarily, if not exclusively, concerned with leases and similar documents which gave rise to penalties and forfeitures and the ability of equity to relieve against such consequences. Bowen LJ expressly confines his observation to the case of 'persons who have contractual rights against each other'. In *High Trees*, Denning J did not expressly confine his statement of the principle to such cases and subsequently when Master off the Rolls indicated his view that the doctrine was not confined to such cases but was applicable to prevent a person from insisting on his strict legal rights 'whether arising under a contract, or on his title deeds, or by statute—when it would be inequitable for him to do so having regard to the dealings which have taken place between the parties.'[1]

Kenny J in holding that the doctrine was not so confined adopted with approval the following statement of the law in the 26th edition of Snell:

'Where by his words or conduct one party to a transaction makes to the other a promise or assurance which is intended to affect the legal relations between them, and the other party acts upon it, altering his position to his detriment, the party making the promise or assurance will not be permitted to act inconsistently with it.'[2]

Kenny J in holding, as he apparently did, that it was sufficient to bring the doctrine into operation for the parties to have been contemplating entering into a contract went further than the other decisions. They appear to have required that there be some pre-existing *legal* relationship, although not necessarily a contractual one. In view of the Supreme Court decision in *Moroney's Case* that promissory estoppel did not arise in the particular circumstances, it must remain an authority of uncertain weight for the proposition stated by Kenny J. Had promissory estoppel been relevant to that case, it might perhaps have been based on the relationship of father and son: the father was no doubt fulfilling what he regarded as his moral obligation to provide for his children as best as he could. Similarly Birkett LJ suggested in *Combe v Combe* that the relationship of husband and wife might give rise to the estoppel.

Accordingly, while the law cannot be regarded as authoritatively settled in this jurisdiction, it may be said with reasonable confidence that the doctrine of promissory estoppel is not necessarily confined to cases where there is an existing contractual relationship. How much further it extends remains to be defined, but it seems reasonable to suppose that it will arise where there is a fiduciary relationship between the parties or where there are existing rights and obligations arising out of the husband-wife or parent-child relationship which while not of a contractual nature are recognised by the law.

1 *Crabb v Arun District Council* [1975] 3 All ER 865 at 871, CA.
2 At 627.

28.09 The unequivocal statements in *Combe v Combe* that promissory estoppel cannot provide a cause of action in itself—sometimes encapsulated in the maxim that it acts as a shield and not as a sword—again reflect the concern of the courts that contracts unsupported by consideration are not enforced in a different guise. But it should be noted that it by no means follows from this principle that the estoppel can only be pleaded by defendants. On the contrary, provided it is not relied on as affording a cause of action in itself, it can also be invoked by a plaintiff to assist in establishing his own case or demolishing the defendants.

One area in which it has been suggested that it has been permissible to use the doctrine as the basis of a cause of action is where there is a fiduciary relationship between the parties and the plaintiff has suffered damage as a result of the representation. This derives some support from an authority of respectable antiquity, *Burrowes v Lock*,[1] decided in 1805 and not subsequently disapproved. In that case, the plaintiff had taken an assignment of the interest of X in a fund of which the defendant was a trustee. In answer to the plaintiff's query as to whether the fund was incumbered, the defendant in good faith but carelessly and forgetfully assured him that it was not. When it subsequently transpired that the fund was already mortgaged to Y, the plaintiff claimed damages in equity and was held entitled to recover. It is not easy to see what the fiduciary relationship was between the parties in that case and it is perhaps difficult to reconcile with the subsequent decision of the Court of Appeal in *Low v Bouverie*.[2] To-day it would perhaps be more appropriate to bring such an action in negligence on the principles laid down in *Hedley Byrne & Co Ltd v Heller & Partners Ltd*. But it has been treated as authority for the proposition that where a representation has been made which binds the conscience of the person who made it and another acts to his detriment in reliance on it, equity will not allow the aggrieved party to be without a remedy.

It might also be noted that while the 'shield, not a sword' theory has won general acceptance in other common law jurisdictions, it has not been universally followed in the United States. Indeed Doyle J found himself in the unusual position in *Shannonside Holdings (US) and another v AMI and others*[3] of deciding that it afforded a cause of action to the plaintiff, a US company who were suing another US company under a contract to be construed in accordance with the law of Florida, because the evidence established that in that state promissory estoppel could provide a cause of action in itself.

1 (1805) 10 Ves 470.
2 [1891] 3 Ch 82.
3 Unreported; judgement delivered 12 March 1980.

28.10 As we have seen, in the case of estoppel by representation, it had to be established that the representee had acted to his detriment on the faith of the representation before the estoppel could arise. While there is some authority for saying that the same applies in the case of promissory estoppel, the better view seems to be that all that is required is that the representee should have altered his position on the faith of the representation in such a manner as to render it equitable for the representor to resile from the representation. This was the view taken by Lord Denning in *W J Alan & Co v El Nasr Export Co*[1] and it is to an extent supported by the statement of Viscount Simonds in *Tool Metal Manufacturing Co v Tungsten Electrical Co* that

'the gist of the equity lies in the fact that one party by his conduct led the other to alter his position.'

But it has been argued that an analysis of the cases demonstrates that in all of them an injustice would have been caused to the representee if the representor had been allowed to resile from the representation and that this amounts to detriment. Thus, in *High Trees* the tenant had remained on in the flat and accepted the obligations of the tenancy, thus altering his position in a way which rendered it inequitable to call upon him now to accept liability for a higher rent and this, it is suggested, amounts to 'detriment' as the word is properly understood.[2]

1 [1972] 2 QB 18.
2 Spencer, Bower and Turner, op cit, p 193.

28.11 In their formulation of the principle, the privy council made it clear that the estoppel was temporary in nature. It was always open to the representor to give notice to the representee that he was withdrawing the concession and, provided the notice was reasonable, the concession was then legally withdrawn. Generally speaking, therefore, the estoppel is not permanent in its effects. Thus, an agreement by a creditor to accept a smaller sum in discharge of a debt remains unenforceable under the decision in *Foakes v Beer*:[1] the creditor is not estopped from claiming the full amount by this promise to accept a smaller one. It is, however, generally accepted that there is a category of cases in which a temporary estoppel may become permanent where events make it impossible to restore the parties to their previous position.[2]

1 (1884) 9 App Cas 605.
2 Spencer Bower and Turner, op cit, pp 399-400.

Proprietary estoppel

28.12 In the leading case of *Ramsden v Dyson*,[1] Lord Cranworth LC laid down the following legal principles:

'If a stranger begins to build on my land, supposing it to be his own and I, perceiving his mistake, abstain from setting him right and leave him to persevere in his error, a court of equity will not allow me afterwards to assert my title to the land on which he had expended money on the supposition that it was his own. It considers that, when I first saw the mistake into which he had fallen, it was my duty to be active and state my adverse title; and that it would be dishonest in me to remain wholly impassive on such an occasion, in order afterwards to profit by the mistake which I might have prevented. But it will be observed that, to raise such an inquiry, two things are required, first that the person expending his money supposes himself to be building on his own land; and, secondly, that the real owner at the time of the expenditure knows that the land belongs to him and not to the person expending money in the belief that he is the true owner.'[2]

In a subsequent decision, *Willmott v Barber*,[3] Sir Edward Fry laid down five criteria which had to be satisfied to give rise to the equity:

(i) The person relying on the alleged equity must have made a mistake as to his legal rights.

(ii) That person must have spent money or done something on the faith of his mistaken belief.

(iii) The person entitled to the legal right must be aware of his own rights.

(iv) That person must know of the other's mistaken belief as to his own rights.

(v) That person must have encouraged the other in the expenditure of the money or the doing of the other acts, either directly or by refraining from asserting his own legal rights.[4]

These criteria have been applied in many subsequent cases and the equity which thus arises when the owner of the land either positively permits another to build on it or at least simply stands by when he does so is well established in our law. Its applicability was considered by Kenny J in *Cullen v Cullen* (the facts of which are set out above) but rejected by him, since in that case M was well aware that he was putting the house on his father's land and not on his own.

In recent years, a broader approach has emerged and it has been suggested that the five criteria laid down in *Willmott v Barber* should not be considered as sacrosanct. Thus, in *Taylors Fashions Ltd v Liverpool Victoria Trustee Cos Ltd*,[5] I Oliver J said the equity should arise where

'it would be unconscionable for a party to be permitted to deny that which, knowingly or unknowingly, he has allowed or encouraged another to assume to his detriment .....'

Another example is *McMahon and Another v Kerry County Council*.[6] The defendants sold a plot of land in 1964 to the plaintiffs in the belief that the latter would build a secondary school on the site. In 1965 the plaintiffs abandoned this plan and did not visit the site again until 1968 when they discovered the defendants were preparing to build on it, whereupon they complained and the building stopped. The plaintiffs never fenced or marked off the site, upon which the defendants subsequently built two houses, the work beginning in 1972. In 1973 the plaintiffs discovered this for the first time and began proceedings, after some delay, claiming possession of the site. The defendants, after the proceedings began, put two tenants in the houses. In addition to those facts, Finlay P found that the site had no intrinsic value for the plaintiffs. The defendants relied on the principle in *Ramsden v Dyson*, but were of course in the difficulty that there was no evidence that the plaintiffs acquiesced in any way in the building and indeed had protested at an early stage against it. Consequently, at least one of the five criteria in *Willmott v Barber* was conspicuously absent. The learned President, however, while accepting that his application of the doctrine of equitable estoppel to this case was novel, considered that it would be 'unconscionable and unjust' for the plaintiffs to recover possession of the site with the two houses. In these circumstances, he granted an order for possession, but, having assessed compensation for the loss by the plaintiffs of their land, put a stay on the order which in the event of the compensation being paid within a specified time was to become permanent.

It may not seem entirely satisfactory that the owners of land should be deprived of their land against their will, even on payment of compensation, in circumstances where their own conduct has been blameless and, specifically, they have not in any way encouraged the trespasser. The facts, as the learned President emphasised, were unusual and possibly unique and the status of the case as an authority is further weakened by the fact that *Willmot v Barber* does not appear to have been cited. It accordingly remains unclear to what extent the broader approach proposed by *Taylor Fashion Ltd* can be regarded as securely established in Irish law.

1 (1866) LR 1 HL 129 at 140, 141.
2 It has been pointed out (Brady, Ir Jur (ns), Vol 20, p 439) that the doctrine had been recognised at an earlier stage by the Irish courts: see *O'Fay v Burke* (1858) 8 I Ch R 511.
3 (1880) 15 Ch D 96.
4 Cited by Finlay P in *Smith v Ireland* (1983) ILRM 300.
5 [1981] 1 All ER 897.
6 (1981) ILRM 419.

28.13 There is a feature of this form of estoppel which is, on the whole, missing in the case of promissory estoppel. The result of the successful invocation of the equity is usually to give the party relying on it a proprietary interest in the land. In some cases, it may entitle that party to no more than a charge or lien on the land for the amount he spent. In others, the owner may be permanently restrained from interfering with his possession of the land, thereby giving him a form of irrevocable personal licence. And there may even exceptionally be cases in which the owner may be required to transfer his interest, or to grant some lesser form of interest, in the land to the aggrieved party. Hence these cases are frequently described as cases of *proprietary estoppel*, although this description has not been universally approved.

28.14 There is another type of proprietary estoppel which closely resembles the category just discussed. This arises where A, the owner of land, either expressly or impliedly promises B that he will give him an interest in the land and in reliance on the promise B spends money on the land or acts to his own detriment in some other manner. Even though the promise may be unsupported by consideration, equity will depart from its usual refusal to assist a volunteer[1] where it would be unconscionable to allow the owner to repudiate his previous assurance.

The leading case is *Dillwyn v Llewelyn*[2] in which a father placed a son in possession of land and at the same time signed a document which was intended to be a conveyance of the land to him but proved not to be sufficient for that purpose. The son with the assent and approval of the father built and occupied a house on the land. After his father's death, he obtained a declaration that he was beneficially entitled to the land and an order requiring the trustees to whom the father had devised the land to convey it to him.

The decision has been followed in many cases in the common law world. Thus in *Plimmer v Wellington Corporation*,[3] the plaintiff had built a jetty into Wellington Harbour, with the encouragement of the government, which was intended to facilitate the arrival of immigrants in New Zealand. He was held entitled to compensation by the Privy Council when the jetty was compulsorily acquired on the ground that he was entitled to an 'estate or interest in the land' within the meaning of the relevant legislation. In a modern case, the same court defined the equity as follows:

> 'where an owner of land has invited or expressly encouraged another to expend money on part of his land on the faith of an assurance or promise that that part of the land will be made over to the person so expending his money a court of equity will prima facie require the owner by appropriate conveyance to fulfil his obligation and when, for example, for reasons of title, no such conveyance can effectively be made, a court of equity may declare that the person who has expended the money is entitled to an equitable charge or lien for the amount so expended.'[4]

This doctrine also arose for consideration in *Cullen v Cullen*. As we have seen, Kenny J in that case refused to grant a permanent injunction to the plaintiff requiring M to vacate the house. He stopped short, however,— admittedly with some misgivings—of ordering any interest to be conveyed to M and dismissed his counterclaim. The learned judge treated the case as essentially one of promissory estoppel which fell short of the criteria propounded in *Ramsden v Dyson* or *Dillwyn v Llewelyn*. It was argued on behalf of M that, on the authority of the latter case, the wife had acquired a beneficial interest in the lands which enabled her to pass some form of proprietary interest to M. This was rejected by Kenny J: since the wife had contributed only £620 in cash to the business and her drawings substantially exceed that sum, it would be grossly inequitable in his view to require the husband to transfer his interest in the land to the wife. His offer to give her the land remained at best an imperfect gift which equity could not perfect.[5]

1 See para 8.07, above.
2 (1862) 4 De GF & J 517.
3 (1884) 9 App Cas 699.
4 *Siew Soon Wah v Yong Tong Hong* [1973] AC 836, PC.
5 For a criticism of the decision, see Brady, 'An English and Irish View of Proprietary Estoppel', Ir Jur (ns), Vol 5, p 239.

28.15   As we have seen, the rights which a person may acquire as a result of the operation of proprietary or promissory estoppel will depend on the particular circumstances. At one end of the scale he will be entitled to a conveyance of the freehold as in *Dillwyn v Llewelyn*. Or he may be entitled to a charge or lien for the money he has spent, as where it is impossible as a matter of title to convey any interest to him. And, as in *Cullen v Cullen* and *McMahon v Kerry County Council*, there are cases in which he will preserved in his occupation of the land for his own lifetime but will not be given any greater right capable, for example, of assignment. Such a right is simply a licence as opposed to an actual estate or interest in the land and is incapable of transfer or transmission on death. But Kenny J, who regretted that on the authorities, as he viewed them, it was not possible for him to order the conveyance of the site to M, suggested that after the expiration of 12 years he would in any event have acquired at title by 'adverse possession' to the land which could be registered in the Land Registry. There are, however, difficulties in this approach also. In the first place, it seems difficult to describe possession as truly 'adverse' when the lawful owner is effectively precluded by court order from asserting his rights of ownership. In the second place, it would seem strange and indeed anomalous that whether M exchanged the strictly personal and inalienable right of a licensee for the full blown status of a fee simple owner depended on whether the land was registered or unregistered.[1]

A similar approach—save as to the last aspect—was adopted by the Court of Appeal in *Inwards v Baker*.[2] In that case, the defendant JB wanted to build a bungalow but had not enough money to buy the site he wanted. His father suggested that he build it on his land, which JB did largely at his own expense. By his will—made long before he acquired the land on which the bungalow was erected—the father left all his property to I, a lady with whom he had lived for many years, and the two children he had had by her. She appointed the two children as her fellow trustees and they ultimately took proceedings to recover possession from JB, claiming that all he had was a revocable licence. The Court of Appeal dismissed the trustees' claim, holding unanimously that JB was entitled to remain in possession of the bungalow for the rest of his life. Lord Denning MR cited a passage from *Plimmer v Wellington Corporation* in which it was said that the equity arising from the expenditure on the land did not fail

· 'merely on the ground that the interest to be secured has not been expressly indicated ..... the court must look at the circumstances in each case to decide in what way the equity can be satisfied.'[3]

In some cases in England, however, it has been said that the equity of the plaintiff to remain in possession in such circumstances may give rise to a proprietary interest recognised by the law to ensure that the requirements of conscience and justice are met. These 'new model' constructive trusts, as they have been called, have been discussed in Chapter 13.

1 In *McMahon v Kerry County Council*, above, however, Finlay P also took the view that at the end of the limitation period the defendants would be entitled to be registered as owners.
2 [1965] 2 QB 29, CA.
3 At 713-714.

Chapter 29

Constructive fraud: undue influence and unconscionable transactions

29.01 From its early days, equity has always given relief to the victims of fraud. But not merely did it give its assistance to those who were the victims of fraud in its more popular sense where it is associated with morally reprehensible conduct. Such fraud, at least where it took the form of deceit resulting in damage to the plaintiff, could be the subject of an award of damages at common law.[1] Equity also concerned itself with cases where the conduct of the defendant might well have been morally defensible and yet had resulted in an injustice which the chancery jurisdiction could remedy where the courts of common law were powerless. This was not to say that where the defendant's conduct was also morally culpable, the plaintiff was without a remedy in equity: but the salient feature of the equitable jurisdiction was that it operated in cases where, however innocent or otherwise the defendant's conduct might have been, the court would consider it unconscionable that he should retain an advantage which he had derived from the transaction in question. It is this species of fraud—frequently referred to as 'constructive fraud'—with which we are concerned in this chapter and we confine our discussion to the two circumstances in which the doctrine has been most frequently invoked, undue influence and unconscionable transactions.[2]

1 *Derry v Peek* (1889) 14 App Cas 337; *Northern Bank Finance Corpn Ltd v Charlton* [1979] IR 149.
2 For more detailed discussion of the Irish authorities, see Sheridan, *Fraud in Equity*, and Dr Robert Clarke's more recent study (published in Canada) *Inequality of Bargaining Power*. See also TS McCann, 'Undue Influence', Ir Jur (ns) Vol II, 205.

Undue influence in general

29.02 The courts do not exist to protect people from the consequences of their own folly. If they choose to give away property in a rash or ill-advised fashion, that is their misfortune: were it otherwise, of course, anyone who thought better of a transaction, whether it took the form of a gift to a friend or relative or a commercial bargain, could rush to court to have it undone, and chaos and uncertainty would follow; Lord Nottingham's celebrated observation that 'equity mends no man's bargain'[1] may seem harsh to the layman, but it enshrines an important legal principle based on the empirical wisdom for which English law is justly renowned.

In the formative period of equity, however, successive lord chancellors made it clear that the court would assert a jurisdiction to set aside a transaction, or decline to enforce it, where, in the words of Lord Eldon, the transaction did not come into being as a result of 'the pure, unsullied will'[2] of one of the contracting parties. If it could be shown that a particular transaction was the result of dominion exercised by one party over the other—if, in short it was the result of what came to be called 'undue influence'—the court would intervene. Obviously, a voluntary disposition of property was the most obvious example of a case where the jurisdiction might be invoked, but, as we shall see, it was by no means confined to such instances.

1 *Maynard v Moseley* (1676) 3 Swan 651 at 655.
2 *Huguenin v Baseley* (1807) 14 Ves 273.

29.03 As was made clear in the leading English case on undue influence, *Allcard v Skinner*,[1] the jurisdiction of equity to intervene in a transaction on the ground of undue influence arises in two broadly different categories. In the first, there is a *presumption* of undue influence arising from the relationship of the parties. In such a case, it will be assumed that the transaction being attacked was the result of the undue influence, unless the party presumed to exercise the influence can prove that the transaction was the spontaneous choice of the other party acting under circumstances which enabled him to make a free decision. The onus of proof, in such cases, in short, moves to the party alleged to have used the undue influence. In the second category of cases, where no such relationship exists, the court only intervenes where the party alleging undue influence affirmatively proves that the transaction was its result.[2]

1 (1887) 36 Ch D 145, CA.
2 The doctrine of 'undue influence' discussed in this chapter should not be confused with the 'undue influence' sometimes relied on as a ground on which a will should be condemned. As a general rule, there is no question of a presumption of undue influence arising in such cases: it must be affirmatively proved by the party claiming that the execution of the will was procured by such influence.

The presumption of undue influence

29.04 In the first category of cases—where there is a presumption of undue influence—two elements must be present in order to give rise to the presumption. First, one party must have derived a significant benefit from the transaction. Most commonly this will arise where there is a substantial gift of property which cannot be accounted for by the motives which ordinarily actuate people.[1] Secondly, the relationship between the parties must be such that the donor placed a special degree of trust in the donee. The law has recognised certain categories of relationships as being of this nature, such as parent and child, guardian and ward, solicitor and client, spiritual adviser and believer, and trustee and beneficiary. The most important of these defined categories are dealt with in more detail below.[2] But the presumption is not confined to any stated form of relationship: it arises in any case where the evidence establishes that the donor placed special trust in the donee.

So in *Gregg v Kidd*,[3] Budd J held that the presumption arose where the undue influence alleged was that of a mother and son, resulting in the transfer of a farm by her brother-in-law, in declining health and with impaired faculties, to the son. The evidence established in the view of the learned judge that the donor was fearful of being left to live on his own and that the requisite degree of trust and confidence had been placed by him in his sister-in-law to bring the presumption into operation.

But it is not every gift that will bring the presumption into operation. It may be of a relatively insignificant nature and hence explicable on ordinary grounds of affection. Nor is it every relationship of trust that will give rise to the presumption. As Fletcher Moulton LJ remarked in *Re Coomber*,[4] the circumstances in which trust and confidence are reposed by one person in another vary from expecting an errand boy to bring back one's change at one end of the spectrum to the most intimate and confidential relationship at the other. Unless the case falls into one of the recognised categories already mentioned—such as parent and child—it is for the court to determine on the facts of each case whether the relationship is of such a nature as to give rise to the presumption.

1 *Allcard v Skinner*, above at 185.
2 See para 29.06, below.
3 [1956] IR 183. Cf *Re Craig* [1971] Ch 95 (secretary companion to octogenarian widower).
4 [1911] 1 Ch 723 at 728-729.

29.05 It should be observed that the presumption will arise in such cases even though the motives of the person exercising the influence may have been perfectly proper and even altruistic. In this it differs from the second category of cases, where no special relationship exists, and where it must be proved that the transaction was the result of some wrongful pressure on the part of the defendant. Thus, returning to the first category, a parent may advise his child to settle property on trust, not with a view to obtaining an advantage for himself, but simply out of understandable concern that the property may be dissipated. Yet such a settlement will give rise to the presumption of undue influence, however kindly may have been the parent's motives, and will be liable to be set aside unless the parent can prove that it was the child's free and informed decision,[1] usually, although not exclusively, by evidence that the child was independently advised before executing the settlement.

Similarly, where a gift to a religious community is apparently prompted solely by the devotion of a particular member and without any evidence of pressure being brought to bear on him by the community, the presumption will arise.[2] In all such cases, whether they come within the categories expressly recognised or are instances of other relationships of trust sufficient to give rise to the presumption, the reason underlying the doctrine is public policy. Courts of equity have traditionally been jealous of such transactions because of the manifest ease with which relationships of this nature may be exploited by a dominant partner and hence have required the person obtaining the benefit to prove that it came to him as a result of a free and informed decision by the other party.

Unfortunately some recent dicta from eminent judges in Northern Ireland and England have tended to cloud this well established and salutary doctine. There is now some support for the view that it is necessary to establish not merely the existence of the relationship but that the transaction was 'wrongful' before the presumption can arise. This appears to have been the view taken by Lord Lowry LCJ in *Regina (Proctor) v Hutton (No 2)*[3] and by Lord Scarman in *National Westminister Bank plc v Morgan*.[4] If all that was intended to be conveyed by the observations in question was that the impugned transaction must have at least been disadvantageous to the plaintiff in some way—and not a perfectly straightforward commercial transaction as in *National Westmins-*

ter Bank plc v Morgan—they would be unexceptionable. But the latter decision seems to go further and suggest that before the presumption arises it must be shown that the transaction was wrongful, in the sense that one person had deliberately taken advantage of another.

In *Allcard v Skinner*, Cotton LJ said of the cases in which the presumption arose:

> 'the Court intereferes, not on the ground that any wrongful act has been committed by the donee, but on the ground of public policy, and to prevent the relations which existed between the parties and the influence arising therefrom being abused.'[5]

Lord Lowry, in *Regina (Proctor) v Hutton (No 2)*, commented on this passage:

> 'The learned Lord Justice was not there saying that a gift would be set aside despite the fact that no wrongful act had been committed between the parties.'[6]

This is, no doubt literally true, but it seems difficult to maintain that Cotton LJ was not drawing in plain terms a distinction between transactions the wrongfulness of which it was necessary to establish, since the presumption did not arise, and those in which wrongfulness did not have to be proved, because of the nature of the relationship.

Lord Scarman in *Westminster Bank plc v Morgan* rejected an interpretation of *Allcard v Skinner* which had found favour in the Court of Appeal and which would allow the presumption to arise where there was no evidence of any disadvantage to the party seeking to set aside to transaction, eg a straightforward commercial transaction such as the mortgage in that case. This is not surprising—there do not appear to have been any other decisions in which the plaintiff was not relying on some disadvantageous feature and in its most characteristic form the presumption arose in the case of gifts—but Lord Scarman's speech is also open to the alarming interpretation that it is not enough to establish the necessary form of fiduciary relationship, together with some element of disadvantage to the plaintiff. It is also necessary to establish positively that one party took an unfair advantage of his dominant position. This comes perilously close to eliminating the presumption entirely from English law, but it is difficult to see what other meaning can be attached to certain passages in Lord Scarman's speech. In particular, he cites with approval a decision of the Judicial Committee of the Privy Council in *Poosathurai v Kannappa Chettiar*.[7] In that case Lord Shaw of Dunfermline stated the law to be as follows:

> 'It is a mistake .... to treat undue influence as having been established by a proof of the relations of the parties having been such that one naturally relied upon the other for advice and the other was in a position to dominate the will of the first in giving it. Up to that point "influence" alone has been made out. Such influence may be used wisely, judiciously and helpfully. But, whether by the law of India or the law of England, more than mere influence must be proved so as to render influence in the language of the law "undue". It must be established that the person in a position of domination has used that position to obtain unfair advantage for himself, and so to cause injury to the person relying on his authority or aid.'

This particular passage was not one of those cited by Lord Scarman in *Morgan's Case* but was not expressly disowned by him. While it may be that Lord Shaw's mind was simply not directed to the presumption which may arise from the relationship of the parties, it is clear that in the unqualified manner in which he laid it down this proposition is unsustainable.

It is submitted that, pace Lords Lowry and Scarman, the law in this jurisdiction remains as stated in *Allcard v Skinner*, ie that where the presumption of undue influence arises the transaction will be set aside in the absence of evidence adduced by the defendant to rebut the presumption, whether or not the plaintiff has affirmatively established that an unfair advantage was taken of him by the defendant. To this the only acceptable qualification is that the presumption will not arise where there is no element of disadvantage, eg where it is a straightforward commercial transaction. This view of the law has recently been reasserted by the Court of Appeal in *Goldsworthy v Brickwell and Another*[8] and, it is thought, correctly so.

1 *Bullock v Lloyd's Bank Ltd* [1955] Ch 317.
2 *Hugenin v Basely* (1807) 14 Ves 273; *Allcard v Skinner*, above.
3 (1978) N1 39.
4 [1985] AC 686.
5 At 171.
6 At 146.
7 (1919) LR 47 Ind App 471.
8 [1987] 2 WLR 133.

29.06 We now consider the more significant relationships which have been expressly recognised by the courts as giving rise to the presumption, again emphasising that it is not confined to such relationships.

(a) Parent and child. A child who has attained the age of majority (now 18) is free to dispose of his property as he wishes. But the law takes account of the natural tendency of children to be influenced by their parents and the presumptions of undue influence accordingly arises when the child enters into a transaction, such as a substantial gift of property, which confers a benefit on the parent.[1] The presumption similarly arises when the benefit accrues, not to the parent, but to a third party as a result of advice or pressure of any sort (however well meant) by the parent.[2] Moreover, while the cases in which the transaction is most likely to be challenged are those where the transaction has been effected shortly after the child has attained his majority, the presumption can also arise in the case of a child of relatively advanced years or one who is married and no longer living under the parental roof.[3] In such cases, it must be established that the child has been emancipated from the parental dominion: otherwise the presumption of undue influence will continue.[4] There is some disagreement, however, as to whether the emancipation from the parental influence must be affirmatively proved in *all* cases: in *Re Pauling's Settlement's Trusts*,[5] the Court of Appeal held that the court was entitled to infer from the respective ages of parent and child that the latter could be regarded as emancipated without evidence. In Australia, the view has been taken that the onus of establishing emancipation must be discharged in every case by the person seeking to uphold the transaction and that the age of the child is merely one of the factors to be taken into account.[6]

(b) Guardian and ward. Similarly the law presumes undue influence in the case of such transactions and the presumption does not necessarily cease with the ward's discharge from wardship.[7] It will be a question of fact in each case as to whether the ward can be regarded as emancipated from the guardian's influence.

(c) Solicitor and client. It is clear that the presumption arises where the relationship is continuous and reasonably close,[8] but doubts have been expressed as to whether it necessarily arises where there has been only slight contact between solicitor and client or where he is just one of a number retained by the client.[9] It is, however, clear that where there has been such a relationship in the past, the presumption will continue even after it has ceased, at least in relation to transactions which can reasonably be regarded as coming within the ambit of the confidence reposed in the solicitor.[10]

(d) Spiritual advisers. The tendency of people to make ill considered dispositions of property under some form of religious pressure is well known and where it is established that someone has entered into a transaction to his own disadvantage while acting under the advice or influence of his spiritual advisor the presumption of undue influence arises. Indeed the two cases which contain the most authoritative expositions of the law on the topic of undue influence were both ones in which gifts of property were challenged on this precise ground: *Hugenin v Basley*[11] and *Allcard v Skinner*.[12] The principle is, of course, not confined to cases of religious 'enthusiasm', as it is called in the older decisions, but extends to the influence exerted by spiritualists and others carrying on similar activities.[13]

(e) Medical advisors. The principle set out in the preceding paragraph also applies to medical advisors, including not merely surgeons and doctors, but also nurses. It has not, however, been extended to dentists.[14]

(f) Other relationships of trust. The presumption, as we have seen, is not confined to the categories just mentioned, but in any other cases the facts must be examined with care in order to determine whether it should arise. It will normally arise, for example, in transactions between beneficiary and trustee.[15] It was at one time thought that it also arose in the case of benefits conferred by a woman on her *fiance*, but the views of Maugham J in *Lloyd's Bank*,[16] where he said that young women placed such trust in their husbands to be that they would sign anything put in front of them were already looking a little old fashioned when the Court of Appeal came to decide *Zamet v Hyman*[17] in 1961. In that case, while it was held that a gift by an elderly woman to the slightly older man to whom she was engaged could not stand on the particular facts, Donovan LJ rejected the suggestion that in modern circumstances any presumption arose from the mere fact of engagement. If anything, this view would have even more force to-day. Nor does the relationship of husband and wife give rise to any presumption—married life would be intolerable if it had to be established that every gift of significance had been the subject of independent advice.[18]

The relationship of banker and customer does not of itself give rise to a presumption of undue influence.[19] It may be, however, that in particular circumstances a banker may place hmself in such a position vis-a-vis a customer that a court will infer that the latter reposed a degree of confidence and trust in him sufficient to give rise to the presumption. This was held to have been the case in *Lloyd's Bank Ltd v Bundy*[20] by the Court of Appeal, but the special nature of the facts necessary to give rise to the presumption was emphasised by the House of Lords in *National Westminster Bank plc v Morgan*.[21]

In the latter case, a husband and wife were in serious arrears with a building society who were threatening to repossess the family home. The husband's business was in serious financial trouble and he was indebted to the bank. The house was the joint property of the husband and wife, and having been told by the manager that the bank would be prepared to provide enough in the way of a loan to stave off the building society, the wife agreed to execute a second mortgage on the strength of an assurance from the manager that the rescue package was confined to the house and that the mortgage would not secure the husband's business debts. In fact, the mortgage in its terms secured all indebtedness, past and future, of husband and wife to the bank: the manager had not adverted to this. In the event, the bank never sought to enforce the security except in relation to the house rescue package. It was held by the House of Lords, reversing the Court of Appeal, that they were entitled to do so: the mortgage transaction was a normal commercial one with no element of disadvantage to the wife. Had it not been available, the building society would have repossessed the house. The relationship of banker and customer did not, of itself, give rise to the presumption, which in any event would only arise where there was some element of disadvantage involved. The wife in this case had clearly failed to discharge the onus of proof which accordingly lay on her of establishing that the transaction was the result of undue influence.

1   *McMakin v Hibernian Bank* [1905] 1 IR 296; *Lancashire Loans Ltd v Black* [1934] 1 KB 380.
2   *Bullock v Lloyd's Bank Ltd*, above.
3   *Lancashire Loans Ltd v Black*, above.
4   Ashburner, *Principles of Equity*, 2nd edn, p 302.
5   [1964] Ch 303 at 337, CA.
6   *Lamotte v Lamotte* (1942) 42 SR NSW 99 at 102-103 per Roper J.
7   *Hylton v Hylton* (1754) 2 Ves Sen 547.
8   *Wright v Carter* [1903] 1 Ch 27, CA.
9   Meagher, Gummow & Lehane, p 375.
10   *Allison v Clayhills* (1907) 97 LT 709 at 712 per Parker J; *Demerara Bauxite Co v Hubbard* [1923] AC 673.
11   Above.
12   Above. In that case, however, the donor was held to have lost her right to recover the gift by laches (see para 3.10, above). *White v Meade* (1840) 2 Ir Eq R 420 appears to be the only reported Irish case where a gift to a religious adviser was set aside. In that case, however, undue influence was held to have been affirmatively proved. See also *Fulham v M'Carthy* (1848) 1 HL Cas 703; *Kirwan v Cullen* (1854) 4 I Ch R 322; *Murphy v O'Neill* [1936] NI 16.
13   *Dent v Bennett* (1839) 4 My & Cr 269.
14   *Brooks v Alker* (1975) 60 DLR 3d 577.
15   *Hatch v Hatch* (1804) 9 Ves 292.
16   [1931] 1 Ch 289.
17   [1961] 1 WLR 1442.
18   *Nedby v Nedby* (1852) 5 De G & Sm 377.
19   *National Westminster Bank plc v Morgan*, above.
20   [1975] QB 326.
21   Above.

Rebutting the presumption of undue influence

29.07   The presumption is rebutted by proof, on the balance of probabilities, that the transaction was the result of the free exercise of the will of the party alleged to have acted under undue influence. While one way of doing this is to show that the party concerned was independently advised by a competent person, that is not the only manner in which the presumption may be rebutted. The law was stated as follows by Budd J in *Gregg v Kidd*:[1]

'The presumption may..... be rebutted either by showing that the donor has had competent independent advice and acted of his own free will or in some other way. As Lord Hailsham says in *Inche Noriah v Shaik Allie Bin Omar*:[2] "the most obvious way to prove that the gift was the result of the free exercise of independent will is to establish that the gift was made after the nature and effect of the transaction had been fully explained to the donor by some independent and qualified person so completely as to satisfy the court that the donor was acting independently of any influence from the donee and with full appreciation of what he was doing." If that method of rebutting the presumption is adopted, and it is not the only method open, the advice relied on must, in the words of Lord Hailsham, "be given with a knowledge of all relevant circumstances and must be such as a competent and honest adviser would give if acting solely in the interests of the donor". The nature of that advice must vary with the circumstances of each particular case.'

The independent advice which may be successfully relied on to rebut the presumption of undue influence does not have to be that of a solicitor, although it frequently is. In some circumstances, a person qualified in another sphere—not necessarily a professional person—may be the one best fitted to give the sort of advice which will enable the donor to make a free and informed decision. Nor is it necessary that the advice should have been acted upon. An observation to the contrary effect by Farwell LJ[3] was expressly disapproved of by Budd J in *Gregg v Kidd*, adopting the views of the judicial committee in *Inche Noriah v Shaik Allie Bin Omar*.[4]

1 Above.
2 [1929] AC 127.
3 *Powell v Powell* [1900] 1 Ch 243 at 246.
4 A different view of the law is taken by Meagher, Gummow & Lehane. Apart from the fact that the weight of authority is in favour of the view stated above, however, it seems illogical to take compliance with advice as a necessary proof of the exercise of an independent will. The decision, if it is to be genuinely independent, must remain that of the donor: one does not achieve that result by requiring that for the gift to be effective the donor must have in essence abdicated his right to make the decision in favour of the adviser.

29.08 An instrument procured by undue influence will be set aside as against a third party if the latter is aware of the circumstances which gave rise to the right to have the instrument set aside. This was also held by Black J in *Provincial Bank of Ireland v McKeever*,[1] applying earlier English decisions of *Kempson v Ashbee*,[2] *Turnbull & Co v Duval*[3] and *Chaplin and Co Ltd v Brammall*.[4] In *McKeever's Case*, the trustees of a farm settled by a will had incurred a substantial liability to the plaintiff bank as a result of expenses incurred by them in running the farm. On their advice and that of their solicitor, who was also their uncle, the defendants, the beneficiaries under the will, executed mortgages securing this overdraft. The trustees thereby obtained a benefit in the strict sense since their personal liability ceased when the mortgages were executed and Black J held that the presumption of undue influence arose. (A good example, incidentally, of how it can arise without any semblance of what would commonly be regarded as wrongful conduct.) He also held that the bank, being aware of the circumstances, could not successfully plead that they were third parties who had not themselves exercised undue influence and did not take under a party who had. The bank who sought to enforce the mortgage deed pleaded that they did not stand in any fiduciary relationship to the mortgagors nor did they take under the trustees who were. Black J held, however, that since they were aware of the circumstances under which the deed was executed, they could not rely on this plea. But on the facts of the case, he held that the presumption of undue influence had been rebutted and the bank succeeded.

1 (1941) IR 471.
2 (1874) 10 Ch App 15.
3 [1902] AC 429.
4 [1908] 1 KB 233.

Undue influence where no presumption arises

29.09 Where no presumption arises, undue influence must be proved by the party seeking to set aside the transaction. There cannot be said to be any general principle relevant to the standard of proof in such cases: where no presumption arises, everything depends on a 'meticulous consideration' of the facts in the particular case, to use the expression in Hanbury[1] cited recently with approval by Lord Scarman in *National Westminster Bank plc v Morgan*.[2] The court has to consider in each case whether a person proferring advice, or even no more than information, may be said to have crossed the borderline between simply recommending a course of action and applying pressure which made the transaction no longer the spontaneous act of the other party. Actual threats—as in *Williams v Bayley*[3] where a father executed mortgages under pressure from bankers who where threatening to prosecute his son—will generally suffice to establish undue influence. But less overt pressure—such as was held to have been exerted by the bank manager in *Lloyds Bank Ltd v Bundy*[4]—may be enough.

1 Hanbury p 613
2 Above.
3 (1866) LR 1 HL 200.
4 Above.

Unconscionable transactions

29.10 Closely related to the doctrine of undue influence but to be carefully distinguished from it is the equitable jurisdiction to set aside *unconscionable transactions*. In essence it means that the court will not allow an improvident agreement to stand where the parties were on unequal terms and the weaker had not been protected. Thus, the court would not allow an agreement to be enforced where a poor or uneducated person had entered into such an improvident bargain, without his interests being adequately protected.

The jurisdiction originated with the concern of equity to protect expectant heirs from entering into what were quaintly called 'catching bargains'. A young nobleman with a taste for high life could be easily persuaded to sell or mortgage his prospective inheritance and where he did so the court would usually require the person getting the benefit of the agreement to prove that it was fair and reasonable. In the Irish case of *O'Rorke v Bolingbroke*,[1] Lord Hatherly in the House of Lords explained it in the following terms:

'My Lords, the Court of Chancery assumed jurisdiction, at a very early period, to set aside transactions in which expectant heirs had dealt with their expectations, when the court was satisfied that they had not been adequately protected against the pressure put upon them by their poverty....'

(Having reviewed the earlier authorities, he went on:)

'It sufficiently appears that the principle on which Equity originally proceeded to set aside such transactions was for the protection of family property; but this principle being once established, the Court extended its aid to all cases in which the parties to a contract have not met upon equal terms. In ordinary cases, each party to a bargain must take care of his own interest, and it will not be presumed that undue advantage or contrivance has been resorted to on either side; but in the case of the "expectant heir" or of persons under pressure without protection, and in the case of dealings with uneducated ignorant persons, the burden of showing the fairness of the transaction is thrown on the person who seeks to obtain the benefit of the contract.'

As the jurisdiction developed, then, it extended to transactions of all kinds and not simply to bargains with expectant heirs. Nor was it confined to gifts of property: it applied to sales of property where the consideration was excessive or inadequate as the case might be, although 'a Court must be very much slower to undo a transaction for value.' As to the nature of the inequality which might bring the doctrine into operation its wide ranging scope is perhaps best summed up by Fullagar J in the Australian decision of *Blomley v Ryan*:[2]

'The circumstances adversely affecting a party which may induce a court of equity either to refuse its aid or to set a transaction aside are of great variety and can hardly be satisfactorily classified. Among them are poverty or need of any kind, sickness, age, sex, infirmity of body or mind, drunkenness, illiteracy or lack of education, lack of assistance or explanation where assistance or explanation is necessary. The common characteristic seems to be that they have the effect of placing one party at a serious disadvantage vis-a-vis the other.'

It was also suggested in that case, on the authority of *Cooke v Clayworth*,[3] that it is not essential that the transaction should be unfair itself. In the latter case, the Court refused to grant specific performance of a contract for sale where the vendor was drunk at the time it was executed, although there was nothing unfair in the terms of the bargain itself. But there seems to have been no case in which a contract for proper consideration, neither excessive nor inadequate, was actually *set aside* because of the inequality of the parties. (In *Cooke v Clayworth*,[4] while specific performance was refused, the party seeking enforcement was left to his remedy at law.)

1 (1877) 2 App Cas 814, HL.
2 (1956) 99 CLR 362.
3 (1811) 18 Ves 12.
4 Above.

29.11 In recent times, an attempt was made by Lord Denning MR to establish in English law a general doctrine of 'inequality of contract'. In *Lloyds Bank Ltd v Bundy*,[1] where the transaction was set aside on the ground of undue influence exerted by the bank manager, he claimed that there existed in English law a general jurisdiction to interfere where there was 'inequality of bargaining power' between the parties. This attempt to bring together a number of different branches of the law under the umbrella of a new doctrine met with a mixed response from commentators[2] and has more recently been roundly condemned by the House of Lords. In *National Westminster Bank plc v Morgan*,[3] Lord Scarman, with whom the rest of their lordships unanimously concurred, emphatically denied the existence of any such doctrine and rejected the suggestion that this was a useful area for judicial innovation. Parliament had been notably active in providing legislative solutions to the problems posed by inequality of bargaining power between large corporate institutions and the individual citizen and Lord Scarman clearly felt that they should be allowed to get on with it. In this jurisdiction, where there has also been legislative reform of this nature and where more may be anticipated, it is thought that a similar approach is likely from the courts.

1 Above.
2 For, Cheshire, Fifoot & Furmston, 11th edn, pp 299-302; against, Meagher, Gummow & Lehane, p 1530.
3 Above.

29.12 The classic ingredients, then, of an unconscionable transaction which will attract the intervention of the court are twofold. It must be improvident and the person getting the benefit must have been in a relatively stronger postion. In the case of voluntary settlements, the absence of any power in the donor to revoke the settlement may be an important factor in determining whether the transaction is improvident. Moreover, as in the case of undue influence, the absence of any independent advice will also weigh with the court in deciding whether to grant rescission.

All these aspects of the doctrine of unconscionable bargains were illustrated in the leading Irish case on the topic, *Grealish v Murphy*.[1] The plaintiff was an elderly farmer in the West of Ireland whom the trial judge (Gavan Duffy J) found to have been feeble minded at the time of the transaction. He went in some fear of his neighbours because of an obscure background of agrarian troubles, including boycotting, and seemed to have thought that the solution to his problems might be to bring in the defendant, a much younger man without any resources of his own, to run the farm. He instructed his solicitors to arrange for the transfer of the farm to the defendant, the only quid pro quo being a covenant by the latter to permit the old man to spend the rest of his days on the farm and provide for his maintenance. There was no power of revocation and no sanctions provided in the event of the young man reneging on his promises. Nor was there any provision for the contingency of the defendant predeceasing the plaintiff. Gavan Duffy J found that there was no presumption of undue influence—the young man was wholly unrelated to the older and they had not known each other for long—nor any positive evidence that the transaction was the result of such influence. On the contrary, it seemed to have been largely the old man's idea. But it was clearly grossly improvident and, moreover, while the plaintiff had consulted his solicitor who prepared the fatal deed, Gavan Duffy J found that the latter was not sufficiently well informed to give the plaintiff the sort of independent advice which might have saved the transaction. It accordingly fell squarely within the principles laid down in *O'Rorke v Bolingbroke*[2] since the parties had not met on equal terms, and was set aside.

1 [1946] IR 35.
2 Above.

Chapter 30

Abuse of confidence

30.01 The equitable doctrine of confidentiality has developed significantly in recent years in Ireland, along with other common law countries, but it must not be thought that the doctrine itself is in any sense novel. As we shall see, the willingness of equity to intervene in a case where one party was abusing the confidence placed in him by another was well established in the first half of the last century. But it has been given renewed vigour in modern times by the growth of the 'information economy,' the greatly enhanced value of 'intellectual property' and the inadequacy, in some areas, of the law of copyright, patents and trade marks in protecting such property from unjust exploitation. Thus, in the leading modern Irish case of *House of Spring Gardens Ltd and others v Point Blank Ltd and others*,[1] the fact that the plaintiffs were entitled to protection for infringement of copyright and had also registered patent applications in respect of the subject matter of the proceedings did not prevent them from obtaining equitable relief under the doctrine of abuse of confidence.

The doctrine, as we shall see, has not been confined to commercial law, but the extent to which it enables governments to protect themselves against alleged breaches of confidentiality by their own officials has given rise to controversy in some highly publicised cases in Ireland and other jurisdictions in recent times.[2] Moreover, developments in the law of confidentiality in what might be called the public domain, and particularly where the topic of telephone tapping and various forms of technological information gathering are involved, have raised constitutional questions as to the extent to which a right of privacy exists in our law and if so the manner in which it may be protected.[3]

1 [1984] IR 611.
2 See para 30.08, below.
3 See para 30.05, below.

The origin and nature of the doctrine

30.02 In its most succinct form, the doctrine of confidentiality was defined as follows by Lord Greene MR in *Saltman Engineering Co Ltd v Campbell Engineering Co Ltd*:[1]

'If a defendant is proved to have used confidential information, directly or indirectly obtained from a plaintiff, without the consent, express or implied, of the plaintiff, he will be guilty of an infringement of the plaintiff's rights.'

This statement was adopted with approval by Costello J in *House of Spring Gardens Ltd and others v Point Bank Ltd and others* and by O'Higgins CJ on appeal in the same case. However, while it states the law with admirable brevity, it naturally requires considerable expansion if the scope of the doctrine is to be properly grasped.

The older decisions — which were also reviewed by Costello J — recognised that, entirely apart from any contractual obligation, which might rest upon a defendant, he could be restrained in equity from committing an abuse of confidence. Thus in *Prince Albert v Strange*,[2] Queen Victoria's consort sought to restrain the publishing of certain etchings by the queen and a catalogue advertising them. The etchings had been sent to a printer so that additional copies could be made and one of his servants passed on copies to the defendant who produced the offending catalogue. The etchings were obviously protected by copyright, but the catalogue was not. There was, of course, no contract between the plaintiff and the defendant, but Lord Cottenham LC held that the etchings had come into the latter's possession because of a breach of the royal confidence reposed in the printer of which the defendant was aware. Hence he could be enjoined against printing the catalogue on the ground that he was in breach of the equitable duty of confidentiality.

1 (1948) 65 RPC 203.
2 (1849) 18 LJ Ch 120.

30.03 Two important features accordingly emerged at an early stage: the duty of confidentiality arose independently of any obligation in contract and was enforceable in the exclusive equitable jurisdiction. Second, it could extend to third parties where they were aware of the confidential basis on which the plaintiff had parted with the information. Thus, the duty of confidentiality may arise, where one party has acquired information of a commercially valuable nature during negotiations which never ripened into a contract.

A modern example is *Seager v Copydex Ltd*[1] where the plaintiff had invented a carpet grip and took out a patent on it. He tried to interest the defendants in marketing the product and during the course of their negotiations gave them details not only of his own grip, but also of an alternative grip. The negotiations failed but the defendants subsequently marketed a product which was based on the alternative grip. Although they were found to have acted honestly throughout — they had simply not adverted to the possibility that the plaintiff might be entitled to profit from the marketing of what was essentially his brain-child — it was held that they were obliged to pay damages for what amounted to a breach of the duty of confidentiality. Lord Denning MR pointed out that

'The law on this subject does not depend on any implied contract. It depends on the broad principle of equity that he who has received information in confidence shall not take unfair advantage of it. He must not make use of it to the prejudice of him who gave it without obtaining his consent.'[2]

Similarly, after a contract has terminated, a person may be accountable in equity for making use of confidential information which he has acquired during the currency of the contract. A contract of employment, for example, will frequently contain terms restraining the employee from in effect competing with his former employer if or when the contract comes to an end. Such a term, unless it constitutes an unreasonable restraint of trade, will be enforced by the courts. Similarly, the contract may preclude the employee from making use of confidential information which he may have acquired during the course of his employment. So in *Thomas Marshall Ltd v Guinle*³ the plaintiffs sought to restrain their former managing director from making use of confidential information which he had acquired during the course of his employment to their detriment. The contract merely prohibited the 'disclosure' of the information and Megarry V-C held that it did not inhibit the 'use' *per se* of the information even to the injury of his former employees. It did, however, constitute a breach of the equitable duty of confidentiality for which he was accountable. But it should be noted that this principle will not extend to a case where the employee has simply improved his own skill and aptitude of which he subsequently makes use.

Nor is the right to relief confined to cases in which the 'information' can reasonably be regarded as a form of property. Clearly in many cases, most obviously drawings and plans, it can take that form, but once it is appreciated that the doctrine is equitable and operates on the conscience of any person who has come into the possession of confidential information which it would be an abuse of such confidence to make use of, it will be seen that it is not necessary that the information in question should itself be capable of constituting an interest in property. It also follows that even where a person comes into possession of the information in circumstances which, in another context would constitute him a bona fide purchaser without notice, he can be subsequently accountable in equity if with knowledge of the confidentiality he makes use of it.

1 [1967] 2 All ER 415.
2 At 417.
3 [1979] Ch 227.

The requirement of secrecy

30.04 It is obvious enough that it is only confidential information that will attract the protection of equity. If what the plaintiff has imparted to the confidant is already generally known, there is no justification for intervention by the court. But difficulty has been experienced in determining whether another publication by the plaintiff has deprived him of the right to restrain others from making use of it.

The publication may, after all, have been partial only, in which case the defendant may be accountable for making use of the undisclosed material. And even a publication of all the elements of a trade secret or industrial process may not deprive the plaintiff of his remedy against someone to whom he has disclosed the relevant information in confidence. If he has learned the details of the process or secret in advance of other competitors, he may have an advantage of which they are deprived: he may already have gone through preliminary stages of tests, detailed designs, 'tooling up' and so on before the information is generally available. In the words of Roxburgh J in *Terrapin Builders Ltd v Builders Supply Co Ltd*,¹

'a person who has obtained information in confidence is not allowed to use it as a spring-board for activities detrimental to the person who has made the confidential communication, and spring board it remains even when all the features have been published or can be ascertained by actual inspection by members of the public.'

This 'spring-board' principle as it has become known, was adopted with approval by Costello J in *House of Spring Gardens Ltd and others v Point Blank Ltd and others*. The circumstances in which prior publication may prevent a plaintiff from obtaining this form of relief were considered by both Costello J and the Supreme Court in that case, which must now be considered in more detail.

The facts are of considerable complexity and can only be baldly summarised. The case concerned the development by one of the plaintiffs of a bullet proof vest for use by military personnel and police officers. He came to a number of agreements with some of the defendants as to the commercial exploitation of the vest. The latter through their personal contacts in Libya obtained a profitable contract with the Libyan authorities for the supply of the vest to the latter. Relations between the plaintiffs and the defendants ultimately broke down, and were the subject of earlier proceedings and ultimately of a compromise. One of the terms of the compromise related to the payment of royalties in respect of any further contract with the Libyan authorities. In circumstances which Costello J found to be cloaked in secrecy and deliberate deception of the plaintiffs, a second contract was entered into by the defendants with the Libyan authorities for the supply of the vests. The plaintiffs' claim was based on breach of contract and infringement of copyright but in addition they claimed equitable relief in respect of what they alleged was a breach of the confidence or trust reposed by them in the defendants.

All the plaintiffs' claims were upheld by Costello J after an exhaustive review of the facts. In particular, he found that, applying the principles already discussed in this chapter, there had been a clear breach of the confidence reposed in the defendants by the plaintiffs. It had been contended on behalf of the defendants that the publication of the patent drawings which necessarily followed the plaintiffs' application for a patent meant that the allegedly confidential information was now in the public domain. Costello J rejected this argument and distinguished an earlier House of Lords decision of *Mustad and Son v Alcock & Co Ltd and another*,[2] on which the defendants had relied: in *House of Spring Gardens*, there was ancillary information disclosed to the defendants which had not formed part of the patented invention. Moreover, *Mustad's case* had been decided in 1928 before the development in England of the relevant equitable principles, presumably a reference to the 'spring-board' rule which was not articulated until 1960. The Supreme Court unanimously upheld the conclusions of the trial judge.

Prior publication then is by no means necessarily fatal to a claim based on an unauthorised use of confidential information. A striking example of the extent to which the courts have been prepared to go in recent times in enforcing the doctrine despite prior publication is *Schering Chemicals Ltd v Falkman Ltd*.[3] In that case, the plaintiffs, a multi-national pharmaceutical company, had produced a preparation intended to be used by women in order to discover whether they were pregnant. As a result of its use, they were confronted with a number of claims that babies had been born suffering from serious congenital defects. The preparation was withdrawn from the market, but the whole affair, including the pending litigation, attracted the attention of the media. Alarmed by the prospect of serious damage to their reputation, the plaintiffs retained the services of the defendants, a firm specialising in protecting and enhancing the corporate image of their clients. They in turn obtained as part of their team an employee of Thames Television, part of whose brief was to ensure that the plaintiffs' representatives knew the most effective way in which to deal with the media. For this purpose, he was supplied with background information by the plaintiffs relating to the development of the whole episode. The defendants' contract specified that all information supplied to them was to be treated as confidential. The Thames Television employee — who remained at all times in the employment of that company — decided to make a television film based on the information he had received for screening by Thames. Having had discussions with him, the plaintiffs concluded that their interests would not be served by the proposed film and declined to consent to its being screened. The employee concerned went ahead with his plans and the plaintiffs immediately sought an injunction to prevent him from so doing.

One of the arguments advanced on behalf of the defendants was that the information supplied by the plaintiffs was accessible to anyone who was prepared to go to the trouble of tracking it down in libraries and other public sources of information. The Court of Appeal (Lord Denning MR *dissentiente*) rejected the submission. Although the information was in theory in the public domain, the employee was in a peculiarly advantageous position, since the relevant parts of it had been collected, collated and digested for his benefit by the plaintiffs so that the defendants might the more effectively carry on the task for which they were retained. That had been done on a confidential basis and it would be inequitable to permit the employee to make use of it for a purpose for which it was never intended. Shaw LJ said that what he described as 'adventitious publicity' was not fatal to a claim based on abuse of confidence. While this has been criticised as stating the law too widely, it usefully underlines the general proposition which can be regarded as acceptable, ie that prior publication even of all the relevant information is not necessarily fatal. The facts of each case must be scrutinised in order to determine whether in the circumstances the plaintiff is entitled to equitable protection.

1 (1960) RPC 128.
2 [1963] 3 All ER 416.
3 [1981] 2 All ER 321.

Invasion of privacy

30.05 The law will also ensure that a person who obtains information surreptitiously from another is not allowed to make use of such information to the detriment of the person from whom it obtained. This is a logical extension of the principle discussed already, that the entrusting of information in confidence gives rise to an obligation enforceable in equity. A person who obtains the same confidential information by stealth — whether by acting as an eavesdropper or by the use of more up to date methods of telephone tapping or other forms of 'bugging' — should be in no better position that the person to whom it is willingly entrusted.

This view of the law derives support from earlier authority, but in Ireland it is substantially reinforced by judicial recognition of a right of privacy which will be protected and vindicated by the courts. Such a right is not expressly acknowledged in Article 40, but its existence as an essential attribute of the human personality which the State must respect was unequivocally recognised by the Supreme Court in *McGee v A-G*.[1] More recently, it was considered in the context of telephone tapping by Hamilton P in *Kennedy v Ireland*.[2]

Two of the plaintiffs were political correspondents whose private telephones had been tapped on the authority of the Minister for Justice. They brought proceedings against Ireland claiming damages for what they alleged was an unconstitutional interference with their right of privacy. The defendants admitted that the tapping was an abuse of the powers conferred on the Minister by the Post Office Act 1908, but submitted that this of itself afforded no cause of action to the plaintiffs. This was rejected by the learned President: the right of privacy which clearly existed in our law included the right to hold telephone conversations 'without deliberate, conscious and unjustified ... intrusion thereon by the servants of the state ...' In the result each of the plaintiffs was awarded exemplary damages.

It is thought that the right to privacy could also be relied on to make private persons accountable for the use of information which they have obtained in a manner which constitutes a violation of the right to privacy as, for example, by some form of industrial or commercial espionage. Nor would it seem right to confine this to cases where the obtaining of the confidential information was planned and deliberate: it would seem reasonable to extend it to cases where the acquisition of the confidential information is the unexpected by-product of more casual eavesdropping. In *Malone v Metropolitan Police Comrs (No 2)*,[3] where the plaintiff was one of the accused in a criminal trial and sought to prevent the police from making use of transcripts of tapped telephone conversations, Megarry V-C held that the imparting of confidential information, whether on the telephone or over the garden wall, is always subject to the possibility of its being overheard. Hence he concluded that the general protection afforded by the equitable doctrine did not extend to the acquisition of that information by eavesdropping or its modern technological equivalents. Even in the context of the equitable doctrine, this is a decision of doubtful authority.[4] In Ireland, it is clear that the constitutional right of privacy will afford a person protection against unwarranted intrusion by the State; and in harmony with the general obligation on the courts to ensure that an appropriate remedy is available to protect constitutional rights,[5] it would seem that they would similarly restrain the use to the plaintiff's detriment of information clandestinely obtained by private persons.

1 [1974] IR 284.
2 Unreported; judgement delivered 12 January 1987.
3 [1979] Ch 344.
4 The Court of Appeal has sought to give Megarry V-C's judgement a more restricted application in a later case, not altogether convincingly: *Francome v Mirror Group Newspapers Ltd* [1984] 2 All ER 408.
5 See para 15.16, above.

The defence of 'public interest' or 'iniquity'

30.06 Equity will not permit the doctrine of confidentiality to be used in order to cloak wrongdoing. If the defendant can show that a breach of the confidence was necessary in order to prevent the commission of a crime or to enable a crime to be punished, this will be a good defence. As Wood VC said, in *Gartside v Outram*,[1] 'there is no confidence as to the disclosure of iniquity.' The English authorities to this effect would presumably be applied in Ireland if a plaintiff sought to rely either on the constitutional right of privacy or the doctrine of confidentiality in a case where the defendant could show that the use by him of the confidential information was necessary to prevent 'iniquity' in this sense. How much further the defence extends is not clear: whether, for example, it can be used because the plaintiff has been apparently guilty of 'anti-social' behaviour remains a matter for debate.[2]

1 (1856) 3 Jur NS 39.
2 Cf *Hubbard v Vosper* [1972] 2 QB 84; *Beloff v Pressdram Ltd* [1973] 1 All ER 241 at 260-261; *Woodward v Hutchins* [1977] 2 All ER 751; *Francome v Mirror Group Newspapers Ltd*, above. A more restrictive view of how far the 'iniquity' defence should extend has been taken in Australia: *Castrol Australia Pty Ltd v Em Tech Associates Pty Ltd* [1980] 33 ALR 31.

Non-commercial information

30.07 Is the equitable doctrine — as distinct from the constitutional protection of privacy — confined to the misuse of commercial information? In *House of Spring Gardens v Point Blank,* McCarthy J in the Supreme Court said

'I would venture the view that the obligation of secrecy whilst enforced by equitable principles, depends more upon commercial necessity than moral duty.'[1]

It seems unlikely that by this observation the learned judge was intending to convey that the equitable jurisdiction was confined to commercial cases. (It was, in any event, *obiter,* since that was a wholly commercial case.) There is certainly ample authority in England for the proposition that the doctrine is not so restricted.

Thus, while the defendant in *Prince Albert v Strange* was actuated by financial motives any commercial loss to the plaintiff was hardly of significance in the context of the case. In more recent times, a plaintiff (the Duchess of Argyll) suceeded in obtaining an injunction restraining the defendant, her former husband, from publishing marital confidences in a Sunday newspaper.[2] Again while the defendant may, apart from any other motive, have been acting for financial reward, the plaintiff was not seeking to protect any commercial interest. Similarly, in *Lennon v News Group Ltd,*[3] a pop star was refused an injunction restraining publication by his first wife of secrets of their married life but solely on the ground that he had indulged himself in comparable public reminiscences and not because there was no cause of action.

1 At 709.
2 *Argyll v Argyll* [1967] Ch 302.
3 (1978) FSR 573.

Government confidences

30.08 Since the duty of confidentiality is not, as has been submitted, confined to cases where the interest sought to be protected is commercial, it would seem to follow logically that a person in the public service could be restrained either before or after the cesser of his employment from a breach of the duty of confidentiality. In many cases, the impugned publication will constitute a breach of s 4(1) of the Official Secrets Act 1963, but the question as to whether, altogether apart from such legislation, publication can be restrained has been the subject of much litigation in recent times in Ireland, England and Australia.

In England in *A-G v Jonathan Cape Ltd*,[1] it was sought to restrain the publication by the defendants of diaries kept by Richard Crossman when a cabinet minister which included graphic and detailed accounts of discussions at cabinet meetings held during the two administrations of Lord Wilson in the 1960s. Lord Widgery CJ (sitting as a judge of first instance) having noted the opinion of Ungoed-Thomas J in *Argyll v Argyll* that the doctrine of confidence was not confined to commercial cases, went on

> 'Even so, these defendants argue that an extension of the principle of the Argyll case to the present dispute involves another large and unjustifiable leap forward, because in the present case the Attorney-General is seeking to apply the principle to public secrets made confidential in the interests of good government. I cannot see why the courts should be powerless to restrain the publication of public secrets, while enjoying the Argyll powers in regard to domestic secrets. Indeed, as already pointed out, the court must have power to deal with publication which threatens national security, and the differences between such a case and the present case is one of degree rather than kind. I conclude, therefore, that when a Cabinet Minister receives information in confidence the improper publication of such information can be restrained by the court, and his obligation is not merely to observe a gentleman's agreement to refrain from publication.'[2]

Widgery CJ, also said, however, that two other requirements must be met before publication can be restrained: the Attorney-General must show ....

> '(b) that the public interest requires that the publication be restrained and
> (c) that there are no other facts of the public interest contradictory of and more compelling than that relied upon.'

This approach was adopted by Mason J in the High Court of Australia in *Commonwealth of Australia v John Fairfax & Sons Ltd*[3] where he said:

> 'The equitable principle has been fashioned to protect the personal private and proprietary interests of the citizen, not to protect the very different interests of the executive. It acts, or is supposed to act, not according to standards of private interest, but in the public interest. This is not to say that Equity will not protect information in the hands of the government, but it is to say that when Equity protects Government information, it will look at the matter through different spectacles.
> 'It may be a sufficient detriment to the citizen that disclosure of information relating to his affairs will expose his actions to public discussion and criticism. It is unacceptable in our democratic society that there should be a restraint on the publication of information relating to government when the only vice of that information is that it enables the public to discuss, review and criticise government action.
> 'Accordingly, the court will determine the government's claim to confidentiality by reference to the public interest. Unless disclosure is likely to injure the public interest it will not be protected.'

---

1 [1976] QB 752.

2 At 770-771.
3 (1980) 147 CLR 39 at 51.

30.09 The extent to which protection on the ground of abuse of confidentiality will be given to governments has been the subject of much litigation in recent times in England, Australia and Ireland in what may conveniently be called the 'Spycatcher' cases. They arose initially out of attempts by a retired member of the British Secret Service, Mr Peter Wright, to publish memoirs in which he made a number of dramatic allegations as to the activities of his former department. An interlocutory injunction was obtained by the English Attorney-General restraining English newspapers from publishing extracts from the book on the ground of abuse of confidence.[1] Mr Wright was now living in Australia beyond the reach of the English Official Secrets Act and a publishing firm agreed to publish the controversial memoirs in full in that jurisdiction. The English attorney also sought but was refused an injunction in the Australian courts.[2] When the book was published in the United States, the English newspapers applied for the discharge of the injunctions granted in England on the ground that the continued restraint on publication was futile and constituted a form of censorship. This view was upheld by Brown-Wilkinson V-C but he was reversed by the Court of Appeal whose decision was upheld, by a bare majority, by the House of Lords.[3] The majority held that the attorney had established that there was a serious question to be tried as to whether the publication was an abuse of confidence: permitting publication in England in the press before the trial would in effect deprive the Attorney-General of the possibility of having that issue resolved in his favour.

While the Australian and English cases were proceeding, an Irish publisher announced the publication of a book called 'One Woman's War' by a deceased lady who was employed in the British Secret Service during the Second World War. The English Attorney-General, presumably sensitive to the charge that he was allowing other retired M15 officials to break the rules, sought an interlocutory injunction in this jurisdiction. It does not appear to have been seriously argued that publication in this instance would damage national security even in England (the author was a comparatively junior officer and the events were long in the past). It was, however, urged that the general principle of confidentiality of information could be successfully invoked to prevent publication. Carroll J had no hesitation in rejecting this argument: in cases of governmental secrecy, the sole criterion was the public interest and the Irish public interest was not in any sense affected by publication. The plaintiff had consequently failed to make out any case and hence did not meet the first requirement for the granting of interlocutory relief. In any event, the balance of convenience was clearly against the granting of such relief, since the plaintiff's constitutional right to freedom of expression was more deserving of protection than the interests of a foreign government.[4]

Since the Irish public interest was not affected by the proposed publication in *A-G for England and Wales v Brandon Books Publishers*, it is not necessarily authority for the propositions accepted in England in *A-G v Jonathan Cape Ltd* and in Australia in *Commonwealth of Australia v Fairfax*.[5] There seems no reason, however, why in an appropriate case governmental secrecy should not be protected where the public interest so requires on the same grounds as those laid down in the two overseas decisions. It would not appear that the constitutional right of freedom of expression would be a bar to the granting of such relief: that article is so heavily qualified (the right exists subject to 'public order and morality')[6] that it would be extremely difficult to contend successfully that, in a case where the executive satisfied the court that national security required the restraint of publication of certain information, there would be any constitutional inhibition against the granting of an injunction. In some common law jurisdictions, such as Australia and the United States, there are now Freedom of Information Acts, but there has been no such legislation in Ireland.

1 *A-G v Guardian Newspapers* (1986) Times, 26 July.
2 At the time of writing, judgement is still to be delivered in an appeal by the Attorney-General against this decision.
3 *A-G v Guardian Newspapers Ltd* [1987] 3 All ER 316.
4 *A-G for England and Wales v Brandon Book Publishers* (1987) ILRM 135.
5 Above.
6 See para 15.16, above.

Remedies

30.10 Where the abuse of confidence amounts to a breach of contract resulting in damages, the plaintiff will be entitled to an award of damages. He may, of course, in any event be entitled to an injunction restraining further breaches. If the breach of confidence is neither contractual nor tortious, the plaintiff may still be entitled to an injunction deriving ultimately from the exclusive equitable jurisdiction of the court. In addition, he may be entitled to such further equitable relief as an account of profits or the delivery up of documents. It must not be thought that because damages is an essentially common law remedy, however, that the court is powerless to order restitution in the case deriving from the exclusive equitable jurisdiction. On the contrary, it is clear that the court has ample powers in its equitable jurisdiction to order restitution to be made.[1]

The remedy of tracing, it has been held in Australia and the US,[2] may also be available in a case of breach of confidence: a person into whose hands the documents incorporating the confidential information has come may be held to be a constructive trustee of such documents although he is not the person originally standing in a confidential relationship to their owner.

1 *Palmer v Monk* [1962] NSWR 786.
2 *Ohio Oil Co v Sharp* 135 F 2d 303 (1943).

Part five

Administration of estates

Chapter 31

Administration of estates generally

31.01 The administration of the estates of deceased persons was at one time exclusively the province of the ecclesiastical courts. When they ceased to exercise that jurisdiction, it was assumed by the court of chancery and many of the doctrine and principles which govern the administration of such estates are purely equitable in origin. Some of the most important have been discussed in Part IV, but we must now survey more generally the manner in which this important jurisdiction is administered by the courts to-day. The office of the personal representative who is responsible for the administration of the estate, his powers and duties, the rules which govern the collection and distribution by him of the assets of the deceased, the payment of debts and legacies: all of these are features of the subject with which it is necessary for the student and the practitioner to be familiar. Since, however, they are fully treated in modern Irish textbooks,[1] we shall content ourselves with summarising the main aspects of the subject, reserving more detailed treatment for those areas which are not so fully dealt with, ie the remedies available to those who are aggrieved by the manner in which the estate is administered or not administered as the case may be, and the particular problems associated with *donationes mortis causa*.

1 Wylie, *Land Law*, Chapter 16; McGuire: *The Succession Act 1965: A Commentary* (2nd edn, ed Pearce)

The personal representative

31.02 When a person dies, all his property vests in his personal representative. This is so whether he has made a will or not. If he has made a will in which he has named a person to act as his executor, that person is his personal representative. If he has died intestate, his property vests in an administrator appointed by the court,[1] who is then the personal representative. The property of the deceased must be collected by the personal representative and applied first in the payment of his lawful debts, with the surplus going to those entitled as beneficiaries, either according to the terms of his will if he died testate or according to statutory rules of distribution among his next-of-kin if he died intestate. At one time under our law, only the personal estate of the deceased vested in the personal representatives: real estate vested in his heir-at-law or in the person to whom he had devised his real estate by his will. Since the enactment of the

357

Succession Act 1965, the rules for the devolution of real and personal estate are the same: they both vest in the personal representative to be applied in the payment of his debts and thereafter to be distributed among those beneficially entitled. The property thus available is called the 'assets' of the deceased and the process by which the personal representative gets in the property and distributes it among those entitled is called 'the administration of assets.'

In the case of a will, the executor named must apply for and obtain a grant of probate of the will before he can begin the administration of the estate. The High Court alone has jurisdiction to grant probate of a will and this is done by the Probate Office of the court or the relevant district probate registry on proof of the due execution of the will and the payment of any duty due to the State. Where the deceased died intestate or appointed no executor in his will, an administrator may be appointed by the High Court under a grant of letters of administration.

There is one fundamental difference between an executor and an administrator: an executor derives his authority from the will itself and not from the grant of probate, whereas an administrator derives his authority solely from the grant of letters of administration. Thus, property vests immediately in the executor on the death of the testator, but in the case of the administrator only when the grant is issued. However, under the doctrine of 'relation back', for some purposes the grant is deemed to be issued on the death of the person concerned.[2]

1 Until the appointment is made, the property is vested in the President of the High Court: Succession Act 1965, s 13.
2 *Tharpe v Stallwood* (1843) 5 Man & G 766.

31.03 The first duty of the personal representative is to collect all the assets. He then must pay the debts and thereafter distribute the surplus. For the purpose of administering the assets, he has wide powers most of which are expressly stated in the Succession Act 1965. The most important are powers:

(a) To sell the whole or any part of the estate whether for the payment of debts or to facilitate distribution of the assets.[1] If it is for the latter purpose, he must give effect to the wishes of all the beneficiaries who are of full age or, in the case of a dispute, of the majority, so far as practicable.[2]

(b) To appropriate any part of the estate, in its actual condition or as invested, in or towards satisfaction of any legacy, share or interest in the estate.[3] Where the deceased's estate includes a dwelling in which his spouse was ordinarily resident at the date of his death, the spouse may require the personal representative to appropriate the dwelling in satisfaction of the share in the estate to which that spouse is entitled.[4]

(c) To make such leases of any deceased's land as may be reasonably necessary for the administration of the estate[5] and to make leases generally for such terms and on conditions as he thinks fit with the consent of the beneficiaries or the approval of the court.[6]

(d) To raise money by way of mortgage or charge, for the payment of expenses, debts and liabilities or the legal right of a surviving spouse.[7]

(e) To carry on the business of the deceased for the purpose of realising it as a going concern or to enable order to be completed.[8] To carry it on for any other purpose or for a significantly longer period requires authorisation either expressly or by implication in the will.)[9]

There is also a provision which protects bona fide purchasers for value of any part of the estate from the personal representative: they hold property so purchased free from debts and liabilities of the deceased (except those charged otherwise than by the will) and from the claims of those entitled to a share of the estate and are not concerned to see to the application of the purchase money.[10]

1 Succession Act 1965, s 50 (1).
2 Ibid.
3 Succession Act 1965, s 55 (1).
4 Ibid, s 56 (1).
5 Ibid, s 60 (1)(a).
6 Ibid, s 60 (1)(b).
7 Ibid, s 60 (3).
8 *Perry v Perry* (1869) IR 3 Eq 452.
9 *National Bank Ltd v Hamrock* (1928) 62 ILT 165.
10 Succession Act 1965, s 50 (1)(a).

31.04 The personal representative holds the estate of the deceased person on trust for those entitled to it, whether as beneficiaries or creditors. The beneficiaries have, in general, no legal or beneficial interest in any of the assets during the course of administration.[1] They only acquire such an interest when, in the case of specific property, the personal representative has assented to its vesting in them, or, in the case of a share of the residue, after the estate has been fully administered by the payment of all debts and legacies, since until then it is impossible to say what their share may be. Until an assent is executed or the administration completed, the sole right of the beneficiary is to require that the deceased's estate be duly administered, if necessary by taking proceedings to that end. An assent by the personal representative to the vesting of any property may be oral,[2] except in the case of any estate or interest in land where it must be in writing.[3] There are provisions regulating the registration of the assent in the Registry of Deeds in the case of unregistered land[4] and the registration of the beneficiary as the owner on production of the assent in the prescribed form in the case of registered land.[5]

1 See para 4.05, above.
2 *Quinton v Frith* (1868) IR 2 Eq 494.
3 Succession Act, 1965, s 52(5).
4 Ibid, s 53.
5 Registration of Title Act 1964, s 61 (3) as substituted by Succession Act 1965, s 54 (2).

31.05 Personal representatives are under a duty to the beneficiaries and the creditors to carry out their obligations with due diligence. Normally they are expected to complete the administration within one year from the death, the so-called 'executor's year'.[1] Until then, they are not bound to distribute the estate and a legatee, for example, cannot require payment before the expiration of the year, even if the testator directed that it be paid earlier.[2] A longer period than a year may be justifiable, depending on the circumstances of the particular administration. If after the expiration of the year, the personal representative has failed, on request, to execute an assent or transfer of any land to the person entitled, the latter may apply to the court and the court may make an order vesting the property in that person.[3]

1 Statute of Distributions (Ir) 1695 s 4; *Dowzer v Dowzer* (1914) 48 ILT 236.

2 *Pearson v Pearson* (1802) 1 Sch & Lef 10.
3 Succession Act 1965, s 52(4).

31.06 In the case of insolvent estates, an order of payment of debts is prescribed and it is also prudent for the personal representative to follow the same order of priority in the case of apparently solvent estates, since it is sometimes not possible to say at the outset whether or not the estate will prove solvent. Leaving aside for the moment the position of secured creditors—who may choose simply to rely on their security and not claim their debt in the administration—the order of payment of debts under the Succession Act 1965 provides for the payment first of the funeral, testamentary and administration expenses.[1] Subject to that the same rules are to apply to insolvent estates as under the law of bankruptcy.[2] Those rules provide that certain debts—known as 'preferential debts'—are to have priority over all other debts. They are as follows:

(1) Rates for one year;
(2) Assessed tax (land, property or income tax) for any one year;[3]
(3) Wages or salary of any clerk or servant for four months not exceeding £50;
(4) Wages of any labourer or workman for two months not exceeding £25;
(5) Sums deducted by employers under the Social Welfare (Consolidation) Act 1981, including PRSI contributions;
(6) Sums deducted by employers in respect of PAYE for the period of 12 months prior to the date of death.[4]

These preferential debts must be paid in full if the assets are sufficient, before the ordinary creditors are paid anything. If the assets are insufficient, the preferential debts must abate rateably.[5] If there are insufficient assets remaining after the payment of the preferential debts, the debts due to ordinary creditors must abate rateably.

It should be noted that at one time it was thought that all debts owed to the State were preferential. It was, however, held in *Re Irish Employer's Mutual Insurance Association Ltd*[6] that this was an aspect of the royal prerogative which had not survived the enactment of the Constitution.

1 Ibid, Sch 1, Part I.
2 See *Bankruptcy Law Committee Report*, (1972) Pri 2714, Chapter 30.
3 The revenue can select the year most favourable to them for this purpose.
4 Income Tax Act 1967 as amended by Finance Act 1968, s 11.
5 *Re Leinster Contract Corpn* [1903] 1 IR 517.
6 [1955] IR 176.

31.07 A secured creditor has the following options: [1]

(1) he may rely on his security and not prove his debt in the administration;
(2) he may obtain liberty to realise his security and prove for the balance owing, if any;
(3) he may value his security and prove for the balance owing, if any;
(4) he may surrender his security and prove as an unsecured creditor.

If the creditor opts for course (3) and undervalues the security, he must refund the difference on the sale to the estate: alternatively, the personal representative may redeem the security at the creditor's valuation.[2] So if the creditor is owed £50,000 and has a mortgage of land which he values at £30,000, he may prove for £20,000 in the administration. But if it is subsequently sold for £40,000, he may be required to pay £10,000 to the estate. Alternatively, the personal representative may get rid of the mortgage by paying the creditor £30,000, ie the creditor's own valuation. Conversely, if the creditor overvalues the mortgage, he may recover the difference out of any assets which have not been distributed.[3]

The bankruptcy rules as to debts which are provable apply in the case of an administration: all debts and liabilities, present and future, certain and contingent, are provable.[4] The rules as to set off also apply: where there have been mutual credits and debts or other mutual dealings, the sums due are to be set off and only the balance found is to be paid.[5]

It should also be noted that not all the bankruptcy rules are applicable. In particular, those rules which have the effect of increasing the assets available for the bankrupt's creditors are not applicable.[6] Thus, it is only the deceased's own property which is available for his creditors: in the case of bankrupts, property in his apparent or 'reputed' ownership is also available. The rules as to the avoidance of voluntary settlements, executions and attachments not completed at the date of adjudication and fraudulent preferences are also excluded.

1 *Ex p Robinson* (1886) 15 Lr Ir 496; *Re Love* (1883) 9 LR Ir 6; *Re Greer* (1877) IR 11 Eq 502.
2 *Ex p Robinson*, above.
3 *Re Hopkins* (1881) 18 Ch D 370, CA.
4 Succession Act 1965, Sch 1, Part 1, Rule 2.
5 Irish Bankruptcy and Insolvent Act 1857, s 251.
6 *Watkins v Lindsay & Co* (1898) 5 Mans 25; *Re Leng* [1895] 1 Ch 652.

31.08 In the case of solvent estates, interest is payable on any debt which carries interest, eg a judgement debt carries interest at the rate currently payable on such debts.[1] A bank overdraft carries interest at the current bank rate on such overdrafts calculated at half yearly rests until the date of death. Thereafter, it carries simply interest only, since the relationship of banker and customer is regarded as terminated by death.[2] In the case of debts on which interest is not payable, such interest will be allowed at the rate currently payable on judgement debts, but only where the other debts have been paid in full together with the interest due in respect of them.[3]

1 Now 11 per cent under s 26 of the Debtors (Ir) Act 1840 as amended by Courts Act 1981 ss 19 and 20.
2 *Provincial Bank of Ireland Ltd v O'Reilly* (1890) 26 LR Ir 313.
3 Order 55, r 42.

31.09 The personal representative may pay a debt barred by the Statute of Limitations 1957: he cannot be compelled to plead the statute.[1] But where an order for administration has been made, the personal representative cannot pay a statute barred debt unless it is owed to the plaintiff in the administration action: the order for administration is made for the benefit of all creditors and any one of them can object to the payment.

1 *Stahlchmidt v Lett* (1853) 1 Sm & G 415.

31.10 The personal representative traditionally had a right of *retainer*, ie a right to pay a debt due to himself in priority to other debts of equal status, the reason being that he could not sue himself in respect of the same debt. This right of retainer is preserved by the Succession Act 1965 but only where the estate is solvent and where the debt is due to the personal representative in his own right.[1] The personal representative also had a right of *preference*, ie a right to prefer one creditor to another provided they were of the same status. This applies even though the effect of preferring one is to leave nothing for the other. The right was left unaffected by the Succession Act 1965, but would appear to be lost where an order for administration is made.

1 Succession Act 1965, s 46(2).

Order of application of assets

31.11 In the case of solvent estates, there is a particular order in which the assets may be availed of for the payment of debts and legacies, viz:

   (i) property of the deceased undisposed of by will, subject to the retention thereout of a fund sufficient to satisfy any pecuniary legacies;
  (ii) property of the deceased not specifically devised or bequeathed but included (either by a specific or general description) in a residuary clause, subject to the retention out of such property of a fund sufficient to meet any pecuniary legacies so far as not provided for in (i) above.
 (iii) property of the deceased specifically appropriated or devised or bequeathed (either by specific or general description) for the payment of debts;
  (iv) property of the deceased charged with, or devised or bequeathed (either by a specific or general description) subject to a charge for the payment of debts;
   (v) the fund, if any, retained to meet pecuniary legacies;
  (vi) property specifically devised or bequeathed rateably, according to value;
 (vii) property appointed under a general power rateably according to value.

This order may be varied by the will of the deceased. It is not to affect the liability of land to answer the payment of death duty in exoneration of other assets. Nor is it to affect the payment of the spouse's share as of legal right.[1]

1 Succession Act 1965, Sch 1, Part II.

31.12 Prior to the enactment of Locke King's Acts, a person who became entitled to land or other property under a will or intestacy which was subject to any charge or mortgage could require the personal representative to pay him off out of the deceased's personal estate. This was changed by the Acts which provided that the property itself was to bear the charge. The Acts were repealed by the Succession Act 1965, but it provides similarly: the rule is that such charges must be paid out of the property to which they are subject, unless the deceased has signified a contrary intention.[1]

1 Succession Act 1965, s 47.

Chapter 32

Remedies

32.01 As we have seen, a personal representative is normally allowed a year from the death of the deceased—the 'executor's year'—to complete the administration.[1] A creditor, however, does not have to wait for the expiration of the year before issuing proceedings. Even if no grant has been issued, the court may proceed to deal with the creditor's claim under Order 15, rule 37[2] in the absence of any personal representative or may appoint some person to represent the estate. But beneficiaries cannot proceed against the personal representatives before the expiration of the year without the leave of the court.[3] Moreover, when the proceedings are commenced, they cannot normally take the form of a simple claim for the payment or transfer to the beneficiary of what he claims to be entitled to under the will or intestacy. As we have already seen,[4] a beneficiary does not become entitled to any share in the estate until the executor or administrator has assented to the vesting of the property in question. Until then, if he is aggrieved by the failure of the personal representative to administer the estate or the unreasonable delay in administering it, his only remedy is to seek an order for the administration of the estate by the court. Creditors and beneficiaries have further rights of tracing property into the hands of persons other than purchasers for value without notice[5] and the beneficiary may also be entitled to take proceedings in personam against the personal representatives and persons to whom he has wrongfully transferred property.[6] Finally, personal representatives themselves may seek the assistance of the court as to questions which may arise during the course of administration.[7]

1 See para 31.05, above.
2 Rules of the Superior Courts.
3 Succession Act 1965, s 62 (1).
4 See para 4.05, above.
5 See chapter 20, above.
6 See para 32.09, below.
7 Rules of the Superior Courts, Order 3(6).

Administration by the court

32.02 This is the remedy which usually must be availed of by a beneficiary who is aggrieved by the personal representative's failure to administer the estate with due diligence or at all. Where the value of the assets other than land does not exceed £5000 and the rateable value of the land does not exceed £200, they may be brought in the Circuit Court.[1] Otherwise, the proceedings must be brought in the High Court. In the Circuit Court, the proceedings are commenced by an Administration Civil Bill[2] and in the High Court by a special summons,[3] unless the plaintiff alleges a breach of trust or wilful default on the part of the personal representative in which case they must be brought by plenary summons.[4] The proceedings may be brought by any person claiming to be interested in the estate of the deceased, whether as creditor, devisee, legatee, next of kin or heir at law, *cestui que trust* or any person claiming to be entitled by virtue of the assignment of any of these interests.[5] It may also be brought by the executors or trustees.[6]

Before any administration proceedings can be commenced, there must be a personal representative, although the Court can deal with a creditor's claim under Order 15, rule 37. The fact that a person has taken out a grant abroad will not make him a personal representative for this purpose if he has not taken out a grant in Ireland.[7]

1 Courts (Supplemental Provisions) Act 1961, s 22 (1), Sch 3 as amended by s 2 of the Courts Act 1981.
2 Rules of the Circuit Court, Order 5, r 1.
3 Rules of the Superior Courts, Order 3(1).
4 Ibid.
5 Ibid, Order 3(2).
6 Ibid.
7 *McSweeney v Murphy* [1919] 1 IR 16; *Re Walsh* [1931] IR 161.

32.03 The claim of a person to have the estate administered by the court may be barred by the Statute of Limitations 1957. Once the proceedings are issued, however, the statute stops running, not merely against the plaintiff, but against any other person interested in the estate whether as a beneficiary or a creditor.[1] The period of limitation fixed by the Act as amended by the Succession Act 1965 for bringing an action in respect of the estate of a deceased person is six years and in the case of interest on a legacy three years.[2] In the case of a legacy, or a share of the estate, the time runs from the date of death, because that is when a right to receive the legacy or shares accrues, even though the legatee or beneficiary cannot in fact bring proceedings until the expiration of the executor's year.[3] A simple contract creditor must bring his proceedings within six years and a specialty creditor (one suing under an instrument under seal) within twelve years.[4] A judgement creditor also has twelve years to sue, whether or not he has registered his judgement as a mortgage.[5] In the case of a debt charged on property, real or personal, the period is twelve years from the date when the right to receive the money accrued.[6] It would seem, however, that a direction by the testator that his debts should be paid out of realty will no longer of itself create a charge on the realty since there is now no distinction between realty and personality when it comes to the payment of debts: all are liable in the same way and hence such a direction is simply superfluous.[7]

As with any other limitation periods, the statute will not run where the claimant is under a disability, eg in the case of a minor it will not start running until he has reached the age of 18.[8] Similarly, an acknowledgement or part payment of the claim will stop the statute running,[9] as will a mistake on the part of the claimant.[10] The statute will also not run where there has been fraud on the part of the personal representative.[11]

1 *Thompson v Hurly* [1905] 1 IR 588.

2 S 45 as substituted by s 126 of the Succession Act 1965.
3 *Dowzer v Dowzer* (1914) 48 ILT 236.
4 Statute of Limitations 1957, s 11.
5 Ibid.
6 Statute of Limitations 1957, s 36.
7 Snell, p 349.
8 Statute of Limitations 1957, s 49.
9 Statute of Limitations 1957, ss 51 and 66.
10 Statute of Limitations 1957, s 72.
11 Statute of Limitations 1957, s 71.

32.04 The form of administration order—called the primary order—will depend on whether the action has been brought by a creditor or someone else, but in every case where such an order is made the judge refers the matter to the examiner to take such accounts and make such inquiries as are appropriate.[1] In a creditor's suit, an account will be ordered of all the property, real or personal, which has come to the hands of the personal representative, of the deceased's debts and of any property which is outstanding. Where it is brought by any other person, the court will in addition order an inquiry as to the legacies left by the will (if there was one) and the persons beneficially entitled to them and, in the case of an intestacy, an inquiry as to the next-of-kin of the deceased. The examiner embodies the results of his accounts and inquiries in certificates which are confirmed or varied by the court on motions for further consideration until the final order is made for payment or distribution.

The parties to an administration action are generally allowed their costs out of the estate. After the payment of the funeral expenses, the personal representative's costs must be paid in priority to all the debts of the deceased, whether preferential or ordinary.[2] He is, moreover, entitled to have them taxed as between solicitor and client.[3] Where, however, any part of the estate is subject to a specific lien, charge or mortgage, the secured creditor is entitled to have his debt paid, so far as the charged property will extend to it, in priority to the funeral expenses and personal representative's costs.[4] Where the personal representative is ordered to bring in any money which he owes the estate, he will not be allowed his costs until he complies with the order.[5] A creditor is entitled to be paid his costs, but only after the personal representative's. He is personally liable for any deficiency in the personal representative's costs if the assets prove insufficient in an action brought by him.[6] Where the plaintiff is one of the next-of-kin or a legatee, he will also be entitled to his costs.

1 For the procedure generally, see Scanlon, *Mortgage and Adminstration Suits*.
2 *Dodds v Tuke* (1884) 25 Ch D 617; *Ramsay v Simpson* [1899] 1 IR 69.
3 *Andrews v Barnes* (1888) 39 Ch D 133, CA.
4 *Hilliard v Moriarty* [1894] IR 316; *Re Cusack* (1903) 37 ILT 152.
5 *Re O'Keane* [1907] 1 IR 223 at 225.
6 *Leonard v Kellett* (1891) 27 LR Ir 418; *Eisenhardt v Talbot* [1909] 1 IR 129.

Actions against the personal representative

32.05 A creditor may always bring an action against the personal representative to recover his debt. A legatee, however, cannot claim his legacy in such an action until the personal representative has assented to the legacy. (He can of course bring an administration action after the expiration of the executor's year.) A person entitled to a share of the residue or on an intestacy can only proceed by way of an administration action.

There are a number of possible defences to such an action against the personal representative. He may plead that he has fully administered the assets and has none left to meet the claim, the plea known as *plene adminstravit* (or *plene adminstrativit prater* where there are assets left but they have been earmarked to meet a particular claim). Or he may plead the statute of limitations. He may also plead that he is not the personal representative or that his grant has been revoked.

32.06 The liability of the personal representative is limited to the assets which he has actually received. But where he has been guilty of a *devastavit*—ie where he has wrongfully applied assets—he will be personally liable for the misapplied assets, as for example where he makes an unauthorised investment.[1] The plea of *plene adminstravit* may therefore be met by a plea of *devastavit*, but a claim for a *devastavit* must be made within six years from the act complained of.[2] The personal representative will also be personally liable if he has been guilty of any wilful default in not getting in assets.[3]

The personal representative will also be personally liable if he distributes the estate without paying a creditor or beneficiary. He can, however, protect himself against such claims by publishing the statutory notice (usually by advertisement) that at the end of a stated period he will proceed to distribute the assets having regard only to the claims of which he then has notice.[4]

1 Chapter 10, above.
2 Statute of Limitations 1957, s 45, as substituted by s 126 of Succession Act 1965.
3 *Blount v O'Connor* (1886) 17 LR Ir 620.
4 Law of Property Amendment Act 1859, s 29.

32.07 Where the personal representative goes into possession of leaseholds, he is personally liable for the rents and the performance of the covenants.[1] But if he wishes to complete the administration and put an end to his liability he is entitled to set aside a sum out of the assets to meet any liability which may arise in the future under such covenants and then assign the lease to a purchaser. He can then proceed to distribute the assets and will be protected against future claims under the lease.[2]

1 *Minford v Carse* [1912] 2 IR 245.
2 Law of Property Amendment Act 1859, ss 27 and 28.

32.08 Where an executor owed a debt to the estate of the deceased, the common law treated it as discharged by his appointment on the basis that a person cannot sue himself. But this was not so in equity, unless the debt had been forgiven by the deceased during his lifetime. Accordingly, the debt remains and is treated as an asset in the hands of the executor for which he can be made personally liable save where it was forgiven by the deceased.[1] In the case of an administrator, his appointment being by operation of the law and not the act of the deceased, the debt was not released by the issue of the grant.[2] This distinction has been abolished by statute in England but not in Ireland.

1 See para 8.10, above. It is sometimes mistakenly said that the appointment of the debtor as executor without more discharges the debt, but this is not so. It was an error into which an Irish Court of Appeal including Palles CB and Fitzgibbon LJ were surprisingly led in

Lee v McGrath (1882) 10 LR Ir 313, their attention not having been drawn to *Strong v Bird* (1874) LR 18 Eq 315.
2 *Re Gonin* [1977] 2 All ER 720.

Liability of recipients of assets

32.09 The right of a creditor, legatee or next-of-kin who has not been paid is not limited to a claim against the personal representative. He can also recover the sum to which he is entitled from any one who has been overpaid. It was held in England in *Ministry of Health v Simpson*[1] that this right could be enforced although the overpayment was the result of a mistake in law on the part of the personal representative. But it will only be available where the claimant has no remedy against the personal representative.

The creditor, legatee or next-of-kin will also be entitled in such circumstances to trace the assets to which he is entitled into the hands of any third party other than a bona fide purchaser for value without notice. This topic has already been fully discussed in Chapter 20.

1 [1951] AC 251.

Chapter 33

Donationes mortis causa

33.01 The orthodox legal method of benefiting a person after one's death is by a legacy. Our law has, however, recognised another means of so doing which has its ancestry in Roman law and hence is called a *donatic mortis causa*, literally 'a gift because of death'. This is in essence a gift of property made by a person in contemplation of his death, but which the donor intends should revert to him if he survives or decides to revoke the gift or if the donee predeceases him. It will be seen that it differs fundamentally from a legacy, since the latter takes effect only upon the death of the testator, whereas a *donatio mortis causa* takes effect immediately. The donee becomes the owner of the property straightaway, but his title is *defeasible*, since the property may revest in the donor in the event of his surviving or changing his mind before he dies.

There are three essentials for a gift of property to constitute a valid *donatio mortis causa*:

   (i)   it must be made in contemplation of the donor's death;
   (ii) it must be made subject to the condition that it will only become indefeasible in the event of the donor's death; and
   (iii) the property must be delivered to the donee.[1]

Each of these requirements will be considered in turn. At the outset, however, it should be noted that such gifts form an exception to the general rule that equity will not perfect an imperfect gift.[2] The donor may not have done all that the law demands to vest the legal title in the donee, but provided the requirements just mentioned are met, it will be a valid *donatio mortis causa*. The statement in Kiely's *Principles of Equity* that 'there is no equity to perfect an imperfect *donatio mortis causa*'[3] is therefore seriously misleading.

1 *Re Mulroy* [1924] 1 IR 98 per Moloney CJ.
2 See para 8.10, above.
3 P 103.

'In contemplation of death'

33.02 Death, as we are sometimes reminded, is the only certainty in life and it is therefore not sufficient that the gift should have been made in the expectation of death. It must have been made 'in contemplation of the donor's death' and the happiest judicial gloss on this expression is to be found in the judgement of Hale J in the Australian case of *Smallacombe v Elder's Trustee & Exor Co Ltd*:[1]

> 'the donor must have been contemplating a comparatively early death from some cause or other, whether it be an existing illness, a dangerous journey or even extreme old age. While an expectation of immediate death is not required, nevertheless something more is required than a mere recognition of the inevitability of death itself.'

Thus, while a *donatio mortis causa* will most frequently be made where the donor is seriously ill, that is not essential. At the same time, the reference in this passage to 'a dangerous journey' should not be misunderstood. It has been held that contemplation of the ordinary risks of air travel is not enough.[2]

A gift made in contemplation of suicide is not a valid *donatio mortis causa*. This was so held by a strong Irish Court of Appeal in *Agnew v Belfast Banking Co*,[3] on the ground that it would be against public policy to enforce such a gift. Suicide was then and still is a crime in Ireland, but it should not be assumed that were the law to be changed (as it has been in England) by the removal of this crime from the statute book, such a gift would then be enforceable. The law would presumably be altered because it is futile and anachronistic to treat suicide as a crime when the perpetrator can never be punished and the other inhuman consequences of suicide have long since disappeared (burial in unconsecrated ground, for example). But it would by no means follow that the public policy against self destruction which was the ground of *Agnew's Case* had also gone.

Where, however, a person makes a gift in contemplation of his imminent feared death from natural causes and then commits suicide, the gift will be enforceable. This was so held by Gavan Duffy P in *Mills v Shields*.[4] In that case, the donor was told that he was in need of treatment in a nursing home which might prove dangerous. He gave some share certificates to a priest with whom he was friendly telling him that it was his wish that he should have the shares in the event of his dying. He then boarded a train for Dublin but left at Mullingar and committed suicide later that evening. Gavan Duffy J, having found as a fact that the donor had taken his own life while suffering from a form of depression severe enough to be described as an illness, held that the gift had been made by him in contemplation of his death and that it was immaterial that his death was self-inflicted while in a state of depression rather than the result of the treatment.

1 [1963] WAR 3 at 4-5.
2 Cf Hanbury, p 138, n 70.
3 [1896] 2 IR 204, CA.
4 [1948] IR 367.

The gift must be conditional

33.03 The gift must be made subject to the condition that it will only become indefeasible in the event of the donor's death. Until then, he retains the power to revoke it and if he has effectively transferred the legal ownership to the donee the latter will hold it in trust for him in the event of the gift being revoked.[1] If he has not transferred the title prior to his death, that event automatically perfects the title of the donee and he does not in general require the assent of the personal representative to the vesting in him of the property. If necessary, however, the personal representative will be compelled to take any steps that may be required to vest the title in the donee.[2]

The condition need not be express: it can be presumed from the fact that the gift was made in contemplation of death.[3]

The gift will be automatically revoked by the recovery of the donor from the illness which prompted the gift.[4] But revocation may also be inferred from the resumption by the donor of dominion over the property[5] or even by his simply giving notice to the donee that the gift is revoked.[6] Where, however, the donor resumes possession and no more—as where the property is given to him for safe custody or for some other reason falling short of a resumption of dominion—the gift will not be revoked.[7] In the case of a post office savings book, for example, the return of the book to the donor to enable him to make withdrawals will not amount to revocation.[8] A *donatio mortis causa,* since it takes effect immediately, cannot be revoked by the will of the donor which takes effect only upon the death.[9]

1 *Duffield v Elwes* (1827) 1 Bli NS 497 at 530 per Lord Eldon.
2 *Staniland v Willott* (1852) 3 Mac & G 664.
3 *Duffield v Elwes*, above.
4 *Gardner v Parker* (1818) 3 Madd 184; *Keys v Hore* (1879) 13 ILT 58.
5 *Staniland v Willott, above.*
6 *Bunn v Markham* (1816) 7 Taunt 224 at 232.
7 *Re Hawkins* [1924] 2 Ch 47.
8 *Watts v Public Trustee* (1949) 50 SR NSW 130.
9 White & Tudor, *Leading Cases in Equity*, 9th edn, Vol 1, p 355.

The property must be delivered to the donee

33.04 There cannot be a valid *donatio mortis causa* of land, whether it takes the form of realty or leasehold.[1] The subject matter must be pure personalty: either chattels (jewellery, paintings, a motor-car etc) or choses in action (money in a bank account or post office, for example). In either case, a delivery is essential to constitute a valid *donatio* but obviously the question as to what constitutes sufficient delivery will depend in the first instance on whether the property consists of chattels or choses in action. And there are some forms of pure personalty which it has been held cannot be the subject of a valid *donatio*.

1 *Duffield v Elwes*, above, at 530, 549, 543, per Lord Eldon. But this has been questioned: see Pettit, p 104; Waters, *Law of Trusts in Canada*, p 170.

33.05 In the case of chattels some form of physical delivery is in general essential to constitute a valid donatio. It is not sufficient simply to say 'you can have my three paintings hanging in my study': the actual paintings must be handed over to the donee.[1] Where, however, dominion over the chattels is exercised by the possession of a key, the handing over of the key will be treated as sufficient delivery.[2] This form of symbolic delivery is illustrated by *Re Lillingston*[3] where the donor handed the donee a key to a trunk, which contained a key to a safe deposit box in Harrods. The box in turn contained a key to a safe deposit locker in other premises. It was held that there had been a valid *donatio* of the contents of all three receptacles, even though the trunk remained at all times in the possession of the donor. Delivery to a servant or agent of the donee—constructive as distinct from actual delivery—will also be sufficient, provided the servant or agent actually delivers the chattels to the donee or acknowledges that he is holding them on his behalf, during the donor's lifetime.[4]

1 *Miller v Miller* (1735) 3 P Wms 356; *Re McWey* [1928] IR 486; *Re Thompson* (1928) IR 606.
2 *Re Mulroy*, above.
3 [1952] 2 All ER 184.
4 *Re Thompson*, above.

33.06 Where the subject matter is a chose in action transferable by delivery alone—such as a bearer bond—delivery, actual or constructive, of the relevant document will suffice. In other cases, the test usually favoured for deciding whether there has been delivery of the chose in action is whether the document handed over would have to be produced by the donor if he was suing on the chose.[1] Documents which have been held to satisfy this requirement include a bank deposit book or pass book,[2] a post office or trustee savings bank book,[3] a cheque by a third party in favour of the donor,[4] a promissory note or bill of exchange[5] and a policy of insurance effected on the donor's life.[6]

More difficulty has arisen with share certificates in a company registered under the Companies Acts 1963 to 1986. Gavan Duffy P held in *Mills v Shields (No 2)*,[7] after an elaborate review of the authorities that their delivery did not constitute a delivery of the shares sufficient to constitute a valid *donatio*. The certificates would seem to satisfy the requirement as to the necessity for production in the event of the shareholder seeking to enforce the chose in action against the company. But Gavan Duffy P applied another test which derives support from some of the authorities, viz that the document should contain all the terms of the contract giving rise to the chose in action. This the share certificate does not do: those terms are contained in the articles of association which are not incorporated, expressly or by implication, in the share certificate. Later Australian authority takes a different view, based on the 'necessity of production' test.[8] It may be, therefore, that *Mills v Shield (No 2)* would not necessarily be followed to-day. It is, of course, the case that delivery of the share certificate will not vest the legal ownership of the shares in the donee—that can only be achieved by the entry of his name in the register of members—but, as we have seen, equity will in the case of an imperfect transfer of title compel the personal representative to take such steps as are necessary[9]—in this case the execution of a transfer—to perfect the title of the donee. There can be no doubt, however, that delivery of a broker's contract note for the transfer of stocks or shares is not sufficient.[10]

1 *Ward v Turner* (1752) 2 Ves Sen 431.
2 *Re Dillon* (1890) 44 Ch D 76; *Birch v Treasury Solicitor* [1951] Ch 298.
3 *Re Thompson's Estate*, above; *Birch v Treasury Solicitor*, above.
4 *Re Mulroy*; above. This is so whether or not the cheque is in fact indorsed by the donor; ibid.
5 *Veal v Veal* (1859) 27 Beav 303 (promissory note); *Re Mulroy*, above (do.); *Rankin v Weguelin* (1832) 27 Beav 309, (bill of exchange).
6 *Amis v Witt* (1863) 33 Beav 619.
7 [1950] IR 21.
8 *Dufficy v Mollica* [1968] 3 NSWR 751 at 759 per Holmes H, JA.
9 See para 33.01, above.
10 *Re McWey*, above.

33.07 Some forms of pure personalty cannot be the subject of a valid *donatio* and here delivery of the relevant document is plainly insufficient. A cheque drawn by the donor on his own account is an example: this is no more than an order to his bank to pay the amount.[1] The same applies to a promissory note signed by the donor.[2] If, however, the cheque is actually cashed by the donee before the donor's death this will be a valid *donatio*. But this does not apply where the cheque is cashed after the donor's death before the bank had notice of the death[3] An IOU cannot be the subject matter of a valid donatio.[4]

1 *Re Beaumont* [1902] 1 Ch 889.
2 *Bouts v Ellis* (1853) 4 De G M & G 249.
3 *Tate v Hilbert* (1793) 2 Ves 111.
4 *Duckworth v Lee* [1899] 1 IR 405.

Index